Mark Twain: The Complete Interviews

STUDIES IN AMERICAN LITERARY REALISM AND NATURALISM

SERIES EDITOR
Gary Scharnhorst

EDITORIAL BOARD
Louis J. Budd
Donna Campbell
John Crowley
Robert E. Fleming
Alan Gribben
Eric Haralson
Denise D. Knight
Joseph McElrath
George Monteiro
Brenda Murphy
James Nagel
Alice Hall Petry
Donald Pizer
Tom Quirk
Jeanne Campbell Reesman
Ken Roemer

Mark Twain: The Complete Interviews

EDITED BY GARY SCHARNHORST

THE UNIVERSITY OF ALABAMA PRESS
Tuscaloosa

The University of Alabama Press
Tuscaloosa, Alabama 35487-0380
uapress.ua.edu

Copyright © 2006 by the University of Alabama Press
All rights reserved.

Hardcover edition published 2006.
Paperback edition published 2020.
eBook edition published 2009.

Inquiries about reproducing material from this work should be addressed to the University of Alabama Press.

Typeface: Minion

Paperback ISBN: 978-0-8173-5995-9
E-ISBN: 978-0-8173-1576-4

A previous edition of this book has been catalogued by the Library of Congress.
ISBN: 978-0-8173-1522-1 (cloth)

*For Louis J. Budd
Scholar and gentleman*

Contents

	Introduction	ix
	Abbreviations	xiii
1.	The Growth of Mark Twain's Early Reputation, 1871–1884 *Interviews 1–20*	1
2.	The "Twins of Genius" Tour, 1884–1885 *Interviews 21–39*	49
3.	The Best and Worst of Times, 1886–1895 *Interviews 40–59*	87
4.	Across North America, 1895 *Interviews 60–81*	151
5.	Across Australia, Asia, and Africa, 1895–1896 *Interviews 82–120*	197
6.	"Ambassador at Large" and Man of Letters, 1897–1901 *Interviews 121–151*	317
7.	Last Visit to Missouri, 1902 *Interviews 152–170*	412
8.	At Large, 1902–1906 *Interviews 171–195*	469
9.	"Dean of Humorists," 1906–1907 *Interviews 196–220*	546
10.	Visit to Oxford, 1907 *Interviews 221–235*	610
11.	The Long Goodbye, 1907–1910 *Interviews 236–258*	647
	Appendix	701
	Index	703

Introduction

According to Louis J. Budd, Mark Twain (aka Samuel Langhorne Clemens) "was probably interviewed more often" than any other author of his time. To be sure, many of these interviews were relatively insignificant but, as Budd adds, "even a slipshod interview may hold a fact or judgment that fits while enriching other sources about his career."[1] The 258 interviews with Mark Twain transcribed in this edition fill a yawning gap in Twain studies. Neither private correspondence nor published writings, they represent another form of "autobiographical dictation" recorded over a period of nearly forty years. They contain the largest body of autobiographical material about Mark Twain still unavailable to scholars and researchers nearly a century after his death. No doubt there are some as yet undiscovered interviews with Mark Twain, but this edition contains all interviews with him that are known to date.

For purposes of this project, I have drawn the following parameters: I omit self-interviews, or humorous sketches written entirely by Mark Twain in the interview form; interviews the author repudiated as grossly inaccurate or imaginary; interviews judged by scholars to be spurious; purported interviews that contain no direct quotation; purported interviews that quote Twain's lectures or other writings as if in answer to questions; and memoirs that ostensibly quote Twain months or even years after the fact. (The one exception to this latter rule: interview 123, based on notes taken during the interview but not published until nearly four years later.) I have also chosen to omit interviews that exist only in versions translated from English for the simple reason that there is no way to verify the accuracy of the translation or, in some cases, its retranslation back into English. As M. Thomas Inge notes in the introduction to such an interview, "the reader should bear in mind that what is provided here is a translation from the Russian of translations from the German of alleged interviews presumably conducted in English. The accuracy of the quotations, therefore, is problematic."[2] I list all known translated interviews in the appendix.

Surprisingly, only a fourth of the interviews in this edition have ever been reprinted from their original sources in late nineteenth- and early twentieth-century periodicals. Budd reprints forty-five Twain interviews in the April 1974 issue of *Studies in American Humor,* the winter 1977 and spring 1996 issues of *American Literary Realism,* and the fall 2003 issue of the *Mark Twain Journal.* Charles Neider reprints twenty interviews in *Life as I Find It: A Treasury of Mark Twain Rarities* (1960). While a few of these items (e.g., Rudyard Kipling's interview with Twain in Elmira in 1890) are well-known to scholars, most of them are lost in a biographical and critical blind spot. This edition is designed to repair this neglect.

In these interviews, Twain alluded to other writers (e.g., Howells, Gorky, Tennyson, Longfellow, Hawthorne, Dickens, Bret Harte) and discussed such topical issues as hazing and civil service reform. They offer rare glimpses of his wife and daughters; his in-laws, the Langdons and Cranes; his employees and domestic staff, especially George Griffin, Katy Leary, Patrick McAleer, Isabel Lyon, and Ralph Ashcroft; friends such as George Washington Cable, Rudyard Kipling, Dan Slote, Horace Bixby, Thomas Wentworth Higginson, and Henry H. Rogers; and other associates such as George Bernard Shaw, Whitelaw Reid, and Albert Bigelow Paine. In them he condemned every variety of imperialism—German imperialism in Africa, Russian imperialism in Asia, American imperialism in the Philippines, the Jameson Raid and the Boer War in South Africa—and scorned corrupt politicians and robber barons. He also discussed more enduring concerns, such as his lecture style, his writings, humor, his bankruptcy, race and racism, woman's suffrage, international copyright, and, yes, even interviews.

Mark Twain usually hated them. Often he required interviewers to paraphrase his comments rather than quote him directly because, as a professional author, he preferred to sell his words rather than give them away. Nor, he insisted, could an interview capture the flavor and nuance of his words. As he once wrote his friend Edward Bok, the editor of *Ladies' Home Journal:* "The moment 'talk' is put into print you recognize that it is not what it was when you heard it; you perceive that an immense something has disappeared from it. That is its soul. You have nothing but a dead carcass left on your hands. Color, play of feature, the varying modulations of the voice, the laugh, the smile, the informing inflections, everything that gave the body warmth, grace, friendliness and charm and commended it to your affections—or, at least, to your tolerance—is gone and nothing is left but a pallid, stiff and repulsive cadaver."[3] Still, Twain understood the utility of interviews for purposes of self-promotion. As Fred Lorch has explained, "In the early years, [Twain] customarily avoided reporters. They took up his time, interfered with his rest, and distorted his statements. They were his natural enemies. . . . But during the world tour his attitude toward reporters softened. He received them as often as his physical condition permitted, and received them graciously."[4] Not surprisingly, the vast majority of these interviews with Mark Twain were conducted during the final fifteen years of his life.

These documents are both oral performances in their own right and offer a new basis for evaluating contemporary response to Twain's writings. Because they are records of verbal conversations rather than texts written in Twain's hand, I have silently corrected obvious errors of spelling, as in names and titles of books, and I have regularized spelling and punctuation. I have also edited extraneous material from a few composite interviews whose focus is not solely on Twain. To avoid unnecessary repetition, when multiple versions of a single encounter with interviewers exist, I have reprinted the most complete version and then added a note for variations or alternative phrasing that appeared in other newspapers. For example, I have codified the press accounts of Twain's return to the United States after receiving an honorary doctoral degree from Oxford University in 1907, when he was met at the gangplank by dozens of journalists, by supplementing the report of the event in the *New York Herald* with versions of Twain's comments published in seven other newspapers. I occasionally found it necessary to exercise editorial discretion in correcting the published text of some interviews rather than merely reprinting them exactly as they first appeared. For example, interview 107 quotes Twain's praise for the "prominent" states-rights advocates "J. C. Cabbon" and "Thomas H. Bentham," when Twain referred no doubt to John C. Calhoun and Thomas Hart Benton. Other mistranscriptions hint at his Missouri drawl, his tendency to swallow the second syllable in a word. For example, in interview 101 the interviewer transcribes "Dane" for "Denny," and in interview 59 an Elmira reporter quotes Twain's references to "Galt" rather than "Galton." Other interviewers (49, 63) identify the same person—a nine-year-old child—by two different names: Effle Eisler and Elsie Leslie. The child actress Effle Eisler (b. 1858) would have been in her mid- to late thirties in the 1890s; but Elsie Leslie (b. 1881), child star of a theatrical version of *The Prince and the Pauper*, was often in the Clemens home in the early 1890s. In all such cases I have corrected the interviewer, and added a note when it seemed warranted.

I am indebted to many people for help and kindnesses in the preparation of this edition: Mark Woodhouse, Gretchen Sharlow, Jane McCone, and Michael Kiskis of Elmira College; Harriet Elinor Smith, Neda Salem, and Robert Hirst of the Mark Twain Project at the University of California, Berkeley; Anne Xu at the National Library of Australia; Matt Teorey, Holly Barnet-Sanchez, Robert Castillo, Megan Hoffman, and Tom Barrow at the University of New Mexico; Horst Kruse at Universität Münster; Sheldon Goldfarb of the University of British Columbia and Craig Howes of the University of Hawaii; Steve Courtney; Tom Quirk; Rebecca Scharnhorst; Anne R. Gibbons; and the staff at the University of Alabama Press. I am particularly delighted to have been able to complete this project with the help and blessing of Louis J. Budd. Upon his retirement from Duke University, Professor Budd donated his papers, including photocopies of newspaper interviews and in most cases transcriptions of them, to the Center for Mark Twain Studies at Elmira College.

Notes

1. *Mark Twain Encyclopedia,* ed. J. R. LeMaster et al. (New York: Garland, 1993), p. 402.

2. M. Thomas Inge, "Ten Minutes with Mark Twain: An Interview," *American Literary Realism* 15 (autumn 1982): 258.

3. Edward Bok, *The Americanization of Edward Bok* (New York: Scribner's, 1920), 205–6.

4. Fred Lorch, *The Trouble Begins at Eight: Mark Twain's Lecture Tours* (Ames: Iowa State University Press, 1966), 201.

Abbreviations

Auto (1959)	*Mark Twain's Autobiography,* ed. Charles Neider (New York: Harper and Row, 1959).
Auto (1990)	*Mark Twain's Own Autobiography,* ed. Michael Kiskis (Madison: University of Wisconsin Press, 1990).
Budd (1974)	Louis J. Budd, "Mark Twain Talks Mostly about Humor and Humorists," *Studies in American Humor* 1 (April 1974): 4–22.
Budd (1977)	Louis J. Budd, "A Listing of and Selection from Newspaper and Magazine Interviews with Samuel L. Clemens, 1874–1910," *American Literary Realism* 10 (winter 1977): 1–30.
Budd (1996)	Louis J. Budd, "Listing of and Selection from Newspaper and Magazine Interviews with Samuel L. Clemens: A Supplement," *American Literary Realism* 28 (spring 1996): 63–90.
Fatout	*Mark Twain Speaking,* ed. Paul Fatout (Iowa City: University of Iowa Press, 1976).
FE	Mark Twain, *Following the Equator* (Hartford: American Pub., 1897).
MT	Mark Twain.
MTE	*Mark Twain in Eruption,* ed. Bernard De Voto (New York: Harper, 1940).
MTHL	*Mark Twain-Howells Letters,* ed Henry Nash Smith and William Gibson. 2 vols. (Cambridge: Belknap, 1960).
MTL	*Mark Twain's Letters, 1835–1919,* ed. Edgar M. Branch et al. 6 vols. (Berkeley and Los Angeles: University of California Press, 1988).
Paine	Albert Bigelow Paine, *Mark Twain: A Biography* (New York: Harper, 1912).

Mark Twain: The Complete Interviews

1

The Growth of Mark Twain's Early Reputation, 1871–1884

Interviews 1–20

During this first flowering of his talent and reputation, Twain enjoyed many of his greatest literary successes, with the publication of *Roughing It* (1872), "Old Times on the Mississippi" (1875), *The Adventures of Tom Sawyer* (1876), *A Tramp Abroad* (1880), *The Prince and the Pauper* (1881), and *Life on the Mississippi* (1883). In addition, Twain collaborated with his Hartford neighbor Charles Dudley Warner on the novel *The Gilded Age* (1873) and began to write *Adventures of Huckleberry Finn*. He also expressed his reservations about his increasing literary celebrity in his satirical sketch "An Encounter with an Interviewer" (1874), in which he flummoxes a young reporter by answering his questions with a string of absurdities.

∽

1

[W. A. Croffut,[1]] "Brevities," *Chicago Evening Post,* 21 December 1871, 4; rpt. Croffut, *An American Procession, 1855–1914: A Personal Chronicle of Famous Men* (Boston: Little, Brown, 1931), 171–72.

"I'm glad the boy's going to get well;[2] I'm glad, and not ashamed to own it. For he will probably make the worst King Great Britain has ever had. And that's what the people need, exactly. They need a bad King. He'll be a blessing in disguise. He'll tax 'em, and disgrace 'em, and oppress 'em, and trouble 'em in a thousand ways, and they'll go into training for resistance. The best King they can have is a bad King. He'll cultivate their self-respect and self-reliance, and their muscle, and they'll finally kick him out of office and set up for themselves."

Notes to Interview 1

1. William A. Croffut (1835-1915), American poet and journalist.
2. MT is commenting on the recent recovery from typhoid fever of the Prince of Wales (1841-1910), who reigned as King Edward VII from 1901 until his death.

2

"Mark Twain as a Pedestrian," *Boston Evening Journal,* 14 November 1874, 2.

The stupendous feat of walking from Hartford to Boston, a distance of about one hundred miles, was, as the public are aware, really undertaken by the adventurous Mr. Samuel L. Clemens, better known as Mark Twain, and his pastor, Rev. J. H. Twichell.[1] It has long been the custom of these two gentlemen to take walks of about ten miles in the vicinity of Hartford for the purpose of enjoying a social chat and exchanging views on nothing in particular and everything in general, the result of which, to use Mark Twain's own words, is that Mr. Twichell sometimes gains ideas from his companion which he embodies in his sermons, and Mark Twain obtains information from his pastor which he works up into comical and humorous stories, and makes note of every joke which unconsciously falls from the clerical lips.

Mark Twain says he and Mr. Twichell always returned to Hartford, after one of these jaunts, with the jaw ache, but never footsore. To put an end to these country walks the "twain" resolved to undertake the trip to Boston, and have enough "jaw" to last them through the winter months. Accordingly they started from Hartford at 9 A.M. on Thursday, intending to keep along the old turnpike road and see the hamlets which the railroads had avoided, and reach Boston on Saturday. At 7 o'clock that evening they found themselves at Westford, having traveled 28 miles, where they passed the night. Before retiring they had a consultation and decided that their undertaking had developed into everything but a *pleasure* trip and was actually hard work, and as they started purely for pleasure and had promised Mr. Howells, editor of the *Atlantic*,[2] to dine at his house in Cambridge on Monday evening they concluded to take the cars at the nearest point and defer their pedestrian tour for a year or so. Friday morning they walked seven miles, drove ten miles and reached New Boston, where they took the Hartford and Erie train, arriving at Young's Hotel at 7 P.M. They subsequently proceeded to Mr. Howells' and partook of his hospitality, and returned to their hotel about midnight.

Mark Twain wishes it distinctly understood that he has not made a failure, and would have continued his trip had Mr. Twichell not have been under engagement to preach in Newton on Sunday morning. Mark says he wants a week to do the job comfortably, and is not anxious to take Weston's laurels away, because he considers that professional about as good as he or Mr. Twichell.[3]

Notes to Interview 2

1. The events of this trip are detailed in Paine, 527–29. Joseph Twichell (1838–1910), minister of the Asylum Hill Congregational Church in Hartford from 1865 until 1910, was MT's closest friend after 1868. He officiated at the marriage of MT

and Olivia Langdon Clemens (1845–1904) in 1870, the marriage of their daughter Clara (1874–1962) in 1909, and MT's funeral in 1910.

2. W. D. Howells (1837–1920), American novelist and critic, MT's closest literary friend, and editor of the *Atlantic Monthly* from 1871 to 1881.

3. Edward Payson Weston (1839–1929), a famous long-distance walker.

3

"Mark Twain: His Recent Walking Feat," *Hartford Times*, 14 November 1874.

As most readers of the *Times* are aware, Mark Twain, known to a select circle of relatives as Mr. Samuel L. Clemens, recently undertook, in company with his friend and pastor, Rev. J. H. Twichell, to achieve pedestrian fame. He started with Mr. Twichell from Hartford at 9 A.M. on Thursday last, intending to reach Boston by way of the old turnpike road yesterday. On Friday they hitched on to a train and reached Boston at seven o'clock in the evening, ahead of the time in which they had proposed to do the journey. Feeling certain that the public would like to know from the adventurous Twain's own lips the details of the journey, a *Times* reporter called on him at Young's Hotel last evening and enjoyed the following conversation with him:

Reporter—Mr. Clemens, the readers of our paper would like to learn the particulars of your journey from Hartford.

Mark Twain—Certainly, sir. We originally intended to leave Hartford on Monday morning and take a week to walk to Boston, just loafing along the road, and walking perhaps fifteen or eighteen miles a day, just for the sake of talking and swapping experiences, and inventing fresh ones, and simply enjoying ourselves in that way without caring whether we saw anything or found out anything on the road or not. We were to make this journey simply for the sake of talking. But then our plan was interrupted by Mr. Twichell having to go to a Congregational Conference of Ministers at Bridgeport, so we could not start till Thursday. We thought we would simply do two days, walking along comfortably all the time, and bring on night just where it chose to come, and about noon, Saturday, we would get a train that would take us into Boston. We got so ambitious, however, the first day, and felt so lively that we walked twenty-eight miles.

Reporter—Did you experience any fatigue at the end of that day's walk?

Twain—Well, at the end of that day when we stopped for the night I didn't feel fatigued, and I had no desire to go to bed, but I had a pain through my left knee which interrupted my conversation with lockjaw every now and then. The next day at twelve past five we started again, intending to do forty miles that day, believing we could still make Boston in three days. But we didn't make the forty miles. Finding it took me three or four hours to walk seven miles, as my knee was still so stiff that it was walking on stilts—or, if you can imagine such a thing, it was though I had wooden legs with pains in them—we just got a team and drove to the nearest railway station, hitched on, and came up here.

Reporter—You could doubtless have accomplished the journey on foot, sir?

Twain—Oh, our experience undoubtedly demonstrates the possibility of walking. By and by, when we get an entire week to make this pedestrian excursion, we mean to make it.

Reporter—When you renew the experiment, do you intend to follow any different plan?

Twain—No, I would just follow the old Hartford and Boston stage-road of old times. It takes you through a lot of quiet, pleasant villages, away from the railroads, over a road that now has so little travel that you don't have to be skipping out into the bushes every moment to let a wagon go by, because no wagon goes by. And then you see you can talk all you want, with nobody to listen to what you say; you can have it all to yourself, and express your opinions pretty freely.

Reporter—Were the opportunities for refreshment by the way good?

Twain—Well, I suppose pretty fair, especially if you are walking all day.

Reporter—Do you intend to lecture in Boston, now you are here?

Twain—No, not at all. I simply intend to go back home again. I shall lie over Sunday to rest, and let Mr. Twichell have a chance to preach at Newton. You may as well say that we expect hereafter to walk up to Boston, and after we get into the habit of this sort of thing, we may extend it perhaps to New Orleans or San Francisco. Really, though, there was no intention on our part to excite anybody's envy or make Mr. Weston feel badly, for we were not preparing for a big walk so much as for a delightful walk.

Mark was holding his napkin between his forefinger and thumb all the time, standing in the doorway of Room 9, to which a select party of his friends were impatiently awaiting his return to the table, and so our reporter abstained from asking him, as he intended and ought to have done, as to whether a bottle-holder would not be a good feature in his next trip, and various other important queries. Thanking him he accordingly withdrew.

4

"Political Views of a Humorist," *New York Herald*, 28 August 1876, 3.

Elmira, N.Y., August 26, 1876—After a rather dusty ride of five miles uphill from Elmira, the *Herald* representative met Samuel L. Clemens (Mark Twain), temporarily residing at Quarry Hill farm,[1] the property of one of the Langdon family, into which Mark happily married. He took me to his studio, an octagonal structure, still further up hill, and commanding a romantic view of Elmira and its surroundings for miles.[2]

Mark was attired in a summer dress of snowy white, not dissimilar to that worn by Abraham Lincoln when the same correspondent interviewed the great lamented at his house in Springfield, Ill., in the memorable campaign of 1860, when Lincoln was first elected President of the United States.

Herald Correspondent—Well, Mark, now we are in your cozy and breezy studio, suppose I interview you in regard to your opinions respecting the present political situation?

Mark Twain—Politics are rather out of my line, yet not outside of my interest. I am not much of a party man, but I have opinions. I should never have pushed them before the public, but if you want to catechise me I will answer, but I want easy questions—questions which a plain answer will meet.

"You shall have them. First, which platform do you prefer?"

"That is easily answered. Platforms are of such secondary importance that I have not thought it necessary to build up a preference. In most essentials the creeds of both parties are good enough for me.

"But there is something back of the written creeds which is important. For instance, inflation and repudiation may be glossed over in a creed, but there are a good many erring people who want these things and would vote for them."

"What do you think is more important than platforms?"

"I think the men are. There used to be a party cry, 'Measures, not men.' That was in an honester day. We need to reverse that now. When you get below the politician scum—or above it, perhaps one ought to say—you will find that the solid men in both parties are equally good and equally well meaning. Both will furnish platforms which the country can survive and progress under. But of what use are these excellent platforms if the men elected upon them shamelessly ignore them and make them a dead letter? A sound and good democratic platform was powerless to save New York from the ravages of the Tweed gang;[3] an excellent republican platform has no more been able to save the country from the ravages of the present administration's highwaymen than the pasting the four gospels on a bad man's back would be to save him from the tropical end of eternity. Platforms are not the essential things now—men are."

"Then how do you judge of your men?"

"Only by common report and their letters of acceptance."

"Which candidate do you prefer upon these grounds?"

"Hayes.[4] He talks right out upon the important issues. You cannot mistake what he means concerning civil service, second term and the honest payment of the national debt. If you can understand what Mr. Tilden means it is only because you have got more brains than I have,[5] but you don't look it. Mr. Tilden is a very able man; therefore I hold that he could have made himself understood. Why didn't he? Because one-half of his party believe in one thing and the other half in another, I suppose, and it was necessary to be a little vague. But Mr. Hendricks is not vague.[6] He is in no hurry to have the national debt paid."

"Is there a democrat whom you would have preferred to Hayes?"

"Yes, Charles Francis Adams[7]—a pure man, a proved statesman. I would vote for him in a minute. I wouldn't need to know what his platform was; the fact that he stood upon it would be sufficient proof to me that it was a righteous one. I want to see an honest government established once more. I mean to vote for Hayes because I believe, from his own manner of talking and from all I can hear of his character and his history, that he will appoint none but honest and capable men to office. I don't care two cents what party they belong to, I never tried to get a political office for but one man and I forgot to ask him what his politics were, but he was a clean man and mighty capable. Mr. Tilden is an old politician, dyed in the wool. History has tried hard to teach us that we can't have good government under politicians. Now, to go and stick one at the very head of the government couldn't be wise. You know that yourself."

"People speak well of both candidates, don't they?"

"I will tell you how it looks to me. I read a lot of newspapers of both creeds every day. The republicans tell me a great many things which Hayes has done; the democratic papers explain why Tilden didn't do a great many things. They keep on apologizing and apologizing all the time. I think that the woman or the candidate that has to be apologized for is a suspicious person. So do you. Now, let me urge you as an old friend to vote for Hayes—a man you don't have to apologize for."

"Well, but what do you think—"

"No, excuse me. You can't get any political elaborations out of me. I simply want to see the right man at the helm. I don't care what his party creed is. I want a man who isn't near sighted. I want a man who will not go on seeing angels from heaven in such buzzards as Delano, Belknap, Babcock,[8] and the rest of that lot, long after 40,000,000 of ordinary people have detected and come to loathe them. I want to see a man in the chief chair who can not only tell a buzzard when he sees it but will promptly wring its neck. I feel satisfied that Mr. Hayes is such a man; I am not satisfied that Mr. Tilden is. There, now, let us take a smoke. My opinions are important only to me. If they were important to others we would spread them all over the *Herald*. Here is your pipe. Now we will talk of things less harrowing."

Notes to Interview 4

1. MT spent almost every summer between 1871 and 1889 and the summers of 1895 and 1903 at the farm on East Hill a mile from Elmira, New York, owned by his

sister-in-law Susan Langdon Crane (1836–1924) and her husband, Theodore Crane (1831–89).

2. In 1874 Susan Crane had an octagonal study built for MT on a bluff overlooking the Chemung River valley about a hundred yards from the main house at Quarry Farm. In 1952 the study was moved to the Elmira College campus for display.

3. William Marcy (Boss) Tweed (1823–78) headed the corrupt Democratic political machine in New York City known as Tammany Hall.

4. Rutherford B. Hayes (1822–93) was elected U.S. president in 1876 in a contested election and served one term (1877–81).

5. Samuel Tilden (1814–86), the Democratic candidate for president in 1876, won the popular vote but lost the disputed election in the House of Representatives.

6. Thomas Hendricks (1819–85), the Democratic candidate for vice president in 1876, advocated a "soft money" policy.

7. Charles Francis Adams Jr. (1835–1915), grandson and great-grandson of presidents, son of the U.S. minister to Great Britain from 1861 to 1868, and brother of the historian Henry Adams (1838–1918), was the chair of the Massachusetts Board of Railroad Commissioners. See also *MTL*, 6:596n2.

8. Columbus Delano (1809–96), secretary of the interior from 1870 until 1875, resigned from Grant's cabinet amid allegations of corruption in the Indian Service; William W. Belknap (1829–90), secretary of war in the Grant administration, resigned in 1876 amid allegations of corruption; Oliver E. Babcock (1835–84), private secretary to President Grant, was indicted in 1876 for complicity in the whiskey revenue frauds.

5

"A Connecticut Carpet-bag," *New York World*, 24 December 1876, 2; excerpted in the *Elmira Daily Advertiser*, 29 December 1876, 2.

Mr. Mark Twain has been "hanging around" New York with a great deal of mischief in his eye for several days. He says positively that he came down from Hartford with no other purpose than to buy a bootjack for the holidays and meekly to eat his atom of the New England dinner,[1] but the officials at the St. James Hotel, where he has retained a bed, affirm that his goings out and comings in have been, if not mysterious enough to excite suspicion, at all events marked, and it is not denied by anyone that the sugar-loaf sealskin cap with which he has seen fit to adorn his head is quite large enough to hold a very fair supply of "papers and documents" in addition to its usual miscellaneous cargo. It is doubtless well remembered that Mr. Mark Twain took what with other men might be called an "active part" in the Republican canvass last fall—so active that Rumor, with her 18,762 tongues, loudly proclaimed his zeal to be begotten of an ambition to be appointed Statistician of Deaths or to some other office congenial with his temperament. His movements since the campaign have therefore been watched with some interest, not to say alarm, by all lovers of political veracity. The exact date of his arrival in this city is shrouded in the deepest mystery. Either he registered under an assumed name, affixed his solemn signature to a napkin and announced his arrival by "chucking" it at the head of the dignified clerk, or, as is quite likely, avoided the form altogether, for certain it is that neither the name nor the well-known initials "M. T." appear upon the hotel records. Possibly he might have tarried here even longer and escaped unperceived but for the absurd dignity of a waiter, who said he'd be vummed [damned] if he was a-going to crawl around on the floor and pull tacks out of the carpet with his teeth, "not to please no gentleman as he ever waited on." This, to use a parliamentary form, "gave him away," and after incessant waiting and watching a reporter of *The World* succeeded in intercepting him, and, it may be said, in frustrating any contemplated nefarious design, as Mr. Twain began rapidly to pack his valise on the instant of the reporter's arrival, and smiling the sad, wan smile of an unearthed coyote, fled with all possible speed to the depot.

At the moment of his discovery Mr. Twain may not have been reading a special dispatch from Zach Chandler,[2] but he was certainly not reading the Bible. It may not have been a note from Kellogg instructing him to indite a hymn for the downtrodden Republican negroes of Louisiana that he crumpled into a wad behind his back on seeing the reporter,[3] and subsequently devoured in mouthfuls, his eyes meanwhile fixed religiously on the gas fixtures overhead, but this by no means proves that it wasn't; indeed, there was an air of guilt about Mr. Twain that no extraneous observations about the state of the Sabbath school in New Zealand availed in the least to dispel.

"Mr. Twain," said the reporter, "what have you to say on the political situation?"

"Sir," replied Mr. Twain, bundling a long white garment into his valise, "it is mixed."

"And?" said the reporter.

"I didn't mix it, and I don't know who did and I can't straighten it, and I don't know who can, and—what do you think, sir, of having Broadway with—"

"Excuse me, Mr. Twain, now there are the Southern outrages—"

"Never heard of them; never, never, never."

"Never heard of them, Mr. Twain?"

"No, sir, I never did (by this time Mr. Twain had one side of his bag packed, and was sitting on it); ain't in my line; let's talk about something else."

"Mr. Twain, I understand you voted the Republican ticket?"

"Yes, sir; where's the whiskbroom? Ah, here it is, in you go. Sir, would you journey through life swiftly and in peace?"

"Yes," replied the reporter; "but Mr. Twain—"

"Never mind the buts. You must make a rule of packing the whiskbroom first. Now for the pipe and the Bible, and there I'm all packed; must go; got to catch a train in three minutes; good bye;" and in a twinkling Mr. Twain was on his way to Hartford.

The reporter turned sadly to leave, when the pensive voice of the Republican politician was again heard, and turning round he beheld Mr. Twain with his body and his head out of the elevator.

"I say, now, you had better not print the information I've given you."

"Why not?"

"Because it's private, and because if you do I'll kill one of the editors you can't spare; I will, I will. Merry Christmas."

Notes to Interview 5

1. On 22 December MT had attended the New England Club dinner in New York and delivered a brief address on "the weather of New England." See Fatout, 100–103.

2. Zachariah Chandler (1813–79), secretary of the interior from 1875 to 1877, managed Rutherford B. Hayes's presidential campaign in 1876.

3. William Pitt Kellogg (1830–1918), Republican U.S. senator (1868–72, 1877–83) and governor of Louisiana (1873–77).

6

"Mark Twain's Tenets," *Boston Globe,* 19 March 1877, p. 3, col. 2; rpt. *New York Daily Graphic,* 20 March 1877, 131.

While the well-known humorist Mark Twain was stopping at the Parker House recently,[1] a reporter of the *Globe* called on him with no particular object in view. After being shown into Room 168 several moments elapsed before the author of *The Innocents Abroad* became aware of his presence.[2] Mr. Twain was seen to be seated in a large easy chair, with a Boston paper before him, smoking a cigar. Finally, the porter who accompanied the reporter in question handed Mr. Twain the latter's card, and Mr. Twain immediately whirled his chair around, told the pleasant-faced porter to withdraw from the room, and asked his caller to be seated. "You see for yourself," said Mr. Twain, puffing away at his cigar, "that I'm pretty near heaven—not theologically, of course, but by the hotel standard." "Your room is rather high up, Mr. Twain, but it appears very cozy. There is an elevator, I believe, is there not?"

Mr. T.—Doubtless there is; all first class hotels manage to have elevators. The fact is, I detest elevators, and I'm not ashamed to own it.

R.—Then you like walking?

Mr. T.—Much better. I do my own walking and talking and write my own books, which is more than every one can say.

R.—You don't believe in plagiarizing then?

Mr. T.—No, sir; I never plagiarize—unless I can do it successfully.

R.—Do I understand that you never have done it?

Mr. T.—No, sir; but that was probably because I wasn't successful at it.

R.—Do you believe everything that you related in *Innocents Abroad?*

Mr. T.—Absolutely everything.

R.—Do you think that the public in general do?

Mr. T.—Of course; why should they not? I related everything as I saw it.

R.—If I remember rightly you mention in *Innocents Abroad* that when you went into a hairdresser's in Paris to get shaved, he loosened your "hide" and lifted you out of the chair. Is that a correct statement, Mr. Twain?

Mr. T.—Certainly, correct to the chair; but you must remember that "statement" don't amount to much in any country—but particularly in this country.

R.—But you believe in them, nevertheless?

Mr. T.—Not even if they have the official mark. I have been trying to believe in the statements, which have been sent from Washington from time to time, but I can't make up my mind. I must tell you right here that my digestion is not so good as formerly.

R.—May I ask you what you think of President Hayes' Cabinet?

Mr. T.—It appears to me that he has made excellent selections; probably if I knew the men he has chosen immediately I might think right to the contrary.

R.—In that case I should think that you would eulogize them all the more.

Mr. T.—I never eulogize except when I don't know a person. It seems to me that the safest way is to eulogize a person you don't know.

R.—May I ask what are your politics, Mr. Twain?

Mr. T.—I am neither a Republican nor Democrat—for any length of time. Vacillation is my particular forte. During the last election, when the country thought Tilden would surely be elected President, I was a strong Tildenite; but as soon as I discovered that everything was against him, I was strong in my support for Hayes.

R.—Mr. Twain, do I infer from what you have just said, that you voted for both men?

Mr. T.—Why, of course; no one recognized me. I did all my voting in New York. I wasn't tolerated in Hartford; as soon as the people discovered that I was exerting all my strength for Hayes, they advised me kindly to leave the State. I went immediately to New York City and cast my vote for Tilden. And yet, people call this a republic!

R.—May I ask what you are now politically, Mr. Twain?

Mr. T.—Politics have completely died out within me. They don't take to me or I to them. Since I have come in possession of a conscience I begin to see through things.

R.—Then you have not had a conscience until lately?

Mr. T.—No, sir; it is only recently that I discovered it. It doesn't prove so great a blessing as I supposed it would. Only a day or two ago I exhausted my second deposit at the bank.

R.—I don't quite understand what you mean.

Mr. T.—Why, simply this: Every one who knows that I have a conscience takes me now for a philanthropist.

R.—Do you refer to bad debts?

Mr. T.—Exactly; or, rather, I might say that they are hotel bills, which I thought were cancelled years ago. As I told you a few moments ago, since I discovered that I had a conscience I begin to see the right and wrong of things.

R.—Do you like Boston, Mr. Twain?

Mr. T.—Very well; but there seems to be a good many issues floating around here; but I suppose this is peculiar to the city. I am going to the Tabernacle this evening.[3]

R.—Are you going merely out of curiosity, or are you going because your conscience says you must?

Mr. T.—I'm going for mere recreation. Religion often times soothes the mind and eases the conscience even if it doesn't penetrate deep into the memory. But I can't talk any more with you today. I have already said too much, I'm afraid, so goodbye.

Notes to Interview 6

1. Founded by Harvey D. Parker in 1855, the Parker House is the longest continuously operating hotel in the United States and one of the most famous hotels in the world. Its guests have included the members of the Saturday Club (e.g., Emerson, Hawthorne, Lowell, Holmes, Whittier, and Longfellow) in the late 1850s and Charles Dickens in 1867.

2. *The Innocents Abroad* (1869), MT's first long work and a popular, commercial, and critical success.

3. The Moody Sankey Tabernacle, with a seating capacity of about six thousand and located about a mile southwest of the Parker House on Tremont Street in Boston, opened 25 January 1877 and hosted a religious revival through May 1877 conducted by the American evangelist Dwight L. Moody (1837-99) and the gospel singer Ira David Sankey (1840-1908). The Boston Cyclorama and the Boston Center for the Arts were subsequently erected on the site.

7

Baltimore Gazette, c. 27 April 1877; rpt. "Mark Twain's Opinion," *New York World,* 28 April 1877, 5.

Last evening a representative of the *Gazette* called to see his old friend Mark Twain at Guy's Hotel. Conversation turned on the war in Europe. Mr. Clemens had "been there"; is on terms of familiarity with all the crowned heads, and seemed to feel pained that he had not been personally advised that the Czar would so soon throw off his coat.[1] "I think Nick might have notified me—by cable at his own expense—so that I might have been in on the ground floor. See what a clever turn I could have made in grain. I'm strongly tempted to get a sutlership in the Turkish army and wreak my vengeance on the Bear."

"Do you think Russia will move first on Silistria or Kalaiat?"

"Well, Nicholas is a long-headed man, but if he doesn't keep a sharp lookout all his fat will be in the fire. But I can't keep the run of the movements by the cable dispatches. Can't locate the places on Krackyourjawoff via Bullyboyyouknow onto Crushemailibet. Then I look on my European map and I don't find the places. A European map is like a blackboard with nothing on it, leaving the industrious student of contemporaneous history to fill in the outlines. The hard part of it is that they'll go on fighting just as though good maps were to be had for the asking."

"Mr. Clemens, I think you are too severe on mapmakers. The *Evening Bugleblast*, of this city, today publishes a most carefully prepared and readable map of the seat of war. I have a copy of it here—"

"Well, I'm sorry for you, old fellow. I didn't know that a strong cigar would affect you that way. You've got 'em on you bad. Why, that's a map of the St. Louis hotel in ruins."

From the war in Europe to the rumpus in the Black Hills was an easy turn.[2]

"Having high times in the Hills, Mr. Clemens?"

"Yes; and I tell you my heart bleeds for the poor prospector. There may be gold there—I suppose there is—but there isn't the big money we hear of. The men who dig gold out of the Black Hills have got to work for it and earn it. The glitter gets into print; the tales of hardships and bitter disappointment don't. When a man comes in and tells about rich finds you must stop to consider what sort of a man he is. If he had been making a dollar or two a day, and hits on ten in the diggings, he thinks he's struck a fortune, and it isn't a bad thing; but a man with a good situation, a paying business or a thriving farm had better keep down to his work. The average man would do better to dig for clams than to go hunting for gold in the Hills. But speaking of mining and getting in big licks—in the best days of California mining, the best of it wasn't worth more than $200 a day to any digger. Now a man would have to hammer away for some time before he could make a fortune even at that and there were not many who struck it that rich. The best-paying mining is in the 'pockets,' and outside of Calaveras County, California—Jackass Gulch and Jackass Hill—there's no other pocket mining in the world. By the way, the scene of our new play—Bret Harte's and mine—is in Calaveras County. There is no other place that would justify *Ah Sin* in picking out such a mass of metal."[3]

"Of course you think you've struck it in *Ah Sin*."

"Well, that remains to be seen. You can't tell anything about a play until you see it played. We know we've got a good character in Ah Sin; whether it is in the right setting is another matter. We've put good work on the play. It may have to be pushed, but expect to make it go. You know we are rehearsing it at Ford's Opera House now,[4] and it promises well, but the test will come when we put it before an audience. We bring it out in Washington on the 7th of May and open in Baltimore on the 14th."[5]

The reporter had something less than half a mile of questions wherewith to rack Mr. Clemens's brain, but he did all the talking, and the reporter had to give him respectful audience. Mr. Clemens saw a way out of the difficulty.

"Just say that you asked me the questions and I couldn't answer them."

Notes to Interview 7

1. MT apparently confuses Nicholas I (1796-1855), Russian czar during the Russo-Turkish war of 1828-29, with Czar Alexander II (1818-81), who reigned from 1855 until his death. The Russo-Turkish War of 1877-78, essentially a conflict between the Balkan states and their Russian partners on the one hand and the Ottoman Empire on the other, ended with a Russian military victory.

2. The Great Sioux War of 1876-77 culminated in the Battle of the Little Big Horn on 25 June 1877.

3. The play was largely based on "A Monte Flat Pastoral: How Old Man Plunkett Went Home" (1874), a story by MT's collaborator Bret Harte (1836-1902).

4. John T. Ford (1829-94), owner of Ford's Theater in Washington, site of Lincoln's assassination in 1865, operated four theaters in Washington and Baltimore.

5. *Ah Sin* debuted at the National Theater in Washington from 7 to 12 May and at Ford's Opera House in Baltimore from 14 to 19 May 1877.

8

Gath,[1] "Mark Twain and His Chinaman," *New York Daily Graphic*, 3 May 1877, 438.

I spent part of my days, or rather nights, with Marcus the Second at Guy's old hotel, where the frogs and fried perch were just in season. Parsloe was there every day—the actor who is to play Ah Sin.[2]

"Look at him," said Mark, "ain't he a lost and wandering Chinee by nature? See those two front teeth of Parsloe, just separated far enough to give him the true Mongrel look."

"Yes," said Parsloe, "when the fellow knocked out that middle tooth some years ago I was mad. But now I ain't mad one bit."

"There," said Mark, "There is the instinct of art. He would lose his whole jaw, his dyspepsia or anything to be an artist. Parsloe's a devoted fellow."

The piece is to rally around the title character. *Ah Sin* will be the title. Nobody but Clemens and Parsloe superintending, Mr. Harte, the associate author, being out of range,[3] they selected Ford's Theatre for several reasons, partly because it was out of the way, and mainly because Mr. Ford is a hard, accommodating, painstaking manager of great experience, whose family has tastes like his own, all of them with the dramatic instinct. Twain works at this piece with a regular, slow, shrewd, journeyman's hand and mind. But I think he will never make a partnership piece again. He has written two characters in it.[4]

Notes to Interview 8

1. George Alfred Townsend, aka Gath (1841–1914), was one of the first syndicated newspaper correspondents.
2. Charles T. Parsloe (1836–98), American comic actor.
3. MT and Harte had quarreled in February 1877. See *Selected Letters of Bret Harte*, ed. Gary Scharnhorst (Norman and London: University of Oklahoma Press, 1997), 145–49. See also n. 5 to interview 84.
4. MT wrote Howells on 3 August 1877 that he had "been putting in a deal of hard work on that play in New York, & have left hardly a foot-print of Harte in it anywhere" (*MTHL*, 1:192). In 1907, however, MT allowed that Harte's "part was the best part of it" (*MTE*, 278). On Howells, see n. 2 to interview 2.

9

"The Start for Germany," *New York Times*, 12 April 1878, 8.

The first name on the passenger list of the *Holsatia*, that called yesterday, was "Hon. Bayard Taylor, United States Envoy Extraordinary and Minister Plenipotentiary,"[1] then followed Mrs. Bayard Taylor and Miss Lilian Taylor, Mrs. Murat Halstead, Miss Jenny Halstead, Master Robert Halstead, Mr. Samuel L. Clemens and family....

The new Minister was smoking another of those large cigars, one eye upon the trunks, with the other watching the wreaths of smoke that puffed to leeward, when a peculiar-looking caravan drove down the pier. It might once have been a coach, but it had been transformed into a sort of pyramid on wheels. As it stopped, and a door opened in its side, a gentleman and two ladies alighted, drawing after them a nurse and a large number of children, whom they carefully counted. The lifting of a few dozen trunks from the top of the pyramid disclosed the Gilsey House coach, shining with gilt.[2] It has brought to the steamer Mr. and Mrs. Samuel L. Clemens, a lady friend of Mrs. Clemens, several children, and a nurse. Mark Twain, the innocent, who was soon to be abroad again, wore a small black silk cap, which, as one of the bystanders said, made him "look like a brakeman." Having checked off his family into the saloon, he came out upon the deck to shake hands with the new Minister.

"Where's Halstead?" said the innocent.[3]

"I don't know," replied the Minister. "I haven't seen him today. I left him about 1 o'clock this morning."

"One o'clock!" echoed Mark Twain. "Why, you ought to have been in bed by that time."

"I know it," replied the Minister, "and I begged Reid not to keep it up the last night,[4] but he insisted; and they were all so jolly, I couldn't get away. I've had a hard time of it the last two weeks."

"I've had just as hard a time," said Mark. "I've been railroading for two weeks and taking mixed drinks. I suppose you stick to one thing all the time—straight."

"Well, I don't know," said Bayard Taylor, "what do you call straight drinks?"

"Coffee," said Mark, "or whisky, if you drink it all the time."

A heavy increase in the shower here rudely broke up what promised to be an important State communication.

Mr. Samuel L. Clemens, while in one of the fits of sober earnest that strike him occasionally, said that he was going to Germany partly for the health of his family, and partly to give him the opportunity to write, which he finds he cannot do well at home.

"I am going to the most out-of-the-way place in Germany I can find," said he, "fifty miles away from any railroad, where I can sleep more than half the time. We have not rented our house in Hartford so, if we get tired soon, there is nothing to prevent us from coming back at any time; but, if we like it, we may stay for two or three years."

On being asked whether he had more *Innocents Abroad* in mind, he replied: "I am going to do some writing. I have been contemplating it for a long time, and now I'm in for it. But it will not be any more *Innocents Abroad*. That is done up and done for."

"You'd better travel this time as the Sage of Hartford," suggested Minister Taylor.

"I will," said Mark, "or the Thyme, or any other herb."

Mark Twain was accompanied to the steamer by the historical character "Dan," with whom every reader of *The Innocents Abroad* is well acquainted. "Dan" is Mr. Daniel Slote, a wholesale stationer, of William street, and the manufacturer of the "Mark Twain Scrapbooks."[5] Dan engaged Mark's staterooms several weeks ago, anonymously, and as he confessed "was warned by Sam that he must be careful what he said to those newspaper fellows."

Dan insisted upon saying that Sam is one of the best fellows in the world, and the funniest; and the latter statement was so evidently true that it carried the other through without question.

"I know him from top to bottom," said Dan. "When we were out on the *Quaker City* expedition, he was the hardest-working man I ever saw.[6] Why, out in Egypt, where the fleas were so thick you couldn't breath without swallowing a thousand, that man used to sit up and write, write, half the night. I used to have go get my clothes off in a second and hustle into bed before any of the fleas had a chance to get between the sheets, and as I was vainly trying to get to sleep, I'd say to Clemens, 'Sam, how the deuce can you stand it to write out there among the fleas?' 'Oh, I'm all right,' Sam would say. 'They've got a railroad track eaten out around both ankles, and they keep in that pretty well, so I don't bother with them.'"

Mr. Taylor went below an hour before the sailing time to avoid the rain that at 1 o'clock came down in torrents. Mark Twain, however, having soothed the youngest baby into a quiet state, went down to the pier to have a last chat with Dan, who by the way is the image of his picture in *The Innocents Abroad*. They were at once surrounded by an army of press representatives, one of whom went so far as to ask Twain, "Are you going to Europe?" a thing that in the most matter-of-fact newspaper might safely have been taken for granted under the circumstances. Somebody spoke of the quantities of flowers the passengers had taken into the saloon.

"Yes," said Mark. "It's all nonsense; they run it into the ground. I was talking with some of my relations about it the other day and told them what I thought about it, particularly at funerals. They said they had intended to give me a good send-off when I died; but if I didn't like the flowers they wouldn't send any. I told them that was all right. I'd rather have ice anyhow."

Our new Minister appeared upon deck again. He walked to the stern and looked anxiously up the street. There was nobody in sight but an old lady selling beaded pin-cushions and a peanut man. It was not either of these that the new Minister wished to see. He kept up his anxious look while Mark Twain, still standing upon the wharf, told how all the ocean steamers feed their passengers well, except one line that he named, which he said still gives its passengers the same fare it did 30 years ago, invariably giving them boiled rice and stewed prunes every Thursday for the benefit of their health. . . .

Notes to Interview 9

1. The *Holsatia*, on which MT enjoyed a "very pleasant trip" to Europe, according to chapter 1 of *A Tramp Abroad*, was built in 1868 and reengined for the Hamburg American line in 1877. See also *Auto* (1959), 292–93. Bayard Taylor (1825–78), travel writer, novelist, and U.S. minister to Germany during the last months of his life. See *Mark Twain's Notebooks and Journals*, ed. Frederick Anderson et al. (Berkeley: University of California Press, 1975), 2:254, 268–69.

2. The Gilsey House was a fashionable hotel at the corner of Broadway and West Twenty-ninth Street in New York.

3. Murat Halstead (1829–1908), editor of the *Cincinnati Commercial*.

4. Whitelaw Reid (1837–1912), managing editor (1869–72) and editor in chief (1872–1905) of the *New York Tribune* and U.S. ambassador to England (1905–12).

After 1882 Reid was often the target of MT's private vituperation. Ironically, Reid as ambassador in 1907 forwarded the invitation to MT to receive an honorary degree from Oxford University.

5. Dan Slote (d. 1882) was MT's cabinmate on the *Quaker City* voyage (see n. 6 this interview) and one of the "boys" in *The Innocents Abroad* (1869), MT's first travel book. Their friendship ended in 1881 in a dispute over money.

6. MT and more than seventy other passengers aboard the *Quaker City*—a sidewheeler weighing some nineteen hundred tons—steamed to Europe, the Holy Land, and Egypt between 8 June and 19 November 1867 in the first organized tour of the region. The fifty travel letters MT published in the San Francisco *Alta California* during the voyage became the basis of *The Innocents Abroad*.

10

Richard Whiteing,[1] "Mark Twain Interviewed," *New York World*, 11 May 1879, 1.

Paris, April 25—The sojourn of a certain distinguished American in Paris ought to receive more notice than I have lately given it. I sent you a meager sketch of a speech made by Mark Twain at a club dinner. I now forward, by way of atonement, a full account of his conversation in a *tête-à-tête*. I called on him at the Hotel de Normandie, one of the brand-new ones near the lately completed Avenue de l'Opera, where he leads a very retired life. He is seldom seen in society and he declines all formal invitations.

I first asked him about the book he is now writing and he gave me the following answer:

"It is a gossipy volume of travel, and will be similar to *The Innocents Abroad* in size, and similarly illustrated. I shall draw some of the pictures for it myself. However, that need not frighten anybody, for I shall draw only a few. I think the book will not be finished in time for the summer season, but will appear in the fall. I call it a gossipy volume, and that is what it is. It talks about anything and everything, and always drops a subject the moment my interest in it begins to slacken. It is as discursive as a conversation; it has no more restraints or limitations than a fireside talk has. I have been drifting around on an idle, easy-going tramp—so to speak—for a year, stopping when I pleased, moving on when I got ready. My book has caught the complexion of the trip. In a word, it is a book written by one loafer for a brother loafer to read."[2]

The mention of the book naturally led to the question of international copyright, of which he said: "I think we can't tell much about the matter yet. I hope the convention of authors, which is to hold its second annual meeting in June, in London, will be able to give it a start.[3] No doubt the authors could have achieved international copyright before this if the publishers had kept their fingers out of the pie. But they wouldn't. I suppose that when you come to look this business fairly in the face the publisher and not the author is the party mainly interested, anyhow, in the life or death of international copyright—on our side of the water. We have only about twenty-five authors whose books are usually republished in England; the works of six or eight of these are usually translated and published on the Continent. Some of these authors write a book a year, some a book in three or four years; altogether they turn out an average of fifteen books a year, say. With a foreign copyright on these fifteen books, the bunch would be worth $7,000 or $8,000 in the English market perhaps. If one author wrote the whole fifteen it would be worth his while to long for international copyright; but he writes only one of them, and his fifteenth of the sum is not a big enough matter to set him wild about international copyright. With our publishers the thing is different. There are only a few of these firms—you may count them on your fingers—and they are not restricted to twelve salable foreign books a year; no, the salable foreign books which they can seize and publish every year without paying for the privilege mount into the hundreds. If English publishers rob American authors of $8,000 a year, under the present system American publishers rob foreign authors of at least $100,000 a year, to put it well within bounds. An American publisher who saves his tenth of this sum annually through the present system will naturally work harder to preserve the system than the American author will to break it down, since he would only get $200 or $250 a year out of England under a new system and only loses that sum annually under the present one. I cannot name six American authors who can say their pockets are perceptibly worse off without international copyright than they would be with it. For our books do not sell enormously in foreign lands. We could not starve an English publisher by compelling him to pay us full copyright; we could not perceptibly enrich him by making him a present of our books. On the other hand, observe what ship-loads of books our publishers turn out yearly bearing the names of Macaulay,[4] George Eliot, Dickens, Thackeray, Tennyson, Reade,[5] Black,[6] Victor Hugo, and others. I have not space for the list even of this order of authors without touching those other long lists of authors who deal in school books, the sciences and the arts. Where an American author is interested 10 cents' worth in compassing international copyright the American publisher is interested a hundred dollars' worth in blocking his project. I speak only of the American author's pecuniary interest in the matter, not his moral interest. Now you see what an uphill game the struggle for international copyright is likely to be. Our publishers are rich. They are a compact body, they have business ability, they know how to use a lobby. Moreover, they are always powerfully backed by a Congress of innocents at Washington whom they persuade without the least trouble that an effect of international copyright would be to raise the price of foreign books. There are some Congressmen whom they can't convince of this but they convince his constituents and that amounts to the same thing. I would like to see international copyright succeed out of simple justice to the foreign authors. It could be of no particular benefit to American authors, for we have no market worth speaking of but England, and she and her publishers give us all the copyright protection we need, partly by law and partly by courtesy. If an American author stands upon English soil when his book is issued in England, his copyright is as good there as it is at home. It is better, in fact, in some minor particulars. Advance sheets usually have the effect of copyright, too. This is by mutual understanding among the publishers. Some of our American publishers respect the advance sheet system also. Two or three of my books enjoy full copyright in England. Mr. Story's books are copyrighted there; also Joaquin Miller's and others whose names do not occur to me at the moment.[7] In Germany Baron Tauchnitz buys my books, and pays for them.[8] On the whole I think American authors are pretty fairly treated by the foreigners. They ought to do all they can to get fair treatment in America for foreign authors, and I am perfectly sure they will. While they have nothing that can fairly be called a pecuniary interest in the matter, they have an interest which is still stronger, the moral one, and the pecuniary interest will come. We shall number a population of a hundred millions before a very great while, and among them some authors who will be widely read abroad. It will be much easier to secure international copyright now, as far as America is concerned, than it will be then."

Finally came the inevitable question, "Why have you never written a book about England?"

"I have spent a great deal of time in England (your question is not a new one to me) and I made a world of notes, but it was of no use. I couldn't get any fun out of England. It is too grave a country.[9] And its gravity soaks into the stranger and makes him as serious as everybody else. When I was there I couldn't seem to think of anything but deep problems of government, taxes, free trade, finance—and every night I went to bed drunk with statistics. I could have written a million books, but my publisher would have hired the common hangman to burn them. One is bound to respect England—she is one of the three great republics of the world—in some respects she is the most real republic of the three, too, and in other respects she isn't, but she is not a good text for hilarious literature. No, there wasn't anything to satirize—what I mean is, you couldn't satirize any given thing in England in any but a half-hearted way, because your conscience told you to look nearer home and you would find that very thing at your own door. A man with a humpbacked uncle mustn't make fun of another man's cross-eyed aunt."

"The English love for the lord, for instance? I don't mean the Lord of the prayer-book, but the lord of peerage."

"I couldn't gird at the English love for titles while our own love for titles was still more open to sarcasm. Take our 'Honorable,' for instance. Unless my memory has gone wholly astray, no man in America has any right to stick that word before his name; to do it is a shame, and a very poor shame at that. At the beginning of this century members of the two houses of Congress were referred to simply as 'Mr.' So-and-So. But this sham 'Honorable' has since crept in, and now it is unlawfully conferred upon members of State legislatures and even upon the mayors and city counselors of the paltriest back settlements. Follow the thing a little further. In England temporary titles are dropped when their time is up. The Lord Mayor of London is addressed as 'My Lord' all through his year of office, but the moment he is out he becomes plain 'Mr.' again. But with us, once 'Honorable' always 'Honorable'; once 'Governor,' always 'Governor.' I know men who were members of legislatures, or mayors of villages, twenty years ago, and they are always mentioned in the papers as 'the Honorable' to this day. I know people who were lieutenant-governors years ago and they are called 'Governor' to this day—yet the highest title they have ever had any right to, in office or out of it, was plain 'Mr.' You see, yourself, it wouldn't quite answer for me to poke fun at title loving Englishmen—I should hear somebody squeal behind me and find I had stepped on the tail of some ex-official monkey of our own. I couldn't satirize the English Civil Service; it was excellent and ours wasn't; it was open to everybody, rich or poor, conspicuous or obscure, whereas ours was only open to scrubs who would do political dirty work for public enemies like Mr. Conkling[10]—'Honorable' Mr. Conkling, to use the obsequious illegal phrase of the day. I couldn't venture to be sarcastic about the horrible corruption of English officials, for how could I know but that something of the same kind, in a minor degree, might be discovered among our own officials at any moment? I could not poke fun at the 'court column' which daily sets forth the walking and driving and dining achievements of kings and queens and dukes, while our own papers have a still longer court column of 'personals,' wherein the movements of half a dozen Permanent Celebrities, a dozen Evanescents and two dozen Next-to-Nobodies are duly and daily recorded. I couldn't satirize English justice, for it was exactly like our own and every other country's. That is to say, there didn't appear to be any particular rule in the matter of penalties. In New York I have known an Irishman to be sentenced to a month's confinement for nearly killing his wife, and another man to be jailed for a dreary long term for stealing a blanket. Now here is some English justice—these two paragraphs are from yesterday's London *Standard:*

Hamley.
A strange case of cruelty came before the stipendiary magistrate this morning. An elderly woman was charged with assaulting her niece. The allegations were that *the child had been beaten with undue severity until she was much bruised, and she was then washed in turpentine and salt,*

causing great agony. The defense was a denial, and that the child was incorrigible. The Bench, commenting on the undue severity of the punishment, imposed a fine of 1s. and costs.

Northampton.
At the Police Court today John Old was summoned by the Society for the Prevention of Cruelty to Animals for gross cruelty to a dog. The evidence showed that prisoner had brutally ill-treated the animal. He was seen to dash it against the stones, and kick it repeatedly in the streets. He afterwards severely wounded it by striking it with a shovel. He was about to bury it while still alive, but was prevented. The animal died soon after from the effects of prisoner's ill-usage. Old was sentenced to *a month's hard labor without the option of a fine.*

"The italics are mine. You see, if you treat a dog inhumanly you can't get off with a fine; you must go to prison for a month at hard labor. But if you treat a little girl inhumanly you catch a scathing lecture from the Bench, and you have to pay a fine of twenty-five entire cents besides and stand the costs on top of that. No, I whittled my opportunities down to this: One could fling criticisms at the ill-matched colors of English ladies' dresses, he could poke fun at the peddling of sermons and reversions of 'livings'[11] and say sarcastic things about various other trifles, but after his book was finished there wouldn't be fun enough in it to keep the reader from dying of melancholy. No, I looked the ground all over; there's nothing funny in England."

"Why, there's the English humorous papers."

"They are not funny; they are pathetic."

"You could have written about the manners and customs?"

"Yes, but only to a certain extent. For instance, I could have written freely about public manners and customs and given instances. I could have said that the innocent and ignorant backwoodsman of the unvisited remotenesses of America is the twin-brother of innumerable well-dressed Londoners in one respect—the disposition to glare and stare into a lady's face in the street and to follow her up, shoulder to shoulder, and crane his head around and still eagerly glare and stare until the poor victim is ready to cry with mortification and fear. I could have written as much as I pleased about public manners and customs and been free to applaud or to blame—but there an end. The real interest would lie in the private and domestic manners and customs, and I had no right to print anything about those, either praisefully or otherwise. I was a guest in many English homes, but when a man takes you into his house he tacitly takes you into his confidence, and it would be a graceless thing to abuse it."

"Mr. Dickens was not so particular with America?"

"No, he wasn't; but he recognized later that he had not done a thing to be proud of, but just the reverse. When he came to America the second time he apologized. But that is neither here nor there. Private matters are private matters and it is not right to meddle with them. We all have our superstitions, and that is one of mine."

This brought our conversation to a close.

Notes to Interview 10

1. Richard Whiteing (1840–1928), English journalist and novelist.
2. MT was writing *A Tramp Abroad,* his third travelogue, based on his trip to Germany, Switzerland, Italy, France, and England between April 1878 and August 1879. The book was finally published in March 1880.
3. The International Literary Congress, part of the Paris Exposition of 1878, was called to develop a "well-considered scheme of international literary machinery devised to protect the rights of authors" ("Foreign Notes," *New York Times,* 9 February 1879, 8). See also *Mark Twain's Notebooks and Journals,* ed. Frederick Anderson et al. (Berkeley: University of California Press, 1975), 2:97.
4. Lord Thomas Babington Macauley (1800–59), English historian and essayist.
5. Charles Reade (1814–84), English dramatist and novelist.
6. William Black (1841–98), Scottish novelist.
7. William Wetmore Story (1819–95), American sculptor and author; Cincinnatus Hiner (Joaquin) Miller (1841?–1913), American Western writer.
8. Christian Bernhard Tauchnitz (1816–85), German publisher of the Library of British and American Authors.
9. MT had planned a book about England along the lines of *The Innocents Abroad* when he sailed to England in August 1872. He soon abandoned the project, however, as he explained in June 1874: "I could not leave out the manners & customs which obtain in an English gentleman's household without leaving out the most interesting feature of the subject. They are admirable; yet I would shrink from deliberately describing them in a book, for I fear that such a course would be, after all, a violation of the courteous hospitality which furnished me the means of doing it." See appendix C to *MTL,* 5:583–85.
10. Roscoe Conkling (1829–88), U.S. senator from New York.
11. Many Church of England parishes permitted landowners to nominate pastors, a practice that led to such abuses as the sale of "livings."

11

"Mark Twain Back Again," *New York Sun,* 3 September 1879, 1.

The only thing about Mark Twain that seems natural is his drawl. That is as nasal and as deliberate as ever. His hat, as he stood on the deck of the incoming Cunarder *Gallia,*[1] yesterday, was of the pattern that English army officers wear in India, and his suit of clothes was such as a merchant wears at his store. He looks older than when he went to Germany, and his hair has turned quite gray. His wife returned with him, and his brother-in-law came on board at

Quarantine.[2] "So," as Mark Twain said, "I shall le—t hi—m ta—ke off my lug—gage and fi—ght it ou—t with the Cus—tom House office—ers."

"I've had a good time," said he," during the seventeen months I've been abroad. You remember I went out on a Dutch steamer—the same one that Bayard Taylor went on.[3] He got out at Plymouth, and I never saw him again. While he was at Berlin I corresponded with him, and we made an appointment to meet in the fall. I stayed on the Continent most of the time."

"How far have you got in *Ollendorf?*" he was asked.[4]

"Oh, I don't speak German," replied the humorist. "It's enough that I've endured the agony of learning to read it.[5] I made two or three speeches in German at Heidelberg—in my peculiar German. I stayed at Heidelberg four months.[6] I could have written my book in German; but then, you see, I want the book read. So I wrote it in English. English is about the cleverest language I ever handled. I like English."

Somebody nudged Mark Twain and introduced to him a man who said that he had heard of him and read his writings, but had never had the pleasure, &c.

"Yes," said Mr. Clemens, "I stayed a long while in Heidelberg and in Dresden and Munich and Venice and Paris, and about four weeks in London. Wherever I stayed a month I went to work on my book. It's finished and will be published in November. I don't know what the name of it is, but I know what it's about. It's about this trip I've taken. No, it isn't fiction—it's about my journey, like *The Innocents Abroad,* all serious—all facts and wisdom. I say it's finished, but it isn't. The first half is done, but I've got to go through the last half and throw whole rafts of it away. After that I may run through the first half and throw away lots of that; then it will be ready for the printer. I'm going to have it published by the same folks that published all my things."

Here a young man intervened between Mr. Clemens and the reporter, and said he'd often read of Mr. Clemens and seen his writing, but that this was really the first time, &c.

"Some of the places I went to," Mr. Clemens continued, "I had been to before, but most of them were new. I suppose New York's changed. I used to go up a block or two above the Gilsey House to see the men work on the elevated railroads—to see how fast they slung the iron together. Before I went away Dan Slote and I parted one afternoon, and next day Dan told me that he wanted to hurry up town, so he started for the elevated railroad—the one in Greenwich street was running then. Well, he got a thinking, and he thought that it was risky for a man with a family and a good business to trust to one of those roads. So he turned on his heel, and walked away to get a 'bus. Well, there was a woman washing windows near the top of a four-story house, and down she came, so close to Dan that her heels took the buttons off his coat and her head greased his shoulder. She was killed, of course, and Dan had a narrow escape. The moral of that is, in my opinion, that a man who is looking out for his life might as well trust to his first impulses."

At this point there was introduced to Mark Twain a robust seafaring man, who said he had often heard of Mr. Clemens, but had never read a word; and then he corrected himself and said he had never had the extreme pleasure, &c.

"When I sailed in the *Batavia*,"[7] said Mr. Clemens to the seafaring man, "I had a different opinion of the Cunard line from that which I now entertain. I objected to the prunes. I suppose you know that when the Cunarders changed from sailing to steam power, they maintained some of their old sailing ideas on the new steam propelled ships. Prunes was one of these old ideas. Why, they had regular days for things—'duff day' was Thursday, and I guess Sunday was a duff day too—that was when they served out puddings, the same as they do to sailors aboard a sailing ship. Then there were Tuesday beans, and Saturday beans, and prunes twenty-one times a week for dessert. They hunted the world for cooks and got the worst there were. Why, you could make up your bill of fare a week ahead—yes, for the return trip—but that's all done now."

Mr. Clemens asked after friends of his, and, in speaking about Mr. Murat Halstead, said that that gentleman went out with him upon a sudden impulse, and took no clothes along. "No," said Mr. Clemens, "I didn't lend him mine, because they wouldn't fit him; and, besides, I didn't have any more than I wanted myself."

"Did you have a pleasant trip—" the reporter would have finished the question, but a burly Custom House officer grasped the traveler's hand and said, "I've often heard of Mr. Twai—Mr. Clemens, and I've read your writings, but I never had the pleasure," &c.

"Oh, yes," replied Mr. Clemens to the reporter. "Lord Dunraven and several other lords and many New Yorkers are on board, and we had a good time.[8] I never express any opinions about people, but Lord Dunraven is an uncommonly clever fellow—nothing stuck up about him. He has brushed up against ordinary clay in his lifetime, and he is very talented besides."

Mr. Clemens had twenty-two freight packages and twelve trunks weighing on his mind, and he went away to get his brother-in-law to look after them. He goes to Elmira today to spend the remainder of the season and to finish his new book.

Notes to Interview 11

1. Built and launched in 1878, the Cunard steamer *Gallia* was "a very fine ship," as MT wrote in chapter 50 of *A Tramp Abroad*.

2. Probably Theodore Crane (1831–89), husband of Olivia Langdon Clemens's

sister Susan Crane, or possibly Olivia's brother Charles Langdon (1849–1916), whom MT had met on the *Quaker City* voyage in 1867.

3. See n. 1 to interview 9.

4. *Ollendorf's German Grammar* was the standard text for instruction in the language in the mid-nineteenth century. According to Paine, 116, MT considered having Captain Wakefield/Stormfield discover a copy of *Ollendorf* in heaven.

5. In "The Awful German Language," appendix D to *A Tramp Abroad,* MT expressed his frustrations with learning German.

6. Most of the first twenty chapters of *A Tramp Abroad* are set in or near Heidelberg. In chapter 2, MT describes Heidelberg as "the last possibility of the beautiful." See also *MTHL,* 1:229–30.

7. MT and his family sailed from England to the United States in November 1872 and from the United States to England in May 1873 aboard the *Batavia.* MT alludes to the ship in chapter 27 of *A Tramp Abroad;* in his essay "About All Kinds of Ships" (1893); and in his story fragment "The Great Dark" (1898).

8. Windham Thomas Wyndam Quin (1841–1926), Fourth Earl of Dunraven and Mount-Earl, Irish politician.

12

"Mark Twain Home Again," *New York Times,* 3 September 1879, 8.

Mr. Samuel L. Clemens, who is much better known to Americans as Mark Twain, the pilgrim who was moved to tears while leaning upon the tomb of Adam,[1] and the nearest surviving kin of the jumping frog of Calaveras, reached this City in the steamship *Gallia* yesterday, after an absence of a year and a half in Europe. Mr. Twain was accompanied by his wife, 12 trunks, and 22 freight packages; and the entire party, after a smooth voyage, arrived in good health and spirits, and were met and welcomed down at Quarantine by a number of friends. During his absence he has visited London, Paris, Heidelberg, Munich, Venice, and a number of other cities, spending most of his time on the Continent, and making prolonged stays in Paris, Heidelberg, and Munich. When Mark Twain went away, it was generally believed that his intention was to familiarize himself with German, that he might prepare one or two scientific works that are still lacking in that language. He not only did not deny these reports, but rather encouraged them, and his taking passage in a German steamer added greater probability to them. It is now certain, however, that such was not his object. He did have some designs upon the German language, but not with the intention of producing a scientific work. A very celebrated Professor in Munich, who has since died, wrote him a long German letter, inquiring about the point of one of the jokes in *The Innocents Abroad,* and Mr. Twain desired to learn enough of the language to explain away the difficulty. After more than a year of study he says he can read German well enough, but that, when it comes to talking, English is good enough for him.

"Yes," said he, in response to questions asked by a group of reporters who surrounded him on all sides, except that occupied by the saloon table, so thickly that he could not fill out his Custom house declaration, "I have been writing a new book, and have it nearly finished, all but the last two or three chapters. The first half of it, I guess, is finished, but the last half has not been revised yet; and when I get at it I will do a good deal of rewriting and a great deal of tearing up. I may possibly tear up the first part of it, too, and rewrite that." With all this tearing up in prospect, the book seemed in such danger of being entirely destroyed that one of the reporters suggested the production of a few chapters in advance in the newspapers, as samples; but Mr. Twain said that the manuscript was in the bottom of one of his trunks, where it could not possibly be reached. He added, however, that the book was descriptive of his latest trip and the places he visited, entirely solemn in character, like *The Innocents Abroad* and very much after the general plan of that work; and that it has not yet been named. It is to be published by the same company that brought out his other books, and is to be ready in November. "They want me to stay in New York and revise it," he continued, "but I cannot possibly do that. I am going to start tomorrow morning for Elmira, where we will stay for some time."

On his outgoing voyage, Mr. Twain had for fellow passengers Mr. Bayard Taylor, the American Minister to Germany, and Mr. Murat Halstead, who started on five minutes' notice, and without any clothes except those he wore. "I did not see Mr. Taylor after we left the ship," he said, "but corresponded frequently with him. His death was a great surprise to me.[2] Oh, no, I did not lend Mr. Halstead any clothes. He could not get into mine; and, besides, I hadn't any more than I wanted for myself."

The age of the author of *The Innocents Abroad, Roughing It,* and *The Gilded Age* has not increased apparently in the last two years.[3] His hair is no whiter than when he last sailed for Europe. He is very much the same man, except that he went away in a silk cap and came back in a cloth hat. He was particularly well pleased with the steamer. "I don't like some of these vessels," said he, "some of them keep a man hungry all the time unless he has a good appetite for boiled rice. I know some steamers where they have the same bill of fare they used to have when the company ran sailing packets: beans on Tuesday and Friday, stewed prunes on Thursday, and boiled rice on Wednesday; all very healthy, but very bad. But we are fed like princes aboard here, and have made a comfortable voyage. We have been in some seas that would have made the old *Quaker City* turn somersaults, but this ship kept steady through it all. We could leave a mirror lying on the washstand, and it would not fall off. If we stood a goblet loose on the shelf at night, it would be there in the morning." Mr. Twain declined positively, however, to say whether a cocktail, left standing on the shelf at night, would be there all safe in the morning. The ship was hardly steady enough for that.

There was a little ponderous silence that no one interrupted, for the returning writer was evidently revolving something in his mind. "I want a ride on one of the elevated railroads," said he, "I've never been on one of them yet. I used to be afraid of them, but it's no use. Death stares us in the face everywhere, and we may as well take it in its elevated form. I have a friend who wanted to ride on the elevated when the first one was built; but when he looked at it he thought of his wife and children, and concluded to walk home. On the way up town a woman who was washing a third story window fell out, and just grazed my friend's head. She was killed, and he had a very narrow escape. It's no use; there are women washing windows everywhere, and we may as well fall as be fallen upon."

"This new book of mine," said he, breaking suddenly off from the Custom house blanks, "is different from any book I ever wrote. Before, I revised the manuscript as I went along, and knew pretty well at the end of each week how much of the week's work I should use, and how much I should throw away. But this one has been written pretty much all in a lump, and I hardly know how much of it I will use, or how much will have to be torn up. When I start at it I tear it up pretty fast, but I think the first half will stand pretty much as it is. I am not quite sure that there is enough yet prepared, but I am still at work at it." The group of reporters and five or six listening cabin passengers stood by waiting for something stupendous in the way of a joke to follow all this serious talk. Several times Mr. Twain's lips moved, as if about to speak, but he was silent. The upper end of Staten Island was passed, and the joke was still unborn. Governor's Island came alongside, the Battery drew astern, the Cunard pier was reached, and yet the joker by profession and reputation kept his audience in suspense. The landing was made, but the joke still lay locked up, with the manuscript, in the bottom of the trunk.

Notes to Interview 12

1. *The Innocents Abroad*, book 2, chapter 26: "The tomb of Adam! How touching it was, here in a land of strangers, far away from home, and friends, and all who cared for me, thus to discover the grave of a blood relation. True, a distant one, but still a relation. The unerring instinct of nature thrilled its recognition. The fountain of my filial affection was stirred to its profoundest depths, and I gave way to tumultuous emotion. I leaned upon a pillar and burst into tears."

2. Bayard Taylor died in Berlin in late December 1878.

3. *Roughing It* (1872), MT's second travel book, based on his sojourn in the American West and in the Sandwich Islands, or Hawaii, between 1861 and 1867; *The Gilded Age* (1873), MT's first novel, a political satire written in collaboration with his Hartford friend and neighbor Charles Dudley Warner (1829-1900).

13

"Mark Twain's Return," *New York Herald,* 3 September 1879, 3.

Mr. Samuel L. Clemens (Mark Twain) arrived in this city yesterday, on the Cunard steamer *Gallia,* after a tour of 18 months through the principal countries of Europe. Mr. Clemens, who was accompanied by his wife and family, appeared in excellent health. "I enjoyed the trip greatly," he said to a *Herald* reporter, "and I learned a great deal that will serve me in after life."

"I am glad to find," said the reporter, "that after so many years of mental labor you at last enjoyed a long respite from your literary avocations."

"Respite!" he exclaimed with astonishment, and then, with a merry twinkle in his eye, he said in confidential whisper, "You don't mean that."

"Why not?"

"If you are in earnest in your remark I can tell you just as earnestly I never spent a busier time in my life. I only wish I could show you the piles of manuscript that are lying in my trunks and then you would have some idea of the work in which I have been engaged."

As he spoke the custom house officers were rushing here and there along the wharf examining the baggage, and seeing them approach the place where his trunks lay he asked to be excused for a few minutes. When the inspection of what he termed his "cargo" was concluded he returned and resumed his conversation. "I feel a deep sense of relief," he said, "in returning to this, the dearest land to me in the world. Many a time—"

Here the conversation was interrupted by a visitor who abruptly remarked "Mr. Clemens, one moment."

With another apology, Mr. Clemens departed, but soon returned, and, taking his seat beside the reporter, said: "You desire to know how I was occupied during my travels. Well, I will tell you. I spent three months in Heidelberg. It is a delightful place. I spent three more in Paris. These were six months taken out of my trip. To tell you briefly, I traveled for the comfort of my family, and wherever I found they could enjoy the attractions and the scenes, there I settled down. I was not traveling in the ordinary sense of running from place to place.

"Do you intend to give a history of your travels through the public journals?"

"Oh, no; nothing will appear concerning my travels till my book is published. I have spent much time and labor on it, and I do not propose to anticipate its publication. It would not be fair to expect that after—

"See, there goes the Earl of Dunraven,"[1] he said suddenly, snapping the thread of his topic, "we have had aristocracy in abundance in company with us on our return trip. The earl is fast becoming Americanized."

"How?"

"Well, you see he has been so often in this country before that he has got a great deal of that aristocratic idea rubbed off him," and the last three words were delivered with an emphasis and a knowing wink that showed how the humorist was engaged in studying character during the voyage. "We had two other lords among the passengers—Lord Caledon and Rodney[2]—but as I had not previously formed their acquaintance I cannot offer any opinion concerning them as representatives of the English aristocracy."

"What will be the title of your new book?" asked the reporter.

"I cannot tell that now," was the reply, "it will take me some time for consideration on that point after I have arranged my manuscript. I have written more and torn up more manuscript after it was written than you can imagine. But it will not take me long to prepare the work for publication."

Mr. Clemens concluded by saying that after remaining a few days in this city he would return to his home in Hartford and there settle down for a few months to the completion of his book.

Notes to Interview 13

1. See n. 8 to interview 11.
2. James Alexander, Fourth Earl of Caledon (1846-97), and Charles Marsham, Fourth Earl of Romney (1841-1905).

14

"Mr. Twain Again with Us," *New York World,* 3 September 1879, 1.

On the eleventh day of April 1878, Mr. Mark Twain, of nowhere in particular—sometimes, though seldom, known as Mr. Samuel L. Clemens, of Hartford, Conn.—set out for Europe on the steamer *Holsatia*.[1] The following day he did the same thing over again, the steamship, for reasons which were explained at the time, having been obliged to come back and take a fresh start. Yesterday Mr. Twain returned. He was one of the passengers on the *Gallia.*

"There," said he, as the ship left quarantine and began her journey up the bay, "the danger is finally passed."

"To what danger do you refer, Mr. Twain?" asked a reporter for *The World,* who had been trying for ten minutes without success to lift the great humorist from a deep and silent melancholy.

"Why, you see," replied the returning wanderer, whose voice has lost none of its querulous plaintiveness by dealing with foreign tongues, "I haven't been at all certain but what we'd have to go back and begin this voyage all over again. I said to my friend Mrs. Clemens the other day, 'If they had to try twice to get us started, what reason have we to hope that they won't find it necessary to try several times before they are able to get back?' It's one of the peculiarities of sea life that, given the same circumstances, you always look for the same results. When the ship begins to roll sideways and kick up behind at the same time, I always know that I am expected to perform a certain duty.[2] I learned it years ago on the *Quaker City*. You might suppose that I would have forgotten my part after so long a residence on shore. But there it is again. It's habit; everything connected with the sea comes down to a matter of habit. You might confine me for forty years in a Rhode Island corn patch, and at the end of that time I'd know just as well what to do when a ship begins to kick up as I do at the moment. The darkest night never confuses me in the least. It's a little singular when you look at it, ain't it? But I presume it's attributable to the solemn steadfastness of the great deep. By the way, how is *Pinafore?*"

"Beg pardon, how is what?"

"*Pinafore;* I understand you have had *Pinafore* in America. I told Sullivan and Gilbert *Pinafore* was sure to be a great success."[3]

"Indeed! Why did you think so?"

"I didn't; that was the reason it was sure to succeed."

It was pleasant to hear Mr. Twain run on in this easy way, but the reporter, realizing that there was much that the public was burning to know, felt compelled to conduct the rest of the interview in a systematic, business-like manner.

"You sailed in the same ship with Bayard Taylor and Mr. Murat Halstead, of Cincinnati, did you not, Mr. Twain?"

"The same craft, all honor to her (Mr. Twain lifted his hat reverently), carried all three of us."

"It was said at the time that you inveighed Mr. Halstead into making the voyage by promising him free use of your linen?"

"Well"—Mr. Twain spoke leisurely—"I did tell Murat that I'd lend him a clean shirt. You see, he didn't expect to go. His wife was going and he'd sort of come down to see her safely launched. You remember the ship ran away with a party of excursionists who had got aboard to bid poor Mr. Taylor goodbye and was obliged to anchor off the Hook all night. During the evening Murat sort of got his sea-legs on and says he, 'Clemens' (he always calls me Clemens), says he, 'Clemens, if you'll lend me a shirt I believe I'll go across.' 'All right,' says I, 'I'll do it.' So Murat he fixed things with the captain and stayed aboard. We got along pretty well with winds a-middling, about nor-nor-west by sou', till we came to latitude 36, longitude 49½, and then Murat wanted his clean shirt—that is, he wanted mine. It was about three bells from noon when I took that garment to the door of Murat's stateroom. 'Here,' says I, 'clothe yourself like a prince of the realm.' At eight bells Mr. Halstead came out of his apartment with his coat buttoned up to his chin and his face as red as a red, red rose.[4] He wore his coat buttoned up to his chin all the rest of the voyage, and I never so much as got a glimpse of my shirt. There was a kind of rumor on the ship that Murat never wore that shirt or any other shirt. I don't know how true it was, but when I came to study the thing it did look to me as if I'd put a rather tough problem to the editor of the *Cincinnati Commercial,* for his neck measures eighteen inches, while mine never footed up more than fifteen, even when I had the mumps."

"Did you see anything of Mr. Taylor after you landed?"

"No, I'm very sorry now, but I was prevented by one thing and another from calling upon him."[5]

"You have written a book since you left America, I believe?"

"Yes, I've sort of put some words together."

"What do you call it?"

"Well, I don't know what I shall call it. I've turned over a good many names in my mind, but none of 'em seem to hit her exactly. You see, she ain't a novel; if she was I'd call her 'Lucy, or the Crescent Cross,' or 'If He Shouldn't Come, What Then?' or some such suggestive title, but the trouble is she ain't a novel."

"What is the nature of the book?"

"It is the history of the travels of a single family. It also resembles *Webster's Dictionary* and Johnson's *Encyclopædia.*[6] You can read any part or all the parts independent of the other parts and be vicariously instructed, open the book where you will. In short she is to be a corker, when she is bound."

"How soon do you expect to have the work before the public?"

"Can't say. I am going right straight to Elmira to finish her up, revise her, &c. She'll be published by the same fortunate beings who have published my other works."[7]

In conclusion, Mr. Twain said that he had enjoyed his seventeen months abroad immensely, having tarried principally in London, Paris, Dresden, Munich, Vienna, and Heidelberg.

Notes to Interview 14

1. See n. 1 to interview 9.
2. To suffer from seasickness.
3. The operetta *HMS Pinafore* by Sir William Gilbert (1836–1911) and Sir Arthur Sullivan (1842–1900) premiered in the United States at the Boston Museum on 25 November 1878 before moving to Baltimore in December.
4. "My love is like a red, red rose": the first line of a poem published in 1794 by the Scottish poet Robert Burns (1759–96).
5. Bayard Taylor died in Berlin in late December 1878.
6. Noah Webster (1758–1843) published the first edition of *An American Dictionary of the English Language* in 1828; Cuthbert W. Johnson (1799–1878) published the first edition of *The American Farmer's Encyclopedia and Dictionary of Rural Affairs* in 1842.
7. The American Publishing Company of Hartford, a subscription press, issued

the first six of MT's major books between 1869 and 1880 as well as *Pudd'nhead Wilson* (1894) and *Following the Equator* (1897).

15

"An 'Innocent Abroad': 'Mark Twain' in Montreal," *Montreal Gazette*, 28 November 1881, 3.

To the casual observer the name of Samuel L. Clemens which was inscribed on the register of the Windsor Hotel yesterday, or rather Saturday, might probably pass unnoticed. A moment's reflection, however, would recall to the minds of most persons recollections of pleasant hours spent in the perusal of certain humorous works, and of ofttimes uncontrollable laughter indulged in over the inimitable drolleries contained in those works, whose author is known far and wide as Mark Twain, the *nom de plume* of what he himself would call plain and simple Samuel L. Clemens, who arrived in this city on Saturday evening, and whom, yesterday afternoon, a representative of the *Gazette* had the pleasure of meeting. Many of our readers are doubtless familiar with the face of the humorist, from the cuts which adorn the front page of many of his works. Suffice it to say that the portrait in question is a fair though not a flattering likeness. In manner Mr. Clemens is rather the reverse of what might be expected. Cool, quiet in demeanor, acting and speaking always with great deliberation. There is little indication of the clever, witty mind which all know him to possess. Nor in discoursing with him is there anything to indicate beyond a stray flash of wit here and there uttered in a dry way which would lead one to imagine that one of the most original humorous writers of the day was speaking. In the course of conversation carried on intermittently between the puff of a corncob pipe, on his part, with our representative Mr. Clemens explained that this was his first visit to Canada; he had skirted round the edge of Upper Canada, he said, in the neighborhood of Detroit and Windsor but had never been in the Dominion. After a brief allusion to his business here, which is in connection with his forthcoming *Prince and Pauper*,[1] something as he explained out of his usual line, Mr. Clemens spoke of some of his experiences with lecture audiences, the subject being brought up by the enquiry as to whether he intended, or could be induced to lecture here. His reply to that query was that in order to be in a position to say he had no lectures, he had some years ago burned all his manuscripts. At any rate he did not care to lecture before a strange audience. "Doors open at 7:30, the trouble will begin at eight" (a familiar line in one of his writings), suggested the reporter. That, said Mr. Clemens, expressed his idea on the subject, and the trouble wasn't over till a quarter past, meaning the work of gaining the sympathies of an audience. It was always a hard ordeal breaking the ice and a shivering task until the hearer was enticed from his frosty reserve. In this connection Mr. Clemens alluded to Mr. Archibald Forbes' lecture on the "Inner Life of a War Correspondent,"[2] which that gentleman delivered in Hartford a few weeks ago. He had sympathized with Mr. Forbes, he said, on that occasion; great as was the interest of that lecture it took fully thirty minutes to thaw the Hartford people out of their frozen attitude. En passant, the humorist observed that he had formed one of the party of journalists, which included the great War Correspondent, at the arrival of that "gaudiest of gaudy frauds," the Shah of Persia.[3]

Naturally one feels inclined to ask a stranger what his impressions of Montreal may be, but the question, in nine cases out of ten, is an absurd one, though, as a rule, every "interviewer" feels it incumbent on him to put it. But in the present case it was obviously useless. Mr. Clemens volunteered the statement that his experience of the city, so far, was confined within the four walls of his room, and his view from the window. He had formed one impression, however, and that was that we were a very religious community. People here, he said, judging from what he could see, went to church about five times a day, and then, in response to an observation, he expressed the opinion that Montreal, more perhaps than Brooklyn, deserved the title of "City of Churches." These remarks naturally led up to a talk on Montreal, its institutions and characteristics. And speaking of the diversified language and the mode of conducting public business in both French and English, Mr. Clemens alluded to his experience of the legislature in Honolulu, Sandwich Islands, where it is also so conducted.[4] There in the Parliament the great majority of which is composed of Hawaiians, are three or four American officials and others. The former know nothing of English, the latter are ignorant of Hawaiian. Nevertheless, this fact is no bar to speech-making. The Americans address their little audience of kindred spirits in their own tongue, and the natives do the same. Here, however, they employ an interpreter, Mr. William Ragsdale, "Bill Ragsdale," as he is familiarly termed, and to him falls the unenviable lot of translating sentence by sentence, the "eloquence" of each speaker, native or American, in turn. "Bill," said Mr. Clemens, "may be said really to have made every speech in that Parliament for years back."[5] Naturally again the reporter suggested a visit to a sitting of our own Council where though no interpreter is employed a somewhat similar scene might be witnessed and some amusement, but little edification it must be confessed, might be gained. Possibly the humorist may take the hint and give to the world a chapter on the Montreal beer garden—City Council, we mean. At this point the announcement of dinner brought the interview to a close, and thanking Mr. Clemens for his courtesy, our reporter withdrew.

Notes to Interview 15

1. MT tried without much success to protect several of his books from British pirates by securing copyright on them in Canada. His visit to Montreal on this occasion was to copyright his forthcoming *The Prince and the Pauper* (1882), his third major novel.
2. Archibald Forbes (1838–1900), British war correspondent.
3. MT had covered the visit of the shah of Persia to England in June 1873 for the *New York Herald*. His five letters on the occasion, written between 18 and 30 June and published in the paper between 1 and 19 July, were later collected under the title "O'Shah" in *Europe and Elsewhere* (1923).
4. MT makes the same point in the first paragraph of chapter 68 of *Roughing It*.
5. MT describes Ragsdale's task in fuller detail in his dispatch from Honolulu to the *Sacramento Union* on 23 May 1866 and published on 20 June 1866. See *Mark Twain's Letters from Hawaii*, ed. A. Grove Day (London: Chatto and Windus, 1967), 110–11. MT began a novel about "Billy" Ragsdale in 1884. See *MTHL*, 1:461; and *Mark Twain's Notebooks and Journals*, ed. Frederick Anderson et al. (Berkeley: University of California Press, 1975), 1:104. MT inquired about Ragsdale in 1895, only to learn that he had suffered a "loathsome and lingering death" in a leper colony years earlier (*FE*, 63).

16

"An 'Innocent' Interviewed: Mark Twain Pays a Visit to St. Louis," *St. Louis Post-Dispatch*, 12 May 1882, 2.

Samuel L. Clemens, Hartford, Conn., registered at the Southern this morning. He did not want a room, and the clerk tossed him off in the usual nonchalant way and paid no attention to him. By and by, a New Yorker dropped in, cast his eye over the register, and said:

"Hello! you've got Mark Twain here, I see."

"Where?" said both clerks, rushing to the register pell-mell.

"Why, here. Sam Clemens," said the wise informer, pointing to the name.

"Him?" said clerk Harvey Willard, with a disdainful smile. "Is that the funny man? Why, he don't look half as funny as I do."

It was Mark all the same, and in his usual good humor. He has not been here since 1864, so that most of the people do not know how he looks. Imagine a middle-sized, stout-built man in a common suit of gray, with coat cut sack-style. A careless, wide-brimmed hat is thrown recklessly over his hair, which is full and long and rather gray. A countenance which shows good living, a pair of gray eyes, and a face entirely smooth, save a rakish gray moustache that gives a slight devil-may-care appearance to the man. He certainly does not look at "all funny," as the clerks put it, and would be mistaken for a serious, matter-of-fact gentleman who would not waste his time on anecdotes and would look down upon a joke with lofty contempt. The most curious thing about him is a reckless, rolling gait, which he probably caught when, as a cub pilot, he swaggered on the upper deck of the *Mary Amandalane* on the lower Mississippi. The aforesaid gait has stuck to him so persistently that it would make a sensitive man seasick to sit and look at Mark meander across the corridor of even so solid a hotel as the Southern.

He also has a remarkable drawling way of speaking, which he most dislikes to see mimicked in print, and which adds quite a charm to his conversation. A *Post-Dispatch* reporter met him in the rotunda of the hotel and was received very cordially. It was only when the possibility of an interview was broached that Mr. Clemens grew slightly restive.

"I guess I haven't got time," he said. "The fact is you can say anything you like if you put it in your own words, but don't quote me saying anything. No man can get me right unless he takes it down in shorthand, very particularly, too."

"You don't love the interviewer, I see, Mr. Clemens."

"No; I don't. I have never yet met a man who attempted to interview me whose report of the process did not try very hard to make me out an idiot, and did not amply succeed, in my mind, in making him a thorough one. They try to imitate my manner of speech, and not being artists, they never succeed, you see. No, I want to fight shy of that class of people."

The reader can imagine the position of a reporter whose fate was fixed that he should write himself down as an idiot, but Twain was assured that no attempt would be made to exhibit his style of conversation, that the present interviewer's weekly rate of compensation did not warrant him to make such flights, and that he was a plain, cheap man used for doing easy police work, meetings of the Board of Public Improvements and elections among the school directors. Mr. Clemens melted a little and said: "I have not been out here since 1864, I think, and I had intended on remaining some time in the city. But I waited too long at New Orleans to catch the *Baton Rouge,* the commander of which was my old master,[1] and in consequence will have to leave tonight."

"You ought not to be in such a hurry. The newspapers represent you as being fabulously wealthy and in living in great splendor at Hartford."

"Oh, there is quite an amount of fiction in that statement. Of course I'm living at Hartford, and I had a house when I left there, but I have not gone into competition with Vanderbilt yet,[2] and I don't think that I'll do so."

"What about the statement that humorous writing is not paying now as it did formerly?"

"That is fictional, too, I think. Is the writing that does not pay really humorous? I'm not talking about myself, but in my opinion good writing of any kind pays always."

"How is it in your case?"

"Well, I don't think that any kind of books will ever yield quite as well as the Bible and indecent works—I might say other indecent works, but that might get the church people down on me. Don't put that in, now."

"No; but, really, is there not a rich harvest in your line?"

"Now, I don't want to make an assignment, and why should I prepare a statement of my assets? I am preparing to try the public again, and my shorthand secretary accompanies me on this trip."

"What is the nature of the new work?"

"I have been writing a series of articles in the *Atlantic Monthly* on subjects connected with the Mississippi,[3] and I found that I had got my distances a little mixed. I took this trip for the purpose of making observations on this subject. I was getting a little rusty about it."

"The new book will treat of your early life on the river?"

"Yes; altogether of that subject."

"When will it be finished?"

"In about nine months."

"And what will you call it?"

"Oh, that is the last thing to be thought about. I never write a title until I finish a book, and then I frequently don't know what to call it. I usually write out anywhere from a half dozen to a dozen and a half titles, and the publisher casts his experienced eye over them and guides me largely in the selection. That's what I did in the case of *Roughing It,* and, in fact, it has always been my practice."

"You have come a little late," said the reporter, changing the conversation. "You should have been here in time for the banquet of the Army of the Tennessee."

"I came very near to jumping on the cars at Cairo yesterday and slipping in on that occasion. As a general thing I dislike banquets, if I am down for a speech. The sense of responsibility weighs me down and destroys all the enjoyment until I have gotten the confounded speech out of my system. But I really had something that I would like to have said last night—a matter that I am really interested in."

"What was that?" asked the reporter. "Why can't you say it now? General [William Tecumseh] Sherman and all the members of the Army of the Tennessee are regular subscribers to the *Post-Dispatch.* Make your speech to them through its columns."

"I wanted to talk to them about Arctic expeditions.[4] I wished to say that, in my humble judgment, we have spent too much money on these trips. Too many valuable lives have been immolated in this search. Even if it is finally successful, what is the good result of it? We could not borrow any money in the North Pole, and I don't think it would become fashionable as a summer resort. Now, I am full of an expedition of another kind. I want the next set of explorers sent in another direction. We have got some doubts [as] to the exact location of hell, and I was very desirous to suggest to the assembled warriors last night, and through them to the government and the American people, that the next expedition go in search of the place I have mentioned. If we ever locate that region, we can make some practical use of it. I had sketched a plan, which is shadowy yet, but I thought it might grow real and practical under the potent influence of champagne."

"Had you any people to suggest as leaders of this trip?"

"Yes, that part could be easily arranged. Of course, I would give my friends all the places of trust. For instance, I would insist on putting Talmage in command of the fleet, with full and absolute control over all arrangements.[5] He knows as much about the route as anybody I could think of, and I assure you I have given the matter some thought. The other officers could be easily selected."

"Would it be strictly in accordance with the fitness of things if the expedition, like those to the Arctic regions, should get stranded and lost, and those who sailed in it should never reach their destination?"

Mr. Clemens smiled broadly and declared that he was not being interviewed and that he really would not answer leading questions. Then his private secretary and a couple of friends got hold of him. He put on his overcoat, tucked his umbrella under his arm and started out to do the town. He leaves here at 4 o'clock this afternoon for Hannibal, the place where he was born, where he intends to make a visit. From that point, he will run up the river to St. Paul and then back East. He says that he never expects to get so far from home again.

Mr. J. H. Carter (Commodore Rollingpin),[6] an old friend of Mr. Clemens, went down the river to meet him last night, escorted him to the hotel, and looked after his comfort during his stay in the city.

Notes to Interview 16

1. Horace Bixby (1826-1912), the "lightning pilot" of the *Paul Jones* in 1857 (as he is described in chapter 7 of "Old Times on the Mississippi"), in 1882 piloted the *City of Baton Rouge*, a luxurious Anchor Line steamer.

2. Cornelius Vanderbilt (1794-1877), American business tycoon. See also MT's "Open Letter to Commodore Vanderbilt" (1869).

3. "Old Times on the Mississippi," serialized in the *Atlantic Monthly* from January until August 1875, was incorporated into chapters 4-17 of *Life on the Mississippi* (1883).

4. George W. DeLong (1844-81) commanded the ill-fated 1879 *Jeanette* expedition

to the Arctic. The bodies of the explorers were discovered in March 1882 and later returned to the United States for burial. The expedition was chronicled by Raymond L. Newcomb in *Our Lost Explorers* (Hartford: American Publishing, 1884).

    5. T. DeWitt Talmage (1832–1902), an American clergyman.

    6. John Henton Carter (1832–1910), aka Commodore Rollingpin, a former steamboat pilot and popular St. Louis journalist and humorist.

17

[Commodore] R[ollingpin],[1] "A Day with Mark Twain" (12 May 1882),
Rollingpin's Humorous Illustrated Annual (New York, 1883).

The boat that was to convey Mr. S. L. Clemens—Mark Twain—northward was to leave St. Louis at four o'clock in the afternoon. It was now ten in the morning, and he proposed the interval be spent in driving about the city and calling on some old time acquaintances. He had already arranged his toilet and added an extra overcoat to meet the demands of a chilly atmosphere, when, running his hand over his face, he suggested the propriety of visiting a barber shop before entering upon the day's program. During the tonsorial performance we carried on a rambling conversation about this trip south, which Mark declared had proved a dismal failure, resulting in nothing but some social interchanges.

"I expected," he went on, "to travel incognito and return east loaded to the guards with solid information about the late flood and other matters of interest concerning the people of the Mississippi river and the valley, but I was discovered the first day I arrived here from the east, and again when I took passage on the boat for New Orleans, and undertook to interview the boatmen. This confounded speech of mine betrayed me to the enemy; and just when the pilot on watch began to 'scape out' in the most beautiful fashion. No, it's all up. I'd have given worlds to have been permitted to pass unrecognized, and stand around and listen to those matchless lies by the hour. But I'm in the hands of Providence, and I suppose Providence does not propose to suffer my morals to be corrupted in that way."

As we emerged from the barber shop, Mark became impressed with the idea that he needed a pair of suspenders, and we at once sought a furnishing establishment for the purpose of making the necessary purchase. When a pair had been selected he divested himself of his three coats, and then his own invention, and which he said was not yet fully perfected in all the intricate minor details, but it soon would be. There was an ingredient yet lacking which had been formulated, and when supplied would make the suspender come into general use by every sensible man in the civilized and barbarous world.

"That suspender," said Mark, holding it up and viewing it admiringly, "will yet hand my name down to posterity as a benefactor of my race. I'm the first man that ever gave his genius to the creation of a practical article of this kind—a garment calculated to fill all the requirements of physical health and esthetical culture. All the rest were idiots. I said when I patented my scrap-book, which cost me years of hard study and sleepless nights, that I would confer another blessing on mankind before I got under my monument, and I will. These buttonholes you notice have worn out, causing the pants to drop down and rest upon the hips. This objection is to be overcome by introducing a rubber band, which will yield to the pressure resulting from the various motions of the body, when the suspender will be ready to go before the country on its merits."

The shopkeeper suggested that the design was very simple, and reminded him of a primitive garment worn by small children, and called in nursery parlance a "waist."

"The design differs radically," said Mark warming. "Don't you see here that the shoulder straps are only three inches wide, whereas they reach from the shoulder to the base of the neck in the child's dress. This is one of the points on which I rest my claim for a patent." Here Mark turned a patronizing look upon the vender, folded the garment, placed it in a pocket of one of his layers of overcoats, when we left the store.

By and by we called a carriage, and giving the driver his directions, settled into our seats. During the drive the conversation ran on books, authors, and literary topics generally. I suggested that his last book, *The Prince and the Pauper,* was his best, and would outlive any of the others that he had written, notwithstanding some of the critics had been rather severe on it as a work of art. Any minor errors or anachronisms that might have unconsciously slipped into the first edition, I urged could readily be eliminated or corrected in a second.

"Not a word will I ever change," was the prompt response. "I never undertake a piece of work until I have thoroughly prepared myself for the task, and when it issues from the press, it is done as well as I can do it, and that's the end of the matter."

We then talked of *The Innocents Abroad* and *A Tramp Abroad,* I maintaining that the later was equally as good a book as the former, though coming after it, could never hope to be so popular.

"A much better book," said Mr. Clemens. "Twelve years ago I could not have written such a book from the same material."

The conversation next turned upon humor generally, and the fatal mistake men of real ability have often made by permitting themselves to express their thoughts in this vein. Oliver Wendell Holmes, I urged, came near swamping a brilliant career by unconsciously falling into this error, and it required years of toil before he could emerge from the unpleasant predicament in which his youthful folly and enthusiasm had placed him; and it was not until the appearance of that matchless work, *The Autocrat of the Breakfast Table,* that his true place in literature was acknowledged.[2] Lowell's *Biglow Papers* stamped him as a man of genius, and the most original of American humorists; but fun and satire, though wielded by a master hand would never have brought him sufficient standing to have sent him as our minister to the courts of Spain or Great Britain.[3] A quarter of a century had to elapse, and the interim filled in with solid work and solemn repentance, before honors such as these could be aspired to. Tom Corwin, one of the most erudite of lawyers, whose wit was as brilliant as his scholarship was profound, and his patriotism undoubted, fell into a similar error, and placed forever a barrier against his advancement to the highest position in the gift of the American people when he condescended to instruct and amuse by the employment of the lighter vein.[4] And so we might run over the long list of brilliant men who have suffered from a like cause. And Mark Twain cannot hope to be made an exception to general rule. He recognizes the inevitable, and bows to it with the resignation of the true philosopher. With all his vast store of common sense and practical capability, he is expected ever to appear in his cap and bells and do the risible.

Such a fame as that which he enjoys it would seem should be sufficient to gratify the ambition of any reasonable person, but Twain is too sensible a man not to realize that humor, of all things, is the most ephemeral, and that which will convulse the world today will appear flat and insipid enough tomorrow.

A quarter of a century ago, Doesticks's fame was worldwide, and his writings in everybody's mouth; and yet who reads Doesticks now?[5] To take up one of his books one wonders why anybody ever did read him. In all his writing there is not to be found a single piece of word painting that cries for recognition and a permanent place in the book stalls. But Mark Twain is a man of real parts, and much that he has done will live. He is endowed with strong common sense, steadiness of purpose, judgment and an insight into human nature, which, if cast in other fields than that which he adopted, would have fitted him for the broader and higher walks of life. No one can read him for an hour without being convinced that while he is a humorist of the first order, that he is something more. There is a breadth and depth of philosophy about his most mirth-provoking pictures, which might be profitably employed in directing the practical everyday affairs of life.

In personal appearance S. L. Clemens is of medium stature, standing rather wide on his legs, and moving about with a careless, swaggering gait. His head is large and well-formed, and may be termed of the massive order of architecture, being well-poised, and having a firm-set chin, which indicates steadiness of purpose and plenty of staying power. The nose is slightly aquiline, thin and pointed at the extreme. The face is smoothly shaven, with the exception of a sandy mustache. Hair slightly gray. He speaks with a drawl and in measured accents, his ideas at times seeming to run into confusion, when all at once his eyes flash with light, when his mind rallies, and he carries his point with vigor.

As an illustration of the peculiar drift which Twain's mind takes when dealing with ordinary subjects, I may cite an incident that occurred on the morning we first met. I had just remarked that the weather was very disagreeable, in fact it was wretched; to which he replied: "Yes, the weather is bad, and if I were dealing in weather it is not the brand that I'd put up in cans for future use. No, it is the kind of weather I'd throw on the market and let it go for what it would fetch, and if it wouldn't sell for anything I would hunt up some life-long enemy and present it to him. Failing in this, as a last resort I should probably take it out on the big bridge, dump it into the Mississippi and start it to Europe via the jetties. I'd unload it someway, and that quickly, too."

On the trip south on the steamer *Gold Dust*,[6] Mark went up into the pilot house and entered into conversation with the pilot, for the purpose, as he himself expressed it, of enjoying some good, old-fashioned, unadulterated Mississippi river lying. The pilot answered all interrogatories with an ease which proved his fertility of resources, while Mark's private stenographer proceeded to take down every word for future use. Questions about the late floods, the changes of the river, and all such matters, were put and satisfactorily answered. At length the conversation turned to piloting, when Mark ventured to inquire of the man at the wheel if he knew Sam Clemens, who at one time was reported to be a pilot. "What! Mark Twain?" said the other. "Yes, that's what they call him," was the rejoinder. "Well, I should say I did! Sam left here 'bout twenty years ago, an' has been writin' books ever since. He's better at that'n he was steerin', for he wasn't much of a pilot. He'd just as like as not go to sleep on watch and run the boat into the bank, head on, if you didn't keep a watch on him. If thar was a snap in the river he'd go miles out of his way to get a whack at it, and was never happy unless he was bouncin' somethin'. Why, you'd think he was gettin' the biggest kind of money from the government to clear the river of snags if you'd seed how he hustled 'em out of the way." "Do you remember his personal appearance?" "Who? Sam Clemens? Yes, I should say so." "What was it?" "Wall, sir, to tell you the truth, to look at Sam Clemens, he wasn't worth sweepin' up!"

Notes to Interview 17

1. Aka John Henton Carter (1832–1910), a former steamboat pilot and popular St. Louis journalist and humorist.

2. Oliver Wendell Holmes (1809–94), American poet and novelist and author of *The Autocrat of the Breakfast Table* (1858).

3. James Russell Lowell (1819–91), American poet and author of *The Biglow Papers* (1848; second series 1867).

4. Thomas Corwin (1794–1865), U.S. senator from Ohio (1845–50), secretary of the treasury (1850–53), and U.S. minister to Mexico (1861–64).

5. Mortimer Neal Thomson, aka Q. K. Philander Doesticks (1831–75), American journalist and humorist.

6. MT refers to the *Gold Dust* as a "Vicksburg packet" in chapter 23 of *Life on the Mississippi* (1883) and to its explosion on 7 August 1882 (chapter 37). MT traveled from St. Louis to New Orleans with his new publisher James R. Osgood (1836–92), whom he later described as "one of the dearest and sweetest and loveliest human beings to be found on the planet anywhere" (*Auto* [1959], 228).

18

"Mark Twain's Travels," *St. Louis Globe-Democrat*, 13 May 1882, 8.

Samuel L. Clemens (Mark Twain), Hartford, Conn., accompanied by James R. Osgood,[1] the Boston book publisher, and R. H. Phelps,[2] of Hartford, the humorist's stenographer, are at the Southern, having arrived in the city yesterday morning from New Orleans on the Anchor Line boat *Baton Rouge*. It was the intention of the party to leave in the afternoon for Hannibal, Mo., on the steamer *Bald Eagle*, but not making the arrangements expected, they deferred their departure until this afternoon, when they will take the *Green City*. From Hannibal they will go to St. Paul, then to Chicago, and by way of the lakes make their way east.

"I go by water," said Mr. Clemens to a reporter last evening, "because I don't like the railroads. I wouldn't go to heaven by rail if the chance was offered me."

The reporter then reminded Mr. Clemens of a chance meeting two years ago, at the time of the reception in Chicago for General [Ulysses S.] Grant, when that distinguished personage was returning from his trip around the world. One of the special features of the elaborate program prepared was a speech by Mark Twain at McVicker's Theatre, on the subject, announced beforehand, of "Babies."[3] The humorist was stopping at the Palmer House,[4] and, in the course of newspaper events, it became necessary to anticipate some portion of what he was to say. A call at the hotel found him still in bed, although late in the morning, with the room properly littered with manuscript.

"I am preparing my address now," said Mark cheerily, when the caller's errand was made known, "and if you'll wait awhile you can take a copy. This is the way, you know, we prepare impromptu speeches."

Mr. Clemens remembered it well and expressed pleasure at the judicious way in which the "applause" was worked in. "I was here three weeks ago," he went on, "and passed twenty-four hours in the city without anyone knowing it outside of one or two friends. Stopped a night right here at the Southern, registering as C. L. Samuels, New York.[5] The three of us were prowling under fictitious names, and we remained here just as long as we dared. I am writing a new book, and a tour of observation down the Mississippi River was necessary in connection with it. To make such a tour incognito seemed best, and so we have been dodging people, making our way by stealth and keeping up a sort of swindle day by day."

"When will your new book be out?"

"Probably about New Year's. I have had a very pleasant trip, and have been much interested in examining the spread of the flood and hearing the stories told in connection with it. I think it would be a capital thing to send a good man down the river and pick up all the yarns told about it. It seemed to me that every time they told some incident they added something to it. Then there are men with theories that we have listened to for hours, and known less when we got through than when we began."

"What do you think of calling your new book?"[6]

"It hasn't been thought of yet. I was in hopes to get away this afternoon, but cannot before tomorrow."

"I've a clean nightshirt at your disposal, if all your baggage is at the boat and you want it," broke in Clerk Keith, who happened to approach.

"I shall want a nightshirt," replied Mr. Clemens, "and I'll take it."

Notes to Interview 18

1. See n. 6 to interview 17.
2. Roswell H. Phelps (1845–1907), stenographer for the Continental Life Insurance Co. of Hartford.
3. McVicker's Theater, first erected in 1857, rebuilt after the 1871 Chicago fire at its original site on Madison street. The speech was delivered on 13 November 1879 in Chicago at the thirteenth annual banquet of the Army of the Tennessee.
4. A fashionable hotel founded by Potter Palmer (1826–1902) in 1875 near the intersection of State Street and Michigan Avenue in downtown Chicago.
5. MT wrote Howells on 16 April 1882 that he planned to register at the hotel in St. Louis under the name "S. L. Samuel" (*MTHL*, 1:401). On Howells, see n. 2 to interview 2.
6. "Old Times on the Mississippi." See n. 3 to interview 16.

19

"Mr. Mark Twain Excited on Seeing the Name of Capt. C. C. Duncan in Print," *New York Times,* 10 June 1883, 1.

Hartford, Conn., June 9—With his strawberries and cream before him and his *New York Times* in his hand, Mark Twain sat upon the portico of his handsome home this morning and made merry. He had chanced upon an item concerning an old acquaintance, Capt. C. C. Duncan,[1] New York's Shipping Commissioner and the father of the three illustrious young men whose powers of absorbing the funds of the United States Government are, as far as is now known, illimitable. "Well, well, well! So the old man's in hot water,"[2] says the author of *Roughing It* and *Tom Sawyer*,[3] with a mock expression of pity on his face as he pushed aside his strawberries. "Poor devil! I should think that after a while he'd conclude to put a little genius into his rascality, and try to hoodwink the public as his little game of robbery goes on. It don't become a scoundrel to be an ass. The combination always makes a mix of things, and if Duncan will persist in his wicked ways somebody ought to have a guardian appointed for him—a guardian with sense enough to throw a little gauze over the work of the gouge. He is still Shipping Commissioner, is he? And his dear noble boys surround him in his old age, supporting his steps, lightening his cares, and helping him to bankrupt the Government. Let us see, what does this item say: A bad man named Root, presuming on his position as a United States District Attorney, is making war on the magnificent patriot.[4] And Root don't like the way in which the funds of the Shipping Commission are disbursed. He thinks it isn't just the thing for the gallant Duncan, after gobbling $5,000 for personal salary, to give a half dollar or so to an errand-boy and then cut the surplus into three equal parts and to each of the scions of the house of Duncan give an equal and exact third. A hard man to please is this District Attorney Root. He may bless his stars and fervently congratulate the Government that Captain C. C. Duncan has not created a deficit, just to give his sons even money, say $3,050, instead of $3,648.30 as is the case.

"I see *The Times* says that just about $2,000 has been turned over to the Government's Treasury by Captain C. C. Duncan during the 10 years he has been Shipping Commissioner. There must be some mistake here. If a single penny in any year, or by any means, has fallen into the Treasury, a doleful error has occurred. Old Duncan never intended it, and I'll wager this new white duck suit I put on this morning that when the old man read *The Times* this morning and saw that a little cash had glided out of his grip, he hurried down town to cook up some job by which he could make the hoggish Government hand that cash back again.

"So he and his three sons appropriated to themselves $15,944.90 of the Government's funds for the work they profess to have done last year. That's monstrous. There's no joke in that. It's scoundrely, it's nauseating, bald, barefaced robbery: but it's Duncan, through and through. Why, my boy, if I wanted to get rich rapidly the one contract I'd most delight in making would be to hire 150 Duncan families by the year, and get just half of this $15,944.90 which Captain C. C. and his noble offspring take, and, as I calculate it, my profits would be precisely the whole amount the Government gave me if I hired them at their true value, for a Duncan of the C. C. stripe is worthless absolutely. Multiply him by 150, or 150 times 150. It will make no difference.

"Enough brains could not be found in a C. C. Duncan family to run the kitchen of a Sixth Ward restaurant respectably. Brains never were there; brains could not be induced to enter there; it is the old story of water declining to climb up hill. As to the matter of honesty, that always was an absent quality with the old man. Where the honesty ought to have been in his make-up an inscrutable Providence provided a vacuum, walled in by hypocrisy and the meanest of meanness.

"It has been my honor to know the old man for a number of years—longer, much longer, than has been to my profit, perhaps. The honor fell to me away back in 1867, when I got my text for *Innocents Abroad* in his gorgeous scheme of an 'excursion to the Holy Land, Egypt, the Crimea, Greece, and intermediate points of interest.' People who have read my tract will remember that I was one of the victims of that excursion. And they may remember, too, how I endeavored to immortalize the fair name of Duncan, though through reverence to truth I was obliged faithfully to note some things which a narrow-minded world chose to set not down to the glory and honor of the man who left New York Harbor a Captain and developed within 24 hours into the ship's head waiter. Queer things happened on that excursion. I performed but my duty to the world and coming generations when I narrated those happenings in words of soberness and truth. But Captain C. C. Duncan felt aggrieved. For years he kept his galled feelings pent up, but finally the time came when somebody advised him to enter the lecture field. He was going to explain all about the Holy Land as he saw it. He departed a little from his program and explained all about me as he did not see me.[5] I smiled and said nothing for a time, and finally only wasted a little ink for a New York newspaper after long and urgent solicitation.[6]

"I don't think Captain C. C. Duncan was any happier when I got through with him than he was before I began. I put on parade one or two of his little frauds that had not been seen hitherto. I called attention to his advertisements that on his big excursion Henry Ward Beecher, General Sherman, Maggie Mitchell, and other celebrities were to be among the passengers;[7] how none of them appeared: how none of them, I guess, ever had any thought of making the trip. I showed up a few other of his thinly disguised frauds and exposed him pretty thoroughly as an old piece of animated flatulence.

"To excoriate the old rascal began to give me fun. I didn't lack for ammunition. What I did not have in stock came to hand readily. I discovered that the world was fairly jammed with folks who had dealt with C. C. and sadly regretted it. A reputable New York law firm supplied me with a big batch of indictments against the humbug mariner. The papers and documents they gave to support their charges were absolutely convincing. There was a long list of offenses. For instance, it was shown that on December 18, 1867, Duncan filed a petition in bankruptcy, submitting his schedule of liabilities, amounting to $166,000, and that among these debts, as sworn by himself, was one of $5,265.28 to J. G. Richardson, of Liverpool, England. This was the proceeds of a consignment of canvas sold by him on account of Richardson and retained by him. He was also obliged to show an item of $634.42 for money collected by Duncan for Hall, Cornish & Co. and not paid over to them. Of course, this was rank dishonesty. There were other equally questionable items in the schedule. But this was not all.

"But, bah! It disgusts me to recite this fellow's manifold offenses. A half-dozen years ago I read a paragraph in the *New York Times* chronicling some of Duncan's wickedness and what I wrote [in response] for publication then I reiterate now![8] I have known and observed Duncan for years, and I think I have reason for believing him wholly without principle, without moral sense, without honor of any kind. I think I am justified in believing that he is cruel enough and heartless enough to rob any sailor or sailor's widow or orphan he can get his clutches upon, and I know him to be coward enough. I know him to be a canting hypocrite, filled to the chin with sham godliness and forever oozing and dripping false piety and pharisaical prayers. I know his word to be worthless. It is a shame and a disgrace to the civil service that such a man was permitted to work himself into an office of trust and responsibility. And I repeat today what I said then, that the act creating the 'Shipping Commission,' concocted by himself for his own profit, was simply and purely an act to create a pirate—a pirate that has flourished and still flourishes.

"I tell you, my boy, Judas Iscariot rises into respectability, and the star route rogues are paragons compared with this same canting C. C. Duncan, Shipping Commissioner."

And Mark Twain resumed his strawberries.

Notes to Interview 19

1. Charles C. Duncan (1821–98), the organizer of the *Quaker City* excursion and captain of the ship and so a figure in *The Innocents Abroad*.

2. On 9 June 1883 the *New York Times* reported that the U.S. attorney general had objected to the "excessive salaries" Duncan paid his sons—exactly $3,648.30 each, as Twain notes—and that "not more than $2,000 or $3,000" of the receipts of the Shipping Commissioner's Office "had found its way into the United States Treasury" over the previous ten years ("Commissioner Duncan's Sons," 8).

3. *The Adventures of Tom Sawyer* (1876) was MT's second novel and the first he wrote without a collaborator; he later described it as "a hymn put into prose to give it a worldly air."

4. Elihu Root (1845–1937) was the U.S. district attorney for the southern district of New York (1883–85), later U.S. secretary of state (1905–9) and U.S. senator from New York (1909–1915). He received the Nobel Peace Prize in 1912.

5. Duncan lectured in Brooklyn on 11 January 1877. In the course of his address, he declared that "one of the first persons . . . who made application for a berth in the *Quaker City* . . . was a tall, lanky, unkempt, unwashed individual, who seemed to be full of whiskey or something like it, and who filled my office with the fumes of bad liquor. He said he was a Baptist minister from San Francisco and desired to travel for his health. I knew him at once, it was Mark Twain, and I said 'You don't look like a Baptist minister or smell like one either'" ("About Mark Twain: His Entirely Disreputable Conduct Aboard the *Quaker City*," *New York World*, 12 January 1877, 5).

6. Twain soon responded to Duncan in a letter to the *New York World* (18 February 1877, 5). To the allegation that when he engaged passage he seemed "full of whiskey," Twain replied, "I hope this is true, but I cannot say, because it is so long ago. . . . I was poor—*I* couldn't afford good whiskey. How could I know that the 'captain' was so particular about the quality of a man's liquor?" Duncan in turn replied in "C. C. Duncan on Mark Twain," an interview with the *New York Daily Graphic*, 2 March 1877, 11: "I am sorry Twain has made such a fool of himself; I have even felt kindly towards him, and am sure he ought to be very grateful to me; for but for me he would never have immortalized himself by his *Innocents Abroad*."

7. Henry Ward Beecher (1813–87), minister of the Plymouth Church in Brooklyn, did not embark on the cruise as was rumored; Sherman originally planned to take the cruise but canceled (*MTL*, 2:24–25); Margaret Julia Mitchell (1837–1918), a popular actress, also canceled her trip on the *Quaker City* at the last minute (*MTL*, 2:407).

8. "The Ship-Owners and Mr. Duncan," *New York Times*, 15 February 1877, 8: "The Ship-owners' Association had also accused Duncan 'of paying salaries to his four sons, and others, grossly in excess of the services rendered, of being arbitrary and unjust in his decision,' etc."

20

"Mark Twain and the Police," *Boston Herald*, 16 November 1884, 16.

Now that Mark Twain is fairly out of the city, it may be safe to tell about his experience with the captain of one of the police stations. Contrary to the usual rule, his experience, as narrated, with the poor demented would-be suicide a few days ago was an actual occurrence, and resulted in his gaining an acquaintance with the workings of the Boston police force, which may be of use to him in the future. After he had followed the somewhat eccentric movements of the poor crazy woman the whole length of the water side of Beacon street up to Charles street, his associate in the deed of humanity which saved the life of the woman met him, accompanied by a police officer. Both brave gentlemen supposed that their duty ended with turning the woman over to the care of the public guardian, and were surprised to be informed that they must accompany the woman and the officer to the police station, and give their evidence as to the attempted suicide, etc. Having given so much time and taken so much trouble in the cause of humanity, they naturally demurred at this additional demand, but finally acceded to the officer's request. Their reception at the station house and their experience there are best told in Mark Twain's own words:

"When we arrived, we found the captain entirely at his ease. His feet were on his desk, and our appearance really seemed a sort of intrusion upon his comfortable leisure. The statement made by the officer that the woman had tried to commit suicide appeared to be a matter of hardly passing interest to him. He seemed absorbed in reading a book, and interrupted himself only to ask the stereotyped questions as to her age, birthplace, condition, married or single, etc., seeming to pay no attention to the fact that she was evidently insane, and incapable of giving any intelligent replies. As for my friend and myself he appeared oblivious of our existence, and we began to feel that we had really committed some criminal act in our efforts to save the woman. She was utterly exhausted, but when the door opened, and a man was brought in charged with theft or some such crime, the captain waved the woman aside, as if at last he had found something of interest. I finally suggested that we might be more comfortable sitting down inside the rail, and the idea seemed to meet with his approval. Having taken our testimony in the matter, a consultation was had between the officer and the captain as to the disposition of the woman, which ended in the former being instructed to take her to the Tombs.[1] This frightened me; I couldn't see that our efforts had been so very commendable after all, if the woman was to be buried anyway—dead or alive. I began to think how we could best save the woman again, when the official kindly explained that the Tombs was a sort of central office, where physicians were in attendance who would decide upon the disposition of the case. I don't want to save any more women from drowning—in Boston."

Note to Interview 20

1. The Boston city jail.

2
The "Twins of Genius" Tour, 1884–1885
Interviews 21–39

George Washington Cable (1844–1925) was an American novelist and Twain's companion on the "Twins of Genius" reading tour. Together, they performed on stage 103 times between 5 November 1884 and 28 February 1885 in some eighty cities, from St. Paul in the west, Louisville in the south, Montreal in the north, and Boston in the east. He often read excerpts from the unpublished *Adventures of Huckleberry Finn* to these audiences. Attendance averaged slightly over five hundred per appearance, and Twain earned in all about sixteen thousand dollars from the tour. As he later reminisced in his *Autobiography,* "a country audience is the difficult audience; a passage which it will approve with a ripple will bring a crash in the city. A fair success in the country means a triumph in the city." During this period he also founded his own publishing firm, best known today for issuing the memoirs of the Civil War general and president Ulysses S. Grant.

∽

21
"Mark Twain as Lecturer," *New York World,* 20 November 1884, 5; rpt. *St. Louis Post-Dispatch,* 20 November 1884, 1.

New York, November 20—Mark Twain, in dress suit, received the correspondent of *The World* yesterday in a waiting room at Chickering Hall.[1] Mr. George W. Cable was giving his recital of Creole life.

"Ah, you are cruel," he said, with an air of utter sadness, "to attempt to interview a man just at the moment when he needs to feel good. You've got to feel good, you know, in order to make the audience feel the same way, but to try to be funny after you've been interviewed"—the thought seemed to overpower him.

"I did not know it was such a physical strain to deliver a humorous lecture."

"Ah, you have never attempted it; you don't know. On a day like this, when we give two performances, I feel like I'm all burnt out after the first performance. As soon as I get back to the hotel, I go to bed. I must get some sleep, somehow. If I don't, I will not be able to go through with the evening performance the way I want to. It's the same thing when you're traveling. The audiences, intelligent newspaper-reading audiences, are responsive enough. They quickly catch the point you are trying to make; often times they anticipate it. Then you are put on your mettle to give a sudden turn to the story so as to bring out a new and unexpected point. If these things don't happen, don't blame the audience; it is yourself who is at fault. The traveling has exhausted you, and, as I said before, you're not feeling good."

"All this you can judge of by the effect you produce on the audience?"

"Oh, yes. If you hear a rustle here or there, or see a particularly stolid face, you can tell that there is something wrong with yourself. The effect, of course, is not general. Heaven forbid! You would then have to stop right off. Audiences have their peculiarities, you know. It is a great inspiration to find a particular individual fairly respond to you as if you were in telegraphic communication with him. You are tempted to address yourself solely to him. I've tried that experiment. Sometimes it is dangerous. Laughter is very infectious, and when you see a man give one great big guffaw, you begin to laugh with him in spite of yourself. Now, it would not do for the lecturer to laugh. His is a grave and serious business, however it might strike the audience. His demeanor should be grave and serious. He should not ever smile."

"You have had ample opportunity to average your audiences on their respective faculties for fun."

"Audiences are much the same everywhere. I have been delighted with all before whom I have had the honor of appearing. In Boston, where Mr. Cable and I appeared before coming *here*, the audiences were delighted with our efforts to please them. You should have witnessed the enthusiasm last evening. Oh, I have nothing to complain of my audiences; perhaps they cannot say the same of me. Our entertainment lasts one hour and three quarters. The fact that Mr. Cable and I alternate makes us able to extend it to that length. Were I lecturing alone, one hour and five minutes is as much as I would dare impose on the audience. The strain on them in the humorous direction would be too much. But now Mr. Cable gently soothes them, then I excite them to laughter, or try to, at least. Then Mr. Cable has his turn and so the change is very healthful and beneficial."

"Your tour will be an extended one?"

"Our agent has booked us to the end of January. I should like to go to California, if I can manage it. You know this is my farewell performance. I so intimated to the audience last evening. I told them that I had not practically

1. Mark Twain and George Washington Cable, 26 September 1884. Publicity photograph for the "Twins of Genius" tour. From J. B. Pond's *Eccentricities of Genius* (New York: Dillingham, 1900).

appeared on the platform for nine years, and that when this term was over I would not appear again—at least, not for nine years. It will do me good; it will do my hearers good. Yet I've known people to give farewell performances for 50 years in succession."

A burst of applause at this juncture announced the conclusion of Mr. Cable's recital and that the time had come for Mark Twain to appear on the stage. As the reporter passed out he heard an outburst of laughter. The humorist had made a point.

Note to Interview 21

1. W. A. Croffut, *An American Procession* (Boston: Little, Brown, 1931), 176–77, also reviewed the performance: "I dodged into the back room of Chickering Hall one evening to get a word with Mark Twain and Cable during their breathing spells. The great American story-teller was on the platform spinning his yarns at the moment,

and the Creole novelist was on tiptoe at the fly, waiting his turn. Almost before a word of greeting and congratulation could be spoken there was a cordial racket of palms and boot heels and our humorist backed upon us through the half-open door. He looked grayer, but not otherwise older than when I first heard him fifteen years before. His abatis of moustache and his porcupine eyebrows were as straggling and bristling as ever, and his rebellious and tousled hair looked as if it belonged to somebody else and had been borrowed for the occasion. I reminded him that the last time I saw him he told me that he hated the whole entertainment business and had quit it forever. "Yes," he said, "but I found I couldn't get along without being amused. No lecturer can be as amusing as an average audience. I shall not keep it up, though. I like audiences, and I like spinning my yarns. It is agreeable. When the evening is over I don't like to quit it, but that accounts for only two hours out of the day. What shall I do with the other twenty-two? That's the question. This business involves too much standing around. If, when I get to a town, I could rush in and play billiards till eight o'clock, it would be fun; but, no, I have to coddle myself. That's what I hate. And I can't accept the hospitality of a friend anywhere. Traveling, too, is an awful trial. If I could be shot all over the country in an air gun, or if I could go to sleep in the morning and sleep all day, that would be tolerable, perhaps, but I haven't any place to go and so I wander around disconsolate. Just hear that last sentence of Cable's; isn't that fine? See there! He's an orator and a genius. Here he comes. Bully for you, Cable! Let's see, what's mine?—Oh, yes, 'The Interviewer'—and he sidled out upon the stage, book in hand, smiling grimly to the audience's salute." MT's sketch "An Encounter with an Interviewer," originally published in *Lotos Leaves,* ed. W. F. Gill (Chicago, 1875), was excerpted as early as 19 November 1874 in the *Hartford Daily Times,* 1.

22

"Mark Twain and the President," *Philadelphia Press,* 27 November 1884, 3.

"I have just been to Washington," said Mark Twain last evening in Association Hall, previous to his going on the stage, to a *Press* reporter. "I read before the President, the first president I ever read before."[1]

"Were you much impressed by him?" asked the visitor.

"I? Him?" drawled the humorist, rumpling up his shaggy hair. "Why! he must have been impressed with me. He ought to have been. It was the first time he ever heard me read."

The readings of Mr. Clemens and George W. Cable were very successful in the afternoon and evening yesterday. Association Hall was filled in the evening, and the awkward, hesitating humor of Mark Twain received equal honor with the pathetic, realistic and linguistic rendition of selections from *Dr. Sevier* and *The Grandissimes.* The best thing done by Mr. Cable was "Mary's Night Ride" from *Dr. Sevier,* into which considerable dramatic power was thrown.[2] But the audience seemed most pleased with the Creole songs, which were very sweetly rendered. After his last number Mr. Cable was called back and sang a song that he had never given before, as he waited to see a lady in Philadelphia, a sister of Gottschalk, by whom he could verify the words.[3] It represented a mother calling upon her child "Salangadon," and being answered by the wind. The effect of the wind-music was perfect and the song itself was very sweet.

Mark Twain, round-shouldered and stooping, slouched onto the stage, and, trying to balance himself on one foot, convulsed the audience with an account of a desperate encounter that he once had with an interviewer, which ended with the reporter going away threatened with mental collapse because of the utter stupidity with which he found Twain afflicted. Twain said he had never had one before and did not know what to do with him, for he understood he had a faculty of making a man say just what he did not want to have divulged, and, as he had committed some crime, he had forgotten just what, he wanted to have nothing to do with him.

After the lecture a reporter, remembering this recitation, advanced into the dressing-room with considerable trepidation and admitted to Mr. Clemens that he felt some nervousness.

"Oh, now you are making fun of me," said Twain. "But that was true. That is just the way it is. I never told the plain, unadorned truth in my life but that all my friends knew I was lying. I have backed it up with affidavits, but they believed it still less. And then I never told the most barefaced lie but what everybody swallowed it whole for Gospel truth. I am always misunderstood."

Notes to Interview 22

1. Chester A. Arthur (1830–86), U.S. president, 1881–85.
2. Cable read excerpts from his novels *The Grandissimes* (1880) and *Dr. Sevier* (1884), including "Mary's Night Ride," chapter 54 of the latter text.
3. Louis Morgan Gottschalk (1829–69), a Louisiana Creole composer.

23

"Mark Twain's Ideas: A Talk with the Humorist," *Baltimore American*, 29 November 1884, 4.

"Yes, we have stood the test very well," said Mark Twain last night, as he sat behind the scenes in the Academy of Music concert hall waiting for the great crowd that had come to hear him read get seated. "To be sure, whenever we would arrive in a town there would be processions and torchlight parades, whether on our account or not I can't say, but they would be there. Yet the political excitement has not hurt us in regard to audiences. We were in places, too, where there was much excitement, and even after the thing was settled the people did not seem to know what to do with their old campaign trumpery, and would get up parades for picnics and socials, just to use it: but the crowd would come to us, nevertheless."

Mr. Twain speaks in a slow, deliberate manner, almost with a drawl. He never seems hurried or excited, but quietly talks, as if he was finding the word to be used in his mental dictionary. Continuing, he said: "It has been seventeen years since I last appeared on the platform in this city. It was in a long hall. I can fully remember it, for I see the people sitting far down in front of me. I have been here since. Once I felt tired and like I wanted a rest. I came here. I got it. I stopped at a hotel—I have forgotten the name—but I stayed in my room all the time and in bed. There, tucked under the covers, I had terrapin, oysters, canvas-back ducks, and lived. No one saw me; no one knew I was here, except George Alfred Townsend.[1] He was roaming about here, and I fell upon him. No, he stumbled upon me, for he found me in bed. Resting? Yes, resting. I don't like traveling. I would, mind, if I could take my family with me; but there are those blessed darlings—the children—and what a trouble children are when they travel! And the average American child when he travels generally makes himself known. Therefore, this is my last appearance on the platform."

The American representative smiled, as he thought of the numerous stars now making their farewell tours, and the smile faded away to almost tears, as he thought Mark Twain was to be added to this list. Mr. Clemens noticed the look, and quickly—well, as quickly as Mr. Twain ever allows his voice to be accelerated, said: "Yes; I mean it, I was forty-nine years of age yesterday; and if I remain off the platform seventeen years, put that to forty-nine, and by that time nobody will want to hear me. I love the platform, and I would like to live on it, but I cannot be traveling about all the time. There is my family at home doing the lonesome. If I could settle down in New York, they could come in and stay there while I talked. Why, look how long a play runs in New York. I don't want such a big hall. I could talk in a small one, and I am sure there would be one man in it to hear me. Why have I got Mr. Cable with me? Well, I don't feel like taking the responsibility of giving the entire show. I want someone to help me. It is a great burden, this awful thought that you alone have to carry everything. Then I want company. Mr. Cable is company, good company. We need not talk all the time. You can be company with each other and not say a word. Sweethearts sometimes sit together a long time and don't say a word. Yet they are company for each other. Yes, the platform has a great fascination. In regard to the way the audiences take the jokes. They say English people are slow to perceive a joke; but you get a large audience before you— why, they catch on to the joke before you have half told it. Yet, you talk to four or five Englishmen and tell them a funny story. When you get through they'll never smile. But next day they'll laugh. Fact. What is the difference between the crowd and the select party? Oh, I think it is a sort of sympathy with the crowd. One laughs, the others laugh with him, not with the fear they have to digest the fun. I was sitting one night in the Savage Club in London with Tom

Hood, editor of *Fun,* and one or two others.[2] I told them a funny story, and not one laughed. Next day I met Hood in the club, and he came up to me and said, 'Twain, tell that funny story you told last night to my friends here.' I told it. Hood laughed loud and long. The other men near smiled. Will you believe it, I told Hood that story five times, and each time he laughed heartier than the preceding time, and the last time I thought he would die. Yet, those who heard it for the first time never smiled. They wanted it to soak in.

"How will F. C. Burnard, the editor of *Punch,* do here on his lecture tour?[3] If I put on a bright flaming red scarf and went out on the platform everybody would look at that scarf. They would have their thoughts distracted by it. They would forget to look at it.

"Mr. Burnard speaks very broad English. How they can call it good solid English I can't understand. I once heard him give a reading, when he described a yachting party giving imitations of the ladies and their efforts to eat off the swinging table. It was very funny, and I enjoyed it, but his pronunciation was so pronounced to me that I noticed it all the time. When Toole came over here he asked me about it.[4] I told him plainly that I did not think his broad English pronunciation would suit the American people. If he would do the red scarf act and come before the people, I do not think he would succeed. We shall see in regard to Mr. Burnard. One day I was talking to George Augustus Sala in London;[5] in fact, he was having a heated discussion in regard to Americans with a friend. I spoke up and defended my countrymen. He quoted as examples the words 'cow' and 'now,' as spoken in one part of the United States with a broad sound. I told him that that pronunciation was only common in one part of our country, and that because it was originally settled by Englishmen. What they are pleased to call Americanisms originally came from England, and it is unjust to us to lay all the vulgar, coarse things at our door. To prove to Mr. Sala that I was right, I said, now I'll call your attention in a few minutes to yourself, for you will use the very pronunciation of the words 'cow' and 'now,' exactly as he had said the Americans used the word."

Mr. Cable, who reads with Mr. Twain, had been exploring the wings, and when it was time for Mr. Twain to go on Mr. Cable remarked: "Look out for the wall as you go in, and don't brush against it, or you'll get whitewash all over you."

"They will have to look out for their whitewash," replied Mr. Twain in his droll manner. "I will take care of myself."

While Mark Twain and Cable were entertaining *The American* representative behind the scenes, the concert hall was rapidly filling up, and when Mr. Cable appeared to read his first selections—one from *Dr. Sevier,* "Narcisse and John and Mary Richling"[6]—the house was crowded, every seat being occupied. Messrs Twain and Cable read alternately, the latter starting off. He was warmly received, and throughout the evening his selections were received with close attention and applause. He read largely from *Dr. Sevier*, the best selection being "Mary's Night Ride," which showed his descriptive powers to the best advantage. He also sang a number of Creole songs excellently.

Mr. Twain, however, seemed to be the star. His appearance was the signal for loud applause, and the people laughed at everything he said. Mr. Twain was funny last night. His *Adventures of Huckleberry Finn*, from his latest work, was his first "reading."[7] It was a happy selection, and made him at home at once with the audience. To those who had read his *Tramp Abroad*, the tragic tale of "The Fishwife and a Trying Situation," taken from it, hardly recognized them, for Mr. Twain told them in his inimitable manner, and gave almost a new reading to them.[8] He was in the midst of "a trying situation," when there was a rustle in the gallery. It grew louder and louder, until the sounds of hustling feet and women's dresses were heard coming down the stairway.

Mr. Twain stopped, and taking out his watch said: "Time to catch a train, I expect."

Just then the form of the principal of a female college near the city appeared at the south doorway and led the troop of thirty or forty girls across the hall, right in front of the stage. The aisle divides the audience equally, and the people applauded terrifically. Mr. Twain looked bored. He was bored, and as the form of the female assistant disappeared Mr. Twain resumed: "You can't always tell the customs of the country. In Boston once it was customary for the people to catch the train at 9:05 o'clock. One night I was reading there, and at that hour everybody in the hall got up and left. I did not know of this tonight. How can one tell of these things?" He finished the story. He was very successful with his short story, which closed the program, and its rendition so wrought up a lady in the audience that when the denouement came she shouted "Oh!"

Mr. Twain and Mr. Cable read at the matinee today and tonight they give their farewell, and retire for good—so Mr. Twain says. There will be a change of bill.

Notes to Interview 23

1. See n. 1 to interview 8.
2. MT was elected to honorary membership in this "gentlemen's club" founded by Richard Savage in London in 1857; Tom Hood (1835-74) was an English humorist.
3. Sir F. C. Burnard (1836-1917), librettist and editor of the English humor magazine *Punch* from 1880 until 1906.
4. John L. Toole (c. 1830-1906), English actor and comedian.
5. George Augustus Sala (1828-95), English journalist.

6. Cable read "Narcisse in Mourning" (chap. 45) and "Kate Riley, Richling, and Restofolo" (chap. 35) from *Dr. Sevier*. See also n. 2 to interview 22.

7. MT's fourth novel, a sequel to *The Adventures of Tom Sawyer,* and by critical consensus his masterpiece (published in England in December 1884 and in the United States in February 1885).

8. "The Fishwife and Its Sad Fate," a satire of gendered German nouns in "The Awful German Language" appendix to *A Tramp Abroad*.

24

"Mark Twain Encountered," *Rochester Herald,* 8 December 1884, 8.

Armed for a "desperate encounter" a *Herald* reporter knocked boldly at room 222 Powers Hotel yesterday afternoon. "Come in," was the response given in a drawling, half-asleep sort of a way, and the reporter knew he had found Mark Twain. Naturally enough the visitor, entering unannounced, felt somewhat abashed to find that the humorist had not yet arisen. It was four o'clock in the afternoon. Mr. Clemens, however, didn't seem to mind the intrusion much and put the reporter at his ease by a cordial greeting, explaining at the same time that on Sunday very often he didn't get up until Monday. The room was in an alarming state of disorder. Articles of clothing, books, letters and various other things were scattered about in the most promiscuous fashion. The humorist's capacious valise, which lay open upon a center table, looked as though it had been struck by a cyclone. Mr. Clemens, in an embroidered *robe de nuit,* lay on the bed, his head propped up with two pillows and a bolster. He was vigorously pulling smoke from a well-burnt cob pipe, and had been writing, his knees serving for a desk. Thanks to the existence of two or three mutual acquaintances in another city, the reporter was able to worry along very comfortably without saying a word about newspapers or interviews.

"How did it happen, Mr. Clemens," inquired the reporter, "that Mr. Cable and yourself combined forces for the season?"

"Well, it makes a pleasant combination so far as we are concerned," was the reply. "Each of us needed company, also somebody to do half the work. I don't mind work much myself, indeed I'd just as soon stand on a platform two hours as anywhere else but I prefer to have somebody to share the responsibility of entertaining an audience. One of us counteracts the other, you know. A counter-irritant often produces good results."

A knock was heard at the door and a chambermaid called out, "How soon will you have your room put in order, sir?" "Oh, never mind," replied Mr. Clemens, "that's all right; tomorrow morning will be soon enough." "I don't feel energetic enough," addressing the reporter, "to get up and move about. The remains of a villainous cold are hanging about me. Every night for the last two weeks I've had to torture my throat with cayenne pepper tea and all sorts of villainous mixtures to be able to use my voice at all. If I can get over this cold entirely I think this campaign will improve my health wonderfully; in fact, in the month we have been out I have gained an appetite—a thing I hadn't known anything about for ten years. Now I eat three meals a day with a fair degree of success. Heretofore I have taken but two meals a day—breakfast at nine, dinner at six and nothing between times. Even at that rate I was rarely able to attack dinner with any show of enthusiasm."

Thus reminded of the wants of the inner man Mr. Clemens called a bellboy and sent down an order for a dinner, delegating to the waiter authority to select the dishes.

Mr. Clemens took occasion to express himself as highly pleased with what he had seen of Rochester and then branched off into an interesting disquisition upon the prevailing styles of architecture in residences. "By the way," inquired the reporter who recalled the appearance of Mr. Clemens' odd but beautiful home in Hartford, "what is the style of your house—what would you call it if you had to name it?"

"Well, I don't know," answered the humorist; "have never invented a name. There are nineteen different styles in it and folks can take their pick. It wouldn't do to call it 'mongrel' for that would be offensive to some. I guess we'll call it 'eclectic'—the word describes everything that can't be otherwise described."

At this point the waiter entered with a heavily laden tray and the reporter started to make his escape. "Oh, by the way, hold on a minute," exclaimed Mr. Clemens rising in his bed, "speaking of architecture reminds me, by contrast, of a thing across the street here. Cable and I have been studying it with a good deal of curiosity but neither of us can get at any satisfactory conclusion. What is it?" Here the humorist got out of bed and ambled across the room to a window, which was raised slightly from the bottom. A gentle breeze was blowing in at the time, and his long night-shirt flapped about his bare legs. "There it is!" he exclaimed, "look there! Am I suffering from some nightmare, or is it a reality?"

"That, sir," replied the reporter, looking in the direction indicated, "is the Cogswell fountain—a gift to the city of Rochester from the famous San Francisco philanthropist, Dr. Cogswell?"[1]

"Oh, yes! Is it possible? It's all clear now. That's a Cogswell fountain! The same philanthropist tried to work one off on Hartford, but we wouldn't have it. And the city of Rochester allowed him to leave one here! That's the best joke I ever heard. What's it made of—it looks like putty?"

"The material, I believe, is monumental bronze."

"It isn't half so monumental," said Mr. Clemens dryly, "as the brass of the donor. I don't feel like interfering in a matter of this kind—purely local you know—but I would like to advise the citizens to turn out and mob the statue to get even. The man looks as if he'd been nine days drowned. It has a putrid, decomposed sort of a look that is offensive for a delicate organism. The only redeeming feature about the doctor, if that is true to life, is his legs—very fair legs those. I would cut that statue off just below the coat skirts and throw the top part into the canal where the water is deepest and the mud in the bottom softest."

"But you must remember, Mr. Clemens," interrupted the reporter, "that 'man and the faithful dog may here find refreshing' and get ice water at that."

"Yes, and you must remember that Dr. Cogswell furnishes neither the water nor the ice."

At this point in the very interesting conversation the waiter who stood by ventured to suggest that the dinner was getting cold and the reporter withdrew.

Note to Interview 24

1. Henry Daniel Cogswell, a temperance advocate, sponsored the erection of statues with water fountains around the country. See Annie Hanmer-Croughton, "The Cogswell Fountain," *Rochester Historical Society* 14 (1936): 320–23.

25

"The Genial Mark: An Interview," *Toronto Globe,* 9 December 1884, 2.

... After the performance, *The Globe* reporter, through the courtesy of Mr. Pond,[1] the manager of the party, had an opportunity of speaking with the entertainers of the evening. Samuel L. Clemens is a quiet, pleasant spoken man, but not "funny" in the ordinary sense of the word. He said it was quite true that he had been elected a member of the Montreal Snowshoe Club, and that he had been specifically invited to attend the carnival, but feared that his lecture engagements would prevent his accepting the invitation.

"How do you reconcile this tour with your vow of which you have written that you would never go on the lecture platform unless driven there by want of bread?" was asked.

"Well, I'd kept that vow so long—fifteen years or so—that I thought it time to break it and make a better one." ...

Note to Interview 25

1. James B. Pond (1838–1903), head of the lecture agency that organized MT and Cable's 1884–85 lecture tour and the North American leg of MT's 1895–96 round-the-world tour.

26

"The Funny Men in Bed," *Detroit Post,* 17 December 1884, 4.

"Is the American taste for humor still growing in your opinion?"

"Yes, I think so. Humor is always popular, and especially so with Americans. It is born in every American and he can't help liking it."

"Is it true that the American style of humor is becoming very popular in England?"

"Yes, the liking for American humor over there has become immense. It awakens the people to a new life, and is supplanting the dry wit which formerly passed for humor. American humor wins its own way and does not need to be cultivated. The English come to like it naturally."

27

"Mark Twain Gets Shaved," *Pittsburgh Penny Press,* 29 December 1884, 4.

Mark Twain's appearance, as he underwent the operation of shaving in his private apartment at the Monongahela House this morning,[1] when a *Press* reporter was ushered in, was strongly suggestive of Dickens' famous character, Cousin Feenix, in *Dombey and Son,*[2] and also reminded the scribe of a badly executed figure on a political transparency without enough light behind it. Time seems to have dealt pretty heavily with Mark of late years, for his hair and moustache are gray. Everybody who has seen him on the platform is familiar with the intense air of being completely, hopelessly and inexpressibly bored, which pervades the whole man, and has doubtless thought that it was assumed, but it is only necessary to meet him in private life to know that the man is really and truly tired of everything. His manner of drawling his words is even more pronounced and noticeable in private than in public, his walk, his look, his way of sitting, or rather lying, in fact his every motion is expressive of one word, boredom.

"How long since you were in Pittsburgh before, Mr. Twain?" asked the scribe.

"About fifty years," was the answer, in a deep, sepulchral voice, that seemed to proceed from the soles of the funny man's boots.

"And how do you like it?"

"As well as I did then," again came the sepulchral reply. At this point a bell boy entered, bearing an autograph album.

"Friend, what have you there?" asked Mark.

"Dis an a'ristocrat book what Massa Kelly done sent up to get you to write in."

"Do you and he expect me to write without a pen?" drawled the humorist.

"I done fo'got de pen. I'll go an' tote one up."

"I've got one. I only spoke of the pen to see if you were true and loyal. Now, let me see; where shall I write in this thing? I can't find a blank page, and it takes a whole page for me. Hullo, here's an outlaw like myself," and, turning the book towards the scribe the latter read, *Bob Ford, the Slayer of Jesse James.* "Bob and I are both outlaws and murderers," Twain continued. "He killed Jesse James, and I am constantly murdering the North American English, so Bob shall be my *vis-à-vis*," and down went the name of Mark Twain opposite that of Bob Ford.[3]

The conversation turned upon magazine literature.

"The literary productions which fill the pages of the magazines nowadays," remarked Twain, "are greatly superior to those of former years. We haven't got any *Autocrat of the Breakfast Table* to be run out;[4] we don't want an autocrat oftener than once in 100 years. Of course, a generation or two ago the magazines had Longfellow, Whittier, Lowell,[5] and some more of those fellows who made literature for one or two generations, but take them out and I think the magazine writing of today much better than it was in their time."

"How do you like the idea of reading in a church?" asked the *Press* man, referring to the fact that Twain and Cable are to appear in the Cumberland Presbyterian Church tonight.

"I don't mind it, but I have always found going to church so conducive to slumber that I am afraid I may go to sleep. Perhaps by the time I have done so the audience, also realizing the fact that they are in church, will be asleep also, and if Cable doesn't disturb us we may spend a very pleasant evening together."

"Can you be funny in church?"

"I guess so, for I shall feel very funny there."

At this juncture Mr. George W. Cable entered the room.

"Here is my partner in crime. Why don't you bore him now?" and poor Twain, with the air of a man to whom death would be a boon as a relief from boredom, heaved a deep sigh, and looked so darkly and intently at the razor with which the barber had been scraping him, that the knight of the lead pencil lost no time in transferring his attention to Mr. Cable, and asked that gentleman what first led him to turn his attention to literature....

Notes to Interview 27

1. At the intersection of Smithfield and Water (now Fort Pitt) streets, a hotel erected in 1839–40 that hosted eleven presidents from John Quincy Adams to William Howard Taft.

2. Chapter 31 of Dickens's *Dombey and Son* (1848): "Cousin Feenix, getting up at half-past seven or so, is quite another thing from Cousin Feenix got up; and very dim, indeed, he looks, while being shaved...."

3. Bob Ford (1861–92), "the dirty little coward who shot Mr. Howard and laid poor Jesse in his grave."
4. See n. 2 to interview 17.
5. Henry Wadsworth Longfellow (1807–82), American poet; John Greenleaf Whittier (1807–92), Quaker poet and abolitionist; James Russell Lowell (1819–91), American poet and author of *The Biglow Papers* (1848; second series 1867).

28

"Talk with Twain," *Pittsburgh Chronicle,* 29 December 1884, 1.

Mark Twain is in town. He did not come here to inspect our manufactories, nor on a pleasure trip. He is to lecture with Cable, the novelist, tonight, at the Cumberland Church, on Sixth avenue. He was sitting in an easy chair in his room, having his hair cut, when the writer called on him today.

"Take off your overcoat and sit down," said he with the air of a man who in his time has overcome many impediments to happiness by courtesy and perseverance.

"Thank you, but I have not time. I merely called to have a five minutes' talk about cosmos."

"Oh, indeed!" he retorted gravely. "Well, I am sorry I cannot oblige you but that is a subject I never speak of except at home after a week's preparation. I always treat light subjects in that way; however, sit down and let us talk. You would not care for a discourse on American art, would you, in place of cosmos?"

"Not just at this time."

"Well, I thought you might. I don't know anything about the subject, but of course that would enable me to be more graphic and entertaining. I met a drummer on a train a short time ago who asked me for my opinion on that matter. I knew he was a humbug in asking it, but I was also a humbug, for I proceeded to tell him what I did not know, but what I pretended to know."

"Suppose you tell me something of what you think about recent American magazine literature?"

"I have not an opinion which would be worth having on that subject. It seems to me, however, that there has been a wonderful advance of late years in the general tone of the magazines. There has been no new *Autocrat of the Breakfast Table,* to be sure, but what do you expect? You do not want more than one 'autocrat' in a century—you cannot hope for more than one. Such men as Holmes, Hawthorne, Longfellow, Fields,[1] and others of that school upheld the literary reputation of two generations, and made the *Atlantic* so brilliant. Most of these men have gone, but the general work in magazines is far superior to that of ten years ago. The trouble is that the two or three magazines which are a good market for a writer, and which can aid him in his work for fame, are overcrowded. The *Century* has perhaps $100,000 worth of accepted articles in its vault which may not appear for years. They are pushed aside by articles on timely topics which cannot be delayed. There are other magazines, it is true, but when you send them an article you send a burial permit with it, for you know that it will be entombed even if it is printed. These combinations of newspapers which print stories and sketches once a week will, it seems to me, give rising and capable writers the field they desire as well as the market. Charles Dudley Warner told me of one of these syndicates which is in charge of Thorndyke Rice, of the *North American Review*.[2] He has fifteen of the leading papers of the country which pay liberally for a page of matter either for their Sunday issues or for another day they may select. The idea is, I believe, to give at least one sketch or story by some very well known writer in each issue, and give other articles on the same page by clever people not so well known. This will bring into Mr. Rice's hands about $10,000 a month to pay his corps of writers. He can pay them just as good, if not better prices than any of the magazines, and besides he can handle matters of passing interest before the magazines get at them. Mr. Rice has written to me and has offered me handsome terms for articles. He seems to think I am a magazine writer, but I really am not."

"He has asked Mr. Henry Irving to write for him also."[3]

"Has he? Well, the idea is to have at his command the men who are eminent in all the branches of art, literature, drama, the sciences, and professions. There are good writers of short stories now, and there have never been very many. Such men as [Edgar Allan] Poe and Aldrich stand out so that you can at once recall them.[4] I do not believe in the decrying of the books of the day, which is so common. I admit I am not a careful reader of novels. I read portions of them, but do not read them through with the care some of them deserve. Much of my opinion is based upon what I hear from men and women of sound judgment whom I know intimately and whom I can rely upon. Take Hawthorne as an example of my peculiar literary bent of thought. It has become quite the custom to speak of him as the greatest of all American romanticists. I read him now and then for his style, the exquisite manner in which he writes, but I do not care for his stories, for I do not think that they are as great as many others by American writers. Howells' newspaperman who is brought before the public a second time in *Silas Lapham*. He is a wonderful creation, a photograph of many such men who do exist, not a cheerful, nice sort of man to sit at a communion table perhaps, but still a strong, living man.[5] I was in Europe when Henry James' 'Daisy Miller' reached there.[6] I chanced to be where there were a great many American ladies, and I must confess I never heard a literary production so roundly denounced as was 'Daisy Miller.' It was called an absurd exaggeration, a gross libel on the American girl, and all sorts of things. Nothing was too bad to say of it. And yet within a few hours I heard these same ladies allude to young American girls who just fitted into the description of that irrepressible young lady. The work has been caviled at and found fault with, but it is true, and just and close to the truth in spite of all that. The blemishes complained of in recent American books are to be found just as readily in English works or those of other countries. The trouble with many authors of books as well as of plays is that they let their work run too long. The interest dies before the story ends. That is the only fault to be found, for instance, with such an admirable book as *Lorna Doone*.[7] I read two-thirds of it with keen relish and interest and then stopped. I felt that there was a disposition to—using a New England phrase—'run emptyings' at the close.[8] I have re-read the first of the book many times, but never have gone through it, yet I suppose this book now has as many people who read it over again annually as *Jane Eyre*, which in many households finds a place between a Bible and the prayer book. The fault perhaps lies in my own taste, which has a strong bent to history and biography."

Mr. Cable made his appearance there for the third or fourth time, and Mr. Clemens, who by this time had come from the barber's hands "a very proper man, indeed," wished his visitor a good morning.

Notes to Interview 28

1. James T. Fields (1817-81), a prominent Boston publisher and editor of the *Atlantic Monthly* from 1861 to 1871.

2. Charles Dudley Warner (1829-1900), co-owner of the *Hartford Courant*, MT's near-neighbor in Hartford, and his collaborator on his first novel, *The Gilded Age* (1873), a political satire. Charles Allen Thorndyke Rice (1851-89) owned and edited the *North American Review* after 1876.

3. Sir Henry Irving (1838-1905), English actor.

4. Thomas Bailey Aldrich (1836-1907), author of *The Story of a Bad Boy* (1869), a model for MT's *The Adventures of Tom Sawyer*, and editor of the *Atlantic Monthly* from 1881 to 1890. For MT's subsequent praise of Aldrich, see *MTE*, 294.

5. Bartley Hubbard, a major character in Howells's novel *A Modern Instance* (1882) and a minor character in *The Rise of Silas Lapham* (1885). On Howells, see n. 2 to interview 2.

6. *Daisy Miller*, a controversial short novel by the American expatriate Henry James (1843-1916), was first published in the British *Cornhill Magazine* for June–July 1878.

7. *Lorna Doone* (1869), historical romance by R. D. Blackmore (1825-1900).

8. Not quite the same as "running on empty," which might describe an internal combustion engine running out of fuel. Rather, "run emptyings" refers to a coal- or wood-fired steam engine running on the ash and dying embers in the boiler.

29

"Mark Twain," *Pittsburgh Post*, 29 December 1884, 4.

Samuel L. Clemens, better known to the sphere of humorous literature as Mark Twain, arrived in this city last evening. He had come from Philadelphia and was immediately driven to the Monongahela House, where the other half of the combination, George W. Cable, was already ensconced. A representative of *The Post* was shown to Mr. Clemens' apartments, and found the noted humorist preparing to retire. Mr. Clemens can hardly be described with his head of roughened, curling hair, just tinged with gray, his vigorous nose, his sardonic mustache and cleft chin, but the humor peeps out of his features nevertheless. When the reporter introduced himself, Mr. Clemens started the conversation by saying:

"Ever since I knew anything I have had a horror of interviewers. The principal reason of that is that reporters have a way of getting at facts that a man does not want to be known. Now, one of these men came to me twice after I had—well, committed a crime. What the crime was has entirely escaped my memory. I have been guilty of so many that I can't keep track of any particular one. I made no note of it, but all the same I did not want to see this interviewer. I wrestled with the problem a long time, and finally offset him with a series of falsehoods that would have knocked any man off his pins."

"Have you met with success this season?"

"We have. You see there are so many people anxious to hear Mr. Cable's readings that I failed to scare them all away. The result is we have had large audiences."

"How long has it been since you left the platform?" inquired the reporter.

His left hand sought the old familiar pantaloons pocket and stayed there, while he leaned with his other arm on the mantle, and proceeded in his slow, nasal drawl.

"It is eight or nine years since I bade good-bye to the lecture platform forever," he said. "But they say lecturers and burglars never reform. I don't know how it is with burglars—it is so long since I had intimate relations with those people—but it is quite true of lecturers. They never reform. Lecturers and readers say they are going to leave the lecture platform never to return. They mean it, they mean it. But there comes in time an overpowering temptation to come out on the platform and give truth and morality one more lift. You can't resist it."

As he closed this remark he looked longingly toward a gorgeous nightshirt that was hanging over the footboard of the bedstead, at the same time saying he had had a very tiresome ride. It would have been cruel not to have noticed these evident signs of distress, and the reporter retired.

30

"The Humorists Interviewed," *Cincinnati Enquirer,* 3 January 1885, 4.

The lecturers, Mark Twain and George W. Cable, with their managers Messrs. J. H. and Ozias W. Pond,[1] were seated at a table in the St. Nicholas dining-room at eleven o'clock last evening when an *Enquirer* reporter was ushered in. Mr. Cable was getting away with some chocolate ice-cream, and Mr. Clemens had before him a half emptied bottle of Bass' pale ale.

"Glad to see you, *Enquirer*," he said, as he extended a hand and introduced the caller to his associates.

"Thought you might be able to say something interesting. You have been both interviewed probably on every conceivable subject, so if you will just rattle away and talk about any thing it will answer. You know how it is yourself."

"You should not expect a fellow to be very interesting after two hours on the platform," said Mr. Clemens.

"You are not expected to say much."

"Do you give a fellow a fair show?"

"Always."

"What I mean by that is, when a man talks to you, do you, in publishing it, eliminate all that he has said that is stupid and retain all that is bright?"

"Well, that is a question of judgment generally. The 'guying reporter' of the paper thought it would be better to interview you without seeing you. How did you used to work it?"

"Well, it's a pretty good scheme. If you know your man pretty well you can size him up about right. Now, I think if you had sat down at the *Enquirer* office you could have written a nicer talk than you can have with me. You, in writing, have time to collect your thoughts and take your choice of words. This especially applies to interviews with statesmen. A reporter cognizant with public affairs and the records of men ought to be able to interview without seeing him nearly any day and report his ideas correctly, using better language than the man himself would have chosen, and making a more entertaining article than if he had really seen him. I used to make reports of speeches in long hand that I could not begin to get the bulk of. I would take the merest skeleton, jot down a word here and there, and then fill it out at the office, using the speaker's ideas and my own language. It made me feel good when they complimented me and said it was better than the original."

"You were what we call a common reporter at one time, then?"

"Oh, yes, in 1862 and '63 I was on the Virginia City *Enterprise,* and in 1864 and '65 on the San Francisco *Call,* besides many other minor journals in my earlier days."

"Were you ever associated with Bret Harte?"

"Not in business. We were neighbors once in San Francisco. Harte was Secretary of the Mint. His office was in the same building with the *Call.* I often met him there, and we became well acquainted. He was editing the *Weekly Californian,* a literary paper, at the same time."[2]

"What is Harte's best work, or at least has brought him the most fame?"

"'The Luck of Roaring Camp' and 'The Heathen Chinee.' 'The Heathen Chinee' nearly ruined him in his own estimation. He was ambitious to shine as a prose writer, and when he found that 'The Heathen Chinee' had caught on and was in everybody's mouth he was disgusted. He did not relish being known as a writer of funny doggerel. It did not do him any real harm, though. Some like 'Tennessee's Partner,' but I don't. Harte could not write dialect."[3]

"I differ from you," said Mr. Cable. "I thought the speech of Tennessee was a grand thing. It was all there. The sentiment is superb."

"There you go again on an argument," returned Mark Twain. "But I tell you when Harte tried to write frontier dialect it was idiocy. Do you mean to tell me there was any literary merit in an effort that contained five or six kinds of dialect? Why, he could have taken it to any miner and had it remedied; but he did not."

Mr. Cable responded by grasping an empty ale bottle and threatening to break it over his companion's head.

"What do you consider your best work?" continued the reporter, addressing Mr. Clemens.

"I play no favorites. I am like the woman with her offspring."

"I think a sirloin steak is his best work. You would have thought so had you seen him this morning," said J. B. Pond.

"No puns," cried Clemens, as he also grabbed his bottle and made a gesture toward his manager. Turning to his inquisitor again he remarked, "*Innocents Abroad* paid in the greatest royalty."

"What about the report that you was for [Grover] Cleveland?"

"Young man, I am lecturing."

"Who got up that story about yourself and Bret Harte removing a newspaper outfit from one town to another long ago, being attacked by Indians, and firing your articles at them?"

"That was a clever story. It originated in the *Carson Appeal*. It said we ran out of ammunition, and began to throw in matter already in type. A half-column leader of mine scattered the Indians, and one of Harte's poems knocked them silly."

"Don't you know those anecdotes of yours about running an agricultural paper in the South and getting mixed up are still talked of a great deal?"

"Yes, and I would sometime like to read them, but the trouble is they have in some places regular agricultural quotations, and would not do on that account."

Mr. Twain looked at his bottle. It was empty. He then gazed sorrowfully upon it for a moment, held out his hand and said: "Excuse me, I must go to bed," and he ambled away toward the stairway. In a slipshod, bent-up sort of manner.

Notes to Interview 30

1. Ozias W. Pond (d. 1892) was James's brother. See n. 1 to interview 25.
2. Harte reminisces about his introduction to MT in the offices of the San Francisco Mint in Henry J. W. Dam, "A Morning with Bret Harte," *McClure's* 4 (December 1894): 47–48. See also *MTL,* 1:312: "The 'Californian' circulates among the highest class of the community, & is the best weekly literary paper in the United States." See also n. 5 to interview 84.
3. MT makes the same point in a letter to Howells in 1879: see *MTHL,* 2:261. See also chapter 7 of *Is Shakespeare Dead?* (1909). On MT's opinions of Harte's early writings, see Bradford A. Booth, "Mark Twain's Comments on Bret Harte's Stories," *American Literature* 25 (January 1954): 492–95. Harte published his dialect poem "Plain Language from Truthful James" or "The Heathen Chinee" in the September 1870 issue of the *Overland Monthly.* On Howells, see n. 2 to interview 2.

31

"A Great Humorist," *Louisville Post,* 5 January 1885, 1.

Messrs. Mark Twain and George W. Cable arrived in the city at 12:30 and registered at the Galt House,[1] Mr. Twain leaving strict orders with the clerk for no one to be shown to their rooms. A *Post* reporter sent up a prayer to be allowed a five-minute talk, and Mr. Twain relented. He sent back a message that he supposed he could spare five minutes.

Mr. Twain was found seated at a table writing, and through the open folding doors Mr. Cable could be seen in the next apartment engaged at the same task. Mark Twain, in appearance, is the typical man of the Southwest. Of medium height, his body surmounted by a big head, covered with a thatch of stiff, curly hair, deeply tinged with gray.

"This is Mr. Twain, I presume," said the reporter.

"I guess it is," replied Twain. "I haven't any reason to the contrary. You may call me Twain."

"Have you and Mr. Cable been successful with your readings?"

"Well, now, we haven't any reason to complain. We have been drawing the people anyhow. I don't know whether we deserve it, but that doesn't make very much difference."

"Have you appeared in Southern cities yet, and have you been well appreciated there?"

"We have only visited one or two places south of the Ohio yet," replied Mr. Twain, with his peculiar drawl, "and we have gotten along all right. They take to us kindly. People of the South can laugh just as loud and as long as anybody, and that's what I'm here to do. I don't want to make them cry."

"But your partner, Mr. Cable, does."

"Oh, well, that is his affair. If he can't do it he is left, not I; but after all our tour has been all that I could wish, and we have had good houses wherever we have gone."

The reporter alluded to the fact that Mr. Twain had brought suit against the house of Estes & Lauriat for advertising his new book, *Huckleberry Finn*, at less than the price.[2]

"I only protect myself," said the author. "That firm doesn't publish my book. It isn't even out yet. Therefore they have no copies, and they can't sell them at what they advertise. It is interfering with my legitimate business, and is a piece of impudence sure to damage me. Therefore I intend to stop it."

"You are a member of the International Copyright Association, are you not?"[3]

"I am. I have just received a letter from Mr. G. P. Lathrop, the Secretary.[4] We are hard at work, and we intend to carry this thing through. We are gathering our forces, our men, and our money, and we are bound to succeed. As for myself, I am always protected in the matter of copyright on my books. I always take the trouble to step over in Canada and stand on English soil. Thus secure myself and receive money for my books sold in England."

"Mr. Twain, I see statements that you are a native of this State. Is it true?"

"I used to see that myself, but not lately. No, I was not born in Kentucky. I am a Missourian. That is, I was; but I live in Hartford now, when I am at home."

"Mr. Twain, I see another statement—that you and your wife are worth $1,000,000. How about that?"

The author of *Tom Sawyer* opened wide his eyes, gazed at the reporter for a few minutes, and with a perceptible lengthening of his drawl, said: "Mr. Cable, did you hear the question the young man asked?"

"I did," replied the latter. "I am awaiting your answer with anxiety."

"I suppose," said the Missourian, "I must acknowledge that I am not a millionaire. It is worse than pulling a tooth, young man, but it must come. No, I and Mrs. Twain don't possess a million dollars that I ever heard of, but I wish we did."

"I am very busy just now," said Mr. Cable, as the reporter turned the conversation upon him. "I wish you would excuse me. Twain can tell you everything."

As the newspaper representative arose to go, Mr. Twain followed him into the hall.

"Come here," he said, with a beckoning of his hand, and speaking in a confidential whisper, "young man, don't you blackguard me in your paper."

"Why not?" asked the reporter.

"It isn't right. Have I ever done any wrong to you or your relations that you should abuse me? No? Then don't do it. We might meet again."

"Has any reporter ever abused you?"

"Perhaps I got mixed up with other articles in the papers and thought they did. But it is all right; I forgive you. Good bye."

Notes to Interview 31

1. Built in 1835 at the corner of Second and Main on the Louisville waterfront, this hotel hosted Dickens as well as seven U.S. presidents from Lincoln to Taft.

2. MT had recently filed suit to enjoin the Boston publishers and booksellers Estes and Lauriat from selling *Huck Finn* for $2.25 a copy, significantly less than its retail price of $2.75, an offer which obviously would depress his royalties. A month later a federal judge refused to issue the injunction.

3. A group of American authors including Cable, Holmes, Julia Ward Howe (1819-1910), and Thomas Wentworth Higginson (1823-1911) founded the International Copyright Association in the mid-1880s to lobby for international copyright.

4. George Parsons Lathrop (1851-98), associate editor of the *Atlantic Monthly* from 1875 to 1877 and son-in-law of Nathaniel Hawthorne.

32

"Cable and Twain: The Author and the Humorist Arrive in the City Today," *St. Louis Post-Dispatch,* 9 January 1885, 7.

While Mr. J. B. Pond[1] was this morning standing in the rotunda of the Southern Hotel with Samuel L. Clemens (Mark Twain) standing on one side of him and George W. Cable on the other, the *Post-Dispatch* reporter present was struck by the touching likeness which the group bore to that beautiful legend which provides a human being with two attendant spirits, one of them of diabolical mien always urging him on to commit felonies and misdemeanors, the other, of angelic aspect, constantly coaxing him to give up his criminal ways. Mark Twain's features, familiarized to the public by several brands of chewing tobacco, cigars, and cigarettes, are so well-known that it only becomes necessary to describe the appearance of his less Mephistophelian companion. Mr. Cable is, or rather, if he were a woman, would be what the society editors describe as a petite brunette. He is short and slender and dark of complexion, and, dressing in black, presents very much the appearance of a clerical gentleman of absolutely orthodox views. His most remarkable features are his eyes and his forehead, the former being very large and dark and intelligent, while the latter is high and broad and gifted with an intellectual bulge which makes him a much more imposing person when he takes his hat off than he previously appears. A long black beard and a still longer moustache, which would be of phenomenal beauty were the beard not allowed to take the wind out of its sails, complete a very interesting, though not particularly strong, face. After the tableau vivant had signed their names in the hotel register they were accompanied by the *Post-Dispatch* reporter to Mr. Clemens' room, where the conversation at once turned upon an accident which had happened to the train they were on just as it entered upon the first of the arches coming from the Illinois shore. Mr. Clemens undertook to supply the descriptive work and at once began as follows in his particular drone which, being a difficult matter to reproduce with the ordinary, copper-faced type as commonly in use among the high class of American newspapers, must be left for the imagination of the reader to supply:

"We had," he said, "just reached that portion of the bridge which overhangs the crystal waters of the Mississippi River when a misunderstanding arose between the forward and rear portions of the train. The engine conceived the intention of leaving the track upon which the rest of the train was and moving upon another one, while the remainder of the train decided to remain where it was. The result was that one of the forward passenger cars was switched diagonally across the track. If we had not been going very slowly at the time the whole train would have left the track."

"Personally, I suppose, you had no fears, being familiar with the river currents?"

"Not in the slightest. It would not have discommoded me in the least to have been tossed into the Mississippi. I know the river thoroughly. It was the other people I was thinking of."

"I noticed that you seemed very anxious about the other people," Mr. Cable remarked with a quiet smile.

"It's no wonder," Mr. Clemens resumed. "There was a continuous kind of jolting which became more and more ominous and suggestive as the train advanced. A sense of crumbling—something crumbling beneath us, where stability was of the highest importance to us all personally—became very prominent. I fully expected the bridge to break down—I have always done so when I crossed it—and my anxiety for the safety of the other passengers led me to leap quite hastily from my seat and make a rush for the nearest exit. I wanted to get out and see what was the matter so I could intelligently supply the required relief."

"And you got there?" the reporter asked.

"Yes, but unfortunately, too late to be of any service. The train had stopped of its own accord. There were not many people hurt in the accident."

"How were they injured?"

"They happened to be in the front when I was going out. I went out in a great deal of a hurry and they were in the way. I'm sorry that I cannot furnish you with a list of the wounded and a statement of where they came from and the nature of the injuries. I did think of getting up such a list and giving the name of prominent men, but it don't do, after all, to play a practical joke on a newspaper. There are so many people who don't understand a joke, however plain it may be, that the possibility of serious results stands in the way of their perpetration."

Turning the subject the reporter offered to sympathize with Mr. Clemens upon the atrocious character of the cuts [woodcut illustrations] which were being published of himself and Mr. Cable.

"They're bad; yes, they're very bad," he said, "but I am glad of it. I would rather have that kind of a picture in the newspapers, because, when people look at us after seeing the picture, we make a favorable impression by contrast. This is a new idea of pictorial advertising and it works admirably. Take the average theatrical chromo; it flatters the subject, and when the latter comes under the gaze of an audience the result is a certain amount of disappointment. If the people we go to see on the stage were as handsome as their portraits they could charge double prices. I think Cable's picture flatters him, but mine does not begin to do me justice."

So much time had already been wasted upon commonplaces that the reporter informed Mr. Twain that he had been entrusted to secure an interview and that if he had no objections—

"Not in the least," Mr. Clemens remarked as he groped nervously through his pockets and finally looked at his visitor with a glance of blank amazement. Then he called out to his partner in the next room: "Cable, have we entirely run out of our Friday interviews?"

"Completely," Cable answered.

"Too bad," Mr. Clemens remarked.

"Give me a Wednesday or a Saturday one," the reporter suggested.

"'Twouldn't do," Mr. Clemens said with a decisive shake of the head. "We can interchange the other days' interviews among themselves, but none of them are with the Friday one. They are too lively. Our Friday one is staid, sober, calm. Cable wrote it and we've had a run on them. They're all gone. Never mind, I'll hunt through my trunk and if I find one I'll bring it around to the office."

The reporter left, but up to the time of going to press neither the humorist nor the interview had arrived at the office.

Note to Interview 32

1. See n. 1 to interview 25.

33

"Two of a Kind: Samuel L. Clemens and George W. Cable," *St. Louis Chronicle,* 9 January 1885, 1.

Mark Twain (S. L. Clemens) and George W. Cable, the humorists, arrived at the Southern this forenoon, and tonight make their first of three appearances here at Mercantile Hall. A *Chronicle* reporter was suavely received by the gentlemen in their apartments, Mr. Clemens remarking in a droll way that it was nothing more than he expected. He was in his shirt sleeves and slippers, his gray-sprinkled, bushy hair left just as he had combed it with his fingers. He is aged 49 years, is 5 feet 8½ inches high, and weighs 143 pounds. "My health is excellent," said he, as he threw a leg up over the arm of a chair—"never was better. We have been two and a half months on the road and will continue until the first of March."

"Where have you had the largest audiences?"

"Naturally in the largest cities."

"With one notable exception," broke in Mr. Cable, who had opened a door from an adjoining room and stood in the midst of it, his Prince Albert [a long frock coat] buttoned tightly around him.

"Yes," said Mr. Clemens, "at Ann Arbor, Michigan, our audience was phenomenal."[1]

"Where have you found the most responsive audiences?"

"Well, take Chickering Hall, New York.[2] One night they will fairly open their arms to you, ready to applaud every utterance all the way through, and the same audience the next night will be severely critical. Then take Boston with, say, an audience of 2500, and when you first come on the stage they receive you heartily. They must have five minutes to examine you in and wonder whether they are going to be pleased with you, and after that they are right with you all the way through, and everything is satisfactory. Then go north to Toronto, Canada, and south to the southern cities, and you have two extremes, geographically, but they are exactly alike. They don't stop to criticize you, but becoming enthusiastic, remain so all the way through. Before the usual northern state audience you must go cautiously and keep yourself well in hand, because they begin criticizing you in the start. Before a southern, Canadian, or London audience you can be thoroughly careless and it's all right; you can go right along and watch nothing. The idea is widespread that an English audience is slow and hard to please, but it is not. They are quick as lightning and see a joke before you get to it."

"Is it not true that an Englishman always laughs after others have gotten over the spasm?"

"Yes, if it is only one Englishman, or five Englishmen. Now, then, take the same five Englishmen and multiply them by 100, and they respond before you want them to. The only theory of this is, I think, that when you are cracking a joke to one Englishman he is more interested [in] setting his reasoning powers to work to weigh and analyze the thought concealed in the joke than he is to laugh at it. I am sure that is it, for the reason they laugh at the same joke so suddenly when in a large audience."

"Your program is?"

"Tonight I begin with a short passage from *Huckleberry Finn,* a book not yet published.[3] Next, two selections from *A Tramp Abroad,* and close with something appropriate, which the hour of the evening determines. Tomorrow matinee I repeat this program, and tomorrow night I read 'A Desperate Encounter with an Interviewer,'[4] and then a fantastic chapter from *Huckleberry Finn,* and close with the only duel I was ever concerned in. Matinee or female audiences are cold because, naturally, women are timid and afraid to laugh right out."

Of his books, Mr. Clemens says he realizes the most money from *A Tramp Abroad* on account of the large royalty, but *The Innocents Abroad* has the largest sale, although not seriously better than *Roughing It.* Of all the books, some eight in number, the sales amount to about 25,000 copies a year. The lecturer has a wife and three little girls, the eldest of whom is 13 years old, and has a good competency.

When the reporter asked Mr. Cable, who only recently came into prominence as a humorist, something of himself, he said in a droll way that would give a cat a spasm, "Now, don't ask me to tell the story of my life, because I have told it so often that I am just sick."

When the reporter said he was familiar with his life and could write it from memory, he said: "Well, for goodness sake don't say I told you."

"Say I told you," said Mark Twain, "and then they know it'll be authentic."

"Yes," said Cable, "say Clemens told you. I am real tired. I will give them as much as they want of me when I get them cornered in the theater."

Notes to Interview 33

1. MT and Cable had performed in Ann Arbor, Michigan, on 12 December 1884.
2. See n. 1 to interview 21.
3. See n. 7 to interview 23.
4. A satirical account of an interview first published in *Lotos Leaves,* ed. John Broughham and John Elkin (Boston: Gill, 1875), 27-32.

34

Fort Madison (Iowa) Democrat, 21 January 1885; rpt. *Iowa Journal of History and Politics* 27 (October 1929): 527-29.

It was Thursday evening. The small 18 x 20 waiting room of the C.B.&Q. Road at Keokuk was filled to overflowing with people of all kinds, sizes and descriptions. There were ministers, advance agents for dramatic combinations, commercial men, stable men. . . . The few dim lights that made an effort to shine out through chimneys made black by constant use and inattention, were only made the more so by the mighty cloud of tobacco smoke that filled the room. The train that should have arrived at 5:50 to bear the subject of this sketch to Burlington (where his other half, George W. Cable, was patiently . . . awaiting him) and ourselves to our destination, Madison, was reported half an hour late, caused by the snow which was rapidly falling and constantly drifting upon the track. A half hour passed and signs there were none of the train. We heard a grunt. Our attention was attracted to a form, evidently that of a man, perched upon a high stool near a lunch counter, upon which doughnuts and other decrepit edibles found slow sale, or more properly an eternal abiding place. We looked at the form. It attracted our attention, perched as it was upon the elevated "settee," with its heels recklessly clinched on the top rung, which caused the knees to come in almost immediate contact with the chin. Closer examination convinced us that it was a man, and the occasional grunts that he was alive, though worried, perplexed, and disappointed. We spotted the personage as Mark Twain. Eleven pair of heavy arctics covered his feet, while a slouch hat, pulled carelessly out of shape, protected his head. From under the brim peered out a few curly locks. Between this and a high collared overcoat was a face. The expression compared favorably with the growling emissions, so we knew that they came from none other than Mark Twain.

An hour later our discovery found the form dismounted and tussling with a huge valise and a smaller parcel. The long expected train had come. The sight of it seemed to lift a wrinkle from the face of Mr. Twain, who made at once for the door of the dingy room, thence to the rear car, the sleeper. We followed him. He walked down the long platform, and with his eyes down bent or half closed caused by the blowing snow. He failed to recognize the fact that platforms, as well as everything else, have an end, and fell headlong into the snow bank, his grips going in opposite directions. We were not far behind and came near meeting with the same fate. At last we ventured to speak.

"Did you lose anything, Mr. Twain?"

"No, I guess I'm all here," he replied.

The car was finally reached and Mr. Twain was assigned a section directly opposite the one we made convenient to occupy. The humorist commenced taking off his outside wraps, and when the task was done he had undergone a complete metamorphosis. He wore a full evening suit of black. The open fronted vest exhibited a newly laundered shirt front from the collar of which article fell a soft black tie. The clear yellow light of the porcelain shaded lamps of the car presented to us a different appearing man than the form before mentioned. Mr. Twain is a man of medium height, light weight, well formed shoulders, heavy curly gray hair, a prominent mustache slightly silvered, and a face that is a study. Perhaps the expression he wore was his best;

for 'twas a compound of expectancy, eagerness, disappointment and regret, certainly one interesting to behold.

Mr. Twain was not in a pleasant position; he knew it, he felt it. He knew that 9 o'clock was but a few minutes distant, and he was only fairly started with forty-three miles to go. Had we better brave the lion in his wrath, thought we; was it wise to interrupt the lethargy into which he had fallen? An interview which to us would be so pleasant, so satisfactory, would to him be dull, uninteresting and stupid . . . and yet that love for "self" quite overcame us. We made the break.

"Mr. Twain, allow us to introduce ourselves. We can readily tell that we are addressing the proper person and believe that we can guess your frame of mind." We handed him our business card.

"Sit down," he said, pointing to a seat in his section and extending his hand.

We sat. He spied the name of "Potowonok"[1] on our card (it was one of some that we had left), and upon inquiry as to its meaning, we told him all that we knew about it, and considerable that we guessed, and the conversation drifted upon the Indian race. He remarked about the scarcity of the red man within the last few years, or at least of his becoming so rapidly civilized, and of so few who kept their blankets, feathers, etc., in constant use.

He conversed on other topics as well. Survived a well meant compliment on his famous volumes, etc., etc.

We inquired as to his success in his present pursuit, and he replied that his reception had been favorable since his commencement last fall. Reaching Velie Station he said, "I must have a porter go ashore and send a telegram; excuse me, please."

We said, "Certainly," and suggested that the message might be called a "Cable-gram."

Whether or not he appreciated the pun we were not able to decide, as we changed our section to the farther end of the car and had only the courage to nod a farewell when the train pulled into the station.

Note to Interview 34

1. "Lone chimney," the Indian name for Old Fort Madison after it was abandoned and burned by the U.S. Army in 1813.

35

"Clemens and Cable," *Minneapolis Tribune*, 25 January 1885, 3.
Samuel L. Clemens (Mark Twain) of Hartford, Conn., and George W. Cable, of New Orleans, arrived at the West hotel yesterday at 11 o'clock, and a few minutes later, in response to the card of a *Tribune* reporter which went up on

the elevator with them, came down to the parlors and gracefully submitted, as a brace of whilom reporters ought to, to the process of being interviewed.

The two gentlemen in appearance present a marked contrast. Mr. Clemens is so like the wood-cut representations in his works, that even the absence of the plaid pantaloons and a certain general flavor of caricature does not destroy the similitude. His rather long hair and moustache are quite gray, but that doesn't seem to account for the stoop in the sloping shoulders and the comical shuffling side-gait of the humorist. Mr. Clemens has a fashion of throwing his head back on one side, folding his hands behind him and putting an intensely solemn expression into his eyes. One would sooner expect a man who looks that way to deliver a weighty opinion as to the existence of the prehistoric man than to perpetrate a witticism of any sort. . . .

"Cable and I started on this raid the day after the presidential election, and have been on the road ever since," replied Mr. Clemens, in his peculiar drawl in answer to a question of the reporter. "Two years ago I got some such plan as this in my head. I wanted to get a larger menagerie together, Howells, T. B. Aldrich, 'Uncle Remus,'[1] Cable, and myself, so that we could all go on the stage together, and each read two minutes or so and pose as 'the happy family' between times. But Howells had to go to Italy on a commission from the *Century*,[2] which will take him a year to fulfill;[3] and the others couldn't join us for one reason or another, and so Cable and I started out alone.

"I suppose I might have gone out on some such expedition all by myself, but I'm afraid it wouldn't be pleasant. I want somebody to keep me in countenance on the stage, and to help me impose on the audience. But more than that, I want good company on the road and at the hotels. A man can start out alone and rob the public, but it's dreary work, and it's a cold-blooded thing to do."

"That is a fact," asserted Mr. Cable. "Last year I traveled and read alone, but it was lonesome."

"Have you another story now in progress?" was asked of Mr. Cable.

"I am not writing anything now, but whenever I am in New Orleans the materials for a new story keep growing up from day to day. There seems to me to be an inexhaustible fund in the Creole life of that region."

"How did you happen upon what so many had missed before you?"

"It was a few years ago that I was assigned by a New Orleans paper, as a free-lance, to write up the religious and educational history of the city. Now, the development of New Orleans is inseparably bound up with the history of the old colonists and their descendants. In this way I stumbled right upon the wealth of material that I have utilized in *Dr. Sevier* (Mr. Cable pronounces it *Severe*, with the accent on the last syllable) and my other novels."

"You have doubtless noticed that the Creoles of New Orleans have taken serious exception to your Creole dialect and your delineation of Creole characteristics, as well?"

"Yes, I have noticed. And I have noticed that all the criticisms have come from the Creoles themselves. Now they are of course insensible of their own errors in the use of English and hence are hardly to be taken as competent critics of my books in that respect. Again, as to their characteristics, the very violence of their attack upon my works only serves to confirm the truth of the characters as I have drawn them."

Mr. Clemens was asked if he was working on a new book, and replied in the negative. "I haven't gotten *Huckleberry Finn* fairly off my hands yet."

"Is *Huckleberry Finn* a creature of flesh and blood?"

"Well, I could not point you out the youngster all in a lump; but still his story is what I call a true story. The incidents are, in the main, facts, and I tried to make a faithful painting of certain phases of life on the southern Mississippi."

"Do you remain in the city over Sunday?"

"Yes; this is the first chance we have had to arrange a new program, and we are going to utilize tomorrow for that purpose. We return to Chicago the 2d of February, and as we have read both our programs there, we have got to have a fresh one for this occasion. It's easy enough to make out a program, but to commit the parts to memory—there's the rub! If I don't know my part perfectly I get all befuddled when I get on the stage, and can't do anything. If I am master of it, why, I often improvise to a considerable extent, as the spirit moves; but when I need to improvise to help out my limping memory, I can't do anything at it."

"I wonder if our breakfast is ready yet," suddenly broke out Mr. Clemens.

"Ah—don't you mean dinner?" suggested the reporter.

"I mean breakfast. We haven't had a bite this day yet, and I begin to feel a goneness here; don't you, Cable?" queried the great American humorist, laying his hand with a pathetic gesture on the region of his stomach.

Just then the waiter appeared and announced breakfast, and Messrs Clemens and Cable, after a pleasant adieu, walked off arm in arm for the dining room to discuss the long deferred meal.

Notes to Interview 35

1. On Howells, see n. 2 to interview 2; on Aldrich, see n. 4 to interview 28. Joel Chandler Harris (1848-1908), Atlanta journalist and author of *Uncle Remus: His Songs and Sayings* (1881) and other dialect tales narrated by Uncle Remus.

2. "Mark Twain Interviewed," *Lafayette (Ind.) Courier,* 6 February 1885, 1, adds the phrase here "on a commission from Roswell Smith for the *Century.*" Smith (1829-92) was one of the founders of *Scribner's* and business manager of Scribner and Co.

3. Howells signed a contract with the Century Co. on 30 March 1882 to write ten

to twelve articles about Italian towns. He lived in Europe between July 1882 and July 1883, in Italy specifically between December 1882 and May 1883.

36

"Talk with Mark Twain," *Milwaukee Evening Wisconsin,* 29 January 1885, 2.

This forenoon a *Wisconsin* reporter who called at the Plankinton House had a very pleasant chat with Samuel Langhorne Clemens, the great American humorist, who, under the nom de plume of Mark Twain, has achieved a worldwide fame. Mr. Clemens is in town in company with George W. Cable, the Southern novelist, with whom he is giving a series of readings throughout the country. The personal appearance of Mr. Clemens is very deceptive. Nobody would ever take him for one of the most humorous writers that ever lived. He is 50 years old, but does not look more than 40. He is of medium size and is an almost perfect specimen of physical manhood, although from habit, he stoops considerably. His features are strong and clear-cut. This statement is particularly true of his chin. His eyes are deep-set under a manly-looking forehead. With the exception of a heavy mustache, his face is smooth-shaven. A fine crop of clustering, curly gray hair covers his head and adds greatly to the peculiar attractiveness of his appearance. Mr. Clemens' manners are brusque but genial and are the result of the varied life he has led. When the reporter found him this afternoon he was clad in an unpretentious gray suit and was hugging the fireplace in his room in an earnest manner that showed he felt the cold.

"How do you like your present business?" asked the reporter, after he had shaken hands with Mr. Clemens and had accepted an invitation to a seat. The question referred to the reading tour of the Twain-Cable combination.

"Very well, indeed," answered the humorist, rubbing his chin. "When we first started out," he continued, "I didn't think I should like the business. I had been off the platform for about fifteen years. But I've got into it now and enjoy it, although the present weather is not calculated to promote one's comfort."

"I understand that you have been doing a very good business."

"Oh, yes. We started out the day after the presidential election and have appeared before the public six times a week ever since. Our houses have, as a rule, been very good. In fact, we have seldom been greeted with any other kind of house. The only fault I find is that the trip blocked out for us is too long. It will take a month yet to complete it." Mr. Clemens rubbed his chin while he was speaking.

"Mr. Clemens, what was the true cause of the public not getting your latest book—I mean *Adventures of Huckleberry Finn*—sooner?"

"Well, you see, the delay was caused by a man employed in the stereotyping department of the New York printing house where the book is being published. This man, with one slight gouge of a graver, made an indelicate addition to a cut of one of my characters. The fact that the picture had been ruined was not discovered until several thousand copies of the work had been printed. When discovery was made, the edition was suppressed and a new one is being printed and will be ready shortly."[1]

"How are your older books selling now?"

"The sale, I believe, ranges from 15,000 to 25,000 every year, in the aggregate. On a rough guess, I should say that 170,000 copies of *The Innocents Abroad* have been sold since it was first published. *Roughing It* is not far behind, with a sale of say 150,000 copies. The sale of *A Tramp Abroad,* a comparatively new book, reached between 80,000 and 90,000."

"Is there any truth in the story that you attempted to establish a residence in Canada in order to get a copyright there?"

"None whatever. An application for a copyright was given me to sign, but I had to swear that I was a resident of Canada, and although told it was only a matter of form, I refused. In some way or other, but how I have never been able to understand, the difficulty was at least surmounted and I now have Canadian copyrights on *Adventures of Huckleberry Finn* and *Life on the Mississippi.* My Montreal publisher managed the affair."

"How have you managed in regard to England?"

"I have never had any trouble there, but have sold my rights without difficulty."

"Do you think that an international copyright law should be passed by Congress?"

"I do. It would be a great step in advance. Our present system is morally wrong. We have now an established literature of our own, and should not attempt to rob foreign authors of the fruits of their labor. It is unjust, to say the least."

Mr. Clemens related to the reporter the manner in which he came to adopt his nom de plume. He was formerly a pilot on the Mississippi River, where a leadman always says "mark twain," instead of "mark two," when he wishes to state that the water is two fathoms deep. "Mark two," Mr. Clemens said, "cannot be heard in stormy weather, but 'mark twain' has a different sound and catches the ear at once." The pseudonym was first used by a Mississippi River boatman who wrote occasionally for a New Orleans journal. When he died Mr. Clemens adopted it. Mr. Clemens lives in Hartford, Conn., "where," he stated to his visitor, "I have led a hermit's life for the past fifteen years." He intends to write another book shortly. The present visit is his first one to Milwaukee. In former years he has been a boatman, a miner, a traveler, and, in a word, has had a rough experience generally. Facts collected on his present trip will form part of his new book. . . .

Note to Interview 36

1. For details about the defaced illustration, see Beverly R. David, "The Pictorial *Huckleberry Finn,*" *American Quarterly* 26 (October 1974): 331-51.

37

"Mark Twain Interviewed," *Lafayette (Ind.) Courier,* 6 February 1885, 1.

A *Courier* representative corralled Mark Twain in the rotunda of the Lahr House shortly after the noon hour today and put the screws to him. . . . [1] "Would you believe it, young man, Cable and I never fail to make a hit. If the audience fail to materialize to any alarming extent, Cable kicks, and I strike the treasurer for all he has in his box. It's a hit every time; if it's not one kind, it's another. You have a very fine city here. I particularly admire the grand canal. I was attracted to it by some invisible influence the moment I arrived. In fact, before I had left the train I knew there was one here. It reminds me forcibly of Venice. Anyhow, there is something familiar like about it. Perhaps it's the odor.

"I thought I saw a gondola fast in the lee, but it proved to be only some misguided animal that had found its way into the water. As Hood remarked:

Oh, it was pitiful,
In a whole city full.[2]

"with the cholera so nigh, or words to that effect. The animal was dead—quite dead—at least I fancied so. There was something peculiar about it

That said as plain as words could tell
—This place is haunted.[3]

"I think the canal is even more attractive than the artesian well, though that is powerful, too. There is a something, however, indescribable about the canal that the artesian well don't have—but you know all that, both speak for themselves—the canal a trifle the loudest perhaps. As a steady intoxicant, I should prefer the well, but in case of sickness where a powerful emetic is wanted, I should recommend the canal—to the other fellow.

"Between them you have a very striking court house—very striking indeed. I should judge that it must have struck the taxpayers a very hard blow. By the way, what is that remarkable object away up on top? At first I fancied the building was not completed and that it might be a derrick sticking out of the tower, but Cable says he has examined it with his spy glass and that it's a part of the building. He thinks it is a statue of McGinley,[4] as he appears in the Police Court. Cable has been there and knows how it is. He has a grievance against Mac, however. He says $13 is entirely too much to tax a man for a police department, and so George is disposed to say mean things about Mac. What do I think of *my* lecture? Well, that is cool! They must keep you on ice, young man. Now, if you want my private opinion of Cable, I'll tell you—'when the bloom is on the rye.'[5] Do you tumble? No? Well, then, when the froth is on the beer—see?"

The reporter caught on. Twain got his beer and continued: "Well, Cable is just *splendid*. But you must ask him about it. He is even more enthusiastic on that subject than I am. I only know he is a powerful card. Would you believe it?—when I, even, fail to exert that soothing influence on the audience, necessary to the real comfortable enjoyment of a lecture or a sermon, Cable can actually close every eye in the hall in exactly five minutes by the watch. I have timed him frequently and always with the same result. But you must come and hear him. We charge members of the press two prices to make them feel independent. We like to encourage free speech on the part of the press. We hope to catch one of them some day for libel, and that would be $5,000 apiece, at least, in our pockets. Good scheme, eh? Ta, ta!"

Notes to Interview 37

1. I omit here a paragraph copied from interview 35.
2. Quoted from "The Bridge of Sighs" (1844) by Thomas Hood (1799–1845).
3. Misquotation from Hood's "Haunted House" (1844): "And said, as plain as whisper in the ear, / The place is haunted."
4. F. E. D. McGinley (1829–1915), the mayor of Lafayette.
5. The title of a popular song.

38

Luke Sharp,[1] "The Re-Mark-Able Twain," *Detroit Free Press*, 15 February 1885, 15.

The city editor said to me Thursday, as he handed me his theater pass: "Most of the boys have to be at the Governor's ball tonight and I wish you would take in the Twain-Cable entertainment."

"I thought the Russell House had taken them in and entertained them. At least they'll think they were taken in when they see the bill."

"If you see Major Pond,"[2] continued the city editor, "just apologize to him and say that I'd have sent up somebody that knew something if it were not for the Governor's snap. Tell him everybody that amounts to anything is on duty there. Try and get it into some sort of shape now. Begin it 'Whitney's.'

If there's a good crowd, it's a 'large and enthusiastic audience.' If there's only a few, it's a 'small but appreciative audience.'"

"Well, I guess I can write up a one-night show," I said.

He sighed and said he hoped so. He's an encouraging man.

I found Major Pond by the door at Whitney's. He should have been called Lake. He is the largest Pond I ever saw. That how he gets his title as differing from the Minor Ponds.

"I would like to go behind the scenes," I said. "I want to write this up from a spectacular point of view. I think that their style of make-up and their general conduct would be most interesting."

"Oh," said the Major, "you're mistaken. The Kiralfy show is next week.[3] This is a reading—a series of recitations."

"I know that," I explained. "I want to study the—"

"That's nonsense," said the Major irritably. "There's no make-up."

"Do you mean to say that the stories are not made up? Why, Twain himself don't claim they're anything else."

The Major refused to talk any more and went round to the stage door to make such arrangements as would prevent my getting in. But the Major doesn't know Whitney's as well as I do. He set a guard at the outside door and the one that comes in from the auditorium. This put me to the trouble of diving down by the fiddler's entrance into the cellar and then up the back stairs to the stage. I sat down beside the fellow who guarded the outside door. Across the stage at the other side my old friend, the Dutchman, was working at the gas fixtures. The view from the wings is rather restricted—you get a section of the opposite box, a full view of the Dutchman, and a complete exposure of how abruptly the shoddy grandeur of the stage-setting fades away into ragged squalor when it passes the point that limits the view of the audience. Several cards on the wall said that the insurance policies of the house would become void if anybody smoked, and that the smoking party would be held responsible—would have the house on his hands, as it were. I put out my cigarette and that is why Whitney owns the house this morning instead of me.

As I said, I drew a chair beside the guard. "Major Pond told me to tell you to keep a sharp look—"

"That's all fixed," said the guard. "That's what I'm here for."

"Bet you $4 he'll walk right past you."

"Bet you $4 he *won't*. No passes at this door. May step over my body, but he don't *pass* me."

"Here he comes," said I. "Now you'll see him try to cheek right in."

The guard stood up. Twain and Cable came in by the front door and walked around the outside of the parquette circle to the curtained entrance by the right hand box. Twain came first. The guard put his hand up against him and said:

"No, you don't. Not *here* you don't."

"Why—why, what's the matter?" drawled Mark, looking in surprise from under his bushy eyebrows. "Isn't the rent of the house paid?"

"It's Major Pond's orders. You can't come in here. You can go to the Russell House and see them after the performance is over."

Just then Major Pond came up and passed the readers in.

Twain took off a fur muffler that was round his neck and stamped up and down the room a bit to see if he still had the use of himself after the cold walk. Cable also shed his wraps and adjusted his white necktie before the glass. Southerner as he was, he didn't seem to feel the cold as much as the Northern author.

Then Mark took a look at the audience. Coming back he said: "The Governor's got 'em, Cable."

"Again?"

"He's got the audience, I mean. We'll have to talk to empty benches, I'm afraid."

"It's not 8 o'clock yet," said Cable. And it wasn't. Before the hour struck the house was well filled. Just then Twain cast his eyes on the program that lay on the dressing-case.

"I knew it," he said, rapping the little sheet of paper with a downward flip of fingers. "I knew it. They've got the program wrong. I marked out myself what it was to be, so of course they got it mixed."

This bothered the readers for a few moments, but they finally adjusted themselves to the changed state of affairs and Mr. Cable walked to the table on the stage and the sound of applause came into the room while Mark was slipping off his rubbers. He looked up in surprise as I stood in the door.

"I came to interview you," I said.

"Then you'll have to take me in sections," said Twain. "You didn't know I had something to do—some little things to say—to the audience tonight. Oh, you *did* know it? Well, I thought maybe you didn't. Some people don't read the papers, you know. That would naturally break up our interview—have a tendency to make it disconnected. I hate anything disjointed like—looks as if a person didn't know just what he was talking about. By the way—"

Here there was a loud burst of applause and Cable came in. "Excuse me," said Twain, and he went hesitatingly, as if afraid he might step too hard on something, and the next moment was before the loudly audible audience.

Mr. Cable was rather taken back to find me there, but he is a gentleman. He made no attempt to eject me. He is under medium height, very straight and very slender. He has a fine, intellectual face. His beard is silky black, and his long moustache is twisted with its end hanging down below his chin, making a bow over his mouth. His nose is straight and small, his eyes bright, black, and piercing, and his forehead high. His hair is the color of jet, and as glossy as oiled ebony.

"I suppose you have no objection to being interviewed?"

"Well—you see," hesitated Cable with a smile, "I could hardly tell you anything in the intervals—"

"Oh, that's all right," I said. "How do you like this terrific cold?"

"It is rather cool," he answered, looking meaningly at me with his black eyes—perhaps dark eyes would sound less John-L.-Sullivanish.[4]

"Don't you feel the cold more on account of living in the South so long?"

"No, I rather like it. The bracing air—"

"Yes, it's bracing."

"I said 'bracing.'"

"I agree with you. It braced a couple of my ears pretty badly yesterday."

"I just said to Cable coming in on the cars today, 'It's astonishing what big contracts the frost is taking this year.'" This was put in by Mark, who had got back. Cable escaped.

"Now to begin where I left off. In the matter of cold weather it is wonderful what a Southerner will stand. You talked to him, I suppose, all the while I was gone, yet he is able to go before that audience again. Now he doesn't feel the cold as much as I do. He likes a cold day—twenty or thirty below or so. You take a good, all-round Southerner, and if he lives through the first winter North, why he'll stand all the cold after that that you can give him. It's like the way they tested that Swiss bridge—put all the people on it that could get there—then, as it didn't break, it was pronounced safe. We tried Cable North one winter, and as he didn't die we felt safe after that—ah, they're after me."

He went on, but Cable didn't come back. He walked around at the rear of the stage. There must have been something interesting back there, for Twain went to see it, too, and walked back and forth slashing his arms around himself to keep up his circulation. Then Pond came in and said the city editor wanted to see me. I couldn't find him, so I started for the office and wrote this up. . . .

Notes to Interview 38

1. Robert Barr, aka Luke Sharp (1850-1912), a popular fiction writer, is perhaps best known today for completing Stephen Crane's romance *The O'Ruddy* (1903).

2. See n. 1 to interview 25.

3. The Hungarian-born Kiralfy brothers Bolossy (d. 1932) and Imre (1845-1919) produced theatrical extravagances, several based on Jules Verne novels.

4. John L. Sullivan (1858-1918), U.S. heavyweight boxing champion, 1882-92.

39

"Mark Twain's Wicked Moments," *Brockville (Can.) Evening Recorder,* 18 February 1885, 1.

Upon the arrival here on Monday evening of Mark Twain and George W. Cable, they were behind time nearly three hours, owing to the snow blockade, and as might be expected, both travelers were in just the proper mood to appreciate the Revere *cuisine.* They were met at the door of the hotel by Major Pond, their manager; and Mr. Daniel Derbyshire, chairman of the property committee, and in a few moments the whole quartette were discussing beefsteak, pork chops, snow blockades, and fast trains. A reference to fast trains generally leads to a discussion of monumental liars and it would seem that the occasion alluded to was no exception to the rule.

"Speaking of the lies being told of fast trains, however," remarked the stalwart representative from the west ward, "reminds me that Canada can boast of a fast train and not encroach upon the liar's domain either. We have a train down on the Canada Atlantic road between Coteau Landing and Ottawa, whose schedule time calls for sixty miles an hour and she makes it right along."

Mark, who was doing his best to demolish a huge slice of beefsteak just at the time, choked for an instant, then recovered himself and without so much as a smile, or even stopping the motion of his jaws, drawled out in his peculiar tone: "Wa'al, I'm not just exactly what you'd call an orthodox Christian, but in my travels around the world I don't think I ever feel so wicked as when I'm going around a curve at sixty miles an hour."

3

The Best and Worst of Times, 1886–1895
Interviews 40–59

Never an astute businessman, Twain parlayed a series of disastrous investments, particularly in the Paige typesetting machine, into fiscal ruin. His disaffection with things financial and technological is evident in his novel *A Connecticut Yankee in King Arthur's Court* (1889). Twain and his family closed their Hartford house and lived in Europe most of the time between June 1891 and May 1895 to save on expenses. He also rushed his last major novel, *The Tragedy of Pudd'nhead Wilson* (1894), into print in a vain attempt to stave off insolvency. Nevertheless, Webster and Co. failed in April 1894, which led inexorably to Twain's personal bankruptcy.

∼

40
"Table Talk," *Boston Literary World,* 15 May 1886, 172.

If common report is correct, Mark Twain is much better satisfied by his career as a publisher than by his literary successes. When asked recently if he would contribute to any magazines this year he said: "No, no. No sum of money however flattering could induce me to swerve from a resolution I have made to enjoy a solid old-fashioned loaf this summer, after which I will visit my country home at Elmira for the balance of the season. Besides there is more money in being a publisher. At any rate that is my experience, and if I perform any more literary work in future it will be only to 'keep my hand in.'"

41
"Mark Twain Abroad," *St. Paul and Minneapolis Daily Pioneer Press,* 30 June 1886, 7.

White plug hat, gray, bushy hair, gray moustache, gray suit of clothes and an Arkansas corn cob pipe in his mouth, from which came wreathing curls of smoke—that was Mark Twain (Samuel L. Clemens) as he stood in the Ryan hotel office last evening, asking to have a cot placed in one of the suite of rooms that he and his family occupied. Said Mr. Clemens to a *Pioneer Press* reporter:

"Glad to meet you (puff). I and my family are on their way to Keokuk (puff), Iowa, to visit my mother,[1] and we have chose the lake route as the most pleasant by which to reach there (puff). The benefit of coming by the lakes was that I got no news. I was (puff) five days in the heart of the United States, and did not see a newspaper. It was refreshing. That's what people take sea (puff) voyages for. To get away from the news; and when the *New York Herald* (puff) proposed to establish ocean life and news bureaus a thrill (puff) of horror went through the minds of many people, because the (puff) news would then go with them on their voyage." Commenting on modern journalism, and its rapid progress, he said: "The metropolitan journalism of my day is the village journalism of today."

Note to Interview 41

1. Jane Lampton Clemens (1803–90), MT's mother, whom he described in his *Autobiography* as his "first and closest friend."

42

"Amusing the Children," *Chicago Tribune,* 9 July 1886, 1.

Mark Twain, traveling incognito, under the name of "S. L. Clemens, one wife, three children, one maid," was at the Richelieu Hotel yesterday. He leaned on the stone steps in front of the hotel, smoking a putative cigar. Mark Twain's literary fame is so great that it has somewhat cast into the shade his abilities as a smoker. He smokes like an artist. He holds the cigar between his finger and thumb and contemplates it in a dreamy fashion. Then he raises it slowly to his lips, draws gently, and closes his eyes. After a judicious interval he removes the cigar, and the smoke rolls out under his long mustache with all the grace of a first dancer drifting on the stage. Then he opens his eyes. Mark Twain looks as little like himself as it is possible for a man to look. He wore a gray suit, a tall white hat, and a wide white tie such as New York brokers affect. His long, drooping mustache, his well-curled hair, and somewhat profuse jewelry made one think of a successful horseman or the manager of a popular burlesque.

But no one ever had such a satisfactory drawl. It established the fact that he was Mark Twain beyond all possibility of quibbling. A woman could "do up" her hair twice while he is pronouncing the word Mississippi. He lingers over it, plays with it, handles it as a young mother does her first baby.

"We came in last night," he said, pulling at the left side of his mustache. "Mrs. Clemens is not very well; neither am I. I have been amusing the children. I have taken them to a panorama. I understand there are three others near here. I will take them there, too. I want to satiate them with battles—it may amuse them." Three little girls, composed of three red gowns, three red parasols, and six blue stockings stood on the steps and grinned.

"Run up and tell mamma what a jolly time you've had and I'll think of something else to amuse you."

When the three little girls had disappeared Mr. Clemens sighed. "Did you ever try to amuse three little girls at the same time?" he asked, after a pause; "it requires genius. I wonder whether they would like to bathe in the lake?" he continued, with sudden animation, hardly pausing five minutes between each word; "it might amuse them."

"Are you on your vacation trip, Mr. Clemens?"

"No; I have just returned from a visit to my mother in Keokuk, Iowa.[1] She is 83 years old and I had not been home for over a year. We came from Buffalo to Duluth by a lake steamer and then from St. Paul down the river to Keokuk. Neither in this country nor in any other have I seen such interesting scenery as that along the Upper Mississippi. One finds all that the Hudson affords—bluffs and wooded highlands—and a great deal in addition. Between St. Paul and the mouth of the Illinois River there are over 400 islands, strung out in every possible shape. A river without islands is like a woman without hair. She may be good and pure, but one doesn't fall in love with her very often. Did you ever fall in love with a bald-headed woman?" The reporter admitted that he had drawn the line there.

"I never did, either," continued Mr. Clemens meditatively. "At least I think I never did. There is no place for loafing more satisfactory than the pilot-house of a Mississippi steamboat. It amuses the children to see the pilot monkey with the wheel. Traveling by boat is the best way to travel unless one can stay at home. On a lake or river boat one is as thoroughly cut off from letters and papers and the tax-collector as though he were amid sea. Moreover, one doesn't have the discomforts of seafaring. It is very unpleasant to look at seasick people—at least so my friends said the last time I crossed."

"It might amuse the children, though," suggested the reporter.

"I hadn't thought of that," replied Mr. Clemens; "but perhaps it might. The lake seems rather rough today—I wonder whether one could get a boat, a little boat that would bob considerable. Yes, it might amuse the children."

"But at such a sacrifice."

"You are not a parent?" replied Mr. Clemens. The reporter admitted his guilt.

"It is strange," continued Mr. Clemens, in momentary forgetfulness of the children, "how little has been written about the Upper Mississippi. The river below St. Louis has been described time and again, and it is the least interesting part. One can sit in the pilot-house for a few hours and watch the low shores, the ungainly trees, and the democratic buzzards, and then one might as well go to bed. One has seen everything there is to see. Along the Upper Mississippi every hour brings something new. There are crowds of odd islands, bluffs, prairies, hills, woods, and villages—everything one could desire to amuse the children. Few people ever think of going there, however. Dickens, Corbett, Mother Trollope,[2] and the other discriminating English people who 'wrote up' the country before 1842 had hardly an idea that such a stretch of river scenery existed. Their successors have followed in their footsteps, and as we form our opinions of our country from what other people say of us, of course we ignore the finest part of the Mississippi."

It might be incidentally remarked that it were worth going fifty miles on foot, if one couldn't get a pass, to hear Mr. Clemens unravel the word Mississippi.

"I suppose we will go East tomorrow," he added, "but I don't know. Mrs. Clemens makes all the plans. Women enjoy that, you know. Of course we never carry any of them out, but that doesn't alter the fact that the plans are thoroughly enjoyable ones. We will pass the summer at Elmira."

"Will you do any work this summer?"

"Yes, I shall probably amuse the children."

"But write—"

"O, yes, I see. Well, I am a private citizen now, and have no immediate intention of turning author. I shall probably set to work on something or other, however. Most of my work is done in the summer."

At this moment the three little girls in the three red gowns and six blue stockings appeared, and Mr. Clemens resumed the shape of an amusement bureau.

Notes to Interview 42

1. See n. 1 to interview 41.
2. Griffith Owen Corbett, *Notes on Rupert's America* (1868); Frances Trollope (1780–1863), mother of the novelists Anthony and Thomas Trollope, was the author of *Domestic Manners of the Americans* (1832), which MT quoted in chapter 27 of *Life on the Mississippi*.

43

"Twain in Court," *Philadelphia Daily News*, 3 August 1886.

... While talking to a *Daily News* reporter afterward Mr. Clemens, with his white high hat on the back of his head and his hands in the pockets of his light sack coat, twisted himself into all manner of shapes and in his familiar drawl and twang gave his opinion of the case.

"It has been settled," he said, "that publishers have a right to sell books as they please, and in this case it is not a question only of whether Mr. Wanamaker shall be allowed to sell a few dozen books or not.[1] We want to know just how binding the contracts with our agents are. If the present contract is not strong enough we'll have one casted, don't you see? It will be worth the powder to us, and other publishers will know just where they stand after we get through with it."

Mr. Clemens took his hands from his coat pockets long enough to light a cigar and run his fingers through his bushy mixed gray hair and said: "Philadelphia is a nice, quiet city, but I must get out of it. I'll go back to Gowen and ask him to tell me how I can get a through train to Elmira."[2]

Notes to Interview 43

1. John Wanamaker (1838–1922) opened the first department store in Philadelphia in 1876. The store was selling copies of *Huck Finn* at a discount.
2. Franklin Gowen (1836–89), former president of the Philadelphia and Reading Railroad.

44

Edwin J. Park, "A Day with Mark Twain," *Chicago Tribune*, 19 September 1886, 12.

Elmira, N.Y., Sept. 17—Among the great hills surrounding the historical Chemung Valley, wherein the City of Elmira is situated, are many romantic spots admirably fitted by Nature for the site of retired country homes. Probably the most romantic and undoubtedly the place of greatest general interest among the number of these secluded spots is the one known as Quarry Farm, the summer home of Samuel L. Clemens (Mark Twain), the most refined humorist that America, and probably the world, has ever known. At the eastern boundary of the city rises a great hill, more properly a mountain, which is called the Great East Hill. Up its steep side, along a rough country road, the visitor to Mark Twain's summer home is obliged to climb for something over a mile. Then, when the summit is reached, the road runs westward for another mile before the home of the humorist is found. The plateau on which the house stands has been reclaimed from the wilderness of refuse limestone which surrounds it, and a broad, well-kept park surrounds the pretty cottage. For many years the knoll at the west of the house furnished building stone for the city, and the place having been laid out and built practically in the abandoned quarry, gives it the romantic title of Quarry Farm. The place is owned jointly by Mr. Clemens and his brother-in-law, Theodore Crane of Elmira, who makes the place his permanent home. Mr. Crane married an adopted sister of Mrs. Clemens, and is associated in business with

Gen. Charles J. Langdon, Mrs. Clemens' brother, who is a very wealthy man, being the head of the great Clearfield Coal Company.[1] The Langdons live in a palatial residence in the city, and are frequent callers at Quarry Farm, where yesterday Mr. Clemens bade me a hearty welcome. Dressed in a négligé suit of gray, with a soft hat placed carelessly on his bushy head, Mr. Clemens was a perfect picture of complacent self-satisfaction. Coming forward to greet me, Mr. Clemens moved with the slow deliberation which indicated an intention never to close his brilliant earthly career by overexertion if he could help it. His vocal salutation was of the same complacent nature as his physical exertion, but the greeting was cordial and sincere. On the large vine-covered veranda, where the cool mountain breeze was a delightful contrast to the heat of the city below us in the valley, Mr. Clemens told my photographer to "go ahead and take all of the place you can get." A grotesque, Chinese-colored cat and three kittens, two of them of the same general appearance and the third the color of slate, were playing about our feet.

"That old cat," reflectively mused the humorist, with his eyes half closed, "is an animal in which I take considerable interest. She was very wild when I found her running about here, but kind treatment and milk have had a wonderfully civilizing effect upon her and she is quite easily approached now." A pause which assumed the importance of a comma, grew to the strength of a semi-colon, reached the full stop of a period, and extended to a paragraph, ensued while the speaker contemplated the feline group. Finally he managed to break the silence by remarking: "I really don't know what to make of that slate-colored animal. The other two kittens are colored all right, but there appears to be some little irregularity about the other one," and he continued to gaze earnestly at the interesting group, his mind apparently full of the strange kitten's paternity. While in this reflective mood, with his hand under his chin and his eyes half closed, the photographer took a snap shot at him, and the result is the picture at the head of this column. It is probably the most unique and original thing in existence. At the suggestion of Mr. Clemens we walked to his study, an octagonal structure of dark brown color, situated right on top of a high pile of refuse stone.[2] It is reached from the residence by a winding walk, and rough, uneven stone steps without lead to its doors, from which a magnificent view of the city and valley may be obtained. The floor was covered with papers and letters, while on the table and mantel reposed a half-dozen pipes, some tobacco and cigars, of which the owner is an inveterate user. He says that his constitution is such that tobacco does not injure him, and, as he enjoys it, he keeps a choice stock on hand.

On the very top of the quarry is a summer house fitted with rustic chairs, hammocks, etc., where, if a breeze is not to be found at the house, the entire family retire to sleep and enjoy the invigorating atmosphere. We climbed up to this delightful spot, and while the stiff breeze blew the humorist's bushy hair into tangled confusion we talked on subjects of mutual interest. He told me of how he had learned to set type in a Western printing office, how he had become a wanderer in the West, and we compared notes on the great strides being made in the art preservative, a matter with which both he and myself were entirely familiar.[3] Our rough surroundings recalled to me the striking similarity to those of Virginia City, which place is so well described in Mr. Clemens' book, *Roughing It*.

"The comparison," said he, "is very timely and apt. At the time I was on the staff of the Virginia City paper the place was similar to this, although on a much larger scale."

Continuing the conversation, I asked Mr. Clemens if he was doing any work this summer.

With a tired expression in his large eyes, he gazed down into the valley for a few moments, and then, as though he had arrived at a very difficult conclusion and felt relieved, said: "No, I am not at work; not doing a single thing; just loafing; that's all. I made up my mind that I would loaf all summer, and I intend to do it. I left all the books I have started on at my home in Hartford, so that I couldn't get at them, and I'm just lying around and resting, and trying to get tired at that. I have started some new books, but I am in no hurry to finish them. I'm not anxious about them. As it is now I am 'at home' to any of my friends, although before this summer I have had to refuse them during office hours, which were from 9 until 4 in the afternoon. But then in the summer, while I am here, you know that there is a good deal of daylight between 4 and 8 o'clock, and I could get around some then. The three summer months which I spend here are usually my working months. I am free here and can work uninterruptedly, but in Hartford I don't try to do any literary work. Yes, as you say," he continued, in answer to my interruption, "this may be called the home of *Huckleberry Finn* and other books of mine, for they were written here.

"Now," said Mr. Clemens, after a rest, "you will see right below us a little building where my children are amusing themselves. My three little daughters have had that stony place fenced off, and they live there about all the time in that building. They call it Ellerslie, and at present they are living retired lives, which they spend in reading *Scottish Chiefs*."[4]

At my host's suggestion we visited Ellerslie, and were assured by the three little maids, who were clustered around a hammock, as shown in the picture, that we were welcome to their temporary home. We passed inside the "house," which consisted of one room, tastefully decorated by the children. On shelves fastened to the side of the room were small dishes of every kind required by the infantile housekeepers, while a little cook stove, which had

94 / Best & Worst of Times, 1886–95

for a foundation an empty soap box, was used for cooking by the little girls. Mr. Clemens found a tin pail containing a half dozen eggs, and after he had examined them carefully for a time inquired of the eldest child if she considered the eggs entirely trustworthy. She said she had some doubts about them, and he sagely advised her to take them back to the house and get some of more recent issue. The two youngest children were induced to sit on the porch of the house, and they are prominent in the accompanying picture of Ellerslie Cottage.

It has become a matter of historical interest that whenever there is an addition to the Clemens family the happy father straightway has erected at the side of the road, near his home, a stone watering trough for horses. On the trough is carved the name of the child and the year of its birth. So far three have been put up.

I asked Mr. Clemens for the names and dates on each of them, and after considerable thought he said he believed they were as follows: "Susie Clemens, 1872," "Clara L. Clemens, 1874," and "Jean Clemens, 1880."

When the photographer took the picture of the troughs I examined the others and found that Mr. Clemens was right regarding the names and dates. He may feel gratified to find that he was correct.

Mr. Clemens doesn't come downtown very often, although he occasionally visits the Langdons and stops in at the Century Club rooms for a game of billiards. One of his nearest neighbors is the Rev. Thomas K. Beecher and the two men are very good friends. It is worthy of remark that one of Mr. Clemens' closest friends and neighbors in Hartford is Mrs. Harriet Beecher Stowe, a sister of the Elmira divine.[5]

When I left Quarry Farm Mr. Clemens was earnestly contemplating the misfit kitten, while the three little maids in three bright Mother Hubbard wrappers waved an adieu from the porch of Ellerslie Cottage.

Notes to Interview 44

1. On Thomas and Susan Crane, see n. 1 to interview 4. Charles Langdon (1849–1916) was Olivia Langdon Clemens's brother, whom MT had met on the *Quaker City* voyage in 1867; he had been appointed commissary general on the staff of the governor of New York in 1880.

2. See n. 2 to interview 4.

3. Printing was considered the "art preservative of all the arts."

4. *Scottish Chiefs* (1810), a historical romance by Jane Porter (1776–1850), was set in Ellerslie, a town in a Scottish glen.

5. Thomas Kinnicut Beecher (1824–1900), minister of the Park Street Congregational Church in Elmira, officiated with Joseph Twichell at the marriage of MT and Olivia Langdon in February 1870. Harriet Beecher Stowe (1811–96) was the author of *Uncle Tom's Cabin* (1852).

45

"The Insolence of Office," *New York World,* 23 March 1888, 4.

Washington, [D.C.] March 2—Mark Twain, having survived participation in the authors' readings, is now playing Rip Van Winkle in revisiting the places in Washington of which he was a habitué twenty years ago. In fact, more than twenty years have passed since Mark, then with little reputation and less money, was eking out a living as the special correspondent of some Pacific coast papers while writing his book *Innocents Abroad,* which was to make him famous and start him on the road to riches. After several passages with the doorkeepers of the House Mark is of opinion that "the insolence of office" is as rife now as it was in his time, to say nothing of Shakespeare's. Presenting his card to one of these officials, the height of whose ambition is to be mistaken for Congressmen, Mark asked that it be sent to Sunset Cox.[1] The doorkeeper disdained to look at the card which he had, as if afraid of contamination, but viewed the humble humorist from head to foot and sized him up for "the country jay" that Mark's drawl and dialect suggested.

"You can't see Mr. Cox."

"Why?"

"Because he is busy."

"How do you know? Is he making a speech?"

"Naw, but he can't see you."

"Well, how can I get in the press gallery?"

"Are you a reporter?"

"No, but I used to be a mighty good one when I lived in Virginia City."

"Well, if you ain't one now you can't get in"; and he pushed Mark aside to be polite to a gentle female lobbyist whose card went in to her member fast enough. Finally the humorist passed the pickets of the press gallery. After he had asked in vain for the dead and gone correspondents who had been his chums Colonel Mann recognized him and gave him *The World* man's seat in the front row,[2] whence he had a fine view of the statesmen of the present generation wrangling over the labor bills. Mark says he will soon publish a compilation of other people's humorous writings and is also engaged upon an original work which he hopes to finish some time next summer.

Having "swapped lies" for a while with the correspondents Mark tried the floor again. This time he was recognized, and Mr. Cox not only went out to see him, but took him on the floor and made him acquainted with all of the Congressional celebrities from Reed of Maine to Martin of Texas.[3] He kept the crowd of members around him laughing until the gavel of the Speaker came to the rescue of order. He says the levee that he had reminds him very much of those he used to see on the Mississippi in the days when he was piloting.

Notes to Interview 45

1. Samuel L. (Sunset) Cox (1824–89), U.S. representative from New York (1869–89), had befriended MT in 1870. See *MTL,* 6:29.
2. William D'Aton Mann (1839–1920), a colonel in the 7th Michigan Regiment during the Civil War and publisher of the weekly *Mobile Register.*
3. Thomas B. Reed (1839–1902), Speaker of the U.S. House of Representatives, 1889–91 and 1895–99. See also Fatout, 349. William H. Martin (1823–98), U.S. representative from 1887 to 1891.

46

"Mark Twain Chatty: He Tells of His Former Life as a Reporter," *St. Louis Post-Dispatch,* 19 May 1889, 20.

Washington, D.C., May 17—I met Mark Twain the other day wandering around the Capitol and looking at pictures 50 years old as if they were new, and inspecting with the interest of a rustic stranger the vivid bronze doors whose Columbian glories had bleared his eyeballs more than two decades ago. He strayed into the press gallery, threw back his gray overcoat, adjusted his gold spectacles on his nose, and looked around.

"A good deal changed," he said, glancing at the life-size photographs of Whitelaw Reid[1] and younger editors which now decorate the walls, "and it seems a hundred years ago."

I asked when he was here.

"I had a seat in the press gallery," he meditated, "let's see—in 1867—and now I suppose all the veterans are gone—all the newspaper fellows who were here when I was, Reid and Horace White and Ramsdell and Adams and Townsend."[2]

"The ones you name happen to all to be gone," I admitted, "some to the control of newspapers and some to where Dr. Potter says there are no newspapers, but some of the real veterans are still here. On those pegs in the corner some of the ancients still hang up their coats—General Boynton and Byington and Uriah Painter and Judge Noah, the king of the Jews and dean of the corps. Most of the old fellows are dead—Whitely of the *Herald,* Crounse of the *Times,* Adams of the *World,* Henry of the *Tribune,* Gobright of the Associated Press. Jim Young is executive clerk of the Senate, John Russell Young is a journalist at large, Ed Stedman has grown to be a banker poet, and Henry Villard—well, you know all about him and his fortunes."[3]

"Yes; some of these men I never knew in Washington; a few of them were here before my time. In fact, I was rather new and shy, and I did not mingle in the festivities of Newspaper Row. Probably most of the men you mention were perfectly unconscious to my existence. The *Morning Call* and the *Enterprise* did not make much of a commotion in the United States.

"I roomed in a house which also sheltered George Alfred Townsend, Ramsdell, George Adams and Riley of the San Francisco *Alta*. I represented the Virginia (Nev.) *Enterprise*. Also, I was private secretary to Senator Stewart, but a capabler man did the work. A little later that winter William Swinton and I housed together.[4] Swinton invented the idea—at least it was new to me—of manifolding correspondence. I mean of sending duplicates of a letter to various widely separated newspapers. We projected an extensive business, but for some reason or other we took it out in dreaming—never really tried it." Here Mark walked into the gallery and looked down at the vacant senatorial seats.

"I was here last," he went on, "in 1868. I had been on that lark to the Mediterranean and had written a few letters to the San Francisco *Alta* that had been copied past all calculation and to my utter astonishment, a publisher wanted a book. I came back here to write it.

"Why, I was offered an office in that ancient time by the California senators—minister to China. Think of that! It wasn't a time when they hunted around for competent people. No, only one qualification was required: You must please Andy Johnson and the Senate.[5] Nearly anybody could please one of them, but to please both—well, it took an angel to do that. However, I declined to try for the prize. I hadn't anything against the Chinese, and besides, we couldn't spare any angels then."

"A pretty good place to write," I remarked as we took seats.

"Some things," he said, "but an awfully bad place for a newspaper man to write a book as the publisher demanded. I tried it hard, but my chum was a storyteller, and both he and the stove smoked incessantly. And as we were located handy for the boys to run in, the room was always full of the boys who leaned back in my chairs, put their feet complacent on my manuscript, and smoked till I could not breathe."

"Is that the way you wrote *Innocents Abroad?*" I asked.

"No; that is the way I didn't write it. My publisher prodded me for copy which I couldn't produce till at last I arose and kicked Washington behind me and ran off to San Francisco. There I got elbow room and quiet."[6]

"It was apparently a wise move," I concurred, "but you could write here now, and this is exactly the place for a man like you. More intellectual society is attainable here than in any other city in the world. The only big mistake of your successful life, Clemens"—for only his intimate friends address him as "Mark"—"is not coming to Washington to live. Why, all over the United States people of leisure and culture are—"

"Yes, I know, I know," broke in Clemens, "but don't tantalize me. Do you take a fiendish enjoyment in making me suffer? I know perfectly well what I am about, and I appreciate what I am losing. Washington is no doubt the boss town in the country for a man to live in who wants to get all the pleasure he can in a given number of months. But I wasn't built that way. I don't want the earth at one gulp. All of us are always losing some pleasure that we might have if we could be everywhere at once.

"I lose Washington, for instance, for the privilege of saving my life. My doctor told me that if I wanted my three score and 10, I must go to bed early, keep out of social excitements, and behave myself. You can't do that in Washington. Nobody does. Look at John Hay.[7] Just fading away, I have no doubt, amid these scenes of mad revelry. My wife, you know, is practically an invalid, too, so that neither of us could keep up with the procession. No, the best place for us is quiet and beautiful Hartford, though there is a good deal of the society of Washington that I should delight in."

"I suppose you have been pirated a good deal," I said to Mr. Clemens. "I do not mean by illegal publication of your works, but by private individuals claiming to write your writings?"

"Oh, yes," he said, "considerably—some scores of cases, I suppose. One ambitious individual in the West still claims to have written the 'Jumping Frog of Calaveras County,' and another is sure that he produced that classic work known as 'Jim Wolfe and the Cats.'[8] I suppose either would face me down with it; and their conduct has led me to conjecture that a man may possibly claim a piece of property so long and persistently that he at last comes honestly to believe it is his own. You know that poor fellow in New Jersey, so weak-minded as to declare that he wrote 'Beautiful Snow,' and going to his coffin with tearful protests? And you know about Colonel Joyce and Ella Wheeler, and 'laugh and the world laughs with you'?[9]

"But I haven't been bothered that way so much as I have been by personators. In a good many places men have appeared, represented that they were Mark Twain and have corroborated the claim by borrowing money and immediately disappearing. Such personators do not always borrow money. Sometimes they seem to be actuated by a sort of idiotic vanity.

"Why, a fellow stopped at a hotel in an English city, registered as Mark Twain, struck up an acquaintance with the landlord and guests, recited for them and was about to accept a public dinner of welcome to the city when some mere accident exposed him. Yet I myself had stopped for weeks at that same inn and was well known to the landlord and citizens. His effrontery was amazing."

"Did he resemble you?"

"I do not know. I hope and believe that he did not. Parties whom I have since been inclined to regard as my enemies had the indecency to say that he did.

"The same thing happened in Boston and several other cities. It was not pleasant to have bills coming in for money lent me in Albany, Charleston, Mexico, Honolulu, and other places, and my calm explanation that I was not there bringing sarcastic letters in reply with 'Oh, of course not! I didn't see you with my own eyes, did I?,' etc., and I resolved that I would follow up the next swindle I heard of. I had not long to wait. A dispatch came from Des Moines, Iowa:

"'Is Mark Twain at home?'

"'Yes, I am here and have not been away,' I answered.

"'Man personated you—got $250 from audience—shall I catch him' came back, bearing the signature of a lawyer.

"'Yes,' I telegraphed in reply, 'have sent you check for expenses.'

"He was a good while catching him—some weeks—perhaps months, and then he made me an elaborate report, giving the route of his labyrinthine and serpentine chase of the swindler, the money he had expended, and the information that he did not entirely and completely catch him, though he 'got near him several times.' I was out some hundreds of dollars.

"I was disgusted; and when I got another dispatch—from New Orleans, I think it was—

"'Man swindled audience with pretended lecture here last night, claiming to be you. What shall I do?' I telegraphed back unanimously, 'Let him go! Let him go!'

"I'd give $100, though, to see one of these doppelgangers who personate me before an audience, just to see what they look like."

Mark Twain comes down every winter to work for the passage of an international copyright law in conjunction with Edward Eggleston, Gilder, and other authors. Senator Reagan of Texas, a friend of Mark's, but an opponent of his pet measure, greeted him cordially last winter with, "How are you, Mark? How are you? Right glad to see you. Glad to see you. Hope to see you here every session as long as you live!"[10]

One of Mark Twain's favorite amusements here, they say, is turning himself into an amateur guide and explaining to his friends the various objects of interest in the Capitol. He is particularly facetious over the pictures in the rotunda and the stone people in "Statuary Hall." Arriving opposite the marble statue of Fulton, seated and intently examining the model of a steamboat in his hands, he indulges in a wide-sweeping gesture and exclaims: "This, ladies and gentlemen, is Pennsylvania's favorite son, Robert Fulton. Observe his easy and unconventional attitude. Notice his serene and contented expression, caught by the artist at the moment when he made up his mind to steal John Fitch's steamboat."[11]

The humorist dresses a great deal more carefully than formerly; this is made necessary by his increasing amplitude, by his vast shock of gray hair, by his boisterous and ungovernable moustache, and by his turbulent eyebrows that cover his gray eyes like a dissolute thatch. And when he talks he talks slowly and extracts each of his vowels with a corkscrew twist that would make even the announcement of a funeral sound like a joke.

Notes to Interview 46

1. See n. 4 to interview 9.

2. Horace White (1834–1916), reporter for the *Chicago Tribune;* Hiram J. Ramsdell, a friend of Walt Whitman, is listed as a "correspondent" in the 1869 District of Columbia *Directory;* George W. Adams (1838–86), Washington correspondent of the *New York World.* On Townsend, see n. 1 to interview 8.

3. Henry Codman Potter (1835–1908), American Episcopal bishop; Henry Van Ness Boynton (1835–1905), Civil War general and newspaper correspondent; A. Homer Byington (1826–1910), former co-owner and publisher of the *New York Sun;* Uriah H. Painter (1837–1900), Washington correspondent of the *Philadelphia Inquirer;* Jacob J. Noah (d. 1897), Washington correspondent of several western papers; Colonel L. A. Whitely (d. 1869), had headed the Washington bureau of the *New York Herald;* Lorenzo L. Crounse resigned as Washington correspondent of the *New York Times* in 1873; Arthur Henry, a Civil War-era correspondent of the *New York Tribune;* Lawrence A. Gobright (1816–79) worked for thirty-three years at the Washington bureau of the Associated Press; Jim Young (1847–1924), head of the Washington bureau of the *New York Tribune;* John Russell Young (1840–99), managing editor of the *New York Tribune* and later U.S. minister to China; Edmund Clarence Stedman (1833–1908), reporter for the *New York World* during the Civil War, opened a New York brokerage in 1869. One of the original fifty members of the American Academy of Arts and Letters, he also coedited the eleven-volume *Library of American Literature,* published by Charles Webster and Co. (1888–90). Charles L. Webster (1857–91) married MT's niece Annie Moffett (1852–1950) in 1875. He entered into a publishing partnership with MT in 1882 and sold his partnership in Webster and Co., a subscription press, and resigned as manager in 1888. The company declared bankruptcy in 1894. Henry Villard (1835–1900), former journalist for the *New York Tribune* and *New York Herald,* chairman of the board of directors of the Northern Pacific Railroad (1888–93).

4. John Henry Riley (1823–72), Washington correspondent of the San Francisco *Alta California.* See also MT's essay "Riley—Newspaper Correspondent" (1870). William Morris Stewart (1827–1909), U.S. senator from Nevada 1863–75, 1887–1905. Stewart recalls his friendship with MT in his *Reminiscences* (New York and Washington: Neale, 1908), 219–24. William Swinton (1833–92), American journalist.

5. Andrew Johnson (1808–75), seventeenth U.S. president, was impeached though not convicted by the U.S. Senate in February 1868.

6. With the help of Bret Harte, MT revised his newspaper dispatches from Europe and the Holy Land into the text of *The Innocents Abroad* while in San Francisco between April and July 1868. As he wrote C. H. Webb on 26 November 1870, "Harte read all the MS of the 'Innocents' & told me what passages, paragraphs & *chapters* to leave out—and I followed orders strictly" (*MTL,* 4:248). Compare with MT's comments in *Auto* (1959), 149.

7. A poet, journalist, diplomat, and longtime resident of Washington, John Hay

(1838–1905) had served as Abraham Lincoln's private secretary (1861–65) and Assistant Secretary of State (1879–81). He would become secretary of state under Presidents McKinley and Roosevelt (1898–1905).

8. MT's sketch "Jim Wolfe and the Cats" was first published in the *New York Sunday Mercury* in 1867. See also *Auto* (1959), 46, for details about its pirating.

9. According to tradition, the sentimental poem "Beautiful Snow" was written during the Civil War by an anonymous woman who died in a Cincinnati hospital. In fact, it was first published in 1870 by Joseph Warren Watson (1849–72).

The first two lines of "Solitude" (1883) by the poet Ella Wheeler Wilcox (1850–1919) were "Laugh, and the world laughs with you, / Weep, and you weep alone." In 1885 John A. Joyce (1842–1915) reprinted the poem as though he had written it in his *Peculiar Poems* (1885). Wilcox offered a reward to anyone who could find the poem in print before she published it.

10. Edward Eggleston (1837–1902), American editor and novelist; Richard Watson Gilder (1844–1909), poet and editor of *Century;* John Henninger Reagan (1818–1905), a congressman (1875–87) and U.S. senator from Texas (1887–91).

11. Robert Fulton (1765–1815) proved the practicality of steam power; John Fitch (1743–98) invented the steamboat.

47

R[obert] D[onald],[1] "Mark Twain and His Book," *Pall Mall Gazette* (London), 23 December 1889, 1–2.

Hartford, Conn., Dec. 3—"Where is Farmington Avenue?" I inquired on arriving in Hartford. "Do you know Mark Twain's?" was the interrogative response, from which it seems that Mark is a more conspicuous object in the topography of Hartford than the magnificent avenue in which he lives. Farmington Avenue is a fine broad street, lined with the American counterpart of the English villa, and stretching away into the country. But for the presence of the cars, and the electric lights, and other signs of advanced civilization, you might imagine yourself in the aristocratic wing of some quiet English town. The world's greatest humorist lives at No. 351. The house stands on a knoll, and is a charming situation in summer. But just now the trees are bare, the creepers on the verandah are withered, and no evergreen shrubs brighten the lawn. Harriet Beecher Stowe lives in the next house to Mr. Clemens's, but the venerable lady's mind is now unhinged, and in her conversation she is no longer the author of *Uncle Tom's Cabin*. Mr. Clemens has also Charles Dudley Warner for a near neighbor,[2] so that the atmosphere of this corner of Hartford is literary.

Two black-and-tan collies were guarding Mr. Clemens's door when I approached, and a pull at the bell brought forth a negro.[3] While waiting for Mr. Clemens I noticed that he has got an eye for artistic house decoration, and that a handsome edition of Browning lay on a table. Mr. Clemens soon appeared, dressed in a light grey suit. His hair is gradually silvering, though it is in as great profusion as ever. It is well tinged with grey in front, but the long tresses which touch his coat collar still lag behind. His moustache clings to its reddish hue, and his heavy eyebrows maintain a harmonious equilibrium. Mr. Clemens was not slow to speak, and commenced the conversation very slowly and quietly. He was to start for Canada in the course of the week, to register at a hotel and to obtain copyright for his new book there and in England. He had a good deal to say about that book and the modifications which he had to make to suit the English market, but as we reached it after going through the copyright question, it will be as well to take the same route. Mr. Clemens was one of the first to agitate the question of international copyright, and started on it as a knight-errant many years ago, but the heroic crusade collapsed for want of support. He took a keen interest in the Chace Bill,[4] which was before Congress last year, but has not much confidence in a Republican majority.

"They are more likely," he said, "to clap on some more protection where it isn't needed, rather than give us a little protection which will do good."

"What," I asked, "do you think of Mr. Stedman's opinion that American literature doesn't now require protection, that it has survived and overcome pirated editions, and is now on its legs?"[5] "That," said Mr. Clemens, "is true, so far as it goes, but it doesn't go far enough. Publishers are constructed out of the same material as other men, and they are not likely to pay a royalty on the work of an unknown author when they can get works of established writers for nothing. But the protection of American authors is not the main thing. The great question is the preservation in this country of a national literature, the spread of national sentiments, national thought, and national morals. What becomes of a few chuckle-headed authors who can go and saw wood, or live or die just as they like, is a mere trifle compared with the colossal national question involved, which is whether our people are going to continue to imbibe foreign ideas, and to take their opinions of American institutions from foreign writers. If I were going to England and delivering myself conscientiously on your royalties—pour out my contempt for your pitiful lords and dukes—no one would publish my book. But an Englishman comes along here, and after looking around for a few minutes, goes home and writes a book in which he abuses our President, jeers and ridicules our institutions, and that book is gobbled up by our American publishers and scattered throughout the country at twenty cents a copy. After that we are told that the Americans are thin-skinned! We are also told that our newspapers are irreverent—coarse, vulgar, and ribald. I hope that this irreverence will last for ever; that we shall always show irreverence for royalties and titled creatures born into privilege, and all that class which take their title from anything but merit.

Merit alone should be the only thing that should give a man a title to eminence. I am sorry that some of our newspapers are losing that irreverence which I wish to see preserved. They talk too much about that miserable puppet, the German Emperor; and the spread of foreign ideas is having its effect on our people. There are American women—well brought up and perfectly respectable—who are ready to sell themselves to anything with the name of a duke attached. There is one railroad thief whom I could name married his daughter to some decayed prince; but you can't expect much from a railroad robber anyway.[6]

Mr. Clemens was quite led away by this onslaught on royalty and titles. He usually speaks very slowly and quietly, but he warmed up, and emphasized his words with expressive gestures. He has a habit when talking with one to stare fixedly at some imaginary object in space, as if he had got hold of an idea and was determined to keep in sight of it. His normal conversation is very slow, and he lingers sometimes over a word, and then accelerates the speed of the next few so as to make up for the delay.

After this he told me something about his new book, and how he had changed it to suit the English market. "I want to get at the Englishman," he said, "but to do that I must go through the English publisher; and your publishers and your newspapers are cowards. I have modified and modified my book until I really couldn't cut it any more; and now Mr. Chatto,[7] who is the most courageous of them, will have to cut it more. I am anxious to see my fate. I have got the preface, and as only the first part remains I presume he has cut it. Yes, cut off more than half my preface," said Mr. Clemens, in sorrowful tones; "and all because of a little playful reference of mine to the divine right of kings."

It may be that Messrs Chatto and Windus will think better of the preface, and reverse their decision; but here is the part which the author thinks is doomed:—

> The question as to whether there is such a thing as divine right of kings is not settled in this book. It was found too difficult. That the executive head of a nation should be a person of lofty character and extraordinary ability was manifest and indisputable; that none but the Deity could select that head unerringly was also manifest and indisputable; consequently, that He does make it, as claimed, was an unavoidable deduction. I mean, until the author of this book encountered the Pompadour, and Lady Castlemaine and some other executive heads of that kind;[8] these were found so difficult to work into the scheme that it was judged better to take the other tack in this book (which must be

issued this fall), and then go into training and settle the question in another book. It is, of course, a thing which ought to be settled, and I am not going to have anything particular to do next winter anyway.

Mr. Clemens also fears that some of the illustrations tell their tale too plainly for the English people. He is delighted with the way the artist has entered into the spirit of the book in executing the illustrations, and pointed to what he considers a very fine portrait of Jay Gould in the capacity of the "slave driver."[9]

"It is four years," he said, in answer to another question, "since I projected this book, and three years since I wrote it. When I write a book I put the manuscript in pigeon-holes for a year or two. I take it out and look at it now and then to see how it is getting on. I began to think some months ago that the time was about ripe for this one. And sure enough it is, for there is Brazil getting rid of its Emperor in twenty-four hours, there is talk of a republic in Portugal and federation in Australia; and, curiously enough, the short proclamation in which my hero abolishes the monarchy is similar—I don't mean the language, but the ideas—to the proclamation establishing the Brazilian Republic."[10]

Mr. Clemens next conducted me upstairs to what appears to be his workshop and a billiard-room combined. He had been standing writing on the billiard table when I called, though he usually writes at a small table in front of the window. He writes a young man's hand, and clearer and better than most young men. Compositors delight in his copy, but then Mr. Clemens has been at the [typesetter's] case himself. He walked up and down the room and smoked a wooden pipe, which he had to refill every few minutes. Mr. Clemens is rarely in New York. He is the head partner in the flourishing and rising publishing business of Webster and Co., of New York, but the details of the business he leaves to his partner, Mr. Hall,[11] who sends him weekly reports. Not that Mr. Clemens is devoid of business capacity! He is a keen and capable business man when he likes, only he cannot be bothered with it when other things occupy his attention. He always sends autographs to the friends who write for them, or, rather, his secretary does it. Mr. Clemens puts his name on several hundred cards every few months, and his secretary mails them to applicants. When he sent them himself he discriminated between two kinds of applicants. "No matter," he said, "whether they sent a thousand cards or a thousand stamps, I never sent it unless they sent an addressed envelope, but I wouldn't write the address. I gobbled the stamps and kept my autograph." The sale of Mark Twain's books is much about the same on both sides of the Atlantic. When a new book is published, about a third of the income comes from England, and two-thirds from America. But when the work falls into the list of old books this order is reversed, probably because the English second editions are much cheaper than the American.

On leaving I asked Mr. Clemens when we might expect another book: "I don't know," he said. "I don't write the book. It writes itself. If there is another book in me it will come out. I shall wait until it is ready."

Thus the evolution of the great humorist's masterpieces is a slow process. They first go through a period of mental incubation, and after they are transferred to paper they lie in pigeon-holes in a chrysalis condition until they are ripe.

Notes to Interview 47

1. Robert Donald (1860–1933), British journalist.
2. See the reference to Warner in n. 2 to interview 28.
3. George Griffin (1849?–1897), MT's African American butler from 1875 to 1891. See also *MTL,* 6:583n5.
4. Jonathan Chace (1829–1917), U.S. senator from Rhode Island from 1885 to 1889, proposed a copyright bill that granted concessions to U.S. typographical unions. The bill passed in 1891 after his retirement.
5. See the reference to Stedman in n. 3 to interview 46.
6. In October 1889, Clara Huntington (1860–1928), adopted daughter of Collis P. Huntington, married the German nobleman Prince Francis Edmund von Hatzfeldt (1853–1910). In his working notes for his fifth novel, *A Connecticut Yankee in King Arthur's Court* (1889; published in Great Britain as *A Yankee at the Court of King Arthur*), MT considered depicting how "American heiresses" buy "rotten dukes"; in particular how "Mr. Skunkington railroad thief-daughter marries Prince Hatfeldt." See Louis J. Budd, *Mark Twain: Social Philosopher* (Bloomington: Indiana University Press, 1962), 115–16.
7. Andrew Chatto (d. 1913) and W. E. Windus, MT's British publishers.
8. Jeanne-Antoinette Poisson, aka Madame de Pompadour (1721–64), mistress of King Louis XV of France from 1745 to 1750; Barbara Palmer, aka Barbara Villiers, aka Lady Castlemaine (1641–1709), mistress of King Charles II of England from 1660 until 1671.
9. Jay Gould (1836–92), an American robber baron, was depicted as a slave driver in a famous illustration in chapter 35 of *A Connecticut Yankee* by Daniel Beard (1850–1941). MT enthusiastically approved all Beard's illustrations.
10. The Brazilian Republic was proclaimed on 15 November 1889.
11. Frederick J. Hall, Charles L. Webster's successor as manager of Charles L. Webster and Co.

48

"'Mark Twain' at Home," *New York World,* 12 January 1890, 14.

"I wonder what Mark Twain at home looks like?" said a young man in *The World* office one day last week. "How does he live? Does he enjoy life or does he groan his way through it as most humorists are believed to do? How does he work? How much stuff does he grind out every day?"

The young man didn't mean any disrespect by calling Twain's happy thoughts "stuff." He was simply expressing a wholesome curiosity as to how rapidly the great funny man produced copy, and unconsciously he used the word familiar to most workers in newspapers offices who are not journalists with a capital J. Every American who reads has frightened off the blues with the aid of the Yankee in King Arthur's Court, or grown young and happy again in the company of Huckleberry Finn; and most of us have reveled in Twain as he fired his solemn and explosive jokes from the platform, or, better still, have laughed with him to the point of tears after dinner. Small wonder, then, that the young man and thousands of other *World* readers wanted to know what Mark Twain, the man, is like, and how he originates the germs of his jokes, and how he hatches them and brings them to a robust and laughter-compelling maturity, and, above all, how he feels while he is doing it and between times.

A *World* reporter was sent up to Hartford, therefore, to find out all that Mr. Clemens knows about himself and a great deal more besides. It is no small thing to beard an author (not one of Mr. Meeson's tame kind[1]) in his den, and it is a still more serious matter to grab a successful publisher after the fashion of the White Knight in Wonderland and tackling the aged, aged man, and cry, "Come, tell me how you live!" Nevertheless, the young man, armed with a letter of introduction from an old friend, took horse and made for Mark Twain's home by the express train.

The City Directory of Hartford, an annual full of the fruits of deep research, contains this interesting paragraph: Clemens, S. L. (Mark Twain), 351 Far.

At first sight this seems to show that the city is so proud of him that it keeps Twain etherealized at a temperature of 351 degrees Fahrenheit. This is misleading. The "Far." is a local synonym for Farmington avenue, a fine, broad, airy boulevard that leads to West Hartford, and No. 351 of it is the home of the humorist. A series of two green and deliberate horse-cars roll to and fro on this avenue several times each week. The shy habits of these cars have made a fine pedestrian of Mr. Clemens, for, although he keeps a few horses, he'd rather walk than wait for the cars.

Near the top of a green, breezy hill stands the long, rambling, red-brick house of Mark Twain. It has more gables, more quaint and unexpected corners than the most enthusiastic Queen Anne house-builder could count.[2] If every one of its windows were filled with stained glass in honor of some saint they would find standing room for all the calendar and a few new saints added. There isn't a vestige of wall or fence of any kind about the lawns which surround the house on every side. Trees and shrubs and beds of flowers are plentiful, whichever way you look. It is strange at first to find a broad porch on the east side of a house, but when you have stood on the western and southern porches, equally broad and spacious, you are reminded that here is the home of a man who has all of the Mississippi's love of air and sunlight, and who wants to be able to sit outdoors under his own roof at any time of day.

A trim young black man in black[3] takes your card and goes on a still hunt for the illustrious ancestor of the Yankee at the Round Table. The door of the reception-room looks out on a roomy hall that occupies the greater part of this floor. In one corner sits a white marble Mercury, his slender, muscular right leg resting carelessly across his left knee, his energies all relaxed—the whole figure a captivating picture of strength and grace at ease. What is that queer helmet, cocked rakishly over his right ear? An old straw hat—and without a ribbon into the bargain. What need is there to ask the statue where did he get that hat. Nobody but Mark Twain would dare to jam such a shocking old hat on the head of Hermes.[4] But there is no doubt that it adds to the expression of serene rest on the god's marble features. The visitor is reminded of the story about Twain's decoration of a marble bust of [John] Calvin a few years ago. That great and good man appeared in marble, his stern features severely smooth. Mark improved him by penciling on a curly mustache and the cutest of cute goatees, after the fashion of the Hon. Bardwell Slote.[5] Mrs. Clemens was horrified when she saw it, but no amount of scrubbing was able to restore Calvin's solemnity.

Presently there comes a soft footfall and the brisk steps of a man of medium height. Somehow S. L. Clemens at home doesn't seem so tall as Mark Twain on the platform. He has just finished breakfast and there isn't a wrinkle in his face. His hand is small, but it takes his visitor's with a firm, nervous grip.

"I'm glad to see you," says he, "and somewhat ashamed to be so late. But we had a little theatre here last night and I find I'm growing old. I don't get up so early as I used to after a night's fun." So saying Mr. Clemens led the way up to his workshop with as springy a gait as a youngster of twenty-five. This room is a treat. A big billiard table with black and gold legs stands in the middle of it. Its windows look to the westward over a festive and noisy brook in a setting of rich, green turf, past clumps of elm and birch and oak and maple. A long line of high blue hills marks the western horizon. On the other side of them is the Farmington Valley. Close at hand the robins' nests on a tall beech seem likely to fall in at the window. It is a delightful spot altogether, just the place for hard work. Mark Twain's desk stands in the southern corner piled with business papers. Shelves of books line the walls of this angle. *Parleyings with Certain People* rubs covers with the *United States Newspapers Directory,* and a commentary on the Old Testament is neighborly and shows no ill-feeling towards Ruskin, who stands near at hand in a red binding.[6] The ground glass of the nearest window is decorated with a beer-stein, gules, two long-stemmed pipes rampant and other devices of festivity. Pipes and boxes and jars of tobacco are tucked in here and there wherever there is room. The pipes are of corn-cob and burned to a jet black by much usage. Portraits of Gutenberg and studies in black and white originals of some famous engravings hang about the wall.[7] At the chimney side hangs the portrait of an aged woman. "In 1833 she taught school near here," says Mr. Clemens, "and admitted two negro girls. This was one of the earliest acts that started the Abolitionist controversy. The parents of her pupils made a great row about her action, but the black girls kept on in her school."[8]

There is a hint of the sailor in the active man who marches up and down the room with the least bit of a roll and a sharp eye to windward as he turns to walk back. He is what a sailor would call "a handy-sized man." Close-knit and a trifle above medium height, small-footed, small-handed, and full of vim. His head is of generous size, the forehead high and full and broad, with shaggy brows of reddish-brown. Mark Twain's hair is plentiful and well touched with gray. It is fine and silky, but every fiber in the thatch stands up aggressively as if in perpetual defiance to the brush. The eyes are neither blue nor gray nor brown, but a combination of all three. They stand far apart and have the power of looking clear through things. Twain's mustache is still brownish-red, with hardly a touch of gray. Possibly he is nearly fifty years old as he pretends, but no observer would write him down for more than forty.

"I'd rather play you a game of billiards," said he, picking up a cue, "than try to instruct *The World*'s readers about myself. I know mighty little about the game, but less about the things you want to know." So many people have spoken about Mark Twain's sleepy drawl that it isn't worth while to say much about it here. He talks rapidly enough, after all, but his solemn enunciation slyly inserts ideas in his hearer's mind, and then bang! goes an unsuspected joke when you have been lulled by that drawl into a state of profound calm. "When do you write?" asked the visitor, with visions of the humorist grappling at midnight with a large idea and slamming around on paper in the old conventional way.

"From 11 o'clock in the morning until 3 in the afternoon," said Mr. Clemens. "I work only three months in the year, when we all go up to Elmira, in New York, where my wife's folks live. I have a little octagonal house made chiefly of glass.[9] It stands on the top of a high hill about three miles from the city. I think it is one of the quietest spots on the face of this globe. Still I have had tribulations in it. Shortly after it was finished and I had begun work on a drowsy summer day, with nothing to break the stillness but the peaceful birr of humble insects, quieter than solitude, I was aroused by a tremendous snorting and squealing and grunting. I looked down the hill and found that our nearest neighbor, a farmer, had established a hog orchard where I could get all the benefit of it. The sounds those hogs made when they quarreled and the smells that floated from them on the soft southern breeze drove me wild. Work was impossible. I went over to the farmer's house and bought all those hogs and his right to keep hogs forever. A few weeks after that another chorus aroused me, and there were six guinea hens squawking to one another in the place where the hogs had been. Well, the farmer said he had paid a quarter apiece for ten hens. . . . I offered him a dollar a head for the lot and reserved the privilege of never seeing or hearing them again. He agreed. Three days later I was disturbed by the same cackling and clattering, but much more of it, and on looking down the hill I found that the farmer had invested my money in four times as many hens. In the haste of my bargain I had overlooked specification as to all future hens. 'Time for a new trade,' said I, and I made it. The farmer, a well-meaning man, next indulged in a flock of sheep that skipped as near my workshop as possible and ate grass and bleated loudly at regular intervals. I bought mutton. The quiet has been preserved around that hill now for some time, but one by one nearly all of that farmer's rights have been extinguished.

"I don't know how much copy I write each day in those three summer months. The amount varies. 'Do a little every day' is my rule. Stick to it and you find the pile of manuscript growing rapidly. If on reading it over I find things I don't like I simply tear up twenty or thirty pages and there is no harm done. Don't be in a hurry to do too much, but work regularly."

"Then you don't wait for inspiration?"

"I don't think the prose writer needs to. If he were to depend upon that support he'd have an inspiration—say once in three months; it would last forty-eight hours, and what would he have accomplished? The poet is a man who works by what is called inspiration, but if he had to sit around and wait for it month after month he wouldn't be much of a poet.

"Well, I work four hours a day five days a week, for three months every year. That is half as much a day as I worked ten years ago. I wrote *Innocents Abroad* in sixty days, working from noon until midnight every day. I wouldn't dare do it now. I'm an old man. It would break me down."

"Didn't it hurt you even then?"

"No; I had just left a newspaper desk and I was used to that sort of thing. But now I go slower. There is a book"—pointing to a bundle of manuscript in a pigeonhole—"that I began in 1867.[10] I'm not sure about the exact date, but I think that was it. I could have been finished any time in the last twenty years by the addition of a chapter. I suppose it could be published as it is; but I'm not satisfied with it yet. Once in a while I take the manuscript out and look at it. There's no hurry for its publication. The time isn't ripe for it. I expect to finish the book if I live long enough.

"It's a different matter when a date is announced for the appearance of a book. Then the author has a contract with the public and he must keep it. On one day the book must appear in England, on another in Canada and on another in the United States. That was the case with this book (*A Connecticut Yankee in King Arthur's Court*). Besides, the time is ripe for its appearance. All Europe, beneath its scum of hereditary kings and royal personages and aristocratic notions generally, is pretty thoroughly Americanized, and America, with its floating scum of fools who are fond of aping aristocratic ideas and actions, is pretty well Europeanized. Besides, I wanted to say some spiteful things in this book, and when a man has that to do it is apt to make him hurry."

The visitor happened to speak of the publication in the newspapers three years ago of the extracts from *The Yankee in King Arthur's Court* that Mr. Clemens read at the Military Services Institution at Governor's Island.[11]

"You enjoyed it?" repeated Mark Twain, with a reminiscent smile. "Well, I didn't. It frightened me badly. I think I was about the worst scared man in the United States. The officer who invited me was an old friend and the invitation came in the summer. I didn't know of that club's custom of having reporters at some of its meeting and I carelessly went down there in November without asking about it, as I should have done. Well, you can imagine how it electrified me to read the papers next morning. There was the chapter I had read printed almost verbatim, but that wasn't all. There was printed in full a rather carefully written synopsis of the whole scheme of the book as I had plotted it out. I thought there was no use of my going on with the work. For the moment I imagined that the book pirate (Mr. Clemens's frown was black) would seize my synopsis and specimen chapter, write the book for me, kindly forge my name on the title-page and help himself to big profits from the spurious edition. I had put myself in a horrible position. There was no help for me. The publication in the newspapers was enough to outlaw any claim I might make for copyright. I guess the old pirate was asleep, for the only thing I had omitted to do was to wake him up and invite him to help himself. How else he could have failed to rob me I cannot conceive. Next day, next week, he had something else to think of and I was safe.

"Speaking of pirates recalls the telegram from Philadelphia I read in the newspapers not long before the *Yankee* was published. It was set forth that I had stolen not only the specimen chapter published in the *Century* from Max Adeler, but that I had pirated all the incidents as well.[12] Mr. Adeler had for some years placed himself in such a position that the imputation of being concerned with humor could be cast at him. But he had reformed now and had become a respectable member of society, devoting his energies to a reputable business. He edits a periodical devoted to the interests of cloth and other solid things. Humor was no more for him. Nevertheless he indulged on this occasion in a convulsion, an upheaval—yes, it might be called a geyser of humor. With the grand air of a man who owns acres of bonds and stocks, he waved his arm magnanimously before the reporter and said: 'Twain has stolen the scheme and incidents of that book from one I published years ago. But no matter. I am through with that sort of thing now. He is welcome to all he has taken.'

"This aroused a great curiosity in me. 'Why,' said I, 'if I have done all Adeler claims, I am the old original boss plagiarist, and hereafter I shall claim pay accordingly.' How the chapter might have lingered in my mind I could faintly conceive, but how he knew that I had stolen from him hundreds of incidents which he couldn't possibly have read because my book was not yet published, was too much for my weak imagination. And where do incidents come from? From the observer himself. Here I had taken a Yankee of today to a remote place and a remote time where everything he saw or heard was startlingly new. I had gone with him step by step, and saw things and heard them as he did. The Englishman of today doesn't know that his cab and carriage and cart wheels are wonderfully thick and heavy and clumsy. He comes here and discovers that ours are wonderfully thin, just as we go to his country and see that his are thick. 'Well,' thought I, 'if I can have stolen unconsciously all of these thousands of ideas from Max Adeler I must have become a worker of miracles.'

"Howells was with me.[13] We went into Lee & Shepard's and I asked for the book,[14] and the grave and white-haired and aged clerk who waited upon us made the altogether unnecessary remark that this was the first copy of the work he had heard called for in all the years he had been there. We carried it over to the Parker House and examined it. It was a book of humor, light, airy, humorous sketches—not a big book, but good. In the middle of it were a few pages telling of an aged Boston man who fell asleep and dreamed of his boyhood, seventy years before. When he tried to strike a match flint and steel were at hand. He tried to light the gas and found he was burning a tallow dip. He rode once more in a stagecoach. It was very funny and brief, and I confess I not only enjoyed reading it, but was much relieved in mind when I had finished.

"Do you suppose this great old world can keep on revolving thousands and thousands of times without turning out the same old thoughts again and again? They will be modified each time by the individual who thinks them, but the germ itself is never new. I laugh every time I hear the idiots jackassing in a charge of plagiarism against somebody or other.

"Why, to repeat another man's thoughts is to pay him the highest compliment you can. It shows what a grip his mind has taken on yours. I never charge any one with plagiarism, for to do so would prove me incapable of gratitude for the highest compliment a man can pay me. I remember that when *The Innocents Abroad* was published a man asked me—he was an old friend and had the privilege of asking such a question—'Why did you steal the dedication of your book from Dr. Holmes?'[15] We stopped at the first bookstore we came to in Broadway and got a copy of one of the earliest editions of Dr. Holmes' poems, a little blue book. There was my dedication not changed so much as one word. Well, I didn't like to make a charge of plagiarism against Dr. Holmes, for he was a much older man than I and I respected him greatly, and besides his book had been published about twenty years before mine. I carried myself back to the time when I had written that dedication, and further. At last I remembered that in 1867 I had been sick for two weeks in a hotel in Honolulu. A copy of Dr. Holmes' little blue book was the only volume in that hotel. You can imagine how I had read it. I knew every poem, I knew the title page, the dedication, the imprint, the first page, the last, the covers even. The dedication had remained. I had absorbed it more thoroughly than anything else. I wrote a letter to Dr. Holmes explaining things, and there was no bloodshed between us."

There may be pleasanter things in this world than an hour's chat with Mark Twain, but if there are the present writer has never discovered any of them. The humor in the man is contagious. No one can hear him five minutes without being surprised into a hearty laugh, and amid all the hubbub it kicks up Twain's solemn conversation drawls serenely along.

"No," he said, in answer to a question about his daily life. "I have not yet begun to cultivate the art of keeping or restoring health. I suppose I'll have to some day. I don't care for riding or driving, but I manage to take a long walk every day. I suppose I ought to have more exercise."

The picture of Mark Twain's library in this story shows Mrs. Harriet Beecher Stowe in the foreground. The inscription above the hearth is: "The ornament of a house is the friends who frequent it." Mrs. Stowe's house is next door to Mr. Clemens', and Charles Dudley Warner's is close at hand.[16] It is odd to hear the people of Hartford call Mr. Clemens Mark Twain. Every car driver, cabman, policeman and messenger boy knows him as Mark Twain, and refuses to speak of him by any other style than his nom de plume in full. Mr. Clemens rarely visits New York, although he is the head of the publishing firm of Charles L. Webster & Co. His partner, Mr. Hall,[17] sends him frequent reports of how things are going, and Twain's keen business instincts enable him to attend to nearly all his affairs in the billiard-smoking workshop in his home. On its northern wall hang in a frame the checks—$200,000 and $150,000—which show Mrs. Julia D. Grant's profits from Mark Twain's publication of General Grant's book.[18]

Notes to Interview 48

1. The title character of *Mr. Meeson's Will* (1888) by the British novelist H. Rider Haggard (1856-1925) describes hack writers as "tame writers."
2. Queen Anne architecture often featured turrets, asymmetrical design, and steep roofs.
3. See n. 3 to interview 47.
4. In Greek mythology, Hermes was the messenger of the gods, protector of travelers, and the inventor of the lyre. He was called Mercury in the Roman pantheon.
5. The Hon. Bardwell Slote, the lead character in Benjamin E. Wolf's play *The Mighty Dollar,* popularized by the American actor William J. (Billy) Florence (1831-91).
6. *Parleyings with Certain People of Importance in Their Day* (1887), a collection of memoirs by the English poet Robert Browning (1812-89). John Ruskin (1819-1900), English essayist and art critic.
7. Johan Gutenberg (c. 1398-1468), inventor of movable type and printer of the Gutenberg Bible (1456).
8. Apparently Catherine Beecher (1800-1878), sister of Harriet Beecher Stowe and founder of the Hartford Female Seminary in 1823.
9. See n. 2 to interview 4.
10. MT had been working periodically on "Shem's Diary" since the late 1860s, to judge from notes and extant manuscripts, though most of this early material remains unpublished.
11. On 11 November 1886 MT read the first three chapters of *A Connecticut Yankee* and summarized the remainder of the book at the Military Service Institution on Governor's Island in New York harbor. See, for example, "Mark Twain's Yankee," *Boston Globe,* 12 November 1886, 2.
12. Max Adeler, aka Charles Heber Clark (1841-1915), author of *The Fortunate Island and Other Stories* (Boston: Lee and Shepard, 1882).
13. See n. 2 to interview 2.
14. Offices and bookstore at 47 Franklin Street, east of Boston Common.
15. MT borrows the dedication to *The Innocents Abroad* from Holmes's *Songs in Many Keys* (1826): "To my most patient reader and most charitable critic, my aged mother, this volume is affectionately inscribed." MT retells this anecdote in a speech at the Holmes breakfast in Boston on 3 December 1879 (Fatout, 135) and in his autobiographical dictation (e.g., *Auto* [1959], 150; *Auto* [1990], 180).
16. See the reference to Warner in n. 2 to interview 28.
17. See n. 11 to interview 47.
18. Julia D. Grant (1826-1902), widow of Ulysses S. Grant. Grant completed his *Personal Memoirs* (published by Charles L. Webster and Co. in 1886) shortly before his death.

49

"Mark Twain's Lawsuit," *Hartford Courant,* 18 January 1890, 1.

Mr. Edward H. House,[1] the author and journalist, has brought suit against Mr. Samuel L. Clemens, alleging breach of contract in relation to the dramatization of *The Prince and the Pauper.* An acting version of the play in question by Mrs. Abby Sage Richardson is announced for next Monday evening at the Broadway Theater, New York, with Elsie Leslie in the parts of Edward VI and Tom Canty.[2]

Mr. House's side of the story appeared in the *New York Tribune* of yesterday.[3] It sets forth that in 1881 Mr. House at Mr. Clemens's request edited the manuscript of the story and suggested dramatizing the work. Nothing came of the suggestion, and he went to Japan and remained four years. Soon after his return Mr. Clemens wrote him, proposing that he dramatize the book and offering one-half or two-thirds of the profits, that he accepted and suggested having the two parts played by one actress, that Mr. Clemens approved the idea, and that in June 1887 he (House) read to Mr. Clemens the first act, that he finished the piece in August of the same year, and in the following February wrote to Mr. Clemens as to newspaper paragraphs that Mrs. Richardson was to dramatize the book. He received no reply, but in answer to a second letter Mr. Clemens wrote, repudiating the whole transaction, but later offered him $5,000 as compensation, which he declined to receive.

A *Courant* reporter called on Mr. Clemens yesterday afternoon. He was found in his cozy billiard room and seemed quite willing to talk about the matter. He said: "Mr. House was never invited to edit the book for me. He asked if he might read the manuscript while lying bedridden for several weeks simply to satisfy his own curiosity. He made one suggestion—which turned out to be a fallacy. I had used in my book some such expression as this: 'This person was kindly entreated,' etc. Mr. House judged it was too late a date to use that form 'entreated' and advised leaving off the first syllable. I do not remember whether I corrected it or not, but afterward found that it was in use in the time of Henry the VIII."

"How about suggesting the advisability of dramatizing the work?" was asked.

"As if that was original!" exclaimed Mr. Clemens. "It needed no suggestion from Mr. House. The story was originally planned for a drama and not as a book. I doubted my ability to write a drama but wrote it purposely for somebody capable of doing so to turn it into a drama."

"He says you offered him one-half or two-thirds of the profits."

"Mr. House did not accept the proposition. In his letter he only entertained it in a noncommittal way. He did not discard the proposition, but there was nothing in his letter that can be construed into an acceptance. The proposition and his non-acceptance are of the date of 1886."

"He next speaks of suggesting the idea of having the two parts played by one actress. How as to that?"

"A suggestion made three years before by Mr. Will Gillette,"[4] promptly returned Mr. Clemens. "I tried to get Mr. Gillette to dramatize the book for me, giving him full permission to do so. Mr. Gillette entertained this proposition in 1888 and went so far as to draft the plot for the play, making liberal alterations of the text of the book. Mr. Gillette has never retired from the undertaking and if an undertaking of that kind can remain in force forever, then it is Mr. Gillette that has a claim upon me and not Mr. House. If I had no right to give Mrs. Richardson permission in 1888 to dramatize, I of course had no right to give Mr. House permission in 1886. Somewhere between 1883 and 1888 I dramatized the book myself, but was assured by competent authorities that neither the living nor the dead could act the play as I had planned it."

"Mr. House affirms," pursues the reporter, "that he read you the first act of the play in June 1887."

"In that part of 1887," continued Mr. Clemens, "Mr. House was a guest for a while at my home. I aroused his sleeping interest in the matter and thought he was going to dramatize the piece; but it was a mistake. He merely showed me a skeleton plan for the first act, with some trifles of conversation put in to indicate the drift of the act. That he wrote a complete act is absolutely untrue."

"Mr. House says in his affidavit that he wrote you that the piece was finished in August 1887."

"A year ago he wrote me the same statement, changing the date of finishing the piece to September 1887. With anybody else this slight discrepancy of dates would count for nothing. With Mr. House the case is different. If he ever wrote me a letter in which he said he had finished the piece, he has a copy of that letter by him and did not need to make that error. Mr. House is a methodical man, an excellent business man, and never destroys or mislays any scrap of writing that comes to him from anyone, or fails to keep a copy of every scrap which he writes himself. I never received any letter from Mr. House saying the play was finished. I was at home again from the vacation as early as October of that year (1887) and he did not mention the play in any way during the many months that followed during his stay in Hartford. Evidently he had dropped the play entirely out of his mind. He was busy with other matters and never made any reference to it. I was thoroughly well pleased with his skeleton of the first act and said so without reservation. But when I recognized that the most I could hope to get from him was a skeleton for me to fill out, my interest in the matter at once disappeared. He was a near neighbor for many months after that. Our intercourse was constant and familiar, he coming to my house and I going to his to talk and gossip after the manner of friends. Yet throughout this cordial intercourse he remained silent as to that dramatization. I believed then and I believe now that with the skeletonizing of the first act Mr. House's interest in the project came to an end. Late in 1888 Mrs. Richardson wrote and asked permission to dramatize the book. I had always been on the lookout for some person willing to do this work, and was not particular as to what the terms might be. So I wrote her promptly and accorded the permission. I also gave her Mr. House's New York address and said that he had once taken an interest in this thing. I suggested that she call on him and see if she could secure his cooperation, as he had practice in dramatic work. She declined, however, preferring to do all the work herself."

"Another matter, Mr. Clemens. Mr. House asserts that he saw it stated in the papers that you had allowed Mrs. Richardson to dramatize the work, wrote you and received no reply. Is that so?"

"Mr. House knew why he received no reply," was the answer. "I was not in Hartford. I told him so when I answered his second letter. Now as regards my repudiation of the transaction: If asking him to send me a copy of any contract or agreement existing between him and me so that I might, as I said, 'undo any wrong suffered at my hands,' is 'repudiating the whole transaction,' then I certainly repudiated it for that is what I wrote. As to the alleged proposition to pay him $5000 as compensation, a proposition that he says he declined, I would only say that is another effort of Mr. House's imagination. I never offered him a penny nor consented to join anybody else in offering him one. Again, he says that 'arbitration was tried without success.' If that was done, I had nothing whatever to do with it. I would not have consented to arbitrate with a man who had no shadow of a claim against me. After about eighteen months of petrified absence of interest in this dramatization, Mr. House's condition instantly unpetrified itself when he found that somebody else was willing to undertake the work. He not only imagines that he has an agreement with me for a dramatization but that the term of it is eternal. It is only fair, then, that the settling of our dispute should be accorded the same liberal lack of hurry. Mr. House is never so entertaining as when he has a grievance. We shall be able to pass the Hereafter very pleasantly. Some of the statements in Mr. House's affidavit are true; but the court will probably give information to amend them."[5]

The *New York Times* of yesterday said: "Mark Twain has given to Howard P. Taylor, the playwright, the exclusive right to dramatize his latest work, *A Connecticut Yankee at the Court of King Arthur*. Mr. Taylor will make a spectacular comedy of it, and when completed it will have its first production at one of the Broadway theaters."[6]

The reporter asked Mr. Clemens if the statement was true, and he replied: "It is a surprising thing, but it is."

Notes to Interview 49

1. Edward H. (Ned) House (1836–1901), playwright and journalist. See also Paul Fatout, "Mark Twain: Litigant," *American Literature* 31 (March 1959): 30–45.
2. Abby Sage Richardson (1837–1900), actress, author, and authorized dramatist of *The Prince and the Pauper*. See Fatout, 256–57; Elsie Leslie (1881–1966), American child actress.
3. "Author against Author," *New York Tribune*, 17 January 1890, 1.
4. William Gillette (1855–1937), American actor and playwright, a native of Hartford, and brother-in-law of Charles Dudley Warner (see n 2. to interview 28).
5. MT lost the case. See "Mark Twain Is Defeated," *New York Times*, 9 March 1890, 1.
6. Howard P. Taylor, MT's friend since their Nevada days and author of such plays as *Snowflake and the Seven Gnomes* (1880), *Jonathan's Courtship: A Yankee Sketch* (1905), and *Wiggins of Pop-Over Farm* (1921). The quotation appears in "Notes of the Stage," *New York Times*, 17 January 1890, 4.

50

"Rudyard Kipling[1] on Mark Twain," *New York Herald*, 17 August 1890, 5.

You are a contemptible lot out there, over yonder. Some of you are Commissioners and some Lieutenant Governors and some have the V.C.,[2] and a few are privileged to walk about the Mall arm in arm with the Viceroy; but I have seen Mark Twain this golden morning, have shaken his hand and smoked a cigar—no, two cigars—with him, and talked with him for more than two hours! Understand clearly that I do not despise you, indeed I don't. I am only very sorry for you all, from the Viceroy downward. To soothe your envy and to prove that I still regard you as my equals I will tell you all about it.

They said in Toronto that he was in Hartford, Conn., and again they said perchance he is gone upon a journey to Portland, Me.; and a big fat drummer [traveling salesman] vowed that he knew the great man intimately and that Mark was spending the summer in Europe, which information so upset me that I embarked upon the wrong train at Niagara and was incontinently turned out by the conductor three quarters of a mile from the station, amid the wilderness of railway tracks. Have you ever, encumbered with great coat and valise, tried to dodge diversely minded locomotives when the sun was shining in your eyes? But I forgot that you have not seen Mark Twain, you people of no account!

Saved from the jaws of the cowcatcher I, wandering devious, a stranger met.

"Elmira is the place. Elmira in the State of New York—this State, not two hundred miles away," and he added, perfectly unnecessarily, "Slide, Kelly, slide."[3]

I slid on the West Shore line, I slid till midnight, and they dumped me down at the door of a frowzy hotel in Elmira. Yes, they knew all about "that man Clemens," but reckoned he was not in town; had gone East somewhere. I had better possess my soul in patience till the morrow and then dig up the "man Clemens'" brother-in-law, who was interested in coal.[4]

The idea of chasing half a dozen relatives in addition to Mark Twain up and down a city of thirty thousand inhabitants kept me awake. Morning revealed Elmira, whose streets were desolated by railway tracks, and whose suburbs were given up to the manufacture of door sashes and window frames. It was surrounded by pleasant, fat little hills trimmed with timber and topped with cultivation. The Chemung River flowed generally up and down the town and had just finished flooding a few of the main streets.

The hotel man and the telephone man assured me that the much desired brother-in-law was out of town and no one seemed to know where "the man Clemens" abode. Later on I discovered that he had not summered in that place for more than nineteen seasons and so was comparatively a new arrival.

A friendly policeman volunteered the news that he had seen Twain or some one very like him driving a buggy on the previous day. This gave me a delightful sense of nearness to the great author. Fancy living in a town where you could see the author of *Tom Sawyer* or "some one very like him" jolting over the pavements in a buggy!

"He lives way out yonder at East Hill," said the policeman, "three miles away from here."

Then the chase began—in a hired hack, up an awful hill, where sunflowers blossomed by the roadside and crops waved and *Harper's Magazine* cows stood in eligible and commanding attitudes knee deep in clover, all ready to be transferred to photogravure. The great man must have been persecuted by outsiders aforetime and fled up the hill for refuge.

Presently the driver stopped at a miserable little white wood shanty and demanded "Mister Clemens."

"I know he's a big bug and all that," he explained, "but you can never tell what sort of notions those sort of men take it into their heads to live in, anyways."

There rose up a young lady who was sketching thistle tops and golden rod, amid a plentiful supply of both, and set the pilgrimage on the right path.

"It's a pretty Gothic house on the left hand side a little way further on."

"Gothic h——" said the driver, "very few of the city hacks take this drive, specially if they knew they are coming out here," and he glared at me savagely.

It was a very pretty house, anything but Gothic, clothed with ivy, standing in a very big compound and fronted by a veranda full of all sorts of chairs and hammocks for lying in all sorts of positions. The roof of the veranda was a trellis work of creepers and the sun peeped through and moved on the shining boards below.

Decidedly this remote place was an ideal one for working in if a man could work among these soft airs and the murmur of the longeared crops just across the stone wall.

Appeared suddenly a lady used to dealing with rampageous outsiders. "Mr. Clemens has just walked down town. He is at his brother-in-law's house."[5]

Then he was within shouting distance after all and the chase had not been in vain. With speed I fled, and the driver, skidding the wheel and swearing audibly, arrived at the bottom of that hill without accidents.

It was in the pause that followed between ringing the brother-in-law's bell and getting an answer that it occurred to me for the first time Mark Twain might possibly have other engagements than the entertainment of escaped lunatics from India, be they ever so full of admiration. And in another man's house—anyhow what had I come to do or say? Suppose the drawing room should be full of people, a levee of crowned heads; suppose a baby were sick anywhere, how was I to explain I only wanted to shake hands with him?

Then things happened somewhat in this order. A big, darkened drawing room, a huge chair, a man with eyes, a mane of grizzled hair, a brown mustache covering a mouth as delicate as a woman's, a strong, square hand shaking mine, and the slowest, calmest, levellest voice in all the world saying: "Well, you think you owe me something and you've come to tell me so. That's what I call squaring a debt handsomely."

"Piff!" from a cob pipe (I always said a Missouri meerschaum was the best smoking in the world) and behold Mark Twain had curled himself up in the big arm chair and I was smoking reverently, as befits one in the presence of his superior.

The thing that struck me first was that he was an elderly man, yet, after a minute's thought, I perceived that it was otherwise, and in five minutes, the eyes looking at me, I saw that the gray hair was an accident of the most trivial kind. He was quite young. I had shaken his hand. I was smoking his cigar, and I was hearing him talk—this man I had learned to love and admire fourteen thousand miles away.

Reading his books I had striven to get an idea of his personality and all my preconceived notions were wrong and beneath the reality. Blessed is the man who finds no disillusion when he is brought face to face with a revered writer. That was a moment to be remembered, the land of a twelve pound salmon was nothing to it. I had hooked Mark Twain and he was treating me as though under certain circumstances I might be an equal.

About this time I became aware that he was discussing the copyright question. Here, as far as I remember, is what he said. Attend to the words of the oracle through this unworthy medium transmitted. You will never be able to imagine the long, slow surge of the drawl, and the deadly gravity of the countenance, any more than the quaint pucker of the body, one foot thrown over the arm of the chair, the yellow pipe clinched in one corner of the mouth and the right hand casually caressing the square chin: "Copyright. Some men have morals and some men have—other things. I presume a publisher is a man. He is not born. He is created—by circumstances. Some publishers have morals. Mine have. They pay me for the English productions of my books. When you hear men talking of Bret Harte's works and other works and my books being pirated ask them to be sure of their facts. I think they'll find the books are paid for. It was ever thus.

"I remember an unprincipled and formidable publisher. Perhaps he's dead now. He used to take my short stories—I can't call it steal or pirate them. It was beyond these things altogether. He took my stories one at a time and made a book of it.[6] If I wrote an essay on dentistry or theology or any little thing of that kind—just an essay that long (he indicated half an inch on his finger), any sort of essay—that publisher would amend and improve my essay.

"He would get another man to write some more to it or cut it about exactly as his needs required. Then he would publish a book called 'Dentistry by Mark Twain,' that little essay and some other things not mine added. Theology would make another book and so on. I do not consider that fair. It's an insult. But he's dead now, I think. I didn't kill him.

"There is a great deal of nonsense talked about international copyright. Are you interested in it? So am I." I don't think that he meant to be crushingly ironical, but I would cheerfully have wrapped myself up in the carpet and burrowed into the cellar when those eyes turned on me.

"The proper way to treat a copyright is to make it exactly like real estate in every way.

"It will settle itself under these conditions. If Congress were to bring in a law that a man's life were not to extend over a hundred and sixty years somebody would laugh. It wouldn't concern anybody. The men would be out of the jurisdiction of the court. A term of years in copyright comes to exactly the same thing. No law can make a book live or cause it to die before the appointed time.

"Tuttletown, California, was a new town, with a population of 3000 banks, fire brigades, brick buildings and all modern improvements. It lived, it flourished and it disappeared. Today no man can put his foot on any remnant of Tuttletown, California. It's dead. London continues to exist.

"Bill Smith, author of a book read for the next year or so, is real estate in Tuttletown. William Shakespeare, whose works are extensively read, is real estate in London. Let Bill Smith, equally with Mr. Shakespeare now deceased, have as complete a control over his copyright as he would over real estate. Let him gamble it away, drink it away, or give it to the church. Let his heirs and assigns treat it in the same manner.

"Every now and again I go up to Washington, sitting on a board, to drive that sort of view into Congress. Congress takes its arguments against international copyright delivered ready made and Congress isn't very strong. I put the real estate view of the case before one of the Senators.

"He said, 'Suppose a man has written a book that will live forever?'

"I said, 'Neither you nor I will ever live to see that man, but we'll assume it.' What then?

"He said, 'I want to protect the world against that man's heirs and assigns working under your theory.'

"I said, 'You think all the world are as big fools as—, that all the world has no commercial sense. The book that will live forever can't be artificially kept up at inflated prices. There will always be very expensive editions of it and cheap ones issuing side by side.'

"Take the case of Sir Walter Scott's novels," he continued, turning to me. "When the copyright notes protected them I bought editions as expensive as I could afford, because I liked them. At the same time the same firm were selling editions that a cat might buy. They had their real estate, and not being fools recognized that one portion of the plot could be worked as a gold mine, another as a vegetable garden and another as a marble quarry. Do you see?"

What I saw with the greatest clearness was Mark Twain being forced to fight for the simple proposition that a man has as much right in the work of his brains (think of the heresy of it!) as in the labor of his hands. When the old lion roars the young whelps growl. I growled assentingly, and the talk ran on from books in general to his own in particular.

Growing bold, and feeling that I had a few hundred thousand folk at my back, I demanded whether Tom Sawyer married Judge Thatcher's daughter and whether we were ever going to hear of Tom Sawyer as a man.

"I haven't decided," quoth Mark Twain, getting up, filling his pipe and walking up and down the room in his slippers. "I have had a notion of writing the sequel to *Tom Sawyer* in two ways. In one I would make him rise to great honor and go to Congress, and in the other I should hang him. Then the friends and enemies of the book could take their choice."

Here I lost my reverence completely and protested against any theory of the sort, because, to me at least, Tom Sawyer was real.

"Oh, he is real," said Mark Twain. "He's all the boys that I have known or recollect; but that would be a good way of ending the book"; then, turning round, "because, when you come to think of it, neither religion, training nor education avails anything against the force of circumstances that drive a man. Suppose we took the next four-and-twenty years of Tom Sawyer's life and gave a little joggle to the circumstances that controlled him. He would logically and according to the joggle turn out a rip or an angel."

"Do you believe that, then?"

"I think so. Isn't it what you call kismet?"

"Yes, but don't give him two joggles and show the result, because he isn't your property any more. He belongs to us."

Thereat he laughed—a large, wholesome laugh—and this began a dissertation on the rights of a man to do what he liked with his own creations, which being a matter of purely professional interest, I will mercifully omit.

Returning to the big chair he, speaking of truth and the like in literature, said that an autobiography was the one work in which a man against his own will and in spite of his utmost striving to the contrary, revealed himself in his true light to the world.

"A good deal of your life on the Mississippi is autobiographical, isn't it?" I asked.

"As near as it can be—when a man is writing a book, and about himself. But in genuine autobiography, I believe it is impossible for a man to tell the truth about himself or to avoid impressing the reader with the truth about himself.

"I made an experiment once. I got a friend of mine—a man painfully given to speaking the truth on all occasions—a man who wouldn't dream of telling a lie—and I made him write his autobiography for his own amusement and mine.[7] He did it. The manuscript would have made an octavo volume, but, good honest man though he was, in every single detail of his life that I knew about he turned out, on paper, a formidable liar. He could not help himself.

"It is not in human nature to write the truth about itself. None the less the reader gets a general impression from an autobiography whether the man is a fraud or a good man. The reader can't give his reasons any more than a man can explain why a woman struck him as being lovely when he doesn't remember her hair, eyes, teeth or figure. And the impression that the reader gets is a correct one."

"Do you ever intend writing an autobiography?"

"If I do, it will be as other men have done—with the most earnest desire to make myself out to be the better man in every little business that has been to my discredit, and I shall fail, like the others, to make the readers believe anything except the truth."

This naturally led to a discussion on conscience. Then said Mark Twain, and his words are mighty and to be remembered: "Your conscience is a nuisance. A conscience is like a child. If you pet it and play with it and let it have everything it wants, it becomes spoiled and intrudes on all your amusements and most of your griefs. Treat your conscience as you would treat anything else. When it is rebellious spank it—be severe with it, argue with it, prevent it from coming to play with you at all hours and you will secure a good conscience. That is to say, a properly trained one. A spoiled conscience simply destroys all the pleasure in life. I think I have reduced mine to order. At least I haven't heard from it for some time. Perhaps I've killed it through over severity. It's wrong to kill a child, but in spite of all I have said a conscience differs from a child in many ways. Perhaps it is best when it's dead."

Here he told me a little—such things as a man may tell a stranger—of his early life and upbringing, and in what manner he had been influenced for good by the example of his parents. He spoke always through his eyes, a light under the heavy eyebrows; anon crossing the room with a step as light as a girl's to show me some book or other; then resuming his walk up and down the room puffing at the cob pipe. I would have given much for nerve enough to demand the gift of that pipe, value five cents when new. I understood why certain savage tribes ardently desire the liver of brave men slain in combat. That pipe would have given me, perhaps, a hint of his keen insight into the souls of men. But he never laid it aside within stealing reach of my arms.

Once indeed he put his hand on my shoulder. It was an investiture of the Star of India, blue silk, trumpets and diamond studded jewel, all complete. If hereafter among the changes and chances of this mortal life I fall to cureless ruin I will tell the superintendent of the workhouse that Mark Twain once put his hand on my shoulder, and he shall give me a room to myself and a double allowance of paupers' tobacco.

"I never read novels myself," said he, "except when the popular persecution forces me to—when people plague me to know what I think of the last book that everyone is reading."

"And how did the latest persecution affect you?"

"*Robert?*" said he interrogatively.[8]

I nodded.

"I read it, of course, for the workmanship. That made me think I had neglected novels too long—that there might be a good many books as graceful in style somewhere on the shelves; so I began a course of novel reading. I have dropped it now. It did not amuse me. But as regards *Robert* the effect on me was exactly as though a singer of street ballads were to hear excellent music from a church organ. I didn't stop to ask whether the music was legitimate or necessary. I listened and I liked what I heard. I am speaking of the grace and beauty of the style."

How is one to behave when one differs altogether with a great man? My business was to be still and to listen. Yet Mark—Mark Twain, a man who knew men—"big Injun, heap big Injun, dam mighty heap big Injun"—master of tears and mirth, skilled in wisdom of the true inwardness of things, was bowing his head to the labored truck of the schools where men act in obedience to the books they read and keep their consciences in spirits of homemade wine. He said the style was graceful, therefore it must be graceful. But perhaps he was making fun of me. In either case I would lay my hand upon my mouth.

"You see," he went on, "every man has his private opinion about a book. But that is my private opinion. If I had lived in the beginning of things I should have looked around the township to see what popular opinion thought of the murder of Abel before I openly condemned Cain. I should have had my private opinion, of course, but I shouldn't have expressed it until I had felt the way. You have my private opinion about that book. I don't know what my public ones are exactly. They won't upset the earth."

He recurled himself into the chair and talked of other things.

"I spend nine months of the year at Hartford. I have long ago satisfied myself that there is no hope of doing much work during those nine months. People come in and call. They call at all hours, about everything in the world. One day I thought I would keep a list of interruptions. It began this way: A man came and would see no one but Mister Clemens. He was an agent for photogravure reproductions of Salon pictures.[9] I very seldom use Salon pictures in my books.

"After that man another man, who refused to see any one but Mister Clemens, came to make me write to Washington about something. I saw him. I saw a third man, then a fourth. By this time it was noon. I had grown tired of keeping the list. I wished to rest.

"But the fifth man was the only one of the crowd with a card of his own. He sent it up—this card of his own. 'Ben Koontz, Hannibal, Mo.' I was raised in Hannibal. Ben was an old schoolmate of mine. Consequently I threw the house wide open and rushed with both hands out at a big, fat, heavy man, who was not the Ben I had ever known—nor anything of him.

"'But is it you, Ben,' I said. 'You've altered in the last thousand years.'

"The fat man said: 'Well, I'm not Koontz exactly, but I met him down in Missouri and he told me to be sure and call on you, and he gave me his card and'"—here he acted the little scene for my benefit—"'if you'll wait a minute till I can get out the circulars—I'm not Koontz exactly, but I'm traveling with the fullest line of rods you ever saw.'"

"And what happened?" I asked breathlessly.

"I shut the door. He was not Ben Koontz—exactly—not my old school-fellow, but I had shaken him by both hands in love * * * and I had been bearded by a lightning rod man in my own house. As I was saying, I do very little work in Hartford. I come here for three months every year, and I work four or five hours a day in a study down the garden of that little house on the hill. Of course I do not object to two or three interruptions. When a man is in the full swing of his work these little things do not affect him. Eight or ten or twenty interruptions retard composition."

I was burning to ask him all manner of impertinent questions as to which of his works he himself preferred, and so forth, but standing in awe of his eyes I dared not. He spoke on and I listened groveling.

It was a question of mental equipment that was on the carpet, and I am still wondering whether he meant what he said.

"Personally I never care for fiction or story books. What I like to read about are facts and statistics of any kind. If they are only facts about the raising of radishes they interest me. Just now, for instance, before you came in"—he pointed to an encyclopedia on the shelves—"I was reading an article about 'Mathematics.' Perfectly pure mathematics.

"My own knowledge of mathematics stops at 'twelve times twelve,' but I enjoyed that article immensely. I didn't understand a word of it, but facts, or what a man believes to be facts, are always delightful. That mathematical fellow believed in his facts. So do I. Get your facts first, and," the voice died away to an almost inaudible drone, "then you can distort 'em as much as you please."

Bearing this precious advice in my bosom I left, the great man assuring me with gentle kindness that I had not interrupted him in the least. Once outside the door I yearned to go back and ask some questions—it was easy enough to think of them now—but his time was his own, though his books belonged to me.

I should have ample time to look back to that meeting across the graves of the days. But it was sad to think of the things he had not spoken about.

In San Francisco the men of the *Call* told me many legends of Mark's apprenticeship in their paper five and twenty years ago; how he was a reporter delightfully incapable of reporting according to the needs of the day. He preferred, so they said, to coil himself into a heap and meditate till the last minute. Then he would produce copy bearing no sort of relationship to his legitimate work—copy that made the editor swear horribly and the readers of the *Call* ask for more.

I should like to have heard Mark's version of that and some stories of his joyous and variegated past. He has been journeyman printer (in those days he wandered from the banks of the Missouri even to Philadelphia), pilot cub and full blown pilot, soldier of the South (that was for three weeks only), private secretary to a Lieutenant Governor of Nevada (that displeased him), miner, editor, special correspondent in the Sandwich Islands [Hawaii], and the Lord only knows what else. If so experienced a man could by any means be made drunk it would be a glorious thing to fill him up with composite liquors, and, in the language of his own country, "let him retrospect." But these eyes will never see that orgie fit for the gods.

Later.—Oh shame! Oh shock! O fie! I have been reading the new book which you also will have read by this time—the book about the yankee animal in the courtyard.[10] It's * * * but I don't believe he ever wrote it; or, if he did, I am certain that if you held it up to a looking glass or picked out every third word or spelled it backward you would find that it hid some crystal clean tale as desirable as *Huck Finn.*

Notes to Interview 50

1. Rudyard Kipling (1865-1936). In 1906 MT claimed he knew Kipling's writings "better than I know anybody else's books." See also *Auto* (1959), 286-88.
2. Victoria's Cross, a British military award.
3. A popular baseball poem.
4. See n. 2 to interview 11.
5. The Langdon family mansion at the corner of Church and Main streets in Elmira.
6. John Camden Hotten (1832-73), British publishing pirate. See *MTL*, 5:165, written between November 1872 and June 1873: "the man has not a personal friend whom a respectable person could dare to associate with."
7. Orion Clemens (1825-97), MT's older brother, began his "Autobiography of a Coward" in 1880. See Philip Ashley Fanning, *Mark Twain and Orion Clemens* (Tuscaloosa: University of Alabama Press, 2003), 180-91.
8. *Robert Elsmere* (1888) by Mrs. Humphry Ward (1851-1920).
9. Large representational history or landscape paintings hung in the manner of the salon (i.e., at eye level and above).
10. *A Yankee in the Court of King Arthur* or *A Connecticut Yankee in King Arthur's Court* (1889).

51

"Mark Twain on Kipling," *New York World*, 24 August 1890, 18.

Most people know by this time what Rudyard Kipling thinks of Mark Twain.[1] The young storywriter of old England has paid his respects in earnest person as well as in luminous prose to the veteran humorist of New England. It is natural for them to wonder what Mark Twain thinks of Rudyard Kipling. And this, as well as something new about the way he thinks his thoughts, Mr. Clemens has told the writer, talking at his best in that easy way in which ideas roll from a brain full.

Mr. Clemens was asked what he thought of Rudyard Kipling's story of his quest for him.

"Why," said he, with the artless frankness of a man too busy to read the Sunday newspapers, "I haven't seen it! I haven't read a line of it, nor even heard, as yet, about it. Tell me what it is. Is it blame or otherwise?"

Then the writer outlined Kipling's vivid story of his drives about Elmira, his search up hill and down dale, and his final discovery of Twain at his mother-in-law's. Mr. Clemens laughed silently, with his eyebrows, and took up the thread of the narrative.

"Yes, I was at my wife's mother's when he found me, and that accounts for a singular, almost unaccountable lack of hospitality on my part. It was just about the luncheon hour when he arrived, and while he and I were sitting talking and smoking the rest of the family were eating. Now, I have a habit of never eating in the middle of the day. As I didn't get hungry the idea of luncheon didn't occur to me, for we were pleasantly engaged, and as I was not in the habit of going to lunch none of the family came to me to announce it. I never once thought of Mr. Kipling's views on the luncheon question; it didn't occur to me that he could have an appetite after his drive!

"Well, when he had gone and I was talking to my wife about his visit she at once recurred to this luncheon business and said: 'Why, do you mean to tell me that after this young man had come all this way to see you and had made such a search to find you, you didn't offer him any refreshments!' And thereupon she berated me for not being 'natural, like other men,' in my habits of eating!" Here Mr. Clemens' eyebrows laughed briskly.

"I thought," he continued, "that was the difference between a natural sense of hospitality and the absence of it.

"The next morning I went down to the hotel to call on Mr. Kipling without taking the precaution to telephone and see if he were still there. He was gone, and I, of course, haven't seen him since. Shall I see him in London soon? No, I don't expect to go to London in the near future; but when I do go I shall call upon him. I shan't wait to have him hunt me up, as you suggest the likelihood of his doing. I shall assuredly hunt him up!"

So much for the episode which Kipling himself has so vividly described, though from a standpoint entirely different to that of Mr. Clemens, whose frame of mind on the luncheon subject evidently insures Mr. Kipling at their next meeting an abundance of creature comforts.

It was not necessary to ask Mr. Clemens what he thinks of Kipling's tales.

"It would be a good thing," said he, "to read Mr. Kipling's writings for their style alone, if there were no story back of it. But, as you say, there always is a story there and a powerfully interesting one generally. How people have gotten to read and talk about his stories! Why, when a young man, not yet twenty-four years of age, succeeds in the way Kipling has succeeded, it simply shows, doesn't it, that the general public has a strong appreciation of a good thing when it gets hold of one?

"His great charm to me is the way he swings nervous English! It is wonderful. That it seems to me is one great secret of the hold he takes on his readers. They can understand what he is at. He is simple and direct."

"Have you any book of your own in hand at present?" Mr. Clemens was asked.

"No, nothing in particular," he replied; "but I have unfinished books on hand nearly all the time, if that is what you mean. I have one book begun seventeen—let me see, seventy-three, eighty-three—yes, just seventeen years ago. And it isn't more than half finished yet!"

"Haven't you abandoned it, or do you still take an interest in it and expect to finish it?"

"I shall certainly finish it, that is—(with a smile)—if I live seventeen years longer! I reckon I am good for that! How old am I now? About fifty-four and a half.

"I began 'The Diary of Shem in the Ark,'"[2] continued Mr. Clemens, and at the drollery of the title and the seriousness with which it was announced the auditors burst into laughter. "Just seventeen years ago," he went on, "I wrote the first six chapters in Edinburgh, when the idea of it occurred to me. I was much interested in it then and am now. But I have laid it down and taken it up perhaps a half dozen times in those seventeen years. You ask if it be more akin to my early or my more recent writings in its conception and style? Well, the plan of the book has changed greatly since I began it in Edinburgh. I have acquired different ideas about it since then and they have expanded and grown and changed."

This led naturally to Mr. Clemens' declaration of his highly original method of evolving a story out of his brain.

"That is a curious thing about stories," he went on. "You have your ideas, your facts, your plot, and you go to work and write yourself up. You use up all the material you have in your brain and then you stop, naturally. Well, lay the book aside, as I do, and think of or go at something else.

"After a while, three or four months, maybe, or perhaps three or four or five years, something suggests your story or your book to you and you feel a sudden awakening of interest in it and desire to go to work at it; and then, lo and behold, to your surprise, maybe, but not to my surprise now—for I am used to it by this time—you find that your stock of ideas and facts and concepts has been replenished and your mind is full of your subject again and you must write, your brain is overflowing, your thoughts are beginning to burn to be put down on paper.

"Is this unconscious cerebration? I suppose so. A most interesting illustration of it, you may well say. The form of the concept of the original purpose may have greatly changed, but the root of it is there in the mind unchanged, and from it, without our being conscious of it at all, has grown a tree, with fresh, new foliage and spreading branches.

"Or, suppose the brain is like a cistern from which you draw off the ideas on the subject in hand as you write, until the cistern goes dry and you have to stop. You busy yourself about something else and put the other behind you and away. By and by from the imperceptible seeping in of ideas, thoughts, facts, fancies, as you have worked or slept or thought of something else, lo, the cistern is once more full to overflowing, and with fresh relish and a wonderful appreciation of the new material you have been acquiring in spite of yourself, you draw off the ideas again and add them to your former stock already committed to writing.

"The field that you reaped and garnered has grown up again and there is another harvest there to reap. The 'think-tank' of your brain overflows once more. The snowball has been rolling all this time without your knowing it and gathering more snow.

"So I take up 'The Diary of Shem in the Ark' with new interest now and expect to do so for years to come. The return is not tedious; the idea of resuming operations on the old lines is conceived with positive relish."

The visitor asked Mr. Clemens when the courts would decide the vexed question involved in the dramatization of *The Prince and the Pauper*. His face grew slightly melancholy. "I expect they will decide as between Mr. House and Mrs. Abby Sage Richardson here in New York probably in October.[3] House never thought of making a play out of my book, in my opinion, until he heard that Mrs. Richardson had done it. He has acted in a sort of a dog-in-the-manger way about it. You ask if I have any doubt about the ultimate decision of the controversy? I can say this: I have no sort of doubt about what the facts are and what the decision ought to be. But I have a good deal of doubt about what the decision of a law court will be, for I believe firmly in the uncertainties of the law.

"By the way, that was an extraordinary opinion which the judge gave when he decided to grant a temporary injunction. It is one of those curiosities of judicial decision, as you suggest, of which we have been reading from time immemorial. The learned Court declared that as Mr. House was a sick man and had been confined to his bed and had time to think and to revolve the facts in his mind and freshen up his memory, his recollection of the facts was probably better than mine, because I was such a busy man and was engaged in so many different things! According to that it would seem that sickness is an admirable way to win a lawsuit."

Notes to Interview 51

1. See interview 50.
2. See n. 10 to interview 48.
3. See nn. 1 and 2 to interview 49.

52

Edward W. Bok,[1] "Literary Leaves: 'Mark Twain' to Live Abroad for Two Years," *Boston Journal Supplement,* 16 May 1891, 1.

New York, May 15—In about three weeks Mark Twain will sail for the other side, not to return to America for two years. The humorist's family will go with him, and, after a month or two of travel, they will seek some secluded and remote French village, where the following two years will be spent. "The children," said the humorist to me a few days ago, "will have their tutors; Mrs. Clemens will enjoy the luxury of a complete rest from housekeeping and kindred evils, while I want nothing but my pipe and my pen. I have no special literary plans in mind, but shall probably do a little something. No, no, I shall not take the 'Innocents Abroad' again; that would mean too much travel, and I can't do what I did years ago. We are going to live in quiet fashion, somewhere away from everybody, where no one knows us, and enjoy each other's company." Passage was engaged some time ago on the French Line by the party under fictitious names, and perhaps the captain of the French steamer sailing from this port on June 6 will learn, from this paragraph, for the first time of the genial company which will be among his passengers.

Note to Interview 52

1. Edward W. Bok (1863–1930), syndicated columnist and later the editor and publisher of *Ladies' Home Journal.*

53

Raymond Blathwait,[1] "Mark Twain on Humor," *New York World,* 31 May 1891, 26; rpt. *New York World* (semiweekly edition), 2 June 1891, 6.

It was on one of the most charming days of this month that I passed through the gates of Mr. Samuel L. Clemens's garden, just off Farmington avenue, in Hartford, and walked up a broad carriage drive to his pretty veranda-circled house. Introduced to the presence of the genial and gifted humorist, I found him knocking about the balls upon an old-fashioned billiard table. As I entered, he at once stepped forward and gave me his hand and a very hearty welcome.

"And how is my dear old friend Charles Warren Stoddard,[2] who has written to me about you? How does he like his curiously secluded life among the priests of the Catholic College at Washington?" he asked in his slow peculiar drawl. "Come and sit down and have a cigar. I myself smoke all the time."

I sat down in a comfortable armchair, lit the cigar he gave me, and it was a very good one, for, as he said, "I always buy my cigars in America, a special brand. I want to take some to Europe with me, for I never can buy a cigar fit to smoke in England, nor, indeed, anywhere in Europe, and there I am going to live for the next two or three years to educate my little girls.

"Yes, it is a great break up, but I do not see how I can avoid it. However, I am reconciled to it now. You see we are in great confusion, as we are more than half packed up. You have just come in time to catch me, and I am very glad to have a chat with you. You shall lead and direct the conversation. That, you know, is the interviewer's business. He must bear the lion's share, or, at all events, his very full half. A good interviewer has in him the makings of a perfect novelist."

I said: "Very well then, Mr. Twain, I should much like you to give me your opinion as to the comparative merits of American and English humor."

The great humorist ran his hands through his mass of fast graying hair, eyed me quizzingly, and then slowly drawled: "That is a question I am particularly and specially unqualified to answer. I might go out into the road there," pointing as he spoke to the pretty, sun-flecked, shadow-stricken pathway, a glimpse of which I gained through the open window, "and with a brickbat I would knock down three or four men in an hour who would know more than I about humor and its merits and its varieties. I have only a limited appreciation of humor. I haven't nearly as catholic and comprehensive an idea of humor as you have, for instance." I demurred loudly to this: "Oh, Mr. Twain, and you who wrote the dialogue in *Huck Finn* between Huck and the runaway Negro about kings and queens."[3]

"Exactly," replied Mr. Twain, as he got up out of his seat and began to pace the room, up and down, while he vigorously puffed away at his cigar, which he almost immediately replaced with his pipe.

"Exactly, and that book, perhaps, reveals the very thing of which I speak. Within certain rather narrow lines, I have an accurate, trustworthy appreciation of humor. It is not guesswork, this estimate of mine as regards the limits of my humor and my power of appreciating humor generally, because with my bookshelf full of books before me I should certainly read all the biography and history first, then all the diaries and personal memoirs and then the dictionaries and the encyclopedias. Then, if still alive, I should read what humorous books might be there. That is an absolutely perfect test and proof that I have no great taste for humor. I have friends to whom you cannot mention a humorous book they have not read. I was asked several years ago to write such a paper as that you suggest on 'Humor,' and the comparative merits of different national humor, and I began it, but I got tired of it very soon. I have written humorous books by pure accident in the beginning, and but for that accident I should not have written anything."

I very heartily remarked that it was an accident by which nations had profited. "The gaiety of nations, Mr. Twain, will be eclipsed when your humor ceases."

Mark Twain bowed slowly and gravely, and went on in a voice that would have made his fortune as an undertaker: "At the same time that leaning towards the humorous, for I do not deny that I have a certain tendency towards humor, would have manifested itself in the pulpit or on the platform, but it would have been only the embroidery, it would not have been the staple of the work. My theory is that you tumble by accident into anything. The public then puts a trademark onto your work, and after that you can't introduce anything into commerce without that trademark. I never have wanted to write literature; it is not my calling. Bret Harte, for instance, by one of those accidents of which I speak, published the 'Heathen Chinee,' which he had written for his own amusement.[4] He threw it aside, but being one day suddenly called upon for copy he sent that very piece in. It put a trademark on him at once, and he had to avoid all approaches to that standard for many a long day in order that he might get rid of that mark. If he had added three or four things of a similar nature within twelve months, he would never have got away from the consequences during his lifetime. But he made a purposely determined stand; he abolished the trademark and conquered."

"To all of which, Mr. Mark Twain," said I, "I can only say in reply that we are all heartily glad that you succumbed to your trademark. And now, in connection with this philosophical chat on humor, I want to ask you why it is that great humor is always found in very solemn people and nations. The Presbyterian Scotchman or the Puritan New Englander are really the most humorous people on earth,"

"Ah, now," replied Mark Twain, "you have put your finger on a great verity. It is, after all, quite natural. I answer in one word that it is reaction. It is a law that humor is created by contrasts. It is the legitimate child of contrast. Therefore, when you shall have found the very gravest people in the world, you shall also be able to say without further inquiry, 'I have found the garden of humor, the very paradise of humor.' You may not know it, but it is true, if a man is at a funeral and broken-hearted, he is quite likely to be persecuted with humorous thoughts. The grotesque things that happen at funerals depend on their solemn background. They would not be funny but for contrast. Take an instance in which you look in vain for fun if it were not intimately connected with a very ghastly occasion.

"Here is the story: A clergyman in New York was requested by a man to come over to Brooklyn to officiate at his wife's funeral. The clergyman assented, only stipulating that there must be no delay, as he had an important engagement the same day. At the appointed hour they all met in the parlor, and the room was crowded with mourning people, no sounds but those of sighs and sobbings. The clergyman stood up over the coffin and began to read the service, when he felt a tug at his coattails, and bending down he heard the widower whisper in his ear: 'We ain't ready yet.' Rather awkwardly he sat down in a dead silence. Rose again and the same thing took place. A third time he rose and the same thing occurred. 'But what is the delay?' he whispered back. 'Why are you not ready?' 'She ain't all here yet,' was the very ghastly and unexpected reply. 'Her stomach's at the apothecary's.'

"You see it is the horizon-wide contrast between the deep solemnity on the one hand and that triviality on the other which makes a thing funny which could not otherwise be so. But in all cases, in individuals, in peoples, in occurrences such as that I have just described, it is not the humorous but the solemn and grave element that predominates, and that affords the strongest background."

"Well, now, Mr. Twain, you, a professional humorist, ought to be very careful how you exercise your humor. You know you greatly horrified some good folk in England when you published your *American at the Court of King Arthur*. They thought you were scoffing at Tennyson's *Idylls of the King*."

Mark Twain sprang up from his seat with more energy than I had supposed him to possess. He looked at me with a sarcastic and sardonic smile, and said:

"Why, a person would waste his labor who would mock at a great poem like that. It would be the art of an idiot. People, you know well, have most confused ideas about reverence and irreverence. Even the dictionary tries to describe 'irreverence,' but it entirely steps out of its jurisdiction. Irreverence is simply scoffings leveled at my ideals, nobody else's, and reverence is simply respect for my ideals, nobody else's. I am not irreverent when I scoff at the image of tar and rags which a naked savage puts up and worships, and that savage is not irreverent when he, from his standpoint, scoffs at my sacred things. Now, if I wished to scoff at Arthur and the knights and at the things which they considered fine and heroic in their day, I am privileged to do so, and I may not righteously be called to account for it. Arthur and his knights were privileged to criticize in any way they chose lower ideals than their own and a lower civilization which prevailed in any other country at their own time and which had prevailed for centuries before, and one is not fairly at liberty to deny them that privilege.

"Our ideals of today will find small respect in the world a thousand years hence, but I shan't climb out of my grave to enter a protest against such procedure of posterity. I do reverence the *Idylls of the King,* but not because I am commanded to do so out of the dictionary, and I should not do so if I did not wish to from an impulse of my own. I reverence achievement, and that only, and so it goes without saying that it isn't any matter to me whether achievement is the work of a person who wore a coronet or wooden shoes. I have no reverence for heredity of any kind. I should have had had I been educated to it, but I have not been so educated. I think that while the titles of Prince, Earl, Duke are high, yet they are not high enough yet to properly decorate men of prodigious achievement, as a recognition by the world of what they have done. I would furnish to such men all the gauds and titles they wanted or would take, but, I would give such things a real value by letting them perish with the winners of them."

All this time Mr. Clemens had been solemnly pacing the room, puffing out great clouds of smoke beneath his thick mustache, gazing at me with keen eyes hidden by shaggy eyebrows, tossing back his plentiful locks of hair, and every now and again emphasizing his remarks with a long forefinger slowly shaken at me as I listened attentively to him. At this juncture of our conversation a manservant[5] came in with a tray of very welcome luncheon. "But you must excuse my joining you," said my host. "I never eat more than two meals a day and that is one too many for me. My ideal of life would be one meal a day, but, alas! conventionality does not always admit of the carrying out of one's ideals."

I noticed the man's kind, grave courtesy of manner, a courtesy which rises to absolute courtliness. Yet report has it that no one can most effectually or most roughly, perhaps, put down an impertinent or an intrusive personage. Verily a man of character and of decision. After my luncheon I resumed the conversation with a remark that *Huckleberry Finn* was my favorite of his books, and I specially commented on the wonderful knowledge of dialect which he displays in that book.

"Yes," he replied, "I was born in one of those States and I lived a great deal of my boyhood on a plantation of my uncle's,[6] where forty or fifty Negroes lived belonging to him, and who had been drawn from two or three States and so I gradually absorbed their different dialects which they had brought with them. It must be exceedingly difficult to acquire a dialect by study and observation. In the vast majority of cases it probably can be done, as in my case, only by absorption. So a child might pick up the differences in dialect by means of that unconscious absorption when a practiced writer could not do it twenty years later by closest observation. But a dialect can be acquired. Take for instance the great traveler, Burckhardt, who must have swindled himself into Mecca.[7] A man who could have escaped the observation of thousands of Arab fanatics must have had a rare faculty for picking up nice accuracies and differences in foreign speech. Clarence King,[8] born and reared here, is an instance. When a grown man, he went to the Pacific coast and in his very first year he wrote sketches filled with Pike County dialect which have never been rivaled for accuracy. Bret Harte went there in his budding manhood and yet with a familiar acquaintanceship of several years with the miners whose speech was that of Pike County, he yet was never able to master even a plausible semblance. *The World* called him the prince of dialecticians, but there is not a dialect sentence of his that will stand examination.[9] This does not mar his work—dialect is not an essential. Why should people find fault with dialect in books? The cunningest things have been said in dialect. It has got to be a mighty poor Scotch story that dialect cannot save. Look at the dialect in *Uncle Remus*.[10] Why, the dialect there is absolutely scholarly. The only one of my own books that I can ever read with pleasure is the one you are good enough to say is your favorite, *Huck Finn*, and partly because I know the dialect is true and good. I didn't know I could read even that till I read it aloud last summer to one of my little ones who was sick. My children all read *The Prince and the Pauper*, but none of the others.

"To go back a moment to our chat on humor, I would like to say with regard to English humor, that your greatest humorist, Dickens, is most humorous to me when he drops into it accidentally. I don't like his humor as a staple. Take, for instance, his *Tale of Two Cities*, which is a beautiful work spoilt for me by that ostensibly humorous character, Jerry. I would improve that book, I would make it all a book should be by leaving out Jerry altogether. I can't read *Pickwick* as a whole, only parts of it. I hold that T. B. Aldrich is the wittiest man I ever met.[11] I don't believe his match ever existed on this earth."

"One more remark and I have done, Mr. Twain. How far, in your opinion, does culture, education, what you will, enter into the making of books?"

"My dear sir, they speak of book culture as being the end of all things. That is applied in criticism upon novels of all kinds, whereas I say it is only applicable to certain classes of novels. Nine out of ten of the qualities required for the writing of a good novel are summed up in the one thing—a knowledge of men and life, not books or university education. If I could write novels I shouldn't lack capital, because I have had intimate acquaintanceship with many groups of men, many occupations, many varieties of life in widely separated regions. It would be impossible for me to use that capital, that culture, for that is really what it is, because I should never be able to acquire the novel-writing art. But it makes me impatient to see that requirement constantly made by the critics that a novelist shall have book culture. I saw the other day that Rudyard Kipling had been called to account under that head. I don't myself see where Kipling's vigorous tales could have been improved by 'book culture' or a university career.

"My *Innocents Abroad* was my first book. I am sure it was not the outcome of book culture. Oh, yes, it was true enough. They really existed. They were only a kind of Cooks' excursionists; only Cook, as Cook, had not then been heard of."[12]

Our conversation was at an end, so I strolled about the room, observing the desk at which he wrote, marveling at the prodigious check which hung upon the wall and which told how, as the publisher of General Grant's *Memoirs,* Mr. Clemens had paid to his family the sum of $450,000, the biggest copyright ever paid on this earth.[13] A phonograph stood close to his desk, and at my request he had let me hear some of the things he had spoken into it and which his typewriter [typist] had subsequently reproduced. But, I could well understand how, as he observed, it was not much of a help to a literary or a businessman.

"When it is perfected it may be so, but at present it will benefit posterity more than it does ourselves," he remarked.

What really interested me very much was a copy of verses that Oliver Wendell Holmes had written to him on his fiftieth birthday, and which hung carefully framed upon the wall.[14]

My visit had drawn to a close. Down the cool dark staircase I passed, preceded by Mark Twain, who paused before a splendid bust of Henry Ward Beecher,[15] which he told me had been done by a young man whom he and his wife had sent to Rome to be educated as a sculptor.[16] "Then," said Mr. Clemens, "we are well rewarded by that bust, which is the best one ever done of the great American preacher."

Notes to Interview 53

1. Aka Raymond Blathwayt (1855–c. 1936), a British journalist.
2. The poet Charles Warren Stoddard (1843–1909) was Twain's private secretary in London during the winter of 1873–74. He taught English at the Catholic University of America in Washington from 1889 until 1902.
3. Blathwayt refers to the so-called King Sollermun passage in chapter 14 of *Huck Finn.*
4. Harte published his dialect poem "Plain Language from Truthful James" or "The Heathen Chinee" in the September 1870 issue of the *Overland Monthly.*
5. See n. 3 to interview 47.
6. The farm of John Adams Quarles (1802–76) near Florida, Missouri.
7. Jean Louis Burckhardt (1784–1817), a Swiss adventurer who, disguised as a Moslem, was the first Christian to enter Mecca. His *Travels in Arabia* (1829) was excerpted in Bayard Taylor's *Cyclopedia of Modern Travel* (1861).
8. Clarence King (1842–1901), author of *Mountaineering in the Sierra Nevada* (1871) and the first director of the U.S. Geological Survey.
9. See nn. 3 and 4 to interview 8 and nn. 2 and 3 to interview 30.
10. See the reference to Harris in n. 1 to interview 35.

11. See n. 4 to interview 28.

12. Thomas Cook (1808-92) founded the pioneering British travel agency Thomas Cook and Son.

13. See n. 18 to interview 48. MT had continued to pay royalties to Grant's family since the publication of interview 48 in January 1890.

14. Holmes published his comic verse on MT's fiftieth birthday in *Idler* for December 1885. It is reprinted in Paine, 826-27. See also n. 2 to interview 17.

15. Henry Ward Beecher (1813-87), minister of the Plymouth Church in Brooklyn.

16. Karl Gerhardt (1853-1940) studied sculpture in Paris (not Rome) between 1881 and 1884 at MT's expense.

54

"Colony of Mermaids: Mark Twain to Exhibit a Lot of Fish-tailed Girls," *Chicago Inter-Ocean,* 15 April 1893, 8.

The next time that Samuel L. Clemens (Mark Twain) comes to Chicago desiring to conceal his identity and to escape the representatives of the press he had better consult a Cook County geography. Yesterday morning he registered at the Great Northern from East Chicago. The name S. L. Clemens was at once recognized as that of the famous humorist, but "East Chicago" seemed to discredit the supposition that it was the great and only Mark. North, West, and South Chicago were accounted for, but it was figured that East Chicago must be somewhere out in the lake. Cards were sent to the mysterious inhabitant of "East Chicago Out in the Lake," and it was suggested that if the person were not really Mark Twain he might at least, from the situation of his homesite, throw some light upon the nature and habits of the sea serpent that has been flapping its tail so much out in that direction. The cards were always returned with the statement either that the gentleman was not in or did not desire to meet anyone. It was toward evening when one of the clerks said: "There is the man who registered as S. L. Clemens." The man had gotten himself mixed up with a crowd of Javanese, Arabs, and Hottentots who were inspecting the lobby and galleries of the big hotel. Mr. Clemens' complexion is dark anyhow. He had been out in the cold and his coat collar was turned up to his ears, and his hat, which did not look unlike a fez dyed black, was pushed down over his bushy head and eyes. People in the lobby gazing at the peculiar-looking foreigners supposed that Mark was one of them, and in fact one of these dark-visaged gentlemen themselves seemed to think that if he were not one of them he was some other kind of foreigner, and jostled him about and talked to him in a most familiar kind of way.

When Mr. Clemens reached the desk he remembered that he was going to sail immediately for Europe, where he would be taken for an American and not an imported freak. He acknowledged then, in his drawling tone, that he was Mark Twain.

"Why did you register from East Chicago?"

"I wanted to escape the press," he answered, "as I did not want to receive callers and correspondents that would ensue. I am on strictly private business, and expect to sail in a few days for Europe, where I have left my family."

In explanation of the location of East Chicago he divulged the alleged object of his visit. He had known that every kind of curiosity, foreign and domestic, human and animal, had been brought to Chicago, so on his way across the ocean he had picked up a colony of young mermaids, who he thought could stand fresh water. These he domiciled in the submarine villa of "East Chicago." Special boats, he said, will be run by the syndicate he represents out to the spot in the lake over the village of the mermaids every evening after warm weather begins. These sirens will float to the top with their æolean harps and make music that will float away on the gentle zephyrs of the lake. Passes will only be given to press representatives and managers of the theaters and the other combinations on Midway Plaisance.[1]

Note to Interview 54

1. An eighty-acre strip of land distinct from the White City and exhibits at the Columbian Exposition at Jackson Park on the lakefront in Chicago between May and October 1893. This entertainment area featured such attractions as the Ferris wheel and the Street in Cairo.

55

"Mark Twain Gone Abroad," *St. Louis Republic,* 1 April 1894, 28; rpt.
"Mark Twain and the Reporter," *Buffalo Express,* 1 April 1894, 9.

New York, March 29—Mark Twain sailed for Europe on the steamer *New York* on March 7.[1] At 11:30 o'clock on the night previous to the vessel's leaving he stood on the deck near the gangplank smoking a cigar with an overcoat thrown loosely over his shoulders. He was leaning over the rail looking at the busy scene on the pier, which reminded him of the old days on the Mississippi, when, as a pilot, he first heard officially the words he adopted as his *nom de plume.* His curly white mop of hair stood out from his head and pressed close up against the broad brim of his black soft hat. His drooping, brown mustache, with but few silver hairs, and his eyes, keen and sparkling, were eloquent with the humorous conceits which are ever flitting through his mind.

He was chuckling with the thought that he was stealing quietly off to Europe without undergoing the cross-questioning of a parting newspaper interview, when a soft and plaintive voice sighed into his right ear the words:

"Pardon me, but isn't this Mr. Clemens?"

He turned his head slowly—he never turns anything quickly, not even a sentence—and saw standing by his side the writer. He shifted his cigar to the other corner of his lips and answered:

"Is that a bug, or what is it on your shoulder?"

It was a bug, and the reporter brushed it off. Then he said:

"Mr. Clemens, I was sent to interview you and to inquire about your European trip."

"One of those bugs got on my shoulder a little while ago," drawled the author. "At first I thought it was a spider; then I thought it was an ant, but I didn't find out."

"Do you expect to remain abroad long?" asked the reporter.

"If I had a light here I could very quickly find out what it was. If you will kindly stand still a moment I will ask the ship's steward to bring a lantern and we can discover whether it was an ant or a spider."

"But Mr. Clemens, if you will excuse me, it's getting late and—"

"If it was an ant," continued Mark Twain in a musing tone, "he is different from any ant I ever saw. I knew an ant once in Nevada who used to come out every evening in clear weather and roll a little pebble along for about—"

"Excuse me, Mr. Clemens, but how long did you say you intended to remain abroad?"

"Five weeks. Exactly why he was continually rolling that pebble or where I never could find out. He was the biggest fool of an ant I ever knew, and I have watched a good many fool ants. Once in the Sandwich Islands [Hawaii]—"

"Are you going to write another book of travels?"

"No; there is no use in writing a book unless one puts hard work into it, and no book can be successful or worth reading unless the author puts his heart and soul into it. I can't do that in a book of travels any more. It is depriving me of a big source of income, too—a big source of income. I think I'll just keep on lying quietly and systematically hereafter. A good lie is always worth writing. A man who can lie well ought never to do anything else."

"Where do you propose to go?"

"Well, I think I shall visit some points in Europe which I have never seen more than once or twice."

"Do you go on business or pleasure?"

"Exactly. I always visit Europe with that idea in view. You see, Europe is a capital place for that sort of thing—much more so than this country."

"Business or pleasure?"

"I haven't thought much about it, to tell the truth, although it opens up an interesting train of thought. Thought is, after all, only an ascription of a mathematical reason for a coexistent plurality, and if we eliminate its cogency we will get right back to the starting place every time, and that reminds me of that bug. What has become of him?"

"Will you do any writing while you are away?"

"That depends upon circumstances. You see, I never write when I am reading, and I never read anything while I write. I find that if I read a book for a while and then begin to write, I can't help borrowing that author's style. Just read Shakespeare for 15 minutes and try to write afterwards and you'll find yourself embarrassed. You'll be trying to describe an ordinary everyday incident in his high and mighty style and you'll be thinking in blank verse. That is one of the reasons why I should advise Herbert Spencer not to read too much of Laura Jean Libbey's works.[2] If the unconscious association of idea should affect his style so that—"

"Pardon me, but won't you tell me, Mr. Clemens, what part of Europe you will visit?"

"Certainly," said he. "I am always glad to oblige a newspaper man. They have invariably misquoted me in the pleasantest and most charming manner and I owe much of my success as a moral instructor to their efforts. If it were not for the newspaper men of America much of the valuable information which I have acquired in the study of—"

"Where did you say you were going?" inquired the reporter in a falsetto voice, to attract Mr. Clemens' attention.

The author reflected for a moment. Then he drew a little book from his overcoat pocket. Opening it, he said:

"I have been thinking of taking a shy at the Holy Land again. Here is a fascinating place where I have longed for years to visit. It has a quaint suggestive name which of itself has always pleased me. I refer, as you may have guessed, to Kibrothhattaavah. I shall probably remain there for a few days for rest, if I go there at all, and then will slide over to Hazaroth. Then I may go to Rithmah and, if the traveling is good, may go on to Rimmon-parez. From there to Libuah, thence to Kehelathath, thence to Mount Shapher, thence to Haradah, thence to Makheloth—"

"But—"

"Thence to Tahath, thence to Tarah, thence to Mitchcah, thence to Hashmonah, thence to Moseroth, thence to Benejaakan—"

"Mr. Clemens, if you—"

"Thence to Hor-hagidgad, thence to Jothathath, thence to Ebrozth, thence to Ezlongaber (that's easy), thence to the wilderness of Zin, then I shall skip a number of unimportant places and go straight to Ije-abarim. From there I will take little excursions to Almondiblathaim, Oboth, and other near points.

"However, I have not yet fully decided upon this route, but may instead begin at Zalmonah and go thence to Punon, thence to—excuse me, but have you a match?"

Mr. Clemens paused to relight his cigar, which had gone out, and the reporter said: "I am afraid I haven't time to get another route before the steamer goes. How long did you say you intended to stay abroad?"

"I had originally made up my mind to remain about five weeks, but my memory is so wretched that I find it difficult to remember how long I had intended to stay. That recalls the wonderful memory that old black cat of ours had. She did have the most remarkable memory of any cat almost I ever knew. Why, once she came into the kitchen and sat down on a hot stove lid, and do you know that ever after that, as long as we had her, she never sat down on a hot stove lid again? She wouldn't even sit down on a cold stove lid. At one time I thought it was her sagacity, but now I know it was her memory. She was like the bull pup that belongs to Miss Apple's old uncle, Ezra Pilkins. He was a wonderful old fellow. Had a bald head all his life from his babyhood. He never did have a single hair on his head, so old Marm Wilson said. Marm Wilson lived in the family, you know, for years and years, and I don't believe she would have left them if it hadn't been for the accident to young Jabel Endicott. That was the most peculiar accident I ever heard of. You see, Jabel was acquainted with Miss Appleby, and he used to visit her house a good deal and people said he was going to marry her. Well, her uncle's bull pup had one of his eyes put out when he was very young, and Jabel bought a glass eye and fitted it into the socket.

"It was not exactly a match to the other eye because the oculist that Jabel got it from only kept human glass eyes. Said he had never kept a stock of bull pup's glass eyes, anyhow. So Elihu Vedder[3]—that was the name of the pup— used to wear the light blue glass eye, and he did have the strongest expression of most any dog I ever saw on the left side of his head—that was the side the glass eye was on. He was mightily proud of that glass eye, though. He used to kind of sidle up with his left side turned to strangers just so that they'd notice the eye and they always did notice it, too. Well, one day—"

"Excuse me, Mr. Clemens, but really about this European trip. If you—"

"Well, I was coming to that. As I said, one day, while Elihu Vedder was feeling so cocky about this glass eye of his and poking it under everybody's nose, so to speak, a strange bull dog came along. He walked up to Elihu in the friendliest kind of way and there wouldn't have been any trouble at all if Elihu hadn't tried to show that eye of his. He turned it suddenly on the other dog and kind of lifted his nose in the air in a superior, supercilious sort of way. That made the other dog mad clean through and he made a jump for Elihu and grabbed him by the throat. Just then Jabel came along to call on Miss Appleby and when he saw her uncle's bull pup being choked by a strange dog he sailed in to separate them. In doing this he jabbed his finger into Elihu Vedder's glass eye and cut it most off. Of course he pulled his finger out again right away, but—"

"Mr. Clemens, I don't like to interrupt you, but if you will tell me just a little about your plans I would be greatly obliged."

"Plans," said Mr. Clemens, "are things that always appealed strongly to me. There is a certain mystery to my mind about plans that is very captivating. I was always a great fellow for making plans. It is a little hobby of mine. I remember a dinner that was given to me in London 25 years ago and of how I had planned to make the great after-dinner speech of my life at it. I found out beforehand just what the man who was to make the welcoming speech to me was going to say and I carefully prepared my answer. It was one of the most perfectly planned speeches I ever heard of and I rehearsed it in the cab on my way to the dinner so that I would have it down fine. The thing would have worked all right if the other man had made his speech, but at the last moment he sent regrets and said he couldn't possibly attend the dinner. George Augustus Sala made the welcoming speech in his stead,[4] and he was wonderfully eloquent. There was thought, history, and oratory in it, for he spoke of my country as well as of me. When I rose to reply I knew I couldn't do anything after such a speech as that. But I made up my mind to take something he had said and use it as a text and lead up to it. So I began in a rambling sort of way, with this plan in my mind, and I tried to work around to the text, but I never got there. I suddenly found that I had talked too long and hadn't come within pistol shot of the text. I told the story of the duel I didn't fight in Nevada at that dinner and Tom Hood, who was editing *Fun*, got me to write it out afterward, and he published it.[5] I believe that I could repeat it word for word today just as I wrote it 25 years ago, and yet there are other things that I cannot memorize at all. There is that jay bird story of mine in one of my books.[6] I have tried again and again to commit that to memory, and the other night I wrote out some catchphrases from it to help me out when I went on the stage at the Madison Square Garden Lecture Hall. But I had to give it up and tell another story. I cannot learn 10 lines of anything so as to be sure of it to save my life. Now I knew a man once in California, who had a second cousin named Zachias M. Botts. This man Botts had a trained horn frog—"

"Mr. Clemens, if you will pardon me, I should like to be able to write only a few lines about this trip of yours. It is getting la—"

"My dear fellow, you may. Just write everything I have told you and submit it to me before the steamer sails. Use all of the information—every bit of it. I don't want the public as a general rule to know too much about my intentions, but in this case I'll make an exception. Give it all without reserve and let me see it before I go. Go into the smoking-room now and write it out."

Mark Twain turned away to speak to the purser and the reporter went into the smoking-room and wrote what he had said. Then he hunted up Mr. Clemens and showed him what appears above. The author read it over carefully and said:

"That's all right. It is all right. It is what I call a perfect interview. Just as incorrect as any interview I ever read. Young man, you understand your business. Keep at it and someday you will be one of us—one of the perfect liars of the world."

Notes to Interview 55

1. Launched in 1888, the *New York* carried as many as 1,265 passengers, 290 of them in first class, on the American line between New York and Southampton.
2. Herbert Spencer (1820-1903), English philosopher and proponent of social Darwinism; Laura Jean Libbey (1862-1924), American author of sensational novels for women.
3. Elihu Vedder (1836-1923), American painter.
4. See reference to Sala in n. 5 to interview 23.
5. "How I Escaped Being Killed in a Duel," *Tom Hood's Comic Annual for 1873*, ed. Tom Hood (London: Fun, 1872), 90-91. See reference to Hood in n. 2 to interview 23.
6. "Baker's Blue Jay Yarn," chapter 3 in *A Tramp Abroad*.

56

"Mark Twain in Town," *New York Sun*, 15 April 1894, 5.

Mr. S. L. Clemens, known to more people as Mark Twain, got back from Europe yesterday on the steamship *New York*, and is now at the Players Club.[1] He said to a *Sun* reporter last night:

"I went abroad to see how my family were getting along, and not for the benefit of my own health, as has been reported. My wife has not been well for some time, and she is now under the care of a physician in Paris. I wanted to see for myself just how she was, and that's the reason I went. I found her to be very much improved, and that's why I didn't stay longer. I've been gone only three weeks, so you see I didn't have much of a visit. But the trip was a glorious one. The voyage back, particularly, was delightful. I hear you'd had a great storm here, but at sea we had nothing of it. The *New York* encountered no bad weather, and only on one day a rough sea, which seemed more like the wash from another steamer than anything else. I shall return to Paris again in just three weeks, to take my family to Aix-les-Bains. Baths are part of the treatment prescribed for my wife."

Note to Interview 56

1. The Players Club was founded by Edwin Booth (1833-93) and other actors in 1888 in a brownstone at 16 Gramercy Park South in New York.

57

"Mark Twain Goes Abroad," *New York Sun*, 16 August 1894, 3.

Probably the most inconspicuous passenger on the American line steamship *Paris*,[1] which sailed yesterday morning for Southampton, was a languid man with fluffy gray hair, who looked as if he had made a mistake in taking passage in the cabin. He carried an old umbrella in one hand and a crush hat done up in a newspaper in the other. A few persons recognized him as Samuel L. Clemens. He apparently was traveling as Mark Twain, professional humorist. He was somewhat late; he might have had to walk to Europe or take the next steamship. Somebody suggested to him that the *Paris* was ready to sail. He answered with his familiar drawl:

"Well, if the boat's ready to go I guess I am. I am going over to see my wife and family at Etretat, where they are supporting a couple of doctors. You see, over there when a doctor gets hold of a good patient he keeps him. They generally take you to a small place and keep you there. Then they pass you along to a friend in another place, and they keep you moving like the Wandering Jew.[2] My wife has been doing this for three years.

"I don't dare to have even a headache after I land on the other side. But I guess I'll bring her back when I come in October.

"This is my tenth voyage in the past three years. I'm getting real fond of sailing now. After the first five or six days I rather enjoy the trip."

Mr. Clemens started up the gangplank. A deck hand, who thought the gingham umbrella hardly in keeping with a first-class ticket, stopped the humorist and asked:

"Are you a passenger?"

Mr. Clemens stammered: "I—I don't—know; but I rather think—so. Wait a minute and I'll see."

Then Mr. Clemens looked over his passenger list and exclaimed triumphantly:

"Yes; I'm a passenger. Here's my name on the list."

The deck hand said something about Bloomingdale,[3] as Mark waved him a stately farewell.

Notes to Interview 57

1. Launched in 1888, the *Paris* sailed between New York and Southampton. MT mentioned it briefly in "About All Kinds of Ships" (1893).

2. A legendary figure who, for mocking Christ on his way to Calvary, is condemned to wander the earth until Judgment Day.

3. A derogatory term for a rude upstart, apparently inspired by Bloomingdale's move from New York's Lower East Side to its tony location at Fifty-ninth Street and Lexington Avenue in 1886.

58

"Mark Twain in Paris," *New York Sun,* 27 January 1895, sec. 3, 4.

Paris, Jan. 5—Mark Twain and his family are installed for the winter in one of the most charming houses in Paris. It is in the quiet old Rue de l'Universite, and is an ideal retreat for a man who is working every day, as Mr. Clemens says he is. The *Sun* correspondent found him there the other day, and congratulated him on the quarters he had discovered. He stood in the middle of the big studio, where he had been reading, and surveyed it deliberately from under his shaggy eyebrows. Then he took his pipe out of his mouth.

"Yes," he said, with his long, peculiar drawl, "it is rather pleasant. It was built by a French artist. That's the reason for this," with a slow wave of the hand. "Studio, you see. Well," putting the pipe back and taking a long puff, "he went away. One day Mr. Pomeroy, New York artist, nice man, came along.[1] He looked around a little, then in his quick [puff] American [puff] way [puff] he said, 'I want that house!' And before the fellow knew what [puff, puff, puff] he was about, Mr. Pomeroy had the lease signed for three years."

Mr. Clemens stopped wearily and walked up and down a while, smoking solemnly. His French felt slippers made no noise on the polished wood floor. Finally he resumed:

"Mr. Pomeroy had to leave Paris for the winter, so we took the house. I was obliged to be here five or six months, any way."

The distinguished humorist made these few remarks with an air of pathetic resignation which said plainly that such explanations were a weariness of the flesh.

"You read and speak French, do you not?" The question was addressed to the back of the famous crop of curls, as Mr. Clemens still wandered uneasily up and down.

"I read it. I don't speak it," he said.

"What do you think about French humor? Is there such a thing among modern French writers as humor?"

His eye brightened. He was interested. He took his pipe from his lips and punctuated his remarks with short, decisive waves.

"Ah! now you ask me something about which I dare not express an opinion. I have thought about that a hundred times, but I have never been able to arrive at a concrete opinion which I would feel I had a right to express. I have even tried to put my thoughts on paper, to see if in that way I could come to a more definite conclusion. But I don't know. We hear so much about 'French wit,' as if it were a particular kind of wit, different from that of other countries. And 'French polish,' too. Now a nation may claim to be the politest nation in the world. And that proves nothing. And it may claim to be the wittiest nation in the world. Only, by advertising the statement sufficiently, the nation makes everybody, including its own people, believe that it has told the truth.

"Now take Saint-Simon.[2] I read three large volumes containing, it is to be supposed, the best things he said and wrote. Well," and the creator of Tom Sawyer and Huckleberry Finn shook his great head slowly, "to me it was a work of despair. Those three big volumes! And I did not find them witty! That's going back a good ways, to Saint-Simon, so let's come down further. There was Talleyrand.[3] There is no doubt that he said brilliant things, but I do not find that his wit differs intrinsically from the wit of other countries. Then, too, one must take into account the man. Every brilliant thing he said was repeated and recorded because Talleyrand said it. Suppose somebody else had said these same things, people would have paid no attention to them.

"'Oh, he never originated that,' they would have said. 'He got it from somebody else.' And so it would have been lost.

"Yes, Talleyrand said good things, but when it comes to brilliancy, why I've heard Tom Bailey Aldrich keep up a running fire of the most inimitable repartee.[4] Talk about wit, why, Tom Bailey Aldrich has said 1,500 if not 15,000 things as brilliant as the things Talleyrand said and which are labeled 'French wit.' And he has humor, too. He can pass from wit to humor, fusing their characteristics. Tom—Thomas Bailey Aldrich," Mr. Clemens hesitated, put his pipe in his mouth, drew a long puff, looked unutterable things through the smoke, and held his peace.

"How about the modern French writers? Do any of them pose as humorists?"

"I believe there are one or two who do, but I don't remember their names."

"And evidently you do not know their work?"

"No."

"Are your books translated into French?"

"*Tom Sawyer* and *Huckleberry Finn* have been translated, but I think that is all."[5]

"Do you know whether French people find your books amusing?"

"I don't think they do," said Mr. Clemens, at last sitting down and treating himself and his visitor to a quizzical smile. "A friend of mine told me of a little conversation he had with a Frenchman, and I feel pretty sure, since then, of the way I strike the French mind. This Frenchman is a great critic and is an authority on all literary matters. I don't remember his name, because I never remember names, but he is an authority. That is what makes it so hopeless.

"'I myself,' he said, 'have read a great many American books, and I have heard the opinions of others who are familiar with your literature. This being the case, and knowing the French mind as I do, I think I may claim to speak for the nation itself in what I say. In the first place, then, we regard Edgar Allan Poe as your greatest poet. The French who know his writings look upon him as a great genius. Bret Harte we think your greatest novelist. He is an artist, a great artist. [Ralph Waldo] Emerson—well.' Mr. Clemens supplied a beautiful French shrug and lifted his heavy eyebrows, 'we don't understand what you can find in Emerson to admire. I believe you Americans think him great, but we cannot understand why. And lastly, there is Mark Twain, but when it comes to him we are in despair, because no intelligent Frenchman can make out your reasons for thinking Mark Twain funny!'"

The pipe had gone out in the course of this recital, and Mr. Clemens tapped it regretfully and laid it down as he got up to resume his pacing back and forth.

"Perhaps we lose the quality of the French humor as completely as they lose the quality of yours."

"Oh, unquestionably," interrupted Mr. Clemens as he lighted his cigar. "That is the reason why I say I am not competent to express an opinion on the subject. A man may study a language for years and years and yet he is never inside of the holy of holies. He must get into the man himself, the man of another country, and he cannot do that.

"But as for French wit being different from any other wit, I do not know about it. To decide a point like that a man would have to gather hundreds of instances and compare them as a naturalist compares his specimens. He would be obliged to sift them, assay them, and find out the real essence of each. Then, if he could say, 'I have among the specimens from this country 500 where the wit turns upon a certain point, while I find no more than fifty similar examples from the specimens from any other country, and those I regard as accidental,' he would be justified in describing that particular form of wit as specially belonging to that one country. But no one has done that to prove that 'French wit' is a unique product of the French brain.

"As for humor, well," wheeling round suddenly, "I don't think any nation that has a sense of humor would go around snivelling over that great Russian bear the way France has been doing.[6] If they could see themselves—but it is like a drunkard. Everybody knows that if a man who gets drunk could once see himself when he is drunk he'd never do it again.

"The French are simply drunk; that's all. In the other case the man does it with whiskey, and in this case it is an intoxication of vanity and enthusiasm; that's all. Of course every Frenchman can see his fellow countrymen, and you would think that he would realize how ridiculous it is. But they are all drunk together, and you know one drunkard doesn't see that he is walking just as crookedly as the other fellow, or even that there is anything wrong with the other fellow. You wouldn't find America playing the ridiculous part that

France has in this Russian craze, and it is for such reasons that I think Americans have a better sense of humor than Frenchmen."

"Do you find American tourists over here any different from what they were the first time you came to Europe?"

"Well, now, you've asked me something I don't like to answer," was the reply, and Mr. Clemens relapsed into his most pronounced drawl. "If I said anything it might be misinterpreted as applying to the American colony at Paris, and I'd rather blaspheme something of—er—even more holy, you know, than accept people's hospitality and then criticize them.

"The man who built and furnished this house had a sort of East Indian fever," said Mr. Clemens as he led the way down the tapestried hall and paused under the shadow of an Oriental god. "It's a way artists have. But it makes a good place to work in."

This is good news to Mark Twain's admirers.

Notes to Interview 58

1. Apparently a joke at the expense of Marcus (Brick) Pomeroy (1833–96), a popular journalist and real estate promoter.

2. MT had read the *Mémoires* of Louis de Rouvroy (1675–1755), Duc de Saint-Simon.

3. Charles Maurice de Talleyrand-Périgord (1754–1838).

4. See n. 4 to interview 28.

5. *Les aventures de Tom Sawyer*, trans. William L. Hughes (Paris: Bibliothèque nouvelle de la jeunesse, 1876), and *Les aventures de Huck Finn: l'ami de Tom Sawyer*, trans. Hughes (Paris: Bibliothèque nouvelle de la jeunesse, 1886).

6. Budd (1974), 20n15: "In the early 1890s France began a rapprochement with Russia; in 1893 a Russian fleet was warmly welcomed in France; in 1895 what amounted to a formal alliance was signed."

59

"The Henry Murder: Mark Twain Theorizes on the Bloody Hand Prints Found," *Elmira Advertiser*, 24 June 1895, 5.

. . . Samuel L. Clemens (Mark Twain) in his recent work on Pudd'nhead Wilson unearths a murder by blood prints of the hand. Pudd'nhead Wilson proved the bloody fingerprints on the dagger were not left there by the accused person in court but were made by a person in court but not accused.[1]

An *Advertiser* reporter called on Mark Twain at the Quarry Farm on East Hill yesterday where he is resting quietly preparatory to starting on his lecture tour around the world next month. In reply to a question as to what value the finding of the bloody prints had on the Henry murder case,[2] he said: "They seem to be in doubt as to which of the two made that handprint, the assassin or the murdered man. I should think that that would be easy to determine.

They have a man under arrest whom they suspect, as I understand it, and I should think that they could easily get a handprint from him and compare it with that bloody handprint and determine whether he made it or not. There is nothing in this case that you or I can suggest that would not suggest itself to anybody's mind. Thus far that handprint has not a value because it is not determinable whose it is. You don't know whether it is valuable until you know that it is not the hand of the dead man. If it is the hand of the survivor it can have some value. If it is a clear handprint, so that the marking of the ball of the thumb, for instance, is distinct and can be followed, here can be a print taken from that and then enlarged by a pantograph ten or twenty times, so that there is no mistaking these lines, because they are clearly defined. Then, unquestionably, they can take as many thumbprints as they want of as many people as they want and they will never find marks corresponding with these until they find the man that left that handprint there. When they have found the man who left that thumbprint they will know him for sure, without any question at all."

"And there will be no need of an expert to determine whose hand made the print?"

"That print will correspond exactly with that hand. When you have got that far you have not arrived at that goal yet. It will be pretty strong evidence but there could have been several people there and you want to know who it was that killed the man. But whether he is guilty or not you won't know. If it were known that there were nobody present but the assassin and the victim then you know you have got the assassin. It is well worth while to follow that clue if they can find that the dead man did not leave that print there. If that body is not decomposed it will be an easy matter to find out whether he made the handprint or not. If he did not that narrows the murder down considerably. I do not say that this bloody handprint can convict anybody, but it can help."

Mark Twain was evidently interested in this subject and had made a study of finger and hand marks. "Galton," he continued, "has made a scientific investigation of this finger marking and from his book one may get all that is known concerning the matter.[3] He has followed it out persistently to more purpose than anybody else and I think, I am sure, he says you cannot find two thumbprints that are alike in the world.

"I wish there was some way I could be of assistance in unraveling this crime but don't see how I can. The papers have urged that the sign manual clue be followed up, and certainly it ought to be. There is a certain value in taking up this clue as it will provoke an interest in the matter of fingerprints. It has been proposed to add the sign manual to the French system of measurements, whereby they say that they can tell when they find a man who has ever passed through their hands. He may disguise himself as much as he like, they can identify him by his measurements. Thus, you see, it is of value in keeping alive an interest in this matter, for people will go ahead as Galton has done and study it further."

Notes to Interview 59

1. *The Tragedy of Pudd'nhead Wilson* (1894), MT's sixth major novel, in which the hero detects guilt and innocence in a murder case through fingerprints.

2. Charles W. Henry of Brooklyn had been murdered in June 1895 under mysterious circumstances, perhaps with an ax found at the scene.

3. Sir Francis Galton (1822–1911) introduced the use of fingerprinting as a means of identification in *Finger Prints* (1893).

4

Across North America, 1895

Interviews 60–81

In order to begin paying his creditors, Twain contracted with J. B. Pond to lecture across North America with a world tour to follow. Under Pond's management, he left his summer home near Elmira, New York, in July 1895 and in the next five weeks performed twenty-four times in twenty-two cities, from Cleveland to the Pacific Northwest and Victoria, B.C. He publicly acknowledged his intent to repay all his debts in full while in Vancouver in August, shortly before sailing for Australia.

∽

60

Unidentified Cleveland newspaper (*Cleveland Leader?*), 16 July 1895; rpt. "Very Much Abroad: Mr. Clemens on Tour," *Australian Star* (Melbourne), 14 September 1895, 7.

... Stopping on the way at Cleveland (Ohio) the noted humorist, who was suffering from what he termed a Pullman carbuncle,[1] was bailed up and interviewed. "I understand," said Mr. Clemens in the course of some interesting biographical details, "that Artemus Ward once lived in Cleveland and worked on a newspaper here.[2] I met him in Virginia City. He was delivering a lecture at the time. That was in—let me see. Well, I can't remember exactly, but I left Virginia City by request, and it was previous to that time. Virginia City, you know, was situated directly over the great Comstock silver lode. I was a reporter on the Virginia City *Territorial Enterprise* at the time, and I used to sit up in the office after midnight. Then I could hear a long, low boom, and then I knew that some fellow was blasting quartz right under me. Parts of the town caved in from time to time, and when I heard that boom I used to feel uncomfortable.

"You have heard it said, I suppose, that I was not a success in newspaper work. What more success could have I had? I was a reporter and then city editor of a paper in Virginia City, and I gave satisfaction. That I was not a success in San Francisco was due to circumstances, or I might say to a circumstance. I was on the *Call,* which had but the one reporter. There was not too much for a man to do, but it required constant exercise and a gift of industry. I won't say that I didn't have the gift of industry, but anyhow it was leaky. My job was a good steady job. It kept me working from 9 o'clock one morning until 2 o'clock the next morning. Finally I intimated to the proprietor of the paper how pleasant it would be if I could have an assistant. He gave me one—a patient, cheerful lad whom the printers nicknamed Smiggy McGlural. I used to tell Smiggy to do the police court, and then a fire or two, and it was Smiggy this and Smiggy that, until it became noticeable that Smiggy was doing all the work. I never was so lazy in my life and never enjoyed it so. Finally the proprietor—well, he asked me to hand in my resignation. The facts were all against me. The case admitted of no argument, and I resigned.

"How did I happen to leave Virginia City?[3] Well, I wonder if I ought to tell. Still, anyone would have left under the circumstances. I was in the full side of my editorial popularity when the editor-in-chief went down to San Francisco to visit some friends and left the paper in my charge. I wrote a very satisfactory editorial about Shakespeare, thinking that it would be news to most of the boys and right away after that I got down to level business, arguments supported by epithets. Every day or two the editor of the rival paper took exception to my epithets, and he answered back.

"It was the custom of the country to call a man out to the field of honor and kill him when he answered back. I didn't want to call the other editor out, but custom made it necessary. I challenged him, naming Colt's navy revolvers the weapons, each to walk 15 steps, turn, fire, and advance firing. That was the way they always had in those days. Duels weren't picnics or Sunday school excursions. 'Twas business. Well, I challenged my man, Sandy Baldwin, the son of the author of *Flush Times in Alabama,*[4] and a prominent lawyer came and routed me out of bed and said to me that the news of the challenge had got to the Governor's ears at Carson City, and that I would be arrested for sending it. The law was new and they wanted to try it on. Of course, I was the first victim. But I preferred that to the duel. Sandy said that he had heard the Governor say that the trial would see that I stayed there until my term expired.

"'Now,' said Sandy Baldwin, 'as you know, the stagecoach leaves at 4 o'clock this morning, and you have just time to catch it. If you have any delicacy about running away like this you can say that you did it at my request.' So my second, Major Gillis,[5] and I took the stagecoach. Governor North was a man whose word was at par all the time.[6] If he said he'd give me two years and let me keep them it was not open to dispute."

Mr. Clemens, in the course of the conversation, told how he came to select his *nom de plume*. "You know the words mean two fathoms, of course," said he. "Well, the oldest pilot on the river was Old Isaiah Sellers. He used to write the news for the New Orleans papers and sign them Mark Twain. I was out in Carson City reporting the legislature when the news came that Sellers was dead. I didn't think there would be any harm in robbing that corpse of that name, and I took it."[7]

The assertion having been made frequently of late that Mr. Clemens is the author of *Personal Reminiscences of Joan of Arc*, which is being published in serial form in *Harper's Magazine*, the reporter asked Mr. Clemens if he had either affirmed or denied the truth of the rumor.[8] He paused for a moment and then drawled out: "That question has been asked me several times, and I have always said that I considered it wise to leave an unclaimed piece of literary property alone until time has shown that nobody is going to claim it. Then it's safe to acknowledge that you wrote that thing whether you did or not. It is in this way that I have become known and respected as the author of 'Beautiful Snow' and 'Rock Me to Sleep, Mother.'"[9]

Notes to Interview 60

1. A bacterial infection, often a staph infection, beneath the skin.

2. Charles Farrar Browne, aka Artemus Ward (1834-67), humorist, journalist, and lecturer, met MT in Virginia City in 1863.

3. MT offers a very different version of his reasons for leaving Virginia City in May 1864 in his "Roughing It" lecture (Fatout, 61-62); in chapter 55 of *Roughing It*; in his essay "How I Escaped Being Killed in a Duel" (1872); in *Auto* (1959), 113-18; and in *Auto* (1990), 71-77.

4. Joseph G. Baldwin (1815-64) was the author of *The Flush Times of Alabama and Mississippi* (1854).

5. Steve Gillis (1838-1918), a compositor on the staff of the Virginia City *Territorial Enterprise* and one of MT's closest friends in Nevada.

6. John W. North (1815-90), surveyor general of Nevada Territory. MT later described North as one of the "unforgotten and unforgettable antiques" of his western years (*MTL*, 2:773).

7. "Mark Twain," *Cleveland Plain Dealer*, 16 July 1895, 8: "When asked how he came to take the *nom de plume* of Mark Twain he said that the well known equivalent for 'two fathoms' on the sounding line had been used as a *nom de plume* for a few marine notes furnished a New Orleans paper by the oldest captain on the river—Isaiah Sellers. 'When the word came out in Virginia City that Sellers was dead,' said he, 'I did not think it would be much of a crime to rob that corpse of that *nom de plume*, and I did so.'"

8. "Mark Twain," *Cleveland Plain Dealer*, 16 July 1895, 8: "So far as *Joan of Arc* is concerned," he said, when asked about the authorship of the memoirs now being published in *Harper's Magazine*, "I have been asked that question several times. I have always considered it wise, however, to leave an unclaimed piece of literary property alone until time has shown that no one is going to claim it. Then it is safe to acknowl-

edge you wrote that, whether you did or not. It is in this way that I have become recognized and respected as the author of 'Beautiful Snow,' 'Rocked in the Cradle of the Deep,' and other literary gems."

9. See n. 9 to interview 46. The lyrics to "Rock Me to Sleep, Mother" (1860) by Elizabeth Akers Allen (pseud. Florence Percy) (1832–1911) and "Rocked in the Cradle of the Deep" (1839) by Emma Hart Willard (1787–1870) epitomized the sentimental ethos MT despised.

61

Detroit Journal, 18 July 1895, 5; rpt. *Mark Twain Journal* 31 (spring 1993): 26–27.

There was one striking figure in the crowd of a score or more persons who stood on the forward deck of the big steamer *North Land* as she drifted up to the dock at the foot of First street yesterday at 4 P.M. It was that of a man past the middle age of life, with bushy gray hair that fell well down upon his coat collar, a moustache of the same color, that was inclined to bristle, and a clear, ruddy complexion. He leaned carelessly over the railing and looked down upon the people assembled on the dock, without displaying any of the curiosity or interest that was evinced by the people who were looking up at him. This man was Mark Twain, the humorist, christened Samuel L. Clemens, and father of Tom Sawyer and Huckleberry Finn.

To a *Journal* reporter, who conversed with him during the steamer's short stay at the dock, Mr. Clemens stated that he had just started on a lecture tour that will take him around the world. He is accompanied by his wife and daughter, and by his manager, Major Pond, and Mrs. Pond. . . .

Questioned about his literary work, Mr. Clemens said: "I am in hopes that on this tour I will have energy enough to start and complete a book. Maybe I won't, but I expect to. I am not under contract to furnish anybody with anything, and am thus free to write or loaf as I please. I am enjoying good health, as far as health goes, but a fellow might as well be on his back in bed as to be burdened with the carbuncles with which I have been afflicted for a few weeks past."

Mr. Clemens was full of praise for the *North Land,* and said there wasn't much about the vessel to remind him of the days when he used to pilot a steamboat on the Mississippi river. "It is the best I have ever seen," he said "in the way of passenger boats. The Fall River steamers are more elaborately decorated, but are more like ocean steamers than the *North Land,* and are not so pleasant and comfortable." Mark Twain's last visit to Detroit was 11 years ago, when he appeared in an entertainment with George W. Cable.[1]

Note to Interview 61

1. See interview 38.

62

"Mark Twain: Something Concerning the Great Humorist," *Petoskey (Mich.) Reporter,* 21 July 1895, 4.

Samuel L. Clemens is as popular with those who know him as Mark Twain as with the world at large. . . . There is an old yarn to the effect that Mr. Clemens got his *nom de plume* Mark Twain while working as a deck hand on a Mississippi river steamer. He may have taken such a job sometime, but unless appearances are very deceiving we don't believe he held it. It affords too many opportunities for hard work. His own story is that one of the old river pilots used to write letters for the New Orleans papers over that signature, derived from the two marks on the lead line signifying two fathoms of water. Mr. Clemens said, "When the news first reached me that the old pilot was dead I was out in Carson City reporting the proceedings of the legislature. I had taken a fancy to that name, and as the original owner seemed to have no further use for it, why I just took it. Yes, it was sort of robbing a corpse, but I had nerve enough for anything those days."[1]

It has been said, and it is undoubtedly true, that Mark Twain is the author of the *Reminiscences of Joan of Arc,* now running in a leading magazine. When the *Reporter* asked him about this he smiled and answered in his drawling way, "Well, now, a Cleveland reporter made that same inquiry of me the other day,[2] and I told him that I never deny the authorship of anything good. I am always willing to adopt any literary orphan that is knocking about looking for a father, but I want to wait until I'm sure that nobody else is going to claim it. I'm willing to admit now that I wrote 'Beautiful Snow,' but the returns are not all in yet on *Joan of Arc.*"[3] . . .

Notes to Interview 62

1. See n. 7 to interview 60.
2. See n. 8 to interview 60.
3. See n. 26 to interview 46 and n. 8 to interview 60. MT repudiated the remainder of this interview in a letter to the editor of the *Reporter,* 31 July 1895, 4.

63

"Not 'Roughing It' Now," *Minneapolis Journal,* 23 July 1895, 6.

The man who is Samuel L. Clemens to his friends and in private life and Mark Twain to the reading public lay in his bed in room 204 at the West hotel this morning and put as pleasant an aspect as he could on the severe ordeal the reporters subjected him to. The great humorist is suffering from a very troublesome carbuncle, which has forced him of late to take a reclining position whenever possible. To the casual observer, as he lay there, running his fingers through his long, curly locks, now almost gray, he was anything but a humorist. On the contrary, he appeared to be a gentleman of great gravity, a statesman or a man of vast business interests. The dark blue eyes are as clear as crystal and the keenest of glances shoots from them whenever he speaks. Although his gravity might make one think him something else than a humorist, the kindly smile that lights up his face and the general appearance of happy abandon proclaim the author who is no bookworm. He talks easily and quietly yet with a marked deliberation.

"Carbuncles are not very obliging things," remarked the author of *Tom Sawyer* as he moved around to get his pet in an easier position, "in fact they are not at all noted for their accommodating customs. Still I ought to be thankful, perhaps, that I've got a comforter on my leg instead of on my neck."

With the remark on boils as a preface, Mark switched off to his travels, which have been extensive in the past four years. "I returned to America," he said, reminiscently, "on the 18th of May, after theoretical absence abroad of about four years. That is the theory, but the facts knock it out to a certain extent. During these four years I have crossed the Atlantic 15 times and have spent perhaps a quarter of the period in the United States. I divided my time abroad about equally between France, Germany and England.

"I am on a long trip now; a regular world better," continued the humorist, as he rubbed his bushy eyebrows and stroked his tawny mustaches. "It will take a year and perhaps more. After making the United States circuit we will go to the Sandwich Islands [Hawaii]; next we will round up the coast cities of Australia, New Zealand, Tasmania, Ceylon, then up the east coast of India, across to Bombay, down to south Africa and last of all to England. I can't say how long I may stay in Europe, but when I come back, I am going to settle down in my Hartford home and enjoy life in the quiet way.

"I have the same program of readings for all my dates in America that I will render at the Metropolitan Opera House tonight. Perhaps I may add another program before I sail for the East, but in Australia I shall give two or three programs."

"Is your daughter Clara,[1] who is with you, the one who was recently quoted as saying that she had never read your works?" inquired the reporter.

"I didn't know that such a report had been sent out," returned Mr. Clemens. "All my daughters ought to be pretty familiar with my works, seeing that they have edited my manuscript since they were 7 years old. They always sided with me whenever Mrs. Clemens thought that I had used some sentence or word that was a little too strong. But," he added, with his delightful smile, "we never stood on that because Madame was always in the majority, anyway. For a long time I used to have Mr. Howells edit all my copy.[2] Ah, but isn't he a charming writer? I believe that Howells is the best we have in America today.

"But, about that report you mentioned. I think that I can, perhaps, guess how in the course of years it was evolved. Long ago, when Effie Eisler,[3] then only 9 years old, had surprised the world with her precocious acting, she dined at my house one day. My youngest daughter, Jean,[4] who was of the same age, sat at the table, too. But in the learned conversation in which the young actress took her part, and acquitted herself as well as her elders, poor Jean understood not a word. She sat there and listened to the conversation of the little actress, every word going over her head, filled with admiration, and, perhaps, envy. At last someone mentioned *Tom Sawyer*. There was a theme that Jeanne knew something about. Speaking up, she said: 'I know who wrote *Tom Sawyer*; Mrs. Harriet Beecher Stowe did.'" Mr. Clemens laughed as he recalled the childish *faux pas*.

Just then big Major Pond, the author's manager, entered and asked in the most solemn way imaginable, "Do you want anybody choked off? If you do I am in prime condition."

The newspaper men arose with one impulse and made for the door, but Mr. Clemens called them back to wish them goodbye and explain that he would like to get a little nap, if possible.

"The most magnetic man I ever saw," declared Major Pond in the hall. "I never saw anything like it. Everywhere we go crowds flock to hear him. Why, on the steamer coming up the lakes the passengers sat around him on the decks all day long in one grand laughing party. I don't believe that there is another man in America that attracts the people as he does." . . .

Notes to Interview 63

1. Clara Clemens Samossoud (1874-1962), the third of the four Clemens children.
2. See n. 2 to interview 2.
3. The reporter apparently confuses the child actress Effie Eisler (1858-1942) with the child actress Elsie Leslie (1881-1966).
4. Jane Lampton (Jean) Clemens (1880-1909), the fourth of the four Clemens children.

64

"Twain," *Minneapolis Penny Press,* 23 July 1895, 1.

"Mark Twain!"

The name for many years has borne a charm to the American, but hardly less than to all other civilized beings in the old and new world alike.

I saw him this morning, as he lay, shrouded by the billowed clothing of his couch, the man whose lightest touch of pen has drawn to him all thinking mankind. No need to tell who or what he is, this Clemens, whose fame outstrips the reach of single publication. With head surrounded by halo of grey and curly locks—the Twain of old—but with added reverence by reason of the whiter touch of Father Time, with manner natural, which can never affect—that was all.

"I seek," said he, with quiet tone, "the climes where I have longed to visit. Australia, Tasmania, Ceylon, Bombay, and Southern Africa. My travels lead hither and I am to see and view the lands that I have often planned to visit."

But America, his native place, he visits first of all.

May 18 Mark Twain returned to the land of the free after four years' absence. His home in France is a thing of the past and at the end of the year which he will occupy in this tour, he and his delightful family, in each of whom the light of genius shines, will be found back in the old home at Hartford, Conn. And here the author Clemens will gather his notes together and write the greatest book of his life with each loving member of his family hearth a critic and editor.

A peculiar man, this Mark Twain, for in this modern age he devotes his warmest and deepest affection for his family. The words seem cold and almost heartless, but there is a truth concealed that is as true as the light that shines from the great sun. An illustration of this occurred this morning, while a group were gathered about the bedside of the author who was resting after a fatiguing journey.

"Mr. Clemens," said one, "there was published a short time ago an article which stated that one of your daughters had never read your works."

A smile flitted over the features for a moment, then the reply: "That must be another of those fairy fictions that start from nothing. My children have edited my manuscript since they were seven years of age; that is, they have had it read to them for criticism. They always sided with their father," with a tender but humorous smile, "and the sentence which mother would say should be stricken out, they would assert should remain. But," with the corners of the mouth curling into half a smile again, and the tone growing delightfully dry, "we did not stand on these little things. Madam was really the best editor of the lot. Before I used my flock of editors at home I sent my manuscript to Howells,[1] but now we don't."

The tones indicated the idolization of his family. There was the father's love in every word.

"I will tell you, though, where the story regarding my daughter might have arisen," he continued. "When one of my daughters was nine years of age. Elsie Leslie,[2] the child actress, who was of the same age, visited her. At the dinner table my little daughter Jean sat and listened to her extravagant conversation, the subject of which was entirely too abstract for her to grasp. She sat there, gazing with admiration, and very likely, envy, too, to hear Elsie taking part in such conversation with such ease. And she waited until something should be introduced about which she knew. In the course of the conversation the book entitled *Tom Sawyer* was mentioned and Jean saw her chance. 'I know who wrote that book,' she exclaimed; 'It was Harriet Beecher Stowe.' You see that this might have been used as a foundation for that story," and the great author laughed noiselessly at the recollection.

Turning to other things, one of those present asked Mr. Clemens if he had ever visited Minneapolis before. He had years before.

"Why," put in Major Pond, the manager of the lecturing tour, a jolly fellow: "I was in Minneapolis when there were no saloons here."

"Well, you didn't stay long," flashed back Mr. Clemens, and the group laughed at the major's expense.

"Don't shoot, Mr. Clemens," broke in an anxious reporter, "but which of your works is your favorite?"

The figure on the bed closed its eyes a moment in a quizzical manner, then replied.

"*Huck Finn.* You see," he replied, "a book is bound to be a favorite that is easy to write, and after it is written you find you have what you want."

The scribes gathered about and bothered him some more and among other things Mark Twain gave forth the following utterances:

"The general tendency, as the years go by, is for a higher plane of humor. Edgar W. Nye's humor I enjoy for it is the frosting on the cake.[3] There is something shining out through it all. This is the true humor that will always prevail.

"Kipling? He is another author whose works I enjoy. I believe that he has reformed in his views of America, has he not? You see, he wrote of the country when he was a young man and first saw this country. We never had a true and vivid picture of India and the life there until it was given us through the pen of this author. (Another query.) Yes, I will write another book. In fact, I am gathering material during this trip. I cannot change my style and it will be of the same class as the others I have published."

Notes to Interview 64

1. See n. 2 to interview 2.
2. See n. 3 to interview 63.
3. Edgar W. Nye, aka Bill Nye (1850-96), American humorist. See also *Auto* (1959), 223.

65

"Talk with Mark Twain," *St. Paul Dispatch*, 24 July 1895, 3.

Mark Twain, the American humorist who has charmed and delighted two hemispheres, administered the tonic of laughter to a large audience in Minneapolis last night, and this evening he will do the same by a representative audience of St. Paul people at the People's church.

Not that he is feeling humorous. Not a bit of it. His health is not what it once was, and his luck has not been of the best; but even these would be bearable were it not for the carbuncle that insists upon being his *compagnon de voyage*. A man does not fully realize what trouble is until he has entertained a carbuncle or a boil, and at present Mark is having a good deal of experience. Nevertheless, he is in trim to amuse and he is able to do it as few men can. This will be evident when he appears tonight and drawls out his inimitable yarns about the jumping frog and other things.

"I am now on my way around the world," he said, "putting a girdle around the earth as it were.[1] After belting this country, I shall sail for the Sandwich Islands [Hawaii], where I shall appear briefly, en route to Australia, the principal cities of which country I shall visit. Tasmania, New Zealand, and Ceylon will be visited in turn and then India, along to Bombay. Then I shall proceed to England, where I shall remain quite awhile. Finally, when my tour is completed, I shall return to my home in Hartford, there to settle down for a rest."

Mr. Clemens chats in a desultory fashion, steering away from himself. His carbuncle and his health keep him quiet and necessitates as much rest as possible.

His program tonight will be the same as that which has been used by him thus far during the present tour, as he does not intend to change his program until he reaches Australia. The features are all favorites, told in his best style and calculated to keep the most solemn man in an ecstasy of merriment.

Note to Interview 65

1. In act 2 of Shakespeare's *Midsummer Night's Dream* the fairy Puck declares that he will "put a girdle round the earth in forty minutes."

66

[W. E. Sterner?] "Mark Twain in Winnipeg," *Winnipeg Tribune,* 27 July 1895, 5.

On Friday afternoon a reporter of *The Tribune* called on Mark Twain at his rooms in the Manitoba. The great humorist was trying to humor a carbuncle, which kept him for the most part in a reclining position. It must be admitted that Mr. Clemens does not seem to make as much of a success in this as in humoring an audience. However, he is rapidly recovering, and in a week or so will be in his wonted health. After talking in a general way about his trips in Europe and the Holy Land, the reporter drew his attention to the very funny incidents which occurred when the Innocents Abroad refused to be astonished or to show any emotion at the stories of European guides.

"Yes," said Mr. Clemens, "they are very amusing when considered in a certain light. When you interrupt a guide in the middle of his harangue, back he flies to the beginning and starts to tell it all over again. And this is not to be wondered at. The repetition of a certain statement a number of times makes it automatic, so at last it tells itself. I know in my own experience, when lecturing fifteen years ago, I told some stories so often that at last they told themselves. Sometimes when I have been very tired, my mind wandered all over; wasn't in the lecture room at all, but my mouth went right along tending to business."

"However excellent these European incidents may be," remarked the scribe, "you doubtless consider the Mississippi your real field of work? You are, so to speak, the prophet of the Mississippi."

"Yes, and the reason is plain. By a series of events—accidents—I was the only one who wrote about old times on the Mississippi. Wherever else I have been some better have been before, and will cover after, but the Mississippi was a virgin field. No one could write that life but a pilot entered into the spirit of it. But the pilots were the last men in the world to write its history. As a class they did not naturally run to literature, and this was made more unlikely by another reason. Every pilot had to carry in his head thousands of details of that great river. Details, moreover, that were always changing, and in order to have nothing to confuse those details they entered into a compact never to read anything. Thus if they had thought of writing, they would have had no connected style, no power of describing anything; and, moreover, they were so engrossed in the river that there was nothing in the life unusual to them. Here then was my chance, and I used it."

In speaking about the spirit of adventure which led people to discover new countries and try new processes, Mr. Clemens suddenly came out with the sentence that the fools in the world were not half appreciated. Going on to explain his meaning, he pointed out that those who discovered new lands or new inventions were always considered fools. The people who put their money into the telegraph, the telephone, and other revolutionizing inventions were always the fools of the age. "Behind every advance you will find your patient and underestimated fool."

67

"A Chat with Clemens," *Free Press* (Winnipeg), 27 July 1895, 1.

Mr. Samuel Clemens (Mark Twain) was seen by a *Free Press* reporter in his room at the Manitoba Hotel. He did not seem to be very much fatigued by his exertions of the night previous, but was enjoying a cigar in bed when the reporter called. Mr. Twain explained that his temperament was naturally energetic, but that he had adopted this mode of life lately out of desire to propitiate a carbuncle which had given him a good deal of trouble in the past month. "The carbuncle was 'born,'" said he, "about the 20th of May, and it is as important a part of myself as anything about me. It does not suffer itself to be overlooked or argued with. I should call its conduct arbitrary—yes, arbitrary."

"You must find it difficult to lecture under these conditions," the reporter said.

"Not necessarily so," said Mr. Twain in his easy drawl. "A good deal of capital can be made in a lecture out of an alert expression of countenance. Perhaps I have that naturally, or perhaps it's the carbuncle. Yet, although we are at present inseparable, we are hardly friendly, and I shall not be sorry on my side when we part."

"Have you formed any special liking for one of your books over and above the rest?" he was asked.

"Well, sometimes," he replied, "I think I like *Huck Finn* best, and sometimes *The Prince and the Pauper*. It just depends on the mood I'm in. *Huck Finn* has this advantage over *Tom Sawyer*, that it was written ten years later, and had that much more experience to its credit. People have spoken kindly of these books of mine, but they have done me the honor of supposing that my boy heroes are myths. As a matter of fact, they are lively human beings. I drew them from life and didn't have to embroider many of the incidents, either. They are only copies of living boys, with a little effect thrown in now and then."

The reporter inquired if Mr. Clemens intended to go to France during this journey round the world, and was answered in the negative.

"Is there not some controversy going on between Max O'Rell and you at the present time?"[1]

"Not that I know of," said Mr. Clemens. "No controversy. Certainly not. Max O'Rell published a very foolish article in the *North American Review* some time ago which I did not answer, but I should not call that a controversy.[2] Max O'Rell, seeking notoriety, or advertisement, took upon himself to interfere in something that was no concern of his. That's all and how many of us make the same mistake with appalling frequency," moralized Mr. Clemens as he finished his cigar.

Notes to Interview 67

1. Lëon Paul Blouet, aka Max O'Rell (1848–1903), French author and journalist.
2. MT had published "What Paul Bourget Thinks of Us" in the *North American Review* 160 (January 1895): 48–62, in which he asserted that "a foreigner can photograph the exteriors of a nation, but I think that that is as far as he can get. I think that no foreigner can report its interior—its soul, its life, its speech, its thought." M. Paul Bourget (1852–1935) was the French author of *Cosmopolis* (1893). O'Rell had replied in "Mark Twain and Paul Bourget," *North American Review* 160 (March 1895):

302–11: "A man of average intelligence, who has passed six months among a people, cannot, it is true, express opinions that are worth jotting down, but he can form impressions that are worth repeating." MT would rejoin in "A Little Note to M. Paul Bourget," first published in *How to Tell a Story and Other Essays* (New York: Harper and Bros., 1897).

68

"An Interview," *Nor'wester* (Winnipeg), 27 July 1895, 1.

The greatest of living humorists, who came to the city on Friday a little after midday, took up his abode at the Manitoba, in the early part of the evening. Mr. S. L. Clemens (Mark Twain) was seen by a *Nor'wester* reporter, to whom he expressed himself very freely in regard to current affairs. Mr. Clemens is a man whose appearance makes him quite a distinct individuality. His leonine head—once seen—is never forgotten. His sixty years of life have left him very hale, well preserved, and at the same time, he bears evident traces of having gone through a good deal of hard literary work. Now and then he becomes quite absorbed in the workings of his own mind, which anyone can see is most active still. He is quite delighted with his present tour so far. The receptions which have met him everywhere have been of the most gratifying character. Harvard,[1] where he resides, he considers a most delightful spot. The society is in every way all that one could desire, and the existence of a university such as Harvard is gives a tone to the town which nothing else could do. Dr. Smith, the president of Harvard university,[2] he considers one of the simplest of men, a most profound thinker, and at the same time one of the purest and most unassuming of men. "I consider myself very lucky," he said, "in having my home where it is." In speaking of his "Old Times on the Mississippi," he said that his early training as a pilot stood him in good stead. "No one but a pilot could ever have written such a book, because no one else could have ever seen the various phases of life and character which are there delineated." He looked back with a great deal of pleasure to his own river-life. Referring to his *New Pilgrim's Progress*,[3] he said he had visited the Holy Land in person before writing it. While traveling there, he had seen so much arrant sentimental humbug that he could not help satirizing it. The conversation turned to the laws and customs of copyright in the United States of America, which he characterized as loose in the extreme, and requiring to be carefully amended. These had done a good deal of harm to literature in general, and to literary men. His reminiscences of Artemus Ward,[4] the genial showman (Chas. Farrar Browne), and other literary men were interesting in the extreme. Artemus he characterized as one of the most lovable of men. The great showman's entertainments took a good deal out of him, and he never was a strong man. Still, when with a few kindred spirits no one was more ready for social intercourse. His flow of animal spirits was perennial, and withal he was one of the most modest of men. In speaking of the appreciation which has met his works in countries outside the Saxon pale, Mr. Clemens referred to an incident which occurred when he was traveling in Germany. He had been dining with the Emperor, and His Majesty had expressed in almost flattering terms the pleasure that had been afforded to him by the reading of Mark Twain's works. "When I returned to my hotel," he said, "I was somewhat astonished to find that the concierge, who had sometimes been a bit grumpy, was as nice as one could desire. Whence the change? He had identified me as the man whose writings had afforded him more pleasure than anything he had ever read. I could not help feeling proud when I thought that I had been spoken well of by the Emperor and by the concierge." His experiences have been of the most varied character. In turn he has been printer, pilot, miner, journalist, and lecturer. An hour spent with him is well spent, for he talks as he writes. He is quite aware of the wonderful power he has exercised, and still exercises, but there is not an atom of self-conceit over it. He has been feted and flattered by the great and the learned all over the civilized world and yet all this has left him entirely free from the airs of the savant and the popular society lion. His own recollections of journalistic work make him a most interesting raconteur to anyone connected with the press.

Notes to Interview 68

1. The reporter apparently confuses "Harvard" with "Hartford."
2. George Williamson Smith (1836–1925), president of Trinity College (not Harvard) from 1883 to 1904.
3. The subtitle of *The Innocents Abroad*.
4. See n. 2 to interview 60.

69

"Mark Twain Talks," *Grand Forks Herald,* 30 July 1895, 4.

Mark Twain (S. L. Clemens) accompanied by his wife, second daughter, and Major and Mrs. Pond passed through the city yesterday morning on the Great Northern train from Winnipeg, on his way to Crookston. A reporter of *The Herald* called on Mr. Clemens in the car, and found him a very entertaining conversationalist, very willing to answer questions as to his opinion of this part of the country, and he asked a great many in return. He stated that he had been unwell for some time; in Winnipeg he was in bed all of the time, only getting up to lecture. "This country of yours out here," he said, "astonished me beyond all imagination. Never in my life have I seen such fields of grain extending in all directions to the horizon. This country appears to me to be as it were a mighty ocean; my conception of it is the same as that of a man who has never seen the ocean before, he sees nothing but water as far as the eye can reach; here I see nothing but oceans of wheat fields. Why it is simply miraculous." He asked a great many questions regarding our city as to its population, buildings, schools, etc. He very much regretted not being able to lecture in Grand Forks, as he had heard that we had a splendid opera house. "I am now on a trip around the world," he said. "Major Pond and wife will accompany us as far as Vancouver. My wife, daughter and myself will sail from there August 16 for the Sandwich Islands [Hawaii]; from there we shall go to Australia. I shall lecture all through there and from there I go to the Fiji islands, then to New Zealand and Tasmania. From there to Ceylon and India, where I shall remain some time, after which I shall sail from Bombay to South Africa, also calling at some places on the west coast of Africa, and then on to London, England. I expect to lecture all through the British Isles and then I will return to New York." . . .

70

"Mark Twain: The Great Humorist Has Arrived in Spokane," *Spokane Chronicle,* 7 August 1895, 1.

Samuel L. Clemens, the world's great humorist who for so many years has entertained audiences and readers everywhere, is in Spokane today. Most of the time he has spent resting from the fatigues of his trip through Montana. But he has found time to greet some old friends and to talk to the newspapermen, besides disposing of a few pretended old acquaintances.

A miner from up the country who evidently had heard that Mr. Clemens and Mark Twain were the same persons concluded to claim old friendship, but made the mistake of putting a "t" on the end of the humorist's name. The miner launched into the discussion of literary productions and then referred to the magazine article which appeared a month or two ago by Clemens concerning James Fenimore Cooper.[1]

"Clements," said the inquisitive friend, "I didn't think it was in you. Did you really write it? Now, honest, did you do it yourself?"

"Well," was the solemn reply, "I got the money for it."

Mr. Clemens is accompanied by his wife and daughter and by his manager, Major James B. Pond and wife.

Major Pond is himself a lecturer of note. He tells very interesting stories about the prominent people whom he has conducted on lecturing tours.

"Yes, I lecture some. I tell what I know about these people," he said. "Not all I know, but some things. I am pleased to find that your book sellers, John

W. Graham & Co., have the complete writings of Mark Twain. I wanted to find some of his works but this is the first place this side of St. Paul where I could find them all."

Note to Interview 70

1. MT derided the Leatherstocking Tales of Cooper (1789–1851) in "Fenimore Cooper's Literary Offenses," *North American Review* 161 (July 1895): 1–12.

71

"Mark Twain Arrives in Spokane," *Spokane Spokesman-Review,* 7 August 1895, 1.

Mark Twain, with his wife and daughter, Miss Clara Clemens, arrived last night from the east, accompanied by Major Pond and wife. At the Hotel Spokane he was requested to receive an introduction to a newspaper man.

"I will receive anything that Spokane has to offer," he replied, with an attempt to smile.

Samuel Clemens is approaching his 60th year. He has a full and ruddy face, adorned with an iron-gray moustache and wears a fluffy shock of grayish hair. In conversation he is deliberate, with only now and then a trace of humor bubbling to the surface. With reference to his financial reverses he said: "I have started on this tour chiefly for the purpose of paying those debts. I did not contract them, but must pay them." For a summer tour, he said, his success had been surprising and gratifying. He intends to sail August 16 from Vancouver, visiting the Sandwich Islands [Hawaii], Australia, New Zealand and Ceylon, the cities of India and South Africa, and will return home by way of London. If he stops to lecture in Great Britain he will be absent about a year.

"Do the English people appreciate American humor?" the reporter inquired.

"Indeed they do," he answered with earnestness. "One has no trouble with an English audience."

Mark Twain's most successful books, he said, are *Roughing It, The Innocents Abroad,* and *A Tramp Abroad.* He still derives a revenue from those works and would be in reasonably comfortable circumstances were there no debts hanging over his head.

"Yes, my health is good," the humorist replied to a question, "with the exception of an abominable carbuncle, and that is improving. I wrote to my friend Carey of the *Century,*[1] giving him a minute description of my affliction. He replied that he was an expert on buncles, and from my description he was convinced that this one did not belong to the ordinary or plebeian family, generally known as carbuncles. He said it must be an aristocratic Pullman car-buncle."

Mr. Clemens paid a high tribute to the steamers between Buffalo and Duluth.

"Twelve years ago," he said, "I was six days making that trip. This time it required only two days on the magnificent new boats, the *Northland* and the *Northwest*. I have never seen any European steamers inland that approached them for speed and comfort. In fact, the European steamers are cattle boats in comparison with these. Then the land travel. After suffering the discomforts and inconveniences for four years abroad I know how to value the home product."

Incidentally Mr. Clemens was told that some enthusiastic admirers of Dan De Quille believe that the Virginia City humorist invented the stories told in *Roughing It*.[2]

"They are cordially welcome to think so," he said. "William H. Wright is one of the noblest men in the world. He was born a newspaper man. I saw his nephew in Chicago a short time ago and he told me that Dan was still grinding away at Virginia City. I wish I could see him. We would have a great time."

"You know Will Visscher and Captain Jack Crawford, the poet scout?"[3]

"I know John W. Crawford, but Visscher—Visscher, did you say? The name is familiar."

"In polite circles he is known as Colonel Will L. Visscher."

"Does he move in polite circles?"

"Oh, yes, he does that."

"Then I guess I don't know him."

Discussing Mark Twain's books, the author was asked which of his sketches he deemed the funniest.

"I have no favorites," he answered. "What is your judgment?"

"The jaybird story, by all odds."[4]

Laughing heartily for the first time during the conversation, he said:

"It was over three years after *Roughing It* was published when I picked up a newspaper and read that sketch. I thought it was funny until I remembered that I had written it. A friend of mine suggested that this would be a good thing for the platform. I embodied it in one of my lectures and the audience fell asleep."

Mr. Clemens' lectures are not in the nature of "readings," but rather are original productions, interspersed with selections from his writings. During his absence abroad he will write another book, which his friend Carey has advised him to call "The New Innocents Abroad," but he is not entirely pleased with that title.

Notes to Interview 71

1. William Carey (1861?-1935?), assistant editor of the *Century*.
2. William H. Wright, aka Dan De Quille (1829-98), a popular Western humorist and journalist and a close friend of MT during his years in Nevada.
3. William Lightfoot Visscher (1842-1924), cowboy poet, Pacific Northwest journalist, and actor; Jack Crawford (1847-1917), Black Hills army scout and poet, author of the verse collection *The Poet Scout* (1879).
4. "Baker's Blue Jay Yarn," chapter 3 in *A Tramp Abroad*.

72

Marie Jousaye, "Mark Twain Interviewed," *Globe* (Toronto), 10 August 1895, 11.

Winnipeg, Aug. 8—I promised to tell you about my visit with Mark Twain. You see I don't call it an interview, as the note book and pencil do not figure in it the least bit. We just sat and talked of different subjects, some of which I will tell you and some of which I intend to keep to myself, for I know he would not like me to put it all in the papers. I will always look back to that two hours' chat as one of the events of my life. I told Mark so, and I just wish you could have seen his face as he drawled out in that inimitable manner, "That's quite right; it is but natural that you should." Like most everyone who has heard of or read of Mark Twain, I had formed a mental photograph of him. I find I am not so far out as to face, but away off as to figure. I have always fancied him as a tall, thin man, with a most pronounced stoop in his shoulders. Why I can't tell, only this was the picture I had in my mind's eye as I stood in the parlor of the Manitoba, waiting, with my heart beating somewhat faster than usual, for this man whose genius and pen have so often had the power to stir my heart, arousing both laughter and tears. It is no stranger whom I am about to greet, but a very old and dear friend, whose acquaintance I made years ago, when myself and a group of bare-footed boys and girls used to gather in the shade of a big woodpile and follow the exploits of Tom Sawyer and Huck Finn with hearts beating in unison with the young scapegraces in all their adventures. I remember a remark made by a favorite brother. I had been reading the adventure on the island, when Tom and Huck and Joe Harper had cast off the shackles of civilization and embarked upon the bold and adventurous life of buccaneers. My audience—mostly boys—listened in breathless silence, and when I had finished Ned drew a long breath and remarked tersely: "That man Twain was boy himself once, and don't you forget it." And we all echoed the sentiment. I am thinking of this incident, when a very gentle and kind voice breaks in on my reverie: "Are you the lady who wishes to see me?" I turn to greet the subject of my thoughts. And this is Mark! You must not think I am so impolite as to call him Mark to his face. I manage to say "Mr. Clemens" every time, but it is with an effort. He has always been Mark to me, and that's what I shall call him in these columns, whatever I may have to call him in our conversation. I find I have not been so far astray in my mental photograph. Instead of being tall, he is rather short, somewhat below the average; but the face I know would look just like that. "Like what?" some impatient reader asks. Well, really you have me there. I could not describe his features if I tried. I guess after all it was his expression which bore out the likeness I had formed of him. But this much I noticed, it was a very kind face, very bright and cheery looking, with clear, keen eyes and framed in by thick masses of hair that has passed the iron-grey stage and not yet reached the silvery white. When you look back at this man's countenance and listen to his tone of voice you realize that this is one who will go a long way out of his path to "help a lame dog over a stile." Such was my impression of Mark Twain at first sight, and I am not afraid but that those who know him will say I judged him aright.

He is not in very good health, he informs me. He has been having a severe struggle with a very bad carbuncle and the result is doubtful. Sometimes it is two to one on the carbuncle. I feel for him from the bottom of my heart, having had experiences with carbuncles myself. There is a great deal of irony in the bare fact of a man with a large and active carbuncle standing on a public platform and helping other people laugh and be happy, and I know of none who would appreciate the irony more so than Mark himself. But you want to know what we talked about. Well, first it was about children and their ways, which are pretty much the same all the world over, whether it is a little pickaninny in Africa or a papoose in an Indian village, or a white child in the more civilized countries. Then we wander off into the ways of grown-up children, and incidentally I ask him if he ever feels a desire to cut loose from civilization, to get away by himself where he can run and yell and kick to his heart's content. A big smile comes over his case. "Why, yes," he replies quickly. "Do you ever feel like that?" I reply in the affirmative, and the second bond of sympathy is established between us, the first being the carbuncles. Then Mark tells me a funny little story about himself and Canon Kingsley,[1] how they were walking along the streets of some city, I forget the name, and he felt the aforementioned impulse coming upon him with irresistible force. I give the story in his own words and only wish I could give the style of relation as well: "And I said to Canon Kingsley, 'I want to yell, I must yell.' And the Canon said, 'All right, yell away; I don't mind.' And with that I stepped back a few steps and throwing my arms above my head let out a war whoop that could be heard for miles, and in less time than you could count Canon Kingsley and myself were surrounded by a multitude of anxious citizens who wanted to know what was the matter. I told them nothing was the matter. I just wanted to yell and had yelled."

As soon as I can speak for laughing I ask: "And did not they run you in?"

"Why, no," says Mark. "They were all men themselves and know how I felt."

I shake my head doubtfully. "It was very good of them, Mr. Clemens; but if you ever come to Toronto and feel that impulse coming on I advise you to get outside the city limits."

A comical little twinkle appears in the keen eyes. "I have heard of Toronto," he says, "and I understand that you are very good and quiet down that way. I promise to behave when I go there."

Then the conversation turns to traveling and packing of trunks and one more bond is established. We both hate packing and looking after luggage. And Mark confides to me how his soul chafes under the cast-iron rules and regulations laid down for him by Mrs. and Miss Clemens, who are accompanying him on his tour around the world. "They mean well," he says dejectedly, "but it is a fearful nuisance. Why, I actually have to wear different clothes for different occasions; and just think of the barbarity of making a man shave when he don't feel like it. Why, when I traveled alone on my lecture tour some years ago I had just a single grip with a few collars and a dress coat in it; the trousers and vest of the dress suit I wore while traveling, and when I buttoned the other coat up nobody could tell what kind of a vest I had on; couldn't even tell if I had a shirt on. I didn't mind traveling in those days. There was nothing to bother me or hold me back. Why, I used to go 'flying light' and if I didn't shave before the lecture it didn't matter; only the first few rows could notice it, and they couldn't tell for sure whether it was want of a shave or bad soap. Those were good times," says Mark, regretfully, "but now—" and he breaks off with a weary sigh.

I say nothing. Obviously it is a time when speech is silver; but silence is golden, and so I sit silently for a few minutes, much the same as those people in the Bible who come to condole with Job. Indeed the presence of the carbuncle makes this illustration a most apt one. All that is needed to complete the comparison is a handful of ashes for me to strew on my head, and a broken saucer for Mark. Presently I recollect a funny incident that took place in the elevator on my way to the parlor. Two gentlemen were in the elevator, and several bags and boxes were piled on the seat. One of the gentlemen pushed the luggage aside that I might sit down, and the top parcel, a very respectable and legal-looking black bag, fell to the floor. There was a sound of breaking glass, and then a most unmistakable aroma greeted our nostrils, as the floor of the elevator became flooded with something much stronger than water. The poor man! I felt so sorry for him. He looked so confused and ashamed, and in the midst of his distress he thought of others. "Mind your dress, madame," he said to me. I thought that was so nice of him, and darted a reproving look at the elevator boy, who was so doubled up with mirth that he could hardly work the hoist. But after I got out in the hall I could not help laughing myself. It was all so comical, and it was such an innocent-looking bag. After this I shall look with suspicion on every black bag I come across. Yea, even though it be on the shoulder of our own Edward Blake.[2] Recollecting the incident, I think it will serve to lift Mark out of his state of melancholy. The experiment proves successful, and, as he listens, a smile steals across his visage. One lovely trait in this King of humorists is his readiness to smile when other folks tell funny things. All humorists are not like this; but then Mark is an exception in more ways than one. He listens attentively until I finish, and then remarks in a regretful tone, "What a pity!"

I mistake his meaning. "Yes," I say, "it was too bad. He seemed so confused, poor man."

"Oh," says Mark, in surprise, "you are thinking of the man. I was thinking of the whiskey."

Naturally I am somewhat taken aback at this, but recover myself sufficiently to say, in my most severe manner, "Do you mean to say, Mr. Clemens, that the shame and exposure would not be worse than the loss of the whiskey?"

"Not to me," he replies, undauntedly. "I tell you, ma'am," and here he stands up and waves his hands excitedly, "if that had happened to me I would have felt so bad I would not have cared where it occurred, not even if it were in a crowded church. I would simply stand up and say, 'Good people, it's no use trying to console me. I refuse to be comforted. The bottle that is broken can never be restored, and the whiskey that is split will never flow again. You needn't even take up a collection for me.'"

I argue the point no longer. Indeed by the time I am through laughing and get the tears wiped away I am too weak and limp to continue an argument. And so I thank him in my best English for the interview, and with a hearty handshake take my departure.

He sails on August 16th, on the good ship *Warrimoo*,[3] from Vancouver, to Sydney. Bon voyage, friend Mark, may you have the finest weather and the jolliest time crossing the seas. May you never be forced to shave once during the entire trip; and when you arrive in Australia may the carbuncle be a thing of the past.

Notes to Interview 72

1. Charles Kingsley (1819-75), Church of England divine and author of such works as *Westward Ho!* and the *Water Babies*. See also Fatout 83-84.
2. Edward Blake (1833-1912), first Liberal premier of Ontario (1871-72) and leader of the Liberal Party of Canada (1880-87).
3. In the first chapter of *FE* (1897), his final travel book, MT referred to the *War-

rimoo, built in 1892 and operated by the Union Steamship Co. of New Zealand, as "a reasonably comfortable ship, with the customary sea-going fare—plenty of good food furnished by the Deity and cooked by the devil."

73

[Lute Pease,][1] "Mark Twain Talks," *Portland Oregonian,* 11 August 1895, 10.

Mark Twain and his manager, Major Pond, left Portland yesterday morning for the Sound, where he will join Mrs. Clemens and his daughter at Tacoma. After lecturing there, and at Olympia, Seattle, Victoria and Vancouver, B.C., he will sail from Vancouver, August 16, with the whole party, for Honolulu.

As was contemplated, Mr. Clemens' tour around the world will take at least a year, and very likely longer. He will be in the hands of his Australian agent some nine months, lecturing in the leading cities of Australia, New Zealand, India and South Africa, after which he will visit the British Isles, where he will doubtless remain a considerable time.

At the Portland, yesterday morning, Mark Twain stood surrounded by a medley of handbags waiting for a carriage to the train. A blue nautical cap confined a part of his big mane of hair, but it bulged out at the sides and behind, a grizzly wilderness. With that bushy growth tumbling over his big head, the bushy mustache and the bushy brows streaming to the right and left, a face rugged as if chiseled by nature's hand from a block of granite, Mark Twain is certainly about as striking and picturesque a character as ever looked out of the pages of any of his own books. And, when to his anything but commonplace appearance is added the originality of his manner, its absolute carelessness, his lazy, cynical good humor, he becomes one of the most interesting men in the world to meet, even if one had never heard of him.

Dozens of people came up to reach over the array of handbags and shake hands with Mark Twain. Most of them claimed to have met him before, and his face wore a rather puzzled look sometimes as he was reminded of various places and occasions where he had met them in days gone by. That genial, courteous gentleman, Major J. B. Pond, was busy with introductions and other matters, but the carriage didn't come, so Mark and the major bundled into the bus, handbags in hand, and were off.

"Portland seems to be a pretty nice town," drawled the author of *Tom Sawyer,* as the bus rolled down Sixth street, "and this is a pretty nice, smooth street. Now Portland ought to lay itself out a little and macadamize all its streets just like this.[2] Then it ought to own all the bicycles and rent 'em out and so pay for the streets. Pretty good scheme, eh? I suppose people would complain about the monopoly, but then we have the monopolies always with us. Now, in European cities, you know, the government runs a whole lot of things, and, it strikes me, runs 'em pretty well. Here many folks seem to be alarmed about governmental monopolies. But I don't see why. Here cities give away for nothing franchises for car lines, electric plants and things like that. Their generosity is often astonishing. The American people take the yoke of private monopoly with philosophical indifference, and I don't see why they should mind a little government monopoly."

"What about that book of travels you are going to write on this trip, Mr. Clemens? Will it be something like *The Innocents Abroad*, or the others?"

"Well, it won't describe the same places by any means. It will be a lazy man's book. If any one picks it up expecting to find full data, historical, topographical, and so forth, he will be disappointed. A lazy man, you know, don't rush around with his note book as soon as he lands on a foreign shore. He simply drifts about, and if anything gets in his way of sufficient interest to make an impression on him, it goes into his book. General Sherman told me that when he made his trip abroad, he found just about what he needed in my old books to guide him to what interested him most.[3] He said it was too much bother to wade through the conventional guide book, which mentioned everything, so he dropped them by the wayside. That's just what makes traveling tiresome, I think—that ever-present anxiety to take in everything, whether you can enjoy it and digest it or not—that fear that you won't get your money's worth if you leave anything mentioned in the guidebook behind. What's the use of making a business of traveling when you are out for pleasure? While I am not going to write a guide book, yet if it can help people to enjoy the same journey, why, I shall think it something of a success."

Mr. Clemens, during this time, had sauntered through the depot, and on into the smoking compartment of the Olympia car, where he settled himself comfortably in a corner.

"There must be some reason," said he, "why a fine town like Portland has not long since built a new depot. What is the reason?"

It was explained to him that the completion of the new station had been delayed through two of the roads interested in its construction having gone into receiverships.

"Well, I haven't had an opportunity to see much of Portland, because, through the diabolical machinations of Major Pond over there, I am compelled to leave it after but a glimpse. I may never see Portland again, but I liked that glimpse."

Someone asked him about the story that was published in one of the San Francisco papers not long since about an old-time Mission street bartender named Tom Sawyer.[4] This individual had asserted that he had met Mark Twain in 'Frisco many years ago with a jolly party and that all went out together and got still jollier, and that Mark had slapped Sawyer on the back with the remark: "I am writing a book about just such a boy as you must have been, and I'm going to name him after you."

"That story lacks a good deal in the way of facts," said Mr. Clemens. "One doesn't choose a name that way. I have always found it rather difficult to choose just the name that suited my ear. Tom Sawyer and Huckleberry Finn were both real characters, but Tom Sawyer was not the real name of the former, nor the name of any person I ever knew, so far as I can remember, but the name was an ordinary one—just the sort that seemed to fit the boy, some way, by its sound, and so I used it. No, one doesn't name his characters haphazard. Finn was the real name of the other boy, but I tacked on the Huckleberry. You see, there was something about the name Finn that suited, and Huck Finn was all that was needed to somehow describe another kind of boy than Tom Sawyer, a boy of lower extraction or degree. Now, Arthur Van de Vanter Montague would have sounded ridiculous, applied to characters like either Tom Sawyer or Huck Finn."

"Both those books will always be a well of joy to innumerable boys, Mr. Clemens."

"Well," said Twain with a smile, "I rather enjoyed writing them. The characters were no creation of my own. I simply sketched them from life. I knew both those boys so well that it was easy to write what they did and said. I've a sort of fondness for 'em anyway.

"I don't believe an author, good, bad or indifferent, ever lived, who created a character. It was always drawn from his recollection of someone he had known. Sometimes, like a composite photograph, an author's presentation of a character may possibly be from the blending of more than two or more real characters in his recollection. But, even when he is making no attempt to draw his character from life, when he is striving to create something different, even then, however ideal his drawing, he is yet unconsciously drawing from memory. It is like a star so far away that the eye cannot discover it through the most powerful telescope, yet if a camera is placed in proper position under that telescope and left for a few hours, a photograph of the star will be the result. So, it's the same way with the mind; a character one has known some time in life may have become so deeply buried within the recollection that the lens of the first effort will not bring it to view. But by continued application the author will find when he is done, that he has etched a likeness of some one he has known before.

"In attempting to represent some character which he cannot recall, which he draws from what he thinks is his imagination, an author may often fall into the error of copying in part a character already drawn by another, a character which impressed itself upon his memory from some book. So he has but made a picture of a picture with all his pains. We mortals can't create, we can only copy. Some copies are good and some are bad."

2. Mark Twain interviewed by Lute Pease in Portland, Oregon, 9 August 1895. Courtesy of Kevin Mac Donnell.

Just then the train started and Mark Twain said good-bye to Portland. A lot of people are sorry he did not remain to lecture another night.

Notes to Interview 73

1. Lucius (Lute) Pease (1869–1963) was a reporter and cartoonist for the *Portland Oregonian* and from 1905 to 1912 editor of the *Pacific Monthly;* he received a Pulitzer Prize in 1948, the oldest journalist to do so.
2. The Scottish engineer John McAdam (1756–1836) invented a process (macadamization) for paving roads with broken stone and tar.
3. William T. Sherman had traveled abroad for nearly a year in 1871–72.
4. See "The Original Tom Sawyer: Mark Twain's Hero That Got into Trouble and Out Again with Huckleberry Finn Now Living in the Mission," *San Francisco Examiner,* 9 October 1892, 15:4–5.

74

"Mark Twain and Major Pond," *Tacoma Union,* 11 August 1895, 6.

... Then Mark Twain (Samuel L. Clemens) joined the party. He slid into a chair sidewise, and on coming so near his eyes did not look so wild as they did at a distance. Twenty feet away they look not unlike burned holes in a blanket and appear to be entirely out of joint with Mr. Clemens' calm and slightly ashy face. However, they seem entirely at home when the expression of pain and perseverance that return to his lips after each smile is taken into consideration. His Paderewski mop of hair,[1] and a commonplace moustache, also had the ashy dust in them, especially the hair which is pretty nearly white.

He had already been pumped dry by the reporters, and evidently took much satisfaction in sliding down in his chair, with his legs on the settee, with his Paderewski for a cushion, to lean the back of his head on the back of the chair. He puffed leisurely at a cigar, while Major Pond tried to make it appear that Mark Twain was only the runnet of the Clemens family.[2]

"You ought to see Mrs. Clemens and Miss Clemens. They constitute the family," Pond said. "You don't know it, but in five minutes I could produce the cleverest person with a piano on the coast. Miss Clemens is a wonder."

Mark Twain smiled coyly. "You're trying to boom the big end of the show by making up the minor parts," he said, after Major Pond had exhausted himself praising Miss Clemens' abilities.

"You can't deny it," Pond urged.

"Oh, no," replied Mr. Clemens, "but it's only transmitted genius."

Someone asked Mr. Clemens if he really enjoyed knocking about the country on one of Major Pond's lecturing tours.

"He's got," put in Pond [before] Twain could reply. "He's got to like it. We won't have it otherwise."

Twain smiled, and seemed glad to have someone else talk for him by proxy. Finally, his attention was called to a remark in the *Seattle Post-Intelligencer* made by John W. McKay, the man who made millions in mines.[3] Mr. McKay had returned from Alaska, and remarked on seeing a picture of Mr. Clemens on a billboard that he used to know him in Nevada in the early days. He left word for the newspaper men to tell Mr. Clemens that a cowboy sort of fellow who was with him in Nevada had passed through town and sent him his regards.

"McKay is a great man," said Clemens. "He is a superb man. Yes," after one of those leisurely puffs at his cigar. "I met him while at work on a Nevada newspaper. Once I asked him how he would like to swap places with me. He was running a little mine broker office, and he asked me how much I was getting. I said $40 per week, and then he said no, he could not swap with me, as my place was worth more than his."

"Too bad we can't see that grand Mount Tacoma,"[4] Major Pond remarked when the conversation, which had taken the bit in its mouth from the start, brought up among the scenery of the Rocky Mountains. "I did not see it when I was here with Beecher, either."[5]

Mr. Clemens took all the snap out of Pond's oration about the grandeur of the Rockies by stating that when he saw Pike's Peak there wasn't snow on it, and then Pond brought in a photograph of Mount Tacoma.

"Mark," said he, "I'm going to give that photo to Mrs. Clemens so that she can write back east and tell the folks how it looks."

Mark Twain smiled, and slid a little farther down in his chair. "It isn't a photograph of the mountain, is it?" he asked. "Sure," replied Pond.

"Thought it was a photo of a painting. It's grand anyway."

Major Pond had stated before Mr. Clemens joined the party that he had been offered most fabulous sums for his forthcoming book, "Around the World, by Mark Twain." He said Mr. Clemens received $100 per page for his magazine work, "twice as much," he added, "as any other writer."

So Mr. Clemens was asked what he proposed to put in his new book.

"It won't be a guidebook," he replied. "When men write guidebooks they give too many details. I will try to give some interesting impressions."

"Don't forget Tacoma. Help us boom Tacoma."

Mark Twain smiled.

He smiled just the same each time, even when he went into details about palmistry. He knew much about the subject, and told how Editor Stead of the London *Review of Reviews* had had his hands photographed once when Twain met him on an Atlantic liner.[6] Twain was making one of the fifteen ocean voyages made by him during the past four years, and Stead was to submit the photos to a man who would read and report on the character of the subject.

Several men examined the photos, and Mr. Clemens said two of them were quite accurate in their reports, others were not so accurate.

But here, as elsewhere, he mixed things up so a wooly west man could not decide with satisfaction to himself when it was proper to laugh. "The laugh" kept bobbing up at unexpected points, and it seemed impossible to decide about its genuineness.

For instance, Mr. Clemens went on to say that when a man looked at your hands and gave you certain information which you know all about yourself, and no one else knew it, not even members of your own family, you had to acknowledge the corn.

Well, one of the experts who examined those Stead photos of Mark Twain's hand reported "this subject has no sense of humor."

Mr. Clemens did not say whether this was so or not.

Then he talked about "doubles," and said all his doubles were around the country lecturing without giving him any of the proceeds. One had secured four bits, he said, at San Francisco by saying he was Mark Twain.

"He got the money in a saloon," added Mr. Clemens, "and I think he was a mighty sharp fellow to raise half a dollar in that way."

He thought Julian Hawthorne had the most remarkable doubles,[7] one of whom died in Australia, and word was thereupon sent to Mrs. Hawthorne.

A. B. Frost is a clever artist in Mark Twain's opinion.[8] Pond talked up some other knight of the brush to illustrate his new book of impressions, but Mr. Clemens clung to the idea that Frost was the man.

About this time a *Morning Union* staff artist was making a sketch of Twain. It was gently hinted that if he put off making a decision regarding the artist who should illustrate his new book he might be favorably impressed with the *Morning Union* genius.

He looked about him, curious to catch a glimpse of the artist, but the bird had flown. The sketch conveys a bored and somewhat piratical expression, which, from his conversation, Mr. Clemens did not intend to wear.

There is a big mounted buffalo in the hotel lobby. This attracted Major Pond, and he proposed to have the women of the Twain party seize it by the horns while he took a snapshot. This he thought would give the people of the east an idea of the thrilling encounter which they could say they had had with the buffalo of the plains.

Mark Twain smiled.

Notes to Interview 74

1. Ignace Jan Paderewski (1860–1941), Poland émigré and piano virtuoso, was well-known for his "long hair" style of music.
2. "Runnet" is a variant of "runt," or the smallest member of a group.
3. John W. McKay (1831–1902), western American mine owner and entrepreneur. See also Paine, 237.
4. Aka Mount Rainier.
5. Henry Ward Beecher (1813–87), minister of the Plymouth Church in Brooklyn.
6. William T. Stead (1849–1912), journalist and editor of the *Pall Mall Gazette* (1893–90) and the *Review of Reviews*.
7. Julian Hawthorne (1846–1934), popular American novelist and son of Nathaniel Hawthorne.
8. Arthur Burnett Frost (1851–1928) was one of eleven illustrators who contributed sketches to *FE*.

75

"The Same Old Twain," *Seattle Post-Intelligencer,* 11 August 1895, 7.

As Mark Twain sat in the smoker of a northbound Northern Pacific train yesterday, on his way from Portland, where he had lectured the night before, and Olympia, where he appeared last night, vigorously puffing a cigar, a *Post-Intelligencer* reporter approached him and soon drew him on to give such a random, jolly, enjoyable talk as only Mark Twain can.

Of course Mr. Clemens was pleased with the Northwest. Of course he was. In expressing himself about it he did not confine his comment to vague superlatives and flittering generalities, but pointed out just those facts and features that have thus far impressed him during this, his first visit to this section of the Union.

"One feature which has struck me as differentiating this section from those other parts of the West where I have passed before," said Mr. Clemens, "is its notable lack of desert lands. In other states the great stretches of sand and alkali lands are neither picturesque nor pleasant. The lands here are all cultivated or cultivable, and vast tracts of pasture land take the place of the California and Nevada deserts."

Mr. Clemens was equally enthusiastic about the scenery through which he is now passing. In speaking of the almost boundless areas of level grain fields about Winnipeg, he instituted a comparison between the scenic effect of such a mass of waving green and that produced by the ocean. Like many of his comments and observations, this comparison was supported by striking arguments and illustrations. He maintained the superiority of the prairie view, first on account of the richness of color, and still more emphatically on account of the impression of amplitude, which, he asserted, contrary to the poets and artists of all ages, is most conveyed by the open sea. His reason for holding to this opinion was that at sea there is seldom any intervening object of known magnitude by which distance can be gauged, whereas the clump of trees or the prairie cabin stand out as landmarks to deepen the perspective and accentuate the reaches of distance that lie beyond them.

"The eye, in fact, cannot judge of distance unless it has some familiar object to set up as a sort of gauge," continued the great humorist; and then, with that peculiar drawl in his voice and twinkle in his eye which stamp him as the prince of raconteurs and herald the flashes of fun for which he has become famous, he went on to tell how once during his early life on the plains he had stood with a group of comrades and gazed at a mass of approaching objects without a single rock or tree on which to base an estimate of distance. Indians, suggested one of the party, a keen-sighted pioneer and experienced hunter. Wild horses, ventured another. Buffalo, hazarded a third. All thought the objects fully two miles away. "And what do you think they turned out to be?" asked Mark Twain, with as much zest and animation as if he were telling a ghost story to a wondering child. Then with his peculiar drawl: "They were nothing more than a lot of j-a-c-k-r-a-b-b-i-t-s."

Then, with all the soberness of a sworn witness, he went to tell how he once saw a man in New Orleans stand on the sidewalk and declare he saw a squirrel moving about in an upper room across the street, and the squirrel turned out to be a louse on a hair hanging from the man's hat. With equal facility he reeled off a yarn from the days when he was a pilot's cub on a Mississippi river steamboat. He and the pilot, side by side at the wheel, each and both distinctly saw one night what they supposed to be a man performing the foolhardy feat of climbing the whistle-pipe, a slender tube that reached far up the side of one of the tall smokestacks of the boat, some sixty feet from the pilot house. They commented on his strange conduct, and, concluding he must be a lunatic, were starting to capture him when he turned out to be nothing but a rat climbing a bell rope only a few feet distant from their eyes.

The mention of those old days of piloting naturally led the reporter to ask Mr. Clemens as to the truthfulness of the current story that tells how he came to take his well-known nom de plume.

"Like many others of its kind," he answered, "the story has become somewhat warped from being often told. The facts are about these: Old Isaiah Sellers, back in the '50s, was by odds the oldest pilot on the Mississippi. He used to write up the changing stages of that fickle stream for the columns of the *True Delta,* and now and then he would intersperse his short reports with startling statements of how things used to be fifty or sixty years before. I wrote my first skit as a burlesque on his reports. It covered a column and a half in the *Delta,* sometime in 1857.[1] It was a crude effort, but it served its purpose. It played sad havoc with some of old Sellers' pet islands and channels, fairly knocking them galley-west, and telling how some century or so ago they used to occupy places in the far interior of the country. The old man never wrote another report. The name over which he used to write was Mark Twain. Time rolled on, and when the news of Sellers' death was borne to me in Carson City, I was doing up the Nevada legislature, embalming the members in a weekly letter. They did not relish some of my criticisms, and they were continually rising to a question of privilege to denounce the man whom they were pleased to call the 'unreliable correspondent of the *Territorial Enterprise.*' From the frequency with which they denounced me, I concluded it would save time if I gave them a shorter phrase than that, and when I heard that Isaiah Sellers was dead, I deliberately robbed his corpse and signed my next letter 'Mark Twain.'"

Among the reminiscences thus told by Mr. Clemens as the train hurried onward was another which, like the foregoing, is of more than passing interest, since it is related to his life as a man of letters. It was the story of how he came to write and publish his first "serious effort in humor." Artemus Ward was going to publish a book.[2] He met Mark Twain in 1865, and asked him to contribute a chapter. Mark promised, but the promise grew six months old before he ran across the story of the jumping frog, which he heard first in Calaveras county. He wrote it out and sent it to Carleton, Ward's publisher. Ward's book was already in press, and Carleton would not take it out. He turned the now famous story ignominiously out, and it drifted into the hands of Henry Clapp, who was then publishing the *Saturday Press.*[3] Clapp pub-

3. Mark Twain at his hotel in Olympia, Washington, 11 August 1895. Courtesy of Kevin Mac Donnell.

lished it at once, but that was the last issue of the paper. "If my story did not kill the paper, it at least assisted at the burial," said Mark Twain laconically.

Thus he talked on in his bright and sunny temper, undaunted by the business reverses that have come upon him in his old age, and apparently not one whit jaded by the long journey which is to keep him a full year longer from home. Seated unostentatiously among the crowd of casual passengers, his plain dark suit and russet shoes, his quiet manner, his modest tone, attracted no notice from strangers, and it was only when the jaunty traveling cap was laid aside that his bushy gray hair crowned his pleasant face and made him look as he does in "the pictures," so that people whispering down the aisle said: "That is Mark Twain."

Notes to Interview 75

1. MT's satirical piece in the New Orleans *True Delta* appeared on 8 or 9 May 1859. It is reprinted in appendix B of Paine's biography. See also Paine, 150.
2. See n. 2 to interview 60.
3. Henry Clapp (1814–75), New York journalist and editor of the *Saturday Press*.

76

[Lute Pease,][1] "Twain Brands a Fake," *Seattle Post-Intelligencer,* 14 August 1895, 8.

When Mark Twain was shown what purported to be an interview with him published in the Washington City *Post*,[2] he sat quietly for a minute yesterday afternoon, puffing his cigar, and then said:

"Well, a fellow oughtn't to be too severe on a man that's as hard up for an interview as that. If he wants to palm that sort of stuff off on me, it's all right—I can bear it. He ought to have made his story a little more plausible, however. In the first place he represents me as collecting, while city editor of the *Morning Call* of San Francisco, which was just thirty years ago, verses which were not in existence until that time, and most of which were simply manufactured by him for the occasion. In the next place, he represents the interview as having taken place in Hartford, when in point of fact I have not been in Hartford for four years."

Having thus disposed of the tombstone poetry that has been floating about the country with his name attached to a sort of running critique on the sentiment contained in the verses, Mr. Clemens sank back on the sofa and meditated. He had come in on the Flyer from Tacoma, where he lectured Monday night, having, as he said, a "delightful audience." Reaching Seattle at 2:45, he was taking a short rest before going aboard the United States steamship *Mohican,* where he was to dine at the invitation of Lieutenant Commander Wadhams,[3] an old acquaintance of his. Resting, he talked, or to put it according to his own logic, talking, he rested. It is easy enough to tell what he said, but not to reproduce his way of saying it. Talking seems to come as easy to him as breathing. He goes through all moods in five minutes, "from gay to grave, from lively to severe,"[4] and it is safe to say that many of his private conversations are fully as rich in thought and humor as his more pretentious efforts on the stage.

"I have a fellow-feeling for newspaper men," he said, "because of my own experience. I have not only written a great deal as correspondent and contributor, but I was at one time city editor of the *Territorial Enterprise* of Virginia City and afterwards of the San Francisco *Morning Call.*

"My lecture tour thus far has been remarkably successful. I had thought before setting out that everybody in the cities would be taking a vacation; but there have been enough to give us large audiences everywhere."

Then very delicately, almost as if speaking of the disaster that had befallen some friend, he spoke of the business reverses that have come upon him, and his listener was reminded of the story told by Thackeray of the great French comedian's consulting a physician, who, observing his melancholy and not knowing who he was, advised him to go and hear himself and laugh away his fit of blues.[5]

"I cannot hope to build up another fortune now," he said. "I am getting too old for that; I shall be more than satisfied if within the next five years I can pay off my creditors. I believe that I can do it, too.

"It is a little remarkable that Scott was just my age, 58, when the great publishing house of Ballantyne Bros., with which he had formed a business partnership very similar to the one in which I was engaged in Hartford, failed.[6] In his successful effort to pay off the vast debt of $600,000 he killed himself by overwork. No other author could have accomplished such a feat, even at the sacrifice of his own life. Dickens would have come nearer being able to do it than any other, but he could not. General Grant's book, bringing the rich return of nearly half a million dollars within seven months, was an exceptional production and does not afford a precedent in the realm of authorship.

"Now, if I have to pay my debts by writing books as Scott had to write them, I might easily kill myself in five years as he did. But I have the advantage of this lecture bureau system, which has grown to such enormous proportions. Instead of killing me, it builds me up physically. The fatigue of travel by easy stages is not great, and the constant change of air and scenery is beneficial. My health is a hundred percent better already than when I started out from home in July."

Just then a small boy happened to pass by, and perhaps attracted and emboldened by Mr. Clemens' kindly bearing, approached him and said, "Say, mister, can you tell me where this place is at?"

Directing the lad with as much care as if he were guiding a caravan to an oasis, Mr. Clemens said: "It is strange, but although that expletive 'say' is so commonly used throughout the West and South, only once have I heard it for any years. I was standing one day with George W. Cable in front of the St. Charles hotel in New Orleans,[7] when we heard a man shout to another, 'Say, where have you been at?' and the odd form of speech gave us food for talk for some time afterward."

Speaking further of Cable, Mr. Clemens said, "There is no truth whatever in the story that has been going the rounds to the effect that the lecture partnership in which Cable and I were at one time engaged was broken up by a quarrel between us. There is no foundation for such a story. I had been off the platform for several years, and was anxious to take a short turn at it again. At the same time I did not feel equal to the strain of a full evening's program. I wanted someone to relieve me of part of the burden. Mr. Cable and I entered into a specific agreement for four months, and it is a sufficient

4. Posing aboard the *Mohican,* 13 August 1895. Courtesy of Kevin Mac Donnell.

contradiction of the story about a quarrel to say that we did not miss a single engagement. We are of exactly opposite temperaments, and on that account perhaps became not only close friends, but the most congenial of traveling companions." . . .

Notes to Interview 76

1. See n. 1 to interview 73. This interview was attributed to Pease in the *Portland Oregonian* for 8 February 1925, sec. 3, 7.

2. Twain repudiates the spurious interview "Twain's Obituary Poems" (*Hartford Post;* rpt. *Minneapolis Pioneer Post,* 24 July 1895; rpt. *San Francisco Examiner,* 18 August 1895, 21). That interview was erroneously attributed to the *Washington Post.* It was nothing more than a revision of his essay "Post-Mortem Poetry" (1870).

3. Albion V. Wadhams (1847–1927), a U.S. naval officer, later a rear admiral.

4. Slight misquotation of Alexander Pope's *Essay on Man,* epistle 4, l. 380: "from grave to gay, from lively to severe."

5. Thackeray opened his lecture on Jonathan Swift: "Harlequin without his mask is known to present a very sober countenance, and was himself, the story goes, the melancholy patient whom the Doctor advised to go and see Harlequin."

6. After the failure of John Ballantyne and Co. in 1826, Sir Walter Scott (1771–1832) pledged to repay the firm's indebtedness of £130,000.

7. A historic hotel on St. Charles Avenue near the French Quarter in New Orleans. On Cable, see chapter 2.

77

"Mark Twain to Pay All," *San Francisco Examiner,* 17 August 1895, 2; rpt. "Mark Twain's Plan of Settlement," *New York Times,* 17 August 1895, 8.

Vancouver (B.C.), August 16—Sam L. Clemens (Mark Twain), who is about [to leave] for Australia, in an interview concerning the purposes of his long trip, said:

"I am idle until lecture-time. Write, and I will dictate and sign. My run across the continent, covering the first 4,000 miles of this lecturing tour around the world, has revealed to me so many friends of whose existence I was unconscious before, and so much kindly and generous sympathy with me in my financial mishaps, that I feel that it will not be obtrusive self-assertion, but an act of simple justice to that loyal friendship, as well as to my own reputation, to make a public statement of the purpose which I have held from the beginning, and which is now in the process of execution.

"It has been reported that I sacrificed, for the benefit of the creditors, the property of the publishing firm whose financial backer I was, and that I am now lecturing for my own benefit. This is an error. I intend the lectures, as well as the property, for the creditors.

"The law recognizes no mortgage on a man's brain, and a merchant who has given up all he has may take advantage of the rules of insolvency and start free again for himself; but I am not a business man; and honor is a harder master than the law. It cannot compromise for less than a hundred cents on the dollar, and its debts never outlaw.

"I had a two-thirds interest in the publishing firm, whose capital I furnished. If the firm had prospered, I should have expected to collect two-thirds of the profit. As it is I expect to pay all the debts. My partner has no resources,[1] and I do not look for assistance from him. By far the largest single creditor of this firm is my wife, whose contributions in cash from her private means have nearly equaled the claims of all the others combined. In satisfaction of this great and just claim, she has taken nothing, except to avail herself of the opportunity of retaining control of the copyrights of my books, which, for many easily understood reasons—of which financial ones are the least— we do not desire to see in the hands of strangers.

"On the contrary, she has helped and intends to help me to satisfy the obligations due to the rest.

"The present situation is that the wreckage of the firm, together with what money I can scrape together, with my wife's aid, will enable me to pay the other creditors about 50 percent of their claims. It is my intention to ask them to accept that as a legal discharge and trust to my honor to pay the other 50 percent as fast as I can earn it. From my reception thus far on my lecturing tour I am confident that if I live I can pay off the last debt within four years, after which, at the age of sixty-four, I can make a fresh and unencumbered start in life.

"I do not enjoy the hard travel and broken rest inseparable from lecturing, and if it had not been for the imperious moral necessity of paying these debts, which I never contracted but which were accumulated on the faith of my name by those who had a presumptive right to use it, I should never have taken to the road at my time of life. I could have supported myself comfortably by writing, but writing is too slow for the demands that I have to meet; therefore I have begun to lecture my way around the world. I am going to Australia, India and South Africa, and next year I hope to make a tour of the great cities of the United States.

"In my preliminary run through the smaller cities on the northern route, I have found a reception the cordiality of which has touched my heart and made me feel how small a thing money is in comparison with friendship.

"I meant, when I began, to give my creditors all the benefit of this, but I begin to feel that I am gaining something from it too, and that my dividends, if not available for banking purposes, may be even more satisfactory than theirs."

Note to Interview 77

1. See n. 11 to interview 47.

78

"Mark Twain Unsuited," *New Whatcom (Wash.) Blade,* 17 August 1895.
When a *Blade* reporter was ushered into the presence of Mark Twain at the Fairhaven Hotel Thursday morning, the great humorist had not yet donned his trousers and was engaged in packing a dress suit; he said that he would "rather be skinned alive than perform such a duty."

"I have not seen anything of the country since the 17th of July, when we left Detroit, on account of this infernal smoke. This is the first time I have ever been in this section of the country but I can't see anything but the ground I walk on, which is like any other ground. I haven't even been able to see your harbor yet, and I know nothing about the country." Mr. Clemens has a very severe cold and it is difficult for him to talk. "The only reason I was able to speak last night was that the hall was equipped with splendid acoustic properties. I fear that I shall have to give it up tonight at Vancouver." Mrs. Clemens was sick and remained in Seattle, but went to Vancouver Thursday.

They sailed from Vancouver yesterday for Australia on their tour around the world, which will take about a year. . . .

79

"Mark Twain Talks," *Daily News-Advertiser* (Vancouver), 20 August 1895, 5.

The scribes found Mark Twain in bed when they called on him last Sunday morning at the Hotel Vancouver by appointment. He was reclining in a sitting posture with his head at the foot of the bed in order to catch the light. There was a cigar between his lips and a copy of the *News-Advertiser* between his fingers. He received his visitors with the utmost cordiality and his voice, though not yet quite free from hoarseness, suggested that sonorousness and volume for which in its natural state it is remarkable. The scribes gathered around the great man, while Major Pond, his celebrated "business manager," assumed a point of vantage with a view of gauging his client's physical limitations.

It would be hard to say what Mark Twain did not talk about. The scribes expressed a hope that R.M.S. *Warrimoo* would convey the humorist and his family in safety to their destination and apropos of the subject mentioned the *Miowera*'s predilection for running on to hidden rocks. At the same time they did not forget to add, no lives were ever lost and beyond the damage to the steamer itself, these several experiences were unmarked by casualties. Mark Twain said he was looking for a ship of that kind—a ship with the rock habit, and one which never allowed such mishaps to disconcert her, but always got off again. The conversation gradually turned on Thursday evening's lecture and the inability of some people to perceive the point of a joke. Thus one well-known citizen would insist on giving the lecturer's flights of fancy a literal interpretation. Mark Twain ascribed the effect of a lecturer, humorous or otherwise, to the audience as much as to the lecturer. "When you have a crowded house," he said in substance, "some subtle magnetic influence seems to permeate the atmosphere, so that the recognition of the speaker's intention by the audience is unanimous. It often happens that when one is telling a joke to three or four listeners, only one out of that number will perceive its meaning, but with a large auditory, it is invariably the large majority. The depressing influence of a small audience is due to several causes. In the first place, the individual members of that audience feel sorry for the lecturer. Mentally they put themselves in his position and sympathize with him—such is the charitable disposition of most people. But should the lecturer become scared and rattled their attitude changes from sympathy to contempt and contempt is fatal. The sympathetic attitude is hard to fight against and the ability to do so only comes with experience. Personally some of my most enthusiastic audiences have been small ones. I remember on one occasion many years ago, I delivered a lecture in St. Louis. The hall was a very large one, with a seating capacity of about 1,600 persons I believe, no galleries, but every seat occupying the same level. The night was terribly stormy and there were perhaps 30 people in the hall and with that exception a vast acreage of chair backs confronted me.[1] The feeling of a lecturer at such junctures should not be despondent. Every man's presence should be regarded as an individual compliment. If there are only 15 people present there are compliments and it surely is not necessary to multiply a compliment by 50 in order to appreciate it. I requested everybody present to come forward and sit in a solid phalanx. It was like lecturing to the disciples on the edge of the Sahara but I started off, and instead of lecturing for an hour and a half only, I kept it up for more than two hours. Among my auditory, as I afterwards learned, was H. M. Stanley, who took down the lecture in shorthand."[2]

The reporters satisfied themselves en passant, as to the authenticity of Mark Twain's story of his terrifying juvenile experience in his father's office, when the moonbeams released the horrible spectacle of a murdered man slain the same day in a street row. "This actually happened to me," said he, "the kind of thing calculated to scare a boy to death."

Major Pond took advantage of a favorable moment to adjust what Mark Twain calls his "cartridge box," to wit a kodak, but before he touched it off at this interesting if unconventional group, Mark Twain removed a wax candle which stood behind his head. "When electricity first came into general use," said he, "I was happy. Formerly, when staying at some hotel I would enter my bedroom and find the gas jet turned down, as I thought, and feeling inclined for a read and a smoke I would attempt to turn it up only to find that the flame was at its maximum. Sometimes I would complain and solicit an amelioration of this state of affairs. Then the hotel people had recourse to a trick, which I soon became aware of and one which has never deceived me since. A waiter would put on a pair of overalls and pretend to be an engineer, or a plumber or some such thing. He would tinker with the gas as long as I remained at the hotel, but never improved it as far as I could see. Consequently I found it useful to travel with a wax candle, and when the electric light was introduced into hotels, I was among the first to rejoice. But recommencing at some meridian the exact position of which is ambiguous and proceeding westwards, the hotels seem to be consumed with a spirit of economy. The electric light is only turned on at a certain hour in the evening and no matter how dark or foggy the day may be—so dark that even those who dwelt in Egyptian darkness would find it impossible to see—unless otherwise provided you cannot obtain artificial light. So even now my wax candle has its uses."

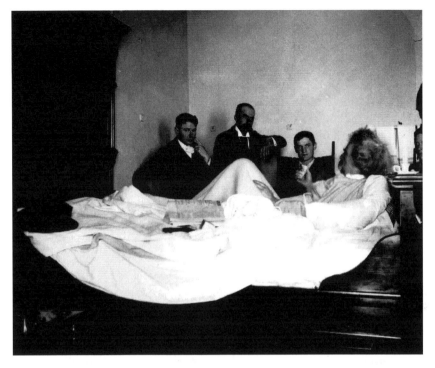

5. Mark Twain and reporters in Vancouver, B.C., 18 August 1895. Courtesy of Kevin Mac Donnell.

Mark Twain talked feelingly and eloquently and on many subjects, while others were dealt with in a lighter vein of badinage which provoked many a laugh, until at length the Major rose and in his capacity of manager declared the interview at an end. "If I didn't," he added, "he would talk all day." Before the scribes departed, Mark Twain presented each of them with a portrait of himself, to which he there and then attached his autograph. Then with a hearty handshake and wishes for a pleasant voyage to the Antipodes, the interview terminated.

Notes to Interview 79

1. MT delivered his Sandwich Islands lecture in St. Louis on the evening of 26 March 1867. According to Paul Fatout in *Mark Twain on the Lecture Circuit* (Bloomington: Indiana University Press, 1960), 72–73, "stormy weather greatly diminished the audience" that evening. See also *MTL*, 4:280n8; and Fatout, 214–15.

2. Henry M. Stanley (1841–1904) covered MT's lecture for the *St. Louis Missouri Democrat*; the American journalist is best known today for finding the Scottish explorer David Livingstone in Ujiiji, a town in Tanzania, in 1871.

80

"Twain's Programme," *San Francisco Examiner,* 24 August 1895, 6.

In connection with Mark Twain's announcement of his financial programme, published in *The Examiner* of last Saturday,[1] the more extended statement which follows is of interest. It was given to his nephew,[2] who is connected with *The Examiner,* and who suggested to him the advisability of taking the public into his confidence through its columns:

> Never mind interviewing me. I've nothing to do; lend me your pencil and let me say it myself.
>
> What am I lecturing around the world for? Your question is easily answered: It is for the benefit of the creditors of the wrecked firm of Charles L. Webster & Co.
>
> I furnished the capital for that concern. It made a fortune the first year, and wasted it in the second. After that it began to accumulate debts and kept this industry diligently up until the collapse came. My wife and I tried our best to save it; we emptied money down that bottomless hole as long as we had a penny left, but the effort went for nothing. When the crash came the firm owed my wife almost as much as it owed all the other creditors put together. By the advice of friends I turned over to her my copyrights, she releasing the firm and taking this perishable property in full settlement for her claim—property not worth more than half the sum owing to her. She wanted to turn her house in, too, and leave herself and the children shelterless; but she hadn't a friend who would listen to that for a moment. And I can say, with what is perhaps a pardonable pride and satisfaction, that there is not a single creditor who would be willing to let her do it. No; I am mistaken. I am forgetting one creditor, a printer. The ruined firm owed him about $5,000. He had made a neat little fortune out of Webster & Co., but that didn't signify; he wanted his money; he could not wait on my slow earnings, so he persecuted me with the law.
>
> No; I must not say anything more about that creditor just now. I will wait till I get time and room. As I understand it, your journal's usual issue contains only sixteen pages.
>
> I earned a good deal of money last year. I have left it all in New York. This money, added to the assets of our defunct firm, will pay off one-half of the firms's debts. A month ago I supposed it would take me a dreary, long time to earn the other half, but my eyes have been opened by this lecture trip across the continent. I find I have twenty-five friends in America where I thought I had only one. Look at that house in Cleveland, in the dead middle of July, with the mercury trying to crawl out

of the top of the thermometer. That multitude has repeated itself in every big town clear across to the Pacific. Did those unknown friends troop to my house in this perditionary weather to hear me talk? No; they came to shake hands and let me know that they were on deck and all was well. I shall be out of debt a long way sooner than I was supposing a month ago, before Cleveland spoke up and set the pace of my jog around the globe.

I shall be sixty years old in November. A month ago it grieved me to be under this load of debt at my time of life, but that feeling is all gone now. Such a burden is a benefaction, a prize in the lottery of life, when it lifts a curtain and shows you a continental spread of personal friends where you had supposed you had merely a good sprinkling of folks friendly to your books, but not particularly concerned about their author.

Consider—we fill the galleries of the opera houses—to hear a lecture! I think that that is a compliment worth being in debt for. The other day in Montana a stranger sent me this word: "You can draw on me for $5 a day until you are out of debt."

When our firm broke, Poultney Bigelow mailed me his check for $1,000 and didn't want to take it back again.[3] Douglas Taylor, printer, New York, said: "Draw on me for $1,000, and if you think you can't find a hundred men to do the like make me a bet and you will see." One dollar bills came in letters from here and there and yonder, from strangers, and I had to send them back. Does all this sound conceited? How would you feel yourself if this had happened to you? Wouldn't you feel pretty grateful and wouldn't you want to talk about it? Well, I am only human, and I like to talk about it. After the Press Club supper the other night in Tacoma one of the boys said: "It doesn't become you to consider yourself a man in misfortune; you are a man in luck; you have lost your fortune and found your friends, and the account is squared. As for the press of the country, look how it has treated you; not five newspapers have said an ungentle thing about you."

And so, let me sound my horn. It doesn't do you any harm, and I like the music of it.

Properly one-third of our dead firm's debts should be paid by my partner—but he has no resources. This is why I must pay them all. If I have time and health I can do it, and I think the creditors have confidence in me. And my wife and children are not troubled. They never knew anything about scrimping before, but they have learned it now; they know all about it these last two years, and whatever murmuring is done I do—not they.

My books? Several of them are in the hands of my pioneer publishers, the American Publishing Company of Hartford—all the others are in the hands of the Harpers. The Harpers will begin to issue them from new plates presently. The books will help pay the Webster debts. I turned them over to my wife to keep them from getting scattered, which would of course destroy their earning capacity—but she will touch none of the profit that can be spared to the creditors.

My trip means a year's lecturing all around the world, and thereafter a lecture trip all over the United States, beginning either at New York or San Francisco—the latter, I expect. My agent was a little afraid of San Francisco in summer. He thought we couldn't fairly expect to get great audiences. Maybe he was right, but I doubted it. It has been one of my homes.

Now that I reflect, perhaps it is a little immodest in me to talk about my paying my debts, when by my own confession I am blandly getting ready to unload them onto the whole English-speaking world. I didn't think of that. Well, no matter, as long as they get paid.

Lecturing is gymnastics, chest-expander, medicine, mind-healer, blues-destroyer, all in one. I am twice as well as I was when I started out—I have gained nine pounds in twenty-eight days, and expect to weigh 600 before January. I haven't had a blue day in all the twenty-eight. My wife and daughter are accumulating health and strength and flesh nearly as fast as I am. When we reach home a year hence I think we can exhibit as freaks.

Mark Twain,
Vancouver, B.C., August 15, 1895.

Notes to Interview 80

1. See interview 77.
2. Samuel Moffett (1860–1908), brother of Annie Moffett. See also reference to Charles L. Webster in n. 3 to interview 46.
3. Poultney Bigelow (1855–1954), American journalist and historian.

81

"Twain Very Ill," *New York World*, 4 September 1895, 8.

Vancouver, B.C., Aug. 28—Samuel L. Clemens sailed yesterday[1] for Sydney, with his wife and daughter and Mr. and Mrs. Pond, on his way around the world. He is in very poor health, and the voyage is undertaken in the hope that change of air and freedom from worry may avert the collapse which appears to threaten him.

After a long period of overwork came the shock of the acutest financial disaster possible for man to encounter—that is, he lost everything and is compelled, at a time when he should be resting as a reward for his years of labor, to start afresh the battle of life. Before sailing, the invalid received a party of newspaper men.

"I am glad to see you," said Mark Twain. "I am somewhat of a newspaper man myself, and we are a hard-up, happy, care-free lot, take us altogether. I do not want to tell you of my business troubles. I have never wanted to do that to anyone since one day years and years ago. The foreman of the horse-bill department of a publishing house with which I was connected printed a card with the legend: 'I have trouble of my own; don't tell yours,' and hung it up where those who ran might read. That card was a corrosion to my soul and seemed to eat into me, and the impression that it made has never been effaced. The whole world knows that I have been in financial difficulties. I have given my newspaper friends for publication a personal statement of how I stand and what I intend to do, so that I need not weary you with any further reference to tales of foreclosures or creditors.

"Just what to talk to you about is a difficult thing to decide," he said. "If I were before an audience I could size them up and know what to say, but you will talk to audiences larger and more diversified than ever was gathered in a hall to listen to me.

"Speaking of audiences," he continued, "a small audience is almost sure to become tainted with a feeling of sympathy for the man on the platform. Let that man become rattled, lose his nerve or in any way show that he is affected by the absence of a large audience, and that feeling is apt to turn to something akin to contempt that is fatal to the entertainer or lecturer, and talk he ever so wisely he cannot overcome it.

"It is necessary in such a case that the speaker should at once disabuse the minds of his audience of the idea that he is at all in need of sympathy, but should let them know that he kept a man to do the worrying over business features, and that he himself is utterly oblivious of the condition of things in the box-office.

"But about audiences. I remember very well, indeed, giving an address in the Exchange Building in the city of St. Louis. The Exchange Building was something like a barn that had gone to seed—one of those great, big, hollow, broad, expansive buildings all on a level. The whole would seat something like 1,500 people.

"The night that I spoke in that hall—it was in 1865, I think—there were twenty people gathered to hear me. I am not sure about their being gathered. I have a kind of an idea that they were people, the kind that lived in the hall— were fixtures, as it were, like the benches. But, anyway, I determined that, fixtures or not, I was going to give them that lecture; so I asked them all to

6. Mark Twain, Clara Clemens, and Olivia Clemens aboard the *Warrimoo,* 23 August 1895. Courtesy of Kevin Mac Donnell.

come and sit on the front bench, and then getting over as near the front of the platform as I could I talked right into their faces.

"Behind them stretched that fearful row of barren benches. It was like talking to people on the edge of the great Desert of Sahara, but we had a good time. The lecture was timed for an hour and a quarter, but we got along so well together and were having such a good time that I talked to those people over two hours, and they were the most enthusiastic audience I have ever had the pleasure of holding conversation with."[2]

Mark Twain here put his hand behind his head and in doing so knocked down the candle set at the foot of the bed. By the way, it may be said that with that charming manner that has always marked his actions, he had his feet in the bed where other people would have their heads. He said that it "kinder" felt more comfortable that way. "There goes that confounded candle again," said he. "I look on that candle as a sort of link between gloom and darkness; it is not very closely connected in my mind with the idea of light. I remember very well when most of the hotels were lighted with coal-oil lamps. They were

7. The last photo before departing for Australia aboard the *Warrimoo*, 23 August 1895. *Left to right:* J. B. Pond, Olivia Langdon Clemens, Mark Twain, Clara Clemens, Mrs. Pond. From J. B. Pond's *Eccentricities of Genius* (New York: Dillingham, 1900).

not bad; and if you could get the hall porter to let you have half a dozen of them you could generally decipher the difference between the outlines of the bed and bureau.

"When gas became more generally used I hailed it as a glorious innovation, but I soon discovered that the economical landlord has a way of dealing with that gaslight that left you a little bit worse off than you were with the lamps. Then came the electric light. I thought that when that came into general use we had at last got into an era of a good bedroom light, but I find that I have again been deceived. They put up a nice electrolier with about four burners on it, but you generally find that three of them have that smoky appearance that betokens a burnt out filament. You send word to the office to have it repaired. For this they keep a bellboy dressed up in overalls so as to look like an electrician. In response to your call up comes this suit of overalls with the bellboy inside of it and monkeys with the burners that won't light up. He pretends to fix them, but he never does. They continue non-illuminant up to the time of your departure.

"Besides that, I find that in most of the towns they run their electric light on a fixed-hour system. The light comes in at a certain time and goes out at a certain time. In this hotel, for example, we have to go to bed as a rule with the candle, because the light quits at 2 A.M. In these fixed-hour towns it does not make any difference how dark or gloomy the afternoon may be or how early the shades of evening gather round, you cannot get your light until a certain hour. If it gets dark at 6 P.M. you have to amuse yourself chasing shadows until 8."

Major Pond then forbade Mark Twain from talking any longer and the humorist dismissed his visitors with a farewell handshake.

Notes to Interview 81

1. Actually, on August 23.
2. See n. 1 to interview 79.

5

Across Australia, Asia, and Africa, 1895–1896
Interviews 82–120

∼

Twain, his wife, Olivia, and daughter Clara arrived in Sydney on September 16, 1895. His 116 performances between September 1895 and July 1896 enabled him to erase between a third and a half of his personal debt of eighty thousand dollars. His memoir of this lecture tour around the world, *Following the Equator,* would appear in 1897.

∼

82

"Arrival of Mark Twain" *Morning Herald* (Sydney), 16 September 1895, 4; rpt. "Mark Twain at Sydney," *Argus* (Melbourne), 16 September 1895, 5.

"Don't forget my soulful eyes. Under the circumstances I shall be unable to twist a diamond of superb brilliance on my forefinger as I talk to you; but don't forget my soulful eyes and deeply intellectual expression."

Thus Mr. Samuel Clemens, otherwise Mark Twain, as he leant over the rail of the *Warrimoo,* as she heaved up and down on the swell of Watson's Bay last night. These were the parting words of the conversation, and were called ironically out as the little launch sheered off for Sydney.

"What are my ideas and impressions in coming to Australia? I don't know. I'm ready to adopt any that seem handy. I don't believe in going outside accepted views. If there are any little things, for instance, that you would like to work off on me, fire away."

Our representative expressed a modest disclaimer to work off anything on the famous humorist, so the author of the "Jumping Frog" craned a little farther over the rail and tried to be as communicative as was possible under the circumstances. The circumstances weren't favorable. A hawser pipe blew off steam at the precise moment that Mark Twain opened his mouth, or if it didn't do that, it gurgled like an asthmatic giant, or else a steam winch started active work. Even a world-renowned laughmaker can't be expected to shine under such conditions.

"I'm going to write a book on Australia," called out Mr. Clemens, in a lull of the infamous noises. "I think I ought to start right now. You know so much more of a country when you haven't seen it than when you have. Besides, you don't get your mind strengthened by contact with the hard facts of things. The hardest facts for people who visit foreign places so as to write books are the local liars. They come out and stuff you with information you don't want, and then they asperse your memory ever after."

Well, we have had several books about Australia, evidently written under the sort of inspiration you describe. No doubt, every bookwriter strikes the native Ananias and incorporates him in his works, and suffers for it afterwards.

"What will be the subjects of my lectures? Well, I shall not take any set subjects. I shall speak of my reminiscences, personal anecdotes of my books, and grow generally discursive about myself and my labors."

Does it pain you much when you write anything humorous, Mr. Clemens?

"Not very much; I try it on the public first, and that takes the first sharp agony of the thing away.

"Yes, I know Max O'Rell was here.[1] I daresay you have heard of our little breeze. But it was he who did all the talking; after I had answered him in his own fashion I let him alone."

Then you are not going to fight a duel?

"No; I can disgrace myself nearer home, if I felt so inclined, than by going out to have a row with a Frenchman. The fact of the matter is I think Max O'Rell wanted an advertisement, and thought the best way to get it was to draw me. But I'm far too old a soldier for that sort of thing.

"Really, I don't know that I can tell you very much more. I didn't see the sea-serpent on the voyage across; but permit me to say that your harbor strikes me as being superb. I haven't seen it yet; but I'm sure it's magnificent from what I've heard about it. Anyway, it seems the correct sort of thing to say on this occasion. I would also add a few words about the beauties of your Post Office, but I don't like to throw my good things away on a quiet night like this. Good night."

And that is the end of the interview with the famous humorist, whom everyone has read, whom everyone has laughed with, except a few unfortunates whose diseases are not known to the pathology, and whom most will flock to see next Thursday.

Note to Interview 82

1. Lëon Paul Blouet, aka Max O'Rell (1848-1903), French author and journalist. See also n. 2 to interview 67.

83
Herbert Low, "Mark Twain: The Humorist's Arrival," *Evening News* (Sydney), 16 September 1895, 4.

Shortly after 7 o'clock this morning the *Warrimoo*, which had been anchored overnight in Watson's Bay, crushed into the wharf at Circular Quay. The crushing was a literal one. The fine steamer had rather more way on than was anticipated, and though a mild wave of excitement passed over the people standing about, the engines were reversed in time to avert serious damage to the wharf. On board the slight concussion was scarcely perceptible. When, sometime later, a representative of the *Evening News* incidentally mentioned the matter to Mark Twain, then quietly breakfasting, the distinguished humorist stood up and remarked dryly, "I suppose I'd better go and look after my traps and get off." Mr. Samuel Clemens, to give him his proper, if less familiar, name is not unlike the portraits of him which have been published. And this is saying a good deal. He is a lightly built man, of average height, with heavy moustache and eyebrows, and a luxuriant head of steel-gray hair. He is accompanied by Mrs. Clemens, a really charming lady, and one of his daughters.

"We had fine weather all the time," said he, speaking of his trip. "I heard people say we had rough seas on two days or rather one day and one night, but I have not heard any trustworthy person say so. My daughter and my wife both said so. But I know we had no rough weather on the whole voyage."

"You've seen our harbor?"

"Oh, yes! Indeed. They told me last night that everybody had to get up and testify about this harbor, and I don't wonder that they are required to do so. There is not a city in the world that would not be infatuated with this harbor, and be able to stand chaffing about it, because it justifies everybody's praises of it. As for anyone to try and convey with a pen what this harbor is, it is impossible. I have read descriptions of it. You get a general idea that there is something unusual about it, but what the harbor is you do not make out at all."

"To whom or what are we indebted for your visit to Australia at this time, seeing that all previous efforts to induce you to come failed?"

"All efforts always did fail because I was rich. Now that I am heavily in debt (that is other people got me into debt!) I am in a way responsible for what these people have done. I must get out, I said, to get money to pay these creditors. The lecture platform is rather hard work, but it is the quickest way to pay these debts and get them out of my way.

"Do I like lecturing? After I am on the platform I do. Lecturing in the United States is no small matter, when in the depth of winter you have to travel from point to point in all kinds of weather except good weather. As a rule about lecturing, you have to get up too late in the morning, and go to bed too early at night. If you could turn things round I should like it."

"Do you think it rather early yet to give your impressions of this country?"

"Well, yes. The country has only been visible to me since half-past 6 this morning. I see you have in mind the average globe-trotter. Now, globe-trotters' impressions are valuable to two sets of people. They are valuable to people who are familiar with the ground and know they are mainly mistakes. That is pleasant reading. There can be nothing pleasanter than the man who tells you something that you know better than he does. The second class of people to whom they are valuable are those who know nothing about the subject. Such a man is in the receptive attitude. He takes in everything, if it is pleasantly and judiciously said, and two things are accomplished—the man is pleasant, and thinks he is being informed. We must never undervalue the globe-trotter's efforts. We must remember, in charity, that we are all globe-trotters, that is to say, if ever we are to see anything."

Our conversation was here interrupted by a call from Mrs. Clemens, who in the bustle of preparing to get ashore required her husband's counsel. The writer begged indulgence for one more question, an indulgence which she granted generously.

"What about the duel between yourself and Mr. Max O'Rell?"

"Max O'Rell had no object in the world in intruding upon a private matter like a magazine article written by me about Bourget.[1] It was infamously offensive and impertinent in a person of Max O'Rell's literary standing (which is a cipher in America and England, I don't know what it is here), to introduce himself into a matter which did not concern him, where he was not invited to appear, and would not have appeared if he had anything above a hostler's manners or breeding. Max O'Rell's twaddle about a duel began and ended in some talk of his in Chicago, when he thought I was in France. I have a family, and some self-respect acquired by great labor and pains, and I cannot afford to sacrifice them in fighting a duel with anybody in this age of the world, and in an English-speaking country. I never saw the day I would risk a life so precious as mine on the dueling field except in the innocent form of dueling that prevails in Max O'Rell's country. Max O'Rell doubtless had that sort of duel in his mind, for to fight a duel with somebody would be of some use to him as an advertisement in America, where he goes to earn his living on the platform, not being able to earn it on the European side of the water. But I did not choose to be his advertising medium. I would not be assisting in advertising him now but for the fact that his lecture season in America does not begin until next winter, by which time these remarks about him will be forgotten.

"As for Bourget, he is a man of great literary reputation and capacity. He was a target worth practicing at for fun, and I said nothing about him that could be construed as a personality. I said nothing offensive about him. He is an entirely respectable person. But I would not go down into the gutter to find somebody to have a literary controversy with, and I would have to go thereto find Max O'Rell. As a literary person I conceive he had no rank whatever.

"Perhaps I have said enough about Max O'Rell. I hope one day to meet him in —," said Mark Twain, rising, his charming wife who evidently divined what he was going to say, smothering the word by placing a delicate hand over his mouth, at the same time telling the writer to be sure not to put that in.

Note to Interview 83

1. Lëon Paul Blouet, aka Max O'Rell (1848–1903), French author and journalist. See also n. 2 to interview 67.

84

[Herbert Low?] "Mark Twain in Sydney: A Further Interview," *Argus* (Melbourne), 17 September 1895, 5.

Mark Twain landed in Sydney today. He is spare and undersized, and there is nothing about him to fill the eye. Physically he is disappointing. Intellectually he is like many another humorist; he seems cast in a somewhat somber mould.

"Life," he said, looking from beneath his fair shaggy eyebrows, "is not at all a humorous thing. I have never found it a joke, and I am serious if nothing else. Man as a normal creature is serious now and then. One of us, say a scribbler like myself, pen in hand, may get a moment of enlightenment. A sudden thought may slip in, and then comes humor. That, however, is a contribution which the gods have sent his way, and which really is not of man. It comes from some place, the key of which he does not possess to open it at his will. Yes, life is serious, and man is the most serious part of it.

"Now you have heard," he continued, "that I am the laziest man in the United States, yet I tell you, and I believe, it is perfectly demonstrable that there is no such being as a perfectly lazy man. Just consider that every man has a gift either large or small. It may be to play billiards or to imitate Paderewski.[1] Whatever that gift is man takes a native delight in exploiting it, and it is a most difficult thing to prevent him from exercising that gift. There are hundreds of interests that the human race possesses. In the case of any particular man ninety-nine out of a hundred of these interests may not appeal to him, so that so far as they are concerned he is the laziest of beings. He is too lazy to do this, too lazy to do that, but when you arrive at his gift he is not lazy. It is difficult then to keep him from working night and day. So I frankly admit that in regard to many human things, I am, if you like to use the term, phenomenally lazy, lazy in every way that you can possible imagine, until it comes to writing a book. Then there is no more industrious man in the world than myself. Let me alone and I will work with my pen until I drop from fatigue. Then the only trouble my family have with me is digging me out of my chair when my day's work is done. To the extent I describe, then, I am lazy or industrious just as you please. Understand, I don't philosophize. I leave that for newspapers to do. I simply state a fact."

Having thus swept away what evidently was looked on somewhat as a personal aspersion Mark Twain discursively alluded to one of his most memorable experiences.

"I was in London for a day," he remarked, "but that day lives with me forever. There is only one London. It is unique. I went there to meet my old friend, Mr. Stanley, and he was good enough to bring some 75 or a 100 of his friends to greet me.[2] There was not one of the men present who had not earned his claim to personal distinction. As I chatted with them the thought was always present, 'This is not the only gathering of the kind in London. There are many more roofs here covering the world's great tonight.' That thought has lived with me, and I want to be told where today is there another city which can produce such a spectacle without effort. The wealth and intellect of the world is centralized there. It is wonderful, and what cannot be said of the nation which has evolved such a city! That day's visit certainly was one of my most memorable experiences.

"Then, if you ask what man has impressed me most, I hardly know what to say. Still I think above all men I would put General Grant. His was a grand figure and his was a noble nature. It was so simple and so beautiful. Standing face to face with him you looked at a man with a mighty record, and yet it was not the knowledge of that fact, but the man's latent power that was so impressive with him. It was just as with the Reverend Thomas Starr King, of San Francisco, who was so renowned a preacher in that city thirty years ago.[3] It was the perseverance of that man that distinguished him above others. So it was with General Grant. Of course, General Grant had great contemporaries. There were Sheridan and Stonewall Jackson, the latter with his deep religious fervor—just such another as Gordon, and the former with his profanity.[4] Oh, my! he could swear. Still, I suppose, after all, that was merely a matter of environment. If he had the same training and the same surroundings as General Jackson I suppose he would have been much the same.

"Do I mind saying what I think about Bret Harte?" said Mark Twain in reply to an inquiry. "No. But mind if I speak strongly it is merely a personal opinion. I detest him, because I think his work is 'shoddy.' His forte is pathos which does not come out of a man's heart. He has no heart, except his name, and I consider he has produced nothing that is genuine. He is artificial. That opinion, however, must be taken with some allowance, for, as I say, I do not care for the man."[5]

Mark Twain uttered this sentence with an emphasis that left no doubt as to his earnestness, and then went on to say, "I have no objection to my views being known. It is purely a personal criticism. I dare say, when I go to London, I shall meet him, but what of that?[6] I am most moderate in my dislikes. There are only three or four persons in the world to whom I have had any antipathy, and the Almighty has removed most of them. It does seem wonderful that I should not have been allowed to get at them before they died. On the other hand, I have devoured what Rudyard Kipling has written. He is wonderful, and, strange to say, I met him before he was known to fame.[7] One day when I was stopped at a country place for the summer I got a card, on which was written that the bearer had come from Allahabad or some such place, fourteen thousand miles way, to see me. Now, this I took to be a tremendous compliment, and then when he was admitted he said he had only traveled from New York. Well, that was 275 miles, so I forgave him his story. His card fell into the hands of my daughter who, impressed with what he had written on it, and the compliment paid me, kept it 12 months. Later, Kipling's name was in everyone's mouth, but I had not the slightest idea that he was the man who had rung in the 14,000-mile fiction on me till I read the account of his tour in the London *World*. Then I realized that he was identical with my visitor of 12 months' before, and sent my daughter to look up the card, which she had fortunately kept. We have met frequently since then, and he is a most interesting personage. We in the United States, of course, look up to Nathaniel Hawthorne as possessing that something which marks genius and makes man live forever. It is always remarkable to me that he should have written such incisive English at a time when that was not the prevailing style of authors, and it is still more remarkable when you travel on the Continent to find that the one book which has been translated as the best type of American literature is *Helen's Babies*."[8]

Notes to Interview 84

1. See n. 1 to interview 74.
2. On Stanley, see n. 2 to interview 79. MT apparently is recalling the Royal Geographical Society dinner in Stanley's honor in London on 21 October 1871. See also *MTL*, 5:199–201.
3. Thomas Starr King (1824–64), a prominent Unitarian minister, pastor of the First Unitarian Church in San Francisco from 1860 until his death.
4. Philip Sheridan (1831–88), Union army general; Thomas J. (Stonewall) Jackson (1824–63), Confederate army general; John B. Gordon (1832–1904), Confederate general, later a U.S. senator (1873–80, 1891–97) and governor of Georgia (1886–90).

5. Harte responded to MT's comments in "Kate Carew's 12-Minute Interview on 12 Subjects with Bret Harte," *New York World Sunday Magazine,* 22 December 1901, 5: "I always considered that we were friends until that trip of his to Australia, and there, it appears, he attacked me in a most savage and unprovoked manner—denounced me as a feeble sentimentalist, and altogether gave it to be understood that Art and I were strangers. I've never been able to understand his sudden change of attitude. It was foolish of him, too, for I have a great many friends in Australia, and it was inevitable that all this should come to my ears." See also nn. 3 and 4 to interview 8.

6. In fact, MT and Harte never met again.

7. See interview 50.

8. The popular novel *Helen's Babies* (1876) by John Habberton (1842-1921).

85

[Herbert Low?] "Visit of Mark Twain: Wit and Humour," *Morning Herald* (Sydney), 17 September 1895, 5-6.

When you sit down to "interview" Mark Twain he makes a remark that recalls the stock observation of the member of Parliament who is about to inflict himself disastrously on time and space. "I have very little to say," he begins. But this is where the simile—which no doubt is as unsatisfactory as similes generally are—begins and ends. Whereas it is found that the "little" of the politician is mostly less than nothing, the case is exactly opposite with Mark Twain. It is his modest way of putting it. As [Francis] Bacon quaintly puts it, he is full of "fruit," and the longer you talk to him the more do you realize the fund of original matter that lies at the base of the composition of the man who has made so many continents laugh. With his cautious American accent, that seems to give the expression of weighing every sentence as it is put forth, Mark Twain is really a brilliant conversationalist, and when you touch a point beneath the good-humouredly satirical armor of reserve that he wears, quick to reveal the more serious side of his nature. The great difficulty is to gather up his points as he branches from topic to topic, for his flight is as discursive as his fancy is untrammeled.

"What is humor?" he says with a laugh, as some suggestive sidewind of conversation takes his mind that way. "What is humor? It is as difficult almost to answer as the more important question put by Pilate.[1] It is easy enough often to say what it is not; but an exact scientific definition—it seems like trying to transfix a sunbeam. I suppose no man ever knew why he had humor, and where he got it from, exactly what constituted a humorous idea, or in what way it first appealed to him. Life has been finely defined as 'a tragedy to those who feel—a comedy to those who think.'[2] That is a very fine definition of the main qualities that go to make the humorist. I maintain that a man can never be a humorist, in thought or in deed, until he can feel the springs of pathos. Indeed, there you have a basis of something material to go upon in trying to comprehend what this impalpable thing of true humor is. Trust me, he was never yet properly funny who was not capable at times of being very serious. And more: the two are as often as not simultaneous. Whilst a man sees what we call the humorous side he must have ever present the obverse; those who laugh best and oftenest know that background."

You don't believe there is such a being who simply laughs, as the poet sings, because he must?

"The true and proper laughter, 'the sudden glory of laughter' as Addison has it, doesn't come in that causeless way.[3] Look at all the humorists and their creations, their subtle contrasts and their exquisite breaks of laughter—can't you see behind it all the depth and the purpose of it? Look at the poor fool in *Lear;* look at Lamb,[4] getting the quaintest, most spirit-moving effects with the tears just trembling on the verge of every jest; look at Thackeray and Dickens, and all the bright host who have gained niches in the gallery of the immortals. They have one thing always in their mind, no matter what parts they make their puppets play. Behind the broadest grins, the most exquisitely ludicrous situations, they know there is the grinning skull, and that all roads lead along the dusty road to death. Ah, don't think there is such a thing as a mere 'corner man'[5] in literature any more than there is in any other department of life. I say that the clown rolling in the sawdust at a circus to the shrieks of the children knows and feels the truth that I have tried to explain. Don't you remember what Garrick said to a friend, 'You may fool the town in tragedy, but they won't stand any nonsense in comedy.'[6] It is so true! Any pretender can cast up the whites of his eyes to the heavens and roll out his mock heroics, but the comedian must have the genuine ring in him. Otherwise he couldn't be a comedian.

"With modern writers of fiction I confess I have no very extensive acquaintance. I read little but the 'heaviest' sort of literature—history, biography, travels. I have always had a fear that I should get into someone else's style if I dabbled among the modern writers too much, and I don't want to do that. As I have never studied any of the great models, I can outrage them all with impunity.

"Among those I have read, though, let me say that [William S.] Gilbert seems to me a perfectly delightful and exquisite humorist. How perfectly charming is the lambent play of his fancy! and when I read his operas I am struck dumb with astonishment. It seems to me marvelous that a man should have this gift of saying not only the wittiest of things, but of saying them in verse! I don't think there are many better examples, in their way, of my philosophisings about humor up above than Gilbert's Jack Point.[7] There you have the humor mingling and floating in a sea of pathos. Lewis Carroll always appealed to me as a true and subtle humorist; but I must fain confess that with the years I have lost much of my youthful admiration for Dickens. In saying so, it seems a little as if one were willfully heretic; but the truth must prevail. I don't know where it is exactly, but I cannot laugh and cry with him as I was wont. I seem to see all the machinery of the business too clearly, the effort is too patent. The true and lasting genius of humor does not drag you thus to boxes labeled 'pathos,' 'humor,' and show you all the mechanism of the inimitable puppets that are going to perform. How I used to laugh at Simon Tappertit, and the Wellers, and a host more![8] But I can't do it now somehow; and time, it seems to me, is the true test of humor. It must be antiseptic.

"Yes, I have often discussed, and often heard discussed, the distinction between wit and humor. I can't say that I have ever heard a satisfactory definition. It is more to be felt than realized and explained. Probably there is an imperceptible touch of something permanent that one feels instinctively to adhere to true humor, whereas wit may be the mere conversational shooting up of 'smartness'—a bright feather, to be blown into space the second after it is launched. I admit it is always difficult to reconcile any definition of the two kindred qualities; but by general, if tacit, consent Wit seems to be counted a very poor relation to Humor. I suppose that [Alexander] Pope was one of the wittiest writers who ever put pen to paper; and yet most of us agree that he was 'artificial.' Now, humor is never artificial."

Mr. Clemens, it has been said more than once that you are the laziest man in the world.

"I think that is a mistaken notion. I don't think there ever was a lazy man in this world. Every man has some sort of gift, and he prizes that gift beyond all others. He may be a professional billiard-player, or a Paderewski,[9] or a poet—I don't care what it is. But whatever it is, he takes a native delight in exploiting that gift, and you will find it difficult to beguile him away from it. Well, there are thousands of other interests occupying other men, but those interests don't appeal to the special tastes of the billiard champion or Paderewski. They are set down, therefore, as too lazy to do that or do this—to do, in short, what they have no taste or inclination to do. In that sense, then, I am phenomenally lazy. But when it comes to writing a book—I am not lazy then. My family find it difficult to dig me out of my chair.

"Oh, yes I have met many interesting men in my wanderings round the world. Not long ago I dined with Stanley in London.[10] There were about 80 guests, and not one of them, I think, was not distinguished in some way. Oh, what a marvelous place London is! I think the most interesting personality I ever encountered was General Grant. How and where he was so much larger than other men I had ever met I cannot describe. It was the same sort of feeling, I suppose that made my friend, Thomas Starr King,[11] whilst listening to a celebrated preacher, turn to me and exclaim, 'Whereabouts in that figure does that imperial power reside.' You had that feeling with Grant exactly.

"Of modern light literature I don't read much, as I have said; but harking back to that topic for a moment I should like to say how I revel in Kipling. A strange coincidence I found out after I had read his first books was that he had come some 275 miles one day for the express purpose of seeing me.[12] I was living in Elmira, and one day Kipling came down from New York and handed in his card. He had written on it 'From Allahabad,' in his laconic way. I felt flattered at the time that he should have come so far out of his way to visit me, and doubly so when I found out afterwards who he was. Bret Harte I consider sham and shoddy, and he has no pathos of the real true kind.[13] The works of Francis Cable I have been reading lately,[14] and they appeal very strongly to me. Some of his scenes are beautiful little vignettes drawn in strong and simple lines.

"About American politics? Well, I have been out of the run of them for some years. Of course, we have found out that an omnipotent democracy is not an unmitigated blessing; but America is not governed by the people, as you seem to think. She only seems to be—it is her politicians who do the governing. Once upon a time, about 14 years ago, we had a strong third party, and that party attracted some of the best men in the country to it. The Mugwumps, as they were called, went down in a subsequent Presidential election before the folly of the people, and it hasn't reappeared.[15] But it's wanted badly enough. It seems to me that you've got right at the basis of things if you have that strong third party with the best men in it. It doesn't matter what their views are, so long as they are the best men. And now," concluded Mr. Clemens, "having thoroughly established my reputation for humor by talking of politics seriously, I shall stop."

And it was necessary to. To properly "do" Mark Twain one would have to bring him out in a serial tale.

Notes to Interview 85

1. "What is truth?" Pilate's words in John 18:38.
2. Horace Walpole (1717-97) in a 1770 letter to Sir Horace Mann.
3. MT misattributes the quotation to Joseph Addison (1672-1719). As Budd (1974), 20n19, suggests, MT cites instead Thomas Hobbes's *Leviathan,* part 1, chapter 6: "Sudden glory is the passion which maketh those grimaces called laughter."
4. Charles Lamb (1775-1834), English essayist.
5. MT is apparently referring to the last man (or sometimes a couple of men at either end, "the corners") in a row of performers at a minstrel show; he would carry on humorous dialogue with the interlocutor.
6. An apocryphal anecdote popular around the turn of the century about David Garrick (1717-79), English actor and playwright. (See Florence M. W. Parson, *Garrick*

and His Circle [New York: Putnam's, 1906], 78.) The story was apparently based on Garrick's lines in the prologue to Oliver Goldsmith's play *She Stoops to Conquer* (1773): "If Comedy forsake us, / They'll turn us out, and no one else will take us. . . . I give it up—morals won't do for me; / To make you laugh, I must play tragedy."

    7. A major character in Gilbert and Sullivan's *Yeoman of the Guard* (1888).

    8. Weller was Samuel Pickwick's servant in Dickens's *Pickwick Papers* (1836-37). MT also refers to Simon Tappertit in Dickens's *Barnaby Rudge* (1841).

    9. See n. 1 to interview 74.

    10. See n. 2 to interview 79 and n. 2 to interview 84.

    11. See n. 3 to interview 84.

    12. See interview 50.

    13. See n. 5 to interview 84.

    14. MT refers to George Washington Cable, whom the reporter mistakenly calls Francis. On MT and Cable, see chapter 2.

    15. Mugwumps were liberal or reform Republicans who bolted the GOP in 1884.

86

[Herbert Low?] "A Ramble with Mark Twain: His Views on Men and Things," *Daily Telegraph* (Sydney), 17 September 1895, 5.

He was standing at the bar of the Australia Hotel. Two friends were with him, and if one might judge from appearance, they were all three drinking whisky "cocktails." Mark Twain, as he subsequently confided to the writer, drinks whisky without any sugar in it. He once found out that whisky with sugar in it disagreed with him. So, instead of abandoning the whisky, as some dull people might have done, he "swore off" the sugar and the lemon, and thus made the discovery that in itself whisky is one of the most harmless, as well as one of the most agreeable, of beverages. He took a sip of the "cocktail," put the glass down on the bar, and went on with his story. The listeners seemed mightily amused. What it was all about is more than anyone beyond earshot would venture to imagine. Mark Twain's hands were moving up and down like two ships at sea, and this was happening by way of illustration to a narrative spoken with extreme "deliberation," and in tones that we are wont to describe as "nasal." The great humorist's hair is thick and bushy, and well streaked with gray; also, innocent of recent acquaintance with the barber's shears. He wears a glossy silk hat, with a rakish curl about the brim; dull-black clothes, of Yankee cut; a small black necktie, fastened in a bow; and tan shoes that he will, perhaps, make up his mind to get polished when the shine begins to grow dim on the outside of the hat. The most conspicuous feature about Mark Twain's face—as, indeed, it is about most people's—is his nose. It is not the kind of nose that seems designed for scenting humor afar off. On the contrary, it is a thin, beaky nose that sniffs the words as they filter through the heavy gray moustache beneath it, and follows the trail in all sorts of quaint and unexpected directions. His eyes twinkle from beneath his bushy eyebrows like a pair of merry stars seen through the boughs of an overhanging tree. They are essentially kind eyes. Indeed, if there is one thing that appeals to you more than his bubbling humor, when once you have got fairly into conversation with him, it is the simplicity and kindness of his nature.

Mark Twain (it sounds more familiar than Mr. Clemens) was just off to Falk's studio to sit for a photograph. He asked the writer to "go along." On the way, there he talked of the Sydney *Bulletin,* a copy of which he had seen for the first time that morning, and *Punch* and *Puck.*[1] He did not understand *Punch,* he confessed. "To appreciate *Punch* I guess one wants to live on the inside of the things they write about," he said. *Puck,* on the other hand, he liked because he did understand it, and because there was a delicacy and an absence of grotesque exaggeration about the drawings. In the anteroom at Falk's the conversation took a political turn. Mark Twain, like Colonel Bell, is a freetrader, as those who have read his *Yankee at the Court of King Arthur* have reason for remembering.[2] "I don't profess to be learned in matters of this kind," he said, "but my instinct teaches me that protection is wrong. Surely it is wrong that on the Pacific Slope they should be compelled to bring their iron from the east when they might get it landed at a much lower price direct from foreign ships at their own door." He added that the chapter bearing on the question in his *Yankee at the Court of King Arthur* was penned at a time when one of the New York papers was publishing a great deal about the progress of New South Wales under freetrade. Later on, speaking of land nationalization, he said: "I have nothing that could properly be called 'views' on the subject. That would be too strong a phrase for a person who thinks so loosely and studies so loosely as I do; but it has seemed to me, from reading Henry George's books and some others in the same vein,[3] that if we could stop now and start again, and let the Government own the land, and lease it to people who would work it, and not leave it lying idle, that would be a measure of justice. But I do not see how so prodigious a revolution like that could be brought about without stopping dead and starting again; and to do that would mean a sort of revolution that is not to be brought about in this world except by bloodshed."

Presently Mr. Barnett, the proprietor of the studios, came in to announce that everything was ready; also to ask that Mrs. Clemens and Miss Clemens would favor him with a sitting. To that Mr. Clemens readily agreed, advising that word should be sent to the hotel for them to come "right up." Ten minutes later two ladies in traveling dresses appeared at the door of the anteroom, and were immediately conducted to the operating room, where the distinguished visitor was still undergoing familiar ordeal. When they had all "got through" Mr. Clemens returned alone, and was preparing to take his departure, when one of the ladies, who had apparently forgotten something, ran back up the stairs again, and, stepping lightly up to him, said a few words in a marvelously soft voice, and once more disappeared. This was Mark Twain's daughter—a beautiful girl, perhaps twenty years of age, with a face like a New England Madonna. Mr. Clemens has two other daughters, both of them at present in America. They do not inherit his gift of humor, he says, but evidently, from the stories he tells of them, they are singularly sweet and affectionate daughters. The youngest of them invaded his sanctum one Sunday morning when they were all living in Paris, and catching him at work on a book gently remonstrated with him for breaking the Sabbath. What would her mother say if she knew about it? Did he not think it was very wicked? Hadn't he better leave off right then? And so on. The reply was characteristic. That was his room—his own particular den. Everybody else was a trespasser there. Whatever she saw there was seen in confidence. On her honor she must not tell her mother. Besides, was he the only person at work in the house? What about the doctor who had just gone upstairs? "Oh, that was different," the girl replied. "The doctor's come to give mamma her medicine." "But I suppose he'll get paid for it?" suggested the father. "Well, a gentleman with a broken leg told me the other day he laughed over one of my books until he forgot all about his broken leg. So remember, whenever you see me at work on Sundays, that I'm preparing medicine for broken legs, and, like the doctor, I'm going to get paid for it."

Downstairs Mr. Barnett showed a photograph of Sir Henry Parkes to his visitor.[4] It was a magnificent specimen of photography—for all the world like a perfect etching, if, indeed, it would be possible for the human hand to trace lines so fine and so soft. Mr. Clemens was delighted with the work, and, commenting upon the subject, said that Sir Henry had a truly splendid head, and that it was hard to believe that he could make the bitter speeches that he had heard attributed to him. "Young men often come to me," said Mr. Barnett, "to ask me to take their photographs in this style; but you can't do it with a young man, you know." "No," said Mr. Clemens, pathetically. "It takes a great many years for Time to get all those things together to put into a human face." From Falk's we strolled across to the Town-hall; and when once in the gallery of the enormous room, with a public speaker's instinct, Mr. Clemens was wishful to try its acoustic properties. So, leaving him in the eastern gallery, the writer went to the platform of the building; and, excepting for the echo, due to the emptiness of the place, heard distinctly the few words that were spoken, as he was afterwards assured, in a conversational tone of voice. "I'm always trying to impress people with the fact," said Mr. Clemens, as he passed out into the street again, "that it's not the size of a building that kills the voice. The size of the building don't count. It's the construction that is everything."

And now Mark Twain divulged the secret that he never ate more than two meals a day—breakfast and dinner; and, consequently, that he had nothing important to think of until 3 o'clock that afternoon, when he had promised to meet a gentleman at his hotel. Accordingly, he set off with the writer for a stroll round the Domain, commenting upon the picturesqueness of Sydney from whatever point of view you looked at it, and inquiring, amongst other things, about the woodblocks with which the street were, to his mind, so admirably paved. A walk round Mrs. Macquarie's Chair is agreeable at any time.[5] On such a day, however, and in the company of such a man, it is an incident of no ordinary kind. From the moment Mr. Clemens and his companion turned their backs upon the city, until they came to their moorings again in the Australia Hotel, he talked without ceasing. This much should be said, however, that Mark Twain's talking is something like his walking—a peculiar amble. He says one word at a time, and makes a distinct pause before he gives utterance to another. Sometimes you think he's finished what he intended to say, and then just as you are about to chip in with a remark you find your mistake out. The way he tells a story, too—in conversation, as in print—is equally his own. None but Mark Twain would dare to break in upon his own remarks (and other people's) with yarn after yarn that seem at the outset, and long after he has got well under way with them, to have no bearing upon the subject, and still to go on meandering farther and farther off into the bush, whilst his listeners are wondering where on earth he will eventually land them. But then, of course, seeing that it is Mark Twain, you know that it will all come right in the end. And in the end it does come right. After carrying you round a vast circle of fact and fiction he sets you down at last on your very doorstep, with more knowledge of your own environment than you ever had before.

On the whole, the conversation turned on serious subjects. Talking of plagiarism in literature, he said that a friend once charged him with having "borrowed" for one of his books a dedication to a volume of poetry by Oliver Wendell Holmes. He denied having "borrowed" anything in that sense for any book he ever wrote. So they went into the first bookseller's shop they came to, and there, sure enough, after seeing his own dedication by the side of Dr. Holmes', he was forced to admit that for practical purposes the two were identical, and that his was not the original. Of course, the coincidence caused him a good deal of worry; and sitting down in his study when he got home, he wrote off to the Autocrat, asserting his innocence and expressing his regret. Oliver Wendell Holmes replied just as anybody would have expected him to reply—but a letter full of generous sympathy. "The fact was," said Mr. Clemens, "several years before writing the dedication to my book I had spent a week or more in bed at a hotel in the country, and the only thing

I could find to read was a volume of Dr. Holmes' poems. I began with the dedication and read them through. I read them backwards and forwards time after time; and, do you know, at the time I wrote my own dedication I had forgotten every poem in the book, and indeed the mere fact that I had read the book at all. The dedication, however, had been lying dormant in my mind all these years, and unconsciously, in providing one for my own book, I had reproduced it. I fancy that we remember things in cycles. Some people's memories are bottomless. Mine is like a basket with a hole in the bottom. Most things tumble through, but now and then one sticks there in the most unexpected way."[6]

Speaking of books, Mr. Clemens said that he had not read *Trilby* yet.[7] He had read two or three chapters in a magazine, but had never read the book as a whole. Nor had he seen the play. Both book and play had been a prodigious success. Kipling and [Robert Louis] Stevenson still hold their own in America, he says. Dickens is read a great deal, but nothing like as much as formerly. "But a decline in popularity must be the fate of every man who ever lived," he continued, "unless one may make an exception in the case of Shakespeare and Walter Scott." Do people read Scott in the States? you ask. "Well, I should say that it is only the middle-aged and the old people who read him much; and there is a good reason for that. The style has changed so much. As a rule, style is not diffuse today, and Scott used a great many words where in our day we would get along with one or two. And yet, you know, Scott's friends in America, whether young or old, are enthusiastic friends. Thackeray is very widely read; and my own books? Yes, I think they are read the same, year in and year out. For many years we have been able to name the income from them a year in advance. The satisfactory thing about it is that it does not fluctuate. That is what distresses one—when one's income begins to fluctuate, because if it gets started it can so easily fluctuate the wrong way, and it might fluctuate a man out of his bread and butter."

Asked whether he considered his own writings to be more correctly described as "witty" or "humorous," Mr. Clemens said without hesitation that he did not think them witty, but that he did think they were humorous. Wit, he thinks, is something that flashes itself upon the hearer, humor something that scintillates and meanders. Wit need not be funny; humor must be funny. Alluding to his method of work, Mr. Clemens says that he begins about 11 o'clock in the morning and writes on without interruption until he is dragged away to dinner between 6 and 7. He is not a particularly rapid writer; indeed, he does not think that rapid writing is, at all events in his own case, an advantage, because when he does write fast he generally waxes warm over it, and finds that what he has written at white heat will not bear the calm scrutiny of cooler moments. He makes a practice, however, of writing, whether he is in the humor or not; and he goes on writing even if he knows that the work he is doing will for the most part have to be done over again.

Notes to Interview 86

1. *Punch* was an English humor magazine founded in 1841; *Puck* was an American humor magazine founded in 1876.
2. George Bell, U.S. consul in Sydney. MT endorses free trade in "Sixth Century Political Economy," chapter 33 of *A Connecticut Yankee*.
3. Henry George (1839-97), who knew MT in San Francisco, best known as the author of *Progress and Poverty* (1879).
4. Sir Henry Parkes (1816-96), Australian politician and five-time premier of New South Wales.
5. Carved stone chair adjacent to Sydney Harbor.
6. For another account of the dedication borrowed from Holmes, see interview 48.
7. *Trilby* (1894), popular romance by the French-born artist and writer George (Louis Palmella Busson) Du Maurier (1834-96).

87

[Louis Becke?[1]] "Mark Twain: A Talk about His Books," *Evening News* (Sydney), supplement, 21 September 1895, 3.

The writer of this having once written a book, which he was told a few days ago had been read by Mark Twain, wrote to the famous author and asked him "straight out" if he (Mark Twain) could spare him time for a talk about some of his own books and various other things—for the benefit of the readers of the *Evening News*. And the great American writer sent word, "Come along at 2 o'clock on Wednesday; will be glad to see you."

So at 2 o'clock the writer was at the appointed place—the Hotel Australia—and in a few minutes Mr. Clemens came out from his bedroom and shook hands.

"How are you?" he said, in his pleasant, deliberate, southern accent. "Sit down and make yourself comfortable. I'm dressing, as you see; but it doesn't take me long. Smoke?" And he dived his hand into a cupboard for a couple of cigars, and lighting one himself, was finished dressing almost at the same time.

"Mr. Clemens, I'm not going to worry you long. I know you're busy and have not much time to talk; but will you tell me something about your books." And then the writer made a clean breast of the fact that he knew nothing about interviewing—couldn't write shorthand, and, indeed, had no business attempting an interview.

The American author laughed good-naturedly. "A square peg in a round hole, eh? Well, I know what it is. I had some experience of that sort of thing. Never mind; we'll get along all right."

Just then Mrs. Clemens came in with a sheaf of letters. "There's someone waiting to see you," she said to Mr. Clemens, after we had shaken hands, and hereupon the writer, seeing Mr. Clemens take out his watch, said he would only keep him ten minutes. "Don't you worry," said Mark Twain. "We can't have much of a talk in that time. Say half an hour." And he let the half hour lap over very generously.

So, the ladies having retired, we began to talk about his books.

"Was C. D. Warner your first and only collaborator?"[2]

"Yes. *The Gilded Age* was the only book in which I had a collaborator.[3] Warner, who is a lawyer, and now in Venice—went into the work in this way: I was to set forth certain phases of western life I was familiar with, and especially to portray the character of a man—the Colonel Sellers of the story—that I knew well, while his peculiarities were fresh in my memory."

"Then Colonel Sellers was no imaginary character?"

"He was a very real personage, and, indeed, the man could not be exaggerated."

"Fed his family and a guest on boiled turnips one day when he was financially stiff, didn't he?"

"No," said Mark Twain, impressively. "You are wrong. Raw turnips, not boiled. I was the guest on the occasion, and have never forgotten the incident.[4] Well, about this collaboration. One solemn stipulation I made with C. D. Warner was that if there was any love making in the book I was not to be asked to do it. He was to do that entirely himself. The book was a great success," this latter remark in a reflective tone, as if implying that this result had been attained from the speaker's abstention from touching upon the subject of love making.

The mention of western and southern life here led to the subject of the war, and the writer asked Mr. Clemens if it were a fact that he had actually taken part in that great struggle. Many people in Australia had the idea that such was the case.

"Yes," he replied, in his slow, carefully accented tones. "That is quite right; I did."

"For any length of time?"

"Just a fortnight."

"What particular operations were you engaged in, Mr. Clemens?"

"I was engaged in retreating. I was a second lieutenant in the Missouri Company in the Confederate service and, as I said, I was engaged in retreating the whole of the fortnight. Then my company became so fatigued that we couldn't retreat any more, and I resigned. I should have got fatigued earlier had the company marched in the other direction."[5]

Speaking of his river experiences as a pilot on the Mississippi, Mr. Clemens said that he was four years at that work—running between St. Louis and New Orleans, a distance of 1300 miles. "The only period of my life," he added, regretfully, "that I ever enjoyed."

"Nearly all my books," he said in answer to a query, "were written in my home. Some few short stories and sketches I wrote elsewhere."

From the subject of his own books we began to speak of other American writers, and Mr. Clemens said that George W. Cable, the author of *Creole Days* and *The Creoles of Louisiana,* has a great hold upon the American reading public. "He writes in such a masterly way. Harris and Thomas Nelson Page also deal well with the subjects which have so distinguished Cable, but Cable is a great writer."[6]

Then, as regards Robert Louis Stevenson's books, Mr. Clemens says that he is a very great favorite in America. He had read *The Wrecker*[7]—which depicts the commercial and social life of San Francisco in such daring colors—but so long ago that he had almost forgotten it, but he remembered that part especially. Did he not think the picture overdrawn in some respects, especially in that portion about the boys' stock-brokering gambling academy? "Well, Stevenson was a great, a very great writer. But," said Mr. Clemens in effect, "a man often oversteps the limits of probability in describing national characteristics, and yet somehow his exaggerated pictures are accepted by sensible people of other countries who don't know that too often these pictures have no more solid basis than that the man who draws them knows a little about the characteristics of the people he had described."

"Did you know Artemus Ward, Mr. Clemens?"[8]

"Charles F. Browne? Another splendid man. Overwork and carelessness cut his life short."

Then having overstayed the allotted time, the writer bid Mark Twain goodbye. He would have liked to have stayed longer, but Mrs. Clemens came in and murmured something admonitory to her husband about resting himself a little.

"I am a very bad interviewer, Mr. Clemens."

"Never mind; you can't help that; interviewing is an art."

Notes to Interview 87

1. George Lewis Becke (1855-1913), aka Louis Becke, British novelist, author of *By Reef and Palm* (1894), short story writer, and frequent traveler to the South Pacific.

2. See n. 2 to interview 28.

3. While technically correct, MT had written plays with Bret Harte and W. D. Howells.

4. In chapter 11 of *The Gilded Age,* the family of the comic character Colonel Sellers enjoys a "plain dinner" of "clear, fresh water, and a basin of raw turnips—nothing more."

5. See "The Private History of a Campaign That Failed" (1885), MT's fanciful version of his two weeks of soldiering in the Marion Rangers, a Confederate militia, in 1861.

6. On Cable, see chapter 2; see reference to Harris in n. 1 to interview 35. Thomas Nelson Page (1853–1922), a champion of the "plantation tradition" in postbellum Southern fiction.

7. Stevenson and Lloyd Osbourne (1868–1947) collaborated on the novel *The Wrecker* (1891).

8. See n. 2 to interview 60.

88

"A Chat with Mark Twain," *Sunday Times* (Sydney), 22 September 1895, 4.

The arrival of Mark Twain, who may be classified as the inventor of the new humor of which *The Innocents Abroad* was the original exponent, may certainly be regarded as marking an epoch in our history. Henceforth the man who has delighted so many thousands of readers by his quaint flashes and coruscations of written comedy will be something more than a mere abstraction to a large proportion of Sydney residents. His characteristic *viva voce*[1] descriptions of life and character will dwell in the memory of a host of delighted auditors, who will associate them with the kindly but rough-cut features which have now become familiar to the majority of our citizens. As the celebrated author has now been a week with us, and it was considered that he might have something of special interest to communicate which could not be well embodied in his ordinary lectures, a representative of the *Sunday Times* called upon him on Friday last at his rooms at the Australia.

It may be premised that Mark Twain is a good subject for the interviewer, but there are certain peculiarities which one has got to get used to. He has plenty to say, but he is not in a hurry to say it, and it takes a little while to find out that when you think he has answered a question he is merely thinking whether he has done so or not, and generally finished by rounding it off, clinching it, as it were, by some sapient or incongruous addendum, these addenda being like a lady's postscript, often the most important part of the communication. Mr. Clemens has also learnt caution, or, at all events, professes to have done so, and appears desirous of weighing his words well before uttering them. For the rest there could not be a more genial, kindly, or unassuming manner. There is a total absence of that "side" which some distinguished visitors consider indispensable to their dignity, but his conversation irresistibly conveys the impression of being thoroughly spontaneous and genuine.

I found him enjoying a peaceful pipe in his private room and opened conversation by expressing a hope that he was not altogether weary of being interviewed.

"Oh, no," was the reply. "The only difficulty is saying things that one should not say."

In reply to a question as to his impressions of the public men he had met here, Mark Twain said: "It is easy to see that they are able men, and remarkable men, or they would not be in those positions. The fact is it may be conceded that when men are politically prominent, no matter whether they are full of virtues or full of demerits, the chances are they are men of large abilities. I have found it so in all countries, and I never expect to see commonplace men in high positions."

"And what do you think of your audience?"

"There could not be a choicer audience or more satisfactory one to me, and I have found the same characteristics here as in England and Canada, that they adopt a friendly and uncritical attitude at the beginning, whereas it frequently happens in America that they only get into that attitude after one is fairly at work. The American audience is delightfully responsive and sympathetic, but not always in the very beginning. Foreign lecturers have noticed that and spoken of it."

"But is not the warmth of your reception chiefly due to your reputation as an author?"

"That may be the case, but I had not much reputation when I lectured in England 22 years ago. I found the attitude of the English audiences exactly the same as here. They give one confidence at once, instead of waiting for one to earn it, but it is impossible to talk much on that subject without thinking it out. It would amount to an essay."

"There has been some criticism regarding your published opinions of Bret Harte's work. They have been referred to as spiteful utterances."[2]

"That's what it was. I said that a criticism of Bret Harte from me could have no value, as it would be tainted with prejudice. That is just one of the infelicities of interviewing—that you in the rush of talk intrude your private feelings upon the public, and no one has a right to do that. If I were writing about Bret Harte, and was betrayed into saying ungracious things of him or his work, that would not disturb me, because I should know that next day this flash of passion would have passed, and that piece of writing would find its appropriate place in the waste basket. No man who is ever interviewed, perhaps, fails to say things which are not proper things to be said to an unoffending public, and I am not less liable to these mistakes than would be the persons who find fault with me, if they were being interviewed without the opportunity to weigh their words. Since I have been out on this tour, now two or three months, I have expressed opinions in a great many interviews about authors foreign and domestic, and I have said no harsh word about any of them but three. It is a good enough average—constituted as I am—and I did not constitute myself. It is no merit that I said no hard things about the others, for there were no harsh feelings concerning them stored up in the place where I keep my bile.

"It would be inexcusable in me to expose my spleen publicly if I did it deliberately and with full opportunity to reconsider the matter and be courteously silent."

Then Mr. Clemens suddenly asked what was the nature of his reported criticisms of Bret Harte, and on the interviewer repeating them to the best of his recollection, observed: "That was stupid stuff to say."

The question was then asked, "Would you wish to modify your published opinions in reference to Bret Harte?"

"I should modify my language, not my opinions. I have a full right to my opinion concerning anybody's literature, and concerning the writer of it also, but I have no right to state those opinions publicly in unparliamentary language. I have known Bret Harte intimately for thirty years, but if I should know him a hundred years my feelings toward him would always make it difficult for me to say rational things about him."

At this point Mrs. Clemens entered the room, and the interviewer having been duly introduced Mr. Clemens mentioned that we had been talking about Bret Harte.

"Ah!" said Mrs. Clemens, with a smile. "I hope it was nothing critical. That was a great mistake you made. I think it would be better if your wife saw your interviews in print before they were published."

"The offence," said Mark Twain, "was committed against the reader; it is that which troubles me, not the offence against Harte himself."

"Do you consider the system of Press interviewing objectionable?"

"No, I have no objection to interviewing, providing the interviewer does not ask me questions which can bring out answers calculated to expose certain large traits of my character which ought to be judiciously concealed. Every man has in his character weak places which he is ashamed of—weak places for whose presence he is not responsible, and which he is always trying to conceal from his friends and the public—and is generally trying to persuade himself that they do not really exist. Fortunate men are like the moon. They never exhibit any but their best side—the rest of us forget sometimes and turn the other side. The man who is interviewed is always liable to expose glimpses of the other side."

In reply to a question whether he found lecturing equally as congenial as authorship Mark Twain said: "I like lecturing when I am on the platform.

There is something very pleasant and sociable about it, and it enables one to get acquainted with a great many people, and often to extend one's list of personal friends; but sometimes one's habits are sorely deranged by the necessity of taking trains at all sorts of unreasonable hours and of making journeys that are so long and hard that they break down one's strength. Except for the hard journeys, I believe I should even prefer lecturing to sitting quietly at home driving the pen."

This naturally brought the conversation to the subject of Mark Twain's works, and he was asked if he had any special preference for any one of them.

"No, I don't think that I have, because I haven't read them—that is, I mean, most of them were written so long ago that I have now only a vague notion of what is in them."

After a pause he added: "I think I prefer *Huckleberry Finn*, but I believe the family prefer *The Prince and the Pauper*."

Notes to Interview 88

1. Orally (lit., by word of mouth).
2. See nn. 3 and 4 to interview 8 and MT's remarks about Harte in interviews 84 and 85.

89

"Mark Twain on Prohibition," *Licensing Guardian* (New South Wales),[1]
late September–early November 1895.

"What do I think of Prohibition? Nothing, for the simple reason that there is no such thing. When men want drink, they'll have it in spite of all the laws ever passed, when they don't want it, no drink will be sold. Without wanting to know the experience of America, you people in Australia have an object lesson in temperance legislation. There is supposed to be no drink sold on Sundays in Sydney and Melbourne. Yet I, a stranger, can see that plenty of it is sold, that the most inveterate boozer can get all he wants while he is able to pay for it. Now, if Prohibition cannot be enforced on one day of the week, it cannot be enforced all the year round, and year after year. If men cannot do without a drink from Saturday night till Monday morning it is certain that they cannot wait longer. The way in which your Sunday closing law is evaded will give you an idea of the so-called Prohibition districts in America. The front door is closed, but the back is opened; instead of open honest drinking, you have sly boozing; instead of having the traffic under the supervision of the law, and conducted in the interests of order and morality, there is no supervision at all, and the trade is conducted under the most demoralizing conditions. The manner in which these absurd liquor laws are broken breeds contempt for law in general. Then, while intensifying, instead of eradicating the evil, these laws give rise to smuggling, and informing, and perjury. So now you see why in the States and Canada, they are often repealed on the very first opportunity. The only approach to Prohibition I have seen is in those English towns where hotels shut during certain hours. There I've seen thirty customers refused and told to wait until the house legally opened. Such a thing would never have happened in Prohibition Maine, where a man gets served at any hour.

"Ah," sighed our distinguished visitor, "Why don't the temperance agitators remember Edmund Burke's words? 'Lawful indulgence is the only check on illicit gratification.'[2] Abolishing matrimony would not stamp out fornication. Well, what marriage is to morality, a properly conducted licensed liquor traffic is to sobriety. In either case, a certain human propensity is regulated so as to be a blessing; while left to itself, or subjected to repressive efforts, it would be a curse."

"You evidently don't believe in Prohibition? What do you think of Local Option?"

"Worse and worse. Why the thing is palpably a fraud. In the first place, it would leave the man who wanted a drink no option at all. In England they now call it local veto, but even at that it was squelched last election. In America and Canada, even the temperance people themselves see the absurdity of shutting up the houses in one locality and driving the drinkers into a neighboring one to get more liquor than if they stayed at home. In fact, the more drink is forbidden the more popular it becomes. Stolen fruit is sweet. The little boy prefers the apples he steals to those he buys. So 'tis with liquor. So absurd is Local Option that now they want to increase the area, some temperance men preferring state prohibition. But I'd decrease the option area, come down from counties to parishes, and from parishes to blocks, until I got to the individual who could be a local option law unto himself. If he decided not to drink he'd do all a man can to stamp out the traffic; if other men followed his example, the traffic would soon be wiped out. That's the only way of meeting the difficulty. As regards either Local Option or Prohibition, I don't see why this matter should come under the direct vote of the people, instead of being dealt with in the ordinary way by the legislature and the executive. Let the principle be applied to other things and people would be forced to spend all their time at the ballot box, as they did in ancient Greece and Rome. No majority has the right to coerce a minority, except in so far as the will of the majority now becomes the law of the land. These direct votes of the people are apt to be misleading. For instance, a vote of the ratepayers, through agitation and wire-pulling, may decide that the licensed houses in a locality are not required. Against that we have the opinions of business men, who invest their time, brains and capital in erecting and conducting such houses. If there were no demand for drink, these people would lose their all. While there is a demand, you may be sure that it will be supplied, even when the houses will be closed. The drinking will go on in a worse fashion."

Asked what he considered the best means of solving the vexed problem, Mark replied, "Ask me something easy. The solution of this problem may come with the Millennium, when there will be no crime, and we'll all be angels with wings instead of sinners in pants, and bloomers, and skirts, divided and otherwise. But no man can now point out a remedy. It is doubtful whether even the Temperance preachers believe in their own remedies. If they did, they would not be so ready to make them known. No man cares to find his own occupation gone. Perhaps the professional Temperance man dreads that universal sobriety which would force him to turn to another calling and keep the lamp of his nose burning by some other means. You must not think that because I'm in the lecture line myself, I'm prejudiced against these Temperance preachers, but if what one hears be true, then some of them are awful shams. If I, or any ordinary man, were to tell such yarns as the preachers, revivalists, and Temperance men are applauded for by their people, why the public would denounce them as Yankee perjuries. Then, some of them drink, but in a sly cute way, after business hours. Some are given to other irregularities, even when they don't drink. In fact, they

> Compound the sins they feel inclined for
> By damning those they've got no mind for.[3]

Of course many, perhaps the majority of them, are sincere and earnest, even to fanaticism. But there is a great objection against even that class. They remind me of one of *Æsop's Fables*, where the fox lost his tail in a trap, and then called all the other foxes together, and told them that the Ward McAllister and the Illustrious personage whom your *Bulletin* calls 'Tummy,' of the fox world had decided that foxes' tails had gone out of fashion, and urged them all to dispense with their caudal appendages.[4] So it is with the drunkard who becomes Temperance preacher. He can no longer drink with enjoyment, or even safety, and tries to make all other men follow his own example. In fact, the temperance people are selfish in one respect, they want a pleasure which they deny themselves, branded as illegal, though it may be agreeable and even beneficial to others. There is a lot of conceited self-sufficiency about these Temperance people. It is gratifying to directly rail at other people's vices, or pity their weakness, and so indirectly extol their own virtues and strength. The union of the churches with the Temperance party will never come off.

The use of wine is sanctioned by the Bible. Teetotalism is supposed to have been invented as a blow at Christianity. Speaking of Mahomet, Schlegel, the German historian, tells us, 'Even the prohibition of wine was, perhaps, not so much intended as a moral precept, which considered in that point of view, would be far too severe as for answering a religious design of the founder, for he might hope from the express condemnation of a liquid, which forms an essential element of Christian sacrifice, that it would necessarily recoil on that sacrifice itself, and thus raise an insuperable barrier between his creed and the religion of Christ.'"[5]

On the connection between the Temperance agitation and woman suffrage he was still more emphatic. "Woman suffrage is favored because likely to add to the voting power of the Temperance Party. But why should women have a vote to put down a practice that does not concern them, except in rare cases? It's the men who drink. Woman now complains of her political bondage, yet would celebrate her liberation by an act of tyranny."

Here Mr. Mark Twain—where is the middle initial of the Yankee name—looked at his watch and said, "Time is pressing; come, let us solve the liquor problem in our own way. What are you going to have? Isn't it curious how drinks always follow the flag? For instance, I take a cocktail wherever I go. That doesn't suit the British constitution. In those German forests where the British constitution was reared, beer, according to Tacitus was popular.[6] Here's luck to *The Guardian* and confusion to teetotalism."

Notes to Interview 89

1. The *Licensing Guardian* was the official paper of the United Licensed Victuallers Association.
2. "Letter to Sire Hercules Langrishe on the Subject of the Roman Catholics of Ireland" (1792) by Edmund Burke (1729-97), Irish-born English statesman and philosopher: "Lawful enjoyment is the surest method to prevent unlawful gratification. Where there is property, there will be less theft. Where there is marriage, there will always be less fornication."
3. MT slightly misquotes two lines from pt. 1, canto 1 of *Hudibras* by the English poet Samuel Butler (1612-80): "Confound for sins they are inclin'd to, / By damning those they have no mind to."
4. Samuel Ward McAllister (1827-95), a social arbiter who publicized a list of the "Four Hundred" most prominent New York City families. The *Weekly Bulletin* (Sydney) (7 September 1895, 18) had referred derisively to the Prince of Wales as "Tummy."
5. Mahomet or Mohammed (c. 570-632), prophet of Islam. MT quotes from *The Philosophy of History* (translated into English in 1869) by the poet and historian Frederick von Schlegel (1772-1829).
6. Tacitus (c. 55-c. 117), Roman historian.

90

Aubrey [Herbert Low?], "Mark Twain," *Evening News* (Melbourne), 26 September 1895, 2.

... I found myself sitting opposite Mark Twain, and we shook hands. He introduced me to two ladies, his wife and daughter, and then observed with a smile, "You have been kind to me, Aubrey. You let me down so easily in your first *interview*." And I lapsed into silence in the presence of the man who had set the world's table in a roar whenever he exclaimed, "Pass the mustard." He looked so tired, with his all-night trip from Sydney, that I contemplated him by way of letting him down easily. What lying jades those cameras are, with their grizzly photographs of our guest. I recognized him from his picture on the cover of his books. Had he written no books he would not have been known! He acknowledged it. The only good point in his likeness is his hair—it is long and gray, but his eyebrows are not shaggy, as they make them, nor yet is his moustache a wisp of hay ruffled and bleached in the sun. It is its natural color—a light brown. He shaves chin and cheeks clean, and his mobile features have full play when he talks. And how he can talk!—quietly and with conviction, which reminds one of the reasons of his popularity. His humor ripples like the light upon the surface of his loved Mississippi, where he spent the most delightful days of his life as a river pilot. It is his expression which is his charm, and tells of depths of pathos whence his joyfulness wells up to delight the giddy swimmers on the surface of modern Society. He dresses—well, what would you expect? He dresses like a cultured American gentleman, who can dispense with formal mode, but doesn't. A serge blue-black, like an Irish girl's hair, is the color he affects in his sac suit,[1] and his peaked hat is a comfortable thing to wear in a railway carriage. He walks with a slight stoop, and attracts attention from the people at the wayside stations. But it is his eyes which are the mirror of his soul. You want to break through all precedent and gush. You *must* come out with: He *has* soulful eyes. They beam on you when he refers to the welcome he has been accorded in Sydney—and when, after a long gaze through the carriage windows upon the speeding landscape, he turns, and, a little above a whisper, says,

"I am learning to love your Australia."

You want to tell him that you love him, too, for the weary moments of Life that he has brightened for you, and for the glimpses of light which have broken in upon the sorrow-darkened corners of your past....

And I look up, and again, as in a dream, I am in the presence of the good fairy of his life, Mrs. Clemens, who, with her daughter, is traveling with her husband.... She is entranced with the beauty of the wattlebloom, and I tell her she has but to express the wish and they will be showered upon her by her husband's admirers. She likes the eternal gumtrees, because they are "so restful to the eye," and the soft coloring of the landscape, which "impresses her like music in a minor key," but above all the "soft ethereal blueness of the sky." There is, she says, "nothing like it in [my] own land."

Then her husband breaks in with his tribute—

"How can one help liking a climate such as this? You cannot overpraise it any more than the magnificent Harbor of Sydney. It is affectation to say that any description of it can be classed as extravagant praise. The man is not born among you who is competent to write about it. Marcus Clarke,[2] who is not read as much as he should be in America, but whose works cannot be kept back in the future, made use of a perfect literary figure when he described the Tasmanian coast as being like molten lead poured into water. *He* might have approached a description of Sydney. Marcus Clarke is making his way slowly in America, but his success is sure."

"I have no literary work in contemplation at present, beyond a book of my present Australian travels. I know that new countries are always a little touchy with respect to their critics. Dickens, in *Martin Chuzzlewit* and his *American Notes,* told us a great many unpleasant truths, but they were truths undoubtedly; and lately, when I have re-read them, I cannot see why so much fuss was made over them. The Americans didn't take kindly to them. Now, however, the case is altered. A lot of foreigners have cribbed Dickens' stale facts, and re-written his disapproval of things which no longer exist! I shall be a mild critic!"

Mark Twain was deeply moved by my next question. "What are your opinions of the British Empire?"

He gazed pitifully upon me and said, "Must I really answer that? It is such a large subject for an infant to try and talk about. I have long wished to receive a considerable gift of prophecy, but, oh, I know so little of politics. Yet it is to be hoped that in the event of trouble the common bond of the English language and literature would lead to practical sympathy in time of need."

"These matters of detail," said Mark, "remind me of a story. I had a friend who grappled with great subjects in a general, comprehensive kind of a manner, which was a sure indication of his grasp of the subject. When trying to explain the otherwise inexplicable, he would seek shelter behind forms and figures of speech. He was reckoning up a political antagonist, and making poor headway in the encounter, when he settled it to his own satisfaction by summing him up as a d—d fool, which he was careful to explain to the fool's friends was a mere matter of detail."

"Your gum trees," he said, in answer to a question, "require long study. I think I should grow fond of them. I know I would try to very, very hard. They look so reproachful, and grave, and serious. I am to be introduced to some of them one day before I leave. So far I have not made any nearer approach than an acquaintance with Bosisto's Eucalyptus oil.³

"It is hard to realize that this is spring at the end of September. I see the bursting buds and the flower blossoms on every hand, and I know that I am in a different country from my own, though the houses and fences and people are alike, and I might be in Kansas or South Carolina. But, then, I have been awake all night, and perhaps that increases the illusion. Fancy American May and Australian September being the same!"

Then with a troubled sigh, he moaned: "Two batches of Spring poets in a single year!"

Somebody read a paragraph from a paper about palmistry, and this reminded Mark that he had sent a cast of his hands to four different palmists, two of whom gave fairly good returns, "written in a manner which might be read either way to suit the client." But there was one virile-minded fortune-teller who was unshaken in his expression that "the man who owned that hand was one utterly devoid of the sense of humor."

"That man started me on a course of reflection. It might be possible that man was right, and that I had been deceiving the people all these years, and deceiving myself! Why not?"

Mark Twain has some misgivings of conscience in connection with one of his works—*The Prince and the Pauper*. It was his intention to publish it anonymously, but his family over-persuaded him, and he is not quite sure that he has not thereby swindled the reading public. It is in many respects different from his other works, and the fact of signing his *nom de plume* would make people think they were going to buy a book of the same brand of literary ware as his other works. Well, they didn't, and Mark's tender conscience condemns him.

Ah! this is something more to the point. Mark Twain and his family will strain every effort to be back in time to witness the Melbourne Cup. We all love him now! His weary expression wore away as he confided this to Aubrey, and he forgot that he had been jolting all night on the rails. . . . ⁴

Notes to Interview 90

1. A lightweight travel suit, often made of linen.
2. Marcus Clarke (1846-81), Australian novelist and author of the penal colony narrative *For the Term of His Natural Life* (1870-72), later revised. MT also alludes to Clarke in *FE,* 214.
3. Medicinal oil extracted from the leaves of the eucalyptus trees mostly indigenous to Australia.
4. Aubrey, "Mark Twain: Going to 'Seymour' of Him," *Evening News* (Melbourne), 27 September 1895, 2: Mark, who admires bravery in the individual, is by some hidden association of ideas impelled to say that "A man who rushes to his fate

unconscious of danger is not necessarily a brave man; and that bravery is a moral quality." He may be thinking of me, or of the officer whom he uses up in an anecdote. "This officer, when going into action, was reproached by his general for his frightened look; and he retorted, 'General'—or probably he said nothing of the sort—'if you were as frightened as I am, sir, you would retire to the rear!'"

91

"The Tramp in Melbourne: A Morning with Mark Twain," *Herald Standard* (Melbourne), 26 September 1895, 1; 27 September 1895, 4.

It commenced with a yawn, did this interview.

"I'll tell you what it is," said the humorist; "I'm really fatigued. I didn't sleep well in the train on the way from Sydney, and when I did at length doze off, they woke me up at five o'clock this morning in order to change trains and bring me on to Melbourne. I must say I believe in early rising—for everyone but myself. Personally, I can always excuse myself for not getting up so very early."

It was Mark Twain who was speaking. He lay back on the leather cushions of the railway carriage and closed the quick, piercing eyes that flash in the cavernous recesses beneath the eaves of his bushy eyelids. It was the Mark Twain of the portraits, undoubtedly; a personality as picturesque in the flesh as it is charming in the pages of the books that have added salt to life for over a quarter of a century. Some who have met Mark Twain in Sydney have professed to have been somewhat disillusioned in regard to his appearance. Why? To the present writer the real Mark Twain was in every sense the Mark Twain of imagination. The brow of the author is lofty, as you see if you note the lien of its summit beneath the white hair that curls over the forehead, and waves in light, undisciplined masses all over the head around the ears, and down to the collar. The moustache that covers the finely-shaped mouth bears even yet some signs of the tawny color of youth, though it is flecked and fringed with the white that age is painting. Mark Twain speaks in a low voice—so low that it is sometimes difficult to hear it as the train rumbles along. He talks slowly, deliberately weighing his words before he allows them to pass the barrier of his lips. One can't fail to note the roguish expression that plays about the mouth, and the twinkle that lights up the eyes when he is about to drop some quaint expression in the course of conversation; the same roguish expression, one could vouch for it, as played around the mouth as its owner wrote that sage piece of advice: "Tell the truth or trump—but get the trick!"[1]

"I can't understand," he drawls, resuming the conversation, "how it is that one has to change trains at Albury. Break of gauge, or something of that sort, isn't it?"[2]

One tries to explain that these colonies are not yet civilized up to the federalizing standard, and that they have not learned to cooperate in trading and traveling affairs for the good of the whole community. But this is a political problem, and Mark Twain confesses: "I am no politician; I haven't a bit of political knowledge in my stock that is worth knowing." So one—like the Australasian Premiers—drops federation.

"How do you like Australian railway traveling as compared with traveling in America?" is a very natural question under the circumstances of the interview. Mark Twain expresses some surprise that the outside car is not in use here for long journeys, though he says that he only found it useful for stretching his legs a bit after sitting a long time in the train. It is remarked to him that the carriage in which we are riding may suggest America to him, seeing that the seats were covered with buffalo.

"Ah," he says, "but not buffalo-buffalo. There are no buffaloes in America now, except Buffalo Bill. A wonderful man is Buffalo Bill, and a very fine show it is that he gives.[3] I can remember the time when I was a boy, when buffaloes were plentiful in America. You had only to step off the road to meet a buffalo. But now they have all been killed off. Great pity it is so. I don't like to see the distinctive animals of a country killed off."

"It is the same in this country. The kangaroo is gradually becoming more and more scarce."

"Ah! I suppose so. And what a queer animal the kangaroo is. I haven't seen one, but I suppose it is. I did see one of your native creatures while I was in New South Wales. That was the laughing jackass. It sat on a tree, and I stood looking at it. But it wouldn't laugh for me. I tried to make it laugh; indeed I did; but it respectfully declined."

"Probably it didn't think you were funny," put in Mrs. Clemens who was sitting in the opposite corner of the carriage.

"Probably not; but I did my best. I found the gas but the bird wouldn't find the laugh. This circumstance and another one I'll tell you about have been setting me thinking lately. Mr. W. T. Stead,[4] who is interested in palmistry, asked me to have my hands photographed. Well, I did, and Mr. Stead, without telling anyone whose hands they were, had them submitted to four people, who professed to be experts. These four furnished reports about my hands. Three of them were of no consequence whatever. They were right out of it. But the fourth one made a remark that made me think deeply. She said, 'The owner of those hands has no sense of humor'! Well, you know, this made me wonder whether I haven't been deceiving the public for the last thirty years or so; and, worse still, deceiving myself! It is things like this that make a serious man muse."

This anecdote amuses everyone in the carriage, but Mark Twain shakes his head as if it is a really serious matter of concern to him. "Just think," he adds, "of the awful deceit I have been practicing for so many years!"

"The public, Mr. Clemens, is quite content that you should go on deceiving them in the same way."

"Thanks. But talking of Sydney, we had a splendid time there. The weather was perfect, and we had some excellent views of the famous Harbor. What did I think of Sydney Harbor? Well, I will say of it that its beauty justifies some of the most extravagant things that have been said of it.[5] The way it is broken up, with its hundreds of little forks and tongues of water breaking into the land—fringed round with blue inlets—reminded me of a figure used by Marcus Clarke in that masterly work, *For the Term of His Natural Life*.[6] The figure I refer to I regard as one of the most striking in the whole of literature. He is speaking of the Harbor at Hobart, you know, and he says—I have always remembered it—that the way the water spread round and indented the land was like 'melted lead spilt in water.' That is, I say, one of the most perfect figures I have ever read. You know how melted lead, when you drop it in water, shoots in all directions—radiates—and that figure came forcibly to my mind when I was looking at Sydney Harbor."

"Is Marcus Clarke's novel read much in the States?"

"By some, no doubt; but it is a work that is bound to be one of the most read as it becomes known, because it is a great work of art."

Then the conversation turns, and Mark Twain asks what news there is in the day's papers.

I showed him the cablegram in last evening's *Herald,* announcing the engagement of Miss Vanderbilt to the Duke of Marlborough, and the settlement of 10,000,000 dollars upon the young lady.[7]

"Perhaps you have noted," I remarked, "that this is the second American heiress this year who has married an English aristocrat. The other case was that of the Chicago girl, who married the Honorable George Curzon."[8]

"Yes, I remember," said he.

"It seems," I added, "that American heiresses are showing a disposition to go after young English aristocrats?"

"No," said Mark. "It is the English aristocrats who run after American heiresses."

"Ah, that is your American way of putting it."

"Well, and the other is your English way of putting it."

No effective reply suggested itself at the moment.

"Do you know," I said, "that if I followed the advice you have put into the mouth of your character Pudd'nhead Wilson, I should ask to see the manuscript of your new book, if you are preparing one."

Mark Twain laughed heartily. He remembered the passage. "You have me there," he said.

The passage referred to is an entry which Pudd'nhead makes in his diary. It reads: "There are three ways of pleasing an author, and the three form a rising scale of compliment; (1) to tell him you have read one of his books, (2) to tell him that you have read all of his books, (3) to ask him to let you read the manuscript of his forthcoming book. Number one admits you to his respect, number two admits you to his admiration, number three carries you clear into his heart."[9]

"Well," Mark Twain continued, "to tell you the truth I haven't done any writing just lately. I haven't had any time. I daresay I shall get time when I get on the steamer again. Of course, I intend to write a book of impressions about this tour, when I get time."

"You haven't given the world any book since *Pudd'nhead Wilson* was born, have you?"

"Yes, one; it was not published under the name of Mark Twain, though.[10] Oh, I am not going to tell you the title of it. That is my little secret at present."

"Then must one read all the anonymous novels of the last twelve months in order to guess which one may possibly be yours?"

"Well," he laughed, "you can do that if you like, you know. You look young; it mightn't kill you, you know. I'll tell you the reason why I published this book anonymously. It is not in my usual vein. It is a story of quite another kind. Perhaps you have read my book *The Prince and the Pauper?* You have? Well, that is a story that is not in my usual vein. At first I intended to publish it anonymously, but I was persuaded not to do so by my family, because they liked it. But afterwards I was sorry I did not. Mind you I like the book myself, but what I felt about it was that the signature Mark Twain is a kind of trademark. The public buying a book by Mark Twain expects to get a book of a certain type. And I felt it was not quite fair to my readers to publish a book of quite another type under that signature. I may be wrong; but that is how I look at it. If a man puts a certain trademark upon a certain brand of cloth he has no right to sell the public another sort of cloth under that same trademark."

"But authors as a rule do not look upon a *nom de plume* as a trademark, do they?"

"Perhaps not, but I do. Mark Twain is my trademark."

"Your Twain Mark one might almost say."

But it seemed to hurt his feelings.

"Talking of authorship, how do American authors regard your copyright law now that it has been in working several years?"

"I think it works very well now. I was at first in favor of giving the British author absolute protection for his books sold in America, but you have to remember that in the course of years all sorts of vested interests are created and have to be considered. There was the vested interest of the printer, and of the publisher, and of all the others who had profited by the free publication, without copyright, of an English authors' books in the States. The Copyright Act passed by Congress was the best Act it was possible to get passed at the time, and, as it gives the protection of copyright to the author who has his books printed in the States it treats him very fairly, I think."[11]

On the same subject, he pays a warm tribute to the honesty of the famous firm of European publishers Messrs Tauchnitz, the head of which died a few weeks back. "Tauchnitz,"[12] said Mark Twain, "was a strictly honorable man, who never published a book by an author without his own consent, or the consent of his representatives. I will give you an illustration in proof. Some years ago, when I was in London, I was asked by the agent of the firm of Tauchnitz to see about arranging for the issue of the novels of Sir Walter Scott in the famous Tauchnitz series of Continental novels. We went to see the firm that publishes Scott's novels in Edinburgh—Black and Co., I think it is—and asked them what their terms were. 'Oh,' they said, 'there is nothing to pay; we can take no money; the copyright has expired and you are free to publish them if you like.' Tauchnitz absolutely refused to publish the novels without paying someone for the right and for a long time because Black's would take no money there was no edition of Scott's novels in the Tauchnitz series. Now, that is what I call being conscientious."

The train rushed along and Mark Twain looked out of the window and studied the landscape. It interested him. The bright warm sunshine cheered and freshened him, and he was evidently enjoying it. The conversation turned, somehow, to the subject of beauty and the treachery it often conceals. Then came a passage in the talk in which the humorist showed what a keen observer of nature he is. He pointed to a creek that was running rapidly down the hillside. "I learned long ago," he said, "that the dangerous part of a current is the part where the water seems gentlest. You see the current of a river, say, hurrying along. It moves swiftly, fiercely. In the middle of it you see a place where the water is quieter. There are gentle circles, constantly forming—thin graceful rings, on the surface—expanding to larger circles, and there is an appearance of pleasant peaceful beauty at that spot. But it is one of the most dangerous points of the river. The current itself is only fierce on the surface; but that quiet lapping at that particular spot indicates that just below the surface there are dangerous rocks hidden. Yes; it is true indeed that very often the greatest beauty indicates the gravest danger."

Then the subject changes again, and the Australian climate is praised. Mark Twain has found the Sydney weather delightful. He has enjoyed no weather so much since he was last in England. "I don't know how it is," he says, "that the English climate should be so much more agreeable than the American climate in the same latitude. I suppose it is due to the warmth of the Gulf Stream. They put everything down to the Gulf Stream that can't be accounted for in any other way!"

As to other Australian literature, Mark Twain gives it as his opinion that Louis Becke's book *By Reef and Palm* is one of the best that has been produced in recent years.[13] "Becke," he says, "is a man who knows the South Seas thoroughly, and has the true feeling for life in those islands. He writes finely, and I think his name is bound to be heard of prominently in literature."

On the subject of his present tour he says that it is the third lecturing season he has undertaken. "And," he quaintly adds, "as my first lecture was given twenty years ago I fancy you will own that is very mild dissipation." The conversation wanders on to a whole lot of subjects of various kinds. He speaks at one moment of his old days as the river pilot on the Mississippi—"the delightfulest life in the world and there never was anything like it," he declares. The British Empires commands his admiration, though, as for his views about it, he considers [it] "a large subject for an infant to talk about." The American civil war he thinks did a good deal for forming the American character by raising up noble men and nerving them to great deeds. And so he talks on, until the train shoots from the environment of the green country laced with silver creeks to the brick and wood-shanty skirts of the city. Then Mark Twain looks out of the window again, and scans the fast-closing landscape curiously. "All suburbs are alike—with differences," he says. "But I like best those ancient towns in the old world where you shoot suddenly into the place, where the city is all bunched up together quaintly. You never see that sort of town in new countries. And as for this railway station"—we are now at North Melbourne, where tickets are collected—"well, it might be a London station. Just like it, in fact."

"Not much like an East End London station," he is reminded.

"No? Well, I don't know the East End of London. I don't frequent theological society.[14] Though I must go down to the East End next time I go there, just to see that East End Palace which owes its existence to Besant's novel, *All Sorts and Conditions of Men*."[15]

And so the train steams into Spencer street station, and farewells have to be exchanged with Mark Twain, who steps out, with his steamer-cap on his head, to receive the welcomes of the Council of the Institute of Journalists.

Notes to Interview 91

1. The first epigraph from "Pudd'nhead Wilson's Calendar" in the first chapter of *Pudd'nhead Wilson* (1894), MT's sixth major novel.

2. On the different rail gauges, see *FE*, 151.

3. William F. (Buffalo Bill) Cody (1846–1917), western American showman.

4. See n. 6 to interview 74.

5. MT elsewhere describes Sydney Harbor as "the darling of Sydney and the wonder of the world" (*FE*, 112).

6. See n. 2 to interview 90.

7. In November 1895 Consuelo Vanderbilt, aka the Duchess of Marlborough (1877–1964), only daughter of William K. Vanderbilt, married the 9th Duke of Marlborough Charles Spencer Churchill (1871–1934).

8. Lord George Curzon (1859–1925), conservative Member of Parliament.

9. Epigraph to chapter 11 of *Pudd'nhead Wilson*.

10. *Personal Recollections of Joan of Arc*.

11. The Chace Act (1891), the first U.S. international copyright agreement, offered authors limited protection on a bilateral basis in a limited number of countries. See also n. 4 to interview 47.

12. Christian Bernhard Tauchnitz (1816–85), German publisher of the Library of British and American Authors.

13. See n. 1 to interview 87.

14. MT's sarcastic comment on the do-gooders who opened religious missions in the East End.

15. Sir Walter Besant (1836–1901), English essayist and novelist; *All Sorts and Conditions of Men* was published in 1882.

92

"Mark Twain: Arrival in Melbourne," *Age* (Melbourne), 27 September 1895, 6.

Mark Twain needs no introduction to the public of an Australian capital, and when he faces his Melbourne audience tonight he will be accorded the hearty welcome of a familiar friend. His personal appearance has lately been made widely known here by some excellent Sydney photographs, which, by the way, he considers "a long way beyond any photographs he ever had made before." This distinguished humorist reached Melbourne yesterday by the Sydney express train, accompanied by his wife (Mrs. Clemens) and one of his daughters, who are traveling with him in this tour round the world. At Spencer-street station he was welcomed by a party of citizens, including the American consul and other Americans, and several representatives of the Institute of Journalists. The travelers took up their quarters at Menzies' Hotel, where Mark Twain was interviewed later in the day by a representative of *The Age*. The fatigue of the night's journey from Sydney was rather too much for him, and this accounted for his receiving the visitor perched in his bed, placidly seeking a renewal of energy in clouds of tobacco smoke. Like a sensible man, Mr. Clemens, whenever he can manage it, sticks to daylight for his railway traveling, and it has been such a long time since he took a sleeping berth that when he got here "he didn't know whether he had slept or not." He had to pull himself together for next evening's lecture, so he rested for the day with the aid of a pipe and a book, which was no other than *For the Term of His Natural Life*.[1]

As a literary workman, Mark Twain has been greatly charmed with Marcus Clarke's best read book. It has given him glimpses of Australian history which he would gladly linger over and follow out himself by personal investigation step by step. But time will not allow him to do more than take an outer view of Australian life and institutions, in which he, nevertheless, has seen much that awakes his sympathy. He notes the uprising of tall city buildings made possible by the use of the rapid hydraulic lift such as they have in America. It is not so in Europe yet, he tells us. "They still stick to the old slow going lift that carries two people and a half, and you arrive at old age on your trip to the sixth floor." But the go ahead fever is not the only temper that is wanted in a community, and the Innocent Abroad warms to us when he sees evidence of worthy sentiments—such as that, for example, which preserves the relics of our early history. "It is a fine thing to have them alongside each other—the sentiment that takes kindly to the swift lift and the electric wire, and the sentiment that preserves the old plough that turned your first sod, or the trees where your explorers camped when they opened up your country." If Mark Twain's feelings in that phase of tradition be of any influence no opportunity of preserving the identities of the nation's past will be lost; for, as he pertinently remarks, "you generally find out that they are very precious when they are gone." He himself is a literary identity of the generation, and happily, in his case, the world has not waited for his funeral to make a god of him. He has enjoyed many years of popular favor in all parts of the English-speaking world, and the public will expect a good deal from him still. Mr. Clemens does not regard the humorous class of books as the most permanent, though his *Innocents Abroad* has been his most popular work. "There is an element of duration," he remarks, "in anything that touches any one side of your nature satisfactorily, and almost every nature has a humorous side; but a humorous book has not the same chance of life as a narrative after all, for it depends on its style, in which the taste changes, while the other holds good with its facts. Such books as *Roughing It* and *A Tramp Abroad* treat of things measurably familiar to the reader, and he gets entertainment in the shape of chaff and substance mixed up together. They have more value than other kinds of books, which no doubt I could write, but which other people could write better." As for that part of his work which is likely to have the most permanent effect, he leans not unnaturally to *The Yankee at the Court of King Arthur,* in which some very powerful, political, and social lessons are cleverly interleaved with the satire of the story. Mark Twain himself does not appear to have closely followed the effect of his book, which, he tells us, was got out in a hurry, at a high price, and went through a comparatively limited edition of 35,000 or 40,000 copies. Yet the incisive force of its pictures should make it a power wherever it was widely read, especially in the democratic colonies of Australia.

Writing books he does not regard as "work," though there is far too much writing for the public that is work, especially the journalistic form which ties men to the ink pot day and night, "while everyone else is having a good time"; and of this Mark Twain has had a share. It is when he feels tired of inaction that he thinks of writing a book. In one of these phases he struck the notion of writing a burlesque on Talmage, which would no doubt have been appreciated in Melbourne after our own experiences of that eccentric individual.[2] "I had seen the reports of Talmage's sermons in the New York papers, and I said 'This is good fun.' I didn't owe Talmage any grudge, but I thought I could burlesque some of his performances without any impropriety, so I bought his book of sermons; but they were altogether difference from what I had read. He had edited the book carefully, and it was quite a reasonable sermon after he was done with it. Yes, he cheated me badly."

Mark Twain intends to write up his impressions of this Australian trip, but he says he will confine himself to outside impressions only. He professes to be fully alive to the folly of those globe trotters who rattle through a country on a three weeks' tour and then write a book "out of their colossal incapacity for the job." As Mr. Clemens puts it, no man can understand the life of a community unless he has lived in it. We would certainly not expect that the writer who sent his hero round the country in the disguise of a peasant, and who nearly hung the King of England in the search for accurate knowledge, would be tempted to hurl dogmatic opinions at a country which he has only seen the fringe of. "The Boss" himself had the rope round his neck, and if Mark Twain gives himself away in this matter there will be no Sir Launcelot with his armored knights to prevent him being pushed off the ladder.[3]

Personally Mr. Clemens strikes one as being well past middle age. His keen, strong face, with bushy eyebrows and full mustache, is crowned by a flowing head of white hair. His manner in conversation suggests deliberate thought; but his utterance, though slow, is free from hesitation or reserve. There are pithy sentences and sparks of humor cropping up occasionally as the subject varies, but the characteristics which have made the great humorist's reputation will best be seen on the lecture platform.

Notes to Interview 92

1. See n. 2 to interview 90.
2. T. DeWitt Talmage (1832–1902), an American clergyman.
3. The reporter alludes to chapter 38 of *A Connecticut Yankee*.

93

"Mark Twain Put to the Question," *South Australian Register* (Adelaide), 14 October 1895, 6.

A quiet, composed, elderly gentleman named Clemens, Christian name Samuel, carefully carrying a large carbuncle of American manufacture arrived by the Melbourne express on Saturday morning, but the people who crowded the Aldgate platform were looking out for Mark Twain, the celebrated humorist, and for a moment did not think of enquiring of Mr. Clemens, who is a personal friend of the celebrated Mississippi Pilot. Mr. Clemens, however, had stolen a march upon the Adelaideans, but not willfully. Mr. Smythe,[1] with Mr. C. A. Murphy, the American Consul, met him at Aldgate with a carriage, and with Mr., Mrs., and Miss Clemens had a delightful drive through the hills amidst scenery which did *not* remind Mark Twain of the Sierra Nevada or the Pacific Slope.

Mark Twain—the familiar name slips more easily off the tongue than Samuel Langhorne Clemens—is so distinctive in face and fashion that it is a toss up whether he is most like the portrait given by us on Saturday or the portrait is most like him. His iron-gray hair is "on its own hook" so to speak. It grows abundantly and wildly in a self-assertive, independent fashion, and under the penthouse of bushy brows the kindly satirist's keen eyes gleam warmly as he talks. It is altogether a striking, masterful head and face, not the sort that one would sketch mentally for the presentment of the most original jester of the age, but quite suggestive of a character.

As we went into the private parlor of the South Australian Club Hotel I remarked that it was very much like introducing a patient into the surgery for an operation, and Mark Twain completed the illusion by extending himself upon a sofa with an air of languor, for his journey had been a wearisome one; he was not well, and his carbuncle bothered him. When I asked him how he managed to smuggle his carbuncle past the Customs officers over the Border, he guessed that they did not know that he had it concealed about his person. "It sits on me like the nation," he said; "it keeps quiet awhile, but at times it gathers itself together and gives an almighty hard twist. It's pretty vigorous." Remarking about the ordeal by interview he said drily, "I think interviewing as an institution is good enough where the man under torture has something to confess, and the torturer knows how to worry it out of him. Now I haven't got much to reveal."

"There is a lot of rubbish forced upon a long-suffering public through the competition in the interview business?" "Just so. It often happens that the interviewed has nothing to say, and the interviewer does not know how to make him say it. So times in despair they write up a lot the man never said, never intended to say, and couldn't say if he thought of it; but an accurate interview is a good thing. The interviewer has his interests to serve, and feels he must get something somehow. It may be that he is no better equipped with material than the man he wants to get the column out of.

"I don't think I ever interviewed any one," he remarked. "It is an American invention?" "Yes; there is a lot of nonsense talked about American reporters sticking a celebrity up, not taking a note nor exchanging half a dozen words, and then working up a column of imaginative matter. It has been done and it may be done, but there are all sorts and conditions of newspapers."

Asked what he thought of Rudyard Kipling, he said he had the greatest admiration for that young writer's poetry and prose. He read his poetry over and over again. It had a grand swing in it, and was truly human. There was a boldness, a dash, a daring, and an originality about it that proved irresistible. "Mandalay" was full of true poetic feeling:—

By the old Moulmein Pagoda, lookin' eastward to the sea;
There's a Burma girl a settin', and I know she thinks o' me;
For the wind is in the palm-trees and the temple bells they say
"Come you back you British soldier, come you back to Mandalay."[2]

"That poem of mingled pathos and humor had the aroma of the Orient, the sound of the sea on the sand and the breezes among the palms in it.[3] Then those barrack-room ballads were true to life, there had been nothing like them written before. For example, that one of Tommy Atkins—

I went into a theatre as sober as could be,
They gave a drunk civilian room, but 'adn't none for me;
They sent me to the gallery, or round the music 'alls,
But when it comes to fighting—Lord, they shoves me in the stalls!
For it's Tommy this and Tommy that, and Tommy wait outside,
But it's special train for Atkins when the trooper's on the tide.[4]

—and so on. In all Kipling's work there was genuine feeling."

"Now, which of your own books do you like best?"

"Well, I think *Huckleberry Finn*."

"I hope you have not killed Tom, Huck, and Jim; we long to hear of them again."

Mark Twain's eyes twinkled, and with a dry chuckle he gave the English equivalent for the Spaniards' "Quien sabe?" who knows, as if that trusty trio were mighty hard to kill.

"You had a capital artist for *Tom Sawyer Abroad* in *St. Nicholas*. I was struck with the beautiful detail, the chasteness and the originality of the drawings of the air-ship and all the scenes."

"Yes; they were real good. The artist is a man named Beard."[5]

In the course of conversation Mr. Clemens said that the details of his books went clean off his memory a few weeks after he had written them.

If any one has a spare appetite he would oblige Mark Twain very much, as he says he never had one in his life. Australians, he says, strike him as being more American than English in their characteristics. There is a frankness, a bluntness, and an absence of self-consciousness about them. The English have a great deal of reserve and stiffness of manner, which he thinks is due to a sort of shyness.[6] The Australian is open, unreserved, independent, and not exclusive. As to Australian journals, he has not paid much attention to them, and will not make comparisons, because it is about the worst way of forming an opinion, and an opinion so formed is bound to be bad. All the stuff said and written about the corruption and unscrupulousness of American journals is rank bosh and bunkum.

"If you make anything and you stick it on a height it becomes conspicuous, and the more conspicuous it is the more notice is taken of it. Hence if a prominent politician or a paper does or says something out of the ordinary there is an unusual fuss about it, and people who haven't anything to think with stamp the whole nation or the whole Press with the character of the individual, which is just about as senseless as it could well be. It is like the silly superstition that Americans habitually carry revolvers and shoot them off promiscuously for pastime, particularly in the southern States. Now, Americans don't know the truth about themselves—a good many of them believe this revolver business. The Northerner believes that the Southerner goes around 'revolvering,' shooting and killing considerable. I tell you it is not a fact. The Southern communities are just as peaceful and religious as the Northern. The Southerner may be more highly cultured, and anything he does is naturally conspicuous. Carrying a revolver is a fad, just a fad of a fashion; but the revolvers are mighty harmless. Of course there are desperadoes on the frontier, but that is not the only part of the world they live in. Their deeds give a false character to their district. I have carried a revolver; lots of us do, but they are the most innocent things in the world."[7]

"What about the racial feeling in America?"

"Well, that's a big question. Much of the talk is exaggerated by windy agitators and stump orators, and does not represent the real feeling. Away back there was talk of deporting the negroes to Africa, and of disfranchising a large number, but you do not hear much of it now. I expect agitators are much the same breed all over the world. Chinamen, the yellow agony; well, most of my acquaintance with them is amongst the washerman class on the Pacific slope; and as for the Japs, those I have met have been highly cultured gentlemen educated in our Colleges. The Jap is a superior person, and wears his English clothes of the latest cut with all the ease of an Englishman born to them. I was never disposed to make fun of the Chinaman; I always looked upon him as a pathetic object; a poor, hardworking, industrious, friendless heathen, far from home, amongst a strange people, who treated him none too well. He has a hard life, and is always busy and always sober, therefore I never could see anything to make fun of in the Chinaman. No, he is not wanted in America. The feeling is that he ought to go, but America is a place for all people, it seems."

"Where is Calvin H. Higbie, the 'honest man, genial comrade, and steadfast friend' who was a millionaire with you for ten days?"[8]

"Oh, he's away down in California, growing grapes."

I did not ask where "John Smith," another dedicatee was,[9] but mentioned Smiley, the hero of the jumping-frog episode. Mark Twain's eyes twinkled, and he said—"He was a real character, and his name was Greeley. The way he got the name of Smiley was this—I wrote the story for the New York *Saturday Gazette,* perishing weekly so-called literary newspaper—a home of poverty; it was the last number—the jumping frog killed it. They had not enough 'G's,' and so they changed Greeley's name to 'Smiley.'[10] That's a fact. Yes, I am going to write a book on this trip round the world. It is such a touch-and-go kind of thing—nothing but a glimpse, but I get material. After doing Australia we are going to Ceylon, India, and South Africa."

I made a reference to Mark Twain's criticism of Bret Harte, and he said—"Let that drop; it was one of those hasty things I had no business to have said, and it should never have appeared. If one criticizes a man one should do it thoroughly." I let Max O'Rell drop, too.[11]

After a pleasant chat and refreshing laughter we parted.

Notes to Interview 93

1. Carlyle and R. S. Smythe, father and son, managed the Australasian leg of MT's speaking tour. See also Carlyle Smythe, "The Real Mark Twain," *Pall Mall Magazine* 16 (September 1898): 29–36.

2. The first four lines of Kipling's 1890 poem.

3. "Mark Twain: Arrival in Adelaide," *Adelaide Advertiser,* 14 October 1895, 7: "Yes, they have an aroma of the Orient, haven't they? You seem to smell the sandalwood, and the lines have a swing and go—there is a snapper at the end of every one of them."

4. The second stanza of Kipling's poem "Tommy" (1892).

5. Dan Beard illustrated *Tom Sawyer Abroad,* serialized in *St. Nicholas* between November 1893 and April 1894; see also n. 9 to interview 47.

6. *Adelaide Advertiser:* "What do you think of Australia?" was a question which the visitor considered covered a good deal of ground. He was delighted with the country, and the people struck him as rather American than English. "In what way?" "Well, in their absence of shyness and self-consciousness. That is American and Australian, but not English. The Englishman has a sort of reserve, and a part of that reserve comes from native shyness and self-consciousness."

8. Mark Twain and Carlyle Smythe in Australia, September 1895. Courtesy of the Mark Twain Project, University of California, Berkeley.

7. *Adelaide Advertiser:* An enquiry about American journalism brought out Mark Twain as a defender of the newspapers of his country from a general charge of venality. "It is like the superstition that Americans all carry revolvers, and are very handy at shooting one another, especially in the southern states. The American does not know the truth about his own country, and how should the foreigner? The people of the northern states all believe that the southern states are inhabited by men who carry revolvers and are always on the shoot. It is not true. The southern communities are just as religious and peaceable as any communities in the world. Yes, it is quite true that in the west, in the early mining days, everybody carried revolvers—even the printers wore them at their work—but they didn't kill anybody. It was a fashion and a fad, and the only people who did the killing were a few desperadoes whom you could count on the fingers of one hand."

8. Calvin H. Higbie (d. 1914), an "Honest Man," "Genial Comrade," and "Steadfast Friend," according to MT's dedication of *Roughing It.* See also *Auto* (1959), 107–12.

9. MT's first book *The Celebrated Jumping Frog of Calaveras County* (New York: Webb, 1867) contains a comic dedication to "John Smith," the most common possible name.

10. *Adelaide Advertiser:* The name "Smiley" was originally "Greeley" but the story

appeared in a tottering weekly called the *New York Saturday Gazette*—"in the last number; it killed it," said Mark, modestly—and as the printers had run out of capital G's the alteration had to be made.

11. On Bret Harte, see nn. 3 and 4 to interview 8 and n. 5 to interview 84; on O'Rell, see nn. 1 and 2 to interview 67.

94

"Interview with Mark Twain," *Courier* (Ballarat, Australia), 21 October 1895, 4.

Mr. Samuel L. Clemens, better known as Mark Twain, being among us, an opportunity was taken to interview him in search of readable "copy." In spite of the carbuncle which Mr. Clemens is now "entertaining," a picture of greater contentment can scarcely be conceived than that which he presented when our representative was introduced to him at Craig's hotel yesterday evening. Stretched at full length on a comfortable couch, his head propped up with a pillow, he lay smoking, and he chatted cheerily in between the puffs. Within easy reach of his hand stood a box of cigars, and an ashtray was conveniently placed. Mark Twain is an inveterate smoker, and when he relinquishes his cigar it is to transfer his attention to a pipe. At the first glance it is apparent that Mr. Clemens possesses a strong individuality, and this is more and more recognized on acquaintance. His features are rugged, a gray moustache partially hides a well-drawn mouth, the eyes are keen and restless, forehead furrowed as though by long study, and the whole backed by a heavy growth of hair, combines to make a personality not easily forgotten. Judging from the manner of speech adopted, one unaccustomed to Americans would conclude that Mr. Clemens is a phenomenally lazy man, one word following the other as though each was being mentally turned over, and its full worth in the sentence weighed. The books which he has given the world—books which are to be found in nearly every house where the English language is spoken—will, however, serve to remove any suspicion of laziness; and besides, the thoroughly lazy man won't talk, while Mr. Clemens, on the other hand, seems scarcely to know where to stop when once he commences. An endeavor was made to induce him to relate some of his early experiences as a miner in California, but he replied:—"All my mining experiences worth giving to the world have been published in my books. There are not many things that happen to human beings in this life—whether life be long or short—that are capable of being worked up into good printable material outside autobiography, and then no incident is too trivial to be set down."

At this stage the fire-bell rang, and Mr. Clemens, looking solemn, breathed a fervent hope that the bellringers at the City Hall would be merciful to him and abstain from practice during the hours of eight o'clock and ten o'clock this and tomorrow evening while he held his "At homes." "I talked against a brass band the other night," he observed, "and found that difficult enough. On another occasion I was speaking in New York, when a full brass band outside opened fire. The day was warm, and the doors and windows were open for the admission of the breeze and the music. I shouted for all I was worth, but soon saw that the audience were getting more fun out of my discomfiture than out of anything I was saying. But," he added, with a smile, "when I found I could not make myself well heard I had a good time, too, by giving them an unspoken speech—throwing in the gestures in a way that would have done for a deaf and dumb asylum."

"Well, Mr. Twain, what do you think of Australia?" "All I have seen of it is from the windows of the railway train. Nay; I did visit the Great Western vineyard!"

"And of course you have been unable to visit any of the mines?" "No; I've been down on the blankets pretty well ever since I arrived, and have done little else—outside lecturing—but study wallpapers. Every kind of wallpaper you possess in Australia has come under my purview, and if I fail as a lecturer, I shall write a book on Australian wallpapers, for I don't intend to be swindled out of everything by a carbuncle."

"While you are here you should take an opportunity of viewing our statuary."

"So far, I have seen nothing; but I recollect hearing this city referred to as 'The City of Statues.' I am not accustomed to see good statuary in the public gardens in America. New York has within its parks a few good pieces of statuary, but it is also disfigured by a number of statues disgraceful in art; in fact, there is nothing suggestive of art about them. They have a statue of Garibaldi in Washington Park.[1] It would be no crime to hang the man who made that statue; and it would be a most meritorious thing also to hang the committee who selected it." And so he rambled on from one subject to another, incidentally expressing a disbelief in faith-healing, giving a disquisition on ghosts, early associations, and a host of other subjects. . . .

Note to Interview 94

1. The nine-foot bronze statue of Giuseppe Garibaldi (1807–82), the republican hero of the Italian civil war, was executed by Giovanni Turini (1841–99) and installed in Washington Square Park in 1888.

95

"Mark Twain: Arrival in Hobart," *Tasmanian News* (Hobart), 2 November 1895, 2.

This morning the Union liner *Mararoa* arrived here from Melbourne,[1] and amongst her passengers was no less a distinguished personage than the great

American humorist, Mark Twain. He was accompanied by Mr. Carlyle Smythe, a son of the "much-traveled" [Smythe Senior],[2] and after a stay here of a few hours continued his voyage on to Maoriland. Mr. Clemens has been very unwell of late, but is gradually being restored to his usual state of health, and hopes the climate of New Zealand will thoroughly restore him. A reporter of the *News* was deputed to interview him and caught the gentleman on the boat surrounded by newly-made friends, who seemed delighted and honored at the opportunity afforded them of speaking to Mark Twain. "It was at first arranged," said Mr. Clemens, "that I would give an 'At Home' here; but owing to the unavoidable alteration in the arrangements I am unable to do so." This fact will be sincerely regretted by many Hobart residents who were naturally looking forward to hearing and seeing this distinguished humorist for themselves. Mr. Clemens is a really brilliant conversationalist and goes from topic to topic with animation and knowledge and drops numberless points, which would fill up far more space than is at our disposal. As to how he likes the colonies, Mr. Clemens quaintly remarked, "I am still in them, and as I am going to write a book on them it will hardly do to tell you, but this I will say, I like the climate very much, while the scenery is also grand." He is a lover of Marcus Clarke's book entitled *For the Term of His Natural Life* and expressed the wish to linger over and follow out for himself by personal investigation the glimpses of Australian life disclosed in that novel.[3] But time is precious, and would not allow him to do more than take what he termed an outer view of Australian life and institutions in which he has already seen much that awakes his sympathy. One of the subjects touched upon was humor, and he maintained that a man could never be a humorist until he could feel the springs of pathos, and the man was never yet properly funny who was not capable at times of being serious. Mr. Clemens' literary capabilities are well known all over the world, and it was not to be wondered that the matter of writing books was remarked during the conversation. He does not regard writing books as work; but it is when he feels tired of inaction that he thinks of writing a book, and he intends to write up his impressions of this Australian trip from an outside view entirely. "No man can understand the life of a community unless he has lived in it," says Mr. Clemens, "and as I cannot do that I intend to confine myself to outside impressions only." Speaking of writers of fiction, Mark Twain said he read little but the "heaviest" sort of literature, and left "modern" writers almost entirely alone, always having a fear of getting into someone else's style if he dabbled among the modern writers too much. Among those he read he spoke particularly in favor of Gilbert, the famous composer of comic operas.[4] He referred to it being marvelous that a man should have the gift of saying not only the wittiest of things, but saying them in verse, and said he had been struck dumb with astonishment when reading Gilbert's operas. He had lost much of his admiration for Dickens, but considered Lewis Carroll a true and subtle humorist. As to the distinction between wit and humor, he admitted it was always difficult to reconcile any definition of the two kindred qualities, but by general consent wit seems to be counted a very poor relation of humor, which is never artificial.

Our representative then asked Mr. Clemens of his wanderings around the world, and the humorist spoke of the many interesting men he had met. He thought London was a marvelous place, and said he had dined with Mr. H. M. Stanley there not long ago, when some 80 guests were present, every one of whom was distinguished in some way or other.[5] One of the most interesting gentlemen he had ever met was General Grant, and he spoke of him in a highly eulogistic manner. He had also met Rudyard Kipling, who traveled some 275 miles for the purpose of seeing him, and considered a very high compliment had been paid him.[6] "Harking back to book-writing," said Mr. Clemens, "I might tell you that when I am engaged [in] writing a book my family find it a hard matter to dig me out of my chair, but unless my taste or inclination leads in some special direction, then I am what you would call lazy. To be a true comedian a man must have the genuine ring about him, otherwise he would not be a comedian, and, as Garrick pertly remarked to a friend, 'You may fool the town in tragedy, but they won't stand any nonsense in comedy.'"[7]

Notes to Interview 95

1. This voyage is mentioned in *FE*, 324.
2. See n. 1 to interview 93.
3. See n. 2 to interview 90.
4. See n. 3 to interview 14.
5. See n. 2 to interview 79 and n. 2 to interview 84.
6. See interview 50.
7. See n. 6 to interview 85.

96

"Mark Twain in Hobart: Some Impressions and an Interview," *Mercury* (Hobart), 4 November 1895, 4; rpt. *Tasmanian Mail* (Hobart), 9 November 1895, 35.

... Mark Twain, with his pilot-cap, his bushy white hair, his cigar, is—very much like his photographs. Those photographs have had such frequent publication of late that I need enter on no other description. When I asked him if he would talk with me for a few moments he looked whimsical and said, "Well, I've nothing to say; but if it's of use to you I'm quite willing to say it." And he led the way (we were on the deck of the *Mararoa*) to a vacant seat apart from the crowd, where for a time, with the strong, invigorating breeze stirring the masses of his hair, he sat in companionable silence, gazing on the kaleidoscopic panorama of Mount Wellington.

"You're really leaving Australia for a time today, Mr. Clemens," I said at length. "Are you sorry?"

"Yes," he said slowly. "I didn't come to stay, but I'm sorry—downright sorry. In this Australian trip the change to me has been delightful. I've met a good many people, and they've all been hearty and friendly. The same thing applies to my audiences, who have all along welcomed me in a fashion which is exceedingly pleasant to a stranger. All my impressions of the country and of the people are of a pleasant sort, for the reason that it is the human element that makes a country beautiful or otherwise. All this now (and he indicated Mount Wellington and its environment)—all this is very beautiful, but it seems to me that this could not be beautiful of itself.[1] Scenery by itself is all very well; but the weather can damage scenery. You must have the pleasant human element to counteract the effects of climate and circumstance. Any country is pleasant, if the people are pleasant; any country is beautiful if the people receive you kindly. There'd be no perceptible beauty to a lone man in a tropical sunset if there were irreconcilable cannibals in the foreground; there is no scenery in the world that could be beautiful in the circumstances. The idea that scenery is beautiful of itself is mere nonsense; in one way or the other it is—it must be—modified by the human element."

With the memory of certain "artistic" discussions hot at heart it seemed to me that we were getting into devious ways. So I changed the subject. "Now you are an American, Mr. Clemens." (He bowed.) "I have heard it said that the people of Australia, and particularly of Victoria, are not unlike your own people. Can you express an opinion on the point? Considered as a British offshoot, would you regard the people of Australia as developing traits of character and manner differing from those of the insular English, and approximating more closely to those that obtain among the citizens of the States?"

"Unquestionably. One notices that at once. In speech and manner you Australians have a sort of frank and friendly way that lacks something of the English reserve. They differ, as you suggest, from the English people in England; and, just in proportion, they develop a certain similarity to the people of the United States. That is so."

"You've seen something of the Press in Australia. Now will you"—

"Wait! Let me anticipate you. I'm not sure that I'm prepared to follow the line of your questioning. I've seen your newspapers, as you say. The *Bulletin*, I'm told, is the most typical paper of the purely Australian type. Well, I think that paper is very brightly written. The men who make the pictures in it have excellent talent. But to go into anything like criticism of your newspapers—I can't do it. Criticism from me could be of no value unless I sat down to my table and put my mind to it. To criticize, I must go to work—and go to work right, seeing the end I want to see. It's an offense to people or things to criticize them without due reflection. The fact that it is a common offense does not warrant me in committing it."

There was another silence here. "Mark Twain" is eminently companionable. Presently he began, inconsequently,—

"Ah, those maps! what erroneous ideas they give one! Before I came over on this tour I'd seen Australia and New Zealand on the maps. Glancing at the maps I had an idea that there was probably a small ferry boat running eighteen or twenty times a day between Melbourne and New Zealand. When I came to inquire about the name of the ferry boat, it was taken as the remark of an ignorant person. That's the trouble with maps: they get a lot of stuff into a small space, and give one an inadequate idea of distance.[2] There was an old lady ran out of a gate to me once in Bermuda—came bounding out of the gate, and said, 'That's your ship that's lying in the offing there? An American ship? You belong in America?' 'Yes,' I said, 'I belong in America.' 'Ah,' she said, 'I've got a nephew there—a journeyman carpenter—and he works down in the lower part of New York City. His name's J. M. White: perhaps you've met him?' And she wanted me to hunt him up. Now that looks silly, but coming from a person who's only looked at a map it was perfectly natural."

"You're going to India, Mr. Clemens. Been there before?"

"Never. But I have received the pleasantest kind of letters from people connected with the civil and military administrations in India for years past. I shall find people in India whom I have not previously met, but who are still my friends."

"As you do everywhere?"

"Well, yes, as I do everywhere, since you are kind enough to put it so. A book? Why, on such a trip as this, one could write a library of books! If I do subsequently write a book it will be an incident consequent on the tour rather than any attempt at dealing fully with the tour itself. Of course on a lecturing tour one has to combine business with pleasure, and I can't say that they harmonize very well. Then I have had a succession of carbuncles—have one, just about spent, on my leg now—and they keep me rather lame. The only good times I have had—times, that is to say, when I have been entirely free from pain—have been on the platform, talking to my audiences. At such a time one's mind is fully occupied, and one has not attention to waste on pain. Yes, I naturally look forward to my visit to the East with anticipation more than ordinarily pleasurable, although I've only heard positively of one Asiatic who took what I may call a literary interest in me. He was a Chinaman, and a friend of mine who was American Consul at Singapore recommended him to read my *New Pilgrim's Progress*,[3] venturing to praise the book as interesting and funny. The Chinaman got a book, written in his own language and illustrated with quaintly forcible woodcuts of fights with Apollyon, Christian's experiences in the Valley of the Shadow of Death, and that sort of thing: it was the original *Pilgrim's Progress*,[4] published sometime ahead of mine, and differing a little in tone and treatment. The Chinaman read it, and seeking my friend the consul (one cannot account for the literary tastes of the Chinese) protested in a pained manner, as one who would deprecate a practical joke, that there was not a funny idea in the book from one end to the other. The consul"—

But at this moment Mr. Clemens was appropriated by a local gentleman with fossils to exhibit, and after a brief leave-taking I saw him no more....

Notes to Interview 96

1. See also *FE*, 281.
2. See *FE*, 151: "On the map the distance looked small; but that is a trouble with all divisions of distance in such a vast country as Australia."
3. The subtitle of *The Innocents Abroad*.
4. The Christian allegory *Pilgrim's Progress* (c. 1668) by John Bunyan (1628-88), English religious writer.

97

Malcolm Ross,[1] "A Chat with Mark Twain," *Otago Times* (Dunedin, N.Z.) 6 November 1895, 4; rpt. *Otago Witness* (Dunedin, N.Z.), 14 November 1895, 37.

... My first glimpse of Mark Twain was as he was pacing up and down the vestibule at Menzies' one evening after dinner; and, as the sporting reporters say, I spotted him at once. He is very like his portraits, only grayer, and there is no mistaking him. Later on it was my good fortune to meet him on the Union liner *Mararoa*, en route to Dunedin, and to have several interesting chats with him in the intervals during which he left his work for a change of scene and a smoke on the upper deck. The stereotyped interview is distasteful to most literary men of any ability, so I discreetly kept pencil and notebook out of view, and the gifted author never dreamt for a moment that he was being "drawn out" for an interview.

Mark Twain, it appears, is a hard worker. He has been living for some few years past in France and Germany. He started out on his present lecturing tour quite unprepared, and with some misgivings on this score. By the time he reached the colonies, however, he was ready to "face the music," and has succeeded beyond expectations. In his spare time he is engaged in writing a book on his present travels, and this will be looked forward to with interest by most colonials. Every day and every night he is hard at work in his cabin, but he is in no danger of becoming "played out," as his method of working is such that there is always a freshness about what he does. As soon as he feels that he has been writing long enough on one subject he leaves it and goes on to another. In the same way with regard to books—when he gets to a point at which writing becomes a labor he immediately throws that book overboard and takes up something more congenial to the inspiration of the moment. He has now two or three unfinished books pigeon-holed in this way. Someday they will be taken up and finished, and will see the light in due course. This is a tip which might be taken with advantage by some modern writers whose "pot-boilers" have been more or less in evidence of late years. At one time this inability to finish a story with the freshness with which it was begun troubled him a good deal, but he found out the remedy, and now whenever he feels a labor of love becoming a task he puts it aside till he is able to do it more justice, and it once more becomes a labor of love.

A friend remarked to me not long ago that he thought Mark Twain was getting "played out," but so long as he works on these lines there is not much danger of this. He cannot, or will not, write to order. At the commencement of his present tour he had an engagement to write a series of articles for the *Century Magazine*, but they wanted them done in a certain way, and Mark Twain got them to let him off the engagement. The cells of his brain supply him with certain ideas, and it is a pleasure for him to commit these to paper. In this way he is able to write for long hours at a stretch without feeling tired beyond the mere physical exertion entailed. This he could not of course do had he to be particular about facts and statistics, or to get up a very difficult subject. He illustrated the difference in the strain caused by his style of work [from] that of the men who had laboriously to get their material together in an accurate manner by citing the case of his friend Professor Fisk, who, while engaged in Florence compiling an Arabic dictionary, overworked his brain to such an extent that he went wandering off about the Continent, no one knew where, till eventually he pulled up in Brussels.[2]

We dwelt for a time on modern literature and the "boom" that the Scotch writers such as Barrie, Crockett, and M'Laren [McLaren] have been experiencing,[3] and I was surprised to hear that these and other British writers, such as Anthony Hope,[4] were now monopolizing the American papers and magazines to the exclusion of many of the more promising American writers. Mark Twain mentioned the case of a friend who had always commanded big prices for his work, and who only the other day had a story returned by a well-known magazine which was full for the next two years!

Mark Twain does not read much modern fiction. He is too busy with his own pen. There are, he says, at present no very prominent novelists in America. Bret Harte is done,[5] and is not likely again to be heard of in the literary world.

Of Kipling, at present in America, he has a very high opinion, and he thinks it possible that we may one day get something from that writer's pen with a flash of New Zealand color in it. Kipling is a man who gets material wherever he is and never misses anything, but it may have to simmer and fester a long time before he uses it.

I found Mark Twain very much interested with Marcus Clarke's writings.[6] He was pleased also with Australasian journalism, notably with the *Melbourne Argus,* which was the paper he saw most of. Some of the American papers, he says are splendid properties. The New York *World,* for instance, returns an income of £60,000 a year. The *Herald* is also a splendid property. Both these papers have an enormous circulation, but their income of course is [two words missing] of advertisements. They also get out Sunday editions of from 20 to 32 pages. These papers, he declares, are a load for any jackass to carry, and only a jackass would attempt to tackle them—which is no doubt very true, but goes to prove that there are a goodly number of jackasses in America as in other countries.

I found Mark Twain deeply interested in details connected with the discovery and early history of New Zealand; also in the Maori race, and it is to be hoped that before he leaves our shores he will have an opportunity of seeing something of Maori character and customs for himself. He marveled at the work done by Tasman and Cook.[7]

He talked for a while of his early successes in literature. It appears *The Innocents Abroad* is the book that has had the largest circulation, though it has been run very close by *A Tramp Abroad.* Both these books have had an enormous circulation at 12 [shillings] and 14 [shillings] per copy. Mark Twain retains the copyright.

Asked which of his books he liked the best, he said he really could not tell me—it was so many years since he had read any of them. In fact, he had only a hazy idea of what was in most of them. I expect, though, if he has really any liking for one more than another it will be for *The Innocents.* "Yes, that was a splendid trip," he said. "Everything was fresh and new then; everything is old now."

From books we came to talk of illustrations and printing, and I mentioned that I had been to see those wonderful machines the linotypes in Melbourne.[8] This led him to remark that he was interested in a type-setting machine in America—a wonderful machine, which, however, could only be produced at a cost of £3000. Ten of these at a cost of £30,000 would be sufficient for a good-sized newspaper, and the Americans would pay the price, but the machine was so wonderfully intricate and so liable to get out of order that it was not a success. Mark Twain lost £40,000 over it.[9] Let us hope that on his present lecturing trip, and with the new material which he will collect, he will get back some share of the capital lost in this unlucky venture.

Mark Twain's present tour is to embrace India and South Africa under the pilotage of the much-traveled Smythe. Smythe, sen., is in quarantine with the *Cozco*'s passengers in Sydney, and his son, Mr. Carlyle Smythe, pilots Mark Twain through New Zealand.[10] The latter is accompanied by his wife and his second daughter, who were delighted with their Australian experience.

While we were finishing our last chat Mark Twain puffed energetically for a time at a briar pipe. Then his hand stole into his breast pocket for a cheroot, which having been sacrificed on the shrine of My Lady Nicotine, was replaced by another, and as the second one was coming to an end I took my leave to jot down these few notes. . . .

Notes to Interview 97

1. Malcolm Ross (1862–1930), New Zealand author and journalist.
2. MT apparently alludes to the missionary Pliny Fisk (1792–1825), who sailed from Boston to the Middle East in 1819, joined the Christian mission in Beirut in May 1825, and completed an Arabic dictionary shortly before his death.
3. Sir James Barrie (1860–1937), author of the play *Peter Pan* (1904); S. R. Crockett (1860–1914); and John Watson, aka Ian McLaren (1850–1907). Barrie, Crockett, and McLaren comprised the "Kailyard school" of writers who sentimentalized Scottish pastoral life.
4. Anthony Hope (1863–1933), English novelist.
5. See n. 3 to interview 8 and n. 5 to interview 84.
6. See n. 2 to interview 90.
7. The Dutch explorer Abel Janszoon Tasman (1603–59) commanded the first European expedition to New Zealand; Captain James Cook (1728–79) voyaged to New Zealand three times (1769, 1773, 1777).
8. Invented by Ottmar Mergenthaler and exhibited in Washington, D.C., in 1885, the first practical modern typesetting machine.
9. The Paige typesetting machine, invented by James W. Paige, failed practicality tests at the *Chicago Herald* in 1894. See also headnote to chapter 3.
10. See n. 1 to interview 93.

98

"Mark Twain: A Talk with the Famous Humorist," *Lyttelton Times* (Christchurch, N.Z.), 13 November 1895, 5–6; rpt. *Canterbury Times* (Christchurch, N.Z.), 21 November 1895, 24–25.

. . . Much may be learned about a man's nature from a conversation with him, and I shall merely record some of the impressions produced by a long talk with Samuel Langhorne Clemens. This conversation was not replete with "funnyisms." He does not distill wit and humor, "even as," to quote himself, "otto of roses distilleth from the otter." Yet is he a brilliant conversationalist, who talks in polished and incisive English, with a decided American quality in the tones of his voice. . . . Mr. Clemens's conversation ranged over a wide field; its subjects were many and diverse; and of all he knew much, and was anxious to know more. He spoke of labor matters in the United States, and remarked that the idea of the Knights of Labor, of consolidating all classes of workers into one body for mutual help in the effort to redress grievances, was a fine one, but that the organization had failed, because its leader could, from the nature of the organization, have no effective control over the members.[1] It has done good, however, for as a result of its action the American State Governments are now turning their attention to Eight Hour Acts and similar legislation, matters to which, Mr. Clemens shrewdly remarked, governments are not inclined to pay much attention unless they are urged thereto by the continual watchfulness of the people—armed with votes.

The American militia system, by which the United States can now put several hundreds of thousands of fairly-trained fighting men into the field at a moment's notice; the negro problem, for which he frankly professed himself unable to see a solution, though he finds hope in the fact that the proportion of whites to blacks is increasing in the southern states; a ghastly story of the French astronomer who bound a book in the skin of a lady friend bequeathed to him by will; the superiority of Maoris to Australian black-fellows; the Mississippi River trade; prohibition; the differing characteristics of the English and Australian novel; the prevalence of crime among foreign residents in America; and the stones of Easter Island were some of the subjects upon which the versatile *raconteur* talked, and talked well and ably. His thirst for information on any matter, however much "out of the way," was striking shown by one little incident. Hearing that there had recently appeared in a Sydney newspaper a full description of the carved stones on Easter Island, those wonderful images, whose origin and purpose have so long baffled research, he exclaimed to his business manager, Mr. Carlyle Smythe,[2] "Now, I must have that as soon as possible: I want to read everything I can get about those."

Mark Twain is pleased with Australian journalism, and has considerable respect for the beginnings of Australian literature; very good beginnings he considers them. In terse and epigrammatic phrase he pointed out what he deems the essential characteristic of the Australian novel, that which differentiates it from the English and American novel. "In an English novel," he said, "the interest centers in the hero and heroine; the surrounding, the manners and customs, the scenery, the local conditions are subordinated to them, to the plot, and are mere accessories. In the Australian novel the reverse is the case; the aim of the writer seems to be to give a picture of the place and times; the hero, and still more the heroine, are subordinate."

The method of work of a celebrated writer is always of interest to his readers. Mr. Clemens's method is peculiar. He begins a book and works at it until he feels that the writing of it is becoming irksome, till he comes to a standstill. He at once lays it aside and begins on another, which in its turn may be put in the pigeonhole. He may thus have several "on the stocks" at once. After a while he takes one out, reads the last chapter or two, finds that his mind will again work freely on the subject, and goes on with the book "as a labor of love." An admirable plan he finds this for keeping his mind fresh and vigorous, and for preventing himself from becoming "played out." He is, as might be expected, a hard worker; and it is whispered that he is occupied on a book dealing with his present travels, a book colonials will look for with a good deal of interest. They need not, however, feel much apprehension that they will find themselves and their countries "slated" in this work, as they have been by some literary travelers. Mr. Clemens was most emphatic in his condemnation of the folly of hasty generalizations, of jumping to conclusions about a whole people because one has seen a few of the individuals composing it. The Americans have had to suffer injustice from that kind of thing, and Mark Twain is particularly anxious to avoid doing like injustice to others.

Though a patriotic American, whose pride in his country is very evident, he has a soft spot, a large spot at that, in his heart for the Britishers. He especially likes an English audience. His best audiences, those whom he felt had "got with him" in the shortest time, were, he said, at Baltimore in Maryland, at London, and at Liverpool. His colonial audiences, however, pleased him well. *Apropos* of his audiences he told a story. His conversation, by the way, does not bristle with stories and jokes any more than that of any other educated and intellectual man. "When I was going over from America to England we had entertainments in the first and second cabins, and I was asked to give some of my pieces. The first cabin was full of Americans, but in the second cabin nearly all the passengers were English. I said to Mrs. Clemens, 'No, you'll find I shall have the most appreciative audience in the second cabin.' She hardly seemed to think so, but I proved myself correct. The Americans in the first cabin were very good, but next night when I gave exactly the same pieces in the second cabin the English people there fairly carried it off with a whoop." . . .

Notes to Interview 98

1. The Knights of Labor, established in 1869, was the first significant U.S. labor union. Its constitution called for an eight-hour workday.
2. See n. 1 to interview 93.

99

"Mark Twain at Home: A Chat with Mr. Clemens," *Press* (Christchurch, N.Z.), 13 November 1895, 5.

Above all things Mr. Clemens—or, as he is more widely known, Mark Twain—is a journalist, one who has passed through all the grades of the great army of journalism, from that of the private to the generalissimo. It was therefore with the greatest possible pleasure that I met Mark Twain, whose quiet incisive humor has made him world-renowned. That one met with a cordial reception goes without saying. Let me just try to give a pen portrait of Mark as he came forward with hand outstretched and cigar in mouth to greet me. The first thing that strikes one is the keen eyes, which look out on you from under penthouse eyebrows as though they would search you through. Yet there is a gleam of fun in them, which broadens and deepens as we talk. A massive head, with a leonine shock of white hair, completes a very remarkable personality. So the first greetings being over, we sat down for a discursive chat.

"You ask me," said Mr. Clemens, "what I think of the colonies. Now, let me say right here that the man who attempts to describe a country which he sees for the first time after a brief visit to it, and before he has time to digest, as I may put it, is wrong. When you are in Rome you go into St. Peter's; there are many other churches about, and all that you know of St. Peter's different from them is that the dome is so many feet high, and so on. You come out, and the facts and statistics do not make much impression on you. By and by the time comes for you to leave. From the car windows you see the city disappear, but rising into the sky, a prominent figure, is the dome of St. Peter's. Now that is just the case with regard to the colonies. I am too close now to give any opinion. By and by, when I get further off—when I get a perspective so to speak of the colonies,—then I can form some idea of the country.

"You ask me what my impressions were of the colonies before I visited them, and whether they have been realized?—Well, I formed an idea of a physical Australia and a physical New Zealand before I left on this tour. You see, I had read a good deal about Australia. That was when it was before the world owing to the gold discoveries. I knew something of mining and mining camps, and though under different circumstances, I could construct pretty well a physical Australia; nor was I disappointed. It was all there as I had pictured it. But I was not prepared to see the populous cities which had grown up since Australia first came before the world owing to the gold discoveries. The writers failed to bring these before my mind, because they did not exist at the time they wrote. Strange to say, I had not conversed with an American who had visited Australia previous to my coming, so that my ideas of the country were purely physical, as I have said. But the growth of the cities I was not prepared for, and I was agreeably surprised. So also with New Zealand. I knew of the New Zealand of Tasman[1] from reading but the New Zealand of today took me by surprise; therefore I may answer your question by saying that I had formed a correct idea of the physical appearance of the country, but there were points which did not suggest themselves to my mind. Men when describing countries give you as a rule statistics—heaps of them, till you are sick and tired of them. There are statistics on all kinds of subjects—extent of land, number of sheep and cattle, and population. But that does not convey any idea—any picture perhaps is the best way of putting it—as to the country as it strikes one when he reaches it. So it has been with me in Australia and New Zealand. I have read barrow loads of books on Australia and New Zealand, but they have not prepared me in any sort of shape or way for the actual appearance of the colonies as I find them today.

"New Zealanders are all enthusiasts—and rightly so—as to their country, which they contend is the finest in the world. From the glimpses I have had I am inclined to believe them. I have seen since I have landed pictures of your alpine and Sound scenery. It seems to me that you have a combination of the fiords of Norway and the scenery of Alaska. There are the same deep crevasses in the mountains, with sea between, that are the charm of the Norwegian Scenery, whilst your glaciers and snowclad mountains remind one of Alaska. The only regret is that there is nothing known of your lovely scenery in America. All that is known of New Zealand is its commercial statistics, its population, &c., those wearying masses of figures to which I have referred, which, after all, convey no true idea of the country to anyone who reads them. I think the scenery which has met my eye from the Bluff to Christchurch is the most charming I have seen. It is not grand, like the Swiss scenery, but there is a quiet beauty which is all its own, and which makes it quite an Eden. It resembles the beautiful English scenery, with its well-kept parks and gardens, hedges, &c., which so enchanted me when I first visited it years ago. I had pictured England before I went there, but the great beauty was far and away before the picture I had drawn in my mind. So it is with the New Zealand scenery I have seen. The sea, with its shade of green in the shoal water and deep blue further out, coming up to the foot of the hills, and the green of the verdure, strikes one with a force which is greater than the grandeur of mountains. Mountains are grand, but they pall upon one; not so the green fields and the trim hedges, with the cottages nestling in a clump of trees.

"What is my experience of colonial audiences as compared with American and English ones? Well, there is a difference, and I will tell you what it is. The colonial audiences at once are friendly with you. They encourage you to give your best. You feel as soon as you step on the platform that they are your friends, that they wish you to succeed, and that puts fire and mettle into you, and puts you at once on terms with them. In Australia, aye, and in New Zealand, too, this was my experience. I went on the platform a stranger, but in a few minutes I found that I had a number of warm friends in front of me who were enthusiastic, and wanted me to do well, and I set to work at once without the least fear of success. This is the same with regard to English audiences. When I first went to London I naturally wished to make a success, and felt a little, well not nervous, but anxious as to the result. But I had only been speaking a few minutes when I felt that I had a houseful of friends, and immediately I was at home. Now, with us in America the audiences are different. They come prepared to demand that you give them the best you have got, and they will therefore feel to you somewhat critical. You must get them when you start in, or perhaps you will not get them again. You must attend strictly to business. They have made a contract with you to give them something and they hold you strictly to your part of the bargain, and all the time they are watching to see that you don't go back on it. But if you find that you don't get them fast at first there is no use in getting fussed. Give them something better a little further on and it is all right. Knowing you have got this then you are sure that in the end the audience will be with you. That is just the difference between an English or colonial—which is one and the same thing—audience and the American. The colonials are warm to you from the first, the Americans size you up and sample what you have got.

"Let a man be what he may, he never forgets that he is a journalist. The rule of that mistress is absolute. Now, looking at your colonial journals, I do so with extreme pleasure. Let me say right here that at home as well as when I am traveling, I only read the editorials, or what you call here leaders. The character of a paper I take it—and I think you, as a journalist, will agree with me—is reflected in the editorials. If they are weak, badly constructed, and illogical, then you may be sure the rest of the paper is run badly. On [one line of type missing in the original printing] well-written, spirited, and logical in their conclusions, the remainder of the paper is also bound to be alive. So the key to the character of the journals is found in the editorials, and that is why, being a busy man, I read these only. Well, taking this view of the Australian papers I have seen during my stay in Melbourne and Sydney, and also of your New Zealand papers I have met with, I am most favorably impressed with the vigor of their style, their scholarly language, and logical conclusions. That a small place like Christchurch, of some 40,000 inhabitants, can support two large daily papers, two evening papers, and two weekly journals is unprecedented in my experience. In the States a town of the same size would probably have a morning paper, one good evening paper, and one inferior. The weeklies such as you have here are unknown with us. The rapidity of transmission of the daily journals prevents this altogether. Still they are most admirable and unique, combining as they do the magazine, the sporting paper, the illustrated paper, and the special features of a daily journal. It shows a real live intellectual community when so many journals are in full swing.

"I want just to say a word as to the hospitality I have received. Everywhere I have gone in the colonies the most cordial and genial hospitality has met me spontaneously. I like it, and appreciate it most thoroughly, and it will be one of the things which I shall remember in connection with my tour through the colonies with the keenest pleasure."

So after a brief and most pleasant and cheery chat on journalism, Bohemianism, and kindred topics, I shook hands once more with Mark Twain, who treated me most cordially, and we said "Good night."

Note to Interview 99

1. The Dutch explorer Abel Janszoon Tasman (1603–59) commanded the first European expedition to New Zealand.

100

"Mark Twain: Arrival in Auckland," *New Zealand Herald* (Auckland), 21 November 1895, 5.

Who has not read Mark Twain? Who has not reveled in his humor? And who has not felt a longing to meet such a man face to face? Auckland people will have that pleasure for a couple of nights or so. A *Herald* representative had that pleasure yesterday evening, at the Star Hotel, where Mr. Clemens (Mark Twain), with Mrs. and Miss Clemens are staying. The provoker of a myriad million laughs is a gentleman who takes a walking exercise while conversing; he has a fine head and a quick eye, and it does not take long to find out that he can talk, to any extent, on almost any subject that may be started in his presence. He did not care about saying how he liked the people of New Zealand, because he said he had been asked that question before. Neither did he seem to care to talk about American humor until someone in the company quoted Lord Rosebery to the effect that it was a new element in literature.[1]

"Ah, yes," he said, "American humor is different entirely to French, German, Scotch, or English humor. And the difference lies in the mode of expression. Though it comes from the English, American humor is distinct. As a rule when an Englishman writes or tells a story, the 'knob' of it, as we would call it, has to be emphasized or italicized, and exclamation points put in. Now, an American story-teller does not do that. He is apparently unconscious of the effect of the joke. The similes used in America may be a little more extravagant than in England, but the method of treatment is modified. The method is quieter, more modified, and more subtle. Josh Billings said 'never take a bull by the horns; take him by the tail, and then you can let go when you want.'[2]

In any other country but America the part at which you should laugh would be put in italics and with exclamation marks."

Americanisms then cropped up in the conversation, for many of these contain a big bulk of meaning, and expressed just what one wants to say.

"Yes," said Mark Twain, "there are many expressions said to be American and slang. Many are local, but here and there a phrase comes that just fits into what is wanted. And many so-called Americanisms come from the English. Take the expression, 'Fire him out,' which has come into use during the last few years. That expression was used by Shakespeare in one of his sonnets."[3] Then most people suppose that everyone who 'guesses' is a Yankee; the people who guess do so because their ancestors guessed in Yorkshire."

Then, naturally, the word "boom" came in, of which the man supposed to have first used it, in a newspaper, has said that he got the idea for the use of the term from the designation given the rise of water in the Mississippi.

"The sound of the word," said Mr. Clemens, elaborating this in his quick way, "has a good deal to do with the adoption of a term. If it has a good strong sound, and that sound seems to express the thing you want, then it has a chance to live."

"You a little while ago said," remarked our representative, "that American writers may be extravagant in the construction of their phrases, while an English writer would use exclamation marks or italics to bring out the 'knob' of his story. Would not the one counterbalance the other?"

"I was not saying that extravagant similes should not be used. Simple extravagance would be utterly reprehensible. But where a thing is happily phrased you do not care whether the figure is extravagant or not. For instance, what fault could you find in this: A captain of a ship is describing the perils his vessel went through; 'Why,' says a listener, 'You must have shipped a great deal of water.' 'Sir,' says the captain, 'we pumped the Atlantic Ocean through my ship sixteen times.' How are you to find fault with that? It is extravagant; but it is good fun, and does no harm."

A most interesting chat having taken place on American humorous writers, from Lieutenant Derby,[4] whom Mr. Clemens considers the father of American humor, he went on to speak of the difference in writing now. If Harriet Beecher Stowe was writing *Uncle Tom's Cabin* now, it would have been written differently—that is, not so diffusively. And the same might be said of Dickens. They wrote for their time.

"And how did the change come?" said he. "That is a change to which every one contributes. These things are contributions of Time. I was once idiot enough to ask the partner of Mr. Bell as to who was the inventor of the telephone. The reply I got was, 'Do you not know that 1500 men had been at work on the telephone for 5000 years—do you suppose that anyone could invent any such instrument in any one lifetime?' It is the same with literature. English writing has been a good deal bound up with conventionalism; American writing has been less so. Though conventions exist in all countries."

The names of a good many American writers having been mentioned, the question was asked, had any American woman developed any capacity for dealing with American humor.

"The only woman I know of," was the reply, "was a writer who wrote, possibly as far back as the '40's, *The Widow Bedott Papers.* These were written by a girl of twenty. The book was a good one, and it lived for say 15 years, or possibly 20 years, and it is a good long life for a book."[5]

"A good many people think you do not show any very great reverence for subjects they regard reverentially. Take your *Innocents Abroad* for instance."

"Yes, I know. I once wrote an article for an American literary journal that has a vast circulation amongst young people. I was asked to change something in that article. I asked the editor what he wanted changed. He said I had put a clergyman in a ridiculous position. My reply was he had put himself there. If he liked to strike the clergyman out he could. But I could put no one in his place. It was a story I would have told in the pulpit, if they would have given me a pulpit to tell it from. The people who object to the backyard of Joseph of Arimathea being spoken of as if it were my own backyard,[6] could not care if I spoke of a Mahommedan's backyard. There are so many curious notions in the world about irreverence."

"Well," said our representative, in conclusion, "I suppose you will be writing a book about us and the rest of the people you see in your travels."

"Yes, I do not think I could do it under better auspices, for I have had not time to see anything. Traveling and lecturing are like oil and water; they don't mix. There are many fine sights in New Zealand that I haven't seen."

Notes to Interview 100

1. The fifth Lord Rosebery, aka Archibald Philip Primrose (1847–1929), a prominent liberal politician and prime minister of Great Britain (1894–95).
2. Josh Billings, aka H. W. Shaw (1818–85), American humorist. See also Paine, 446.
3. The concluding couplet of sonnet 144: "Yet this shall I ne'er know but live in doubt, / Till my bad angel fire my good one out."
4. George Horatio Derby, aka John Phoenix, aka Squibob (1823–61), pioneer western humorist.
5. Frances M. Whitcher (1811–52), author of the posthumously published *Widow Bedott Papers* (1855).
6. Joseph of Arimathea was the wealthy Jew who received Christ's body from Pilate and prepared it for the tomb (Matthew 27:57–60).

101

R. A. L., "A Chat with Mark Twain," *New Zealand Mail* (Wellington), 12 December 1895, 51.

Mark Twain arrived from Wanganui last night at 10 o'clock, and was kind enough to receive me after supper. He received me with the urbanity of a journalist and the courtesy of a man of the world. The light of humor that began to shine in the world some thirty years ago; whose brilliancy several continents have been enjoying for the whole of that period, as it was thrown out from books, after-dinner speeches, lectures, and every vehicle known to the humorist, the man of descriptive power, and the thinker—what sort of man is he? That was my thought. The outside of him I found quite easy to understand. A man of vigorous physique, who walks rapidly to and fro as he talks to you, shaking his vast head of wavy gray hair, looking at you with keen eyes peering from the shade of shaggy brows; eyes which light up a strong determined face, the lower part under the prominent nose hidden by a heavy moustache, and ending in a square chin; a calm self-reliant face, which belongs to a self-contained thinker and close accurate observer, who finds time to be genial and pleasant withal, who sets you thinking as he talks, and laughs silently while you laugh loud—such I found Mark Twain to be. Thirty years ago and more he captured Europe and America. It is something to see him; and a privilege to be allowed to draw him on the history of the achievements which have built up his reputation.

We talked journalism a little at the outset, as common ground. "You were kind enough, sir, in some of your talks in the South of this country to speak well of our journalism."

"Oh, yes." Mark Twain had said things of that kind and he had seen reason not to alter his mind as he went further north.

"You spoke well of the leading articles [editorials] in the colonial newspapers."

Yes. He had a respect for the leading articles. He had done some leading articles himself once. It was for a week, a whole week. "My editor, you see, went away one morning at four o'clock, down to San Francisco for a holiday. I got up at about the usual hour, say noon, and it very soon settled down upon me with great solidity that I had to write a leading article that day."

"Was that the time you discovered that the turnip, with proper care, grew into a handsome forest tree?"

He waved his hand with a gentle deprecating gesture. "Oh, that was an agricultural experience."[1] And he paused as if to indicate that I was referring to one of his humorous efforts. "The week I refer to was serious journalism, sir. The pressure of my first leading article weighed with more and more solidity, until I remembered that it was the 22nd April 1864. Tomorrow would be the 23rd, the third centenary of Shakespeare's birthday. There was my subject."

But as every day was not the third centenary of the birth of the immortal bard, the practice of the daily article proved sufficient after a week to satisfy his modest wishes. He was glad when the week was over.

My friend suspected that the leading article was somewhere within my line, and he chose to put the thing thus flatteringly. I reciprocated by mentioning his many books; he increased the pace of his walk to and fro, and said rapid words about the said books, bursting out in clear cut sentences which seemed to come at will. He called them from the "vasty deep" of his thought, and they came.

"Roughing it"; yes, that was the coach journey across the Continent. A very hard journey, hard old days, a great experience.

"I took that trip for pleasure, for three months, just to put in a good time with my brother out West."

"That was after your experience as a Mississippi pilot?"

He nodded a pleasant yes, as much as to say "You have it." "You see, sir, the war had put a stop to the whole of the traffic in that great river, and the war was supposed to last for just three months; so I just took three months' holiday. You remember Mr. Lincoln called for 75,000 men for three months."

Two turns of the room rapidly, and he extended his hand.

"A curious thing happened—General Grant and I came very near meeting.[2] You see, I myself tried to put down that rebellion; thought I'd do it in two weeks by taking service in the Confederate Army as second lieutenant. But I found I couldn't do it."

Another couple of turns, another extension of the hand and—"Grant and I were very coming into violent collision during that two weeks."

"How was that prevented?"

"By my retreating. When we got to that point there was another point in view—somewhere out of danger," he said, after a long reflective pause—"and I retreated to that point. I was very fond of exercise in those days; had to be to keep in health. But fourteen retreats in two weeks; two retreats a day was too much exercise. I wanted less violent exercise, so resigned my commission as second lieutenant and went off to have a good time with my brother in the West. Knocked about for a year, and stumbled somehow into journalism."

At this point, when I had recovered from the fit of laughter into which his droll accent and dry manner had thrown me, I asked after the birth and life history of "The Jumping Frog," which had enlivened the young bloods of the world some time in the sixties.

He saluted the name with a certain comic air of parentage. "Oh!" said he, "I gave 'The Jumping Frog' to Artemus Ward who wanted something to fill up one of his volumes. But the volume was got out before 'The Jumping Frog' arrived. So Artemus Ward's publisher passed it on to Henry Clapp, the proprietor of the *Saturday Press,* a New York weekly journal. He said he could have it for nothing, which was lucky, as Henry Clapp never could pay for anything. On which terms 'The Jumping Frog' was published."

"With your consent?"

"With my consent."

"You were not like some folks in these parts who won't begin to enlighten the world under a guinea a column."

He nodded assent pleasantly, took a couple of turns in rapid energetic silence, shaking his shaggy locks, and then he said abruptly—"But 'The Jumping Frog' got even with Henry Clapp. After that Saturday that paper of his never appeared again. It was the very last issue. Henry Clapp announced that in that number. He couldn't help it; he had to."

The bright eyes under the thick brows twinkled over the fate of the unhappy frog. But better times were in store. The frog after all jumped, and jumped to some purpose. He did it in company with a volume of sketches which was published two years later, in January 1867. Don't we remember them just? Those were the days when we were young and could laugh. And then?

Then came *The Innocents Abroad.*

I remembered the sensation in Melbourne when the book came out there in 1870. The public were astonished at the cheap edition. Still more when they found it was not nasty.

How keenly the eyes twinkled at this I cannot hope to describe.

When I got with the book to New Zealand, I found several clever fellows who declared that there was never any ship called the *Quaker City,* who insisted that the book was just vamped out of books of travel and encyclopedias.

"I have heard that very thing said eighteen times in a week," said the author of the *New Pilgrim's Progress,*[3] rousing.

"These fellows said it was very easy, sir."

"I wish I could do it," says he directly. "I wish I could do all my traveling that way."

And then he came out of his dream. "You see there's a Freemasonry about dealing with things you see yourself which can't be counterfeited. There is an ease and certainty of touch in describing what you see which you can't get artificially."

Having laid down the axiom, he pauses. I fill the pause with "Defoe is the only man in the whole range of literature who is credited with the feat which you very properly declare impossible."

He is at once briskly alert, and has prompt words, which he shoots at me as he paces to and fro, laying off his theory with unswerving precision.

"And how did Defoe write his plague of London?[4] He knew London as well as you know this city of Wellington, every spot and corner of it. He had nothing in the way of local color to supply; it was all there before him. He got his details of the plague at first hand, from people who had seen. He made his studies in hospitals and by sick beds. What he saw he described, only changing here and there features of disease to suit the accounts of the plague. Defoe described what he saw, and added the equivalents which he had observed, and so he got his wonderful study. But to do a book of travel in that way, you would have to know every city in the world as well as Defoe knew his London. Only in that way could you get the firmness of touch, the Freemasonry I have spoken of, the thing which depends on your personal observation. How could a man describe that battered and faded Last Supper of Leonardo de Vinci's who had not seen it?[5] His touch would be uncertain, his grasp weak, his description faulty. To describe the thing properly he would have not only to go to the works of other men, but to take their very language."

"And the volcano Kilauea," I venture to remark, which I protest (though not in that presence) is the most masterly, lifelike, and vivid description in the English language.[6] He assents with the modest assent of a great artist who knows what good work is.

He throws further light on this problem as he walks about in more hurried eagerness. I had mentioned the Mississippi pilot, referring to the changes on the face of that great stream, and the perpetual watchfulness of the steersman. "Yes, you can see the ripples," he says, "and the eddies and all the moods of the rapid river. But you can only see as an amateur. There is a light line of ripples, which no amateur can understand: a harmless-looking line of ripples, quiet and easy, which to the pilot means the death of his ship if she gets there. You must see these things with the pilot's eye if you want to do justice to them."

The reality of the *Quaker City* and its pilgrim passengers thus established, we presently find ourselves, my friend going briskly back and forth the while, in the famous "street called Straight."[7]

"How did you square up with Mr. Haskett Smith?" I ask.[8]

He laughs his silent laugh, with eyes that twinkle, and teeth that shine and face that coruscates. "It was at supper," says he, "in Christchurch. 'We must settle this matter,' says I, 'Mr. Smith. You have kind of reduced my reputation for veracity. Let's settle at once.' 'With all my heart,' says he. 'Now what did you have to drink,' says I, 'when you went on that street?' 'Nothing,' says he. 'I had something different,' says I, 'and that settles it.'"

But this was one of his broad jokes. The real reason is the guide. The pilgrims had a day to spend; they depended on the guide. They checked the guide by their Murray;[9] ticked off the places of interest they were bound to see. They didn't know one from another, of course. The guide, realizing that they had certain places to see, shortened the journey by simply pointing to what they liked. But Mr. Smith lived in Damascus for months; went about with his camera. He had the instrument that can't lie, and no guide could fool him.

About the ways of guides he tells a story. It happened in Jerusalem. The guide stops before a wall, points to a high stone polished by the kisses of eighteen centuries of pilgrims. "That is the stone that our Savior said cried out"—

"Stop," says Colonel Denny, one of our party. "The sacred writing does not say 'cried out,' but 'would have cried out.'"[10]

"All right," says the guide. "The stone you see before you, ladies and gentlemen, is the stone that would have cried out," &c., &c., &c. So much for the guides and the controversy about the "street called Straight."

After that we drift through the books with Mark Twain upon them, and we stop at *The Prince and the Pauper*. "When I wrote that book I intended it should come out anonymously, but my family dissuaded me."

I venture to say I am very glad they did.

He gives his reasons. They were two: "First, I wanted to test the value of the book on its own merits, and in the event of success I should have put my name to it. Second, the distinctive badge 'Mark Twain' was a trademark which advertised a certain class of goods—low comedy goods all of them. I had no right to introduce tragedy under that mark and swindle people."

"But the book was very successful and much appreciated."

"Oh yes, that's true enough. There were only a few who protested. Some here and there in America said they had paid their three dollars under false pretenses and made a fuss. But the thing went all right after all."

From books to which I have no space to further allude, we get to newspapers, and we wander through the vast field of American journalism. Journalism is largely news there: "With fifty States and a few Territories to draw from,[11] and the rest of the world, the papers must be large to publish all that the agencies collect."

One story he tells of editorial enterprise. "'Mr. Clemens,' said a New York editor in chaff, 'will you write us your obituary?' 'Much obliged,' says I. 'But I would rather leave myself in the hands of your staff.' 'Well, if I give you 250 dollars will you give us your last words?' 'Right you are.' So I gave him my last words. But I haven't done with those last words yet. I am always improving on them, telling the fellow to strike that out and put in something better which I am sending them. And I intend to send him the last yet awhile."

I sincerely hope he will not. It reminds me that my turn has come for last words so far as this interview is concerned. So I say them with what speed I can, which is not much, for one word leads to another, and there are so many with the Mark Twain stamp, and all so interesting and full of cordiality and kindness, and by no means of the low comedy order, that the interview will not end readily. It does at last, to my regret, and we shake hands. . . .

Notes to Interview 101

1. The allusion is to MT's "How I Edited an Agricultural Paper" (1870).
2. As MT asserted in "The Private History of a Campaign That Failed" (1885), "In time I came to know that Union colonel whose coming frightened me out of the war and crippled the Southern cause to that extent—General Grant. I came within a few hours of seeing him when he was as unknown as I was myself." However, there is little evidence to support MT's claim.
3. The subtitle of *The Innocents Abroad*.
4. Daniel Defoe (1660-1731) described an epidemic of the bubonic plague in *Journal of the Plague Year* (1722).
5. In chapter 19 of *The Innocents Abroad,* MT described the da Vinci painting at length: "'The Last Supper' is painted on the dilapidated wall of what was a little chapel attached to the main church in ancient times, I suppose. It is battered and scarred in every direction, and stained and discolored by time, and Napoleon's horses kicked the legs off most of the disciples when they (the horses, not the disciples,) were stabled there more than half a century ago. . . . After reading so much about it, I am satisfied that the Last Supper was a very miracle of art once. But it was three hundred years ago."
6. MT described Kilauea volcano in Hawaii in chapter 74 of *Roughing It.*
7. One of the main streets in ancient Damascus, mentioned in Acts 9:11 and chapter 44 of *The Innocents Abroad.*
8. Haskett Smith (1857-1906), British novelist and religious writer.
9. First published by John Murray III in 1836, the most popular guidebooks for British travelers in the nineteenth century numbered some 270 separate volumes in 1913.
10. William R. Denny (b. 1823), a former Confederate colonel. The allusion is to Luke 19:40. MT recounts the anecdote in chapter 54 of *The Innocents Abroad,* though he does not identify Denny there by name.
11. There were only forty-four states in the Union in December 1895.

102

"Mark Twain: His Tour through New Zealand," *Telegraph* (Sydney), 20 December 1895, 6.

Among the passengers who arrived by the *Mararoa* from New Zealand on Tuesday was Mr. Samuel L. Clemens (Mark Twain).

Asked what opinion he had formed of New Zealand generally, Mr. Clemens said that he had not formed an opinion at all. "I just went through the country at a fast pace, and had not time to form an opinion. I thought the people there were particularly fortunate in living in a country with such a grand climate. When we arrived there the weather was very pleasant, and we were informed that the New Zealand summer had just started. The only unpleasant weather that we met with was at Timaru, where a slight gale blew for about two hours after our arrival. I guess if I had left Timaru before the gale abated, my opinion would have been that that was a windy place."

"Did you see much of the country?" "No, it was mostly the edges that I saw. When we did travel overland, I only caught cursory glimpses of the country from the car windows as we went dashing by. I was very much struck with the beautifully verdant appearance of the different places. I think the cities are admirably situated. Dunedin, Christchurch, Wellington, and Auckland are in very choice situations."

Mr. Clemens further said he had not noticed if the people of New Zealand were in any way different from the people of the other colonies. At the lectures which he had delivered no difference was noticeable in those who attended. With regard to politics in that colony, "I have no impressions," said Mr. Clemens. "If I had, they would just likely be erroneous ones. I don't think it is right to hurry through a place and form impressions. I have none—no publishable ones, anyway. If you want to give impressions you must sit down with a pen and ink and go at it. You can't give them verbally. That is what I object to so many people doing with regard to America. They just hurry through the place, and then venture an opinion on the nature of the country and the characteristics of the people, and they just know nothing. I didn't detect any difference among the different colonists at all."

"Did you see many of the beauty spots or other features of interest in New Zealand?"

"No, I hadn't time. I meant to see the Hot Springs and some other features in the Auckland district that are highly spoken of, but did not have time. I also wished to see some of the glaciers at Milford Sound, but the time was too limited. A great deal of traveling had to be done in getting to the cities that we desired to visit, and that, added to a certain amount of work, prevented us from seeing several places that we would very much have liked to have seen."

In reply to a further question, Mr. Clemens said that it would possibly be 12 months before he returned to America, as there were a number of other places to be visited.

103

"With Mark Twain," *Bulletin* (Sydney), 4 January 1896, 8.

... I went to interview him at his hotel and, sending up my card, received this reply:—"Mark Twain is in bed, tired, and likes it so much that he is going to stay there all day." But I caught him next time.

He sat up in his chair and said: "Max O'Rell,[1] like some other hastening globe-trotters, has written a book on Australia—so he may think. He forms decisions, conclusions, quicker than I; he has been going about for, say, 10 or 12 years, whereas I have been traveling, and watching, and listening—waiting for each subtle sense of suggestion—since I was 14. Now I am 60. How could he, or I, or anyone, from glances snatched in a fleeting passage, hope to divine what is real, what is fundamental in the character of this young nation? I have caught impressions—mere impressions—just as a bird would skimming over a forest—but what could that bird learn of the life and spirit underneath?

"I would not like to say what I think is my best book, for I like them all; and I could not say what I think is my worst, for I don't think there is one of them like that. But the book of mine which gave me the greatest pleasure is *Huckleberry Finn* because years after I had written it, and long after it had been wholly erased from the pages of my memory, I took it up and read it to my daughter, who was ill. It was new to her; it was new to me. As the reading progressed, I didn't know what to expect—a surprise came as a genuine surprise—a genuine pleasure.

"The books which gave me the hardest time to write were *Tom Sawyer* and *The Prince and the Pauper*. In the middle of both I came to a dead stop—a blank wall. Couldn't get on at all; rooted round a long time—a damnation long time, for incidents, for ideas—couldn't strike any. Gave it up—gave it up for twelve months. Came back then with the tank full, broke down the wall, story flowed on. The other books were written fairly easy—working daily from 11 to 3 five days a week—tearing the work up, if necessary, afterwards—and always keeping Saturday and Sunday sacred. *The Yankee at the Court of King Arthur* was as easy as any. *Life on the Mississippi* is my biography; it is a collocation of facts. As I have shown in that book, it is marvelous how the memory can be developed. When I ceased piloting and started reporting I could go all day, remembering everything. And when I brought my catch in towards evening I had it all there in my mind—every trifling detail, every figure. I had only to empty it out. But as the fashion was for reporters to use notebooks, I took up with one, and the first time I put a note down in that notebook, I wrote the death-sentence of my memory."

Asked about his ghastly story of the corpse watcher in the deadhouse, Twain couldn't recall it at all. It was new to him, he said, that story of the thumb-print; of the murderer being brought in a state of trance into the deadhouse, waking up amid corpses, cold, and horrors, and seeing in front of him during three hours of dying the avenger holding the brandy, torturing his foe.[2]

"But my books are all founded on facts; every character was a living being; every incident or germ of that incident has occurred; every plot had actually grown, or nearly grown, within my experience. There was selection, grouping, blending. And in writing a book its characters lived always; day and night, day and night. I'd go to bed, but they'd stay up talking, talking, talking; acting, acting; always in character—spoiling my sleep, yet never doing or saying anything that was rational or valuable or even usable.

"I read very little fiction; I read history and biography. I think *For the Term of His Natural Life* is the finest Australian novel, and Gabbett, the cannibal, as strongly-drawn a character as I ever met.[3] But what gave me the greatest pleasure in reading that book was that all the time I felt that I was reading history. And the chief charm of Louis Becke's stories for me is that the author seems to be chronicling facts and incidents he's seen—things he's lived amongst and knows all about.[4] I've noticed that Charles Reade, in writing about anything he's witnessed or felt, does it with remarkable success, but when he gets his matter second-hand he makes an awful botch of it.[5] I don't remember a book in its particulars very long, and gradually everything in it fades out of my mind.

"It is not true that owing to my lack of humor I was once discharged from a humorous publication. It's an event that could very likely happen were I on the staff of a humorous paper—but then I'd never get into a fix like that. I'd never undertake to be humorous by contract. If I wanted my worst enemy to be racked I'd make him the editor of a comic paper. For me there must be contrast; for humorous effect I must have solemn background; I'd let my contribution into an undertaker's paper of the London *Times*. Set a diamond upon a pall of black if you'd have it glisten.

"Dreams are more vivid than realities. The dreamer sits beside his glass of wine and accidentally causing it to begin falling lives seventy years, then stops his wine falling—drinks. Give Zola's *Downfall* to the day's imagination![6] how feeble are the reproduction of those blood-stained photographs of war's horrors! But at dead of night, when the reason is locked in the seclusion of oblivion, how the dreamer's imagination flashes upon the sensitive plate of the mind—armies, charges, battle scenes and incidents, perfect, horrible, magnificent.

"Periodically I dream that I'm a soldier—don't know why—never wanted to be a soldier. Was one once; found I was on the stronger side; left it to equalize things and give fair play. But in this dream I'm a soldier, in battle, in the very thick of it, the very crash. Soon realize it's not healthy and get back a little—about three miles. Seeing a large wagon, crawl under it to prevent it being taken in case the battle comes that way. By and by an enemy's shell lights on the wagon, and just as I'm congratulating myself upon my generalship, wagon turns out to be full of shells—and hell-fire and explosion—the elements are earthquake and conflagration—and I wake up either dead or alive—can't tell which.

"And I have dreamt of something so exquisitely humorous that the seventh heaven of bliss could be only a side-issue to it—and the ecstasy of it has awakened me. And sitting up and taking pencil and paper, I have there and then written out that subtly humorous thing—lain back, deliciously happy, and gone to sleep. But in the morning what a reversion! That paper! that paper! gave me not a precious treasure, but words, words, words—creatures of irrationality—jotted down—strung together—meaningless—hopelessly meaningless.

"I have seen one ghost. I was seated at a window and saw a man enter the gate, walk up the path and begin mounting the steps. Suddenly at the eighth step he disappeared. I arose instantly, went outside, looked round the garden, round the house, up and down the road. Couldn't see a sign of that man—of that apparition which dead sure was on my tracks. I went inside and asked a servant had she seen a man about. She replied she had just let one in. He never reached the door, I said; he came only halfway up the steps. She said—that servant, that old servant in whom I trusted—said: 'Sir, he did; I let him in; he's waiting for you now.' Sure enough I found him waiting, sitting in a chair. Fact is I dropped off to sleep—getting too tired watching that man mount those steps. That's my only apparition, and he's genuine.

"I have a passion for the theater but seldom gratify it, for whenever I go there is sure to be someone before, or behind, or beside me who persists in talking loudly to his neighbor and ruining my pleasure. It is the same in America, in England, in Australia. There is always the human beast that talks; that is destitute of every artistic feeling, and of every sympathy with artistic feeling. Often have I thought of Sir Walter Raleigh's peaceful happiness in jail;[7] often have I thought it a bitter thing that a man must first exterminate a talker in a theater, must become a criminal in order to gain seclusion."

Twain listened to a story of a Queenslander who, attending the second last farewell lecture in Sydney, was disappointed at Twain having traveled nine hours in a train on a scorching day and being too tired to lecture well. The Bananalander said: "I've come 3000 miles to hear that man, and, blow me, if the heat hasn't taken all the gas out of him." Replied Twain: "He was right to be disappointed; I have always found that whenever an audience is not pleased with me it's my fault or my manager's. Altogether I have been delighted with my Australian audiences."

Notes to Interview 103

1. See nn. 1 and 2 to interview 67.
2. The reference is to "A Dying Man's Confession" in chapter 31 of *Life on the Mississippi* (1883).
3. See n. 2 to interview 90.

4. See n. 1 to interview 87.
5. Charles Reade (1814–84), English dramatist and novelist.
6. *La Débâcle* (1892) by the French naturalist Emile Zola (1840–1902).
7. Sir Walter Raleigh (1554–1618) was jailed in 1603 on a trumped-up charge of treason. He spent the next thirteen years writing and conducting scientific experiments.

104

"Mark Twain in Colombo,"[1] *Overland Times of Ceylon* (Colombo), 14 January 1896, 56.

Our American friend Mr. S. L. Clemens, better known as Mark Twain, the principal humorist of the world and author of so many diverting books, arrived in Ceylon today from Australia, having traveled up in the P.&O. steamer *Oceana*,[2] which arrived very shortly after twelve noon. Though there were only a few passengers on board, for a short time I looked in vain for the man I had specially gone to see. At length, however, he made his appearance and there was no mistaking him.... I introduced myself with the statement that I assumed he was Mr. Clemens, and all doubt, if any remained, was set at rest as soon as he replied with a drawl that there was no mistaking. In response to queries as to his health and the voyage up, Mark Twain said he and his wife and daughter (Miss Clara Clemens—his second daughter) were all well, and they had had a splendid voyage throughout, unattended by storm or untoward incident, and they were all three in good health. He spoke most highly of the steamer, which, he said, was a splendid vessel. Asked how long he meant to stay in Ceylon he replied: "Only a very short time, I'm sorry to say. I am going on to India, and I am booked to transfer to the *Rosetta*[3] here and go on in her to Bombay tomorrow." Asked if he would hold one of his "At Homes" here tonight, Mr. Smythe had a word to say, and that was that he did not think there was time to arrange it.[4] I assured him that the afternoon would allow of time for sufficient announcement to insure a full Public Hall, but Mark Twain said: "Personally, I would rather not speak tonight, but I should have liked to do so tomorrow night. I've got a slight cold on me; it's not a complete cold; only what's left of one; but what there is, I think, I could kill in about 24 hours, and I could speak tomorrow night if the steamer permitted of it; but I am coming back this way later on from India, and then I can speak perhaps two nights."

So the matter had to be left....

Mark Twain began to think of getting his luggage transferred to the *Rosetta* and of coming ashore for a while. Leaving Mr. Smythe to make the necessary arrangements, he dropped up to the ship's rail and there began to take a great interest in the diving boys and the native craft. The catamarans of the former interested him at first, but it was the outriggers that finally engrossed his attention. "Those boats there are just the queerest things in the way of boats that I ever saw," he drawled. "I should say that the man who first designed them was real clever. A man who could build a boat like that could build a three-story house it seems to me, if he only made the outrigger long enough. It's all very interesting, and so are the natives. You only see things like this in places like Fiji and places of that sort, and even there they are different. Those boats and those dresses of the natives are quite novelties.[5] In most places you see them following European customs and ways in the matter of dress, and customs of that sort, but I should class the dresses here, and those boats, as distinctly original." As he turned at last to leave for shore he said: "I must say I'm very sorry to leave that scene. I never saw anything like that anywhere." Just then he was met by Pilot Henderson and the old Mississippi steerer shook hands cordially with him on learning his calling, his handshake being heartily returned by the local pilot.

A little later Mark Twain left the *Oceana* for the shore, and he was the cynosure of all eyes at the Bristol (where he and his wife and daughter took rooms) about tiffin [luncheon] time. He was unable to obtain accommodation at the G.O.H., which had already filled up; but he soon met friends there, including Dr. MacGregor, the ex-M.P.[6]

Bidding adieu to a party of admirers at Adelaide on the 31st December Mr. Clemens said: "Let me congratulate you on your climate. Perhaps your climate has become commonplace to you, but it is not commonplace at all. I am not accustomed to climates like this, where you have beautiful spring weather in midwinter, and where snow is unknown. We who come from the overworked regions of the earth cannot describe the pleasure of finding ourselves in this restful Australia, where it is always holiday. And when you have no holiday, or nothing else to do, it is always a horse race. It is a peculiarly blessed land, it seems to me. And then you have an arrangement which cannot be overpraised; you place your holidays not only to dates but to what suits your own comfort. I was through Australia when they celebrated the Prince of Wales's birthday. They celebrated it on the 8th, the 10th, and the 11th, and skipped the 9th altogether. I suppose there was a horse race on the 9th."[7]

Notes to Interview 104

1. "An Oriental town, most manifestly; and fascinating" (*FE*, 336).
2. A "stately big ship, luxuriously appointed," with "spacious promenade decks" (*FE*, 331).
3. A "poor old ship" that "ought to be insured and sunk" (*FE*, 345).
4. "Mark Twain in Colombo," *Ceylon Observer*, 14 January 1896, 3: "When our representative met him Mark Twain was in the unenviable position of not knowing where to lay his head for the night, the influx of passengers having filled up the hotels.

Amid the bustle of looking after luggage the conversation was naturally of a hurried and disjointed nature. 'What! you are not going to lecture in Colombo?' asked the pressman with astonishment. 'Well, not at present. I am going to fool round India a bit first.' Fortunately at this stage Mr. R. S. Smythe of Melbourne, who is traveling with Mr. Clemens, came to the rescue; and from him we were kindly favored with an outline of the tour." On the Smythes, see n. 1 to interview 93.

5. "And such stunning colors, such intensely vivid colors, such rich and exquisite minglings and fusings of rainbows and lightnings! And all harmonious, all in perfect taste" (*FE*, 340).

6. The G.O.H. was the Grand Oriental Hotel, which opened in 1875. Dr. MacGregor was probably Sir William MacGregor (1846–1919), a physician who served as Fiji's chief medical officer from 1875 to 1888 and as administrator of British New Guinea from 1888 to 1898.

7. "The holidays there are frequent enough to be bewildering to a stranger. I tried to get the hand of the system, but was not able to do it" (*FE*, 189–90).

105

"Mark Twain on His Methods of Work," *Gazette* (Bombay), 23 January 1896, 5.

"It would have served me right to be left alone as I was for twelve hours, and then to be drowned as an idiot!" Mark Twain passed this severe judgment on himself because of his indiscretion in contracting a severe cold by lying asleep on board ship in an exposed place, and the words were uttered yesterday afternoon in a room of Watson's Hotel overlooking the University Gardens, where the humorist has been confined since his arrival in Bombay last Saturday evening. "I have seen nothing of Bombay," continued the great humorist, advancing to the window and pointing outside, "all the time I have been here, excepting these trees, which sadly need dusting, two or three cabs, and those towers. Yes, I am decidedly better than I was, and might even venture out now, but I shall not do so; neither shall I leave my room tomorrow, as I don't want a recurrence of this cough, and want to make sure of being all right on Friday."

The prominent points about Mark Twain's personal appearance are his long untidy hair, and ferocious moustache; and the grey eyes that are not ferocious, but kind, and gentle, and pathetic; and the deep furrows falling outwards, from the thin beaked nose to the sides of the mouth, which are the external and visible signs of the nasal drawl that characterizes the very thoughts of the man before he has given utterance to them. The humorist is beyond middle age, but his energy is that of a man of perpetual youth. During the whole hour and a quarter our representative spent with him, Mr. Clemens was seldom still for a moment—he would sit for a brief space in his chair, preparing his pipe for a smoke, then he would rise, and after standing in his place a moment would pace up and down, talking in a low tone as though thinking aloud in the presence of familiar friends. Although seen under unfavorable conditions, Mr. Clemens gave one the impression of being still strong and vigorous, and that he is capable of doing much more both as a lecturer and a speaker to add to the laughter of the whole English-speaking race. He incidentally mentioned that up to the time of his visit to Australia, he had had no illness of any account for many years.

After Mark Twain, with characteristic hyperbole, had assured our representative that for five hundred years it had been the dream of his life to visit the Golden Orient, a reference was made to the new book for which he is now collecting material. In answer to a question respecting his methods of work, the famous American said: "I have what would be called pretty lazy methods in the matter of preparation for my books. It is a troublesome thing for a lazy man to take notes, and so I used to try in my young days to pack my impressions in my head. But that can't be done satisfactorily, and so I went from that to another stage—that of making notes in a notebook. But I jotted them down in so skeleton a form that they did not bring back to me what it was I wanted them to furnish. Having discovered that defect, I have mended my ways a good deal in this respect, but still my notes are inadequate. However, there may be some advantage to the reader in this, since in the absence of notes imagination has often to supply the place of facts.

"I said just now I was lazy in preparation," said Mr. Clemens, "but I won't admit that I am lazy in writing. No, I don't write rapidly, for when I did that I found it did not pay. I used to spend so much time next day correcting the manuscript, that it went to the printer a veritable forest of erasures, interlineations, emendations, abolitions, annihilations, and revisions. I found I should save time by writing slowly and carefully, and now my manuscript gives the printer no cause to blaspheme. You ask me how it is I have not written more largely. Well, the fact of it is that for many years while at home, in America, I have written little or nothing on account of social calls upon my time. There is too much social life in my city for a literary man, and so for twenty years I gave up the attempt to do anything during nine months of the twelve I am at home. It has only been during the three months that I have annually been on vacation, and have been supposed to be holiday-making, that I have written anything. It has been the same during the five years that I have been away from America. I have done little or no work. I wish now," he added regretfully, "that I had done differently and had persisted in writing when at home. I could easily have done it, although I thought I could not. I seemed to think then that I was never going to grow old, but I know better than that now. In my vacation I have steadily done four or five hours' work every day at a stretch; and if they would only have let me alone, I would have done seven hours a time without getting up from my chair."

Asked the amount of copy he turned out during these vacation periods, Mark Twain pondered deeply, and having half-aloud worked out a problem in mental arithmetic, continued: "Well, my average would be from ten thousand to twelve thousand words a week. But I have numerous interruptions, and so, instead of turning out from forty-five to fifty magazine pages per month, I do not do more than thirty. Yes, I am very fond of literary work, and nothing would please me better than to be allowed to be kept at a book for six months. You ask me what my opinions are with regard to the respective merits of my books. Well, I could easily point out which are the worst, but I am not going to do that. I cannot say on which book I have spent the most time simply because my methods have been very erratic. For instance, in writing *Tom Sawyer* I got up to the middle of the book and then did not touch it for a year or two, and it was the same with *Prince and Pauper*. It has been like this for many years, owing to my stupid notion that I could do no work at home."

"It has been said that the reason you have not published more works is that you did not desire to tire your public. How far is that correct?" asked our representative.

"Well, I have always kept that in mind, but I like literary work for its own sake, and I am sorry that I did not make time to write, and not to publish. I should like to have half-a-dozen works in manuscript just for the pleasure of writing them."

After assuring Mr. Clemens that anything that he might write would not be allowed to remain in manuscript after his death, unless he strictly interdicted its publication, our representative asked him whether he had as great a fondness for lecturing as for writing, and in answer received an emphatic shake of the head. "I like the platform when I am there, but the thought of it makes me shudder," said Mr. Clemens, momentarily collapsing into his chair; "the prospect of it is dreadful."

"Then I presume you prepare carefully for your lectures?"

"Yes, I am not for one moment going to pretend I do not. I don't believe that any public man has ever attained success as a lecturer to paid audiences (mark the qualification) who has not carefully prepared, and has not gone over every sentence again and again until the whole thing is fixed upon his memory. I write my lectures, and try to memorize them, but I don't always succeed. If I had a better memory it would be worse in some respects, for when one has to fill up an ellipsis on the spot, there is a spontaneity about the thing which is a considerable relief. I ought really to write the whole thing beforehand, but I don't do it, as I prefer to use material which has appeared in my books. The extracts, however, are seldom exactly the same as they are printed, but are adapted to circumstances. No, I don't localize, because to do that you want to be well posted up, and know exactly what you are about. You must be exactly prepared beforehand. I never pretend that I don't indent on my books for my lectures, for there is no object in doing that. It is all very well to talk about not being prepared, and trusting to the spirit of the hour. But a man cannot go from one end of the world to the other, no matter how great his reputation may be, and stand before paid houses in various large cities without finding that his tongue is far less glib than it used to be. He might hold audiences spell bound with unpremeditated oratory in past days when nothing was charged to hear him, but he cannot rely on being able to do so when they have paid for their seats and require something for the money unless he thinks all out beforehand.

"You ask me whether my memory has deserted me on the platform sometimes? Yes, it has sometimes entirely. And the worst of it is that, as I prefer to select things from my books, my remarks are often in the narrative form, and if you lose yourself in the narrative it is not very comfortable, because a tale should have an end somewhere. Still I have generally managed to get out of the difficulty in some way or other. It is really very curious to see what a man can do on the platform without the audience suspecting anything to be wrong. A case in point occurred in Paris a year ago. I began some opening remarks at one of my 'At Homes' there with an anecdote, as for some reason or another I wanted to fill up the time. I began telling the anecdote, but I found when half-way that my memory regarding it had gone. So I switched on to another line, and was soon leaving the half-told anecdote far behind. My wife and daughter were present, and I afterwards asked them whether they remembered the breakdown. They replied in the negative. I then asked whether they heard the finish of the anecdote with which I had begun my remarks, and they at once replied they had not. As you say, if anyone would be likely to discover a flaw, it would be my wife or my daughter, and when I found that they were unaware of the defect, I was quite satisfied that the audience in general knew nothing about it."

Conversation then followed on the copyright law of England and America and on Mr. Clemens' impressions of Australia. He also gave his opinions on the relations between England and America, but we reserve an account of that conversation to another issue.

106

"Interview with Mark Twain," *Times of India* (Bombay), 23 January 1896, 5; rpt. *Times of India: Overland Weekly Edition*, 25 January 1896, 4; *Calcutta Hindoo Patriot*, 31 January 1896, 3; and *Johannesburg Times*, 11 May 1896, 4.

Of all things possible with Mark Twain, there is one thing that is wholly impossible: you cannot reproduce the man in any kind of representative embodiment which is afforded by the shallow resources of cold printing type.

Manner, voice, gesture, and the indescribable something which, in manifold ways, is always characteristic of genius, can never be set down even with the most facile of fountain pens. After all, perhaps, it matters but little, since everybody will see Mark Twain in *propria persona* at the Novelty Theatre at half-past five tomorrow afternoon, when the worldwide humorist gives his first lecture in India. A representative of this journal called upon Mr. Clemens at the Esplande Hotel yesterday evening and found him very nearly recovered from the severe cold which has kept him within doors since his arrival here on Saturday last. "I suppose, Mr. Clemens," he said, after congratulating him upon getting "fit" again, "that by this time you are getting pretty tired of being interviewed?" and probably he is; but in this instance he manifested a most genial disposition to talk.

"How did I make my first start in journalism, you ask? Well, I first stumbled into it as a man falls over a precipice that he is not looking for. I wasn't, as far as I could see, intended for a journalist, but out in Nevada in those early silver days it was a struggle—a scramble from pillar to post—and one had to get a living as best he could. I was invited to take a place on the staff of a daily newspaper there—the *Territorial Enterprise*—and I took it. I should have taken command of a ship if it had been offered, for I wasn't particular in those days. I had had no training, but yet they offered me the post of first officer, not the Chief Editor, but a subordinate post, and I remained in the journalistic profession for four years in Nevada and San Francisco together. On the *Territorial Enterprise* I was what they called the City Editor. It was a large title, but the pay was not correspondingly great; in fact, the name was merely for style. In reality the City Editor should have been called the local reporter. The post was, so to speak, flung at me. I didn't ask for it. There was a Chief Editor, a news-Editor, and a telegraphic-Editor, and in those days they gathered in from the San Francisco and Sacramento papers a good part of the reading matter of the journal. We were expected and supposed to furnish facts pure and simple for the columns of the *Enterprise*, but there were not facts enough to fill the required space, and so often the reading material was largely a matter of imagination—sometimes based on fact, but not always. After about four years in these parts I went off to the Sandwich Islands [Hawaii] to write a series of letters concerning the sugar industry there for the *Sacramento Union*. I was gone about five or six months, and when I came back I concluded to deliver a lecture or two on the Sandwich Islands, and I did so. It seemed an easier way of making a living than by journalism; it paid better, and there was less work connected with it, so I dropped journalism and took to the lecturer's platform for two or three years. Then I went on an extended tour in Europe, which lasted for five or six months, and when I returned I was asked to write a book. I did so, and from that time on I have written books mainly. Up to the present I have stepped out of silver-mining—that, by the way, was my first start in Nevada—into journalism, from journalism into lecturing, and from lecturing into book-making, each of these steps being not forced in any way, but the one leading to the next by a short of natural sequence."

The conversation having turned to his method of work, Mr. Clemens remarked: "I work very regularly when I work at all. I work every day and all night from after breakfast till late into the night until the work is finished. I never begin to work before eleven in the morning, and I sit at it till they pull me away from table to dress for dinner at seven at night. They make me stop then for a while, as they think I might overwork myself, but I don't think there is any fear of that, for I don't consider the kind of writing I do is work in any way: it is in no sense a labor with me. The mere physical work would not hurt me or anyone else, you can sleep that off. The mental part of it is nothing but amusement: it's not work. I always write my own copy. I have tried a typewriter and also a phonograph, but I couldn't get along with either."

"You do not find dictation any help, then?"

"I couldn't learn the art. I could conceive that for commercial correspondence it would be easy to do, but there's no inspiration about that. There's nothing to help inspiration or whatever you may call it like the sight of your own work as it goes along. I am not a *very* rapid worker, but when I sit down to it I get through a fair amount in a day. For instance, take *The Innocents Abroad:* it contains 650 octavo pages with about 200,000 words on them. That book I wrote in a good deal of a hurry. The contract compelled me to furnish the manuscript complete on a certain date, therefore I worked every day from one o'clock in the afternoon till midnight, and I got it finished in sixty-two days. I must have written on an average 3,000 words per day."[1]

"What do you find most helpful in your work?"

"Tobacco," replied Mr. Clemens, picking up a capacious briar-root pipe which was kept busily engaged as he paced up and down the room, enveloped in a rich cloud of smoke. "I always smoke when at work. I couldn't do without it. I smoke by necessity. I did stop smoking once for a year and a quarter, but in that year and a quarter I didn't write anything. I have no works in contemplation just now, but as soon as I get at leisure I shall go to work again. There are two or three things I want to write and I may—no doubt shall—write some sort of book on this excursion, but I always leave myself quite free in these matters. I never make any promises to myself or anybody else, because I don't like being hampered by the feeling that something as to be done when perhaps I am not in the mood to do it."

Passing from Mark Twain's own works to those of other authors, the name of Rudyard Kipling was mentioned. "I have met him several times," said

Mr. Clemens, "and I like him very much.[2] I admire his work prodigiously. There is no question as to his genius; that must be confessed by everyone. He has genius and plenty of it, and if there is any fault found with him it can only be as to the accuracy of his presentation of Indian matters. There is sure to be criticism of detail; every author has to put up with that. His accuracy of detail may be criticized here, but we in other parts take his accuracy for granted. We don't know anything about that, and besides we don't read his work for fact anyhow; we read it for the pleasure of it. I have an amazing fondness for his *Plain Tales*,[3] and I think that some of his ballad work is inimitable. I don't see how anyone could possibly surpass it."

The blessing or otherwise of "interviewing" as a prominent feature of modern journalism having been of late considerably under discussion, the opinion of Mr. Clemens as one coming from the land where the interviewer practically had his birth was naturally worth canvassing, and there is a good deal in that opinion which the "interviewing" fraternity may ponder over. "Of course," he dryly observed, "everyone has his moods and tenses and I have mine, but when I am going round about at leisure, as I am now, why, dear me! I would as soon be interviewed as not. At the same time there are, it must be confessed, a hundred thousand objections to interviewing, and the first one is naturally this, that when you put before the whole world in print anything out of your skull, it should, by the very nature of the case, be something worth reading. Now how many men—and I don't care how practiced they are even with the pen—can sit down on a sudden call, hunt round their head, find a subject, and write acceptably on that subject? I could not do it, and I don't believe anyone could do it. Interviewing necessarily has that blemish, it is surface talk; it is mere fluff and foam; there is no substance to it. It has no value; it has no right to go into print; it is a waste of the time of a man who sets out to read it. A man sits down and talks in an interview, and he is ostensibly saying something worth printing, but he knows all the time that he is not: it would be a most dazzling action if he ever did say anything worth printing in such circumstances. Interviewing would be quite justifiable if the public would grant that when a man is being interviewed he is not to be expected to say anything worth the interviewer's trouble in recording. If that be understood, no harm would be done. The interviewer is not a bit of trouble to me or to anyone else for the matter of that, for anyone can talk. The difficulty is that talking offhand no man is likely to say anything worth preserving. Haven't you heard a thousand men called on their feet at dinners to speak, and it is the most uncommon thing in the world to find them saying anything that is worth listening to. If they had known they were going to be called on they would make quite a different show and so it is with interviewing. I don't know of any other objection to it. In the first place there is nothing on the spur of the moment worth talking about, and in the second place there comes the question of phrasing, and it is phrasing that makes a piece of literature valuable. How are you going to do your phrasing, unless you get time to think it over and get it ready? Phrasing is the difference between good literature and poor, commonplace literature."

Speaking of his visit to India, Mr. Clemens observed, "I am expecting a great deal. I haven't seen anything yet, for I've been shut up in the house ever since I arrived, and I haven't had even a glimpse of Bombay. My wife and daughter overwhelm me with the fascinations of Bombay, and so make my imprisonment all the harder to put up with, but I hope to be released shortly, and then I shall certainly see all that it is possible for me to see. The only glimpse of anything akin to India that I have yet had was in Ceylon, where I spent the most enchanting day I ever spent in my life. Everything was absolutely new—all that beautiful nakedness and color, all those costumes which one hears of but never sees, and which if you see them on the stage you never believe in. It beggars all description: one simply laughs at the painter's brush; it is impossible for him to reproduce it."

During the above interview Mr. Clemens received a letter from H.E. [His Excellency] the Governor inviting himself and Mrs. and Miss Clemens to luncheon at Government House today. His Excellency incidentally mentioned that he had once had the pleasure of meeting Mark Twain at the Garrick Club,[4] and the recollection of the occasion was evidently very welcome to Mr. Clemens, for he at once recalled it, remarking, "Why, it must be twenty years since then," and he then went on to recall the names of several people present on that occasion, observing after a moment's thought that although the party was not a large one he could remember four members of it who were still alive, which was "not a bad average."

Notes to Interview 106

1. See n. 6 to interview 46.
2. See interview 50 for an account of Twain's first meeting with Kipling.
3. Kipling's *Plain Tales from the Hills* (1898). See also *Auto* (1959), 288.
4. A London club named after the English actor David Garrick (1717-79).

107

"Mark Twain on the Relations between England and America," *Gazette* (Bombay), 24 January 1896, 5.

Although Mark Twain is of the opinion that remarks made to an interviewer on the spur of the moment are mere surface talk, unworthy of being printed, we venture to assert that the observations he made to our representative on

Wednesday, respecting the relations between England and America, so far from being looked upon as of little or no value, will be generally regarded as important contributions to the discussion now raging around the Monroe doctrine and the Venezuelan question.[1] As they form the first recorded utterances of this celebrated American on the question since it entered into an acute phase, they are deserving of wide publicity, especially in his own land. For there, instead of a local prophet being without honor, the pulpit and the platform wield an immense, not to say paramount, influence in determining national policy in times of great excitement. It is a far cry from Australia to Venezuela, and yet the conversation between Mr. Clemens and our representative drifted most naturally from the one topic to the other. Mark Twain was speaking in high terms of the Australians whom he described as "a live bright people, energetic and modern, in every way up to date"; and said they reminded him of the Canadians. "I am intensely interested in them," he added, "as one ought to be in any community that speaks the English language, because they are becoming growingly important in the shaping of the world's destinies. When you think what the English race is today compared with one hundred years ago and how much ground it has since covered, and the immense influence it wields amongst the peoples of this earth, you cannot fail to be struck with how much it has accomplished in a very short time. Now, on the other hand, look at the case of France. There were, if I remember rightly, twenty-eight millions of people in that country at the time of the French Revolution. But this number has not since doubled; it has only gone up by fifty per cent. At that period Great Britain had a population of eighteen or twenty millions; it is now thirty-nine millions, and her sons have overflown into all parts of the globe. France had just as good opportunities as England, but has allowed them to slip from her grasp. America has progressed in a still more marvelous manner. A hundred years ago we had a population of three millions in the United States, and now we have seventy millions. We have in that period flung in two Frances and the United States has now three times as many people as France had a century ago."

This monologue on the greatness of the British naturally brought the conversation round to the existing relations between England and America, and Mark Twain, walking vehemently backwards and forwards, spoke in this wise: "I think it would be criminal now to interrupt the old friendly relations. I cannot conceive of any greater disaster to the world than a war between these two great countries. There can never be a sufficient excuse for so great a crime; neither the Monroe doctrine or anything else. Whatever the Monroe doctrine may require, it cannot ever require what the statesmen of the first countries in the world would call unjust. If the meaning of the doctrine is properly threshed out, it will be found that when it was enunciated it was a legitimate and justifiable one and nobody found any fault with it. I have seen speeches of two prominent men made a long time ago. One was J. C. Calhoun, the well-known statesman, and the other, Mr. Thomas H. Benton,[2] and they both said that the real meaning of the Monroe doctrine is that the United States desired that no foreign Government should colonize its people on the continent of America or form a Government over there on the same line as that of the United States. We were to keep free from complications with other Powers and not to go shouldering anybody's and everybody's quarrel in the way President Cleveland talks of."

"Then you think, Mr. Clemens, that most of the American people are of this opinion? You must have read that your friend, Mr. Stanley,[3] after touring in America, has stated that there is an intense anti-English feeling in America—that is, the America outside New York and its money market?"

"I do not believe that the people of America as a whole are unfriendly," said Mark Twain decisively. "All that I can make out of Mr. Stanley's remarks given in the *Bombay Gazette,* the other day, is that the explorer got his information where you or I would get ours if we were traveling abroad, that is to say, from the newspapers, which are not always a safe guide to public opinion."

"At any rate in America?" suggested our representative.

"In any country governed on party lines," was the prompt reply. "You know that almost every journal in America has made a party question of President Cleveland's message.[4] I have just received a file of American papers, the first I have seen for some months, and I find that discussion all goes on party lines. I notice that it is the sound and influential journalists who are opposed to the jingo policy of the President. There is no anti-English feeling in the towns among really solid folk. People that Stanley would hear or you or I would hear if we were traveling in America would be the most noisy people. They are the ones that get themselves heard in any and every free country in the world. Now, in my own town of Hartford, which has a population of sixty thousand people, I know every sound and valuable citizen. But I cannot call to my mind one of these men who would talk in such a way as to give Mr. Stanley the impression with which he returned to England. What is the case in Hartford is the case elsewhere; and travelers mistake the noisy clamor of a few men for the voice of the people generally."

Mark Twain is one of those rare American authors of note who have no grievance against the English [publishing] pirates, notwithstanding his immense popularity in Great Britain. He explains the reason thus: "From 1861 to 1878 I did not get any remuneration for the copies of my works printed in England; but it was my own fault. I could have got copyright of my works, but was ignorant of the fact. There was no precedent to guide me; for up to that time American writers had had no market in England. Yes, Fenimore Cooper was an exception.[5] He had an immense audience in England and all over Europe, as he still has today, but he had long ceased to be a figure in the world when my literary fame reached England. His experience as an author had already been forgotten before I gained a reputation. When American writers complain of the English pirates, I tell them that it is their own fault. They will not believe it, however, and say that there is no English law to provide for American copyright in England. They remark that all I go upon is some dictum of an English judge, whose name I forget for the moment, on a case that was not before him.[6] It was in this way. A case in which an American author tried to procure English copyright was before the Judge, who, when dismissing the case, made this remark: 'It seems to me that if the plaintiff had a copyright of his book in England before it was copyright in America, if only for a few moments, he would have been protected from piracy.'"

Our representative observed that the American authors ought to erect a statue to the judge instead of forgetting his name, as the one who had profited most by his dictum appeared to do.

"Yes," replied the humorist, "but they ought first to erect a statue to their own stupidity for not protecting themselves from piracy when they have opportunity for doing so. I have always told them that when they see an English publisher flying the black-flag they can make him keep his hands off provided the book is copyrighted in England before it is published in America. And what do you want more than that. It serves my purpose admirably, and would also serve theirs. Although, as they say it was only the remark of a judge, my experience is that it has always had the force of law. Since that date I have always been well paid for my books in England. Chatto and Windus have paid me the same royalty as if I lived in London and was a subject to the Queen, and they also look after my rights on the Continent.[7] No American author has a right to grumble about not being paid for his works in England, when he neglects to avail himself of the opportunities which exist for protecting himself from piracy."

Notes to Interview 107

1. Budd (1977), 97n36: "In July 1895 the United States protested that Great Britain was violating the Monroe Doctrine in its stand on the boundary dispute between Venezuela and British Guiana." This doctrine, promulgated in 1823 by James Monroe (1758–1831), fifth U.S. president (1817–25), asserted that the Americas were no longer "to be considered as subjects for future colonization by any European Power."

2. John C. Calhoun (1782–1850), champion of states rights, U.S. vice president (1825–32), U.S. senator from South Carolina (1833–43), and U.S. secretary of state (1844–45). Thomas Hart Benton (1782–1858), U.S. senator from Missouri (1821–51).

3. See n. 2 to interview 79.

4. President Grover Cleveland sent Congress a message on 17 December 1895 threatening war with England to settle the boundary dispute between Venezuela and British Guiana.

5. See n. 1 to interview 70.

6. MT "may refer to the Report of the Royal Copyright Commission in 1878 and to the Digest by Sir James Stephen that was appealed to it; this Digest accepted the legality of copyright by simultaneous publication in the United Kingdom and a foreign country and made no reference of residency stipulations" (Budd [1977], 98n39).

7. Andrew Chatto (d. 1913) and W. E. Windus, MT's British publishers.

108

"Sporting Notes &c.," *Asian* (Calcutta), 7 February 1896, 398.

... Mr. Clemens, or as he is better known by his *nom de plume* of Mark Twain, arrived in Bombay last week. He has been most enthusiastically received, and has been delighting crowded audiences with his bright and humorous lectures. Mr. Clemens may be safely said to be one of the greatest laughter raisers of the day. Till, however, you get accustomed to his dry and caustic style, he is somewhat difficult to follow. With a slow and distinct enunciation, tinged with a slight American accent which gives piquancy to his delivery, he pours forth a flood of most graphic word painting. You are almost completely bewildered, and when he has this audience completely in touch with him, then comes the flash which illumines the whole story. Quick as lightning, pungent as red pepper in perhaps a dry aside it strikes you, and in a moment from grave and patient attention, everyone is rippling with light and joysome merriment. Such is his method and from the constant bursts of laughter at his sallies it has proved to be a very successful one.

I had the privilege of spending an afternoon in his company, and though one cannot attempt to set down on paper one-tenth part of the good things he said, yet, perhaps, a few gleanings from the sheaf of humor may be acceptable to your readers. It is impossible through the poor medium of printer's ink to attempt to reproduce his inimitable drollery and light-heartedness. The merry twinkle of the eye, the preternaturally grave face, the power and command of language and the polished smartness of his conversation must be heard to be appreciated to its fullest extent. Mr. Clemens is a finished speaker and one of the best raconteurs it has ever been my privilege to meet. My first question naturally was, "Well, Mr. Clemens, what do you think of India?" Pat came the answer: "Well, you can't show me much in climate and scenery"—this, to a man who has passed years of his life amongst the Rockies and been grilled upon the prairies of the West, is quite possible. "But, sir, the people—the people—the brilliant colors, the heterogeneous mass of humanity, the constantly recurring yet ever changing kaleidoscopic views, the never ceasing stream of types of so many different nationalities and race, that you have gathered up in this great city of yours. Why that is enough to make a man long to sit down and write about it all till he is quite tired."

Directly after this Mr. Clemens in his best manner started upon a recent experience of his. "I came down from Poona this morning, and got upon the cars before daybreak in the beautiful bright soft Indian moonlight. Shortly after we had started the sun got up, and the whole panorama was changed. Looking out of the window I said to my companion, 'Why, this can't be the same country we came through yesterday. Are we going the same road? Yesterday afternoon the whole country appeared to be a dry arid sterile waste—this morning it is a beautiful, glossy, green, and rolling prairie. The hills yesterday, which stood out bleak and bare, without a particle of vegetation, are now a mass of verdure.[1] How do you account for it?' He immediately pointed out that the blue glass of the window, acting upon the old gold color of the sandy tracts we were passing through, caused the optical illusion. 'Well, then,' I said, 'When I want to trade off a back-lot of this country, I shall see that the man who prospects it wears blue glasses.'"

At luncheon the topic of precedence came up, and we said that in England the custom was to write the names of the guests on slips of paper and put them on the table, the host telling the various men who they were to take in. Mr. Clemens said that in America it was the habit to give each man an envelope containing a plan of the table and the name of his partner. "That reminds me," broke in Mr. Clemens. "When this fashion first started in New York I was invited to a big dinner. At the entrance stood a colored servant with a silver tray on which were a quantity of envelopes. I thought it was a lottery and would take a chance anyhow. So I took one and slipped it into my vest pocket. I found the next morning that it was the name of some lady I was supposed to take into dinner, but I didn't that time anyway—I hope she got on all right without me."

Shortly after this conversation turned upon fame and notoriety, Mr. Clemens said: "I thought I was pretty well known at any rate in America, but I found it wasn't so. The other day in New York I went into a store that was simply plastered from cornice to floor with photographs of celebrities: I asked the young man running that store if he had a photo of Mark Twain. He ran his eyes up and down the walls and then drawled out 'I don't know. Where is she playing?'"

Mrs. Clemens capped this by another experience in which she used the *nom de plume* with equal ill success. Having bought some things in London and giving the man directions, she said "that as they were going by the Cunard line he had better send the goods for Mark Twain." "Very well, Mum," he said. "When does she sail?"

One could go on almost indefinitely recounting the good things that Mark

Twain gave utterance to that afternoon. You will shortly have an opportunity of judging for yourselves in Calcutta. Anyone who misses the treat in store is like him who hath not music in his soul and is fit for treason, conspiracies, and *thugs*. I trust that I have been able to show in some small degree the light vein of humor that runs through the conversation of this great humorist and which makes the hours passed in his presence seem to be the very briefest moments.

Note to Interview 108

1. *FE,* 460: "Out in the country in India, the day begins early. One sees a plain, perfectly flat, dust-colored and brick-yardy, stretching limitlessly away on every side in the dim gray light."

109

"Mark Twain Interviewed: First Impressions of India," *Englishman* (Calcutta), 8 February 1896, 5; rpt. *Hindoo Patriot* (Calcutta), 10 February 1896, 3; and *Weekly Englishman,* 12 February 1896, 11–12.

"Mr. Macaulay,"[1] a titled lady is said to have once remarked to the Essayist, "I am so surprised by your appearance. I thought you were dark and thin, but you are fair, and, really Mr. Macaulay, you are stout." Some such surprise was afforded an *Englishman* interviewer who called upon Mark Twain at his hotel yesterday afternoon. He was as familiar with the portraits of the great humorist as anyone, and from these he had gathered the impression that the original was stern, dark, and a martinet in his appearance. In reality he found him fair, with a ruddy complexion, a gray moustache, and a pair of shaggy eyebrows, whose somewhat severe effect was counteracted by the friendly blue eyes which twinkled beneath. A man of middle height, with erect, well-set up figure, and abundant head of gray hair, Mark Twain paces up and down the room in a leonine fashion as he converses. He had just arrived from Benares that morning, and told his interviewer that he hadn't been able to leave his room since he entered it through a wretched cold which he had caught on the journey.

"I can't go out at all," he said, in his measured, American way. "I have got to stick right here and nurse myself. I haven't been able to go out to the Tournament today, and I reckon I shan't manage to get to it tomorrow either. It closes tomorrow, doesn't it?"

"In consequence of the unprecedented success of the Grand Military Tournament," quoted the interviewer, "two extra night performances will be given on Monday and Tuesday."

"Just so," assented the humorist. "But Monday and Tuesday night I'm engaged to give my 'At Home,' you see."

"I hope your cold will be better by that time. When did you catch it?"

Mark Twain replied that he had caught it in the train coming from Benares. It was the old story. A draught was playing upon him, but he could not make up his mind to shut the window, and while he was trying to form his resolution he fell asleep, and the mischief was done. This naturally led up to a question as to his experience of Indian Railways.

"How do you find, Mr. Clemens, that Indian Railway journeys compare with similar journeys in the States?"

"I find them very comfortable. I don't know what it may be like traveling straight through from Bombay to Calcutta, but there is certainly nothing to complain about in the journey from Bombay to Allahabad."

Asked what his impressions were of the country as he was traveling through, Mark Twain said, "I saw for the most part great plains like the prairies you pass over in the States. On the whole I should say Indian scenery is the more interesting of the two. Still from Benares west, and from Missouri to the Rocky Mountains you get very much the same kind of rolling, grassy plains. In India there are more trees, which relieve the monotony of the landscape. Now and then, it is true, I saw deserts such as those which lie behind the Rockies."

"You have just come from Benares. Would you mind—"

"Certainly," replied Mark Twain, knitting his brows, and speaking with more than his usual deliberation. "I think Benares is one of the most wonderful places I have ever seen. It has struck me that a Westerner feels in Benares very much as an Oriental must feel when he is planted down in the middle of London. Everything is so strange, so utterly unlike the whole of one's pervious experience."[2]

"The Brahmani bulls, for example.[3] How did they behave themselves?"

"Those that I saw—very fine-looking cattle, too," said the humorist with a sly twinkle, "were peaceable enough. They certainly had a fine, lordly way of going where and taking what they liked."

"Did you ever have to make room for them?"

"Well, yes. I will make room for a bull any time—Brahmin bull or not. Very different creatures these from the poor, starved cows you see in the villages. It's a wonder to me how these animals manage to keep on their legs.

"We went to see a recluse," continued Mark Twain. "A man who is worshipped for his holiness from one end of India to the other. On the way we saw various images of this saint, and when I saw him coming out of his hut, I at once recognized him from the really excellent likenesses which these images afforded. Look here. This is a portrait of the man, and this is his book."[4]

He showed the interviewer the book. It was the Vedic translation by Sri

Swami Bhaskara Nand Saraswati, with a photograph of the translator as a frontispiece. The holy man is represented sitting cross-legged and scantily clothed. He is said to be over sixty and is certainly a well-preserved man, with a keenly intellectual face. The *Englishman* representative remarked on this.

"Yes," said the humorist. "That man started with a grand head on his shoulders, and after thinking and reading and improving upon his initial advantages he came to the conclusion that the greatest object in life is—that."

He pointed to the photograph, but neither in mockery nor contempt. It may surprise his many readers, but when Mark Twain is serious he is very serious. He described in graphic language how he stood at the hut of the hermit, and wondered what there was in him to worship.

"Suddenly a man came up who had traveled hundreds of miles for this very object. As soon as he approached near enough he prostrated himself in the dust and kissed the saint's foot. I had never realized till then what it was to stand in the presence of a divinity.

"Because," Mark Twain pursued, with great animation, "he is a divinity. Not even an angel. At the age of seventeen, I am told, he renounced his family ties and embraced the asceticism in which he has lived these forty years and over."

"And what effect have these practices had upon him? Is there anything peculiar in his voice, his talk, or his actions?"

"Nothing at all. It is just as though you had taken a very fine, learned, intellectual man, say a member of the Indian Government, and unclothed him. There he is. He is minus the trappings of civilization. He hasn't a rag on his back. But he has perfect manners, a ready wit, and a turn for conversation through an interpreter."

Turning to the fly-leaf of the book, Mark Twain pointed to certain Sanskrit signs and relapsed into the humorous vein.

"That is his name," he said. "He is so holy, that before his name can be written it must be repeated 108 times. I thought that too much even for a god. I made 104 times do. We traded autographs. I said I had heard of him, and he said he had heard of me. Gods lie sometimes, I expect."

"On the contrary, it is extremely probable that your books may have cheered him up in his loneliness."

Mark Twain laughed. "Hardly, because they would require to have been translated into Sanskrit first."

"In that case, Sanskrit is almost the only language, I should suppose, in which they have not appeared."

"This face," said the humorist, again regarding the portrait, "is a strongly legal one, is it not? You have heard of W. M. Evarts, formerly Secretary of

State, and one of the greatest minds America has ever produced.[5] Well, this face at first reminded me strongly of Evarts. But when I looked into it, I found that it resembled the face of another noted American."

"Who was—"

"Dr. DeWitt Talmage.[6] But the head is more intellectual than that of Talmage.

"The subject of caste," the humorist proceeded in reply to further inquiries, "seems to me a great mystery. It's a fascinating mystery. Anything more uncongenial to the Western mind and training could not be conceived. When I am told that this man will not drink out of that man's *lota* [water jug], because if he does so he will be defiled—these are simply so many words to me. I can't grasp the idea. When, again, you say that the man with a special cord round his neck is a Brahmin, and twice born, and that because of the cord and what it implies he is to be groveled before, I ask how is it? And I can't for the life of me imagine.

"When, too, I see a Hindu—the very man, perhaps, who fears defilement so much through the other man's *lota*—when I see him going down to the muddy, filthy Ganges, and washing himself in and drinking out of water only fifteen yards away from where a dead body is lying—I can't help thinking he is at least sincere."

"That, I believe, has never been denied."

"You read about these things," said Mark Twain, "but here you see them actually going on before your very eyes. You get a glimpse of what India was in the far-off days, before the British power was heard of."

"I take it, however, that you, as a Westerner, and particularly as an American, are more interested in the progress which the country has made in various directions under British Government, than even in the antiquities of Benares?"

"That is not so—" with a decided shake of the head—"I have no hesitation in saying that in all my travels I have never seen anything so remarkable as Benares or anybody so wonderful as that recluse. These modern improvements have been familiar to me for years, but such an experience as the other is only met with once in a lifetime.

"Not that, of course, I, or anyone else, can deny the obvious advantages which the British have conferred on India. When one looks at the industrial and educational activity which has been set in motion all over the country, and when one considers its security and prosperity one cannot help coming to the conclusion that the British Government is the best for India, whether the Hindus or Mohamedans like it or not."

"They themselves are generally willing to acknowledge it as a benefit."

"I can quite believe that," said Mark Twain. "I have myself heard it from the lips of members of both communities. It is my belief that in the development of the world the strongest race will by and by become paramount—the strongest physically and intellectually. Now if we look round upon the nations we find that the English [race] seems to possess both these qualifications. It has spread all over the earth. It is vigorous, prolific, and enterprising. Above all it is composed of merciful people, the best kind of people for colonizing the globe. Look, for instance, at Canada.

"Look at the difference between the position of the Canadian Indians and the Indians with whom the United States Government has to deal. In Canada the Indians are peaceful and contented enough. In the United States there are continual rows with the Government, which invariably end in the red man being shot down."

"And to what cause, Mr. Clemens, do you attribute this difference?"

"I attribute it to the greater humanity with which the Indians are treated in Canada. In the States we shut them off into a reservation, which we frequently encroached upon. Then ensued trouble. The red men killed settlers, and of course the Government had to order out troops and put them down. If an Indian kills a white man he is sure to lose his life, but if a white man kills a redskin he never suffers according to law."

"Is not the negro difficulty somewhat allied to the Red Indian question?"

"No doubt. But I am of [the] opinion that in course of time that difficulty will settle itself. The negroes at present are merely freed slaves, and you can't get rid of the effects of slavery in one or even two generations. But things will right themselves. We have given the negro the vote, and he must keep it."

"Is there, then, any likelihood of intermixture?"

"Not the slightest. The white and the black population, however, will in time learn to tolerate each other and work harmoniously for the common good. They will co-exist very much as the different races in India have done for centuries."

"You have, then, been struck by the distinctive races who inhabit the continent of India?"

"One cannot help that. Take the Parsis in Bombay. What a fine race they are. How intelligent, how accomplished, how proficient in English. I must say the same, however, of most of the Native princes we saw, notably the Gaekwar of Baroda.[7] And my wife tells me that the women are equally proficient."

"Have you yet come across the Bengali Babu?"[8]

"No," said Mark Twain, looking as though he had reserved his brightest smile for this question. "Not yet in the flesh, but in literature can I ever forget him?"

He flaunted the immortal biography of Onoocool Chunder Mookerjee in our representative's face. "I am renewing my acquaintance with this book," he remarked. "I read it when it first came out, but have not seen it for years. Now I am coming back to it with fresh zest.[9]

"And yet," Mark Twain said, growing grave again, "and yet it is astonishing to recognize the fluency of the writer. Here is one sentence which in expression and construction is faultless English. Yet in the next Mookerjee tumbles into bathos. It is more remarkable even than it is funny."

Mark Twain certainly had a shocking cold. The *Englishman* representative could not help noticing it, intent though he was upon the humorist's words. He had been fatigued, too, by the previous night's journey, and taking pity upon him on account of both these considerations the interviewer shook hands and departed. . . .

Notes to Interview 109

1. Lord Thomas Babington Macauley (1800–1859), English historian and essayist.
2. MT describes his visit to Benares in chapters 50–51 of *FE*.
3. The Brahman bulls (*Bos indicus*) are the "sacred cows" of India.
4. Bhaskara Nand Saraswati, trans. *Upanishad Prasada, i.e., An Easy Translation of 10 Upanishads* (Benares: Bharat-jiwan, 1894). MT recounts his visit to the holy man in *FE*, chapter 53, and quotes the book in chapter 61.
5. William M. Evarts (1818–1901) was a U.S. attorney general, secretary of state, and U.S. senator from New York.
6. T. DeWitt Talmage (1832–1902), an American clergyman.
7. Gaekwar of Baroda (1863–1939), one of the richest and most influential princes of India.
8. The stereotype of an educated, nouveau riche, effeminate, urban Indian gentleman, the parallel to a British fop or dandy, featured in Kipling's *His Chance in Life* (1888).
9. Mohindro Nauth Mookerjee, *The Memoir of the Late Honourable Justice Chunder Mookerjee* (1873; rpt. Calcutta: Thacker, Spink, 1884, 1889).

110

"Mark Twain in Calcutta," *Statesman* (Calcutta), 8 February 1896, 3; and *Friend of India and Statesman* (Calcutta), 12 February 1896, 18.

"The great interest in every country and among all peoples is the human interest," said Mr. S. L. Clemens to a *Statesman* representative, who called upon him yesterday at the Hotel Continental to express a hope that three weeks in an Indian climate had not sufficed to merge Mark Twain, the author, into Mr. Clemens, the invalid. It was pleasant to shake hands with the author of so much laughter, and to see the face so familiar in the photographer's window, with its framework of white hair, and its deep-set genial eyes. . . . Can this quiet, reposeful-looking person, whose cultivated look and deliberate manner are indicative of the habit of introspection and of acquaintance with books, have really spent some of his earlier years in heaving the lead—

and shouting "Mark Twain!"—on steamboats of the kind with which other American humorists have made us familiar—where, in order to get up sufficient steam to race a rival, hams are thrown on the fires, and a "nigger" is seated on the safety-valve? Surely, if this be a natural development from the miner of Nevada, then Bret Harte[1] has been unjustly reproached with idealizing his dashing adventures of pine woods and mining camps. Incredulity, however, melts away at the recollection that Mr. Clemens has the honor to belong to a country where every man is, at any rate in sober British conception, a "quick change artist," equipped more thoroughly for the battle of life than most people of effete Europe.

"The fame of your fever reached us from Bombay, Mr. Clemens. We were almost afraid there would be no chance of welcoming you to Calcutta."

"Yes, I was in bed for seven days, though I had at first, of course, no idea of going there; but we missed the Calcutta boat at Colombo. However, I have no fever now, and hope to be quite equal to my work here. I shall not stir out for the next twenty-four hours."

"India has charmed you already, has it not?"

"If I have seen anything like India anywhere before, it was years ago—perhaps in the Holy Land. But here there is so much life and color; it is all on such a big scale; everything is so thoroughly alive. I spent two days at Benares, and found the place full of interest. Ceylon has been my nearest approach to the tropics. I have never before been so close to the equator, if I except a short visit to Fiji. I hope to return to Ceylon before I go to Africa."

"From here you go—"

"To Delhi, Cawnpore, Lucknow, and Agra. I hope to go to Ceylon afterwards from Bombay. Also to see something of southern India."

"You will not go to one of our hill stations?"

"I should have liked to see Darjeeling, but I am afraid it will be too far. I am told that the Himalayan scenery is on a much grander scale than that of Switzerland, for instance, but I think that impression must be largely aided by one's knowledge of the actual figures. You can't tell the size of things by looking at them. You remember the tale of the three men on one of the plains of America. There was no bush or anything to gauge distance by, and they saw far away something which one of them thought was a troop of mounted Indians; another took it for a herd of buffaloes. It turned out to be a big rabbit."

"What is your program for Calcutta, in the matter of sight-seeing?"

"The interest of Calcutta is, of course, chiefly historical—Clive, Warren Hastings, and the Black Hole.[2] I mean to see as much as possible. The Indian interest has been greater elsewhere."[3]

"Have you found traveling in India pleasant?"

"The American sleeping-car is a model of luxury and magnificence; in the Indian car there is not a suggestion of either, yet the Indian carriage is more comfortable. One has plenty of air, and a night's rest is refreshing. On the whole, I appreciate the Indian train, though I caught my cold in it."

"Your book may presumably not be expected for a year or so?"

"Quite that. I am taking a heap of notes, but I have still a tour of several weeks in South Africa before I even go to England to begin it."

The interviewer would willingly have added a question or two, for so important a personage does not often come his way in these latitudes; but though Mark Twain is, in general—so he says—amenable to such little attentions, his present want of perfect health demands consideration; and he was left in peace.

Notes to Interview 110

1. See n. 3 to interview 8 and n. 5 to interview 84.
2. Robert Clive, first Baron Clive (1725-74), statesman and military leader instrumental in establishing British India by the Treaty of Paris (1763). Warren Hastings (1732-1818), first governor-general of British India (1772-74). The Black Hole was an eighteen-foot-square chamber where 146 British subjects were confined the night of 20 June 1756 on orders of the Nabob of Bengal. All but 23 died. See also chapter 54 of *FE*.
3. *FE*, 522: "There was plenty to see in Calcutta, but there was not plenty of time for it."

111

"Mark Twain in Calcutta," *Indian Daily News* (Calcutta), 26 March 1896; rpt. *Madras Mail,* 31 March 1896, 7.

Mr. and Mrs. S. L. Clemens and Miss Clemens arrived in Calcutta yesterday morning and put up at the Hotel Continental. During the afternoon they embarked on board the B.I.S. Co.'s steamer *Wardha,*[1] en route to Ceylon, the Mauritius, and Cape Town, where the great humorist will make a somewhat lengthened stay. One of the members of our staff called on him yesterday, and found him in the office of the hotel, comfortably ensconced in an easy chair and smoking a Meershaum, black with age. In answer to a question, Mr. Clemens said he had recovered his usual health. Miss Clemens, however, was suffering from a slight attack of malarial fever, but was much better. Their medical attendant had advised their immediate departure from Calcutta, where the heat was very trying, to sea, the breeze of which would soon restore her to her usual health. Questioned as to a statement made by a local contemporary that he had parted with the copyright of his forthcoming work for £10,000, Mr. Clemens said there was no truth in it, and he did not know how it had got abroad. It was unlikely, he added, that he would sell, outright, the copyright to any of his works, as he claimed and readily obtained a royalty on the sale of every copy of his works. It was all a gamble, he went on to say. For instance, when he was an almost unknown author, an American publisher offered him £2,000 for the copyright of *The Innocents Abroad;* he refused the offer, as he did not know how the book would take, and he had now no desire that any publisher should lose through him. If Du Maurier was now to write a new book, after the success of *Trilby*,[2] he would never dream, Mr. Clemens continued, of selling its copyright outright. He (Du Maurier) had sold the copyright of that work to Mr. Harper, who had made such a good thing out of it, that they were giving donations over and above the price paid for the copyright. He thought he now recollected how the newspaper paragraph about the sale of his new book came about. An American publisher had made him an offer of £4,000 for it, £3,000 to be paid down at once, and the remainder on the sales. He had refused this offer, and was now considering other contracts, but he certainly would never part with the copyright of any of his works. His book would, perhaps, be worth more than £10,000. He had a large mass of notes he has taken during his trip in India, which from want of time he had not yet been able to touch; amusements and business having kept him fully occupied during his Indian tour. He did not even hope to get the book out in six months, and would, perhaps, commence work at Cape Town. He was afraid to say anything as to the impression he had formed in India of things Indian, as they were so vast and complex and required time to digest. He repeated that publishing books was all a gamble, self-interest, of course, guiding both the author and publisher.

Notes to Interview 111

1. The *Wardha,* operated by the British India Steamship Co., was built in 1887.
2. See n. 7 to interview 86.

112

Standard (Madras), 1 April 1896; rpt. "Mark Twain in Madras," *Reis and Rayyet* (Calcutta), 11 April 1896, 176–77.

The British India Company's S.S. *Wardha,*[1] which arrived off Madras about eight o'clock on Monday night and was piloted into the harbor at day-light yesterday, carries the immortal Mark Twain and Mrs. and Miss Clemens away from India to Cape Town via Colombo and Port Louis. A Calcutta daily giving him the tip as to the celebrated humorist's departure from the City of Palaces on Thursday night last, a representative of the Madras *Standard* proceeded on board yesterday afternoon to interview him. Our reporter confesses to a sense of disappointment as he first set eyes upon the distinguished globetrotter because of his advanced years and a drawn paleness of countenance that suggested anything but the aspect of an active tourist anxious to take graphic notes of all he saw and heard. So far from impressing him with the vigor of middle manhood at least, and an active desire to know all about everything around him, Mr. Clemens appears to have given his interviewer the idea that he meant to take the rest of life as easily as surrounding circumstances would permit. The veteran author, then, was on the saloon-deck buried behind the pages of a Madras paper, reclining in an attitude of repose well into a deep cane-bottomed chair. It seemed almost a cruelty to disturb this *dolce far niente* [pleasant leisure] but pabulum the pressman must have when he has set his mind upon it! And this is how the ice was broken:—

"Mr. Clemens, I presume," said our representative laying his card upon a handy tea-stand within focus of Mark's glasses.

"The same, sir; glad to meet you, I am sure; sit down."

"Not wearied yet with interviewing, I hope."

"Well, no, I have the last three or four days myself [been] occupied nursing a cold, and I don't mind meeting press people anywhere. We are brought up to regard interviewing across the water as part of our lives, you know. Yes, thank you, my daughter has much improved, but I cannot make out why I am so troubled with this cold. It has stuck to me in spite of everything, even two weeks spent in bed, but I must say that, notwithstanding this inconvenience, I have enjoyed my tour. When this boat leaves Madras today, I suppose I will be leaving India quite behind me. Let me see, I landed at Bombay in the middle of January and here is the 31st of March. It seems such a short time and India is such a large place to study. You are right, we call at Colombo and Port Louis and then push on to Cape Town. All going well, I hope to reach America again next September. Ah! about the price I have been offered for my book. It is not true that I have been offered £10,000 for it, because no publisher, at least I have never heard of one, offers what he considers an author's possible share in a lump sum, but the statement may have grown out of the fact that a publisher offers you in advance one-fourth of what he considers will be your ultimate profit on the book. I said in Calcutta that I was offered that quarter, but I have not and shan't make any contract. I don't usually make a contract as regards a book yet to be written. That £10,000 you speak of would not be good business—it wouldn't be wise of the publisher to offer it, but to offer you one-fourth would be rational, and it would be also rational to the author to have it—rational because it protects his book from being neglected. A publisher is only a human being. He might get a book worth pushing more than yours and the chances are that he will neglect your book if no money has been paid, and so silence his conscience; he won't attempt to do that if he pays you down something.

"Did I find India precisely the place it was represented to be? Well, hardly.

You seem to know of course that this is my first visit to India. I came here like many others with only a very vague idea of the country, and I am bound to confess that I did not find it the immensely wealthy place it has been described as. But I am not surprised at that at all, because it is the showy side of the globe that reaches the remotest region, whether that showy side exists or not. In California, for instance, people have an idea that the gold dust is merely to be scooped up. Go there and you realize the nakedness of things. A feature that has struck me very forcibly in India is the poverty of the country. This was something I knew of only vaguely before. It is poverty compared with the poverty I have been acquainted with, and it is also a poverty based upon a certain value which does not exist in the country I come from. Somebody on this very ship told me that it doesn't make any difference how low wages in India are, the working-man will save something out of it. He said don't deceive yourself when people talk to you about low wages. Take the case of a man who earns Rands 7 a month[2]—he pointed out one to me—and lower than that sometimes, I should think it would cost that man all that to live and yet leave him something to lay by. Wherever that is the case, then I would not say it was abject poverty, but then this is looking at it all through a false medium—the values are not the same here as they are in other countries. We think the Italians are very poor until we have lived in Italy; then we readily find that there are really no poor Italians. When you come to examine their circumstances they have enough in life to live upon and to save. It is not possible for a stranger to tell what widespread poverty is. I know though from reading Buckle on India that it is the very home of poverty and he's an authority, I suppose, we should respect.[3] All the aspects of the country are poverty; a stranger could never mistake it for anything but poverty. It is the Anglo-Indian who calls your attention to the fact that the wages do not prove poverty. It would be the same in Europe or America as here if the conditions were the same. You can't create a famine in Europe or America, but you can here, and the people die off from actual want of food, a thing which can't happen in Europe or the United States—only in Ireland! You want to know how famines can be created? I mean that in those countries there is no failure which is universal—no failure of foods which keep people alive. Here the failure of the crops is universal at times and when a district can't be approached in time by railway, famine prevails and the mighty masses die of sheer starvation. Here is Madras with a population of 35 millions, I think,—that means half the population of the United States, and I consider the area they occupy would represent about half the territory of the United States; now fancy that great mass to have to supply food to! I took particular interest in the appearance of the land between Bombay and Calcutta and I do not think that much of it is allowed to go waste. Wherever water is accessible the soil seems to have been diligently tilled, and as regards General Booth's scheme, I have read something of it, but I do not think he can hope to succeed if he means to sandwich the religion of the Salvation Army with his peasant-settlement scheme.[4] It may amuse you to know that I first believed General Booth's scheme was intended to import paupers and the milder sort of criminals from among the surplus population of England. I do not think any country would like that unless the settlement was removed some considerable distance from decent habitations."

(A slight fit of coughing here interrupted the interview, then Mr. Clemens proceeded:) "I am killed with this cold since morning. We went ashore and breakfasted at the hotel near Spencer's shop intending to drive around Madras afterwards, but I found I could not manage it. I wasn't equal to the heat with this cold, so I left my family to do that. By the way, who is the Roman General on horseback on one of your broad roads? Sir Thomas Munro, did you say?[5] Ah, that takes one way back in your history to Clive.[6] Yes, I recollect now, he was one of your early Governors. And that just reminds me Lord Wenlock was your last governor.[7] I remember reading of him in the *Pioneer* and one or two other papers. The *Pioneer* made him out a failure. I think it a mistake myself to send out your landed noblemen to administer this vast country. They are not cut out for administrative work and are better left on their wealthy estates. You want men who are born to govern and who have made statesmanship a lifelong study. Your new Governor comes up to that mark, I am told. And what is that very telling structure there by that lighthouse? The High Court of Madras? Ah! it is so pleasant to see that. It has a proper look, as if it belonged to the country. This distinctly European architecture over here (the G.P.O. [general post office]) is a false note, too European altogether. I like Oriental architecture in its place. You ask me a very large question when you say 'have I made the acquaintance of the National Congress as an Indian institution?' Well, I have read of it, here a little and there a little, and all I can understand is that the men composing it, want a little more independence than they now have. I know little of their aims, but with the scholarly qualifications of the Hindus who sit in this Congress, I have been very much struck. I have recently read a book by Mr. Skrine, who has just been promoted to a Commissionership in Burma (Chittagong), dealing with the merits of a Hindu friend of the higher caste.[8] Mr. Skrine makes certain quotations from letters written by his friend and that Hindu was so much a master of our language—he went into such excellent niceties—which you couldn't expect except in a man born English and bred to his own mother tongue. Now this Hindu was a born native of this country, and educated in this country; he was very learned in Western educational sciences and his

English was flowing, easy and ever so idiomatic. This great aptitude on the part of the native of this country to excel in the English language is what one is confronted with all the time. There is, however, one good quality they lack as a nation—I believe they like to be called a 'nation'—and that is, inventive genius in the various practical arts. England, as you know, has attained greatness chiefly on account of the inventive genius of her sons. There are many who suppose that America is the home of inventions. This is a mistake. We rank, but falsely, as the inventors of the world, but we do what is worth a great deal more; we take up an invention and work at it till it results in something perfect. 'Promoters of Inventions' would be the proper way of describing us Americans, and there is a reason for it. England invented Colt's revolvers three or four centuries ago; she invented the application of steam power to machinery 'way back in Charles the Second's time; England invented the telegraph 60 years ago, but she has thrown away her great inventions for the reason that she has had no patent law to protect them. England had Wheatstone's system of telegraph,[9] but because she did not stick to it, Morse in America worked at it,[10] and a hard time of it he had too, till he developed the present electric telegraph, but then he had the patent law to protect him. It was only during the past 15 or 20 years that England has had a patent law worth anything.[11] It is true that men in America waste fortunes on patents that turn out failures, but it is also true that they make larger fortunes on patents that turn out successful.

"Yes, I have been interested in the recent 'situation' between England and America, but I never doubted for a moment that the warlike talk was based upon nothing.[12] The latest news is, I see, that they are getting into a rational and satisfactory state. Arbitration is to be resorted to after all. I knew that common-sense would get the advantage of all concerned presently. It was absolutely silly to think that America and England would ever fire a shot at each other.

"I hope to reach Colombo on Friday. I am engaged for two 'At homes' there I believe—not three. Thence I go on to Mauritius and South Africa. This boat I am in just suits my mood at present. I am in no hurry to get along. The more salt air I breathe the better I feel. We had a fine passage down from Calcutta except for a current that took about 30 miles off the rate of our travel each day. The *Wardha* is not one of those boats that cover 500 miles a day, but without running away from herself she keeps in the neighborhood of 200.

"Thank you very much for your kind wishes. I have had nothing else all over India, and will carry the best recollections of this country home with me."

Concluding the interview thus, Mr. Clemens strolled to the other end of the deck to watch Harmston's menagerie being hauled inboard.[13]

Notes to Interview 112

1. The *Wardha,* operated by the British India Steamship Co., was built in 1887.
2. An amount roughly equivalent to five U.S. dollars.
3. Louis Rousselet and Charles R. Buckle, *India and Its Native Princes: Travels in Central India* (New York: Scribner, 1876).
4. William Booth (1829-1912), founder of the Salvation Army.
5. Sir Thomas Munro (1761-1827), appointed governor of Madras in 1819.
6. See the reference to Clive in n. 2 to interview 110.
7. Beilby Lawley, Third Baron of Wenlock, governor of Madras, 1891-96.
8. Francis H. B. Skrine, *Journalist: Being the Life, Letters, and Correspondence of Dr. Sambhu C. Mookerjee* (1895).
9. Sir Charles Wheatstone (1802-75), inventor of an electric telegraph.
10. Samuel F. B. Morse (1791-1872), artist and inventor of an electric telegraph.
11. The Patent Act of 1883 basically codified existing law in England.
12. See nn. 1 and 4 to interview 107.
13. The Harmston Circus toured throughout Asia from the 1890s through the 1930s.

113

"Mark Twain in Durban," *Natal Mercury* (Durban, South Africa), 8 May 1896, 3; rpt. *Natal Mercury Weekly Edition,* 8 May 1896, 5989; *Natal Witness* (Pietermaritzburg), 9 May 1896, 6; and *Press* (Pretoria), 15 May 1896, 3.

"He's staying at the Royal; you might get an interview with him."

"With whom?" queried the reporter to whom the remark was addressed by his editor.

"Why, Mark Twain."

"Oh, the Y.M.C.A. young man, you mean?"

"No, I don't; you're thinking of Mark Mee. I mean Samuel Langhorne Clemens, the author of the 'Jumping Frog'"—which appeal to the early reading days of the journalist brought him to a sense of the urgency of the mission, and straightway he sallied forth to meet in the flesh the man who had erstwhile been such a familiar spirit in the sparkling pages of *Roughing It,* or the perennial *Innocents Abroad.* The *Mercury* man at the Royal Hotel sought out Mr. Carlyle Smythe[1], who is acting as agent to the distinguished tourist, and was, through him, introduced to Mark Twain in bed. It was approaching noon, but the fatigues of travel, on a constitution which is not by any means so vigorous as it once was, had rendered it advisable that Mr. Clemens should take the rest he had been for the previous day or two deprived of.

The veteran author spoke first of all of his visits to India and Australia, and said he had received nothing but kindness from the people of both countries. "I have had a delightful time in India. I only wish my stay could have been extended two or three years longer; but," he added with regret, "the heat came and drove us out. During our three months' stay there, however, we had an opportunity of seeing the region stretching between Bombay and Calcutta."

"Your tour began when?"

"I left America on the 23rd August last year."

"And you have been wandering about ever since?"

"Well yes; we have been knocking about since then, but extensive traveling has never been a proclivity of mine. I never have enjoyed it; it has never been my own desire"—and the reporter thought of the never-ending fund of enjoyment those unenjoyable travels had afforded most people in the world.

"Then, of course, you were away during the Venezuela scare."[2]

"Yes; I heard of it while in Australia."

"What did you think of it?"

"I think it was a foolish thing. I could not imagine how so near approach to a breach between England and America could have happened upon what seemed to be such slight, such inadequate grounds; and I can't now any more than I could three months ago. I cannot still understand where there was occasion for a talk of war."

"You don't think the feelings of the American people are inclined that way?"

"To my mind, it would be impossible for the American people to desire a breach with England, and I do not think it will ever come to that"—and there was a tone of earnestness about the remarks of the speaker which bore the stamp of sincere conviction.

"Will you tell me, Mr. Clemens, how you came to take to writing?"

"I entered journalism simply without intending it. It is just what happens in all frontier towns and in all new places. Half your time your vocation, if you have one, has no place there, and you must seek another; and you're apt to find it by accident. I found a vacancy in a newspaper office when I wasn't looking for one. That was in Nevada, in the silver mining days."

"And your newspaper work developed into book writing?"

"I was asked to write a book, and I did it. Otherwise it would never have occurred to me. After a time I went to Europe. The tourist business had not begun then, and so that sort of thing was novel enough to make a publisher see that a book on it might have a commercial value. So at his instigation I wrote."

"And you have written how many books?"

"About 14 or 15 altogether. I know it is very slow work, for I have been writing between 29 and 30 years, but I never worked very diligently."

"The book you have in hand—"

"Will be descriptive of my tour. I have got a mass of material for it, but I do not exactly know when it will be published. Delays may arise through waiting for the season."

"It will be published in England, I presume?"

"For the purpose of securing the copyright."

"How do you find the new international copyright agreement between England and America works?"

"It works very well, for the reason that, if a book is likely to have a big sale, the mere setting of it up in America is nothing at all. As you know, in order to secure a copyright in America, the work must be set up and printed in the States. No English publisher would send the sheets of a book 3,000 miles unless it were probable that the work was going to have a big sale; while if an enormous circulation was from the first assured, no publisher would scruple about the slightly additional cost of having the book set up in America. So you see, it only acts as a check upon works of a trifling commercial value."

"How does it affect Canada?"

"As far as I know, Canada has her own copyright laws, and the convention between England and America does not really affect her. Yet Canada has had always a sort of double privilege, and has been able to reprint both English and American books without regard to the copyright. But of course it would not pay her to reprint a book unless she got information before its publication that it was going to be a great success; and even then it would be only conditional upon her getting advance slips of the work. Take a case as an illustration. If the Prince of Wales announced his intention of writing a book, there would be the assurance of an enormous demand throughout the world, and if Canada could manage to get an early copy she could flood the American market with a cheap edition and destroy the regular publication, but if John Smith or William Jones, or some person of no prominence, were to announce a novel, Canada would be asleep, and, when it hit the public taste under some sudden impulse, would be unable to step in. A book which had that kind of fortune was Wallace's *Ben-Hur*.[3] That lay on the shelves in Harper's warehouse for a couple of years, and no sale at all took place till President Garfield delivered his opinion of the book in highly complimentary terms.[4] Then started up a sudden and prodigious call for *Ben-Hur*, too late for Canada to meet, and Harper's supplied a million copies to the public of the United States. The case of *Trilby*,[5] however, is a curious one. It was very apparent long before it was finished in *Harper's Magazine* that the book was going to have a great sale, and it was a circumstance which, in the light of former practices, Canada should have taken advantage of. The Copyright Law," continued Mr. Clemens, as he warmed to a subject in which he is naturally well versed, "is to encourage local literature and discourage the imported article. Now, just consider what happens in England today. Zola, or any prominent French novelist, can flood the English market with his books, and the only result is that they 'Frenchify' the morals of the readers, and inflict a mighty serious damage. International copyright ought to go beyond the mere dollars and cents involved; it should shut out pernicious literature, and copyright should only be extended to books that could be approved of."

"What do you think of the general leaning of the literary taste of today?"

"Taste for a while, as you will be aware, leant towards the romantic—uncleanly, erratic scurf—which was undoubtedly created by the wide dissemination of French novels in England and America. But that seems to have run its course, and there seems to be a sort of lull in the matter of taste. *Trilby* is the only book I can now call to mind as having 'caught on,' and I think the reason of its great popularity is merely that it gives a felicitous view of a sort of artistic Parisian life which was fresh to the world, and taking. It was most happily done, and out of the common of what people were reading."

"But take Rudyard Kipling?"

"Kipling's books were out of the common. His field was new, and his gifted treatment of it gave it interest that commanded a wide, wide popularity. And deservedly so."

"We are looking forward eagerly to your new book, Mr. Clemens; and we shall all await your opinions on the South African situation."

"Well about that," smilingly replied the humorist, "I shall have to ask you to furnish me with news. I did hear of an outbreak in Johannesburg just as we were leaving Melbourne, and we were told by cablegram that Jameson had crossed the line with 700 men?[6] Well, for a moment we did not know what line he had crossed, and wherever we have been since there have been such wide intervals between the scraps of information we got that it has been almost impossible to follow the course of events. At Delagoa Bay we heard that some cipher correspondence had been discovered, and that it had changed the complexion of things; but that was about all we knew."

"Still, you can tell me what you thought of Delagoa Bay?"[7]

"We had little opportunity of observing it. But it is just every bit what one would expect where Portugal is the paramount authority. Portugal doesn't seem to be able to take care of herself in a very effective way, let alone manage a Colony. The same incompetency is shown by the Spaniards in Goa. It is almost a farce. Last January the news would come to us every day at Bombay how some Spanish prince, with 300 soldiers at his back, had endangered his life in battle against 36 natives. It seemed to me that Delagoa Bay at the time of the creation was intended for an important port in Africa—the most important port in Southern Africa—in energetic and intelligent hands; but to remember that it is in the possession of the Portuguese is to recognize that it is not in energetic and intelligent hands, and that its development to the importance which it ought to possess is never to be expected."

"You came from Delagoa in the *Arundel Castle*, I think?"[8]

"Yes."

"What do you think of her?"

"She is really a perfect passenger boat. Everything that one could hope for; and the table is most excellent. I only remember once coming across so good a cuisine, and that was on a French boat between Newhaven and Dieppe, where, if you would expect anything, it would be good cooking."

"Then when do you complete your tour?"

"After leaving South Africa I shall stay, I think, some months in some corner of England—some village, perhaps—and get on with my book."

"Which we all hope will be successful," remarked the Pressman as he shook hands with the laughter-maker and bowed himself out.

Notes to Interview 113

1. See n. 1 to interview 93.
2. See nn. 1 and 4 to interview 107.
3. Lew Wallace (1827–1905) was the territorial governor of New Mexico and author of the historical romance *Ben-Hur* (1880).
4. When Wallace resigned as territorial governor in March 1881, President James A. Garfield (1831–81) was reading *Ben-Hur*. As a result, he appointed Wallace the U.S. ambassador to Turkey so that he might "draw inspiration from the modern east for future literary work."
5. See n. 7 to interview 86.
6. A group of about 600 British irregulars under the command of Leander Starr Jameson (1853–1902) tried and failed to spark a rebellion against the Boer government in South Africa in late December 1895–early January 1896. The raid was planned and supported by Cecil Rhodes (1853–1902), an English businessman and founder of the Rhodes Scholarship. (See MT's comments on Rhodes in interview 116 and n. 2 to that interview.) The raiders were jailed in Pretoria and subsequently released upon payment of an indemnity by the British government. See also *FE*, chapters 66–67.
7. Budd (1977), 98n48: "Delagoa Bay, on the Southeast coast of Africa, had been at times under British control; but it had been awarded to Portugal by arbitration in 1875.... The British had continued to feel that they could administer the area more efficiently." See also *FE*, chapter 64.
8. *FE*, 630: "The *Arundel Castle* is the finest boat I have seen in these seas. She is thoroughly modern, and that statement covers a great deal of ground." Built in 1894, it was operated by the Castle Mail S. P. Co.

114

"A Chat with Mark Twain," *Star* (Johannesburg), 18 May 1896, 4.

Ushered into the best bedroom of the Grand National (writes a *Star* reporter, who spent an hour in the company of Mark Twain this forenoon) one finds the famous humorist still in bed, enjoying his pipe and his paper. In order to express his thorough unconventionality, he has propped himself up with pillows, with the "head-piece" from which have proceeded Huck Finn, Tom Sawyer, and dozens of others we all know and like, at the foot of the bed instead of the top. From a mountain of bed-clothes, a pair of kindly grizzly eyes look out at you. The mouth is clear and firm, but with a tell-tale twist at the corners which proclaims the man for what he is. The forehead seems benignity itself, and is unusually broad and lofty. You are heartily bidden welcome, and before many moments have passed Mark (you may say "Mr. Clemens"; but you think of him as "Mark") is telling you that, as a man who knows Western America reasonably well, he scouts the idea of there being an American people there quite different from the Easterners—a people who are virulently anti-English.

The possibility of war between England and her mighty offshoot he dismisses as being not worth serious discussion.[1] They were made to help and stand by each other, those two nations, he goes on to say, and he adds that had England decided to fight for the sake of the Armenians the American nation would have backed England with all her might.[2] He does not agree with you, though, that there is a party in America who makes it its business to be always pulling the lion's tail. When messages like the famous Cleveland dispatch are sent, he says, they are honestly meant by the people who send them; but he does not think that at the back of the senders' mind is the idea of proceeding to extremities. Mr. Cleveland, he maintains, is a statesman, and has made very few blunders.[3] He adds rather sadly that there are no Websters or Calhouns in American politics today;[4] but, he repeats, Mr. Cleveland is a statesman. Mr. McKinley he regards as an excrescence.[5] He is the top of a wave, that is all; and Mark does not seem to take him seriously. Mention of McKinleyism brings you naturally to the subject of the American Presidential election, and you ask who will come out at the top of the poll. "Well," Mark returns, very solemnly, "you know that reminds me of a tale of Browning. Somebody read a line of 'Sordello' to him, and asked what it meant. Browning said that once there were two who knew, but one was up there (pointing to the sky) and he was not the other.[6] "Now I suppose there is One up there who knows; I am not the other. Still, I should say the Republicans will win unless they commit some very bad blunder—and blundering is the prerogative of the Democrats."

Coming to more personal matters, you ask him what sort of an experience he has found traveling in South Africa to be; and he replies that except for the stretch from the Natal border into Johannesburg he has found it not only endurable, but enjoyable. Asked if he had found us unusually stolid in South Africa, he says "far from it"; and goes on to say that wherever he had addressed English-speaking people he has found a quick and appreciative response to his efforts to amuse them. In this connection he says that one of the things he cannot understand is the popular reputation of the Scotch as regards the appreciation of humor. No one, he says emphatically, *enjoys* anything humorous more intensely than a Scotsman does. You are reminded of the saying attributed to a Scotch member of the present Parliament, that it is only English jokes which need to be let into the skull of the Scot by means of a surgical operation. He thinks that just as public taste in novel reading has advanced wonderfully during the past twenty years, so it has advanced in regard to humorous writing. The public demand that its jokes shall be sharp, clean, pointed.

Asked what is his favorite book among his own writings, Mark replies drily that he really isn't familiar with them, and must be excused from replying. He says he has only taken up one of his books to read, after writing them, and that was *Huckleberry Finn*. He read that once to a little girl in his family, and—he owns it shamefacedly—he laughed over it, whereupon his young critic sharply reproved him for laughing at what he had written himself. That experience, he says, was so discouraging that he never ran the risk of repeating it. His most popular books—"that is, judging by the sales, and that's a consideration, you know"—are *Roughing It* and the first *Innocents Abroad*. Then comes *The Prince and the Pauper*. By and by the talk turns upon some of the American authors he knows, and you mention the brilliant little group which includes Curtis, Howells, Cable, and Stockton.[7] This gives him the opportunity of launching into an exquisite bit of criticism of Howells. "Howells," he says enthusiastically, "is one of the very best literary men America has produced; there is no bludgeoning with him. His is the rapier method. You English don't like him because he once adversely criticized Dickens, and I believe even Thackeray![8] But we honor him as a man who delivers his verdicts after weighing the evidence most carefully; a man who dispatches this aspirant or that not hurriedly or with passion, but slowly, deliberately, almost lovingly. Howells is a gentle, kindly, refined spirit; he is too good for this world. In my opinion there is never a trace of affectation or superiority in either the man or his books, though he is accused of both."

Discussing some recent literary phenomena, Mark tells you that one of the remarkable things of the century, in his opinion, is the Bellamy "boom." He knows Edward Bellamy well, and he is perfectly convinced that nobody was more surprised than the writer of *Looking Backward* himself when it was made clear that hundreds of thousands of people in the United States had accepted that book as a new Gospel.[9] Nor did the publishers expect much of it, "for the first edition," says Mark, "was about as scrofulous-looking and mangy a volume as I have set eyes on." Yet in a few months a quarter of a million copies had been sold; and the publishers were turning out two thousand copies a day. In all probability the sales constituted a record. *Trilby* and *Ben-Hur* have been the only things like it.[10] Many other subjects does Mark touch upon; and all in an interesting way, but other callers are pressing and you take your leave with a cordial handshake—and an expression of the wish that succeeding visitors may take up less of your host's time.

Notes to Interview 114

1. See nn. 1 and 4 to interview 107.
2. Budd (1977), 98-99n49: "In 1893 Turkey had begun to suppress brutally the Armenian nationalists; Great Britain, France, and Russia tried to intervene; in 1895 Great Britain had favored the use of force, but the other two nations had balked. In 1896 the Sultan renewed the brutality."
3. MT supported the Democratic candidate, Grover Cleveland, against the Republican candidate, James G. Blaine (1830-93), in the 1884 presidential campaign.
4. Daniel Webster (1782-1852), Whig politician from New England; see the reference to Calhoun in n. 2 to interview 107.
5. The Republican candidate, William McKinley (1843-1901), was the U.S. president from 1897 until his assassination.
6. The British poet Robert Browning (1812-89) published "Sordello" in 1840.
7. On Howells, see n. 2 to interview 2; on Cable, see chapter 2. George William Curtis (1824-92) and Frank Stockton (1834-1902) were American writers and editors.
8. Howells criticized Dickens and Thackeray in his controversial essay "Henry James, Jr." in *Century*, 25 (November 1882), 25-29.
9. Edward Bellamy (1850-98), author of the utopian novel *Looking Backward* (1888), which MT considered "the latest and best of all the bibles."
10. On *Trilby*, see n. 7 to interview 86; on *Ben-Hur*, see nn. 3 and 4 to interview 113.

115

"Mark Twain: Mr. Clemens on the Rand," *Standard and Diggers' News*, (Johannesburg), 18 May 1896, 4.

Mark Twain arrived last night by the Natal train from Durban. . . . It is impossible to feel otherwise than at ease with this unaffected courteous gentleman, and the treasured recollection of glorious evenings spent over *A Tramp Abroad* and *A Yankee at the Court of King Arthur* faded into dimness before the spoken words of the great humorist.

"Mr. Daly sent for me—" Mark Twain was saying when he was interrupted. Greetings over, the pleasant voice resumed.

Yes, Mr. Daly, the great theater-manager, wrote a note and sent for me, asking me to come and see him.[1] He gave me most minute details as to how I was to reach the backdoor of the theater down a little lane, through a cigar shop, and so to the rear entrance of the building. I had been reading then about a great bench show [a competitive dog show] down at New Haven where they had a great St. Bernard, the prize-dog of the United States. As I understood it, it was about the height of an ordinary table and weighed some 180 lbs. Its dimensions every way were extraordinary, and I was becoming impressed, although, mind you, I was no judge of bench shows—had hardly ever seen one.

Well, I followed my directions, went through the cigar shop, down the lane, and reached the little backdoor where a mighty big Irishman was located. I pushed the door open but the Irishman said "Wait!"

I waited.

Then he said, "What do you want, anyway?"

I said I wanted to see Mr. Daly.

"You can't."

"But he invited me, sent me a letter to come."

"To this door?"

"He did—to this door."

"Well, you can't see him, and I say, don't smoke, put out that cigar."

I put down that cigar, and took out my letter. He looked at it—upside down, and handed it back.

"Ye might just read it, will ye? My sight's not much."

I read it to him and he didn't seem impressed.

"What name do you call yours?"

"Mark."

"Whole of it?"

"No, Mark Twain."

"What's your business?"

"Oh, I'm in the show line."

"Oh, you're in the show business, are you? In what line?"

Well, I hadn't quite made up my mind to what my show-business was, but a great St. Bernard just then came by—a large dog, quite the height of the table, so I said:

"Running a bench show!"

"Is that so? Where at?"

"Down at New Haven."

"Are you running the big bench show at New Haven? Where the big St. Bernard is?"

"That's so."

"Been in the business a long time?"

"Yes, most of my time."

"And you've got a big dog there? What about this one?"

Well, I sized that dog up and he looked a powerful big animal, so I said: "127 lbs."

That Irishman got up, and he said: "Man, you've beat it. It weighs 125 lbs. Man, you are a judge of dogs. Just 2 lbs. over. Well, I say, light your cigar; here's a match. And it is Mr. Daly you were wanting to see?"

"It was."

"Well, come away up this way. Mind your head. These stairs might be pesky." And he showed me into Mr. Daly's room. Daly turned around and said:

"Oh, by the way, about that man. I forgot to tell you about him. How did you get in?"

"By the back way."

"By the back way? Well, you're the first man that's got past that Irishman in 18 years. I thought General Grant and a battery of artillery would fail to get past that hall-keeper."

"It was an accident, but it saved me some trouble."[2]

Mr. Clemens ceased speaking, and the sound of his Missouri tongue seemed to have opened infinite possibilities to the understanding of books that one had read so long ago.

Mr. Clemens enjoyed his journey from Maritzburg, and managed to shorten the way marvelously by the help of two well-primed travelers who invaded his compartment.

I tried to explain that the car was reserved for Royalties, but as they only saw two princes, they refused to be impressed. First thing they asked was what my business was. I said "writing books." They thought I said "keeping books," so to encourage me they said:

"Well, there's a countryman of yours here, one Hammond who's done well.[3] He might manage to get you a job. Where did you keep them last?"

"In New York, with the Standard Oil Co."

Then they began to call the Standard Oil Company for everything they knew. It seems one of them had a small grocery store out'n New York, and he'd dropped money over the Company. I got nervous in case they asked too much. Evidently they looked on the Standard Oil Company as a sort of cuttlefish or anaconda, or whatever they fancied swallowed most. One of them asked—

"What's the finest Florida?"

This rather got me, but I ventured 40 cents.

"What? Wholesale?"

"No, no—retail. It's only 20 cents wholesale, but it's been fluctuating—fluctuating."

I found 7 cents was enough, but I got away from that subject.[4]

The conversation turned to Italy, and Mr. Clemens had much to say of the pleasure he found in his ten months' stay in Florence.

"I lived three miles outside the city wall. I used to watch the sunsets there from the esplanade. The sun set exactly behind the Palazzo Vecchio.[5] How I reveled in the rose-tinted mist! It seemed like a dream city, so that one could not believe it real. Every evening for ten months that marvelous prospect never failed us."

It came out in the conversation that Mr. Clemens had crossed the Atlantic fifteen times in the last five years, on visits to his family in Germany and Paris.

Later the talk turned to the troubles of the Transvaal, and Mark Twain had something to say of the locust swarms he had passed through on his way from Maritzburg.

"It was 10 o'clock when we saw them first. Then they grew thicker and darker. I'd never seen locusts that thick before. When I looked on the great clouds with the sun shining on them, they seemed like burnished silver. At one place there were great silver-plated acres of veld, all due to the locusts. When you looked at them against the sun, each black silhouette was distinct, when the sun shone on their gauzy wings they made the best imitation of a snowstorm I have ever seen."

Locusts were not the only topic of conversation.

"Yes, you have had a fearful time here lately," Mr. Clemens said, "what with wars, revolutions, rinderpest, locusts, drought, and me—I guess you can go no further with plagues. Now that I've come you must take a change for the better."

Under no happier auspices could this be done than those of Mark Twain.

Notes to Interview 115

1. Augustin Daly (1838–99), theatrical impresario and playwright. See also *MTL*, 6:206–7.

2. MT retells this story in chapter 45 of *FE*. See also Fatout, 222–24.

3. MT had met John Hays Hammond (1855–1936), mining engineer and collaborator with Cecil Rhodes in gold and diamond mining in South Africa, in Hartford in the mid-1870s when Hammond was a student at Yale. Hammond reminisced about MT's visit to South Africa in his *Autobiography* (New York: Farrar and Rinehart, 1935), 398–400. On Rhodes, see n. 6 to interview 113; see also MT's comments on Rhodes in interview 116 and n. 2 to that interview.

4. MT's dialogue with the two "well-primed" (i.e., drunk) travelers is obviously absurd and nonsensical.

5. A palace adjacent to the Uffizi Gallery and the Ponte Vecchio.

116

"Mark Twain on the Rand," *Times* (Johannesburg), 18 May 1896, 5.

.... Last night the Natal train, by which Mark Twain was expected, arrived in fairly good time.... In the course of a conversation with the *Times* representative Mark Twain showed that he took a very keen interest in the local political situation. "Years ago," he said, "I was going from Southampton to New York, when I met Mrs. John Hays Hammond, whose husband was on the Reform Committee.[1] I found she and I had much in common. She was born in Missouri; so was I. She had lived a long time in California; so had I; and we were therefore fellow Americans. When I at last decided to come to Africa, I tried to recall the name of the pleasant lady I had met on-board the ocean steamer, but I could not succeed. You know," explained the speaker, "I am such a wretched hand at remembering people's names. I even forget my own at times, and often have to give a fictitious name to the police. I was terribly aggravated at this unfortunate lapse of memory, and it was only when stopping at Durban three days ago, when I saw a telegraphic message stating that Mr. John Hays Hammond was a political prisoner in the jail at Pretoria, that the name came back to me. I understand that Mrs. Hammond is not here, but I will certainly make a point of going and renewing the acquaintance."

"How did you like the journey up from Natal?" put in the Pressman.

"The carriages on the Natal line are all right. I like them. But I seldom can sleep in a train anywhere, and when I do sleep it does me little good, as it is not at all refreshing. I see in the papers that one of the Reform prisoners has committed suicide. It is a most terrible case, and is really infinitely pitiful," said Mark Twain pathetically. "You know I take a great interest in the political situation, but at the same time I consider politics here are in an inextricable tangle."

"Good expression," put in the Pressman.

"The first I heard of the Jameson raid was when in Albany, Western Australia; it was just the bare fact of the incursion having taken place. At Colombo we got nothing further that was definite beyond the fact of the defeat, and we were without any more news till we got to Bombay, although it was aggravating to reflect that particulars were passing under the sea along the wire we were passing over. From that day to this I have been getting more and more bewildered through missing weeks of news at a time. From Calcutta to Mauritius I was in a state of handsome suspense, until at last I heard that the leaders were all in jail, and I could not for the life of me make out what it was for."

"You will hear enough about it in Johannesburg," put in the *Times* man.

"I believe you have no municipality here. Isn't that curious?" said the man from America.

"It is one of the many peculiar customs of the country," put in the Pressman diplomatically. "What do you think of Cecil Rhodes of Africa?"[2]

"Well," said the interviewed one, "if you take the newspaper accounts of him you get two sides only, a good side and a bad one. Never what one might call a rotund picture of the man—only that which is worst and best. There is one main point, however, on which everyone seems unanimous, namely, that he is a most extraordinary man. I did wish to see Cecil Rhodes before I left, but am afraid he is too far away to be got at. In my opinion to have seen South Africa, without having met Cecil Rhodes, is to have seen only a part of the country, but by no means all," said Mark Twain emphatically.

"Mr. Stead says that Rhodes and Olive Schreiner are far and away the two greatest figures in South Africa.[3] What is your opinion of the latter?"

"I read *The Story of an African Farm* when it first came out, in a casual sort of way, yet it left a definite impression upon me, which was chiefly derived from the first chapter. The book is good literary art, and gives a clear, definite picture, I believe, of the country where the scene is laid. It is full of the sentiment and atmosphere of the region described, and I had then a great opinion of this young girl's gifts. I read the book again on the ocean, this time as the literary critic examining the workmanship, and found the greater part to be written crudely, and to be formless and without any distinct aim. It was a plenty good enough book for a girl her age," said the American, "and anybody could see there was a gift there beyond the ordinary that gave large promise of great things in the future, which were not fulfilled in her first effort. I have a great belief in W. T. Stead's opinion, and although he is not always right, if he says a thing is good he is certain not to be very far wrong."

Mr. Clemens, although just off a long sleepless journey, was brilliantly conversational, and, did space permit, much that is interesting could be written of the racy stories he related last evening of his adventures in South Africa and elsewhere.

Notes to Interview 116

1. Natalie Harris Hammond was the author of *A Woman's Part in a Revolution*. MT refers to her book in *FE*, 660. On John Hammond, see n. 3 to interview 115.

2. Cecil Rhodes (1853–1902), British financier and African colonialist. MT expressed a grudging respect for Rhodes in *FE* (pp. 708–10) before concluding: "I admire

him, I frankly confess it; and when his time comes I shall buy a piece of the rope for a keepsake." See also n. 6 to interview 113.

3. Olive Schreiner (1855–1920), South African novelist and author of *The Story of an African Farm* (1883). See also *FE,* 684, 689, 697. On Stead, see n. 5 to interview 74.

117

"Mark Twain at Queenstown," *Diamond Fields Advertiser* (Kimberley, South Africa), 10 June 1896, 6; rpt. *Diamond Fields Advertiser Weekly Mail Summary,* 13 June 1896, 4.

An occasional contributor who interviewed Mark Twain at Queenstown remarked to the humorist:—"You will have some difficulty in making the book descriptive of your present tour as entertaining as your *Innocents Abroad.* You have not the old institutions to serve as a butt for your humor." "No," he said, "I guess I know the limitations of this book, but if one had time to do such a tour in a leisurely fashion, one could write five books on it without much trouble." During the interview, Mark, speaking of the penalties attached to being a distinguished humorist, said: "The public are more prone to believe a lie than a truth, and if a man begins to paint in a certain style, he must keep it up or his public will forsake him."

118

"Mark Twain in Port Elizabeth: An Interview," *Eastern Province Herald and Port Elizabeth Commercial News* (Port Elizabeth, South Africa), 19 June 1896, 3.

Nor every successful author has also the reputation of being a successful lecturer, so that when the two accomplishments are combined in one fortunate individual the measure of public esteem must necessarily be liberal and widespread. As an author the widespread reputation of the humorous Mark Twain, although a product of the other side of the Atlantic, had reached South Africa long ere his coming hither as a lecturer was foreshadowed, his works having had delighted readers anywhere within 300 terrestrial miles of the Cape, almost since the time when he first "rushed into print." In the course of his peregrinations he has now come amongst us in order to derive profit and pleasure from a study of our characteristics by means of social intercourse, and to impart to his literary admirers the additional gratification of being personally "at home" with the genius who contributed *A Tramp Abroad* and other gems to their book shelves. That Mark Twain is always and every where "at home" with English-speaking people was a conviction soon forced upon a representative of the *E. P. Herald* who had an interesting interview with him at the Grand Hotel on Wednesday afternoon. The man of letters reached Port Elizabeth late on Tuesday night by the R.M.S. *Norham Castle,* on board of which he had come from East London, and it will be a matter of surprise if he does not, before his departure next week, largely draw upon, as elsewhere, the characteristics of the town and neighborhood. He has the liveliest impressions of his welcome to South Africa, and Johannesburg in particular; but those impressions are much better conveyed in his own words.

"I could not have come to South Africa at a better time," he said, "excepting that I should like to have arrived say four months earlier, and been 'on the spot' throughout the whole crisis. As it is I have had it handed to me in chapters, and the whole make up of an interesting, I may say exciting, novel. The first chapter came in the form of the briefest telegrams published on a slip of paper about so big (forming a square with the forefinger and thumb of both his hands). These telegrams, which were handed into the steamer at Albany, the last port of call as we were leaving Australia, merely stated that Dr. Jameson and 700 men were crossing the Border, and were making for Johannesburg.[1] Nobody could tell where this 'Border' was, or how long Jameson would take to cross it. We had a long interval to wait for the second chapter—until we reached Ceylon. Then we got the telegraphic announcement that Jameson had fought his way so far, and had surrendered, and he and his men been taken prisoners. The next chapter we got at Delagoa Bay,[2] where all the details and the sequel were to be had—Jameson sent home, and the Reform Committee arrested and on their trial. After that we had other chapters—the sentences to death of the big four, and the subsequent commutations. The story has unfolded just like a novel."

"The completion of the novel, so far as you were concerned, was still more interesting?"

"Yes, indeed; I was fortunate in being in Pretoria just then, and had a good time with the Reformers in jail."

"Did you hear any complaints from the prisoners as to their treatment?"

"Oh, no; I have been in many worse jails in America. All that I heard objected to by some of the Reformers who were first released was the treatment of the natives by the Boer jailers. These colored prisoners were separated from the white on opposite sides of the jail premises. Some white prisoners strongly objected to being under the same roof with the niggers, and I have known young men in the jails of the Southern States who thought it a worse degradation to be imprisoned with negroes for whatever offense than to be with whites who had been convicted of murder or other 'respectable' crimes."

"What is your opinion of the newspapers of South Africa as literary productions? Did you have an opportunity of viewing their production in Johannesburg?"

"Well, no I didn't. You see the whole town was an open house to me, and I felt I was a particular guest, so that one couldn't very well air one's opinions on these matters; and being a journalist myself I couldn't very well talk 'shop' without appearing to set up my opinions against others."

"You are an experienced traveler, Mr. Clemens; how do you like the passenger service on the South African railways?"

"Oh, I don't mind the slowness very much. If I had particular business on hand that required dispatch I might perhaps complain; but then you see I am in no hurry. If it were cold and miserable, or hot and disagreeable weather I might not relish it, but the weather since I have been in South Africa has been simply perfect. I have thoroughly enjoyed the traveling, and as soon as I have stepped on board the train I have made myself very comfortable indeed. One can well understand the reason for the slowness. The Government controls—it is always the same, where there is Government control—the paying goods traffic. If the passenger traffic were remunerative some means would be found, under whatever systems, to increase the speed of the trains and otherwise encourage that branch of traffic. Another cause for the slowness is the lack of competition, as in France and Germany. When compared with traveling in England and America it is very slow indeed." Mr. Clemens incidentally mentioned a somewhat painful experience of traveling in France some little time ago, when one of his daughters was taken ill in the train before reaching Amiens, and although their destination was in Paris the authorities would not allow the family to break their journey without forfeiting the six tickets, which had to be done. He stated that for £250 a through ticket, extending over six or nine months, to cover the round-world journey could be had at any of the big railway or steamboat "pools" of America or England. The same journey, taken piecemeal (as he was doing), cost many times as much. He thought nothing could beat for cheapness the round-world excursion ticket.

"Do you think the idea of forming a permanent board of arbitration to settle disputes between England and America likely to take effect in America? It is rather a large order, but what, as an American, is your opinion of this? I presume you are pretty well able to estimate public opinion on your side of the Atlantic?"

"I say, unhesitatingly, that such a Board of Appeal between the two great English-speaking nations is bound to come at some time or another. A Board comprising four or six of the best representatives of the nations could not fail to be respected by those nations, and their decisions accepted without further serious dispute. You know Arbitration could deal with difficulties as they arrive with a matter of say £100,000 to consider; but there is no pitched battle to be fought for less than a couple of millions in money, and an outpouring of human blood, to say nothing of the national hatred that would take a century to wipe out."

"Were you in the States when the Venezuelan war cloud rose?"[3]

"No, I was in Australasia at the time, and for the life of me I cannot understand what could have been in President Cleveland's mind when he sent that memorable address to Congress."

"Then you don't consider it a Wall Street or Tammany Hall move?"

"Oh, no, not at all. If the late Mr. Blaine had been in the President's seat I should have said at once it was a political move to influence the next election of President.[4] But I cannot think that of President Cleveland. He is a clear-headed and much experienced statesman, and as such has a worldwide reputation; and I don't think for a moment he would stoop to a political job of the kind. If I were in America I should get the idea in view firsthand from the President himself. But now there is no reason to my mind for the extraordinary attitude he has taken up towards England in the matter of Venezuela, and so it will remain until I get back. I cannot understand it at all. I am not surprised that Lord Salisbury put his back up, but I believe there is a tacit understanding between England and America now to submit the point to arbitration, and so it should be. Arbitration must be conducted on a liberal basis, and the nations concerned must be prepared to give as well as take."

And so the conversation turned on many important subjects of the day, the replies to the interviewer being by no means fluently given, but with the free and easy drawl in characteristic American style. When once under weigh with his sentiments the genial Mark left no doubt that these were the intelligent and settled opinions of a thinker who knew what he was talking about. At the same time he was "discussing" the inevitable cigar, and when rising to depart, his inquisitive visitor ventured to extract from him, as an expert, a judgment upon the Transvaal weed. He said: "I have tried several kinds, but I best like the mixture of Transvaal tobacco next in grade above the heaviest and coarsest make. It reminds me very much of the flavor of the tobacco sold to the Italian peasantry for about 2 francs per pound and done up in 2 ounce packets. To some people the Transvaal tobacco is like friendship—the liking is more lasting through taking the longer to form."

Notes to Interview 118

1. See n. 6 to interview 113.
2. See n. 7 to interview 113.
3. See nn. 1 and 4 to interview 107.
4. See n. 3 to interview 114.
5. Robert Arthur Talbot Gascoyne-Cecil (1830–1903), Prime Minister of Great Britain.

119

"Midland and Local Gleanings," *Midland News and Karroo Farmer* (Cradock, South Africa), 30 June 1896, 4.

Mark Twain, with his wife and family, arrived here on Saturday and stayed at the Victoria Hotel until last evening, when the party left for Kimberley, where the celebrated humorist and worldwide known writer will give two "At Homes." Mark is a decidedly striking personality, with his wealth of bushy hair, mobile face, and his yankee drawl with an accent as strong as a Waterbury watch.[1] In the course of a long and enjoyable chat with him, he evinced great interest in the early history of the Colony, the relative positions of the two European races, and the customs and manners of the black and colored races. On being shown the last telegram from [Lord] Salisbury, he drily remarked, "Strange, how that number, 2,000 natives, recurs in every paragraph. Never more—never less!"

Note to Interview 118

1. An inexpensive watch with a loud tick.

120

"Mark Twain on Tour: Arrival in Cape Town," *Cape Times* (Cape Town, South Africa), 7 July 1896, 7; rpt. *Cape Times Weekly Edition*, 8 July 1896, 3.

The gentleman known to the English-speaking world under the *nom de plume* of Mark Twain, the quaint reminiscence of old pilot days on the Mississippi, is at present a visitor to Cape Town, and will on Thursday night make his appearance on the platform of the Opera House in the capacity of a lecturer. His visit to South Africa has fallen in the midst of exciting times, and it would have been difficult for anyone interested in the development of a new country, as any American naturally would be, and particularly such a keen observer of men and manners as Mr. Clemens, to have chosen a more suitable period for a peregrination through Austrel Africa than the present year of grace. Though his tour through the country has been a brief one of two months' duration only, Mr. Clemens has had the opportunity of witnessing the sequel to a peculiar phase of the country's history, and his stay in the Transvaal, where some of his old friends and compatriots were in durance vile, was invested with a peculiar interest. With the object of ascertaining some of his impressions of the country he is soon to leave and his views on the remarkable political situation recently developed, a representative of this journal called on the famous author yesterday and had the inevitable interview, which in his own country is an indispensable adjunct, real or artificial, to the arrival of strangers of distinction.

"The trouble with the outsider in the Transvaal," he remarked in reply to a question, "suggests the simile of a person walking around a monument which changes its aspect with every step he takes. It changes its form and its expression, and by the time he gets around to the point he started from he is likely to say that he had a wrong focus, and at the same time he must admit that, his time being short and his eyes not as good as the eyes of men on the spot and familiar with the matter, he has probably still got a wrong focus.

"When I first arrived in the country it was in absolute ignorance of what had been going on, and the whole affair of the Jameson raid was a big surprise.[1] Since then I have moved through a tossing sea of varying opinions and information, and for a while I supposed that, if the Jameson raid had for its purpose the overthrow of the Transvaal Republic, it was inexcusable. By this time I have considered the peculiar grievance of the 'uitlanders,'[2] which make that position uncertain and pretty nearly untenable. Of course an outsider looks at a matter of this sort from a judicial and, to some extent, privileged standpoint. Now I ask you, does it not look like a fair and square opportunity for a revolution?"

"Unquestionably, and does it, may I ask, suggest any analogous case in the history of your own country?"

"It is very like our old quarrel of the American Revolution 100 years ago, which is a sort of parallel case I should say. The three millions of Americans who existed in that day, and who were really Englishmen and regarded themselves as such, were really 'uitlanders.' To put it in a single phrase, it was the old story, taxation without representation. That is just the exact trouble at Johannesburg. In America they were hampered in all sorts of ways. The country—such as it was—was run solely in the interests of the Mother Country, and finally there was a Jameson raid at Concord and Lexington, in Massachusetts, on April 19, 1775.[3] We had a little fight and the 'uitlanders' won. They were more fortunate than Jameson. The object of that raid, however, was not the overthrow of the English Government, but it was the beginning of that sort of a revolution where the persons beginning it cannot foresee the lengths to which it is going to reach. It was a year or more after that before anybody dreamed of throwing over the British rule. They wanted their rights under the British Government, that was all that Lexington and Concord were fought for, and if the English Government had acted wisely it would have gone no further. If they had allowed those American prisoners certain perfectly fair privileges which they asked for, the United States of America would be a province of the British Crown today. It is one of those vast political mistakes which Governments can make, and which the Transvaal Government can easily make. That Government can drive the 'uitlanders' into revolution if they go on and just follow the English example in the matter of the revolution in America.

"That has been the case with every revolution in this world. The thing could have been stopped if it had been taken in hand at once. There was no necessity for the French revolution, which would never have happened if the Crown had made concessions."[4]

"Kimberley and Johannesburg," continued Mark Twain in reply to the usual question, "are the striking features of South Africa. I have seen plenty of gold-mining towns, but Johannesburg does not look like any I have seen, because it is so substantially built. Kimberley is of course different. In the old California days when the gold-washer washed out two or three ounces of gold it had a distinct value. It is not so with diamonds, and they would have ruined the diamond business if everybody had been in it. I went over the Kimberley mines and very interesting it was. I found a diamond about as big as the end of my finger, but there were so many people watching me that I did not bring it away"

"Where was that?"

"Where they sort, where the final skirmish is. Kimberley is a very interesting show, and it has a personal interest for me, because I sent a man out there twenty-six years ago to gather up diamonds for himself and for me.[5] What I really meant him to do was to make notes and come back and give them to me for a book. He came back with voluminous notes but died almost at once. I wish I had those notes now; they would be interesting.

"Yes, I suppose things are permanently quiet now," observed Mark Twain, replying to a question on the recent Anglo-American war scare.[6] "It looked ugly for a while; but I never believed that the two countries which stand peculiarly for common sense in these modern times—they think they do, anyway—would allow so foolish a thing as a war to spring up. But at such times you hear all the noisy people. They are always in the front, but they are not at all the people who are going to transact the business. With regard to South Africa, everybody has dropped in here during the last ten years and grabbed a slice of land, and it would seem to promise disputes and war some time or other. The colony has got the permanently best part of South Africa. I suppose Matabeleland may be a valuable part of Africa, too. Then there is the Transvaal—that is a valuable country—what there is of it. I wish I could look into the future and see what was going to happen, but I suppose it does not need any prophetic instinct. There is the prophecy of facts, and the facts point to a continually increase of the 'uitlander' population until it will have so augmented that by its own weight it will carry its desires without any war."

"How do your South African audiences seem to you?"

"Very delightful audiences; in fact, you get an exceedingly bright crowd here. The bulk of the audiences are people who have been all round. They have traveled in fact. I have seldom met anybody who has been able to say that he has not been out of Africa. I played billiards with a man in Kimberley whom I met only once before, and that was over a billiard table twenty-five years ago in America. The guard of a train reminded me that he crewed in the steamer with me twenty-five years ago. Captain Mein, one of the political prisoners, I knew very well thirty-two years ago, and John Hay Hammond I have known for many years."[7]

It's interesting to note that the trip which Mark Twain is just concluding will furnish the material for a book, the appearance of which will be looked forward to by South Africans with unusual interest. Mark Twain returns to England with his wife and daughter by the *Norman* on Wednesday week.[8]

Notes to Interview 120

1. See n. 6 to interview 113.
2. Dutch settlers in the southern African Cape Colony.
3. The initial battle of the American Revolution.
4. In light of his repeated praise for the French revolution, MT's comment here seems uncharacteristic.
5. In 1870 MT had commissioned John Henry Riley (1823-72), Washington correspondent of the San Francisco *Alta California,* to visit South Africa to research a book on the diamond mines there. Riley embarked from England in February 1871 and returned six months later, though the project died aborning when his health began to fail. See also *MTL,* 4:250-54, 258-66 and MT's essay "Riley—Newspaper Correspondent" (1870).
6. See nn. 1 and 4 to interview 107.
7. Thomas Mein (d. 1900), a civil engineer who worked for Cecil Rhodes's companies in South Africa, later president of the Union Hill Consolidated Mines in Nevada County, California. On Rhodes, see n. 6 to interview 113; see also MT's comments on Rhodes in interview 116 and n. 2 to that interview. On Hammond, see n. 3 to interview 115.
8. The 7,537-ton Union Line steamship *Norman* was launched in 1894.

6
"Ambassador at Large" and Man of Letters, 1897–1901
Interviews 121–151

After the death of his daughter Susy in Hartford from meningitis on August 18, 1896, Twain remained in Europe to mourn and travel. He finally returned to the United States in October 1900 after spending most of the previous nine years abroad and promptly launched a verbal assault on American imperialism abroad and the corrupt Tammany Hall political machine in New York. He repaid the last of his creditors in 1898.

∽

121
Frank Marshall White,[1] "Mark Twain Amused," *New York Journal*, 2 June 1897, 1.

London, June 1—Mark Twain was undecided whether to be more amused or annoyed when a *Journal* representative informed him today of the report in New York that he was dying in poverty in London.[2]

He is living in comfort and even luxury in a handsomely furnished house in a beautiful square in Chelsea with his wife and children, and has only this week finished the narrative of his recent travels in Australia, New Zealand, India, and South Africa, which is to be published at once by the American Publishing Company of Hartford. He only today settled finally upon the title, which is to be "Another Innocent Abroad."

The great humorist, while not perhaps very robust, is in the best of health. He said:

"I can understand perfectly how the report of my illness got about. I have even heard on good authority that I was dead. James Ross Clemens,[3] of St. Louis, a cousin of mine, was seriously ill two or three weeks ago in London, but is well now. The report of my illness grew out of his illness.

"The report of my death was an exaggeration. The report of my poverty is harder to deal with. My friends might know that unless I were actually dying in poverty I should not live in poverty when I am receiving offers to lecture by every mail. The fact is that I was under contract to write the book that I have just finished or I should have accepted these offers."

Mr. Clemens expects to spend the summer in London, and the fall and perhaps the winter in Austria, where he will pursue his literary labors.

Notes to Interview 121

1. Frank Marshall White (1861-1919), journalist and writer.
2. For other perspectives on this famous interview, see *Mark Twain's Notebook,* ed. Albert Bigelow Paine (New York: Harper, 1935), 327-28; and *MTE,* 252-53.
3. MT's cousin James Ross Clemens, M. D. (1866-1948), a pediatrician and author.

122

"Mark Twain Smiling through His Tears," *New York Herald,* 13 June 1897, sec. 4, 1.

"Of course I am dying," Mark Twain smiled grimly. "But I do not know that I am doing it any faster than anybody else. As for dying in poverty, I had just as soon die in poverty here in London as anywhere. But it would be a little more difficult, because I have got quite a number of friends, any one of whom would be good for a month's provisions, and that would drag out the agony a fairly long time.

"No, I assure you I am as well as ever I was. You see you must not attach too much importance to my wife's remark that I was not in a condition to receive visitors. That simply means that I was in bed. Now most women think that if a man does not get up before twelve o'clock there must be something wrong with him, and as I never get up before then, my wife thinks that I am not in good health. As a matter of fact when you were announced I told her to have you shown up to my room, but you can never persuade a tidy woman to show a stranger into an untidy bedroom, and so that did not work.

"I said to her, 'Show him up, send some cigars up. I am comfortable enough!'

"'Yes,' she said, 'But what about him?'

"'Oh,' I said, 'if you want him to be as comfortable as I am make him up a bed in the other corner of the room.' That did not work, either, so I thought the best thing to do was to get up and come to see you.

"Poverty is relative. I have been in poverty so often that it does not worry me much. A more serious matter is the money owing to other people, not by any fault of mine, and yet owing to them by me. But I do not trouble about the rumors that go about in regard to me. Why should I? The rumor will die itself if you will only give it three days. Start any rumor, and if the public can go with its curiosity unsatisfied for three days something else will spring up which will make the public forget all about the first one. Therefore when people talk about my dying, or as really happened a few days ago, about my being dead, I do not take the slightest notice. I know perfectly well that the public will forget all about it if I let it alone. I keep on ploughing away and working and working and hoping and hoping, but the idea of being in poverty does not either trouble me, or frighten me."

What are you working about, just now?

"Oh, my journey about the world. Everybody has done his little circumnavigation act, and I thought it about time I did mine, so I have been getting it ready for the press since I have been here, and therefore, for the matter of that, the book is just my impressions of the world at large. I go into no details. I never do for that matter. Details are not my strong point, unless I choose for my own pleasure to go into them seriously. Besides, I am under no contract to supply details to the reader. All that I undertake to do is to interest him. If I instruct him that is his fate. He is that much ahead."

What is to be its name?

"I had thought of calling it 'Another Innocent Abroad' but following advice, as the lawyers say, I have decided to call it 'The Surviving Innocent Abroad.'

"Now, my wife said, 'But that is not true, because there's so-and-so in Cleveland, and that and the other in Philadelphia,' but I said to her, 'I will fix that': so I am going to put a little explanatory note to that title pointing out that although there are still in existence some eight or ten of the pilgrims who went on the *Quaker City* expedition some twenty-eight years ago, I am the only surviving one that has remained innocent.

"In fact that title *The Innocents Abroad* could only be strictly applied to two even at the time it was written, and the other is dead."

When do you expect the survivor to appear?

"Oh, about Christmas. Christmas is a good time to bring out a book. Everybody is thinking about Christmas presents, and the pious are praying that Divine Providence may give them some clue as to what to give for a present, and the book if it comes just at the right time is about as good a thing as one could desire. It must come just at the right time though. In other words the opportunity to secure the present must happen just at the moment when the impulse to give one is felt.

"Similarly, we make a lawyer study Blackstone and statute law and common law,[1] and we try him before a jury and see what his skill as an orator is, but we never ask him the crucial question—Have you ever committed a crime? Have you ever undergone a term of imprisonment? Because that has been done, a man is not fit to sit in judgment upon his fellow creatures. It is such a little thing that stands between all of us and crime at one time or another of our lives.

"As I said about charity, if the impulse to kill and the opportunity to kill always came at the same instant, how many of us would escape hanging? We have all of us at one time or another felt like killing something, and we have all of us at one time or another had the opportunity to kill something, but luckily for us, impulse and opportunity did not coincide. If a man is rich and he does want to kill something he can take his gun and go out and shoot. He lets off steam in that way, and the sore place gives over hurting. I used to have a rage and let it expand in the letter box.

"If anyone had done something to me that annoyed me or put me out, I would sit down and write a letter to him, and I would pour out all my thoughts and all the bitterness and anger and contempt and indignation and invective in my heart, and when I had cleaned myself out thoroughly I would put that letter in the box and my wife would see that it did not go.

"She used to say when she saw me sitting down: 'What are you going to do?'"

"'I am going to answer this letter. I would—'

"'But you know you won't send it.'

"'I know that, but, by George, I am going to write it.'

"I have been very sorry many a time that those letters were not kept, because when a man is in a thoroughgoing temper, he finds things to say worth preserving."

Note to Interview 122

1. Sir William Blackstone (1723–80), English jurist whose four-volume *Commentaries on the Laws of England* (1765–69) became the standard Anglo-American legal textbook in the nineteenth century.

123

William T. Stead,[1] "Character Sketch/Mark Twain," *Review of Reviews* (London) 16 (August 1897): 123–33.

"Personal Reminiscence"

It was my good fortune some four years ago to cross the Atlantic in the *New York* as a fellow passenger with Mark Twain. It was in the early months of 1894. I was returning from Chicago. Mark Twain was hastening from New York to rejoin his family at Paris. We had a capital passage, and, as we were neither of us inconvenienced by *mal de mer*, we used to have long and pleasant conversations every day on deck. Before I left the ship I dictated notes of our talk, and from these notes I venture to draw freely for the purposes of this sketch. For they were jotted down while the presence of the man was still with me, when his quaint sayings were still murmuring in my ears. I do not suppose that Mark Twain has changed much since 1894, although he was then at the zenith of his fortune, while now plaguy Fortune, with her revolving wheel, has landed him otherwise.

Mr. Clemens is a man below the average height, with bushy, shaggy gray hair, and a somewhat shambling gait. He has a moustache, but no beard or whiskers. The face is fresh-colored, the eyes gray and kindly-looking. When on board the *New York,* he had a slight cold, and for the most part wore an overcoat, which he threw off his shoulders halfway down his arms when he was in the sunlight, and pulled over his shoulders again when he was in the shade. He smoked a briarwood pipe, and then three cigars, before twelve in the morning.

For the most part he kept himself to himself, writing regularly every morning a certain definite quantity of copy, and devoting the rest of the day to reading, revising, or conversation. At an entertainment in the saloon on the eve of our arrival he gave a reading from his works, selecting the story of his experiences as a courier. No one could have been more kindly, more friendly, or more obliging when communications were opened, but for the majority the opening never came.

The first word I heard from his lips was an amusing anathema upon the recalcitrant match, which, despite all he could do to the contrary, obstinately refused to light his pipe. The way he condemned that match, the pathetic solemnity of his protest against the ignominy of being "insulted by a mere inanimate thing" lingers with me to this day. It was the genuine keynote of *The Innocents Abroad.*

We had much talk about his books, and I was delighted to have the opportunity of saying to him in person how much I felt indebted to him for many a laughter-lifted hour. He said that laughter was a very good thing, but for himself he scarcely got two laughs a month, and this was natural, because every humorist dwelt upon the serious side of life. All true humor was based on seriousness, and hence the humorist, who often made other people laugh, laughed least himself. He said it was so in his own case anyhow.

On my saying that I thought I had laughed more over his description of the German language in *A Tramp Abroad* than over anything else, he said that probably appealed very much to those who were struggling with German.[2] As for himself, he had never been able to master the mysteries of a foreign language to his own satisfaction. He had done his best, but it had been no use. For seven years he used to put himself to sleep by constructing German sentences. He got on fairly well on those occasions, when there was no one to listen, but he had never been able to stand up and face a human being and air his German more than two words at a time without coming to a dead stop.

A short time before he came on board he had made a speech on George Washington. He said that the Washington joke had always been one from which he had made a great deal of fun. The usual way he got it off was by remarking that there were many points of difference between himself and Washington, only one of which he need specify. He used to say, "Washington could not tell a lie, I can" then he would pause until they took in the joke, and then would add, "but I won't."[3]

Talking about his books, he said that for the last sixteen years he had a regular yearly account from Chatto and Windus which specified how many of each of his books in each edition had been sold, how many sets were in hand, and who had them all.[4] He was able to tell at a moment's notice what the sale of his books had been, both in England and in India—for there is an East Indian edition. He said that some years ago he had taken the trouble to total up how many copies Chatto and Windus had sold. He found up to that date they had sold three hundred and eighty thousand copies of his various books. There were five other publishers who published his earlier works who gave him no royalties, so that there must be a pretty considerable sale for his books. A fact which pleased him as much as the receipt of money was the universal recognition which this circulation secured him wherever he went.

He said that *A Tramp Abroad* was the greatest favorite of his books, then *Roughing It*, and after them *The Innocents Abroad*. At one time *The Innocents Abroad* was the most popular, but now his works stood in the above order. In England *A Tramp Abroad, Huckleberry Finn,* and *Tom Sawyer* were the most popular. He could not say whether *Roughing It* was as popular in England as in America. Humor, he remarked, could not be served up alone, it needed something with it. It was like embroidery, very good as an ornament, but one could not dress in embroidery; you needed something else to keep the cold out.

He said that of the American humorists there were very few who were doing any work at present. One whom he named was still working but he was the bond-slave of a syndicate, for whom he had to pound out jokes whether he had anything in his mill or not, and no one could do that and not suffer. "M. Quad" of the *Detroit Free Press* is also extremely vain.[5] Writing people, like other folks, have only a certain amount of capital, and when that is done they have nothing more to go on with. Burdette had done very good work, but for some time past he had not done anything.[6] He did not know of any new man who was coming on.

When he was asked to sign his name on the back of a steamer-ticket, I said they could keep it as an autograph. He said, "Yes, it ought to be worth 25 cents." He said that Aldrich had come in one time with a catalogue of autographs to Howells and said with great glee, "Here is fame indeed! I find that my signature is valued in this catalogue at 25 cents. There is glory!" Howells turned over the pages, and then said, "Yes, I see. Here is Habberton who wrote *Helen's Babies*[7]—his autograph is worth 75 cents, three times as much as yours."

The color of the sea being green led him to remark that we were in shoal water. He did not know why the water should be green in shoal water, but it was so. Certainly after we got out of sight of land it became deeply and beautifully blue. I asked him about the Mississippi. He said that the color of the Mississippi was the color of coffee when made up with a very great deal of cream; that it was a varying shade of brown, changing according to the quantity of rain. I asked him if they drank it. He said, "Yes, and people who drink it never like to drink any other." If he went back to the Mississippi, he would as soon drink that as any other water. It was very strange the taste people acquired for drinking Mississippi water. To a person accustomed to drink it, clear water is positively distasteful. If you took a glass of Mississippi water and allowed it to stand for a little time, there formed a sediment of about an inch deep at the bottom. If you are accustomed to Mississippi water, you stir it up before drinking in order that you may have the sediment in solution. Was it not very unhealthy? No, he said, it was good alluvial loam, and the utmost that it would do would be to line you inside with more aluminum than would otherwise be the case. I asked him about the river. He said you could always see both sides of it, and that both banks were flat, with the exception of the Chickasaw Bluffs and the Bluffs before Memphis; but they were very small. The only impression that he got from the river was one of immense solemnity, such as you got from the desert or any other immense wild place.

He said that when he was in St. Louis, Chicago was not considered to be the rival of that city. Then for about ten years the rivalry continued; but after the census of 1870, when Chicago had 350,000 population, St. Louis dropped behind. There has never been any more talk about rivalry between the two cities. Speaking of Chicago, he said he thought there was a greater mixture of all nationalities there than in any other place excepting Hell. Speaking of Chicago, he laughed heartily over the story of the contest between the Chicago liar and the St. Louis liar, which was won by the St. Louis man, who began by saying, "There was once upon a time a gentleman in St. Louis—" whereupon the Chicago man gave up and declared that no one could possibly tell a greater lie than that. Twain said: "A Chicago man was once in St. Louis and sent a telegram to some place in Missouri. He was charged so heavily for it that he protested. 'Great Scott,' he exclaimed, 'Why, in Chicago it does not cost so much to telegraph to Hell!' 'No,' said the operator quickly, 'that's in the city limits' "—an unpremeditated and unconscious sarcasm, which is always worth much more than a premeditated one.

When we got upon the subject of clothes, Mark discoursed learnedly and at much length upon the sinfulness of apparel. It had come in with the Fall and was the badge of depravity. No one ought to wear more than a breech-clout, and even that ought some day to be dispensed with. The worst of it was that when people simplified their clothes to the extent of a breech-clout, they seemed to find it necessary to do other wicked things to make up for the virtue of dispensing with garments. They took to scalping and other abominations, which for their neighbors were even worse than their clothes. Cycling, he said, was doing good service in tending to simplify woman's costume, and in making clothes to be adapted to the necessities and use of life.

I asked him if he ever cycled. He said yes, he had, but it was a long while ago. It was in the days of the high cycles. He had never ridden, but he used to take lessons from a professor in cycling, who after watching him for some time remarked judicially: "'Clemens, it seems to me that you have the art of falling off in a greater variety of ways than I had ever conceived it possible for any one to fall off.' I suppose it was so, for although I never happened to break a limb, I raised a large bump upon my head and the skin on my legs hung in festoons." He was all for a bicycle; a tricycle, he thought, was a miserable compromise.

I had some talk to him about Chicago and about monopolies. He said he had thought a great deal about monopolies, and thought that it was impossible to do anything excepting very slowly, and that it would take one hundred years to do it. "You see," he said, "they have such a hold upon all the agencies by which you can express public opinion. There is a great deal of cowardice, if you like to call it so, but cowardice is not the right word. It is a great principle in the human heart. I am not going to do anything that will deprive my wife and children of their daily bread, and as long as men are not willing to sacrifice their wives and children as well as themselves in denouncing millionaires, the millionaires will have things pretty much their own way. There are some things upon which you can get public opinion roused. For instance, if it were to be proved that gas were so deadly as to poison people, nothing would be easier than to get up an agitation to pass a law sentencing any man who had a gas-jet in his possession to instant death. That would be easy enough, but the case of the monopolist is very different, and it is very difficult to see what can be done."

Mark Twain himself was then contemplating no less a monopoly than the exclusive contract for the typesetting of the world.[8] For many years past he said he has been engaged on a typesetting machine. I asked him how he was getting on. He said they were about to place the machine upon the market. Two machines had already been built, nine were almost finished, while forty were in process of construction, when the cyclone of the financial disaster struck the country last year and compelled them to postpone everything. He said he was very glad it was so, for by his old arrangement there were two companies, one of which had granted a concession to another. The second company was a business-like concern, but the other was of moonshine and water. When the crisis came last year the moonshine one had to disappear, and the two companies were amalgamated into one. He said that he had struck oil. The two companies amalgamated into one had a capital of five thousand dollars instead of seven and a half millions, and were then ready to go ahead.

I asked him what kind of machine his was. He said it was a perfect machine. "It is made of blue steel, polished, graceful, and beautiful; a thing of beauty and a joy to the eye. You could place it upon the finest carpet in the house without fear of any dirt or broken type. It is a machine which to know is to love; a machine which the men who were making it were so fascinated by that they said that if I had not money to pay their wages, they would go on working at it as long as they had anything left to pawn in order to keep them alive. They are now being gathered together from where they have been working. They will come back any distance in order to work at the machine. It is a fascination," he said. "To be allowed to work on that machine is enough for them. When that machine is in the market all other machines will disappear; 65,000 compositors in the United States will be thrown out of work, or will have to find other work to do."

He then entered into an elaborate explanation of the immense superiority of his machine over all others, and especially over one, which, he declared, seemed to develop more unscientific lying and bad spacing than any other machine invented. He really feared that it was possessed by an evil spirit. Whereas other machines cheapened the cost of composition by 25 percent., his machine would cut it by 90 percent.

"My machine will enable a man to do the work of 10, 15, 24 men. With my machine an ordinary instructed man can set 10,000 ems an hour, a smarter man could do 15,000, and the capacity of the machine, if it were worked by the supreme expert, is 24,000 ems an hour.[9] Some time ago I could not believe that a type-setting girl could do 46 words a minute until I saw it done before my eyes. Since then, 100 words a minute is by no means unusual, while the supreme expert will sometimes do 120 words a minute on superior speed machines. So it is with our machine. With the evolution of the supreme expert we will get up to the maximum speed. We do not, however, expect anything more than 10,000 or 15,000 ems, which gives us a margin of 4,000 ems an hour over the maximum claimed by other machines."

The way they would put the machine upon the market is as follows. They would not sell any nor would they lease them at an annual rental. They would simply go to anyone who was using either hand composition or the Linotype machine, and ask them how much their present composition was costing them. "Take your best man and your best machine and cipher it out exactly, and we will undertake to put our machine in and charge you less for the best work than for the poor results which you obtain from your existing machines. We shall be able to bring down the cost of composition to five cents per thousand ems, and we shall be able to attain a perfection of composition in the way of exact spacing to which hand composition cannot compare. We have nine different sized spaces so that we can space to the breadth of a hair. The machine makes no mistakes, but it adjusts the spaces after the line is set."

I said I did not see how this was possible until he had constructed a machine which could think. "But," he said, "it does think. That is one of the beauties of the machine. Suppose," said he, "you have a line of 27 ems to space, the words varying from 6 to 7 ems. When the operator is striking the keys at the end of each word, he strikes the space key, but no space drops. All he does is to remind the machine that the space ought to come in that place. He sets straight on, and when he has filled up his 27 ems, the machine takes the line of type and measures off 27 ems so as to make the word either fall rightly or turn correctly. It then fills in exactly the spaces which are required to make the line fit. This it does with mathematical accuracy. The ordinary compositor has only spaces of four sizes; we have nine. As I said, we can adjust to a hair.

"When our space bar is struck a space is left large enough for the insertion of any size that may be required, but the thickness of the space is not calculated until the whole line has been set, when the machine measures it automatically and takes up the spaces as they are wanted. Our machine distributes the type as well as sets it." I remarked that I thought there would be a great deal of difficulty in distinguishing between the various spaces. He said that was all done by the machine, and it knew what to do.

"Another great advantage of our machine over existing type-setting machines is that it does not have to depend upon gravity for getting the type into the right place. That is to say, it does not have to depend upon the weight of the type and the degree of friction it may have to overcome. Then again, in the old machines, you have to have a perfectly smooth type and a clean groove or your type will not fall easily. Hence in the gravitation machines type continually falls at varying rates of speed with resulting irregularities and frequently a block. Nothing of this takes place in my machine. Nothing is left to the uncertain action of gravitation. Every type from the moment that the keyboard is struck is clutched by the mechanism and thrust into its place. Hence there is no danger of that block, and no irregularity."

"I suppose you work it as a typewriter does?"

"Yes, with this exception, that whereas a typewriter must strike every letter in rotation, in our machine you can strike several keys at once—a whole word can be struck simultaneously."

"What about correction?" I said.

"We have no corrections," he said. "People may think that strange. But ask a good pianist how many false notes he strikes in playing a piece of music. He strikes none; he is not expected to strike any. So it is with our machine. It can be played as correctly as a piano, and the corrections are not due to errors and do not amount to two literals in a column. That is, of course, when you have good copy, as is the case in all reprints. In fact, we do not reckon anything for corrections. Author's corrections, of course, are different, but what may be called compositor's corrections disappear in our machine."

Of course, if his machine would do all he said it would be an earthquake. Labor-saving machines in the long run increase employment no doubt, but in their immediate effects they inflict great hardships on multitudes.

He admitted this, but the process of introducing a new machine was always slow. It took seven years for the Linotype even to attain its present position, so that there is a period of grace allowed to compositors to clear out and adapt themselves to other functions. "For instance, my machine is bound to throw out of work 65,000 men in the United States. That is to say, it will enable their work to be done better than it is done now, but it will lead to the employment of many more than sixty-five thousand men by the impulse which it will give to the multiplication of printed matter. There will be more men wanted in paperworks and in the manufacture of printers' ink, and more women and girls in binderies, and the result will be that it will give work to two or three for every one it throws out of employment."

I said I had no doubt but that was true in the long run. What was wanted was some kind of Industrial Insurance Society which would enable workmen to tide over the transition period.

He said he did not see how it was to be fixed up. The same thing has always occurred in every department of life. Take, for instance, crinolines. There was a great industry which employed hundreds and thousands of men and women. Suddenly, in the twinkling of an eye, crinolines went out of fashion and all these people were thrown out of work.

I said this was true, and hence the social reformer always considered that changes of fashion were of the devil, producing great hardship with no compensating advantages.

He said, "Look at the wood-engraving trade! There were thousands of men making their living by engraving in wood. Then the Morse process came in and away they went. There still remained the better class of wood-engravers, but then came photography and other processes, and cleared out the rest of them. Take the cotton gin, which enables one man to do the work of 2000, and the spinning jenny, and all those means of production. The world adjusts itself to them, and people find that they can make their living all the better. In fact," he said, "it is the discovery of these labor-saving machines which have brought about the great increase of population. It is wonderful to think that England and Scotland remained for centuries with such small populations, and then a hundred years ago suddenly blossomed out into their present millions."

In his domestic life Mark Twain has been almost ideally fortunate. He told me that during the twenty-four years of his married life whenever his wife had been absent she had written to him with the punctuality of a planet, every day of the week. He had written to her every mail with one exception, which caused him great grief. Some mutton-headed idiot, he said, had told him that the quickest steamer sailed on Thursday, whereas it sailed on Wednesday. He wanted to add some more to his letter, and so missed the mail. She was greatly grieved, and he has been getting letters full of despair ever since. When she first left he wrote once, twice, or thrice a day, until he discovered that the mail only went once or twice a week. He still wrote every day, but he kept them till mail day. He put everything into the letters that came into his life, writing with a freedom which was utterly impossible when he was writing for a magazine or a book. "From a literary point of view," he said, "these letters to my wife in the last six months satisfy me much better than anything I have ever written; there is a lightness of touch and a vividness of description, and altogether a lightness which I try for in vain when I am writing for magazines or books."

He said on an average his letters were twenty-five pages, each containing from four to five thousand words. These were sent twice a week, so that in the six months he must have written some 200,000 words to her. "I was telling Walker, of the *Cosmopolitan*,"[10] he said, "the other day what I had been doing. He said, 'What a waste, what a waste to send all those letters to your wife, when you know I would give you a thousand dollars apiece for them.' So I wrote to my wife, and told her I was afraid I had been guilty of much waste, and that I must ask her to send me my letters back, inasmuch as Walker of the *Cosmopolitan* would give me one thousand dollars apiece. She replied she would not give them up for one thousand five hundred dollars apiece." I suggested he might get that from Walker. "No," he replied, "she would go up again." I said it would be well if in a few years he published these letters, altering the names and places. He objected that it would make them unreal. They were a picture of New York as it is today. "There is nothing that I have written or read compared in value to these letters to my wife." . . .

Notes to Interview 123

1. See n. 6 to interview 74.
2. See n. 2 to interview 10.
3. MT refers to the apocryphal "cherry-tree incident" in the juvenile biography of George Washington first published c. 1800 by Parson Mason Locke Weems (1759-1825). MT also refers obliquely to the incident in chapter 35 of *Tom Sawyer.*
4. Andrew Chatto (d. 1913) and W. E. Windus, MT's British publishers.
5. Charles Bertrand Lewis, aka M. Quad (1842-1924), newspaper humorist long affiliated with the *Detroit Free Press.*
6. Robert (Bob) Jones Burdette (1844-1914), a minor humorist.
7. The popular novel *Helen's Babies* (1876) by John Habberton (1842-1921).
8. See n. 9 to interview 97 and headnote to chapter 3.
9. An "em" is a unit of measurement used in typesetting.
10. John Brisben Walker (1847-1931), American publisher of *Cosmopolitan* from 1889 to 1905.

124

"Mark Twain in Vienna," *New York World,* 13 December 1897, 6.

Vienna, Nov. 29—Mark Twain is the literary lion of Viennese society this winter. His fame as a man of letters and humorist is great, but the man himself is voted as charming as one of his books. He has been sought after by the most cultured circles in the exclusive society of this capital, but he has made little use of his social opportunities. He is working all the time, studying life or describing it, which is his excuse for not availing himself of a large part of the invitations showered upon him.

On the occasions of the recent riots in the Reichsrath he obtained without difficulty the eagerly sought privilege of being present.[1] When I first sought him he was ill—too ill to be seen. But a few days later I did see him—still in bed and suffering from what he called the toothache in his big toe. I came, saw, and was conquered. What a revelation that splendid head of his with its silver crown of wild curls, is! And the sweetness of his manner, the tolerance of his great understanding for the deficiencies in individuals, in nations!

He had been three days in Vienna and already was a prey to journalists, photographers (amateur and otherwise), and to that modern pest, the autograph-hunter. But it all amused him. The journalists did not know English, which was a great hindrance to lengthy interviews.

On the other hand, the humorist, who is very fond of German, tried to get some practice out of them, and that drove them away. He was shy as to photographing, but he did not deny his autograph to those who asked for it, and was particularly touched by the request of a woman who wrote on a postcard from the other end of Galicia, describing herself as a week-young wife whose husband called her silly, but who wanted to show him that she was clever enough to wheedle an autograph out of Mark Twain. All this was merely because the papers had announced his arrival.

But when the public learned he was going to stay a whole year in Vienna, that he suffered from gout, was anxious to have a house to himself and would study the peculiarities of the country and its inhabitants, then it was that letters poured in upon him. Most people were glad to hear he mastered the German language sufficiently to read the papers in the morning, and these wrote in German. But some were anxious to show their proficiency in English, and these letters Mark Twain considered worth keeping. There are two categories of letters—those whose writers have an interested motive and those which are dictated by admiration of the humorist. Among the latter are quite fifty ways of curing the gout.

In the first notice the *Neue Freie Presse* published on Mark Twain[2] there was a reference to his wish to use his observant powers as long as they were quite fresh, by standing at some street corner where the tide of men and women flowed past, and to see with an eye to which all is new the difference between these men and women and those of other busy cities. On the Sunday following Pötzl, the Vienna humorist,[3] one of the few who write the dialect to perfection, showed Mark Twain what a queer city he had come to. He placed him on a bridge with a notebook and pencil and set all the characteristic figures of Vienna streets—the errand boy, the commissionaire, the bootblack, the chestnut vender, the woman who washes the cabs, the cabmen and the police—to guess who the stranger was and what he wanted. This was done with so much good humor and good taste that a friendship has resulted from it between Mark Twain and Pötzl, though they cannot talk much together, which is a pity.

Mark Twain was popular when he came to Vienna, but the number of his friends increased enormously after he had attended the supper given him by the press club of Vienna, the Concordia. It was a so-called "Festkneipe," and the ladies were excluded. If the women had been allowed to come there would have been no room large enough to hold the assembly.

The most eminent actors and artists had been invited by the journalist to meet the illustrious American, and the United States Minister and Consul-General were there also. Mark Twain was warmly welcomed, but he called forth enthusiastic applause when he addressed the company in his quaint, childlike German, mastering the difficult language to perfection, but protesting vehemently at the same time against its peculiarities.

Mark Twain attended the historical long sittings of the Austrian Reichsrath, and was so much interested in the menagerie that acted its violent scenes before him that he stayed far into the night both times. It soon became known in the house that he was there in a reserved box in the second gallery, and there was not a member, from the Ministers to the attendants, who did not take a good look at him.

But Mark Twain was not aware of the sensation he was creating as hour after hour he made notes on the scenes before him.

In the lobby the speaker of twelve hours, Dr. Otto Lecher,[4] was introduced to him and asked him if he had ever seen the like of this parliament.

"Not quite!" said Mark Twain. "A scene I witnessed in America once was what approached it most nearly. It was when one gentleman had gone off on another gentleman's horse—by mistake—and was caught and brought back. Well, there was an assembly then something like this Reichsrath that began by hanging the accused and then sat in judgment over him afterward. I daresay a good deal of the language then used was like what I heard tonight, but which, to my regret, I did not always catch correctly."

The Viennese are an artistic people, and the beauty of Mark Twain's features and head strike their fancy most particularly. Artists have applied for permission to reproduce the head, and Mark Twain very good-naturedly sat for his bust to a sculptor of fame,[5] who has finished the head in clay and will exhibit the cast from it at Christmas.

Notes to Interview 124

1. See MT's "Stirring Times in Austria" (March 1898) on the riots among legislators in the Austrian Reichsrath in November 1897 and the fall of the Badeni government. See also *MTE,* 91.

2. "Ein Besuch bei Mark Twain," *Neue Freie Presse* (Vienna), 1 October 1897, 1; translated and reprinted in *American Literary Realism* 10 (winter 1977): 77–78.

3. Eduard Pötzl (1851–1914).

4. Otto Lecher (1861–1939), Reichsratabgeordneter, or Austrian parliamentary representative.

5. The Russian sculptor Theresa Feodorowna Ries (1874–1956) had executed an alabaster bust of MT.

125

"Mark Twain Proud and Happy," *New York World,* 13 March 1898, 7.

Vienna, March 12—Mark Twain was asked by *The World* correspondent today whether he would say for *The World* readers how it felt to be out of debt.

"Oh," he answered, gaily, "you can tell them I'm glad it's over. What a worry it has been."

Then he opened a drawer and proudly took out the receipts, copied by typewriter, just as they had been sent to him.

9. Posing for Theresa Feodorowna Ries in Vienna 1898. Collection of Gary Scharnhorst.

"There were ninety-six creditors," he went on. "I would have paid them all in full at once to have done with it, but friends advised me to pay them in three monthly installments—December 6, January 6, and February 6.

"What I hate as much as anything is to have the public regard me as unwise in business. I consider that the contrary was proved by the way I published General Grant's book in 1885, which could not have been done by a bad businessman.

"However, one of my greatest pleasures now is to be able to look forward to the day when I can return home and live in the house which I and my family so dearly love."

126

"Mark Twain's Bequest," *Times* (London), 23 May 1899, 4; abridged in *New York Journal and Advertiser*, 4 June 1899, 42; rpt. *New York Tribune*, 10 June 1899, 8.

Vienna, May 22—Mr. Samuel Langhorne Clemens (Mark Twain) has been obliged to postpone his departure from Vienna until the 26th inst. in consequence of a flattering communication which has just been made to him through the United States Minister, Mr. Addison Harris.[1] The Emperor Francis Joseph will receive the distinguished American author in audience on Thursday next.[2] Mark Twain, whose works have long vied in popularity in the German-speaking countries with those of the best-known native contemporary writers, has, during his two years' stay in the Kaiserstadt, become quite a familiar and welcome figure to the humor-loving Viennese and a great favorite in Austrian society. The American colony, headed by the official representatives of the United States, have missed no opportunity of doing honor to Transatlantic literature in his person, while all classes in Vienna have been eager to welcome a writer who is not only a prophet in his own country, but whose name is one to conjure with among gentle and simple, from schoolboys to courtiers and princes, in the lands of the German tongue. It may be fairly said that the prestige of literature has been considerably enhanced when, as in this instance, its representative may take formal leave of the chief of a State of which he has been the guest, particularly when that chief is the head of the House of Hapsburg and that State Austria. The American newspapers have been calling Mr. Clemens "the Ambassador at large of the U.S.A."; but humorists in their hours of relaxation have a habit of taking jokes seriously. That apparently is Mark Twain's way. Mr. Clemens and his family, who will reach London about the beginning of June, will probably spend a couple of months in England prior to their return to America in October.

Mr. Clemens has kindly given me permission to telegraph to *The Times* some particulars of a pet scheme of his to which he has already devoted a great deal of his time and which will occupy a great part of the remainder of his life. In some respects it will be unparalleled in the history of literature. It is a bequest to posterity, in which none of those now living and comparatively few of their grandchildren even will have any part or share. This is a work which is only to be published 100 years after his death as a portrait gallery of contemporaries with whom he has come into personal contact. These are drawn solely for his own pleasure in the work, and with the single object of telling the truth, the whole truth and nothing but the truth, without malice, and to serve no grudge, but, at the same time, without respect of persons or social conventions, institutions, or pruderies of any kind. These portraits of men and women, painted with all their warts, as well as with every attractive feature which has caught his eye, will not be written in the style of Mark Twain's books, which their author anticipates will be forgotten by the time his gallery is published. Any humor they may contain will be entirely unsought. It must be inherent in the subject if it is to appear in the portrait.

In Mr. Clemens's opinion, a work of the kind he proposes is only possible under the conditions he has laid down for himself. To use his own words: "A book that is not to be published for a century gives the writer a freedom which he could secure in no other way. In these conditions you can draw a man without prejudice exactly as you knew him and yet have no fear of hurting his feelings or those of his sons or grandsons. A book published 100 years hence, containing intimate portraits, honestly and truthfully drawn, of Monarchs and politicians, bootblacks and shoemakers, in short, of all those varieties of humanity with which one comes in contact in the course of an active life of 50 years, cannot help being then valuable as a picture of the past. I have written a great deal of this book since I came to Vienna. During the rest of my life I mean to write in fresh portraits whenever they come vividly before my mind, whether they be of the present day or old acquaintances. To make such a book interesting for immediate publication it would be necessary for me to confine myself to the men of note. As it is, I choose them from my whole circle of acquaintances and the undistinguished have about as good a chance of getting in as the distinguished. The sole passport to a place in my gallery is that the man or woman shall have keenly excited my interest. In 100 years they will all be interesting if well and faithfully described. We have lost a great deal in the past through a lack of books written in this way for a remote posterity. A man cannot tell the whole truth about himself, even if convinced that what he wrote would never be seen by others. I have personally satisfied myself of that and have got others to test it also. You cannot lay bare your private soul and look at it. You are too much ashamed of yourself. It is too disgusting. For that reason I confine myself to drawing the portraits of others."

Notes to Interview 126

1. Addison C. Harris (1840–1916), U.S. chief of mission to Austria-Hungary from 1899 to 1901. See also *MTE*, 53.
2. Franz Josef (1830–1916), crowned emperor of Austria in 1848 and king of Hungary in 1867.

127

"Mark Twain in London," *Chronicle* (London), 3 June 1899, 3.

Mark Twain has just arrived in London, and he gave me an audience yesterday, as the Emperor Francis Joseph gave him one before he left Vienna. "Mr. Clemens," said Mr. Chatto, his publisher, and I fumbled for the German oration which I had prepared. Alas! I had forgotten it at home, and all I could do was to explain that.[1]

"No matter," replied the American humorist, with easy gravity, "we'll do without it."

He sat down in one chair, I taking another; then he pulled out a cigar and got it alight. By the time it was blowing freely he was on his feet again, and walking up and down the room. While he walked he talked.

"Well, now," I had asked him, "what brings you to London—why have we such luck?"

He seemed to like it put that way; anyhow, I thought I caught a twinkle in his eye. It was banished almost before it had arrived, and I argued with myself, "Why, he is serious enough for a Scotch humorist."

He was, for he went on, "You see, my American publishers are about to issue an *edition deluxe* of my books in twenty-two volumes. I have come to London to arrange for the issue of a similar edition through my publishers here, Messrs. Chatto [and Windus]. The volumes will include all my writings, which I have revised for the purpose.[2] The publishers are trying to make the books nice—as fine books as they can. The two editions will be limited to a thousand copies each—limited, mark ye!

"Yes," he soliloquized, "I fancy it's the limitation to a thousand copies that is the chief charm and value of an *edition deluxe*. I don't expect to read this *edition deluxe* myself, although you needn't tell that to anybody else. Frankly, you know, I don't suppose that anybody ever reads an *edition deluxe*. No one puts bric-à-brac to any very practical purpose. There's some human instinct which makes a man treasure what he is not to make any use of, because everybody does not possess it."

Next, he gave me an instance in proof, taken from his own experience with Sir Walter Scott.

"What trouble didn't I go to when I was in Edinburgh in order to get hold of an original Waverley Edition? Naturally, I had to pay a fancy price for it, which is a detail. The point is that it stands in our bookshelves to this day untouched. We have handier volumes of Scott, and read them and admire the others. Part with that edition? Not at all; it's a possession, an asset."

Here was a chance to introduce the subject of those wonderful memoirs which Mark Twain is preparing for the readers of a hundred years hence. I did so, by way of a sly question as to what were his literary plans. He took the inquiry as cheerfully as could have been expected, seeing that it referred to a doomsday book. Nay, he chatted on it freely, merely interrupting himself when he had to rout out another cigar.

"No," were his words, "I'm not expected to write any more for publication. You naturally ask why. I have been writing diligently for thirty years, and I had arranged to stop some time ago. However, I was so situated that I was obliged to keep that pot-boiling pen going. The man is entitled to a holiday for the rest of his life who has written for twenty-five years, or been a soldier that long, or made himself useful or ornamented in any capacity for such a period. My holiday will consist in writing two books, simply for the private pleasure of writing. One of them will not be published at all; the other is written for the remote posterity of a hundred years hence."

Curiosity was strong in me to exclaim, "Won't you give us some of the contents now?" Mark Twain must have seen this, since he went on to say what the book, which is to be published, will not be.

"Although the *Chronicle* thinks I'm going to write harsh things about people, that is an error. I said originally there would be no malice, and that is the truth. I want to set down the facts about people, and in some cases the facts may not be pleasant. But they will at least be void of malice. The *Chronicle* pronounces the idea not to be original. I did not contend that it was. I knew it was not. There has not been an original idea in the world from Adam's time until our own.

"What I mean," he resumed, "is that no man produces an idea out of his own head. The idea first comes from the outside; you cannot grow an idea. Why, Adam could not invent the idea of modesty. He went naked until he learned from the outside that to be naked was immodest. I'm not attaching any large importance to this, for I have a sense of modesty, although Adam hadn't. I got it from Adam; I did not invent it."

We fell upon a historical precedent of Talleyrand, vouched for by Mark Twain. He left, didn't he, a book to be published when he should be dead fifty years.[3]

"Ah," observed Mark Twain, "that was a political and historical work. The value of the book which I propose is of another sort; it presents merely portraits of folks with whom I have come in contact—humble folks and otherwise. That, precisely, may not have been done before, but, as I have remarked, I don't claim any originality. It has been intended a thousand times." He added, what I must not forget, that he has arranged for the preservation of the manuscript. It was all I could do to refrain from asking the name of his literary agent.

"Part of the manuscript," he assured me, "is already written, and I shall so arrange matters that it will be to somebody's interest to publish the lot when the time comes. I know how to manage that, too."[4]

So far, I had managed not to ask Mark Twain, "What is the real story of that German speech of yours which was to be delivered to the Emperor Francis Joseph, but which you forgot?" It was useless to bottle the question down any longer.

"Necessarily," he almost rebuked me, "anybody prepares for an audience with an emperor, because it is essentially formal. You prepare yourself to say the right thing in the best words. I made that preparation, and there were only eighteen words in the sentence. That was very short for a German sentence, which generally covers a good deal of ground. Mine was a compressed sentence."

"You had rehearsed it all beforehand—gone over the field, so to speak?"

"Wouldn't you? But, you see, the Emperor at once began to talk in an entirely informal way, and I didn't remember, until some little period after, that I had a speech in stock. We were indulging in a pleasant talk; no ceremony about it. Then I recollected, and I blurted out to the Emperor that I had memorized a very good speech, but that it had gone clean out of my head. 'Oh,' he said, agreeably, 'it isn't necessary.' Strangely enough, I can't recall the seventeen words yet, though a minute ago I fancied I had them."[5]

My suggestion was that perhaps they would recur to him before he had finished his doomsday book. Meanwhile, I got him to give me what I may call a brief appreciation of the Austrian Emperor.

"Yes, indeed," it ran, "he struck me as a very fine fellow altogether. Necessarily, he must have a great deal of good, plain, attractive human nature in him, or he could not have unbent in the easy manner which I have described. You and I could not unbend if we were emperors. You agree. We should feel the stiffness of the position. Francis Joseph is just a natural man, although an emperor."

"You were impressed with him both as a man and as an emperor?"

"Why, certainly; I was greatly impressed by him. I liked him very much. I had seen him on several occasions when he was performing public functions. I had not met him before. His face is always the face of a pleasant man, with a kindly good nature. He is a man as well as an emperor—an emperor and a man."

"Humor—has he humor?"

"He has a sense of humor. One is incomplete without that. The Emperor of Austria has a sense of humor easily discernible by the sparkle in his eyes. For the rest, throughout the Austro-Hungarian Empire this is recognized—that in these times it is the Emperor's personality, and the confidence all ranks have in him, that preserves the real political serenity in what has the outside appearance of being the opposite."

After the Emperor, Vienna and the Viennese, and Mark Twain testified handsomely of both. He had chatted of the Emperor in words as ready as they were hearty. He tackled the Emperor's capital with an equal flow of expression.

"You cannot live a couple of years in Vienna," he said, "without becoming pretty thoroughly saturated with the fascination of both the people and the city. The disposition of the citizen of Vienna is commonly described by the German word 'gemüthlich.' This is not quite translatable into English, but perhaps our nearest word to it is 'genial.' One soon becomes contented in Vienna, and is never quite willing to go away again."

Finally, I asked Mark Twain, as one who had viewed it from the distance, what he thought of the great coming together of England and America? He straightened himself up, feeling the whole Anglo-Saxon man, lit a fresh cigar, and delivered [his] verdict.

"It has always," his words were, "been a dream of mine, this closer relationship between England and America. I hardly expected to live to see that dream realized, but it has gone far enough towards realization to furnish me with contentment. As far as the English people are concerned, I knew that this friendly feeling was already blossoming four years ago—when I was in Australia."

"During your tour round the world, of course?"

"Yes. Mr. Cleveland had just issued that proclamation which threatened for a moment to embroil the two countries.[6] But the people in Australasia and in India were as friendly and as hospitable to me as if there were not a suggestion of gunpowder in the air. Neither in social gatherings nor in the lecture hall did anyone say anything which could remind me that friction existed between England and America."

"You might have been at home?"

"Practically. The Australian and Indian papers never spoke of this episode with anything like bitterness, but were always moderate in tone, rational, kindly. Therefore, as I say, this English feeling is not a new birth, but is already four years old as evidenced in my personal experiences. Dear me! I could find more than one incident to suggest that it dates much farther back. It was a commander of a British warship at Havana, I should say as much as thirty years ago, who saved an American vessel's crew from being shot down, without trial, by the Spanish Government of Cuba on an uninvestigated charge of coming there with filibustering intentions."[7]

"Then the American feeling?"

"I have spoken of the English attitude. The attitude of native-born Americans has been of this friendly sort towards England as long back as I can well remember. If there has been a feeling of any other sort I chanced upon it so rarely that it made no impression on me."

Mark Twain stood for a few moments silent, thinking. Next, he addressed me in words deeply felt, quietly uttered, which I shall make the final ones here.

"I am glad," they were, "that the present feeling between the two countries received an added and powerful impulse from a literary source, the handicraft of the pen, my guild—the English-speaking world's outburst of sympathy when the life of Rudyard Kipling was threatened."[8]

Notes to Interview 127

1. An inside joke. See MT's remarks later in this interview and in interview 128. Franz Josef (1830–1916), crowned emperor of Austria in 1848 and king of Hungary in 1867.
2. Both the American Publishing Co. of Hartford and Chatto and Windus of London issued a limited deluxe edition of *The Writings of Mark Twain* in twenty-two volumes in 1899. None of the works were revised, though MT did write a brief autobiographical sketch published at the end of volume twenty-two signed by his nephew Samuel E. Moffett (1860–1908).
3. Charles Maurice de Talleyrand-Périgord (1754–1838) left his autobiography in manuscript at his death with instructions it should not be published for thirty years. In fact, it was not published until 1888.
4. MT indicated in the margins of his manuscript autobiography that some parts of it were not to be published until fifty or seventy-five years after his death.
5. A small joke: MT forgets even the number of words the forgotten sentence contained.
6. See nn. 1 and 4 to interview 107.
7. The *Quaker City*—the same ship on which MT had traveled to Europe and the Holy Land in 1867—was seized in port in New York by federal authorities on the insistence of Cubans in May 1869 on the grounds it had been equipped to sail to Cuba with American filibusters aboard. It was released to sail to Jamaica only after the British consul in New York proved the ship was the property of a British subject and was authorized to sail to Jamaica on legitimate business. See "Seizure of a Steamer," *New York Times*, 26 May 1869, 2; and "The Quaker City," *New York Times*, 28 May 1869, 7.
8. Kipling had nearly died in a New York hotel from lung congestion in February 1899.

128

Dr. Johannes Horowitz, "Twain's Farewell to Vienna," *New York Times*, 11 June 1899, 19.

Vienna, May 30—Mark Twain has left Vienna after a twenty months' stay, and no other town has ever seen him depart with more regret. He had become well known to everyone. Wherever there was a festivity or something interesting to be seen or heard the famous humorist was to be found. There are few persons here of any importance whose acquaintance he did not make. A farewell audience was quickly granted by his Majesty Francis Joseph.[1] Mr. Clemens had expected to be received on the ordinary audience day, and his surprise was great when he was informed hat he would be received in private audience.

Conscious that the Emperor's time is precious, Mark Twain had written out a little German speech which he had learned by heart. But when he was in the imperial presence he was unable to utter a word, having simply forgotten his whole speech! However, the Emperor cordially shook hands with him and began an interesting conversation. He inquired about the author's stay here, and Mr. Clemens replied he had never felt so comfortable anywhere else, declaring Vienna to be a wonderful and delightful city, beautiful despite its enormous size, and from which he was carrying away many a fruitful idea that he hoped later on to turn to account. His majesty referred to the efficiency of the American Army and Navy. After a rather long audience the Emperor dismissed the American most graciously, and the latter declares the audience will always remain one of his pleasantest memories.[2]

To the many people who asked him about the work he had done in Vienna, Mark Twain replied that he had written a book about present-day persons which, however, was not to be published till a hundred years after his death. He left Vienna with a joke on his lips. Mark Twain's last words to the well-known Viennese humorist, Herr Pötzl, were: "The New York papers have asked me about my audience, and I have telegraphed the following, which I consider quite nice, because it is dignified and does not give any information: 'It was only a pleasant, unconstrained private conversation on matters unconnected with international policy. I very much wanted to explain my plan, now in the hands of the Secretary of State in Washington, for insuring universal peace, but I feared his Majesty would laugh, or else consider it too radical.'

"Now," Mark Twain went on to say, "all the newspapers in America will telegraph to the Secretary of State to know what my plan is, and then they will learn that I have discovered a method of suddenly depriving the air of its vital principle, and thus of killing off the whole human race in four minutes."

Notes to Interview 128

1. Franz Josef (1830–1916), crowned emperor of Austria in 1848 and king of Hungary in 1867.

2. MT's audience with Franz Josef occurred on 25 May. According to the *Neues Wiener Tageblatt,* cited in the *New York Sun* ("Mark Twain Saw the Emperor," 26 May 1899, 1), the audience lasted about twenty minutes. MT "was so embarrassed when he entered the room that he forgot every word" of his prepared speech in German. "The Emperor laughed heartily and said: 'Don't trouble yourself. If you will say it in English I will translate it for you.'"

129

Curtis Brown, "Mark Twain Talks," *Buffalo Express,* 30 July 1899, 1; rpt.
Elmira Gazette and Free Press, 2 August 1899.

London, July 20—Mark Twain has just set out for a sojourn in Sweden with his wife and two daughters, and will not get back to London till fall, when he will rent a furnished house or find apartments somewhere and stay until late in the winter or early in the spring, and then, at last, return to the United States.

At least, those are his intentions; but, as he observed, in a rather extraordinary talk I had with him the other day before he left, "I am full of intentions. I don't believe I've had an intention in months that I've fulfilled. Why, it isn't safe to have an intention. You mustn't have anything more than just the vaguest germ of an idea that maybe you'll do something or other if when the time comes you don't happen to do something else. You mustn't be a bit more definite than that, and if you get as far as having a real intention you are lost."

Mark Twain isn't often interviewed. He is always a hard man to find, in the first place. System and regularity are not numbered among his sins; and in the second place, after he has talked awhile to a favored newspaperman, he is likely to say, as he did on this occasion: "Now, see here, it won't do to publish any of that. I ought not to be telling about my affairs. It isn't quite right. It doesn't look well."

Whereupon I argued, and with fervor enough to win consent to the publication of some of the talk, although Mark Twain reiterated that he didn't believe the public would care much about his "fool intentions." He added: "You see, it's the vanity of the thing that worries me—that everlasting vanity that every mother's son of us has. If you can manage to cover it up somehow—if you can be deceiving enough to make it appear that the vanity wasn't there—why, go ahead and print some of the things I've been saying; but don't you print all of 'em." He pulled one hand from under the bedclothes and shook his finger impressively, thrusting the warning home with a sharp glance from two of the keenest blue eyes that were ever put into the head of man.

Mr. Clemens was in bed taking a bite now and then from his morning roll, and getting a sip of coffee between times, although it was 11 o'clock in the morning. He had been having the same sort of experience in London that Mr. Choate has had,[1] and which led that distinguished gentleman to explain to the Savage Club[2] the other night that in order to be an ambassador a man's chiefest need was a stomach, and that if anyone had told him he could dine out 50 nights in succession and live he would have thought it a good joke. Mark Twain has been in as much demand as Mr. Choate, and to catch up on lost sleep he said he had put in 32 hours in bed in the last three nights. "The surprising fact about it" (and he's vain of it), he said, "is that I haven't been really tired."

Naturally, one of the first questions was about the remarkable book which Mr. Clemens is writing, but which is not to be published for 100 years. It evidently worries him to think that he can't be taken seriously. "It's no use talking about it," he said, slapping his hand down on the bedclothes and giving the pillow an extra hitch. "There isn't a living soul, so far as I can discover, who can understand my purpose. My best friends don't grasp the idea. I begin to think even my family don't quite understand me. You couldn't get the idea either. Nobody could. And yet I suppose that the one thing I could do was to talk plainly. I don't use any big words. I don't sprout any flowers of speech, and yet I suppose I have read comments about it in 50 English and American papers, and not one of 'em seemed to know what I was driving at. And yet I have made it a rule to say exactly what I meant to say. I try to be clear, and let all the other graces go.

"When I say I have earned a vacation and am going to spend it in my own way, they get up and say to me, 'But what a waste of time it is to write a book that you won't sell!' Oh, the sordidness of the idea! And yet I am not pretending to work for nothing. I am no better than anybody else. I shall get my pay in pleasure. I have a right to get my pleasure in my own way, haven't I? Now, it is my idea of a good time to write a book that nobody now living shall ever see. If it is expensive to write a book that I shall not let anybody buy in my day, all right. It's my little copper penny, and if I want to spend it in a new way it doesn't need to worry a man who might spend his little copper penny some other way.

"Some say I want to advertise myself. What should I want to advertise myself for? I'm through writing for publication. Anyway, that's my intention, although it isn't safe to have an intention.

"Some say: 'That's not a new idea; Talleyrand did it.'[3] Why, there isn't any such thing as a new idea. There isn't a man alive who ever had a new idea. Nobody ever did have a new idea. Adam himself never had one. When a critic goes to a play and then goes and writes about it that it wasn't based on a new idea, all he should mean is that the old idea didn't have a new coat of paint, that it wasn't rearranged. The mind of man isn't capable of producing a new idea. All it can do is to take the material already at hand and work it over into a little different form. We can't even boss the job. We can't tell our minds what to do and what not to do. All we can do is just to stand around and admire the workings of our mammoth intellects and think how moderately smart we are.

"If Talleyrand did what I am going to try to do it's about time it was done over again. Why, an idea is brand new if we merely didn't see it yesterday, and all that makes life endurable is that all the old things become new about once in so often. But my book has no resemblance whatever to Talleyrand's or to any other book, but the difference is something that I can't get anyone to understand.

"We all think we are swimming out vigorously on the ocean, while, as a matter of fact, we are each of us paddling around in our own little mud puddle. If you try to get a man out of his private, individual mud puddle he is lost. No man can swim in another man's mud puddle, so when I have a plan that is different from other people's plans they can't understand it, and I have to swim around alone in my own puddle.

"However, I'll tell you what it is I want to do. The difference between what I am writing and the ordinary biography is as marked as between an ordinary flat photograph and one of those—what-d'ye-call-'em—cinematograph pictures [motion pictures]. Biography is a patchwork of flat photographs, each of them giving the prejudiced view of some particular observer. Perhaps one of the photographs would be the prejudiced recollections of the hero's mother, another the prejudiced observations of a man who hated him, another the stories told of him by Tom, Dick, and Harry—all of them distorted by some sort of prejudice. Along comes the biographer to patch all of these prejudiced views together, and, lo, he, too, is prejudiced. The cinematograph picture, on the other hand, shows the man complete, all around and in action.

"But you can't show all sides of a man without prejudice while he is living or while his friends or children are living. If he is a friend, you are inclined to paint him up a little, whitewash him a little; if he is an enemy, you are inclined to put a little black paint on him. If you know a story about him that reveals one whole side of his character, but that would hurt the feelings of his family, you will not be able to compel yourself to use it; but if it isn't going to be published for 100 years, it can be told without offense to yourself.

"Now, I'm writing on this book at odd times—and I have been at it for several months—just as if I were writing about people I had known 100 years ago, and as if they and their children were buried. I'm writing as much as possible, as if time had smoothed down all my prejudices; as if I'd got far enough away from my subject to see it in the proper perspective. Yes, I'm writing as if I were a Rip Van Winkle, and as if the things I remembered as having happened yesterday had really happened 100 years ago.

"If a publisher should come along and offer me an incredible sum I should say, 'Get thee behind me, Satan!' Why, that would spoil the whole thing. I am unhampered now, but as soon as the idea of publishing that book in time for anyone now living to read got into my thoughts, anyone can see that I couldn't go ahead as I had started out.

"I'm not going to write autobiography. The man has yet to be born who could write the truth about himself. Autobiography is always interesting, but howsoever true its facts may be, its interpretation of them must be taken with a great deal of allowance. In the innumerable biographies I am writing many persons are represented who are not famous today, but who may be some day.

"Let me see if I can't make a kind of parallel that will show one side of my idea. Supposing there was a shoemaker who lived in Stratford-on-Avon in Shakespeare's time. Suppose that shoemaker had neither chick nor child and concluded that he would entertain himself by setting down every night for his own amusement, and not for anybody else to read, his observations of the people who came into his shop, made a record of the things they did and said that seemed to him significant of the time in which he lived. He would have something in about the saddler and the baker and the candlestick maker, and might also have something about a man named Shakespeare, who lived in the town and who was said to have some sort of a reputation in London, but who wasn't considered as anything extraordinary by the townspeople who had always known him. If he were a wise or a fortunate shoemaker he would probably find when he had his book written that this man Shakespeare occupied an unexpected amount of space in it, not because he was as important as some of the town dignitaries, but because he seemed to say brighter things and to do more that seemed worth putting down than anybody else who came into the shop.

"If that shoemaker's book had been put away in a safe somewhere for 25 years it would have become pretty valuable. In 50 years it would have become precious. In 100 years it would have been worth its weight in diamonds.

"Just think, if the meanest, most insignificant man in all the town in Shakespeare's day were to walk out on the streets of London this morning with his memory as fresh as if Shakespeare had passed him on the corner the night before, how precious every word he had to say would be!"

The Clemens conscience was much troubled at the time of the interview by the hat of Canon Wilberforce.[4] The American humorist and the famous English divine had been fellow guests at a dinner two nights before, and Canon Wilberforce was called away early by his Parliamentary duties, and when Mark Twain came to go later on he found that his hat was gone. "I tried every hat in sight," he said, "and at last found one that fitted every idiosyncrasy of my cranium. It is a strange and mysterious circumstance that it turned out to be the property of Canon Wilberforce. After I had had it a day I was obliged to write hastily to the canon and explain that my family had become seriously alarmed by my condition. Ever since wearing the canon's hat I had been unable to take property that did not belong to me; had found it impossible to stretch a statement beyond the bounds of truth and had shown such a complete change in morals that the advisability of sending for a doctor for me was being seriously considered.

"When I reflected that this was, no doubt, the influence of the clergyman's hat, I became badly frightened at the thought of what must be the effect of my hat upon him. He must have been telling lies right and left, ever since he picked out my hat—'Mark Twain' was written in it, too, in big letters; I wrote it myself. Judging by the number of moral beauties brought out in me by the canon's hat, the number of vices awakened in his bosom by my hat must have been appalling, and I must get up this minute, have that hat nicely ironed, take it down to Westminster and get mine away from the canon before it plunges him into some awful disgrace, if it has not done so already."

The incident pleased Mr. Clemens so much that he told a somewhat different version of it at a dinner that night.

Notes to Interview 129

1. Joseph Choate (1832–1917), U.S. ambassador to Great Britain from 1899 to 1905.
2. See the reference to the Savage Club in n. 2 to interview 23.
3. See n. 3 to interview 127.
4. Albert Basil Orme Wilberforce (1841–1916) was appointed chaplain of the House of Commons in 1896 and Archdeacon of Westminster in 1900.

130

"Mark Twain Says He's Discouraged," *New York World*, 17 June 1900, E1.

London, June 16—"I have postponed sailing for home until October," said Mark Twain to *The World*'s correspondent yesterday. "Then you have abandoned your Presidential candidacy?" "Well, you see, it's so discouraging. I had a letter from a friend in America the other day saying there were all kinds of candidates for the Presidency in the field, and every sort of crank except myself seemed to have some following; but he could not discover any one who followed me. He suggested that I should withdraw, but my candidacy will withdraw itself at the proper moment." "What plans have you formed as to your future movements?" "I am going home for good this time. I don't anticipate leaving America again. I should have gone back this month, but my younger daughter's health has been benefited so much by our stay here that we have postponed our departure on that account. But unless some such reason should arrive I won't leave home any more." The world-famous humorist is himself in excellent health. He has been steadily working on his new book during his stay in London, living very quietly and keeping away from society so as not to be interrupted in his writing. Seeing the reverence and affection in which Mark Twain is held in this country, this self-denying ordinance is typical of his quiet determination.

131

"Mark Twain Returns after Nine Years," *New York Herald*, 4 October 1900, 3.

London, Wednesday—Mark Twain will leave London on Saturday, to make his home in the United States, after a nine years' residence in Europe. He returns, he says, feeling like a boy, rejuvenated in body and inspirited in mind.

The great humorist will spend the winter in New York, and will go back to his old home, Hartford, Conn., in the spring. He was found today taking treatment in a massage establishment.

"I am not here for my general health," he said, "but for lumbago. It isn't the ordinary kind of lumbago, either, but what is called 'private hotel lumbago.' One gets it from the beds. They are unnecessarily firm and their main characteristic is of a geological nature. They are composed of Silurian, superimposed upon red sandstone, and still contain the imprint of the prehistoric man. The English private hotel was once the best in the world. It is still the quietest, but its other merits are in decay. It is lingering upon its bygone honorable reputation. Many elderly English people still cling to it from inherited habit and arrested development. Rich Americans frequent it through ignorance and superstition. They find in its austere solemnity and Sabbath repose a charm which makes up for the high charges and mediaeval inconveniences. Pretenders who can't afford to live in Dover street at all affect the lumbago because it conveys the impression that they live in private hotels there."

Mark Twain added that nine years' contact with Englishmen and Continentals had assured him that the Anglo-American pact existed in everything but writing.

"England," said he, "is the best friend we have got in Europe and we are the only friend she's got on earth. No one ventures to suggest a formal offensive and defensive alliance, but it is [in] our mutual interest and sentiment along that line should grow in the hearts of our people. The time is coming when each of the two great peoples will need it in their business. It is out of my line to be pessimistic, but I think that the Chinese concert, which has already become a comedy, is likely to end in tragedy.[1] When the crash comes it will be best for England, best for America and best for the world that the Union Jack and the Stars and Stripes should wave together."

Note to Interview 131

1. Resistance to the Western presence in China climaxed with the Boxer Rebellion (1898-1901). See also MT's comments about Christian missionaries in China in "To the Person Sitting in Darkness," *North American Review* 172 (February 1901): 161-76.

132

"Mark Twain, the Greatest American Humorist, Returning Home, Talks at Length to *The World*," *New York World*, 14 October 1900, 3.

Mark Twain, aboard the *Minnehaha*, is due at this port now.[1] He is returning after many years' absence abroad to dwell permanently in his native land. He talked with *The World* correspondent in London, who gives this interesting account of what he said:

London, Oct. 6—If it were the good fortune of the journalist to have only Mark Twain to interview his lot would indeed be cast in pleasant places.

When *The World* correspondent called upon him today at his London hotel he was received with that charming courtesy and dignified geniality which are the outward stamp of the noble personal character of the greatest living humorist. The inevitable Brobdingnagian pipe was produced and lit, and throwing himself back on the smoke-room couch at Brown's Hotel in Albemarle street, Mark Twain began in that dreamy New England accent of his with its delightful musical cadences: "Why, of course I am very glad to speak for *The World*. Whenever I arrive in a new place or whenever I leave it I always make it a point to answer as well as I can any questions that may be put to me by the boys. But between seasons I never talk. The same rule guides me in connection with public appearances. I have to work, and I like to do it as systematically as I can."

"Have you been busy with your pen amid the distractions of London?"

"Well, London, you see, doesn't distract me. I find it about the best possible place to work in. I like it too as a place of residence better than any I know outside Hartford, where I am always happiest and feel best. Here I meet men of my own tongue and I have many friends. For although seemingly I live a retired life here, I am constantly going out to dinners. You can understand that at the close of a day's work it is a big luxury, a great relaxation, to dine in pleasant company, in absolute privacy, where you can say what you like with the knowledge that it will not get into print. These dinners I enjoy; it's the luncheons that break in upon your time and upset your working arrangements. But dinners! Why, I can do with millions of dinners!"

"Is it true that you have resolved never to leave the United States again?"

"Not a word of truth in it. Perhaps we may spend the rest of our days at home. I don't know and no consideration on earth could induce me to give a pledge about that or anything else. That is another of my rules of life. I never give pledges or promises about things of that sort. If I felt myself under the constraint of a pledge the situation would become so irksome to me that only on that account alone, I should be irresistibly compelled to come away again. No—as far as I am able to speak about a subject on which other people have the controlling voice more or less—I propose to stay the winter in New York, and then go back to Hartford in the spring."

"But do you really think it possible that such an indefatigable traveler as you have been can settle down at home? Won't you feel restless?"

"An indefatigable traveler! That's where I am misunderstood. Now I have made thirty-four long journeys in my life, and thirty-two of them were made under the spur of absolute compulsion. I mean it—under nothing but sheer compulsion. There always was an imperative reason. I had to gather material for books or sketches, I had to stump around lecturing to make money, or I had to go abroad for the health or the education of my family. For love of travel—never any of these thirty-two journeys. There is no man living who cares less about seeing new places and peoples than I. You are surprised—but it's the gospel truth. I had a surfeit of it.

"When I started out in 1867 for a six months' tour in the *Quaker City* I was a voracious sightseer. With nearly all the rest of that gang I said to myself: 'This is the opportunity of my life never again shall I have the chance, the time or the money to see the Old World.' We lived up to that idea. We went in for seeing everything that was to be seen. In a city of inexhaustible treasures like Rome we got up at 6 in the morning and throughout the whole day, in rain or shine, we made a perpetual procession through picture galleries, churches, museums, palaces—looking at things which for the most part did not interest us one cent but which we thought we had to see. And we saw them. If our meals interfered with our seeing any old thing our meals were put aside. At 9 or 10 at night we returned to our hotel, our brains and our bodies reeling with fatigue and utter exhaustion. My head used to ache, my eyes to swim, but I would not succumb to the terrible temptation to throw myself on the bed, as if I did so I could not rise from it again before morning. I had to resist because we had to see something else by moonlight or because there was no moon or some other foolish reason. The only rest we had was when we went a short voyage from one port to another in the Mediterranean, and then I slept all the time. What was the result of this insensate sightseeing? Why, that I was so fagged that I lost the capacity to appreciate most of what I saw or to carry away any coherent idea of it. Since then only hard necessity has ever driven me traveling. When I went around the world, five years ago, it was because I wanted money to pay off debts that were a nuisance to me— they burdened my conscience. People say that it was to relieve my creditors. Not at all. It was far more to relieve Clemens than creditors. I could not be happy until I got rid of that debt. I have never recovered from the *Quaker City* surfeit of sightseeing, and don't think there is any reasonable prospect of my doing so now."

"Don't you find theatres as much of a relaxation as dinners?"

"No: that is another mistake. I had a surfeit of theatres, too. My family are fond of the play and go very often, but they don't enjoy themselves as much as they otherwise would when they persuade me to go with them. You see, when I was a reporter on the San Francisco *Call* I always had a full day's work. I had to do all the police reports, together with any other odd assignments that might turn up, always finishing up by going to seven theatres every evening. I had to write something about each of them, and as a reporter yourself you can understand that with the fag end of my day's work to finish and seven critical notices of high-class performances of the most varied kind to write up, I could not devote that leisure to each play that as a conscientious dramatic critic I should like. Ten minutes here, a quarter of an hour there—that was all I could afford, because there might be a couple more night assignments waiting me at the office. I was very hurried all the time. The result is that when I go to a playhouse now and I have been there about fifteen minutes or half an hour, I begin to fidget around, thinking, 'I shall get all behind if I stay here any longer; I must be off to the other three or four houses, and I have still that murder story to write.' So that the family don't care much about my company at the theatre. That is another example of how bad a surfeit is."

"How long did you continue to keep the San Francisco *Call* going?"

"Let me see—just about twelve months. At the end of that time I was reduced to such a pitiable condition of mental destitution, was so completely worn out and impoverished in mind and body by the responsibilities of my position, that the editor invited me to resign. I didn't want to be ungrateful to a man who had allowed me to learn so much of different kinds of newspaper work in so short a time, so I resigned. And, mind you, there was very little chance of another job, either—in fact it was three or four months before I got one."

"Have you been doing much lately with that autobiography that is to be published a hundred years after your death?"

"Oh; yes; I have added a good deal to it from time to time. I only write it when the spirit moves me and don't lay myself out to keep it regularly going. I find it one of the most interesting works I have ever undertaken. There is something very pleasant in thinking that what you are writing won't be published until the person you are writing about and every one who can have any personal affection for him or her is dead. I find I can take such large, calm views of people, so free from flattery on the one hand and from any taint of malice on the other, when I am writing my own unvarnished, unbiased opinions and impressions. There has never been an autobiography or biography or diary or whatever you like to call it that has been written with quite the detachment from all anxiety about what the readers may think of it or its writer as this one of mine. Pepys, you might be disposed to think, was a miracle of candor even at his own expense, but even Pepys wrote with the consciousness that his contemporaries were looking over his shoulder, and despite all he could do he was fettered by a sense of restraint that consciousness produced. I am free from all that and I think that any work undertaken in that spirit and with that intention of quietly and frankly giving a faithful picture of the men of this or any time will be of interest to posterity. It should be a human document of value provided it is reasonably intelligent and above all wholly true to life as the writer sees life and judges it."

"Is it your method to describe events or only men?"

"You can't do one without touching upon the other. When I meet a man or a woman who interests me, and I feel I can write something about them that would be of interest or value to people a hundred years hence, I jot down my impressions. It is just as the fit takes me."

"Have you been watching the elections here with any interest?"

"Not very much. I have not had time to read the papers. But from what I can judge the system of appealing to the country here is preferable to ours—I mean it is less of a strain on the country. The dissolution is proclaimed here one day, and the next the arrangements for the elections are in full swing, while by the end of the week a good many members of the new House are elected. We have the elections on one day, but our candidates are nominated way back in June and are not elected until November. I think the strain and dislocation of business here is less. When one district elects its member there is an end of the turmoil as far as that one is concerned, and its constituents just go about their business as usual, looking on at the fight as it proceeds elsewhere. But what I don't understand is why this dissolution has been proclaimed just now. The Government had a big majority, the Opposition had nothing particular to say against the settlement in South Africa that the Government intended,[2] and now after it all it seems that they will get about the same majority that they had before."

"And what do you think about the American campaign?"

"Well, you see, I have only read scraps and snatches of news in the papers here, not sufficient to stir my prejudices or partialities. I am going back to vote—I mean, I shall vote, as I shall happen to be there when the election comes on. I have been paying taxes all the time I have been away, so I suppose I am entitled to exercise the franchise.

"You ask me about what is called imperialism. Well, I have formed views about that question. I am at the disadvantage of not knowing whether our people are for or against spreading themselves over the face of the globe. I should be sorry if they are, for I don't think that it is wise or a necessary development. As to China, I quite approve of our Government's action in getting free of that complication. They are withdrawing, I understand, having done what they wanted. That is quite right. We have no more business in China than in any other country that is not ours.[3] There is the case of the Philippines.[4] I have tried hard, and yet I cannot for the life of me comprehend how we got into that mess. Perhaps we could not have avoided it—perhaps it was inevitable that we should come to be fighting the natives of those islands—but I cannot understand it, and have never been able to get at the bottom of the origin of our antagonism to the natives. I thought we should act as their protector—not try to get them under our heel. We were to relieve them from Spanish tyranny to enable them to set up a government of their own, and we were to stand by and see that it got a fair trial. It was not to be a government according to our ideas, but a government that represented the feeling of the majority of the Filipinos, a government according to Filipino ideas. That would have been a worthy mission for the United States. But now—why, we have got into a mess, a quagmire from which each fresh step renders the difficulty of extrication immensely greater. I'm sure I wish I could see what we were getting out of it, and all it means to us as a nation."

"Have you any literary plans for the future?"

"No, but I have some work on hand which I'm getting along with now and then. I have a book half finished, but when the other half will be done the Lord only knows."[5]

"I need scarcely ask how you are—you look the picture of health."

"I have been to the doctor lately—nothing more serious than lumbago. I have invested all the capital possible to produce a good, prosperous lumbago. It is not my fault that it didn't succeed."

"What are your plans on returning to America?"

"Our original plan was to stay in New York, as I said, for the winter, and go to Hartford in the spring. I heard today, however, that there is a chance of this being altered. I do not complain. I only ask that I shall be told in time to arrange. This is my last day here—we sail in the morning from Tilbury on the American Transport liner *Minnehaha*. I could not get on one of the fast steamers—they are engaged over and over again. But I don't mind. I like the long voyage, although it is not so agreeable to the family. I am never seasick. Now I must be off to see my friend Poultney Bigelow in Chelsea.[6] I hope the rain has not made it impossible to go on the top of a bus. That is the mode of conveyance I prefer in London."

And so, with a hearty handshake and good wishes, Mark Twain departed.

Notes to Interview 132

1. The sixteen-thousand-ton *Minnehaha*, built in 1900, plied the route for the Atlantic Transport line.
2. The Boer War (1899–1902), between the British and the descendants of the Boers, Dutch colonialists in South Africa, eventually led to self-government.
3. See n. 1 to interview 131.
4. After the U.S. liberated (and purchased) the Philippines from Spain in 1899, President William McKinley decided the islands were unprepared for self-rule and ordered their occupation, precipitating an insurgency that officially lasted until 4 July 1902.

5. The "half-done" book MT mentions was almost certainly "The Mysterious Stranger." See also *Auto* (1959), 266.

6. Poultney Bigelow (1855–1954), American journalist and historian.

133

"Mark Twain Home, an Anti-Imperialist," *New York Herald*, 16 October 1900, 4.

Mark Twain, sometime known as Samuel Clemens, returned home last night after an absence in the outside world of five years, and landed on his native shores with a smile of good-natured fun on his lips that even the terrible experiences he has passed through could not dim. The great humorist has triumphed over his own misfortunes, as well as those of others, a thing which is said to be impossible even for philosophers.

"I have had lots of fun," remarked Mr. Clemens, as he came down the gangplank. "I have enjoyed myself, except for a twinge of dyspepsia now and then, in every country and under every sky.[1] Fun has no nationality. It has the freedom of the world. But I think I had most fun in Vienna, with the poor old Reichsrath.[2] I was there for a year and a half, and had plenty of time to take it in. It was one of the biggest jokes I have ever seen, and I enjoyed it immensely.

"Fate has its revenge on the humorist," said Mr. Clemens, after he had got well ashore and felt his legs more secure under him, and could risk a more serious tone. "Now, I have lied so much, in a genial, good-natured way, of course, that people won't believe me when I speak the truth. I may add that I have stopped speaking the truth. It is no longer appreciated—in me.

"I have found that when I speak the truth, I am not believed, and that I have never told a lie so big but that some one had sublime confidence in my veracity. I have, therefore, been forced by fate to adopt fiction as a medium of truth. Most liars lie for the love of the lie; I lie for the love of truth. I disseminate my true views by means of a series of apparently humorous and mendacious stories.[3]

"If any man can do that, and finds that he can disseminate facts through the medium of falsehood, he should never speak the truth and I don't.

"The English, you know, take everything that is very serious as an immense joke, and everything that is really side splitting as terribly dull. They even pretended to think me jesting when I spoke about writing a history to be read one hundred years after it was written.

"If ever I spoke truth—and at that time I had not given up the habit of resorting to it occasionally—I spoke it then. I was in dead earnest, but of course the English set it down as a great joke.

"Am I really going to write that history? I have never said that I would, and if I said so now no one would believe me. I merely suggested that it would be an ideal sort of narrative that could slash away at sores without fear of hurting any one—not even the author."

"Mr. Clemens, have you had time to give any thought to the grave question of imperialism?" I asked.

"It is most too grave a question for one of any temperament, but I have taken a try at it. I have thought of it, and it has got the best of me.

"I left these shores, at Vancouver, a red-hot imperialist. I wanted the American eagle to go screaming into the Pacific. It seemed tiresome and tame for it to content itself with the Rockies. Why not spread its wings over the Philippines,[4] I asked myself? And I thought it would be a real good thing to do.

"I said to myself. Here are a people who have suffered for three centuries. We can make them as free as ourselves, give them a government and country of their own, put a miniature of the American constitution afloat in the Pacific, start a brand new republic to take its place among the free nations of the world. It seemed to me a great task to which we had addressed ourselves.

"But I have thought some more, since then, and I have read carefully the treaty of Paris, and I have seen that we do not intend to free but to subjugate the people of the Philippines. We have gone there to conquer, not to redeem. We have also pledged the power of this country to maintain and protect the abominable system established in the Philippines by the Friars.[5]

"It should, it seems to me, be our pleasure and duty to make those people free and let them deal with their own domestic questions in their own way. And so I am an anti-imperialist. I am opposed to having the eagle put its talons on any other land.

"But I want to say that I cannot conscientiously support Mr. Bryan.[6] I am not so much of an anti-imperialist as that. I have been told that I cannot vote in this election, but if I could I should not vote for Mr. Bryan. As to what I would do I cannot say, as I am a mugwump, and a mugwump won't vote until he has had plenty of time to look the thing over.[7]

"And then, I don't want to commit myself too far, as, if I find that I cannot vote, I shall run for President.[8] A patriotic American must do something around election time, and that's about the only thing political that is left for me."

"Have you any books about ready for publication?"

"No; but I have several on the way.[9] I wrote myself out in the line of anecdotes and humorous sketches in my last book. I ran short even in that and could barely find enough material to fill it. I am now falling back upon fiction;

but, as I have said, my fiction is different from the fiction of others. No matter what I write in that line people will think that I am hiding some truth behind the stalking horse of a story."

"Will you have an American story?"

"You see, I write the story and then fill in the places, like blanks in a railway form. The places don't count so much. The story is the thing."

"But you will give your people some of their own types, with characteristic dialect, will you not? And won't that require you to select your scenes first?"

"No, not entirely. Even that can be filled in. It is astonishing how much can be filled in. I rewrote one of my books three times, and each time it was a different book.[10] I had filled in, and filled in, until the original book wasn't there. It had evaporated through the blanks, and I had an entirely new book. I shall write my story, and then lay the scene where I want it, and, if necessary, change other things to suit the places.

"I shall very probably write a story with the scene laid in this country, or I shall place the scene of one of my present uncompleted stories here. This can be done rather handily, after the whole story is written.

"But I am not going to publish another book for at least a year. I have just published a small one, and a book every two or three years is enough."[11]

"Will you have any more like *Huckleberry Finn* and *Tom Sawyer?*"

"Perhaps," and Mr. Clemens smiled as he thought of these creations. "Yes, I shall have to do something of that kind, I suppose. But one can't talk about an unwritten book. It may grow into quite a different thing from what one thinks it may be."

When I asked Mr. Clemens to tell some of his experiences of travel, he replied: "That is another old story, and almost everything I saw or thought or imagined during my trip around the world has been told in my books.

"I had a very unusual and pleasant experience in Australasia. I was traveling through Australasia and lecturing in the larger cities during the time of the excitement over the Venezuelan boundary dispute.

"When Mr. Cleveland's sizzling message came I thought that the people of the British colonies would feel a little chilly toward me.[12] But I was mistaken. They didn't let it interfere with our relations, and laughed at my jokes just as much as ever.

"I even think they strained a point to laugh, or they laughed sometimes where I didn't intend that they should. I found that they had learned to like me a little through reading my books, and that friendship was warm enough to carry me smilingly through President Cleveland's crisis.

"In Pretoria, also, I had some little fun. It was with the Jameson raiders, who were in jail when I reached there. They were very disconsolate, expecting to be shot, or something of the sort, every morning. I went down to cheer them up a bit.[13]

"I talked to them. I told them that they didn't seem to appreciate the privilege of being confined in a jail. Bunyan, I told them, would not have written the *Pilgrim's Progress* if some one had not shut him up in a cell, and that we should not have had the pleasure of reading *Don Quixote* if Cervantes had not spent several years in prison.[14] Some of the fellows smiled sadly. They didn't appreciate the point of view. I told them that some men went through life without having the privilege they were enjoying."

Mr. Clemens said that five years ago, when he sailed from Vancouver, he was in bad health and spirits, and that there was but one thing that cheered him up—his debts.

"They were so many, that I could afford to be cheerful after I got used to them," he said. "I was determined to pay them off, to the last cent, and I have done it. I finished paying the last debt that I owed to any man about two years and a half ago, or in a little more than two years after I set myself the task of meeting my obligations.[15]

"I had estimated that it would take at least five years, but with good luck and with a far greater appreciation of my efforts to please than I had any right to expect, I was able to pay off every cent in far less time.

"They are gone now, and when they fell from around my neck, I felt like the Ancient Mariner when the dead albatross fell into the sea.[16] I became a new man. I think the hope of paying them made me funnier than usual, for the English people laughed at all my stories."

"I ought not to overlook Mr. Krüger, especially at this time, when he has become almost as interesting a personage as Napoleon at St. Helena.[17] I saw the heroic old man at his capital, Pretoria, at the time of the Jameson raid.

"I had heard so much about him everywhere, read so much about him in every newspaper and magazine of the world, had painted his picture in my brain so often, that I knew him before I saw him. He did not astonish me. He was exactly as I had fancied him.

"He treated me very graciously, and I had a long talk with him. He is just the stalwart old fellow one would imagine, who has read his life story—a great rugged character, that will live."

Mr. Clemens says that he has made his plans for at least a year. "I shall spend the winter in New York, making my home at the Earlington Hotel. I shall spend the time very quietly, doing nothing but reading and writing a little on my books, and doing some little work for the magazines."

"I do not expect to see much of the bright side of the city; that is, I shall not go out much to the theatres and other places of amusement.[18] I expect to keep close and devote my time to reading, smoking and as little work as possible.[19]

"In the spring I shall return to Hartford, Connecticut, where Mrs. Clemens, my daughters and myself will settle down for some home life, after nine years of wandering up and down on the earth.[20]

"No, I shall not lecture. I have abandoned the lecture tour that I had almost arranged. I did want very much, at one time, to go through the Southern States, where I have not done much traveling, and lecture in the big cities. But I withdrew from the engagement, although $50,000 was offered to me for a hundred lectures.[21]

"I don't want to lecture again, and will not unless forced to do so. I am tired of it and want to rest."

Mr. Clemens is looking as young as he did nine years ago, when he left this country on his first extended tour abroad. His face has as few wrinkles, and there does not seem to be one in that kindly countenance that has not been traced and graven by good nature, fun and laughter. His hair and mustache are a shade whiter, and his form is a little more bowed, but he seems to be in better health than he was in 1891.

He has acquired or accentuated some tricks that accompany the humorist. His drawl is a trifle longer and more pronounced, and he has a trick of bending his knees and throwing back his head as if in preparation for a good story. It is equivalent to one of President Lincoln's "That reminds me."[22]

He left America in 1891 and went to the baths of Aix-les-Bains;[23] then, in a few months, to Berlin, where he lectured. In 1892 he lived on the Riviera, then retreated again to the German baths, and in 1893 went to Florence, Italy, where he lived for several months, and while there completed *Joan of Arc* and *Pudd'nhead Wilson.*

After this he spent two years in France, where he says he wrestled, like Jacob, day and night, but in vain, with the intricacies of the French grammar. He gave it up.[24]

In 1895 he returned for a short time to this country. Then he started on another tour, which embraced Asia, Africa and Australasia.[25]

When the *Minnehaha,* of the Atlantic Transport Company,[26] reached her pier last night at nine o'clock, there were only a handful of persons on the deck. Most of those had come down to see Mark Twain, but they did not make up a good sized reception committee. When Mr. Clemens came down the gangplank there was some applause and some cries of "Welcome," and nearly every one on the pier came around him and pressed his hands, and hung about in the hope of catching a ray of fun.[27]

They were not disappointed, for the genial humorist, who left his country under clouds of disappointment, came back with sunny smiles, and in a humor that was good natured enough and broad enough to make the whole world sharers in his mood.[28]

Notes to Interview 133

I have supplemented this interview as reported in the *New York Herald* with versions of Twain's comments published in other newspapers. All newspaper citations below are from 16 October 1900.

    1. "Mark Twain Home," *New York Tribune,* 1–2: "My health . . . was not good at all until nine months ago. It was a pretty shaky, dyspeptic kind of existence. I am not dyspeptic now."

    "Mark Twain Talks," *New York Mail and Express,* 3: "The only thing that worries me," said he, "is that I may be told to move on. I've been around so much that I have none of those little prejudices against other countries. Neither is it that I am not comfortable. I am. I'd be comfortable in a coal cellar if they would only let me stay there. But before I get accustomed to my surroundings I would be obliged to move somewhere else. Still, I would be an ingrate to the various countries whose hospitality I have enjoyed and under whose flags I have lived if I did not appreciate the kindness with which I was received abroad."

    2. See n. 1 to interview 124.

    3. *New York Tribune:* "I never told the truth that I was not suspected of lying, and never told a lie that I was not believed."

    "Mark Twain Home Again, Hale and Hardy at 75," *New York World:* "I never yet told the truth that I was not accused of lying," was the solemn answer, "and every time I lie some one believes it. So I have adopted the plan, when I want people to believe what I say, of putting it in the form of a lie. That is the difference between my fiction and other people's. Everybody knows mine is true." . . . "Isn't [your autobiography] all a joke?" "That's just it—a joke? Never. Whenever I want to tell the truth people think I'm lying, and whenever I lie there's somebody sure to think that I'm talking gospel truth. Some people write facts that are taken for fiction, but whenever I write fiction it's taken for truth. This time I'm writing facts and everybody thinks it's going to be fiction. Anyway, there'll be a lot about people of today that other people will read when they and we are all dead."

    "Mark Twain Wants to Be President," *New York Press,* 3: When finished telling of his travels he was asked if it was a fact that he was writing an autobiography of himself, to be published 100 years after his death. "When I told about that," he answered, "I spoke seriously, and it was taken for fiction. Now that's the difference between the fiction I write and that written by others. When I disseminate truth from fiction it is taken for the latter and vice versa. So when I want to be believed I lie."

    "Mark Twain Home Again," *New York Times,* 3: Some one in the crowd asked him about his autobiography that is to be published 100 years hence. "It is true I am writing it," he said. "That's not a joke, is it?" "No; I said it seriously; that's why they take it as a joke. You know, I never told the truth in my life that some one didn't say I was lying, while, on the other hand, I never told a lie that somebody didn't take it as a fact." "Well, it's not wrong, anyway, to tell a lie sometimes, is it?" was a question someone asked in a very conciliatory way. "That's right, exactly right. If you can disseminate facts by telling the truth, why that's the way to do it, and if you can't except by doing a little lying, well, that's all right, too, isn't it? I do it."

4. The armada of Admiral George Dewey (1837–1917) destroyed the Spanish fleet in Manila Bay on 1 May 1898 in the decisive naval battle of the Spanish-American War.

5. The Treaty of Paris ending the Spanish-American War and ceding the Philippines to the U.S. for $20 million was signed on 10 December 1898. Some twenty-six hundred friars, all of them European, most of them Spanish, effectively governed the Philippines at the turn of the twentieth century, a form of clerical colonialism.

New York Press: "I will not vote for William Jennings Bryan, but will, if permitted by the law, vote for Mr. McKinley. I did, before reading the Treaty of Paris, favor imperialism, but since reading it I have changed my views."

New York Tribune: "Once I was not anti-imperialist," he said. "I thought that the rescue of those islands from the government under which they had suffered for three hundred years was good business for us to be in. But I had not studied the Paris Treaty. When I found that it made us responsible for the protection of the friars and their property I changed my mind."

New York Press: "The treaty provides that the United States care for the friars and their property in the event of giving the Filipinos their freedom. This I don't believe in. If the inhabitants of the Philippines are to be released from what they have suffered for 300 years, I do not see why we should assume the responsibility of the friars and their belongings. Let their freedom be unconditional, and for that reason I am an anti-imperialist. Notwithstanding this fact, I would not vote for Mr. Bryan, but owing to my long absence from home I do not think that the election laws will permit me to vote. In that event, I see nothing else to do but become an independent candidate for that office."

New York Times: "As near as I can find out, I think that I am an anti-imperialist. I was not though, until some time ago, for when I first heard of the acquisition of the present Pacific possessions I thought it a good thing for a country like America to release those people from a bondage of suffering and oppression that had lasted 300 years, but when I read the Paris treaty I changed my mind."

New York World: "You've been quoted here as an anti-imperialist." "Well, I am. A year ago I wasn't. I thought it would be a great thing to give a whole lot of freedom to the Filipinos, but I guess now that it's better to let them give it to themselves. Besides, on looking over the treaty I see we've got to saddle the Friars and their churches. I guess we don't want to."

6. William Jennings Bryan (1860–1925), Democratic candidate for president in 1896, 1900, and 1908.

New York World: "If you get a vote, will you cast your ballot for Bryan?" "I guess not. I'm rather inclined toward McKinley, even if he is an imperialist. But don't ask political questions, for all I know about them is from the English papers."

7. Mugwumps were liberal or reform Republicans who bolted the GOP in 1884.

New York Tribune: "I have not decided who I am going to vote for. I have paid taxes in Hartford for nine years, and I suppose I am entitled to vote."

New York Times: "I am a Mugwump. I don't know who I am going to vote for. I must look over the field. Then, you know, I've been out of the country a long time, and I might not be allowed to register.... But I should have to look the ground over," he said; "at present I know nothing about it. I am a Mugwump, and we Mugwumps have to think over the matter of how we shall vote; we want to know which man will best suit us."

New York Mail and Express: "I've been a mugwump these many years," he said. "I am a mugwump now. I shall be a mugwump until I die—and afterward. It is the only entirely respectable party that ever existed.... I understand that I am the only living member of it. I will maintain its respectability to the end. Do you know what the mugwump platform is? It has one plank. Out of howsoever many candidates there may be before the public, select the best man. Don't pay any attention to principles. If I had a vote on November 6 I would inquire into the character of McKinley and of Bryan and vote for the one who had the soundest morals. Everybody has some principles, I suppose, but I'd rather support a man with morals and without principles than a man with principles and without morals."

New York World, 1: "I'm a Mugwump, and a Mugwump has to make up his mind before he votes. And I guess they won't let me vote. So I won't have to make up my mind. But I'll know a lot more about that the day after tomorrow."

8. *New York Times:* "You are still a citizen of the United States, are you not?" interposed a member of the party. "Well, I guess I am. I've been paying taxes on this side for the last nine years. I believe, though, a man can run for President," laughingly inquired Mr. Clemens, "without a vote, can't he? If this is so, why, then I am a candidate for President."

"Mark Twain Home Again," *New York Sun,* 2: But perhaps the registration laws will bar me out. Then I won't have to think over the matter. Besides, I am an independent candidate for President myself; if I can't vote, I'll run. I've paid taxes a good many years." "Then you haven't made up your mind about the Presidency?" "No, I may run as an independent candidate myself."

9. *Auto* (1959), 265–66, 277.

10. *New York Tribune:* "You can't tell what a book is going to be ... until after you have written it. I found that out after writing one over three times. Every time it was different." MT no doubt refers to *Pudd'nhead Wilson* (1893).

11. *New York Tribune:* "I am not contemplating publishing a book immediately. One book in two or three years is all a man can do well.... My literary projects are yet unborn," said he, "and as yet there has been appointed neither a birthday nor a christening. I always refuse to discuss personal affairs. Generally I make some sort of an answer to a question of that kind, but what I say doesn't mean anything."

12. See nn. 1 and 4 to interview 107.

New York Times: "This was at the time of the famous Venezuelan message of President Cleveland, and it did my heart good to see that the animosities engendered by that message did not affect the affection of a people in a strange land for me."

New York Press: "While we were there [in Australia]," said Mr. Clemens, "Cleveland made his famous Venezuela speech, but the natives showed no [ill] feeling toward me, as they knew me either personally or through reading my books."

13. On the Jameson raiders see n. 6 to interview 113.

New York Press: "I arrived in Pretoria in '96, while the Jameson raiders were in jail. ... Thinking they might be lonely, I asked permission to speak to them. The privilege was allowed me, and I told the prisoners not to feel uncomfortable, as they were just as well off there as in any other jail. I also told them that much had been done in jails. Bunyan wrote *Pilgrim's Progress* while a prisoner and the author of Don Quixote was in the same predicament when he wrote that famous book. Some laughed at my consoling words, and they all appeared good natured, notwithstanding the fact that some did not even smile at my joke on them."

New York Times: "At this time the Jameson raiders were in jail, and I visited them and made a little speech trying to console them. I told them of the advantages of being in jail. 'This jail is as good as any other,' I said, 'and, besides, being in jail has its advantages. A lot of great men have been in jail. If Bunyan had not been put in jail, he would never have written *Pilgrim's Progress.* Then the jail is responsible for *Don Quixote,* so you see being in jail is not so bad, after all.' Finally I told them that they ought to remember that many great men had been compelled to go through life without ever having been in a jail. Some of the prisoners didn't seem to take much to the joke, while others seemed much amused."

"Mark Twain in America Again," *Chicago Tribune,* 5: "The Jameson raiders were all in jail. I went down and looked them over. I informed them that *Pilgrim's Progress* never would have been written if John Bunyan hadn't been locked up in jail; and I asked them if *Don Quixote* would ever have been produced if Cervantes hadn't been jailed. I tried to cheer them up by telling them that many men had spent their entire lives without having had such an experience."

New York Sun: "I made a little speech to them during my call," he said. "I told them that I thought I could comfort them some. I told them that they were as well off there as they would be in any jail in any country. I assured them that they did not realize the advantages as they ought to do. 'Why, the *Pilgrim's Progress* and *Don Quixote* would never have been produced if their writers had not been in jail,' I said to them, and I dwelt upon how many people had to go through life without the advantages that they enjoyed. Some of them laughed, but they didn't seem altogether to like it, somehow."

New York Tribune: "I went to the jail to visit them," he said. "I thought I might comfort them a little. I told them that they were as well off in that jail as they would be in any, and that lots of people went through their entire lives without once having the experience of being in jail. They laughed, but they didn't seem to like it."

14. John Bunyan (1628-88) reputedly wrote *Pilgrim's Progress* while in jail for twelve years after the Restoration in 1660. According to tradition, Miguel de Cervantes Saavedra (1547-1616) wrote the first part of *Don Quixote* (1605) while in prison at Argamasilla in La Mancha. MT also alludes to *Don Quixote* in chapter 3 of *Huck Finn.*

15. *New York Sun:* When a question was put to him last evening whether he had accomplished the purpose with which he set out, and as to the amount of the debts, he said: "I did, some time ago. The amount is not the question; it is the load upon a man, and whether he can live to work it off. I was afraid I could not live to do it. I did not think it could be done in four years; it was done in a little more than two years. It was finished in 1898."

New York Tribune: "I accomplished my object in paying off my debts in two years. Oh, but my creditors treated me very well. The main thing, whatever the amount may be, whether large or small, is to have the load relieved. I did not think it could be done in four years, but I did it in two years and a half."

New York World: "I resolved," said he last night, "to clear it up in three years. I did it in two years and a half. I started the latter half of 1895 and finished in the early part of 1898. I'm clear now."

New York Mail and Express: "You say I've been compared with Scott in the payment of the debts of the publishing houses in which I was interested? Nice, but purely personal." On Scott, see n. 6 to interview 76.

16. Twain alludes to *The Rime of the Ancient Mariner* by Samuel Taylor Coleridge (1772-1834).

17. Paul Krüger, aka Oom Paul (1825-1904), a prominent Boer resistance leader against British rule, first president of the Transvaal Republic in 1880.

New York Sun: "I had heard about Paul Krüger," he said, "about his beard and long pipe and all that, and he corroborated my impression of him."

Chicago Tribune: "I had read all about old Krüger and he was just like what I had read—silk hat, old pipe, and everything. There had just then been the trouble in the Transvaal."

After his defeat at Waterloo, Napoleon was exiled to the south Atlantic island of St. Helena until his death in 1821.

18. *New York Mail and Express:* "A certain amount of dining is fit and proper," he said, "but if you go too far somebody gets up and says, 'Oh, thunder, that man talks too much.' I don't believe it has ever been truly said of me—truly said—that I talked too much, and I don't mean that it shall be. I have three dinner appointments, made some time since, and I intend to be discreet about the rest."

19. *New York Mail and Express:* "I was born into the leisure class," said he, "but that is the most courteous name I have ever heard it called by. Usually it is called by a pretty rude name. I have been charged with being lazy, but from this time forth I shall claim my place in the ranks of the leisure class."

20. *New York Tribune:* "I shall remain in New York for the winter," he went on. "Then, in the spring, I shall go to our old home in Hartford. The house has not been closed during our nine years' absence, but has been in charge of servants."

Chicago Tribune: "Are you going to stay here now, Mr. Clemens?" "I guess so," replied the author. "This is a pretty good place. I'm going to stay in New York all winter, anyway, and I'm going up to Hartford in the spring. That's the best place in the world." "Are you going to vote there?" "Now you've got me. I don't know. I pay taxes there, but I've been away for nine years."

New York Times: "I'll see you again. I'll be at the Earlington all the winter. I am not going to Hartford till next year."

21. *New York Tribune:* "Three years ago," he said, "I accepted a proposition from Pond to lecture one hundred nights for $30,000, but I withdrew from that. I was not feeling well."

New York World: "But I'll never lecture again," he added, "if I can help it. Major Pond offered me $50,000 for 100 nights. But I'm getting old and it meant traveling all over the United States during the winter and I got out of it. But I expect to keep on writing right along."

New York Times: "I am absolutely unable to speak of my plans," he replied, "inasmuch as I have none, and I do not expect to lecture." . . . It had been Mr. Clemens' plan when he went away to make a final lecturing tour of this country when he came back, but this has been abandoned. Major J. B. Pond offered him a contract of $50,000 for a hundred lectures and it was Mr. Clemens' intention to visit the Southern States where he has never been on a lecturing tour. But he does not want to lecture any more unless he has to. "I could cancel that contract, so I did," he said. "I want to give up lecturing."

22. Abraham Lincoln often began a joke or story with the formulaic phrase "that reminds me of."

23. Resort town in southeastern France. See also MT's essay "Aix-les-Bains" (1891).

24. The biblical Jacob wrestled with an angel (Genesis 32: 24–27).

New York Press: "I did not learn French," he said, "and do not yet know how to speak the language, but my daughter studied it."

25. The Polish-born Theodor Leschetitzky (1830–1915) taught piano in Russia and Austria.

New York Sun: "Tell us some of the incidents of your tour of the world." "There aren't any except what I put in my book, and there weren't enough of them to go 'round," he answered.

New York Press: "After leaving there we next visited Southampton and Guilford, England, where we spent ten months, and then went to Switzerland and Vienna, where we remained until '99. While there my daughters were taught music by a man named Leschetitzky. He was a Russian and a man of talent. We then spent the balance of the time in Sweden and London."

New York Times: "Now, that's a long story, but I suppose I must give you something, even if it is in a condensed form," he said. "I left America June 6, 1891, and went to Aix-les-Bains, France, where I spent the fall and winter. After that I went to Berlin, where I lectured, giving readings from my works. After this my next stop was the Riviera, where I remained for three months, going from there to the baths near Frankfurt, where I remained during the cholera season. Most of 1892 I spent at Florence, where I rented a home. While there I wrote *Joan of Arc* and finished up *Pudd'nhead Wilson*. For the next two years I was in France. I can't speak French yet. In the spring of 1895 I came to the United States for a brief stay, crossing the continent from New York to San Francisco [actually, Portland, Ore.] lecturing every night. In October of that year I sailed from Vancouver for Sydney, where I lectured, or, more properly speaking, gave readings from my works to the English-speaking people. I also visited Tasmania and New Zealand. I then proceeded to India, lecturing in Ceylon, Bombay, and Calcutta. I then sailed for South Africa, arriving at Delagoa Bay in April 1896. In South Africa I visited Kimberley, Johannesburg, and finally Cape Town. I met Oom Paul. I had heard and read all about him—hat, beard, frock coat, pipe, and everything else. The picture is a true likeness. [On Oom Paul see n. 17 this interview.] All this time my family was with me, and after a short stay at Cape Town we took a steamer for Southampton. On arriving in England we went to Guilford, where I took a furnished house, remaining two months, after which for ten months our home was in London. All this time I was lecturing, reading, or working hard in other ways, writing magazine stories and doing other literary work. After London came Vienna, to which city we went in September 1898, remaining until May of the following year, in order to allow one of my daughters to take music lessons from a man who spelled his name Leschetitzky. He had plenty of identification, you see, and withal seemed to be a pretty smart fellow. After Vienna, where, by the way, I had a lot of fun watching the Reichsrath, we returned to London, in which city and Sweden we have been until our departure for home some days ago, and now I am home again, and you have got the history of a considerable part of my life."

New York Tribune: "I am not fond of traveling and I did not travel for pleasure, but because duty and my financial obligations compelled me. I was deeply in debt, and determined to pay my creditors. I sailed from New York on June 6, 1891, going first to Aix-les-Bains, where I took the baths and got rid of my indigestion and rheumatism. Then I gave readings from my own works in Berlin and on the Riviera. Most of the year of 1892 we spent at Frankfurt, and then we spent ten months in the suburbs of Florence, where I wrote *Joan of Arc* and *Pudd'nhead Wilson*. . . . After Florence we spent two years in Paris, and in the spring of 1895 we returned for a few weeks to the United States. I crossed the continent from New York to San Francisco [actually, Portland, Ore.], lecturing every night. . . . October 15, 1895, we sailed from Vancouver to Sydney, and I lectured, or, more properly speaking, gave readings from my own works to the English speaking people in Tasmania, New Zealand, and Australasia to the end of the year. . . . On January 1, 1896, we sailed from Melbourne to Ceylon, where I gave readings to the English speaking people. From Calcutta we returned to Ceylon, sailing thence to the Mauritius and thence to Delagoa Bay, where we arrived April 1896. . . . From Delagoa Bay we went to Kimberley, Johannesburg and finally to Cape Town, where my readings seemed to please every audience. We left Cape Town for Southampton, and took a furnished house in Guilford for two months, and then I took another furnished house in London for ten months. . . . I was working hard all this time, reading, lecturing, writing magazine articles and doing other literary work. We reached Vienna in September 1898, and remained until May 1899, as one of my daughters was taking music lessons from Letschetitzky. Later we went to London and Sweden."

New York Sun: "My daughter had a music teacher at Vienna," Mr. Clemens said. "His name was spelt L-e-t-s-c-h-e-t-i-t-z-k-y, but he was a good music teacher. I believe he was a Russian."

26. Lyman J. Gage (1836-1927) was U.S. secretary of the treasury from 1897 to 1902.

New York Sun: Mr. Clemens wrote Secretary Gage that he was coming home: "I told the Secretary," he said, "that I had quite a good many things, but that there was nothing good enough to pay duty on, while it was all too good to throw away."

New York Times: "I wrote to Secretary Gage telling him that my baggage was on a 16,000-ton ship, which was quite large enough to accommodate all I had, which, while it consisted of a good many things, was not good enough to pay duty on, yet too good to throw away. I accordingly suggested that he write the customs people to let it in, as I thought they would be more likely to take his word than mine."

27. *Chicago Tribune:* "No, I didn't get off on the other side of the boat," he said to the people there to greet him, and impatient because he was nearly the last one off.

New York Sun: Another reporter confided to the author that his city editor had sent positively the worst equipped man in his office to interview a humorist. "My boy," said Mark Twain, "I don't know about that. Humor is so serious. When you sit down to write humor go at it seriously; if the humor doesn't come, don't write it."

New York Mail and Express: "When I said that if I once got ashore in the United States I'd break both my legs so that I couldn't get away again," remarked Samuel L. Clemens this morning in his easy, pleasant drawl, "I meant to register a protest against having to pack up a satchel and go somewhere."

New York World: "I told my friend, Colonel Bass, who's on the boat, that if I once got ashore again in the United States I'd break both my legs so that I couldn't get away again."

Edgar Wales Bass (1843-1918) was professor of mathematics at the U.S. military academy from 1878 to 1898.

28. *New York Mail and Express:* "You were quoted abroad as saying that there was an Anglo-Saxon fact in everything except writing." "Well," Mr. Clemens drawled, "Very—likely—I—said—it. At times I say anything, whether it is true or not, but I

wouldn't say a meaningless thing. That sentence hasn't any meaning. It starts out as if it meant a great deal, but when you examine it, it doesn't mean anything. Of course there is a copyright now. What I do believe is that there should be a perpetual copyright. There is no man alive who can make a good argument against perpetual copyright."

134

"My Impressions of America," *New York World*, 21 October 1900, E5.

The World's clever caricaturist, Kate Carew, was sent the other day to get Mark Twain's impressions of America.[1]

"As he has been away from the United States for some years," said the editor, "you might get him to express himself just as if he were a foreigner coming here for the first time.

"Have him tell what he thinks about the bay, the Statue of Liberty, the policemen, the manners of the people, the hotels, the cabs, bootblacks, fashions, the theatres and everything else that has interested him in New York."

Here is the interview which Miss Carew obtained, in which he talks about nearly everything else.

"The trouble with us in America," said Mark Twain, "is that we haven't learned to speak the truth."

He was sitting at breakfast opposite an exceedingly embarrassed young woman who was taking pains to keep her pencil and sketchbook below the level of the table, because she did not wish to excite the curiosity of the waiter—though he would be a bold waiter that betrayed curiosity in the presence of Samuel L. Clemens.

What led up to the remark about truth was that others were clamoring to see Mark Twain, and the embarrassed young woman had ventured to say: "Don't you find that one's time is more respected on the other side?"

"Well, yes," he replied, after a pause occupied in carefully breaking the end off a roll—and I wish I could convey the solemnity of utterance and the long, oft-broken drawl. "Well, yes. I guess—perhaps—it is. Now—in London I always had—a—regular time set for myself. But there—I'd—go—'way down into the—city—and people—would know where to find me, and wouldn't—know—my other—address."

He had just come downstairs, and, after trying vainly to get a London paper at the newsstand and contenting himself with a local one, meandered breakfastward. A fresh, spotless little old man, good to look upon and suggesting spring water and much soap, with the more metropolitan advantages of shoe blacking and starched linen. On closer acquaintance he proved not such a very little man, not so very shrunken and not so very old as he seemed at that first glimpse. Great, unaffected dignity he has, great poise, great simplicity and strength. White hairs are not always admirable, I have heard, but Mark Twain's are. They are also beautiful.

"Except friends, of course—but then—no one would think of calling—at—ten in the morning—there; and if—they did—one wouldn't hesitate—to—say—'I'm at—breakfast'—or—'I'm—about—to breakfast.'

"But here—well, of course—our—friends are anxious to see—us, and they—come—whenever—they think they can—find us. And—the trouble with us in America is we haven't learned how to—speak the—truth—yet.

"If we had it would be—a—pleasure for me to—tell—my friend—that he was intruding, and he would be—benefited—and not injured.

"Now, it is an art—high art—to speak the—truth—so that the object does not object—does not become offended. The trouble is—with—our social laws. The only—way to get reform is to—educate—both sides—one to—give, the other to—receive; one to tell the truth, the—other to—listen to it without —getting—mad."

A pause. A longer pause than usual. An abominably protracted pause. A pause hovering on the abyss of irretrievable silence. Heavens! Would he say no more? He whom it had been so much trouble to coax into speaking at all? It was a desperate chance. I broke in, hardly knowing what I was saying: "But I always thought that the art was in telling lies, and telling the truth seems so easy!"

The waiter flitted forward, and then vanished, like a wraith, with an empty dish. Mark Twain took a mouthful of coffee and carefully dabbed his mustache with his napkin. I was admiring his hands delicate, pinky-white hands matching the pinky-white cheeks of a wholesome old man.

"Don't believe it," he said, dropping his napkin to his knee. "Lying—is not an art—not that I have ever been able to—discover—and I have—tried—hard all my life. It is a—device—of primitive intelligences. The best—liars—are savages and—children. The most cultured—people—speak the truth as often as they—think about it, and enjoy—hearing it spoken by—others. In heaven I shouldn't wonder but they—use—the truth most of the time."

I had been listening too hard to do much work, though there was never a more tempting head for pencil or brush than this silver-crowned one. He observed my inertia, and inquired, with a touch of fatherly reproof: "Are you getting—what—you wanted?"

"Not much," I replied, all confusion. "Only a few notes."

"Notes!" He half rose from his chair. "Notes!" There was a sudden drawing down of his shaggy eyebrows.

"An artist's notes, you know," I hastened to explain. "Just scratches on the paper—an eyebrow, a wrinkle, a coat collar."

He sank back, much relieved.

"Make all the notes—that kind of notes—you want to," he said. "So long as—you—don't interview me, I—don't care. I won't be interviewed. I don't—approve—of interviews; don't like them—on—principle."

This was not a very good omen for further conversation. I tried him on Vienna, having caught a glimpse of him there two years ago. This recollection of mine did not excite him perceptibly. I remarked that it was a beautiful little city. Yes, beautiful, he confessed into his mustache. I told him how my traveling companion and I had felt tempted to speak to him, but had found ourselves incapable of taking such a liberty.

"You might—just—as well," he said, with a vague look in the eyes which suggested memories of other traveling Americans who had been less diffident. "That would have—been—all right." He waved a reminiscently hospitable hand. "I would not have hurt—you."

Of his experiences in Vienna and his friendships there not a word. Paris, London the same.

New York? If I could only get this most taciturn of humorists and philosophers to tell his impressions of America—not a whole budget of impressions, just one or two tiny ones that might escape his determination not to be interviewed!

Ah, what a master of the art of silence is Mark Twain! The skyscrapers? Not a word. The torn-up streets? Not a word. Rapid transit? Not a word. Politics? Not a word. Noise? Let me see.

"Don't you find New York very noisy after the quiet of European cities?" I ventured.

"No; it doesn't annoy me," he said. "I don't—hear it. You don't have to hear—noise—unless you want to. The only time I hear the elevated—is—when it—stops."

The waiter flitted back with a note. Another caller.

"They don't do this—sort of—thing—in London," he remarked. "There one can—breakfast—between 10 and 12 in beautiful—safety. I don't know why I breakfast at—the same hour—here. It's just habit, I guess. The early breakfast habit is one of—the American institutions—I admire most—when I am abroad.

"But these early morning—calls—are meant in a kindly spirit. They touch my heart, even when—the coffee—gets cold."

It would be impossible to exaggerate the composure and gravity with which Mark Twain utters his quaintnesses—and I'm sure he wasn't in much of a mood for quaintnesses that morning. There is no afterglow of self-appreciation, no swift glance to see how his point has "taken." I am sure he does not try to say funny things, only he sees life through a glass that distorts every fact into a paradox. Or perhaps it is the serious people that have a distorted view of life. I wish Mark Twain would say what he thinks about it.

You can't imagine anything more solemn than the atmosphere he carries with him. I, in my innocence, had pictured to myself one who would be surrounded with faces wreathed in smiles. In fancy I had heard waiters giggling behind their napkins and seen the hotel clerk with a broad smile repeating "Mr. Clemens' latest" to an admiring circle.

But, bless your heart! they all walk on tiptoe and speak in awed whispers when Mr. Clemens appears. His long residence abroad has taught him to expect the ministration of servants whose parents were servants, who will be servants all their lives, and whose children will be servants. Europe spoils many good Americans for the free and easy "help" of their own dear land, and I fancy that Mark Twain finds it so.

He had occasion to send for the head waiter and ask him why something hadn't been done, or why it hadn't been done sooner. He didn't scold, he just said: "You understand, it's better—for me to—know—about these things, so I'll know what to do about it next time."

The tremulous head waiter explained that there had been something the matter with the speaking-tube by which the original order had been transmitted.

"Oh, that was it, was it?" said Mr. Clemens. "I just wanted to—know." And then, turning to me, he added: "I don't suppose we—have a right—to know as much as cooks and—waiters, anyway."

They know him now, after having him with them for a week, and it's safe to say that there isn't a person in New York better waited on than Samuel L. Clemens, who has made more people laugh than any other living man.

Note to Interview 134

1. Mary Williams, aka Kate Carew (1869–1960), caricaturist and interviewer for the *New York World* beginning in 1890.

135

"Wouldn't Work 30 Minutes for $500," *New York World* supplement, 21 October 1900, 5.

Mark Twain cares less about the almighty dollar than any other man in New York. He is out of debt, the royalties on his books will provide an income for himself and family for many years and he has no more contracts for the future than he cares to fill.

The following incident best shows Mr. Clemens's utter disregard for the coin of the realm.

A reporter of *The World* on last Tuesday afternoon was directed to visit him and make arrangements if possible to have Mr. Clemens attend the [William Jennings] Bryan mass meeting at Madison Square Garden and write about what he saw for *The World*.

Mr. Clemens was found at the Hotel Earlington, in West Twenty-seventh street, where he is stopping with is wife and daughter.

"*The World* has directed me, Mr. Clemens," said the reporter, "to offer you $500 if you will go to Madison Square Garden tonight and tell its readers what Mark Twain thought of the Bryan meeting. A carriage will take you over there, you will have a good box seat, and after the meeting you will be driven back to the hotel, where a stenographer will take your dictation."

"That is a very flattering offer and I want you to thank *The World* for the compliment, but I would rather not work tonight," said Mr. Clemens in his peculiar drawl.

"Why, there won't be any work about it," said the reporter. "This meeting will be something worth seeing. It will be the greatest thing of the kind that has happened during this [presidential] campaign and it will interest you mightily aside from the money consideration."

"Yes, but I hate to work when it is not necessary," replied Mr. Clemens. "I admire other people who are industrious, but I am the laziest man alive. I hate work. It would destroy all my pleasure at the meeting if I knew I had to do some work after it was over."

"The work will not take long. In thirty minutes after the meeting you can dictate all that you will care to say. Practically you will be getting $500 for thirty minutes' work."

"That is true, but I'm tired and sleepy and would rather go to bed and get some of the sleep I missed last night when I got back from Europe. You don't know how lazy I am and how much I dislike doing work of any kind. No, if you talked to me an hour it would not change my decision. I fully appreciate the compliment, but I only work when I have to."

136

"What Mr. Clemens Said," *Hartford Courant*, 26 October 1900, 10.

When Mr. Clemens was in the city to attend Mr. Warner's funeral this week he was seen by a *Courant* reporter and began at once to talk of Mr. Warner and his death.[1] He said:—

"This was expected any time this year or two, but it has carried with it a shock proportional to an altogether unexpected thing. We have had our warnings, and frequent warnings, that Warner must pass away. But no matter. When your telegram came the other night, it smote me just as if I was not thinking of such a possibility. I kept it from the family until next morning so that they might sleep. I told the mother the first thing in the morning, but we kept it from the children as long as we could. They only learned it in the evening by accident. Going up on the elevated late in the afternoon somebody spoke to me and I said, 'Yes; it's a staggering blow to us all,' and before I thought I had uttered Warner's name. My daughter asked me 'What is it, papa?' I had said enough to start the inquiry. The children, as little things, were pets of the Warners, and Warner himself was always to them 'Cousin Charley' and Mrs. Warner 'Cousin Susie,' and this had made a sad time for them all.

"It brings back the Monday Evening Club to me afresh and I can see all those men as they were in those days talking upon all subjects and regulating the affairs of this planet—Warner, Robinson, Judge Pardee, Hammond Trumbull, the elder Hamersley, Dr. Bushnell, Dr. Wright, Dr. Burton, Dr. Wainwright, and the rest.[2] It amounts to this, that the Monday Club is assembling in the cemetery. That is our honorary membership and we are all taking our places in that procession and arriving one by one. The club life and the Saturday afternoon walks through the autumnal tints, and the constant communion back and forth between Warner's home and mine were things that made the intimacy very close and of the daily sort. And, although we have been away so many years and that intimacy in the bodily presence has been so long interrupted, this death affects us as would the death of a member of the family who had been living in another state. He was a beautiful spirit and a gracious presence, but I don't need to say what Warner was. Everybody knew his lovable character and how much he was to all the country, high and low, rich and poor."

Mr. Clemens suddenly recognized that he was being interviewed and said he had told the reporters when he arrived at New York that they might question him all they wanted for twenty-four hours and then he was through. "But today," he said, "I am in Hartford. When I return to New York I shall resume my silence and this silence is not for my benefit but for the benefit of the general public. I don't wish to destroy my welcome with my tongue."

Asked what were his plans Mr. Clemens said: "I am arranging to spend the winter in New York if I can find a furnished house that will not bankrupt us. Beyond that we have no plans. But we have the hope that we can then come to Hartford and live in our own home among the friends whom we have reared from their childhood to their old age, and have reared them properly and on lines which make them fit society for the elect."

"It is a surprise to see you looking so youthfully fresh and robust," said the reporter. "It was reported, last year, that you were a shadow."

"It was true," said Mr. Clemens, "but I am in sound health, now. I had an eight years' persistent dispute with dyspepsia, but got rid of it last January by adding plasmon to my other food, and have had no return of it since.³ Plasmon is a food; it is pure albumin extracted from milk, and was discovered by Siebold, the chemist, in Vienna, when I was there two or three years ago.⁴ I did not eat it for indigestion, but for nourishment, and because it was cheap. In Europe the dyspeptics are aware, now, that it cures without the help of medicine, and so [are] the physicians, but they did not know it then. The *Lancet* and the other medical journals informed them. I ordered it from the druggist here. In Europe, from the grocer or the baker.

"But tell me about politics. Is the vote going to be close here?"

"The politicians say not in this state," said the reporter.

"Then I shan't come up to vote. If I could tip the scale I should like that distinction and would exploit it, but to swell a majority or a minority isn't a patriotic necessity when a person is hard driven by other stress upon his time."

Notes to Interview 136

1. See n. 2 to interview 28.
2. The Monday Evening Club of Hartford, founded in January 1869, met twice a month between October and May. MT was elected a member in February 1873. Henry C. Robinson (d. 1900), a prominent Hartford attorney and former governor of Connecticut. Dwight Whitfield Pardee (1822-93), associate justice of the Connecticut Supreme Court from 1874 to 1889. James Hammond Trumbull (1821-97), Hartford philologist. William Hamersley (1828-1920), state attorney for Superior Court of Connecticut. Horace Bushnell (1802-76), American theologian. George Frederick Wright (1828-81), Hartford artist. Nathaniel J. Burton (1824-87), Congregational minister. W. A. M. Wainwright (1844-94), Hartford physician.
3. Plasmon was a food supplement of powdered skim milk.
4. Siebold patented his invention under the name "Plasmon-Milch-Eiweiss."

137

"A Day with Mark Twain / Funniest Man in the World / Pictorially Told by Vivid Snap Shots at America's Famous Humorist," *New York Journal and Advertiser*, 11 November 1900, magazine supplement, 18; rpt. "How Mark Twain Cheered Up the Prisoners at Pretoria," *San Francisco Examiner*, 25 November 1900, magazine supplement, 7.

Mark Twain disapproves of interviews, but in his talk with a correspondent the other day he said some things that were as interesting and full as a nut is of meat of the unique quick wit of the author of *Tom Sawyer* and *Huckleberry Finn*.

To everyone who tries to interview him, Mark Twain explains why he objects.

If the impression he intends to convey is as various as the reports of it set forth by his interpreters, he is armed against them cap-a-pie.

That, he explains, however, is striking evidence of his unfailing courtesy.

He maintained this reputation at 10 one morning last week.

"The coffee is freezing on the table," he said, "the bacon is getting hard and dry—"

His mustache drooped pathetically, his shoulder followed the same line; he was as apologetic as the reporter who begged him to return to the dining-room.

An hour later he explained himself. He did it slowly, with a melancholy drawl.

"I thought it all out on the Continent," he said. "I made up my mind that it wasn't good for me to scatter impressions broadcast. So I got the thing down to this basis: When I arrive at a place I will talk about my trip, etc. On the wharf or at a railroad station what I say goes out to the world as a quick impression, a flashlight. I'm not held responsible for it. Neither is the interpreter. It lives one day. That's long enough.

"But when it comes to a serious interview—I feel—er—as though I might be able to write my impressions as well as the reporter.

"And—er—make more money."

A little later Mr. Mark Twain gave painful evidence of his lack of enthusiasm for American newspapers.

"Now, Sunday morning," he said, in his slow drawl, "I wanted a paper to read while I was eating my breakfast. I am such a tremendously hearty eater that it takes me more than a week to eat enough to last me from breakfast to lunch time. I said so to the man at the news stand when he showed me an enormous stack of paper.

"'One copy!' he cried, and then, seeing I was green, added, 'costs 5 cents.'

"'Oh, I don't want the whole thing,' said I. 'It's too expensive, and besides, I haven't my carpetbag here to carry it in. Just give me a little installment of it that I can carry into the dining-room by myself. Let me pay for it in proportion. I guess about a cent's worth will do me today.'

"But actually he wouldn't do it!

"'Why not?' said I. Then, to persuade him, I added: 'If you're saving any particular part for someone else I don't care; I'm not particular. Give me anything; a little bit "off the top," the outside, the inside, or anything you've got handy.'

"Still he said he couldn't do it.

"The result was we couldn't strike a bargain and I couldn't read a Sunday paper."

Mark Twain's opinion of newspapers recalls the time when a reporter was sent to interview him as the leading author and striking example of the literary value of newspaper training, of which in his early manhood Mr. Twain had had a considerable amount.

He received the reporter with his customary politeness and elusiveness. The reporter, however, summoned all his wits and asked the question which was to point his article.

"Mr. Twain," he asked, "to what one thing, most of all, do you owe your marvelous success in literature?"

He waited for the humorist to answer "My newspaper training."

Instead Mr. Twain burst forth decisively:

"To the fact that when I was young and very ambitious, I lost my job."

"May I ask what was your job, Mr. Twain?" exclaimed the puzzled reporter.

"Certainly, sir, certainly," replied the humorist, with great suavity. "I was a reporter."

However, if Mr. Mark Twain doesn't care for our journalistic methods, he does approve of us in other ways.

On the train going to Hartford, he spied a water cooler and drinking from it he said:

"Ah, there is one of the great foundations of American health, wealth, and happiness. In no other country in the world do you find a water cooler on board every train, or indeed any train. Why? Because the people of other countries haven't found out yet that water is good to drink. They admit that for cleansing purposes it is a success, but for drinking—never. But in dear old America every car has its cooler. It doesn't matter if the water is clean or dirty, warm or cold; it is water, and when you're thirty, it tastes good.

"Now, ordinarily, very few intelligent, hard-headed businessmen with a keen understanding of the value of money would think of preferring a cup of muddy water to a ten dollar gold piece. But you put a man on a little raft in mid-ocean for a day or two with nothing to eat, and see how quick he would take that water instead of the money if he had his choice."

During the first week after his arrival in America, Mr. Mark Twain rejoiced over the weather.

"I always bring either sunshine or rain or pestilence, plague or famine wherever I go," he said cheerfully.

As part palliation for not being willing to be interviewed, Mr. Mark Twain kindly consented to be snapshoted. The photographer caught him, as he has here set forth, having his shoes blacked, and talking with his wife and his friend Major Pond.[1] The humorist has refused to be interviewed, but he couldn't be forever silent. He made remarks with absolute gravity, never as though he was saying anything that would in the least bear repetition.

On one occasion he said, lugubriously: "I hope I'll get to be such an old story soon that the photographers will leave me alone."

"Oh, that's only one of the little annoyances of fame," answered his companion.

"Yes," he replied, "there are always more or less drawbacks to fame, as the man said when the sheriff was chasing him."

On one or two occasions the humorist became interested in the photographer's work and examined it keenly. He paused before one which showed only half of him.

"Well," he said to the photographer, "you didn't miss me altogether, as the sheriff of the jail at Pretoria did. I visited there and tried to cheer up the prisoners by telling them that if they weren't in that jail they'd probably be in some other. I told them they ought to be thankful that they didn't have to worry about where their next meal was coming from—as I did.

"The sheriff liked me so well he wanted to keep me for a year or two, but I told him that I had promised to patronize home industries when I needed any jails.

"He said he was sorry, for he'd rather have me for a prisoner since he had heard me lecture than anyone he knew."

It was on his first visit to the Pretoria jail, to see the Johannesburg reformers, that Mark Twain said it had been the dream of his life to get into jail, but misfortune dogged his footsteps. Whenever he had committed anything it always happened that no witnesses were around, and he never had sufficient reputation for veracity to get himself convicted without corroborative evidence.

"There is no place on earth," he said, "where a man could get such uninterrupted quiet as in jail. *Pilgrim's Progress* would never have been written if Bunyan had not been in jail, and Cervantes was privileged to suffer in durance vile, and thus enabled to write *Don Quixote*. These two roamed about on the wings of imagination describing perils and enjoying the intoxicating delights of war without personal danger."

Mark Twain ended by telling the prisoners that the insidious charms of jail would increase the longer they remained in jail. He said he felt this so strongly that he meant to ask Oom Paul to extend their sentences.[2]

He had said a few days before that he was the laziest man in the world, with a supreme contempt for the almighty dollar except in the case of necessity. Up to a certain point he seemed to be the most indifferent. The photographer gently urged him to pose. He looked frightened to death.

"I?" he cried. "I? Don't ask me—I wouldn't have the nerve."

He looked so frightened that the subject was changed to catch him unawares.

He was asked if he was an enthusiast about golf.

"Well, no, I can't say I am," he answered. "I saw part of a game once about thirty years ago. But I have forgotten some of the fine points since."

Notes to Interview 137

1. See n. 1 to interview 25.
2. See n. 17 to interview 133.

138

"Sure Mark Twain's in a Crooked Game," *New York World,* 12 November 1900, 12.

Mark Twain has left the Hotel Earlington and has taken a house at No. 14 West Tenth street. The clerk at the Earlington got the impression that the house was No. 14 East Tenth street, and there's trouble.

"It does not make much difference to me whether it is East or West," says Mr. Clemens, "but it seems that it does to the housekeeper at No. 14 East Tenth street."

This housekeeper is a blue-eyed, large-faced woman, with a deep voice. The owner of the house is Ambrose Henry, member of an old New York family, and a well-known Wall street banker and broker.[1] The Henry family is still at Tuxedo, and Mr. Henry goes to No. 14 East Tenth street only about once in two weeks. So he has not heard of the terrible doings at his New York home.

"In the last three weeks more than fifty people have called here and asked if a Mr. Mark Twain lived here," the housekeeper told a *World* reporter yesterday. There seem to be two men going around telling that they live here. One is this Mr. Mark Twain—whoever he may be—and the other is a Mr. Clemens. People are calling here all the time and asking for them. And they have had letters come here, too.

"I give all the letters back to the mailman, and he takes them away. And then last week there was an order of cabbage and vegetables and groceries left here. The delivery man said they were for Mark Twain. I told him no Mark Twain lived here. He looked at me so funny! I bet there is something queer about that lot, Clemens and Twain."

When Mark Twain was told of the perplexity of the good woman he laughed all over.

"Hurrah for Mrs. Faithful!" he said. "She is a jewel, and my friend Ambrose Henry is lucky to have such a good housekeeper. And how refreshing it is to know that she never heard of me. I begin to feel like a respectable citizen again. Fifty people asked for me at her door? No wonder that she thought that Clemens and Twain were trying some crooked game.

"But say, don't print a word of what I have said. It is my trade to gabble, and if I talk to reporters for nothing where's my bread and butter coming in? I will not say a word to a paper unless they pay me. Why, I could peter myself out in two months by talking against a reporter's pencil so that I couldn't sell a thing.

"Ideas are worth money, young man. If you have got one, hang on to it till you can sell it. Don't give it away. Conserve your energies and turn your ideas into gold. But don't come stealing mine. This world is mighty hard and grasping and suspicious—just notice that housekeeper now. You want to make everything you do count."

"How did you happen to miss the hour of that dinner at the Lotos Club the other night?" he was asked.[2]

"Didn't miss it. I was just gabbling. The house was full of visitors, and when I looked at my watch to see if it was time to go to the Lotos Club, why I mistook the hour, as any one might. If I hadn't been talking for nothing with a lot of friends here I shouldn't have mistaken the hours on the face of my watch."

Notes to Interview 138

1. Ambrose Henry (1863–1939), a prominent New York stockbroker.
2. The Lotos Club was a New York literary club founded in 1870. MT once referred to it as "the ace of clubs." See also Fatout, 265.

139

"'This Beats Croquet,' Said Mark Twain at Football Game," *New York World*, 18 November 1900, 3.

Mark Twain, as the guest of Laurence Hutton, the writer, was an interested spectator of the Yale-Princeton football game.[1] Mr. Clemens left Friday afternoon for Princeton and was driven immediately to Mr. Hutton's residence. He held an informal reception there during Friday evening.

Just before 2 o'clock yesterday afternoon Mr. Clemens, Mr. Hutton, and several Princeton professors were driven to the football field. Some Princetonians in the crowd recognized Mark Twain and he was the recipient of several long-drawn out "Sis-boom-ahs" as he climbed up the seats of the east stand. This was the stand where the Princeton singing societies were congregated. They were gathered near the northern end of the stand, and the mighty volume of sound they put forth seemed to delight Mr. Clemens, who smiled at their enthusiasm.

Mr. Clemens wore a huge yellow chrysanthemum in the left lapel of his long black overcoat. This tribute to the college was appreciated by the students nearby, who throughout the game gave an occasional "tiger" [or roar] for "Mark Twain."

Mr. Clemens appeared deeply interested in the contest. It was the first college football game he had ever witnessed. He asked many questions of his friend Mr. Hutton and of others nearby concerning the plays and the players. He quickly mastered the main principles of the game and easily detected the superiority of the team from New Haven.

In the early part of the contest, when Princeton surprised her admirers by the strong resistance she put up, Mr. Clemens cheered lustily in unison with the other rooters for Old Nassau. He looked gloomy and sympathetic when Gould made an easy touchdown for Yale soon after the game began. But when Mattis shortly thereafter dropped a pretty goal from the field Mr. Clemens laughed loudly, clapped his hands, and exclaimed: "That's good! That's good! Perhaps Princeton will win after all."

When the first half closed with the figures standing 11 for Yale and 5 for Princeton, Mr. Clemens was one of the most eager of the mathematicians figuring how Princeton might yet pull the game out of the fire. After the ten minutes' intermission were up, Yale's giants came lumbering on the field for the second half, and Mr. Clemens, who had been standing up and stamping his feet to keep warm, sat down again with a broad grin of anticipatory joy.

"Here's where Princeton gets even!" he remarked jovially to his friends. But Princeton didn't get even.

As the second half progressed and Yale's big fellows ripped the light Princeton line to pieces for long gains Mr. Clemens' face was a study. He apparently was a sincere adherent of Princeton, yet he could not refrain from making remarks complimentary to the physique of the Yale eleven.

When the gigantic Perry Hale and the huge and gritty Gordon Brown,[2] the captain of the blues, or the almost equally stalwart Stillman slammed into the Tigers, bowling them over on all sides, Mr. Clemens made such remarks as:

"I should think they'd break every bone they ever had!"

"Those Yale men must be made of granite, like the rocks of Connecticut!"

"Those young Elis are too beefy and brawny for the Tigers!"

"Well, say, this beats croquet. There more go about it!"

"That Yale team could lick a Spanish army!"

"The country is safe when its young men show such pluck and determination as are here in evidence today."

The eighteen thousand cheering people were a revelation to Mr. Clemens. As the Tigers were trawled deeper and deeper in the mire, when the score was standing 29 to 5 against them, toward the very close, the cheering clubs gave a grand exhibition of the "never say die" spirit for which Princeton has always been famous. Without letup they sang all the songs in their repertoire with a vim and an energy that were inspiring, and waved the yellow and black flags on high.

Yale might beat their football team, but the pluck of the Princeton men was undaunted. It was this feature which particularly impressed itself upon Mr. Clemens. He said, after the game, that the contest was one of the events of his life, and that he was proud to have been present at a game where Princeton men made such a splendid exhibition of spirit. He said he was proud of Yale, too, for Yale is in his State. He spoke of the splendid courage displayed by all of the Yale men, particularly Brown, who repeatedly hurled himself at formations and broke them up in a manner that overwhelmed the lighter Jerseymen.

Mr. Clemens said he was sorry football, as it was played today, was not in vogue during his schooldays, as he believed he would have liked to play it. He gave it as his opinion that it was the grandest game ever invented for boys—one which showed all their best qualities to advantage, and a game that must necessarily build up the mind as well as the body.

The sport made such a favorable impression on Mr. Clemens that he said he believed he would attend the Yale-Harvard contest at New Haven next Saturday. Mr. Clemens will return to New York today.

Notes to Interview 139

1. Laurence Hutton (1843-1904), American editor, author, and lecturer (1901-4) in English literature at Princeton University.
2. F. Gordon Brown Jr. (1879-1911), captain of the 1900 Yale football team, which won all twelve of its games and outscored its opponents 336 to 10. Brown was inducted into the College Football Hall of Fame in 1954.

140

"Mark Twain Bests a Grasping Cabman," *New York World,* 23 November 1900, 12.

Seriously, semi-tragically, the plaint of Mark Twain against the cabmen of New York was told to the Mayor's Chief Marshall at noon yesterday, and as a result Cabman William Beck now has no license.

In his role of reformer the humorist charged that the citizens of New York are criminals because they submit to extortion.

With Mark Twain came Kate Leary, who for eighteen years has been a maid in his family, and Sherman Everett, butler for the Clemens household, who did the detective work in locating the cabman after he had given a false number. Richard Watson Gilder also accompanied Mark Twain.[1] It was for Kate Leary, the maid, that the author made his protest. She sat by Mark Twain during the hearing. The Marshal did not question her, for it was apparent that she was badly frightened and on the point of bursting into tears at the most exciting points of the controversy between Mark Twain and Michael Byrne, who conducts the hack line to which William Beck, who overcharged the author, belongs.

Mark Twain, who is in mourning, wore black. He learned forward in his chair and began deliberately: "The salient features of the case are these: That this maid servant came to my study the evening of the 20th at 6 o'clock— along there some place—and said she had been brought from the Forty-second street station to my house, No. 14 West Tenth street, in this coupe, and that the driver required a dollar and a half for the service, and I went down to see about it, and he required the dollar and a half from me. I judged it to be an overcharge."[2]

Marshal David Roche called the attention of Mark Twain to the fact that the distance was thirty-four blocks, and that the legal charge for the hackman was only fifty cents a mile.

"I haven't finished yet," interrupted the author. "There is another charge. I inquired of him his number. Instead of exhibiting his number, he gave me a false one with his mouth. Those are my two charges."

The Marshal wished to know how Mark Twain ascertained the false number.

"I ascertained it," replied Mark Twain, "through my colored man who serves us.[3] I sent him down to the carriage to ascertain. I suspected when he did not show me his number that he was not telling the truth."

Marshal Roche asked the cabman to produce his license. When this was read Beck, the cabman, started in to make his defense. He said: "He engaged me from Grand Central Station down to No. 14 West Tenth street. I took the maid down there and thought I was entitled to $1.50, being as the ordinance reads that any conveyance that carries two persons is deemed as a carriage."

The Marshal scowled at the cabby. "It was an overcharge," he announced.

The cabby quailed and looked at Byrne—a strapping six-footer. Byrne doubled his fists and looked wickedly at the author.

"Well, Mr. Marcus—I mean Mr. Twain," said the cab owner, "you know that we are all more or less selfish and that a man driving for wages is trying to get all that he can. I admit that there was an overcharge of half a dollar but I got only one dollar."

"Well, he said you required him to pay $1.50," answered Mark Twain.[4]

Marshal Roche then delivered his sentence midway in the hearing.

"This man was required to exhibit his license and he failed to make his number known," said the Marshal. "It is against the ordinances and therefore we will have to suspend your license, my dear man, for this action. I will go further. I will hear out all the evidence and pay particular attention to this case."

Mark Twain smiled. It was the only time during the hearing that his deep seriousness left him.

W. Winston, Secretary of the Hack Owners' Association, took the floor to inform the Marshal and Mark Twain that he was glad the charges had been brought. He informed them that his organization intended to cleanse New York of corruption and extortion.

The hearing appeared to be finished. Mark Twain had reached under his chair for his silk hat.

"I don't think the case warranted this publicity," spoke up the cab owner.

"May I speak?" suddenly asked Mark Twain, turning to the Marshal. When an affirmative reply came the author settled back in his chair, closed his eyes as if he was soliloquizing, and said: "Now, my dear sir, this is not a matter of sentiment. It is mere practical business. You cannot imagine that I am making money wasting an hour or two of my time to prosecute a case in which I can have no personal interest whatever.

"I am doing this just as any citizen who is worthy of the name of citizen should do. He has no choice. He has a distinct duty. He is a non-classified policeman, and every citizen is a policeman and it is his duty to assist the police and the magistracy in every way he can and give his time if necessary to help uphold the law. Now if nobody comes forward you have this result:

"Here is a man who is a perfectly natural product of an infamous system in this city. It is a charge upon the lax patriotism in this New York that this thing can exist. You have encouraged him in every way and allowed him to overcharge. No fault has been found with him. He is not the criminal here at all. The criminal is the citizens of New York and the absence of patriotism. They ought to be ashamed of themselves to allow such a state as this to grow up; and if they allow, it will continue forever.

"I am not here to avenge myself on him. I have no quarrel with him. My quarrel is with the citizens of New York that have encouraged overcharging in this way.[5]

"Now you say it is not necessary that there should be publicity. In church and state and everywhere always the defense of a man with a weak case is to conceal.

"The only way to bring such things out and make them practical and give them force is to remove all concealment; make it a public offense when a citizen neglects his duty—when he should bring forward a charge.

"I believe that if the public knew how simple it is here to spend a few minutes and prove a case or lose it, they would do so. They don't appreciate that you take care of these things. If they knew that you were here always ready to carry out the law, more complaints, I am sure, would come to this office."⁶

Byrne, the cab owner, said: "We are, to a large degree, liable for the men in our employ who make these overcharges. In every part of the city these corporations, like railroads, get the best of special privileges. We have to compete with this unfair competition. You may think we are making lots of money, and we probably would if we could overcharge, but we cannot. Of course, sometimes these cabmen have to stand in one place a long time; then they want to make up for this loss of time. He reduced your fare to a dollar and a quarter, you say?"

"I paid only a dollar," answered the author gruffly.

The cab owner took a step forward. Mark Twain straightened in his chair.

"There are two sides to a question," said the cab owner.

"There is only one side to a moral question," answered Mark Twain. "A legal question is a moral one. There are not two sides to a moral question."

The voice of the humorist was loud.

"Years and years ago," he continued, "when I am sure there was nothing of the outside competition that you speak of, you created it yourselves by your extortionate charges. I took a hack at the ferry of the Delaware and Lackawanna Railroad a good many years ago, when I went to the Gilsey House.⁷ I had a hand satchel with me, and the driver's charge was $3—probably more than he was entitled to charge. He insisted upon it. I didn't ask for the tariff charge. I sent for the proprietor of the Gilsey, expecting him to take my side, which he didn't do, and I never saw any hotel proprietor in the world that would take your side, for the hackman brings in custom to him. The proprietor advised me to drop the case there. I said, 'I will take it into the police court.'

"He said, 'You will be flung out like that' (with a wave of the arm). I presume he was right. I did not prosecute that case then, but now I will prosecute every case that comes to my notice, at any time or any place.

"This charging of extortionate rates caused the formation of the Pennsylvania hack service and the New York Central hack service, and after a time there will be no room at all for other hackmen."⁸

"There is more back of this case," said the cab owner.

"What?" asked Marshal Roche.

"Well, if they get all the special privileges we must do something," said Byrne. "Why don't they give us some of the business those other people get?"

Mark Twain bristled up. His eyes flashed. "The pirate can make that argument," he interjected.

This caused laughter. The cab owner did not take it as a joke. His face became livid.

"You have been repeating parrot talk yourself," he exclaimed.

10. Katy Leary in Jean Clemens's room at Twenty-one Fifth Avenue in January 1905. Courtesy of the Mark Twain Project, University of California, Berkeley.

Mark Twain did not notice that "pirate" had been twisted into "parrot."[9]

Marshal Roche was hammering on his desk for order. Several policemen who were outside edged in toward the room.

"Well, it's all over," said Mark Twain to the maid. "Let's go home."[10]

He left by the side entrance to the City Hall with Mr. Gilder and Kate Leary, the servant.

Notes to Interview 140

I have supplemented this interview as reported in the *New York World* with versions of Twain's comments published in other newspapers. All newspaper citations below are from 23 November 1900.

1. Catherine (Katy) Leary (1856–1934) worked for the Clemens family from 1880 until after MT's death in 1910. Richard Watson Gilder (1844–1909), poet and editor of *Century*.

2. "Mark Twain Is Avenged," *New York Times*, 7: "The maid servant came into my study on the evening of November 20 and said that she had been driven by this cabman from the Grand Central Station to my house, at 14 West Tenth Street. The hackman demanded $1.50 for that service. I went down to see him, and he also asked $1.50 of me."

"Plaintiff, Mark Twain," *New York Sun*, 5: "The salient points in this matter are these.... This maid-servant came into my study on the evening of the 20th and said that this cabman wanted to charge her $1.50 for driving from the Grand Central Station to my house, No. 14 West Tenth street. I went down to see the cabman. He insisted on his charge."

"Mark Twain's Wit Is Cabby's Woe," *New York Herald*, 4: "The salient features . . .

are these:—A maid servant of mine came to my study on the evening of November 20, at six o'clock, saying that she had been brought in a cab from the Grand Central Station, in Forty-second street, to my home, at No. 14 West Tenth street. She said that the driver required $1.50, which she thought was too much. I went to the door and he demanded the $1.50 from me."

3. *New York Times:* "I have not finished yet," said Mr. Clemens. "When I asked for his number he gave me a false one." "How did you learn the right one?" asked Marshal Roche. "Through my other witness."

New York Sun: "May I say something more? I have not yet done. . . . Well, I asked this man his number," continued Mr. Clemens, "and he gave me a false one." "How did you find that out?" asked the Marshal. "By my witness here, a colored man in my employ. I sent him out to get the right number. I thought it very likely the cabman might give a false one."

New York Herald: "That is not all that I have to say. . . . I judged that $1.50 was an overcharge, and I required the man's number of him. He gave me a false number."

4. *New York Sun:* "Now, may I ask the gentleman one question?" said Mr. Bryne. "Now, you will admit," he continued, addressing the complainant, "that we must get what we can?" "I inferred as much from the charge this man made," replied Mr. Clemens in a slow melancholy tone.

"The Humorous Cab Owner," *New York Tribune,* 9: "Now, Mr. Clemens," said Mr. Bryne, . . . "we are all more or less selfish, and are looking for all the money we can get." "Yes, it looks very much like it," said Mr. Clemens.

New York Herald: "Mr. Twain," said Bryne, . . . "you are a man of common sense. You know that we are all human. We are all selfish, and cabmen want to get all they can." "It does look like it," rejoined Mr. Clemens.

5. *New York Times:* "This is not a matter of sentiment, my dear Sir. It is simply practical business. I am doing this, just as any citizen who is worthy of the name of a citizen should do. He has a distinct duty. He is a non-classified policeman. It is his duty to aid the police and magistracy. Here is a man who is a perfectly natural product of an infamous system. It is a charge on the lax patriotism in this City of New York that this thing can exist. You have encouraged him in every way you know how to overcharge. He is not the criminal here at all. The criminal is the citizen of New York and the absence of patriotism. I am not here to avenge myself on him. My quarrel is with the citizens of New York who have encouraged him. I should not be excused for failing to bring a charge against a man who assaults me with a club to rob me. If this man attempts to rob me without a club, then why should I refrain from making the charge?"

New York Sun: "Well, I think we might have got along without so much publicity in this matter," continued Mr. Byrne. "Publicity!" retorted Mr. Clemens with animation. "Why, in Church and State and everywhere else, the only defense of a weak cause is secrecy. If I am clubbed and robbed in the street and I say that maybe the man needed the money and make no complaint, is that acting the part of a good citizen? Here this man comes without a club and tries to rob me. I would be as bad a citizen if I did not complain as I would if I kept quiet about being clubbed and robbed. Now, I have no feeling against this man. I have no quarrel with him. My quarrel is with the condition of society that makes him possible. The New York public are responsible for such men as he. They submit to the extortions and encourage them by their submission. Every good citizen is a private policeman. It is his duty to assist and cooperate with the authorities in sustaining the law and in bringing violators of the law to justice. I am here in no other capacity than that. I am not seeking any revenge. I simply am here as a good citizen trying to do my duty to society as such. . . . I blame the public for encouraging your practices and for creating just the condition which makes extortions possible."

New York Herald: "May I speak?" asked the humorist, solemnly. . . . My dear sir, . . . I see no reason why this matter should not be public. You cannot imagine that I may make any money coming down here. It is a case in which I have no personal interest. I am doing this simply as a citizen. A citizen worthy of the name has no choice in such a matter. He is an unclassified policeman. It is his duty to make complaint when he sees a violation of the law. He should give his time to the enforcement of the law. Here is a man who is a perfectly natural product of an infamous system. These cabmen are encouraged to overcharge. They will continue to do so if the citizens of New York submit to such extortion. I do not come here to avenge myself on this man. Not he, but the citizens of New York who created him should be prosecuted. You say that you do not wish publicity in this thing. That is always the defense of a man with a weak cause. If I am beaten and robbed in the street, should I be excused from making a complaint, even if in so doing I risk my life? A man comes without any club and proposes to rob me. Why should I not prosecute him and the city of New York as well?"

New York Tribune: "I do not see any reason why it should not be public. I come here as any other citizen should who is worthy of the name. Every citizen is an unclassified policeman. Every citizen should give time to the enforcement of the law. Here is a man who is a perfectly natural product of our infamous system. These cabmen are encouraged to overcharge. The public submits to it. I am not here for the purpose of avenging myself. Not to want publicity is always the defense of men with weak causes. They always have something to conceal. If I were clubbed in the street and robbed, should I be excused from making a complaint, even though I might do so at the risk of my life? Now, a man comes to me without any club and proposes to rob me. Why should I not prosecute him and the city of New York at the same time?"

6. *New York Times:* "It seems to me that if the people only knew how easy it would be to come here and receive consideration at this official's hands, if they only knew your stand, Mr. Marshal, they would feel more at liberty to present their grievances to you."

New York Herald: "If the public only knew. . . . They may think that you do not receive these things pleasantly."

7. The Gilsey House was a fashionable hotel at the corner of Broadway and West Twenty-ninth Street in New York.

8. *New York Sun:* "Well, why don't you look into the other side of the case, then?" said Mr. Bryne. "There are two sides to every story. Now competition is such that we cannot go a block without running into some sort of a combination that we have to run against. We have to stand for hours in a place and not get a fare, and when we do get one we try to make him pay for the lost time." "Now, you ought not to come into a place like this with such a confession as that," said Mr. Clemens mildly; "that's the whole case. And that competition you speak of, it is you who are responsible for it. I remember years and years ago I came to the ferry from over the Delaware and

Lackawanna road. There wasn't any competition then. A cabman charged me $3 for driving me to the Gilsey House. I spoke to the landlord about it. I had not much faith that the landlord would take my side. Landlords never do. They take the side of the cabman. The cabmen bring them business. Well, the landlord of the Gilsey House took the cabman's side in this case. I was inclined to go to court with it. But he told me I would not have a ghost of a chance, so I let it drop. It's you," repeated Mr. Clemens, "who are responsible for the competition you complain of. You charge extortionate prices and the people try in every way to get out of your clutches. They build elevated roads and tunnels and trolleys, and then there is the Pennsylvania Cab Company and the New York Central Cab Company, and there won't be anything left of you after a while." . . . "You said the proprietor of the Gilsey House sided with a cabman that overcharged you. Now, I know the proprietor and I know he did not do it." "You impeach my word?" "Yes, I do," retorted Mr. Bryne hotly. "Oh, well, I suppose I can stand that. But I don't think you are in a position to impeach anybody or anything after your confessions here today."

New York Tribune: Mr. Clemens replied, "This is a moral question, and there cannot be two sides to a moral question. You brought all this upon yourselves by these double and these treble charges—the surface roads, the overhead roads, the Pennsylvania cab service, the New York Central cab service. Keep it up and there won't be a living left for any cabman in New York."

New York Herald: "Hotel proprietors always do [take the side of the cabman]," continued Mr. Clemens. "The cabman brings their patrons and takes them away. . . . You keep it up," said he, "and there will be no living for any hackman. . . . You impeach my word, sir?" "I do!" responded the cab owner. "That does not disconcert me," replied the author. "You have made confessions which put you out of court."

9. *New York Times:* "A pirate might advance that argument," said Mark Twain, with droll emphasis.

New York Sun: "We have to do the best we can," said Mr. Bryne, with some heat. . . . "Why, a pirate might say that," interrupted Mr. Clemens, gently.

New York Herald: "Give us a chance to make a living," said Mr. Bryne. "Why should we not make a living as everybody else does?" "My dear sir," responded Mr. Clemens, "the pirate makes that same argument."

New York Tribune: "The pirate makes that argument," said Mr. Clemens.

10. *New York Times:* Mr. Clemens tipped his hat and said: "Good afternoon, Mr. Marshal."

141

"Mark Twain on Hazing," *New York Times*, 20 January 1901, 1.

Washington, Jan. 19—Mark Twain, in an interview today, spoke about hazing at West Point, and denounced the practice as a brutal one and the men who indulge in it as bullies and cowards. "Why," he said, "the fourth class man who is compelled to fight a man from the first class hasn't a show in the world, and it is not intended that he should. I have read the rules provided to prevent such practices, and they are wholly deficient, because one provision is omitted. I would make it the duty of a cadet to report to the authorities any case of hazing which came to his notice; make such reports a part of the vaunted West Point 'code of honor' and the beating of young boys by upper class men will be stopped.

"I am not opposed to fights among boys as a general thing. If they are conducted in a spirit of fairness, I think it makes boys manly, but I do oppose compelling a little fellow to fight some man big enough to whip two of him. When I was a boy, going to school down in the Mississippi Valley, we used to have our fights, and I remember one occasion on which I got soundly trounced, but we always matched boys as nearly of a size as possible, and there was none of the cowardly methods that seem to prevail at West Point."

142

Pendennis,[1] "Mark Twain Bearded in His New York Den by a Camera Fiend," *New York Herald*, 20 January 1901, sec. 5, 3.

Mark Twain in his study, a brown study, can be a very serious man. There is about him a calm, benevolent dignity, a practical belligerence toward those misguided human beings who have everything to get, as it were. He feels a parental sympathy tempered with a judicial tendency for the depravities of human nature.

He approaches each phase of human weakness with an earnest, kindly care that explains the world wide affection his books have gained for him.

When I talked with him the local atmosphere of New York city was dark with depraved conditions. The shadow that had threatened the decencies of life for so many years in this city had but just been illumined by indignant men and women.

The night before Mark Twain had stood up with Bishop Potter in defense of clean politics.[2]

It was quite understood that he was not to be interviewed in New York. Mark Twain is a disciplinarian; he subdues all difficulties with fixed iron-bound rules.

For the first twenty-four hours that he arrives in a new city he receives everybody, and will talk to every one who asks for an opinion; after that, as he himself puts it, "Never again, in that city, forever and ever."

This fact was emphatically impressed upon me by the author in the hushed atmosphere of his study.

Mark Twain's study has never been presented to the public eye before, nor has it ever been possible to secure so faithful a record of this author actually at work, until now. The special interest in these pictures is their faithful record of Mark Twain in a serious mood—Mark Twain, as he sits at his desk, conspiring against the evils of human nature.

Realizing that I was not supposed to obtain any opinions, I took a seat beside the desk, looked into the pleasant, cheerful countenance of a wood fire, and silently resigned my curiosity to the camera.

There it stood, on its three long legs, staring greedily at the great man, who silently ignored it with patient tolerance.

So we three sat in silence some five minutes, Mark Twain, Mark Camera, and myself. The room was very quiet, particularly suited to studious reverie. Somewhere beyond the door we heard the occasional rustle of a feather duster, a whispering voice, and far off, as far away as possible without going into the street, some one was practicing vocal music.

Slowly the author opened his letters with a paper knife and turned his correspondence inside out.

At last, moved by a sense of companionship, or a desire to share the literary musings of a quiet half hour, he leaned back in his chair, and, turning a closely written four page letter over and over, that no pen stroke of it should escape investigation, he spoke.

But, alas! it was in the forbidden city of New York, one of the cities where he would not be interviewed, "Never again, forever and ever."

While the artist has faithfully recorded a reminiscent study of Mark Twain as I saw him in his den in New York, the actual spoken thoughts of the man himself had been given me under bond of secrecy, as it were, the social seal of privacy stamped upon them.

"Is there no place where we can revive the memories of this half hour in vivid type?" I asked, as I was leaving.

He told me he was going to Boston on the 14th of the month, discovering that this would be his first trip there since his return from Europe.

I determined to make a geographical compromise, rather than lose a pen and ink sketch of Mark Twain in a serious mood.

So it was agreed that we should meet on the train at Worcester, and there resume the inspiration I had gathered from the author in his study. It so happened when I boarded the train that the author was looking over his mail and enjoying his latest pipe, patented in Ireland.

I turned my back upon the landscape as we sped by, watched the author attentively, and felt as if we were together in his study in New York, as we had been a few days ago.

"There's a strange thing," he said slowly, and read aloud portions of a letter. It was from the daughter of an old friend. She recalled having seen the celebrated author at her father's house when she was a little girl. She had been married since then and lost her father. Also, she had been unfortunate, and was in destitute circumstances. She possessed a painting by the animal painter, Beard,[3] which her father had purchased for $500.

Would Mark Twain buy it for $150?

Slowly and deliberately the author answered this communication aloud, addressing his correspondent with practical kindliness, as if she were there before him.

"Well! If I could buy a painting by a famous artist that was worth $500 when he was alive, I should certainly not pay a cent less for it after he was dead. It seems to me it ought to be worth more, since he has passed away. I remember seeing a picture of his of some bears. They were wonderful; the creatures were human beings in everything but their shapes."

Up went the value of Beard's picture, and a momentary resentment of reducing the value of this particular one showed itself in the author's countenance.

"Women are impractical in the face of trouble sometimes!" I suggested.

"Yes, they run to extremes both ways. They either ask you four times as much as a thing is worth, or not half enough. Of course I can't buy the picture, but I should think the Museum of Art ought to have it."

A reflective pause followed, in which the commercial instinct which is no small factor in Mark Twain's success crystallized.

"Of course, if the Museum of Art in New York can get this painting for $150 they won't pay any more for it.[4] As a corporation, it would be their duty to pay no more for it," argued the author, then, tempering his worldly reason with sympathy for the writer of this letter, he laid it aside, saying, "I will not send it to the Museum of Art. I'll see if I can't find some one who will pay full price because he knows it is worth it."

It was evident that if Mark Twain had not been gifted as a writer he would have been a successful business agent.

Two more letters were opened and laid aside with the faintest suspicion of a sigh.

"I can't do it. There isn't money enough in New York or Boston to go round."

He hadn't spoken to me, but had answered a condition of depravity in human nature that his letters had revealed.

"I suppose they can't help it; it's a dreadful habit, though."

"More requests for money?" I asked.

"Yes. I don't mind helping people I know; friends should depend on each other when the world doesn't treat them well, but no wonder the figures of Charity are made to look so haughty and stuck up in statues."

Mechanically he took a puff or two at his big pipe, and looking out of the window, surveyed human nature comfortably.

"We're all beggars, more or less, the whole lot of us. It is a depraved condition in all of us. One man, in good clothes, asks a favor, another asks for a quarter because he's hungry. I asked a man to give me the address of another man. He mailed it to me. I might just as well have found it out myself, but by begging I saved myself exertion and trouble.

"I remember a certain day in San Francisco, when, if I hadn't picked up a dime that I found lying in the street, I should have asked someone for a quarter. Only a matter of a few hours and I'd have been a beggar. That dime saved me, and I have never begged—never!"[5]

He was distinctly proud of this fact, not for his own strength of achievement, but for a fortunate escape from violation of his principle. A good deal of fun has been made of Mark Twain's endeavors to arouse New Yorkers to a sense of their rights of citizenship. His recent resentment of a cabman's attempted extortion was only a shade of the principle and uprightness that make the ideal American citizen.[6]

There is no one living in New York today who is more sanely equipped with an insight of the depravities in human nature than Mark Twain. His nature is so strong in its original simplicity that he bristles at the mere suggestion of an abuse as a cat will at the sight of a dog.

The Postmaster of New York city loomed up in the unpleasant guise of an autocrat to the author's vision.

"Why do we have to go down to the Post Office and present an official with a carefully revised edition of our family tree before we can get a registered letter?" asked Mark Twain, glancing at me, as if I were the Postmaster.

"Abominable!" I said, soothingly.

"I didn't do it. I refused to do it. I received a notice that a registered letter had got into the United States for me, from Europe, and a request to go down town and confide the secrets of my family history to prove that I was not attempting to defraud the authorities. I sent my colored boy down with a note and got the letter."[7]

"You were favored," I suggested.

"Why should I be? Why should the Postmaster break a rule that he considers necessary for the proper transaction of his official business for one man, and enforce it for others? Something wrong about the rule."

"Local tyranny," I suggested.

"No such trouble in Europe. A registered letter means important letter to the authorities over there, and they can't get it into your hands too quickly. Not only that, but you're not obliged to receive it if you don't want it. Nearly all begging letters abroad are sent by registered mail, so that you can't say you didn't receive them. I never accepted a registered letter unless the handwriting was familiar to me after awhile."

"Do they write begging letters in Europe?"

"Oceans of them. They have a habit of enclosing soiled and timeworn letters and documents of recommendation, signed by famous people who are not on earth to deny them. I used to leave them with the hall porter of the hotel, with a note thanking them for the opportunity afforded me of reading their testimonials, and stating that they could receive them intact from the hands of the porter."

I suggested that these letter writers made a mark of celebrated men, who had been poor themselves, relying on fellow sympathy and so on.

"All the professional beggars, or rather the men and women afflicted with the complaint, need are a name and address. They scan the newspapers for arrivals at the hotels, and labor diligently in this way to make a living."

He handed me a letter on which was printed the statement that the sender, having a "nice collection of autographs," would be quite willing to add Mark Twain's to the collection. A stamped envelope, addressed to Bloomington, Ill., completed the bargain so far as he was concerned.

"What gorgeous type," mused the author, grimly.

"There's another phase of human depravity, the organized autograph hunter. Now, I don't object to answering a letter if the writer will show me the common courtesy of using pen, ink and notepaper to address me, but when he goes to a printing machine, and seems to begrudge the time he must spend to write me personally, I don't feel compelled to answer him. I can't afford a printing press in my establishment to turn out my correspondence in colored inks, bound and folded automatically. I still have to use the primitive methods of correspondence. He's too rich for my blood," and he laid the letter aside.

"How often have you been photographed?" I asked, as I showed him the pictures taken in his den in New York.

"Twenty-three times in twenty-three minutes the day before yesterday," was the answer.[8]

"Harpers wanted to be sure to get something lifelike," explained Mark Twain. "I felt as a moving picture must feel going at full speed. It's wonderful how ugly we are sometimes, too, when we get a real, good, faithful likeness. No one would have believed a horse was such a homely acting animal till we got a picture of him in action.[9] It won't do for us to be too self-conscious in these snapshot days of inquiry. Now, I said a thing last night in a speech that I didn't mean to say. It just slipped out because I had been writing an article on the subject. I didn't intend to say it there."

It was in reference to the Presidential policy in the Philippines. I showed him the paragraph as reported in the daily papers.[10]

"There it is, sure enough. Now, I don't believe in saying a thing that is an opinion but once, in one way, at one time and in one place, and I did not intend to say it last night, though I have substantially written about it, fully."

"You do not approve of the policy of the administration in the Philippines?" I asked indifferently.[11]

"If we desire to become members of the international family let us enter it respectably, and not on the basis at present proposed in Manila. We find a whole heap of fault with the war in South Africa, and feel moved to hysterics for the sufferings of the Boers, yet we don't seem to feel so very sorry for the natives in the Philippines."

"Another phase of depravity," I suggested.

"That's it. Human nature is selfish, and it's only real noble for profit."

"Have you been to the opera?" I asked.

"Once; the other night." He spoke with the slow utterance of reserved thought and a little sadly, I thought.

"You don't like it?"

"Yes and no. I think opera is spoiled by attempting to combine instrumental and vocal effects. I love instrumental music and I love a good voice, but I don't like them together. It's too generous. I can't fully take it in. Either the instruments spoil the voice or the voice spoils the instruments."

He got up, restlessly shaking off discordant operatic memories, and picked up a book.

"Here's an illustration of what I mean. This is a Scotch story, sent to me by a lady who is the authoress, and when I began to read it, I found that she had got a man to tell the story for her. I expected to hear a simple Scotch tale from the lips of a charming woman and I get a duet, as it were, with a man. The surprise of finding so much more than I expected was a disappointment. And yet I approve of her idea in one way. You see, the story is all about an old lord, and as it required a very constant and intimate companionship with him to tell the story at all, it was absolutely necessary that a man should be employed by her to figure in her stead. She had a truly Scottish sense of the proprieties. It would have been quite improper for an authoress to tell so much about an old lord, except through another's lips."

I showed him one of the photographs taken at his desk.

"Now, if Mrs. Clemens had come in and seen that desk being photographed in this shape she would have been aghast at its apparent disorder. But that is not disorder. I know exactly where everything is, top and bottom, from a telegraph blank in its hiding place to a manuscript or a letter. What looks like disorder to some people is the best of order to others.

"My mother had the same disordered sense of order that I have. I might buy her reams and reams of the most magnificent note paper, blue, green, red, pale peacock, anything you like; it was no use. She never would write on anything but odd scraps. Many's the letter I've received from her written on uneven scraps of paper, different colors and qualities all bunched together in an envelope and unpaged. My mother's letters were as hard to understand as any problem book I ever read."

For the first time since we had been talking Mark Twain laughed at his loving reminiscence of her tender frailties.

Mark Twain is great because of his simplicity, his honesty and his intelligent antagonism to even the minor "depravities of human nature"—and his objection to being interviewed.

Notes to Interview 142

1. W. de Wagstaffe, aka Pendennis.
2. Henry Codman Potter (1835-1908), American Episcopal bishop.
3. The American painter William Holbrook Beard (1824-1900).
4. The Metropolitan Museum of Art in New York, founded in 1870, moved to its present location at Fifth Avenue and Eighty-second Street in 1880.
5. In chapter 59 of *Roughing It,* MT reminisces about a two-month period in San Francisco when he "had but one piece of money—a silver ten cent piece—and I held to it and would not spend it on any account." Later in the same chapter, he narrates the adventure of a "mendicant Blucher—I call him that for convenience," who "had been without a penny for two months" before he finds a silver dime in the street and worries how to spend it.
6. See interview 140.
7. Sherman Everett was MT's butler at the time.
8. Some 650 photographs of MT are known to exist.
9. MT refers to the motion studies of the pioneering photographer Eadweard Muybridge (1830-1904) who published serial images of a trotting horse in 1878.
10. See "Anti-Spoils Party Wanted," *New York Sun,* 5 January 1901, 2. On 4 January 1901, MT spoke at a meeting of the City Club of New York, an anti–Tammany Hall group dedicated to civic reform. Toward the close of his speech he commented on the recent presidential campaign: "I don't know anything about finances, and I never did, but I know some pretty shrewd financiers, and they told me that Mr. Bryan wasn't safe on any financial question. I said to myself then that it wouldn't do for me to vote for Bryan and I rather thought—I know now that McKinley wasn't just right on this Philippines question, and so I just didn't vote for anybody. I've got that vote yet and I've kept it clean, ready to deposit, at some other election. It wasn't cast for any wildcat financial theories and it wasn't cast to support the man who sends our boys as volunteers out into the Philippines to get shot down under a polluted flag." According to the *Sun,* "The statement about the President, his Philippines policy and the polluted flag was not received with enthusiasm" and the applause when MT sat down was "in marked contrast to that which he received when he got up." The next speaker, the author and editor St. Clair McKelway (1845-1915), chided MT for his remarks: "I cannot agree with him in his estimate of the able and dignified President of the United States and I cannot agree with him that our soldiers are fighting behind a dishonored musket and under a disgraced flag on the other side of the seas." McKelway's "sentiment was received with great applause" by the audience while MT on the dais "simply puffed away at a stub of his cigar." See also Fatout, 372.
11. See n. 4 to interview 132.

143

"Mark Twain, Expert on Trade Marks, Has Fun," *New York Journal and Advertiser,* 14 March 1901, 1.

"I hope you gentlemen will let me go soon," sighed Mark Twain, as he seated himself in United State Commissioner Shields' private office yesterday.[1] "I have a most important engagement." And the lovable humorist resignedly settled himself in a chair and looked unhappy.

Presumably Mr. Clemens was called as an expert on the copyright law and literary trademarks, with which he has had some sad experiences. Rudyard Kipling's suit against R. F. Fenno & Co., alleging infringement of copyright, was to be heard, and A. T. Gurlitz, Kipling's counsel, had called Mark Twain.[2]

Mr. Gurlitz began to question him about the trademarks used by Kipling's publishers.

"I object!" exclaimed Mr. Rives, counsel for Fenno & Co., and "'Bject!" "'Bject!" "'Bject!'" sounded after each of Mr. Gurlitz's questions.

"They don't seem to want me to talk at all," plaintively observed the man who wrote *The Innocents Abroad,* and he added, looking at the Commissioner, "I think I might smoke if I can't talk."

Mr. Shields, smiling, offered him a cigar. Mr. Clemens looked long and solemnly at the cigar, then at Mr. Gurlitz, then at Mr. Rives. Waving the cigar away from him, he said: "No, no. I guess I'd better not take it. They would ''bject,' I know. But"—regretfully—"it looks like a good cigar."[3]

"Oh, there will be no objection, Mr. Clemens," the lawyers declared.

Looking much relieved, Mark Twain slowly put on his steel rimmed spectacles, lit the cigar, learned back contentedly, puffed away, then exclaimed: "Now, go on, gentleman. I'm ready to meet all your objections."

"Have you written in your career?" asked Mr. Gurlitz.

Mr. Clemens seemed as surprised as if the thought of writing had never suggested itself to him. Recovering himself, he replied, with mock modesty:

"A few stories."[4]

Q. Do you consider that a book of stories of an author, published under a title selected by the author, can reasonably and generally be regarded as a book written by that author?

Mark Twain drew a deep sigh, as if to say, "That's a hard one."

"I should say yes. But it's no business of mine. I don't know whether that's a legal answer," he hastily added.

Q. Do you consider that a publisher, other than the one who originally published such a book, has any right to issue a similar volume of the same works?

"No, that wouldn't be square," answered the most entertaining of experts. "Nothing square about such a proceeding."[5]

"A manufacturer who put up soap, beer, whiskey"—Mr. Gurlitz began.

Mr. Clemens, most temperate of men, pretended to be delighted by the mention of whiskey and looked around as if he were athirst.

"Put up soap, beer, whiskey, under the label previously used by another manufacturer would be guilty of counterfeiting, too?" the lawyer finished his question.

"Yes, no difference between counterfeiting, be it whiskey or a book," Mr. Clemens replied.[6] "There's no substantial difference. I might be permitted, by the by"—this with much significance—"to explain why I think so. But you understand why."[7]

Mr. Rives cross-examined Mr. Twain, who didn't seem to mind it.

Q. You once brought a suit, did you not, in which your views as to the right of an author were expressed?

A. (yet more sadly) I did.

Q. The decision was adverse to your interests, was it not!

A. (despairingly) It certainly was.[8]

To Mr. Gurlitz, Mr. Clemens said he understood that, since his own suit, trademarks have become more valuable to authors. When his testimony was over Mr. Rives most politely said, to enable Mark Twain to keep his engagement, he would waive verification of his testimony nor need Mr. Clemens sign it.

"I will get Mr. Clemens to read it and make any needed corrections," suggested Mr. Gurlitz.

"You will have a hard time to get me to read it," retorted Mark Twain, gathering up his hat and coat.

"Don't you ever read your own productions?" laughed Mr. Rives.

The answer came like a flash, as Mark Twain hurried away: "Not when I can get a proofreader to do it."[9]

The hearing was adjourned for a week.

Notes to Interview 143

1. John A. Shields (1840–1914), U.S. commissioner for New York since 1869.

2. Augustus T. Gurlitz (d. 1928), Kipling's attorney. See also *The Letters of Rudyard Kipling*, ed. Thomas Pinney (Houndsmills: Palgrave, 1996), 3:49–50. Kipling sought an injunction against the New York publishers R. F. Fenno & Co. to prevent them from issuing a "Library Edition" and a "Pocket Edition" of his works. Kipling lost the suit, however, because none of the titles in the Fenno editions were covered by copyright.

3. "Mark Twain a Witness," *New York Times*, 14 March 1901, 3: "and it's too good a cigar to have to refuse."

4. *New York Times*: "Have you written in your career?" asked Mr. Gurlitz. "Oh, yes. A number of stories and the like." "Have you later collected the same and had them published in book form?" "Yes." "Give me some of the titles used by you." "Oh,

there were a number of them. I don't recall just this minute. The first, I guess, was *Sketches, Old and New, The White Elephant,* and—well, that's enough, isn't it?" MT refers to his collections *Sketches, Old and New* (1875) and *The Stolen White Elephant, Etc.* (1882).

    5. *New York Times:* "Consider," said Mr. Gurlitz, "a book of stories of an author, arranged and published under a title selected by an author. Do you consider that that could reasonably and generally be regarded as a book written by that author?" "I should say yes," replied Mr. Clemens, positively. "Do you consider that another publisher than the one bringing out such a book would have any right to issue a similar volume?" "What's that? Give me that again," said the witness, waving his hand about his head and blowing out a great cloud of smoke. The question was repeated. "No. That wouldn't be square. Nothing square about such things."

    6. *New York Times:* "It might be called—piracy," said the witness. "Would you call it counterfeiting a book?" "Yes, I think so—decidedly."

    7. *New York Times:* "Do you think it is an important thing for an author to preserve control and title of his books?" "I certainly do," replied Mr. Clemens positively. "I consider it very important."

    8. See interview 49 and n. 5 to that interview.

    9. *New York Times:* "You'll have a hard time getting me to read it," said Mr. Clemens. "Don't you ever read your own productions?" asked Mr. Rives. "Never, when I can get a proofreader to read it for me," was the rejoinder.

144

W. B. Northrop, "Mark Twain in the Woods," *New York World Sunday Magazine,* 21 July 1901, 1–2.

On the borders of Lake Saranac, in the heart of the Adirondack Mountains, Mark Twain has taken up his summer home. Far from the madding noises of New York, within the depths of a forest primeval, he lives the life of a recluse. The circle of his society is narrowed to the members of his own family, consisting of his wife and two grown daughters. He reads no daily papers. Even his mail is left stacked up and uncalled-for at the nearest post office. No one could take a vacation more seriously than does the world's greatest humorist.

    Though on the borders of a lake stocked with fish, the rod and reel possess for him no charms. Though employing an Adirondack guide, the pathless woods, the airy mountain-top, hold out for him no allurements. Seated in a little tent beside the borders of the lake, Mark Twain spends the largest portion of his time in work. Systematically, brooking few interruptions, he applies himself from four to seven hours a day. It was only after much persuasion, seconded by the kindly offices of Mrs. Clemens, that I obtained an interview with him and succeeded in taking photographs which accompany this article.

    On the south shore of Lake Saranac, literally buried in a deep forest of fir and pine trees, stands "The Lair," Mark Twain's cottage. Though the dictionary defines a lair as the couch of a wild beast, it is only in the sense of its seclusiveness and inaccessibility that the name is apposite as the dwelling-place of the famous author.

Dean Swift longed for

A house to entertain a friend,
A river at his garden's end,[1]

but Mark Twain has more than this. The beautiful sweep of a whole lake stretches out before him.

From the outside Mark Twain's house looks like a Swiss cottage, such as one sees perched on the side of the Alps near Lake Lucerne. The wood of which it is built is rough pine, the bark of the tree being left on the outside.

Within, the idea of rusticity is further emphasized by leaving the cross-beams of the ceiling covered with native bark. The upper portion of the doors and windows are finished in the same fashion. The high mantelpiece of the reception room is made of a huge pine log, with the bark left on, the upper surface being planed flat. The tables, chairs, and other furnishings are rustic, even down to the inkwell on the writing desk which stands in the northeast corner of the room.

So closely is the house surrounded by trees that the long branches protrude far across the verandas and look impudently in at the windows of the second story. The tops of the trees seem to lock arms above the roof, and when the wind blows the trunks rub against the eaves.

Save for the rippling of the waters of Lake Saranac or the sighing of the wind through the trees, there is nothing to disturb the profound quiet which reigns about "The Lair."

It was a sentimental unwillingness to break through the quietude that made me at first hesitate upon calling on Mark Twain in his Adirondack retreat. It seems almost a species of sacrilege for an outsider to enter the monastic nook in which he has buried himself.

After rowing up and down several times in front of "The Lair" I at last overcame my reluctance and grounded my canoe on the little boat landing which juts out into the lake a few rods to the left of the house.

A short walk over soft moss, strewn with pine needles, and I found myself on the veranda of "The Lair."

I was met at the door by Mrs. Clemens, a woman of sweet face and charming manner. She explained to me that her husband was very, very busy—that he had even neglected to send for his mail at the post office.

It was about 1 o'clock when I first called. Mrs. Clemens said it was one of his busiest hours. If I would return after 6 o'clock, she added, he would see me—perhaps. Deep shadows were creeping across the lake when I again made my way Lair-ward. Seated in a high-back cane chair on the veranda, in an easy position, with one leg crossed over the other, was Mark Twain. He wore a loose-fitting suit of grayish blue, a negligee shirt, low, turned-down collar, and wash tie. Comfortable slippers were on his feet. Floating on his mass of white hair, rather than fitting his head, was a flat-top Panama hat.

He arose to greet me as I approached and waved me to a seat beside him. The book he had been reading—Bismarck's autobiography[2]—he placed on a settee nearby.

I asked Mark Twain how he employed his time on his vacation. "I suppose you enjoy the deer and other hunting to be found in these parts?" I said.

"No," he replied, "I never hunt. I have never taken any pleasure in shooting down birds and animals."

"Of course, you go fishing?"

"No, I do not fish, either," he responded, with a smile.

Mark Twain then explained to me that his life in the Adirondacks was not one devoted to pleasure. He went there mainly for the purpose of working. "Quiet is essential to me in order to do satisfactory work."

Mark Twain then talked freely about books, Anglo-Americanism, incidents in his life at home and abroad, his private system of philosophy, answering my every question with open candor. He expressed a desire, however, not to be quoted on any of these subjects in the form of an extended interview.[3]

He said he had no objection to my describing his Adirondack life. With slight variation, here is Mark Twain's daily program at "The Lair." Rising between 7 and 8 in the morning, he dresses leisurely and breakfasts about 9. After breakfast he enjoys a cigar, either sitting on his veranda or strolling by the lake. At 10 o'clock promptly his working day begins.[4]

To the right of his house, about fifty feet away toward the lakeside, is a small tent. This tent is Mark Twain's literary camp. He works there regularly each day. The floor of the tent is covered with boards, which in front are extended outward toward the lake, forming a small platform, railed off at the end. The sole furniture of this tent is a high-back cane chair on the seat of which are a couple of cushions. Seated in this chair, which is placed either within the tent or on the little platform, Mark Twain produces each day the humorous phrases which make the whole world laugh.

Perhaps you think his humor is dashed off with little thought and that his sentences drop from the pen point as water flows from a fountain? Not so. No sentence ever leaves his hand without undergoing rigorous inspection. No word is used without first weighing its every import.

Mark Twain makes it a rule to write four hours each day. Four hours of writing may mean seven or eight hours of thought and meditation. So, after all, there is little time left for recreation when his self-imposed daily task is done.

After writing steadily from 10 in the morning until 2 in the afternoon, Mark Twain partakes of a luncheon in his house. The remainder of the day is devoted to reading and recreation.

His afternoons are varied according to circumstances. At one time he will patronize a hammock which swings between two trees far back in the woods. He explained to me that he had acquired the art of being able to remain in a hammock as long as he desired.

At other times, either accompanied by his daughters or alone, he will take a canoe trip on Lake Saranac. The canoes are as light as feathers and it takes scarcely any effort to propel them.

Very frequently his afternoon is spent with some favorite book by the lakeside. Here, sitting on some old moss-grown log, he will spend hour after hour, reading at times, at others gazing in reverie out over the waters of the lake. After his dinner at 6 o'clock he sits on his veranda till bedtime—about 10 o'clock.

For a literary man the life Mark Twain leads at his Lair is ideal.

It is difficult to imagine how one can work in so beautiful a place, where everything lulls to rest. The lapping of the waves on the shore and the moaning of the winds through the pines would enchant an ordinary mortal from all tasks, however exacting.

I asked Mr. Clemens if he would permit me to take photographs of him through the course of one of his typical days. He consented to this audacious request with a kindliness which I was far from expecting.

On the morning of July 6 at 9 o'clock I presented myself at "The Lair," camera in hand. It takes a courageous man to pose for an amateur photographer, and I almost feared Mark Twain would back down from his agreement. But he was once a Confederate soldier and knows no fear. He had not changed his mind.

Presently he seated himself in a chair on his veranda. With great simplicity and without any apparent effort he assumed the most natural of "poses," as the reader will, I think, admit on inspection of the photographs accompanying this article.

The deep shadows cast by the trees surrounding the house made necessary somewhat lengthy "time exposures" in order to obtain effective photographs. Mark Twain was patience itself, even permitting me to take again certain pictures in which I feared I had not obtained just the desired result.

From the house we then walked over to his workshop in the tent. Standing at the door of this tent, he paused a moment in a reflective attitude, which the camera was fortunate enough to catch.

The expression in this picture shows Mark Twain just as he would appear had he risen from his chair a moment and stepped to the door of the tent in order to think of a word or to formulate a nicely balanced sentence.

Very frequently, when his day's work is done, Mark Twain seats himself on a large rock near the lakeside and enjoys an hour or two of meditation while gazing out over the placid waters. It was my privilege to photograph him in this favorite haunt.

This particular spot is a veritable sylvan grotto. One would not be surprised to see elves and fairies flitting in and out among the branches of the trees which cluster thickly by the water. Moss-grown stumps of old trees, water-worn logs, bending boughs of leafy green and rocks over which the waters ever tumble make a picture of wondrous harmony. If Mark Twain is able to work at all in such a place it is singular that he does not produce inspired verse instead of humorous prose.

As canoeing forms part of his day on rare occasions, Mr. Clemens kindly consented to let me photograph him indulging in this pastime.

The day on which the picture was taken was a windy one, and the waters of the lake were rather tempestuous. Nevertheless, the venerable writer got into the frail Adirondack craft with the agility and alertness of youth, rowing out on the lake and keeping the boat quite steady, with its head to the waves.

When I had taken all the photographs I desired, Mr. Clemens said, "You have taken so many photographs of me that I intend telling Mrs. Clemens I let you photograph me climbing a tree. You may depend on it. I shall be roundly lectured for allowing myself to be photographed in so undignified a pose. The children will have to help me out in my little joke."

As I took my departure from "The Lair" I asked Mr. Clemens how he had discovered so ideal a spot. He said it was the result of a long search and added, pointing across the lake, "I came very near choosing a house way over there. But at the last moment, I discovered it was quite near neighboring houses. It is not well to be within caterwauling distances of another house if you desire absolute quiet.

"Yes, it is certainly very quiet here," he continued reflectively. "We have no excitement. We do not even read the daily papers. I take one paper—a weekly. It gets here about once every two weeks."

Notes to Interview 144

1. A slight misquotation from *Imitation of Horace* by Jonathan Swift (1667–1745): "A handsome house to lodge a friend, / A river at my garden's end."
2. Otto von Bismarck (1815–98), *Gedanken und Errinerungen* (1898), trans. *Bismarck, being the Reflections and Reminiscences of Otto, prince von Bismarck* (London: Smith and Elder, 1898; New York: Harper, 1899).

11. Rowing on Lower Lake Saranac, 6 July 1901. From W. B. Northrop's *With Pen and Camera* (London: Everett, 1904).

12. On the porch of "The Lair," Mark Twain's summer home in the Adirondacks, 6 July 1901. From W. B. Northrop's *With Pen and Camera* (London: Everett, 1904).

13. Musing by the shore of Lower Lake Saranac, 6 July 1901. From W. B. Northrop's *With Pen and Camera* (London: Everett, 1904).

3. Northrop, *With Pen and Camera* (London: Everett, 1904), 39: "I don't think I care to be interviewed," he began, "as I'm averse to that sort of thing. . . . You see, it's this way about interviews. . . . It is seldom you can say just what you wish said, and when it appears in print, it all looks so different from what you intended. Besides that, I'm under contract not to do any work save for one firm of publishers, and I do not know but a formal interview would look like an infringement of the contract. . . . However," he continued, noticing my disappointment, "if you wish to describe how I live up here and to take some photographs, I can see no objection to that."

4. Northrop, 39–40: "We'll go down in the woods, and I'll show you where I work. . . . Every morning about nine," he said, "I come to this tent and work. I write up to about two o'clock in the afternoon, and then I go to lunch. I usually turn out about two thousand words a day. I do not use a typewriter; nor can I dictate anything. I think I can best express myself with a pen. . . . You see," he continued, "I keep office hours with myself. I do this work every day, systematically, rain or shine; and I never let anything interrupt it, unless it is a little interview, perhaps, like yours," he added, reassuringly.

145

"Why Mark Twain Is for Seth Low," *New York Evening Post,* 8 October 1901, 3.

All of Mark Twain's doubts as to his eligibility to vote—he having recently taken up his abode in the Appleton homestead at Riverdale[1]—are now dispelled. The policeman who tramps periodically up and periodically down the roadway before the graystone manse dispelled these doubts. He was the first one to whom Mr. Clemens applied for enlightenment. He said: "Sure, you've got a vote," and Mr. Clemens, more than half convinced, sought legal counsel, which confirmed the dictum of the wayside sage. Moreover, Mr. Clemens is going to vote for Seth Low.[2]

But there is one thing he is not to be prevailed upon to do, that is to make any speeches during the campaign.[3] Several friends have urged him to take the stump, but Mr. Clemens declares he dreads speeches, particularly those he makes. However, Mr. Clemens says he intends doing all he can to further Mr. Low's election, according to his abilities at campaigning, which, and he wishes this clearly understood, do not include speechmaking.

Mr. Clemens, pipe in hand, in his study, in the Appleton homestead, surrounded by books, papers, letters, boxes of manuscript—the orderly confusion of a busy man of letters—was asked today as to his politics, his view of the coming campaign, and the intimation that he might take the stump for Mr. Low. He drew deeply upon his pipe for a moment, clouding himself in smoke, and said, after a prolonged pause: "First of all, I've learned that I have a vote. I've taken counsel of an expert in such matters, and he assures me I have a vote in Riverdale."

"For what reason did you doubt your eligibility?"

"Ignorance," Mr. Clemens replied. "Step up to a man and ask him if you can vote, telling him the circumstances of your residence, and he'll say to you, 'Yes, you've got a vote'; but he'll not be able to tell you why. That's why I pursued matters with the policeman who passes here every day. He asked me how long I'd lived here, where I'd lived before, and various other searching things, and then he said to me, 'Sure, you've got a vote.' He went a bit farther than the other people I've asked and told me that before election I would have lived here the legal time, and could vote as well as any man. And he's right, too. Really, I hadn't much doubt about the voting matter, but I wanted to be legal and proper above all things. My legal expert clinched matters for me."

"How will you vote, Mr. Clemens?"

He was striding up and down the big, sunny room. Once he stopped abruptly, put down his pipe, and said: "I shall vote the Low ticket. I am only interested in voting this ticket, what ever it may be. I'll vote for anything that opposes Tammany Hall. I'd rather have Mr. Low than Satan on the ticket, but I'd vote for Satan himself if he were on the Low ticket; indeed, I would." Here the walk was resumed as far as the corner of the worktable, when Mr. Clemens stopped long enough to pry open the lid of a cigar-box.

"I've known Mr. Low personally for seven years and I think he's one of the finest men I've ever met, but this voting of mine is not to be a matter of personalities. I'm going to vote against Tammany, and I'm glad it means voting for Mr. Low.

"Up to four years ago I thought as many another thought, that Tammany was unconquerable, but I'm bravely over that belief now. The showing that Mr. Low made in 1897 with the ticket split demonstrated what he could have done if there had been no split, and what he will do this year.[4] Tammany is not unconquerable, but it was this belief among the good people of this city that gave the organization all its strength. I know that I spent lots of time planning what might be done to overcome Tammany, but I had to give it up with the other incapables. You see, all of us were possessed of the idea that you couldn't beat Tammany, and that was where Tammany opened its sleeve and laughed heartily in it, which certainly was disconcerting, to say the very least. Yes, Tammany's strength has been in the stupidity of the other parties. But now, with the fine Low ticket, Tammany is going to be taught several things this year; you see if it isn't. The 1897 election demonstrated it."

"You do not intend to make any speeches this campaign?"

"No." The negative was determined. "I'll not speak, but I'll do all in my power for the success of the Low ticket; that is, all I can by the methods that are suited to my abilities. I dread a speech because if I do prepare one I never can remember it when the time comes for me to deliver it. For this reason when I get up I'm there without anything to say, or only with something that has occurred to me during the speech of the preceding orator. But that's bad; it isn't good speaking, as it leads a man to say foolish things that don't look well in print next day. Several persons have asked me to make a few speeches in the campaign, but I'll not do it."

A few minutes later, as Mr. Clemens was walking slowly across his great hallway and along the roadway to the rough steps that climb his encircling wall and give ingress and egress to his place, he said: "Have you ridden up Madison Avenue lately? Have you ever been able to tell where you were? Certainly not by any aid given you by the lampposts. They talk about sermons in stones, books in running brooks; what about lessons in lampposts? I tell you, the lampposts, those dilapidated, useless things in Madison Avenue, are a commentary on Tammany. Car conductors have far too much to do to tell people where they are; the lampposts should do it—and what do they do but blot the scene? A good, honest, thoughtful city government will remedy this grievance. It is only a small thing, perhaps, but when you add all the grievances, you have an array of mismanagement that is staggering."

At the over-the-wall steps Mr. Clemens paused and pointing to a tall chestnut tree, flanking his house, said: "As the small things are the commentaries, let me tell you of a squirrel that lives in that tree. He's as much of a commentary as the lampposts—only a good one. I saw the little fellow opening a burr this morning. I stood near him, and as he had his back to me he continually glanced over his shoulder to see what manner of man I might be. I did not move, and, finally the small animal carried the nut to the grass plot over there and buried it. Just before he covered it up he used his nose as a pile-driver, and, plump—plump—plump—packed the nut into the hole. Then he scraped the dirt over the place and patted it down. When quite satisfied with the job, he cocked one eye at me, just as if to say, 'You've seen where I put it, but I guess you're all right, so here goes!' and he sped up a neighboring tree.

"Now, that is just as much of a commentary as the lampposts. It tells one that the people who were here before me had humanity—were kind, gentle people. What do the useless lampposts tell me and you, and every one?" And Mr. Clemens put his cigar between his lips and went back to his house.

Notes to Interview 145

1. The American publisher William H. Appleton (1814-99) was the first in his family to own the house. See also Paine, 1141.

2. Seth Low (1850-1916), president of Columbia University, a reform candidate elected mayor in 1901, was defeated for reelection in 1903.

3. MT would introduce Low at a campaign rally on 29 October 1901.

4. Budd (1977), 99n58: "In 1897 Tammany had elected its candidate for mayor through a mere plurality because the Republicans ran their own candidate instead of endorsing Low, nominated by the Citizens' Union; also, the Henry George Democrats ran a candidate."

146

"Mark Twain Won't Be Stump Speaker," *New York Press*, 8 October 1901, 3.

For a few glad hours yesterday it was believed that Mark Twain would take the stump for Low. At the mere announcement staid citizens chuckled in expectancy and ordered their head clerks to watch carefully in the newspapers for the printing of Twain's campaign itinerary. Everybody knew that with the humorist afield—veiling sarcasms under that inimitable drawl of his—this would be the reverse of a dull fall.

Tammany heard the rumor, too, and at once there was a search among the faithful to find one who was Twain's equal in the shooting of arrows of wit. Maurice F. Holahan was suggested.[1] It was pointed out that his famous "hunting-the-wayward-son" story was one of the most humorous things in all literature. It was decided to enlist Mr. Holahan at once as an offset to Twain.

Still, more talent was needed. Somebody mentioned the name of the gentleman who used to sign himself "Tammany Tim."[2] A whole American Ice Company of frigidity was dumped on this proposition. It was pointed out that Mr. Croker,[3] to put it mildly, had been displeased with "Tammany Tim" since that chronicler, in another guise, had printed an interview that wasn't so.

"Nothing funny about that guy," growled one of the faithful.

It was decided that Commissioner Keller,[4] who, as "Chollie Knickerbocker" used to display a sprightly fancy, might be a good offset to the author of *The Innocents Abroad*. There the matter rested for the day.

If the worried wigwamites could have met Twain they would have realized that they were arming against a phantom foe. For Mr. Clemens is not going on the stump. He said so last night, and, although it is hard to tell by his drawling voice and his grave glance just when he is fooling, he seemed in earnest in this announcement.

"Yes," he said slowly, as if a great affair of state had been settled; "yes, I find I have a vote. I was in doubt at first, but a careful study has settled that point. I learn that I have lived in Riverdale, up here in The Bronx, long enough to cover the thirty-day clause.

"I've joined a Seth Low club up here. I am with the other youths" (Twain certainly is a perpetual fountain of youth himself, despite his gray hairs) "in wanting to elect Mr. Low.

"But speaking? Stump speaking? I—(pause)—don't—(longer pause)—think so. You see, I'm a poor talker."

Memories of many after-dinner speeches, in some of which Twain had scarified Tammany, made his questioner enter dissent to this self-depreciation.

"Yes, really," said the "Jumping Frog" inventor. "I never was much at talking."

Then he brightened up, as if he had discovered some hitherto-hidden redeeming quality in himself, and added: "But I'm a whole battery of Gatling guns at voting,[5] and I'll turn loose for Low on Election Day."

And with this statement—which, of course, he didn't intend to be taken as meaning that he would become a "repeater"—Twain signified that he had settled finally the course of the campaign as far as he was concerned.

Notes to Interview 146

1. Maurice F. Holahan (1847-1905), former president of the Board of Public Improvements of the City of New York, whose political career ended when he was arrested in a poolroom raid. He claimed he was only there to look for his son.
2. "Big Tim" Sullivan (1862-1913), Tammany boss.
3. Richard Croker (1841-1922) led Tammany Hall from 1886 to 1902.
4. John William Keller (1856-1919), a New York journalist and Tammany politician.
5. An early type of machine gun named for its inventor, Richard J. Gatling (1818-1903), first used during the Civil War.

147

"Mark Twain Will Vote and Work for Seth Low," *New York World*, 9 October 1901, 3

Samuel L. Clemens, known to fame as Mark Twain, yesterday announced his intention of voting the Low ticket and working for its success. He believes that the desire of the vast majority of voters to do away with Tammany Hall corruption insures victory for the man of his choice.

Mr. Clemens has recently established himself in a beautiful old mansion at Riverdale, surrounded by charming grounds and overlooking the Hudson. It is his first permanent home since his trip around the world.

"It is true," he said, "that I have decided to vote the Low ticket. I'll vote for anything that opposes Tammany Hall. I'd rather have Mr. Low than Satan on the ticket, but I'd vote for Satan himself if he were on the Low ticket. I've known Mr. Low personally for seven years, and I think he's one of the finest men I've ever met, but this voting of mine is not to be a matter of personalities. I'm going to vote against Tammany, and I'm glad it means voting [for Low]."

Asked if he intended making any speeches, Mr. Clemens replied:

"No, I'll not speak, but I'll do all in my power for the success of the ticket; that is, all I can by the methods that are suited to my abilities. I dread a speech, because if I do prepare one I never can remember it when the time comes for me to deliver it. For this reason, when I get up I'm there without anything to say, or only with something that has occurred to me during the speech of the preceding orator. But that's bad; it isn't good speaking, as it leads a man to say foolish things that don't look well in print next day. Several persons have asked me to make a few speeches in the campaign, but I'll not do it.

"Have you ridden up Madison avenue lately? Have you ever been able to tell where you were? Certainly not by any aid given you by the lampposts. They talk about sermons in stones, books in running brooks; what about lessons in lampposts? I tell you, the lampposts, those dilapidated, useless things in Madison avenue, are a commentary on Tammany. Car conductors have far too much to do to tell people where they are; the lampposts should do it—and what do they do but blot the scene? A good, honest, thoughtful city government will remedy this grievance. It is only a small thing, perhaps, but when you add all the grievances, you have an array of mismanagement that is staggering."

148

"Mark Twain Will Warmly Greet Robbers," *New York Journal and Advertiser*, 11 October 1901, 1.

Mark Twain offers a warm welcome to the burglars who, for two months and more, have been defying the police and preying on the rich and fashionable residents of Riverdale and Kingsbridge. Having been robbed, W. H. Appleton moved out of his fine house at Riverdale[1] and Mark Twain now occupies it. His voice was sympathetic, coaxing, even seductive, as Mr. Twain said yesterday:

"If I were a burglar I would feel very much hurt that my confidence in the persons who occupy the residence around here should be so abused. Any decent burglar is entitled to something for his pains."[2]

Mr. Twain here opened a drawer in his desk and fondled a highly polished revolver, repeating, "Something for his pains." Then he continued:

"It is unkind to deceive these industrious burglars by putting plated ware where they can get it, when everyone knows they put themselves to the trouble of breaking into houses to obtain solid silver. The burglar, like anyone else, must make a living. I believe it unkind to discourage him in his peculiar efforts; perhaps he has a family to support."[3]

At the thoughts of the burglar's family Mr. Twain seemed about to weep. But just then three great dogs, with large, white, sharp teeth came bounding into the study.

Mr. Twain restrained his tears, patted the dogs' heads, felt the sharp points of their teeth, and murmured, "What a pity it would be if the burglar's family should be deprived of his invisible means of support." Then he continued:

"Sic 'em!" shouted Mr. Twain of a sudden. With distended, dropping jaws, the huge dogs hurled themselves into the grounds around the house.

"Or I may tie the burglars up, so that my dogs may not be interrupted in the repast," drawled Mr. Twain.[4] . . .

Notes to Interview 148

1. See n. 1 to interview 145.
2. "Riverdale Burglar-Ridden," *New York Sun,* 11 October 1901, 1: "If I were the burglars," said he, "I should feel very much hurt that my confidence in the persons who occupy these handsome residences should be abused. Any decent burglar is entitled to something for his pains. He should not be deceived by putting plated ware where he can get it. It must be known that the poor man comes for the genuine article."
3. *New York Sun:* "A burglar, like everybody else, has to make a living. I believe it unkind to discourage him in his peculiar efforts, especially when you consider that he may have a family to support. I haven't yet had the honor of a call, but certainly if they do visit me and give me timely notice I will welcome them with more consideration."
4. *New York Sun:* "The last time they called on me at my home in Hartford they taxed me for luncheon, but I feel sure that they were not satisfied with the brand of wine in my icebox. Now if the burglars will only let me know when they intend to grace my new home with their presence I will see that they have a full assortment of good wine on the ice and a full cupboard. I will also tie my dog so that he will not disturb them, and no plated ware shall be passed off on them."

149

"Mark Twain Would Convert Tammany Police," *New York Herald,* 14 October 1901, 5.

Mark Twain has declined regretfully to take the stump for Seth Low, because, he says, he cannot persuade folks to take him seriously, even in his most lofty flights of spellbinding eloquence.

Among his new neighbors up in the pastoral suburb of Riverdale it is whispered, however, that Mr. Clemens is conducting a subtle still hunt in the interest of the fusion ticket. He has set himself the herculean task, they say, of converting the rank and file of the Tammany police force to reform principles between now and election day, and in his mildly insinuating manner has made already astonishing headway.

For the purpose of persuading Mr. Clemens to report progress a reporter for the *Herald* called upon him in his charming new home in the Appleton Mansion, overlooking the Hudson River. It is a spacious stone house, with a roomy hall in the centre, in which appear many of the humorist's cherished trophies, gathered from all parts of the world. Standing back from the road, the house is shaded by fine old trees, on whose limbs countless squirrels were romping in the autumn rainfall. Mr. Clemens and his family moved into the Appleton Mansion on October 2, and since then have been enjoying the enchanting atmosphere of their rural home.

"Sh-h-h! Not so loud," said the author of *Tom Sawyer*, with a warning finger at his lips. "Yes, it is too true, but if I am discovered I am lost.

"You see, I have undertaken this proselytizing effort wholly on my own responsibility, and with only the tacit support of the fusion Campaign Committee. I understand that 'Billy' Leary was not even consulted about it.[1] The fact is, my advisers thought it would be better so. In this way the Campaign Committee does not have to pay heavy sums for my services, and in the event of my imperfect success the disgrace of failure falls upon my own head alone and does not dishonor the cause. The report that the enemy has tried to buy me off by offering a life interest in the profits of the Police Department is a base canard.

"I violate no confidence when I say that I have not yet been approached either by Mr. Croker or Senator Sullivan.[2] I have entered upon this crusade without promise of reward or emolument, either by Mr. Low or Mr. Shepard.[3] It is a labor of love.

"I will tell you in confidence that I am much encouraged. I began my campaign on a Tammany policeman whom I met the other day at my gate. Personal suasion is my long suit. I am more successful at that than I am on the stump, though I used much good cart-tail [simple and direct] eloquence on this particular policeman, and I could see that he was impressed. I convinced him that there was no authentic record of any Tammany man ever having gone to heaven. But, while he seemed measurably pleased by my attentions, I noticed that he appeared to restrain his enthusiasm. I soon saw that this was a very judicious policeman, the kind who does not blurt right out all the things that may be in his mind and so does not get transferred oftener than twice a week.

"Well, now, I'm willing to bet you a squirrel's nest that if this policeman were watched on election day he would be found voting for Seth Low. If I were a policeman I should do just what I think this policeman intends to do. I should let Tammany think I was with them right up to the time I marked my ballot, and then I should vote according to my conscience, but I should be careful not to make any improper exposure of my conscience to the public view beforehand.

"I don't know just when I will be able to approach the other men on the force, but I regard this particular policeman as a rather promising convert. At least, I have impressed him with a sense of my interest in his personal salvation, and I am pleased to think that he may keep a special eye on these premises, for you know there has been a band of burglars operating around here rather actively of late, and I have no means of knowing with which party they are affiliated.

"I am really fearful that Tammany may have heard something of my political activity up here. Certain of my new neighbors who are democrats are throwing out dark hints that they will challenge my vote if I attempt to poll it on election day. They even insinuate that I am no better than any other vulgar thirty-day colonizer, and have just come up here to electioneer and then get in my vote. Of course it is a fact that I have not been thirty days in this district, and this may subject me to suspicion in the eyes of a partisan. I have tried to assure my neighbors that I am above such sordid motives, and that I will have lived here a full month before election day, but still they look at me askance and talk about watching the house to see if cheap cots are being carried into it.

"In one of the daily papers I saw a notice—not in agate, nonpareil or minion type, which is soft and soothing—but in the heavy, blackface characters which jar one, to the effect that I dare not register nor vote, because the last registration day is October 19, and unless I perjure myself I could not swear on that date that I had lived thirty days in Riverdale. Now, I do not wish to perjure myself unless there be strong provocation, and, being a good republican, I feel great respect for Mr. McCullagh's deputies.[4] So I think of asking Mr. Croker to grant me a special dispensation and permit me to register all by myself on October 31."

When Mr. Clemens' attention was called to the rumor that Mr. Croker thought of taking a house in Riverdale for the winter, and so might become one of his neighbors, the author smiled delightfully, and said, with a twinkle of the eye:—"Wouldn't that be charming? I should then certainly ask the Tammany chief to take my family as lodgers and boarders. I should feel so much more secure from burglars, sneak thieves and second story men if I could only feel that Mr. Croker's protecting aegis were spread over us and our household gods. Think what such an arrangement would save me in the cost of burglar alarms, special watchmen, firearms and patent electric doormats!"

Becoming more serious, Mr. Clemens said that while he did not intend to make any speeches for Mr. Low during the campaign, he had written an article on Tammany and Croker for the November issue of the *North American Review*.[5]

"Apart from the suspicion that I may be a thirty-day colonizer," added the humorist, "I have been 'pleasantly welcomed by every inhabitant' of Riverdale, except the little squirrels in the trees about my house. These little chaps seem to resent my invasion of their playground. They chatter and scold at me incessantly, as though they would say, 'We don't like the way you are acting around here, Mr. Clemens. We were here long before you, anyhow, Mr. Clemens, and don't you think you are just a bit of an interloper?'

"Lord bless you," the genial merrymaker concluded, with a toss of his long, gray shock of hair and a parting handclasp, "these little squirrels have a heap of sense.

"Now, don't betray my police still hunt to the public," was his final injunction. "Shepard and Croker and Devery[6] might bring such pressure to bear upon the structure of my moral integrity as to cause some of its girders to buckle under the strain."

Notes to Interview 149

1. William Leary (1854–1939), formerly secretary of the New York Parks Department, later secretary of the New York Fire Department.
2. See nn. 2 and 3 to interview 146.
3. Edward Morse Shepard (1850–1911), Democratic candidate for mayor of New York in 1901.
4. John McCullagh, first New York City police chief (1898).
5. "Edmund Burke on Crocker and Tammany," first delivered as a speech at the Acorns dinner at the Waldorf-Astoria hotel, 17 October 1901. The piece was not published in the *North American Review*, however; it first appeared in the *Harper's Weekly* supplement, 19 October 1901, 1602.
6. William S. Devery (d. 1919), second New York City police chief (1898–1901).

150

"To Challenge Mark Twain," *New York Sun*, 14 October 1901, 6.

Mark Twain is worried over the threat of a Bronx Tammany man that if he attempts to vote on election day he will be challenged as a colonizer. Mr. Clemens rented the house at Riverdale-on-the-Hudson, which is the home of W. H. Appleton, head of the publishing firm.[1] He took possession on October 2, which entitles him to register and vote. He said to a *Sun* reporter:

"I tried to convert a Tammany policeman out at my gate the other day. I used all the eloquence of a cart tail [simple and direct] campaign orator on him to show him how foolish he was. I tried to prove to his satisfaction that there was no record of any Tammany man ever going to heaven. He didn't seem to get enthusiastic. He was a very judicious policeman; one of those fellows who never let you know what they are thinking about.

"I'll bet a squirrel's nest that if he is watched at the polls on election day, he'll be found voting for Low. If I were a policeman I would do just what this Tammany cop did, when I tried to get him over to my way of thinking, and then vote according to my conscience. But never expose that conscience to public view.

"The next time I see that policeman I'll tackle him again. I must admit, thought, that for the last few days I have felt a cold chill run down my spinal cord whenever I think that I will be only a little more than thirty days in the district when election day comes, which subjects me to suspicion in the eyes of my fellow-countrymen that I am a colonizer, just coming in here to register and vote. I assure my neighbors and friends that I am above such practices.

"Within the last day or so I have been debating whether I can vote here at all. In one of the daily papers I saw a notice, not in agate or minion, which is soft and soothing, but in heavy, bold-faced type, to the effect that I could not vote unless I had lived in the district thirty days. As the last registration day is the 19th of October, I cannot unless I perjure myself, declare that I have lived in the district thirty days, when as a matter of fact, I have only been here three weeks."

The reporter assured Mark that the thirty days runs back from election day, not from any registration day.

Note to Interview 150

1. See n. 1 to interview 145.

151

"Twain Would Be a Bill Poster!" *New York Tribune,* 31 October 1901, 3.
Mark Twain appeared yesterday at the headquarters of the Citizens Union in the role of a bill poster. The humorist has been reading so much about the feud which has sprung up between the Tammany and anti-Tammany bill posters in the fight to get possession of the boards along the route of the rapid transit tunnel that he had decided, he said, to spread a little paste himself.

"Give me a brush and a pot of paste," he said as he entered the room where Captain Arthur F. Cosby was seated.[1]

At the sight of Mr. Clemens, standing with one hand outstretched by way of greeting and the other forking over his long white hair, Mr. Cosby was so nonplussed that he answered with somewhat of a stammer: "Why, how t'do, Mr. Clemens. A paste pot! What?"

"That's it," was the answer. "I want to cover up those Tammany posters along the tunnel. The tunnel does not belong to Tammany, but to the people, and Tammany does not represent the people."

Mr. Cosby was still so surprised that the author of *Innocents Abroad* added: "I am a good friend of the policeman, so you need not worry about my getting arrested. I have made it a point to be friendly with the police and the clergy, so I shall not get into jail either in this world or the next. Haven't you some paste, Mr. Cosby?"

"I'll send for Winans,[2] our chief bill poster," said the captain at last. "He can fix you out, I guess."

A search was made for Mr. Winans, but he could not be found. The only things in the office that would stick were the mucilage on the press agent's desk and a half dozen "new converted" fusionists from the lower West Side.

"Too bad," said the captain, at last, "but I can't find any paste."

"Then I will come again," said Mr. Clemens, with evident disappointment. "But it's too bad. Those Tammany signs ought to be covered up. Their arguments touchin' on and appertainin' to Mr. Shepard and rapid transit are as much out of place as a wet hen on a nest of warm duck eggs."[3]

Then after a moment's thought the hero of *A Tramp Abroad* added: "Well, after all, maybe it's just as well. I'll bring Jerome along with me next time.[4] He is an artist at pasting—Tammany."

Notes to Interview 151

1. Arthur Fortunatus Cosby (b. 1872), a member of Teddy Roosevelt's Rough Riders wounded at the battle of San Juan Hill; he was appointed deputy attorney general of New York City by Governor Roosevelt, and later wrote the *Codes of Ordinances of the City of New York* (1908).

2. Probably William Winans (1875-1949), future New Jersey state assemblyman. Perhaps Edward R. Winans (1857-1942), constable in the Fifth Judicial District in New Jersey.

3. Edward Morse Shepard (1850-1911), Democratic candidate for mayor of New York in 1901.

4. William Travers Jerome (1859-1934), New York district attorney. See also MT's endorsement "Jerome Reviews His Official Years," *New York Times,* 8 May 1909, 2; and Fatout, 643-44.

7
Last Visit to Missouri, 1902
Interviews 152–170

Awarded an honorary doctor of laws degree from the University of Missouri on 4 June, Mark Twain was feted in St. Louis, Columbia, and Hannibal during his final visit to his home state.

152

"Mark Twain Laughs in Grain Pits," *St. Louis Star,* 29 May 1902, 1, 7.
Mark Twain was given a big reception on 'Change. He arrived at the Merchants' Exchange at five minutes to twelve, and after a brief view of the pictures of old Exchange members about the walls, was escorted through the crowds of brokers on the floor. Recognition was instant on all sides, and hand-clapping broke into cheers. Soon Mr. Clemens was surrounded by a mass of yelling men, and shouts for a speech went up on every hand.

Mr. Tansey[1] then came forward and, taking Twain's arm, escorted him to the rostrum. Dashes for close points of hearing ensued among the members on the floor, and the two gentlemen on the stand were well nigh enveloped in humanity.

Mr. Tansey, in his few words of introduction, uttered the pleasure he felt in welcoming back to Missouri the man who had been honored by so many countries, and under so many flags; the man who eased the world's pain with laughter, and who never penned a line to bring the sting or blush of shame to any reader's cheek.

Hearty applause followed Mr. Tansey's remarks, and increased as Mark Twain stepped forward. He began by saying that the sudden class had taken him without a text.

"I wish now," said Mark, "that I were the clergyman I once started out to be, but I am not like the clergy.

"They are always talking for others, and not for themselves. Always seeking the salvation of others, and incidentally putting in a stroke for themselves. Had I followed the course of a clergyman, as mapped out when I was young, things might have resulted without the slightest disaster to you—and to myself.

"President Tansey has said lots of good things about me. Such good things said about me always go to my heart. There is nothing so welcome as a compliment.

"Some men can pay compliments. But the one you are quite sure of is the one that comes along like the ones President Tansey uttered. He said some good things about me, and thought a lot of things, too.

"I hope to deserve all such things as I go along. I am on my way to Columbia to receive a degree of Doctor of Laws.[2] The colossal part of this is my degree will cost me nothing, whereas other folks have to earn theirs. But Missouri is granting this degree to her most deserving son.

"After June 4 I shall be a doctor, and maybe I shall call on you good folks for your practice.

"I am glad to be back in Missouri, the State that gave me birth, and trusted me for it, never knowing how I would pay her back.

"Thank you, gentlemen, for your reception."

Mark Twain, who is one and the same person as Samuel Clemens, the dear, delightful, genial, grand old man of American literature, arrived in St. Louis Thursday morning.

He came in shortly before 8 o'clock, over the Big Four, and went to the Planters' Hotel.[3]

But from the time the train touched St. Louis, Mark was surrounded by admirers and friends and up to 11 o'clock he had not reached the room which was reserved for him at the hotel.

They gathered around him solidly and hung on his words, reminding one for all the world of those devout groups one read about that gathered around the oracles and sages in old Greece.

Mark, genial, affable, continuously saying whimsical things, took the adulation with quaint dignity. He wasn't blasé nor worn out. Everything he said or did was spontaneous and humorous and kept the group constantly in a ripple of smiles. . . .

Clemens has many manners that he must have acquired in his boating days years ago on the old Mississippi.

When he arrived at the Planters' Hotel he wore the familiar big, broad, black soft hat. He wore a pepper and salt business suit, neatly pressed and roomy. It wasn't a la mode nor was it conspicuously different from other suits. The celebrated author just looked like a prosperous Western business man in town for his autumn buying.

He wore a low turndown collar and a black tie and patent leather shoes.

He stood talking to his cousin, Dr. Clemens.[4] Mark looks the picture of his photographs. The white, silvery, curly hair is beautiful, and his face is poetically aquiline. You feel immediately that he is a tranquil, whimsical old man, who has worked hard, but is now resting.

There was a large group around the author when a messenger boy thrust a slip of paper into his hand.

He looked for his glasses, but he couldn't find them. Mark turned to a reporter.

"Will you please read that?"

It was a summons to the long-distance telephone. Mark Twain was wanted. The author called his cousin:

"Will you please see what they want?"

It was a message from New York, but nothing would move Mark to leave his chair. He insisted that the message should be given to the cousin.

Mark Twain never gets excited. And he is always smoking big black cigars. They come somewhere from the inside of his pocket. The pocket must be spacious, for one witness saw at least six come from the pocket within an hour and a half. He reminds you for all the world of a yarning old mariner. When he begins to talk in that slow, slightly ponderous way he has he throws his arm out and his head back in the storyteller's familiar way. His eyes are large and blue. Have you ever been in close contact with Paderewski or Kubelik or Verestchagin or Sir Henry Irving?[5] There is that very same thing which for the lack of a better word might be called electrical in the mobile pupils. They have depth and sensitiveness.

Mark usually lowers his lids and peers through in a quizzical way. His nose is beautifully modeled. As the world knows, it is decidedly Roman. It makes a strenuous effort to touch the broad, solid old chin, but the whimsical, deep-seated human sympathy and generosity of the author prevents hardness and sharpness. His eyebrows are heavy and bushy, straw-colored. The mustache is an enlarged duplicate of the eyebrows. His skim is as pink and fine as a child's.

"You look hale, hearty, and healthy," someone remarked.

"Offensively healthy," replied Mark Twain.

"But why offensively?" was asked when the laugh subsided.

"My dear sir, when you are healthy, or rather when you look healthy, and have reached the 67th year of life, like I have, you will remember that healthiness entails responsibilities. You bear the responsibilities of your duties to your fellow men and to the government, and there are hundreds of things that you ought to do.

"Now, my boy, you know that our natural inclination is not to do what we ought to do, but what we like to do.

"Nature made us lazy. Look at me. I don't know but what I ought to be doing something else now. I can't even find the excuse for my conscience that my age has brought frailty and disease. I am thoroughly healthy and ought to do my duty.

"But I am not worrying. I don't think that I am the only solitary soul living this lazy life. In fact, I know that there isn't a soul on earth that has done, is doing, or will do the one-hundredth part of what it ought to do.

"If you can wake up in the morning and say, 'Well, Bill, or Hank, or Jim, or Red, or whatever your name may be, I've done my full and entire duty to mankind,' let me tell you whatever your name may be that you are an innocent liar.

"Our great trouble is that we never do what we know we ought to do but we do what we think others expect us to do. We are always working for the applause of our neighbors or the people among whom we move. Don't you know if we would do more what we knew to be just the right thing to do we would be more thoroughly individual because the other people would be what you call 'knockers.'

"Our inclination is to win the approval of others by thinking as they think and doing as they do."

At this point a slim, wiry man with a short, cropped gray beard appeared at Mr. Clemens' side.

"Why, hello, Bixby," the author exclaimed.[6]

"Sam, Sam, old man," said Captain Bixby. "I didn't think you'd know me. Why, it's been more than twenty years since I met you last."

Captain Horace G. Bixby is known as one of the best river pilots alive today. He is the one who taught Mark Twain to guide a boat. Mark insisted that the old fresh water sailor should sit down beside him.

"This man talks about my not knowing him," said Mark, throwing his arm back in a reminiscent mood. "Why, he taught me the river. Do you know that he is one of the greatest pilots this old Mississippi has ever known? That he is, this same old Captain Bixby.

"How old are you, Bixby?" he said, turning to the old pilot, who was embarrassed by the glare of distinction which had fallen on him.

"Why, I am 62," said Captain Bixby.

"Lord, man, you were 62 it seems to me when I first met you in 1857," replied Mark. "Do you know that when I first met Bret Harte, years ago in California, with that crown of white hair, he seemed 62 years old and when he slipped away from us in London the other day, I read in the paper that he is only 62 years old.[7] It's a wonderful old world," sighed Mark, who is almost 70 himself.

"That reminds me," he continued, "a fellow's responsibility does not cease until he supports a monument.

"I expect I will be supporting one very soon. I've come to New York not to live, but to die. I know perfectly well that my allotted time is coming to a close, and all the things you boys can say doesn't make a bit of difference. But I always feel happy except when someone reminds me that I am still writing books.

"Now, do you know I am always writing new books. Not one book, but many books. The trouble is my interest ceases, and I find a new theme, and I start a new book, and I can't get the other book finished. I'm always starting new books, but I don't know when I shall publish one."

Someone wanted to know which was his favorite book.

Mark thought it over a minute and replied, without moving a muscle:

"Indications in the usual way make me think that *Huck Finn* and *Innocents Abroad* are the books most favored by the public. I mean, of course, by the financial returns. I have no favorite of my own.

"In fact, I don't know what's in my books. I haven't read one of them for years. Do you know that when I write the book and get it out of my hands and finish with the printer and proofreader I am sick of it? So sick that I don't want to see it for a year."

"Are you going to stage one of your books?" a reporter asked.

"Now, really, I don't know," replied Mr. Clemens. "As a matter of fact, *Huck Finn* will be put on the stage next season, with Arthur Dunn in the title role."[8]

"Did the river look familiar?" asked Captain Bixby.

"Old man," said Clemens, "it looked new in places. You know I came over the other bridge—not the Eads bridge.[9]

"Well, I saw one old boat, a Wiggins Ferry boat, that I knew. I knew it because I had been on it often years ago. I think I even piloted it. I can't think about its name. But it was the boat, all right. Some men were painting it. If it had been painted before I reached here I wouldn't have known it at all.

"Now, do you know I didn't see the riverfront. Just about the time I was ready to take a look at it a pretty young lady whom I knew was bidding me good-bye, and she was so pretty that I forgot to look at anything but that young lady.

"The city is entirely new. I don't recognize any of it. Do you know that I did not even take a look at your Union Station? Whenever I get off a train there is a group of men who know me, and they all shake hands and we talk and then we get into carriages and I don't see a thing."

"Is your memory good?" inquired a reporter.

"No, not particularly. Indeed it's faulty. I don't know faces or names. But that should be excused, because I've been lecturing to 5,000 and 6,000 people for weeks and weeks and meeting many of them.

"Once I was out in Australia, when a big burly strapping specimen of English [masculine] beauty came up to me and assured me that he knew me very well. Do you know I couldn't place him, try as I might? Well, he kept on speaking and trying to make me think of his name and so finally he recalled it to me this way.

"About 20 years before I had been in Belfast, Ireland, at a gentleman's house. At a billiard table I met a young man just out of college. A splendid, trim, slim young man, who interested me much.

"Well, I remembered him immediately. He was a sheep rancher and had an immense place, and was a grandfather himself now.

"Bixby, does the river still rise in June and December? I saw it rising as I came along this morning," said Mr. Clemens.

"I've been all over this small world—in India, Australia, Africa, way up in Iceland, down in South America, but do you know there never was such an old river as the Mississippi? It's been since '84 or '85 since I've been as far west as the Mississippi. It's good to be back again. But I'm not going to talk about the river until I get a better look at it.

"My family, you know, has been in Europe continuously for ten years. We've lived everywhere. I've made seven trips to America since they lived in Europe. We'll stay now."

Someone wanted to know what Mark Twain thought about the probable candidacy of Mark Hanna for the presidency.[10]

"My friend, there are newspapermen around. I'm in the craft and I'm going to be very careful not to say anything until I get ready to write it.

"Now, when I get ready to talk about Mark and his presidency, I'll write it on a piece of nice white paper and give it to the newspapers." . . .

Notes to Interview 152

1. George Judd Tansey (b. 1865), president of the St. Louis Transfer Co.
2. MT was awarded an honorary doctor of laws at the University of Missouri in Columbia on 4 June 1902.
3. Historic hotel opened in 1841 at the corner of Chesnut and Pine in downtown St. Louis.
4. MT's cousin James Ross Clemens, M.D. (1866–1948), a pediatrician and author.
5. Ignace Jan Paderewski (1860–1941), Poland émigré and piano virtuoso; Jan Kubelik (1860–1910), Czech violinist; Vessilli Verestchagin (1842–1904), Russian artist; Sir Henry Irving (1838–1905), English actor.
6. See n. 1 to interview 16.
7. Harte died from throat cancer on 5 May 1902 at the age of sixty-five. On Harte, see also nn. 3 and 4 to interview 8 and n. 5 to interview 84.
8. Arthur Wallace Dunn (1859–1926), actor and playwright.
9. A 1,520-foot steel bridge on stone pillars over the Mississippi at St. Louis designed by James Eads (1820–87) and completed in 1874.

10. Mark Hanna (1837–1904), U.S. senator from Ohio (1897–1904) and Republican political boss.

153

Robertus Love,[1] "Mark Twain Here as St. Louis' Guest for the First Time since 1861," *St. Louis Post-Dispatch,* 29 May 1902, 1–2.

Mark Twain is here.

That is, he was here until 2 o'clock, when he boarded a train for Hannibal.

While in St. Louis he took a nap at the Planters' Hotel.[2] On the way downtown from Union Station he remarked: "St. Louis reminds me of several cities—Philadelphia and other places."

Then he went to sleep.

But it must not be taken for granted that Mark Twain went to sleep because St. Louis reminded him of Philadelphia. He courted a siesta because he was sleepy. He was sleepy because he needed sleep. It was the most natural thing in the world.

Mark Twain had been on a train two nights and a day. He left New York night before last. He didn't sleep well on the train. That was not the fault of the train. It was due to the weather.

The first night he was too cold. The second night he was too hot. He said so himself, and he never lies.

"The only real liar in this world," said Mark Twain to me on the train Thursday morning, somewhere this side of Litchfield, "is the practical joker. I hate a practical joker. His aim in life is to deceive. I never was a practical joker—except when I was a boy, and a boy has not sense. The practical joker is a boy who never has grown up. His head is full of stewed oysters instead of brains."

"Is Mark Twain aboard?" I inquired of Hi Jenkins, the merry-mouthed Ethiope who pilots the New York sleeper as head porter.

"Yes, sah," replied Hi, wondering why on earth any man should want to see Mark Twain.

It was just about daylight—a raw, chill dawn on the Illinois prairies, January jabbed into June, a latter May morning with March mercury.

Still, it was the end of the night when Mark Twain got so hot that he couldn't sleep.

"Yes, sah, Mistah Twain is on dis train. He's jis' puttin' his clo'es on, in de drawin' room. Say dat gentleman mus' be rich. He had de drawin' room all de way through."

"Will you carry my card into Mr. Clemens' drawing room?" I requested.

"Into who?" asked the porter. "Say, I thought you wanted to see Mr. Twain."

Meekly I explained that Clemens was Mr. Twain's home name.

"What's he travelin' under one o' dese yere a-lie-asses fur?" asked the porter.

"Mr. Clemens," said I, "is a writer, a man who writes funny books, and he uses Mark Twain when he writes."

"Say, mistah," the porter said. "I thought dat man was a writer. He laid awake all night befor' las' a-readin' a great big book. Funnies' man I evah did see. Say, he didn't sleep a wink, dat man didn'. Whah'd you know dat man?"

This necessitated another explanation that Mr. Clemens was bound to Missouri to receive the degree of LL.D. from the Missouri State University at Columbia.

"He's going to be doctored," said I.

"Say, look-ee yere, mistah," said Hi. "Dat man don' need no mo' doctorin' than I does; his skin's as pinky as a baby's. He's de healthies' man, fur an ol' man, I evah see yit."

"How is Mr. Clemens' appetite?" I inquired.

"Mighty po,' sho's yo' bo'n," replied the porter. "I don' see how he keep up laik he does, eatin' so little. W'y, dat man hain' been outen de drawin' room but oncet sence we lef' New Yo'k. He come out to eat lunch. All de res' o'time he been inside a-readin' outen dat great big book."

"As soon as you get my bed made, so there will be room for two Missourians in this pigeon hole, you can admit the gentleman," said Mark Twain to the porter.

When I was admitted, Mark Twain was enjoying coffee, bread, and butter, his breakfast. He gave a duplicate order for himself and insisted upon his visitor eating what he wanted.

The porter came in to take the second order, and Mark Twain paused between mouthfuls to look up at the smiling car pilot and remark: "Where's the bill? Now, don't you forget the bill."

"Sho, I won't, Mistah Twain," replied the porter.

"But you look to me like a man who would forget it," insisted the humorist. "You have the forget face. I'm very much afraid you'll never present me that bill."

Then Mr. Clemens took occasion to explain how he happened to be cold on a reasonably warm night and hot on a cold night.

"The first night I was aboard," said he, "the porter thought it was going to be a hot night, naturally, because it is summer time. I had only one blanket on my bed. I got chilly. It was so chilly that I was uncomfortable, so I lay awake and read a good part of the night. That porter was mistaken—I did sleep some.

"Last night I determined to be prepared. So I ordered an extra blanket, which the porter brought me. But some offspring of an idiot turned on the heat, and I almost suffocated."

That is why Mark Twain went to sleep shortly after reaching St. Louis—not because the town reminded him of Philadelphia.

"The fact is," said Mr. Clemens, "I don't know anything about St. Louis except from memory. I haven't been here since 1861. That is to say, I haven't been here really to stay any time. I have flitted past once or twice. In 1885 I lectured here, in the old Mercantile Library Hall, but that wasn't a visit.[3]

"In fact, I merely flitted past. I flit into many cities and flit out. I don't see the places, I just flit. I'm a flitter and have been one for a good many years."

"But this time, Mr. Clemens, you are not going to flit. You will stay with us for awhile, won't you?"

"I'm going up to Hannibal this time, but I want to come back by way of St. Louis and stay a day or two, if I don't get a telegram calling me back to New York. I have some relatives here whom I have promised to visit.

"But Hannibal is my main point. I am determined to see Hannibal this time. Practically, I may say that I have not been back to Hannibal, where I grew up, for 50 years. I have not been back there long enough to see the town and the people.

"Twelve years ago I went to Hannibal to bury my mother,[4] but I was there only a day or a part of a day.

"Now I am going to see the place—perhaps for the last time. When a man gets to be 67 he is about ready to wind up. I don't feel old, but the years are upon me. There was Bret Harte. I was with him in San Francisco many years ago. He was 69 when he died the other day, though the newspapers said he was 62.[5] Bret Harte was two years older than myself, so much older that I deferred to him on account of his age. But I suppose if his ghost could be interviewed it would be glad to accept the newspaper estimate of 62.

"There's Charley Warner—Charles Dudley Warner," Mr. Clemens was quick to add, evidently fearing that I would not recognize in the familiar "Charley" the distinguished Hartford litterateur who was his close neighbor for many years.[6] "He's gone, too. Most of the men I chummed with out on the Pacific coast are gone. Noah Brooks and Charles Warren Stoddard are left."[7]

Mr. Clemens showed heightened interest when his train reached the Mississippi river. He craned his neck to look up and down the stream, once so familiar to him as a steamboat pilot.

"See those ripples and curlicues," said the author to a young woman who entered his drawing room to get his autograph—and she got it, too, with a smile and a pat on the shoulder.

(N. B.—I promised not to mention this. Mark Twain says he has writers' cramp and is scarcely able to make his "mark." Autograph hunters, he thinks, should respect age, unless they are unusually pretty girls.)

"Those little curls on the surface," said the humorist, "are quite familiar to me. They are distinctive of the Mississippi. There is no other river I know of that has so many of them."

Here was the old pilot cropping out. The Mississippi river pilot must know all those curves and curlicues; otherwise, he is likely to run into "mark twain" water—only two feet deep—and hang up his craft on a bar for seven days.

The ripples and curls show the depth or shallowness of the water, just as the smile curves or frown angles on a man's face show his character.

"By the way, Mr. Clemens," I remarked, "an old raft pilot on the upper river told me the other day that you never made a good pilot. He thought you might have been a pretty fair one if you hadn't quit the business just about the time you had it learned and begun writing. It takes a man, he said, about 10 years or so to learn the business."

Here was where Mark Twain woke up. He saw a challenge and accepted it.

"I'll venture that man," he said, "was a mud clerk. I'll venture he never knew me, and had no opportunity to know whether I was a good pilot or a bad one. I'll venture he's a no account pilot himself, or he would not have shown his ignorance by making that remark.

"Rank on the river those days was very strict. The captain and the pilot had a rank of their own, at the top. Those under them never met them on terms of equality. There was one grade—and I guess your raft friend belonged to that—which was made up of mud clerks, cub pilots, and strikers. The mud clerk was the apprentice clerk. The cub pilot was the apprentice to the pilot, and knew nothing about the business till he spent several years at it. The striker was the engineer's apprentice. Those three were equals. They never got near the captain or pilot in rank.

"Your man was on the upper river, you say. Where did he see me? I was on the lower river altogether. What did he know about the lower river?

"Some men never did make good pilots, it is true, but that was because they didn't have the faculty. They were in the wrong business. They were not born to be pilots. Others made good pilots naturally.

"There was a Horace Bixby, who taught me the business.[8] He was a pilot. But one of his assistants, whose name I can't recall, though he had a license, never was a pilot. He had been at the business 22 years, and still Bixby used to do part of his work and draw part of his salary, because he couldn't steer a boat under all conditions.

"Whatever your raft man may think, I reckon a man who could draw his own salary and part of another man's knew enough about piloting to get along, and I did that."

Changing the subject, lest I should be compelled to give the name and town of the raft pilot and carry him a challenge to mortal combat on Bloody

Island, I asked Mark Twain why it was that he was popularly supposed to be the author of the famous jingle:

"Punch, brothers! punch with care!
Punch in the presence of the passenjare!"[9]

"When Isaac H. Bromley, editorial writer on the *New York Tribune,* died a few years ago, his friends claimed that he was the author of the lines," said I.

"So he was," replied Mark Twain; "he and Noah Brooks. I saw the lines floating about in a newspaper, after having read the street car placard which inspired them, and used the jingle in a sketch I wrote for the *Atlantic Monthly,* published in February 1876.

"I told how they had run in my mind until I was well-nigh crazy, then I gave them to a preacher friend of mine, who carried the jingle in his brain until he delivered a funeral sermon in the singsong rhythm of the 'punch' rhymes and had the whole audience bowing and swaying in time to his rhythm.

"I never made any claim to the authorship of the verses, but Noah Brooks writes me twice a year demanding to know why I am trying to steal his lines."

These are the lines to which reference is made:

Conductor, when you receive a fare,
Punch in the presence of the passenjare!
A blue trip slip for an eight-cent fare,
A buff trip slip for a six-cent fare,
A pink trip slip for a three-cent fare;
Punch in the presence of the passenjare!
Chorus:
Punch, brothers! punch with care;
Punch in the presence of the passenjare!

In April 1875, the New York and Harlem street railroad, horse car route, posted in its cars the following placards, announcing that the punch system was adopted:

The CONDUCTOR, when he receives a Fare, must immediately PUNCH in the presence of the passenger.

A blue trip slip for an eight-cent fare,
A buff trip slip for a six-cent fare,
A pink trip slip for a three-cent fare.
For Coupon and Transfer Tickets, Punch the Tickets.

"This was the real father of the jingle," said Mark Twain. "I have told Noah

Brooks that I don't see how I could be accused of trying to claim the authorship of verse which the horse cars might have written, so musical was the jingle in the placards."

Among the parodies of this famous jingle it may be appropriate to mention one in *The Western,* a St. Louis magazine of those days. This publication appeared with a Latin parody, addressed to "Marco Twain," with this chorus:

Pungite, fraters, pungite!
Pungite cum amore,
Pungite pro vectere,
Diligentissime pungite!

Algernon Charles Swinburne made a French reproduction of the jingle—but let us talk Missouri.

Mark Twain is proud of the proffer of an LL.D. degree from the Missouri State University.

"What do I think of such a degree?" he said. "Well, you can see that I think enough of it to travel more than 1000 miles each way, in my old age, to get it."

"But isn't it a fact, Mr. Clemens, that its value is enhanced because it comes from Missouri?"

Mr. Clemens tried to hedge on this question, but when I asked him if he would go 1000 miles up in Canada to receive an LL.D. he replied, with his honest smile: "You can rest assured I wouldn't."

The honesty of Mark Twain's smile is its chief characteristic. One never has any suspicions about that smile. When the Mark Twain smile comes around, one doesn't think of locking the doors and hiding silver under the parlor rug. That smile is just what it purports to be—strictly honest, no humbug.

Mark Twain wore the smile when he reached Union Station. He was thinking of the past.

"Once I flitted into St. Louis," he said, "with James R. Osgood, the publisher.[10] That was in 1880, when I came here to take passage down the river on a boat, to gather material for my book *Life on the Mississippi.* I wanted to go under an assumed name, so the captains and pilots would tell me lies about the river; otherwise, I fear they might have told me the truth, if they knew I wanted it for a book.

"I went into the Southern Hotel and registered as 'James R. Smith.' The clerk looked at me and yelled: 'Front! show Mr. Clemens up to room 256.'"

Mr. Clemens was much amused because the Pullman porter was not acquainted with his fame.

"When I was swindling the public on the lecture platform with George W.

Cable, about 15 years ago," said he, "Cable bet me that we could not find a person who had not heard of Mark Twain. I took the bet. We went at once into a store on Broadway, New York, where pictures of all sorts of celebrities, actors, singers, and authors were kept.

"'Let me see the latest picture you have of Mark Twain,' remarked Cable to the young woman at the counter.

"The girl looked puzzled, but she glanced up and down the long line of pictures on the wall and, turning to Cable, asked:

"'Where does she sing?'"

Mr. Clemens' remarks anent the practical joker, quoted early in this narrative, were called forth by a question as to the truth of a story about the presentation to him of a pipe by the printers on the Virginia City *Enterprise,* when he was a reporter there in is earlier days. Mark Twain's pipe, called "The Remains," smelt so vile that the printers determined to get rid of it. One night they bought a new pipe for 30 cents that did not look like 30 cents in the gaslight. It looked like $30, but it was as much of a fraud as the $2 Panama hat.

With touching speeches they presented this pipe to Mark Twain, who responded feelingly and threw "The Remains" out of the window. That was the only time that Mark Twain ever was known to descend to pathos.

The cheap pipe split in twain—mark that—the first time the recipient smoked it, and Mr. Clemens went out in the yard and hunted up "The Remains."

"Yes," he said in the train, "that story is true, and I'm mad about it yet. It was a practical joke, and the cheapest form of wit is the practical joke. I wouldn't have cared if the pipe cost 30 cents or $30, but when they came to me seriously and made the presentation as a costly pipe, when it was a cheap affair, that was another thing."

At Union Station Mr. Clemens was met by Dr. J. Ross Clemens of St. Louis,[11] a cousin, whose guest he will be for a day or two after June 4, when he returns from Columbia as Dr. Samuel Langhorne Clemens.

The "first Missourian" took a carriage for the Planters', where he looked over his mail. Then he visited the *Post-Dispatch* office and looked through the plant. He was much pleased with the office.

"The last printing office I knew anything about," he said, "was the *Hannibal Weekly Courier.* That was in 1852. Maybe I'll visit it again when I go up to Hannibal this time."

Then he went over to the Planters' and took a nap.

Notes to Interview 153

1. Robertus Love (1867-1930), popular western biographer, poet, journalist, and author of *The Rise and Fall of Jesse James* (1926).

2. Historic hotel opened in 1841 at the corner of Chesnut and Pine in downtown St. Louis.

3. MT and Cable appeared in St. Louis on 9 and 10 January 1885. See chapter 2.

4. Jane Lampton Clemens died in 1890 at the age of eighty-seven.

5. In fact, Harte was sixty-five. See n. 7 to interview 152. See also nn. 3 and 4 to interview 8 and n. 5 to interview 84.

6. See n. 2 to interview 28. See also interview 136.

7. Noah Brooks (1830–1903), American journalist. On Stoddard, see n. 2 to interview 53.

8. See n. 1 to interview 16.

9. This jingle was written by Isaac H. Bromley (1833–98), American journalist, and Noah Brooks with the chorus by W. C. Wycoff and Moses P. Handy. MT published the jingle in "A Literary Nightmare," *Atlantic Monthly* 37 (February 1876), 167–70. See also Paine, 556.

10. On MT's visit to St. Louis in 1882 with James R. Osgood, see interviews 16–18, especially n. 6 to interview 17.

11. MT's cousin James Ross Clemens, M.D. (1866–1948), a pediatrician and author.

154

"Mark Twain's Visit," *St. Louis Globe-Democrat*, 30 May 1902, 9.

Samuel L. Clemens, oldest and [only] surviving member of a trinity of quaint characters which Missouri has given to the world, consisting of himself, Eugene Field, and Sol Smith Russell,[1] was in the city yesterday for several hours, which he spent around the Planters' hotel lobby,[2] meeting old acquaintances, swapping stories and harking back a half century or more to the time when he first came to St. Louis from his home in north Missouri and gazed in wonder at the four and five story skyscrapers of that city.

"I knew I was in St. Louis the moment I looked down from the bridge and saw the old ferryboat plying across the river. Do you know, it has been nearly seventeen years since I saw that boat, and yet I recognized her at a glance. I see by the paper that she has been sold."

In this fashion Mr. Clemens went on the whole morning, greeting each old and new acquaintance with some whimsical remark in his drawling tone, and never failing to raise a laugh. Captain Horace E. Bixby, who "learned" Mark Twain the river, and Captain Dan Able,[3] led the contingent of old rivermen who pounced down upon the great humorist and completely swamped him with their attentions. "Yes, I have met nearly everybody I used to know in connection with the river," said Mr. Clemens as he was preparing to leave the hotel. "That is to say, all that are left. Ever and anon I hear of the death of some old comrade of the river, whose name recalls the fragrant memories of other days."

Instead of hiding himself in a room and having callers send up their cards, Mr. Clemens remained in the hotel corridor all morning. He said he wanted to get a room to take a nap, but the hotel people wouldn't trust him. However that might be, he lounged around in a big armchair, like any ordinary hotel guest, regarding the crowd of curiosity seekers which gathered around him with amused content, and kept up a running fire of comment upon men and things. "This gentleman," someone remarked, in presenting a friend, "is from Pike county." The old humorist regarded the newcomer closely from under his shaggy brows, remarking, "that's what they used to say about every Missourian you met out in California. If a man got in trouble out there and wanted to gather a crowd to fight his battles, all he had to do was to proclaim that he was a Piker. The enemy generally took to its heels without waiting for further developments." . . .

Notes to Interview 154

1. Eugene Field (1850–95), American poet; Sol Smith Russell (1848–1902), American comic actor.
2. Historic hotel opened in 1841 at the corner of Chesnut and Pine in downtown St. Louis.
3. MT piloted the steamboat *White Cloud,* captained by Daniel Able, in October 1858. On Bixby, see n. 1 to interview 16.

155

Robertus Love,[1] "Mark Twain Sees the Home of His Boyhood," *St. Louis Post-Dispatch,* 30 May 1902, 1.

Hannibal, Mo., May 30—Mark Twain at 10:30 o'clock visited and identified the old house on Hill street where most of his boyhood was passed.

"Yes, this is the house," he said, while a large crowd of adults and children gathered about him.

"I couldn't recognize the picture, but I recognize the house." He tarried only long enough for a photographer to preserve the incident to posterity's eyes, then entered a carriage with Mrs. John H. Garth, widow of an old-time chum,[2] and was driven to Mt. Olivet Cemetery, where he saw the graves of his parents and brother.

Mr. Clemens did not emerge from his room until 9 o'clock, clad in a fresh suit of clothes to match his hair and a real Panama hat of the circular type. He walked downstairs, remarking that he had slept unusually well. He had remained in his room 16 hours. This afternoon he was to attend the Memorial Day exercises at the Presbyterian Church and tonight he will present diplomas to 15 girl graduates and 3 boys of the Hannibal High School class of 1902.

He promises that he will make a speech if he can think of a subject. At breakfast he was visited by Dr. F. A. Bishop and other members of the Labinnah Club, who made arrangements to tender him a public reception in the clubrooms at 8:30 o'clock Saturday.

Many old-timers crowded about the great man to shake his hand in the hotel office. Among them were W. H. C. Nash, Charles W. Curts, and Edwin Pierce, all of whom he identified as old playmates.

"How are you doing, Eddie?" he inquired of Mr. Pierce.

"Like yourself, Sam," replied the schoolmate, "like a cow's tail going down." With a light and springy step, Mark Twain walked up the street with his old cronies to the Farmers and Merchants' Bank, where an informal reception was held. Here he met other old boyhood chums, among them W. R. Pitts, John L. RoBards, J. B. Brown, J. J. Cruikshank,[3] and A. R. Levering. Mark Twain, whose hair is whitest, looks the youngest of them all. Some of them he remembered as soon as they gave their names. In the case of others he required a memory search.

"Hello, Sam," said one old man; "I'm Lippincott, and used to play marbles with you, but probably you remember my brother, Dave Lippincott." Mr. Clemens could not recall the Lippincotts.

"You and Dave and I and Charley Buchanan used to—"

"Ah, Charley Buchanan," said the humorist. "Yes, indeed, I remember Charley." Mr. Buchanan now lives in New Franklin, Missouri.

Mark Twain says he will remain in Hannibal until Monday. Tomorrow he will visit the cave and other points of boyhood interest.

Mark Twain, the prodigal son, returned home at 5 o'clock Thursday evening, but as his father, Hannibal, did not see him coming from afar off, the fatted calf was not killed and cooked in time for supper.

However, the veal feast was ready for the slaughter—it has been penned up and cornfed these 50 years—and so the prodigal who has wandered so long and so far will eat his fill of the fatted calf of universal affection at his old home.

If the father and his family, Hannibal's 15,000 people, had known of the near approach of the prodigal, Mark Twain would have been filled so full of the chops and cutlets of the people's long pent-up admiration when he stepped from the tail end of the train that he would have been heavier than the shotted frog of Calaveras County.[4]

Hannibal had no idea that Mark Twain was coming when he did. He was expected next week, after Missouri's LL.D. shall have been added to that of Yale.

"If we had known he was aboard that train," remarked a citizen, "the Union Depot platform would not have been big enough to hold the chairmen of committees."

Possibly this explains why Mr. Clemens did not write to any of his Hannibal friends that he was coming to pay a visit to the home of his adventurous boyhood.

As it was, the few scores of persons on the depot platform "spotted" him at once, and he was compelled to shake hands with two at a time.

Mr. Clemens walked the one block to the Windsor Hotel, where he registered and gave his trunk to the negro porter.

"Does the gentleman want his trunk put in the sample room?" inquired the Ethiope. Will Sutton, the hotel clerk, remarked: "Mr. Clemens, I was born close to your birthplace at Florida, and have been in the house where you were born, often."

"I was not born often—only once," responded the humorist, "but I'm glad to see you, all the same."

Thus early in his visit Mark Twain learned that he was back among the home folks.

Three or four others introduced themselves.

"I never saw you before," said one, "but I recognized you by your picture in the *Post-Dispatch*."

"I am a railroad engineer," said a young man, "and my mother-in-law went to school with you in her girlhood—Artemisa Briggs."

"Of course I did," replied Mr. Clemens.

"She sends you an invitation to call," said the engineer.

Ten minutes after his arrival Mark Twain went to bed. Room 27 was assigned to him and the porter took his leather traveling trunk thereto, having learned that it did not contain samples.

"I feel as if I ought to go out and walk around and see the people," said Mr. Clemens, "but I'm a little tired and will rest. Perhaps later in the night, when everybody is abed, I may go out and take a walk."

By invitation, I knocked on the door of No. 27 two hours later and found the great son of Hannibal lying on top of his bed covers, feet to the headboard, dressed for the night, with a long black cigar between his teeth and Mont Pelle puffs of smoke arising.

He was not asleep, but he was dreaming. It was a dream at sunset—and 67.

The mild blue eyes of this man who has viewed the rivers and mountains, the creeks and crags of many lands, were turned toward a high hill half a mile to the south, plainly visible through his one window.

At the eastern crest of the hill, far above the river, arose a rounded yellow bluff out of the foliage of green trees on the slope.

"That," said Mark Twain, beckoning me to the window, "is Lovers' Leap. Many times when a boy I have climbed that hill and dangled my legs over the precipice. It has not changed—not that. It is handsomer than I thought."

"Now is the time for the reporter to withdraw and leave the great man to his memories," thought I; but then came the recollection that Mark Twain himself was once a reporter, and it occurred to me that if Mark Twain, reporter, had retreated from an opportunity to observe the most famous humorist in the world lying upon his back in a hotel bedroom, gazing at the Lovers' Leap of his boyhood, in a sunset's gilded glow 50 years after, and retreated through a mere consideration of sentiment—that biographer of his who wrote on one page that he was "not a successful journalist" and on the next that "he was an ideal reporter" would have omitted the latter statement.

The news of Mr. Clemens' arrival permeated Hannibal rapidly.

"Mark Twain is here," said every second Hannibalite to his neighbor, and presently the streams of people began to flow toward the Windsor Hotel.

Old and young and middle-aged, they arrived afoot, by street car, and in carriages. To each the hotel clerk gave the disappointing information that the guest had retired and must not be disturbed.

During the evening a delegation from the Labinnah Club (spell Hannibal backwards) called to consult the humorist's wishes in regard to a reception which the club desires to tender him. . . .

There are more "originals" of Huck, Tom, and Becky in this town since Mark Twain arrived than one would expect to meet in a staid old town with 23 respectable Sunday schools and a Salvation Army.

You don't need to bait your hook if you go fishing for a Huck. Just make a cast anywhere around town, and there's your Huckleberry.

"I've lived in this town 71 years," remarked one reputable native, "and I never was accused of being Huck Finn until last night. I submit that my reputation has been good, and if I ever was Huckleberry Finn, I can't recall it. It's a base slander to put upon a man in his old age."

Each man, woman, and child in Hannibal seems to have agreed upon a different Huck, Tom, and Becky. The variety is choice, but bewildering.

To the outsider who has known but one Huck, Tom, and Becky each, it is amazing to learn the cold and naked truth—that every Tom, Dick, and Harriet in Hannibal is a Tom, Huck, or Becky.

Any man or woman here who has reached the age of 65 is subject to the Huckleberry, Thomas, or Rebecca aspersion. Most of the old folks remained indoors last night to escape the overhearing of such remarks as: "There he is—that's Huckleberry Finn. Run an undertaking shop after he reformed and settled down."

Another thing strikes me as being out of the ordinary. I learn that Mark Twain has 18 or more "first sweethearts" in Hannibal. They were remarkably healthy, too, for all are living now. Mark Twain must have chosen buxom lasses for his 18 first sweethearts with an eye to longevity.

But how he managed to manipulate the 18 so that each was the first is beyond comprehension. Here is where human reason runs up against a stone fence and flattens out.

14. Posing before his boyhood home on Hill Street in Hannibal, 30 May 1902. Collection of Gary Scharnhorst.

Notes to Interview 155

1. See n. 1 to interview 153.
2. MT's childhood friend John H. Garth (1837–99), one of the models for Joe Harper in *Tom Sawyer,* married Helen Kercheval in 1860. See also *Auto* (1959), 71.
3. John L. RoBards (b. 1838), younger brother of George RoBards. See also *Auto* (1990), 210–11; *Auto* (1959), 71, 202–03. John J. Cruikshank (d. 1924), wealthy Hannibal lumber merchant.
4. In MT's "Jumping Frog" sketch, a stranger fills the frog "Dan'l Webster" with quail-shot "pretty near up to his chin."

156

"'Mark Twain' Comes Back to Missouri," *St. Louis Republic,* 30 May 1902, 1–2.

Samuel L. Clemens, who as Mark Twain is the friend of all, who as plain "Sam" or as "Mr. Clemens," is at once the friend of anybody whose good fortune it is to meet him, was in St. Louis yesterday.

Old associates and one-time river comrades gathered round him by the score to shake hands and talk a moment of the days that are gone. Admirers, young and old, crowded the lobby of the Planters' Hotel hoping to see him,[1] wishing to exchange a word or two with the distinguished author, who is known wherever books are read, who is and who emphatically announces himself a Missourian.

Perhaps the most touching incident of Mark Twain's stay—let us call him that, it is most familiar—was his meeting with Captain Horace Bixby,[2] the Bixby in *Life on the Mississippi*, the Bixby prominent among river men of St. Louis, the Bixby who for almost two years way back in the fifties was his teacher—pilot teacher—when young Mark was the victim of overwhelming desire to master the intricacies connected with guiding Mississippi River steamboats.

Captain Bixby has just passed his seventieth year, yet his slim, wiry figure is unbent and he appears not more than 45. Mark Twain is almost 67, but his hair is gray to whiteness, his figure slightly stooped, though his color is healthy and much reserve strength seems still present. The two grasped hands with fervor and said the latter:

"Why, Horace, you're as young as ever."

They met last in 1884 upon a street in New Orleans. Then the former cub pilot's remark must have been of the same nature, for at the time he wrote of the Captain: "It is a curious thing to leave a man 35 years old, and come back at the end of twenty-one years and find him still 35."[3]

Now almost forty years had passed and "Cap Horace" was but ten years older. Captain Bixby met Mark Twain at the train and went with him to the Planters' Hotel. There they had a long chat together.

They talked of the halcyon days of the river traffic, when three tiers of steamers extended a mile along the levee at St. Louis. Men who are now in their graves were recalled to their memories.

Incidents and anecdotes of the past were revived. A bygone time was clothed with new life by virtue of the famous writer's vivifying imagery.

Later in the morning Mark Twain descended into the lobby of the hotel. He held a continuous reception. One would have supposed that some official dignitary was visiting the city. Elderly gentlemen who evidently were not used to so much exertion would come puffing up to the clerk one after another.

"Where's Mark Twain?" they would shout. "I mean, where's Sam Clemens?" A glance around, however, and it was not difficult to locate the object of the inquiries. Always a knot of persons was gathered near him, and his long, wavy hair and mustache, often seen in pictures, gave his personal appearance strong individuality.

He stood most of the time, talking in a low voice and smoking black cheroots—very black ones, very many black ones. With friends of old the talk was all personal—"How's your health?" "How's your wife?" "You've been a long time gettin' out to poor old Missouri, Mark." "You won't find the river as it once was." "By George, I'm glad to see you, Sam," etc.

Being a humorist, it was apparent that many persons expected Mark Twain to be funny. He did say amusing things occasionally, but nothing which was obviously intended to be funny—he was too natural to act "funny now."

About 11 o'clock he went across Fourth street from the Planters' to the rooms of the Pilots' Society. There the river men had gathered in force, and royally they welcomed back a long-lost brother. A short address was made and a handshake exchanged all round.[4]

At noon, George J. Tansey, president of the Merchants' Exchange, escorted Mark Twain to the exchange, where he was introduced to many, and where he made a short address. He said that the sudden call upon him had found him without a text upon which to base his remarks. Of Mr. Tansey's introductory words, the humorist quaintly said:

"It is very embarrassing to listen to personal compliments, but doubly embarrassing when the recipient of them feels that they are deserved. Mr. Tansey said very many nice things about me, but there are many other things which he might have said, but which, no doubt, slipped his mind."

After hastily lunching at the Planters', Mark Twain took a cab for Union Station, where he departed for Hannibal, his boyhood home, at 2:15 p.m. He looks forward with much interest to his two or three days' stay in Hannibal, and hopes there to meet many other old friends, and perhaps seek out the localities which are the setting for much of *Huckleberry Finn.*

Asked before leaving what he thought of St. Louis, he replied that it was like coming to a strange American city.

"Everything is changed," said he. "The high massive buildings have made quite a different place of it. When I was here last, in '84, there was still some vestige of the old city which I knew before the War. These are now gone."

As his train sped along the elevated tracks and the broad river came within view, he gazed upon it pensively. Asked what he thought of it now, he replied: "It's very natural, it's the same river."

He seemed impressed with the dignity of becoming a Doctor of Laws, which degree is to be conferred upon him June 4 by Missouri State University, and he was especially flattered since he did not have to work for it. "That is the colossal thing about it," said he.

"Have you ever doctored laws?" he was asked. "Yes, cab laws," he said. Further explanation requested, he continued.

"I doctored the cab laws in London and New York. The cabbies overcharged and I simply made them come down by calling official attention to the fact.

"The truth is, however, that the laws do not need to be doctored so much as the enforcement of them needs to be doctored."

Mark Twain emphatically denies that he was a bad pilot. Asked concerning this report, he said: "Who is it that claims I was a bad pilot? The fellow that said that never was a pilot himself. He don't know anything about me or piloting. He don't where the Missouri empties into the Mississippi. He don't know a lumber raft from a packet."

The story of Mark Twain's years upon the river, when he sought to rise high in the ranks of pilotism, is the story of a man with a sense of humor who tackled a "tough proposition."

There are more kinks in a pilot's business than kinks in the Mississippi itself, yet in addition the pilot must know all these twists of the river—which Mark found out to his sorrow. He had some notion of the printing business when he met Captain Bixby on the Ohio River in 1857. Having left his Hannibal home in search of both a career and adventure, he had landed in Cincinnati, and at Cincinnati had conceived the idea of a voyage to Central America, or South America, either one, with a vision of an expedition up the Amazon prospecting for Eldorado or some more tangible gold mine.

He set out upon his voyage with $30 capital. He was to go from Cincinnati to New Orleans upon the steamer *Paul Jones*, which many years after he dubbed an "ancient tub." "For the sum of $16," said he, "I had the scarred and tarnished splendor of 'her' main saloon principally to myself, for she was not a creature to attract the eye of wiser travelers."

Nevertheless, dawdling down to New Orleans on the *Paul Jones* must have awakened fascination for the great yellow torrent of mud, which is facetiously named the "Father of Waters." In *Life on the Mississippi* Mark Twain explains that South American fortune seemed farther away at New Orleans than at Cincinnati, that his $30 capital was almost exhausted, and that he was forced to look about for a ready money job. Probably for the several reasons indicated, when he found that his friend, the *Paul Jones*, was about to start for St. Louis, he "besieged a pilot," with whom he had scraped up an acquaintance on the down trip, and "after three hard days" the pilot surrendered. This pilot was Captain Bixby.

The Captain had his own way of telling of this siege. "A pretty good looking young fellow," said he yesterday, "was always hanging round the pilot house. Said he was going down in Central American or somewhere. But when we got down to New Orleans he came round to me and said that he thought he'd like to learn piloting; didn't think he'd go to Central America after all;

asked if I wanted to teach him the river. I said that young fellows like him round were more trouble than use; couldn't think of it.

"He kept after me anyhow, and finally I agreed. He was to pay me $500 for teaching him the river between St. Louis and New Orleans. We drew up a contract, which was put away in the safe of the boat and neither he nor I have seen it to this day. Well, I was with him pretty much all the time for the next three years, or until he got his certificate as pilot. I know some say he didn't make much of a pilot, but I think he was about as good as any young fellow of his age—he was about 20 when I first met him.

"He was a quiet sort of boy at the time. Of course, he had some of that famous drollery and humorous way of looking at things which is celebrated in his writings. I remember when I undertook to teach him I questioned him about his antecedents and other matters.

"'How are your habits?' I asked.

"'Fair,' he mumbled.

"'Do you chew?'

"'No, don't chew,' very deliberate.

"'Do you drink?'

"'No, don't drink.' At this he seemed a little uneasy, and with a slight twinkle of the eye, he continued, 'But I must smoke.'

"He must smoke to this day."

"After he left me in the latter part of '59 I saw little of him. He was on board the *Alonzo Childs;* was caught by the Confederates and had quite a time of it. Then he went out to Nevada and California, then to Honolulu, then to New York, and all over the world."

"How about the five hundred?" *The Republic* reporter asked Captain Bixby; "did he pay that?"

"Paid three hundred," responded the captain. "You see, the war came on and there wasn't much money to be had. He didn't have any and I didn't. So we just called the other two hundred off."

Life on the Mississippi is Mark Twain's true narrative of his experiences on the river, and Captain Bixby's name frequently enters. Like Captain Bixby, Mark Twain has his own way of describing that three years' grapple with the science of piloting.

"I supposed," said the humorist, "that all a pilot had to do was to keep his boat in the river, and I did not consider that that could be much of a trick since it was so wide."

But it proved to be more of a trick and nearer a science than the pilot novitiate thought. Each eccentric bend in the stream had a name, each of hundreds of reefs had a name, to say nothing of the innumerable lands, which had names. The would-be steamboat guide was expected to load his mind with all these names, and with a mass of extraneous but practical information about each locality. Moreover, the river's course was constantly changing, new reefs were forming, and there were an endless number of boat-destroying snags which were sure to find positions, bayonet-like, in the most unexpected places.

At times, Mark Twain was moved to give up the task of acquiring so much dry information. But he was encouraged by Mr. Bixby, who according to Mark said: "When I say I'll learn a man the river, I mean it. And you can depend on it I'll learn him or kill him."

Notes to Interview 156

1. Historic hotel opened in 1841 at the corner of Chesnut and Pine in downtown St. Louis.
2. See n. 1 to interview 16.
3. See also *Life on the Mississippi*, chapter 48.
4. Among the pilots who greeted MT were John Henton Carter (aka Commodore Rollingpin), a former steamboat pilot and popular St. Louis journalist and humorist, and Sobieski (Beck) Jolly (d. 1905), captain of the *John J. Roe*, which MT piloted in the fall of 1857 (see also chapters 16 and 24 of *Life on the Mississippi*). See also *Auto* (1959), 79.

157

Robertus Love,[1] "Mark Twain Dines with His Sweetheart of Old Time Days," *St. Louis Post-Dispatch,* 31 May 1902, 1–2.

Hannibal, Mo., May 31—This visit of Mark Twain to Hannibal is no joke. It is a serious matter.

The solemnity of the occasion grows upon one as the hours pass. One sees it in the face of Mr. Clemens himself.

Those kindly blue eyes mirror the solemnity. A new quaver in the buoyant voice tells it aloud.

And yet the humorist, upon occasion, fulfills his lifelong part. He laughs with indubitable heartiness when laughter is due. He smiles with indisputable pleasure when he ought to smile. He says many things which erupt the laugh-craters in his auditors.

And yet—well, there is nothing at all funereal about this visit. Mark Twain is having a good time. He is enjoying the visit because he is doing his duty. Sixty years ago he did not enjoy doing his duty, but age has altered him. There is no doubt Mark Twain came here because he felt it to be a sort of sacred duty to come back to the starting point and review the journey.

How he feels about it, now that he is here, may be judged from what he said to me Friday noon while waiting for the hotel people to move his baggage into two connecting rooms nearer the bathtub than is No. 27. He was just back from the cemetery.

"It is very beautifully situated, that cemetery," said Mark Twain. "If I had the time I should look for the boys out there. That is where they are. I came here to see the people.

"I have met a good many more than I expected to meet. I find about 20 surviving, and am moved with gratification and gratitude for that.

"But most of them are out there in that cemetery. I could pick them out if I had the time to walk about and read their names.

"I came this time for the reason I was invited by the university of my native state to go to Columbia and be made a doctor of laws. I think I am well fitted for that avocation, and I am glad of the invitation to come and get an honorary degree which I have not earned. The chiefest of all the preparation I have had for the LL.D. I acquired in the old schoolhouse here that Mr. Cross used to take care of.[2] He qualified me to be an LL.D. There were difficulties connected with it two generations ago. Here tonight I see a great advance in matters of intellectual taste over the schools of my boyhood. Two generations ago the quality of school oratory was bombastic, a pretentious, inflated oratory, words, abounding words, and words delivered with an immense energy, when the ideas were weak.

"The modern oratory, which deals with grace of expression and felicity of ideas, I heard in the Presbyterian pulpit for once in my life in Hannibal. Many is the time when, as a boy, I went to the Presbyterian Church by request.

"The desire I had to stand in the Presbyterian pulpit just once and help instruct those people the whirligig of time has gratified and the ambition of nearly two generations ago has been satisfied. The character of those school exercises you have listened to tonight shows a great improvement. In those boyhood times we had children in school of all ages up to 25 years and of a dozen sexes, year after year, and there was only one Latin pupil. That was George RoBards and he was the envy and admiration of all the school.[3]

"He occupied that great and solitary eminence, that alpine summit of isolation, of the one Latin scholar in Hannibal school. In the old commencement exercises there was not a single line of original thought or expression. The programs were made up of recitations and nearly always poems, exciting poems. But these young ladies tonight had delivery, graceful and expressive, and they had written their own ideas. Here are the young gentlemen, too, and I don't see why the so-called superior sex is in such a limited quantity. This commencement is a mighty advance on what we did on the public square 60 years ago. If a boy then showed any original thought the people suspected that something was the matter with him.

"As I said, everything was recitation and those recitations were not selected from the wide field of English literature. There were three or four poems used and only one prose piece and that we had always heard every week. It was 'Give Me Liberty or Give Me Death.'[4] I never ventured that. And the poetry—well, these three pieces of poetry were never neglected.

The Assyrian came down like [the] wolf on the fold,
And his cohorts were gleaming in purple and gold.[5]

"And this one—

Lochiel, Lochiel, beware of the day
When the lowlands shall meet thee in battle array.[6]

"But the standby of all, the boy that saved Hannibal to intellectual life, recited always 'The Boy Stood on the Burning Deck.'[7] Today it has been so pathetic for me to meet, shake hands and look into the eyes of old white-headed men whom I knew as boys in the old school and I could not help but imagine them repeating again 'The Boy Stood on the Burning Deck.'

"I shook hands today with half a dozen who used to recite 'The Boy Stood on the Burning Deck,' always in the same old way. They never tried to invent ingenuities and new departures. It is hard for me to conceive of taking that as a method to identify a Hannibal boy, but seven years ago coming in a ship from Ceylon to Bombay in the Bay of Bengal—no, let me see, my geography was learned here—in the Arabian Sea, on the deck stood a man who yelled, 'Hello, Mark.' 'Hello, yourself,' I said. 'Who are you?'

"'Don't you remember,' he said, 'the old Cross school in Hannibal?'

"'Yes,' I replied.

"'But who are you?'

"'Why,' he said, 'I'm the boy that used to recite 'The Boy Stood on the Burning Deck.'"

"There wasn't a boy in Hannibal that didn't do it. It was a cold day when he didn't have half a dozen boys standing on the same deck. In this presence tonight is that old mariner, Billy Nash.[8] I have stood on the burning deck with him a hundred times, without fire insurance or anything."

Here Mark Twain stared ruefully at a bunch of rolled diplomas tied with red and blue ribbons on a table in the wings. He continued: "I never distributed diplomas in my life, and don't know how to do it, but a person can do a thing with more confidence if he doesn't know how. To know how to do a thing is a great sapper of confidence.

"I'll distribute these diplomas as they come to hand and let the graduates toss up for a choice. There will be no underhanded work about this. It will be frank and open. I am going to punch in the presence of the passenjare."[9]

Amid a roar of laughter from graduates, undergraduates, and the packed theater, Mark Twain picked up the bunch of diplomas and extending them end foremost, he passed along the semi-circle and invited each graduate to take one.

"There, don't take but one," he said to a pretty girl near the center. "If you do there won't be enough to go round and then Billy Nash will blame Sam Clemens for making a bad job of it."

By this method Miss Lottie Bulkley, valedictorian, happened to get the diploma belonging to Charles Seibel, and no graduate received his or her own diploma. There was a great jollification when the distribution was rectified, Mark Twain joining—and thus ended the most memorable commencement in Hannibal.

Rain began falling early Saturday morning and continued until noon. Mark Twain's coffee was sent to his rooms and he remained therein resting and recuperating for the Labinnah Club reception tonight.[10] Last midnight he remarked to me:

"In the course of time this sort of thing might make a man a little tired." It has been a day of memories for Mark Twain. His memory has ransacked the past, and one can observe without an effort that he is trying to live it over again, to bring back out of the drift and swirl of time the events of his boyhood and the old familiar faces. Though he cannot, like Charles Lamb,[11] lament:

Gone, all gone, the old familiar faces,

he finds that the faces of the few survivors have so greatly altered that there is little left of the familiar look.

There is one face, however, in which Mark Twain—no, Sam Clemens, aged 15—sees some of the old familiar aspect. "That old sweetheart of mine"—he saw her Friday evening, though the romance did not turn out as in the Riley rhyme.[12]

Sam Clemens and Laura Hawkins,[13] both aged 15, ate dinner together Friday evening. They were guests of Mrs. Helen Garth at her costly mansion on South Fifth street.[14]

Sam, who, in the future is destined to be one Mark Twain, genial humorist and one of the most famous men in the world, and Laura Hawkins, whose star of fortune reads that she will become the Widow Frazier and serve as matron for the Home of the Friendless in Hannibal—these two, playmates in

1840, schoolmates in 1845, and pledged sweethearts in this present year of 1850—met Friday evening at dinner, with Mrs. Garth as chaperone.

Strange to say, Sam was staying at the Windsor Hotel on Main street instead of at his mother's house on Hill street. This Hannibal boy of 15 is reveling in the splendors of two connecting rooms, with a whole bed to himself and a wardrobe for his clothes. Just why he left home the Hannibal people—the whole 700 of them—are not quite sure, but it is hinted at Brittingham's drug store, around the corner from the Widow Clemens' house, that Sam has found at last a large quantity of the buried treasure in Loop Hollow, north of Holliday's hill, and is enjoying the luxuries.

Eddie Pierce, Tom Nash and Billy Nash, Charley Curts, and the other boys of his village are speckled all over with green envy, and Eddie Pierce declares that if he were as big as Sam Clemens he would waylay him some dark night and get some of the gold.

"Ain't I helped Sam dig for that gold all spring?" says Eddie, "and didn't I whitewash his old fence for him?"

Well, at any rate, Sam Clemens returned to his rooms in the Windsor Friday evening and dressed himself in evening clothes from head to foot. In swallowtail coat, low-cut, white vest, creased trousers and patent-leather shoes, with a white bow tie, he entered his carriage and was driven to Mrs. Garth's.

"O, you think you're the Prince of Wales, Sam Clemens, but we know you!"

Suffice it to say—all curtailed tales must end so—Sam found Laura smilingly awaiting him at the chaperon's house.

"Gee whiz!" Sam cried. "It seems like I ain't seen you in 50 years, Laura."

Youth's enthusiasm! Sam knew well enough that he had waited outside the Presbyterian Church only last Sunday night to ask Laura Hawkins if he couldn't take her home, and Billy Nash had tried to cut him out when the girl appeared.

The dinner was a success. All good dinners are. Sam and Laura talked—

But let us draw a veil over this scene. Very good veils can be bought for a bit a yard.

Mark Twain, whose claim that he wept at the grave of Adam has been questioned,[15] shed tears in Hannibal Friday afternoon.

Of that there is no question.

A thousand reputable citizens saw him wipe the tears away with a big handkerchief when he arose to address the G.A.R. men and the other persons gathered for the Memorial Day exercises in the Presbyterian Church.

He was tottering with emotion when he arose. His voice was broken—almost sobbing—during the utterance of his first sentence: "As is quite natural, I am profoundly touched by this welcome. I am not easily moved. I wish I were more easily moved.

"But I am deeply moved this time, as I have been several times in the 24 hours that I have spent here, by the reception I have met from the old men and women still living here and from later citizens.

"The expressions in their face and the hand grasps and the words that have greeted me have been something more than friendship, and that something is affection, the proudest thing an old man may possess, and in granting me that this city of my earliest time has stirred me with the profoundest compliment."

Notes to Interview 157

1. See n. 1 to interview 153.
2. MT attended Sam Cross's frame schoolhouse on the square in Hannibal. See also *Auto* (1959), 31.
3. George RoBards was the only Latin student in MT's class at the Cross school and is mentioned incidentally in chapter 21 of *Tom Sawyer*. See also n. 3 to interview 155.
4. In March 1775 Patrick Henry (1736-99) protested British tyranny. Tom Sawyer attempts to recite the speech in the school declamation scene in chapter 21 of *The Adventures of Tom Sawyer*.
5. "The Destruction of Sennacherib" by the English poet Lord Byron (1788-1824).
6. "Lochiel's Warning" by Thomas Campbell (1777-1844) about Donald Cameron of Lochiel (c.1700-1748), who was a highly regarded Highland chief.
7. "Casabianca," better known by its incipt, "The Boy Stood on the Burning Deck," by the English poet Felicia Dorothea Hemans (1793-1835). MT also refers to the poem in his essay "Miss Clapp's School" (1864), and in *Tom Sawyer*, chapter 21.
8. MT also refers in chapter 15 of *The American Claimant* (1892) to "tall, raw-boned Billy Nash, caulker from the navy yard."
9. See n. 9 to interview 153.
10. Labinnah is Hannibal spelled backward.
11. Charles Lamb (1775-1834), English essayist.
12. The American poet James Whitcomb Riley (1849-1916).
13. Anna Laura Hawkins Frazier (1837-1928), MT's childhood friend and the model for Becky Thatcher in *The Adventures of Tom Sawyer*. Also the name of one of the principal characters in *The Gilded Age*.
14. See n. 2 to interview 155.
15. See n. 1 to interview 12.

158

Hastings MacAdam, "Attention of Old Friends Moves Mark Twain to Tears," *St. Louis Republic,* 31 May 1902, 1.

Hannibal, Mo., May 30—Touched by the deep attention which this community has evinced for him, before an audience assembled in the Hannibal Presbyterian Church to celebrate Decoration Day by religious observance, Mark Twain wept. Sobs choking him, the man of laughs, in deep, heart-touching seriousness expressed his appreciation of the tender regard in which he is held. He wept manly tears. The audience, many of whom were old like himself, yet had been young with him in Hannibal, likewise was carried away by deep feeling, the truest expression of which was tears.

"I am profoundly touched," said the speaker, "by my reception here. I have not only been moved, moved a number of times, by the cordiality of my reception by the old, old men and women who knew me here when I was a boy. I am overcome by the something more than friendship which has entered into my reception—an evidence of true affection. Affection! That is the proudest thing anybody can acquire in this world, and in granting me that this city of my early life has paid me the highest possible compliment."

Then Mark Twain spoke of patriotism, a theme appropriate to the day, and his words were earnest and true.

"The patriot is the conscience-instructed man," said he, "the man who is true to his convictions."

His theme led him to the Civil War, and one of Mark Twain the author's inimitable narrations followed.

"My conscience directed me to take up the Confederate cause," said he. "I labored for that cause just two weeks. In that period I tried to help Confederate affairs. I think it was in the second week of June 1861 when Ed Stevens,[1] Sam Lyons, and a lot of young fellows marched out of Hannibal and camped at New London. We walked the ten miles in four hours. We might have done it in three and a half, but were not practiced up yet. We camped, as I said, and had a council of war—to see what we could do toward inducing the Northern States to behave themselves. We didn't do any fighting, but we didn't see that we could aid the Confederates' cause any by being harassed by General Grant's soldiers—he was Colonel Grant then, Colonel of the Palmyra Regiment. We did no fighting because we couldn't get into a fight. General Grant's soldiers never showed their faces. They never got that near to us, though I think if they had there would have been trouble. After two weeks, we thought there wasn't any use bothering with the problem anymore—it was too big for us. We went down in Louisiana and dissolved ourselves.[2] I still think that, if we'd have met Grant and that Twenty-first Illinois Infantry of his, there would have been trouble."[3]

At the invitation of W. C. H. Nash, Mark Twain consented to attend the commencement exercises of the Hannibal High School.

He gave the diplomas to the sixteen graduates, three of whom were young men and thirteen young women. In the course of the exercises he spoke briefly, expressing his gratitude that he had arrived in Hannibal at a time that made this pleasant service possible. Last year he had been invited to attend these exercises, but was unable to do so, and he said that he was grateful that the opportunity had now been given him to remedy his unavoidable default the year previous.

Before the limits of his visit expire, Mark Twain expects to visit all the old landmarks to which he is attached by the bonds of youth. He will go to the famous cave, three miles south of the city in the depths of which Tom Sawyer and his beloved Becky were lost, and in which Mark Twain, then young Sam Clemens, was himself lost—the same cave to which attaches memories of the dread Injun Joe, his crimes and death by starvation imprisoned in the endless vault.

Mark Twain has stood once more within the shelter of the home of his boyhood where he was raised, whence he went to school, whence he went forth into the world to become printer, pilot, reporter, newspaper correspondent, lecturer, writer of books and Missouri's most famous man. Worthwhile it is to note, too, that many years before young Sam, the future Mark, went forth, a watermelon sailed from the second-story window of the house and landed squarely upon the head of the man who sold that melon. For the melon was rotten, and the boy, Sam Clemens, had paid his last 10 cents for it—perhaps planning to enjoy it with the original Huck Finn. According to boyhood's sense of justice, the melon should return unto its owner, and it did, unexpectedly.

Mr. Clemens, or Mark Twain—one is in doubt what to call him here; his identity is equally divided between himself as Clemens and himself as author in the minds and talk of his old comrades—stood for a long time gazing upon the little frame building which was his home. He did not talk much. Even the ever-present playful smile that hovers at the corners of his mouth was gone. He was thinking—of the days that are dead, of men and women who are dead, perhaps of hopes that are dead, and likely enough of the fact that he had come back home upon what will likely be his last visit—that he must soon bid final farewell to this gray old house which was his shelter many, many years ago.

Finally he turned away from the little cottage so familiar, and his eye took in the surroundings. At the corner of Main and Hill streets, the southwest corner, is an old frame structure known as the McDaniel confectionery for the last fifty years.

"I think I know that building," said he in his slow manner. "Ah, yes, there are those pilasters which grill it like a broiler. They convict it. Yes, yes, it's McDaniel's place. I bought sweets there long ago."

Just then an old man with long, gray whiskers down to his waist strolled up bashfully. He took a position directly in front of Mark Twain. The celebrated man looked at him intently for a while and then exclaimed: "What, it is Jimmie!"

"Yes, it is," replied Jimmie.

James McDaniel was the newcomer,[4] son of the McDaniel who had sold Mark sweets. They talked for several minutes. Mark asked if Jimmie remembered such and such an occurrence at such and such a time.

"It wasn't then," said Jimmie. "It was, Jimmie." "It wasn't."

"You swear it, Jimmie." "I swear it," said James.

"If you swear it, all right," said Mark.

After drinking in these sights, Mr. Clemens—he must be so called in this connection—went in a carriage to Mount Olive Cemetery. There are buried his parents and two brothers, Henry and Orion—the former of whom was killed in a steamboat explosion in 1859, and the latter of whom died several years ago in Keokuk, Iowa.[5]

I went into the one-time Clemens home. It seemed that Tom Sawyer was here, and Tom's tricks without number were called to mind. It seemed, too that Huck Finn was outside, "meowing" to the Black Avenger of the Spanish Main to come forth, show himself, and be a good fellow. Looking up the narrow flight of stairs, upon the steps of which the youthful Clemens it is said wrote his first effusions, one half expected to see Aunt Polly start from out one of the upper rooms and cry, "Tom, you Tom!"

Out back of the house was a jumble of shed, and one particularly high hip roof, joined to a rear second-story window of the main structure. Upon this, of course, Tom Sawyer crawled from home at Huck's caterwaul summons, and from it he dropped to the woodshed, and from the woodshed to the ground, where stood never-to-be forgotten Huck himself. On one such occasion Huck had a dead cat—and this was the time of the spine-curling graveyard scene.

Out in this not overlarge backyard is the fence—the whitewashed fence. There is now a coat of whitewash on it, but it is confidently said here that the whitening is not the same which Tom Sawyer with the assistance of a gullible boy Ben put upon it. Then, too, across this fence, further north, is Huck Finn's home. This place is now old and decayed and will soon cease to be—like Huck himself, for they tell in Hannibal that the real Huck has gone to his last accounting.

Hannibal teems with stories about Sam Clemens, about Tom Sawyer (the original for whom say those who should know was Mark himself), about Huckleberry Finn. It is beyond doubt a Twain town. So greatly is the "Prophet" honored in his own country that a dozen men here claim to be the one and only original Tom Sawyer. So, too, is it with Huck. But Huck Finn's identity is established by Ed Pierce of this city, and Huck's name was Tom Blankenship.[6]

Pierce, who is a few years younger than Mark, was his friend and Blankenship's friend in boyhood and through him the Huck Finn home was pointed out to me. It stands a dingy, three-story frame structure which appears about to fall into ruins. Now occupied by negroes upon a street which has degenerated to an alley, it must have called up again said memories to the mind of Mark Twain.

"Oh yes, I know the swimming pool where Tom Sawyer played 'hookey,'" said Pierce. "It was there that Sam Clemens and I played 'hookey' many a day. More than a mile back of town it lay, and near it also was 'ghost hollow.' Now the pool is no more. The course of Bear Creek has been changed and where stands the most substantial part of Hannibal ran that stream.

"Sam, or Mark, I get his names mixed, was a queer boy, but we all thought he was 'too durned slow.' Maybe he was slow, and maybe he wasn't—depends on how you look at it. Say now, I remember where Sam and I first went to school. It was old Cross's school—an old log hut. Cross was cross. 'Cross is his name,' we used to say, 'cross is his nature. Cross jumped out of a raw potato.' Well, one day Sam and a lot of the boys locked old Cross out of school. Well, there's not much more, except that Cross got in and hammered us all good. I never did see a man so mad."

William Robbins, old river man, remembers much concerning Mark. One incident refers to a time when, in excess of spirits, the youth is said to have started an immense boulder which almost obliterated a sawmill, down Holliday Hill, just north of town. Such anecdotes are without number. . . .

Notes to Interview 158

1. MT had described Ed Stevens in "The Private History of a Campaign That Failed" (1885) as the "son of the town jeweler,—trim-built, handsome, graceful, neat as a cat; bright, educated, but given over entirely to fun."
2. Louisiana, Missouri, about twenty miles downriver from Hannibal.
3. See n. 2 to interview 101.
4. On James McDaniel, see also *Auto* (1959), 74; *Auto* (1990), 212-13.
5. Henry Clemens (1838-58), MT's younger brother. On Orion Clemens, see n. 7 to interview 50.
6. Tom Blankenship (b. circa 1831). *Auto* (1959), 67-68: "ignorant, unwashed, insufficiently fed, but he had as good a heart as ever any boy had."

159

Hastings MacAdam, "Mark Twain Visits His Old Sweetheart," *St. Louis Republic,* 1 June 1902, sec. 3, 1.

Hannibal, Mo., May 31—"I'm afraid we'll have to put a hoop around Mark Twain's head before he leaves Hannibal," said Mrs. Laura Frazier, Mark's first sweetheart, now matron of the Home for the Friendless at Hannibal.[1]

"I'm afraid he'll be spoiled," she continued, "but I suppose if there was any danger of that it would have happened long ago."

Mark's first sweetheart, who is believed to be the original of Becky Thatcher in *Tom Sawyer,* is now a matronly lady whose memory is still clear concerning those early times.

"We lived right across the street from the Clemens family," she said, "and I saw Sam, as he was known to us then, nearly every day. Yes, as children we were attracted to one another. I remember the last time I saw him. It was just before we parted for the last time; we were skating on Bear Creek, and I can distinctly recall that I had trouble in getting on one of my skates, and Sam performed the service beautifully for me.

"I have a little remembrance of a date much later. It was the time when he was married. He sent me a wedding card, but did not know my husband's name, and sent the card to my brother, addressing it 'Mrs. ——, to my first sweetheart, whom I knew twenty-nine years ago.'"

Mrs. Frazier still has this card, which she prizes highly.

Last night Mark Twain met Mrs. Frazier at dinner at the home of Mrs. John H. Garth,[2] and the talk reverted to the incidents and the friends of their youth. This afternoon he visited Mrs. Frazier at the Home for the Friendless.

A story attaches to a visit made by Mark Twain yesterday, of which no word has yet been said. When Mark was Sam, and perhaps Tom Sawyer to boot, he knew a girl whose full name was Azelia Erminie Cordelia Tranquilla Emilie Emerine Penn. Her father owned Mark's birthplace, a house in Florida, Mo.

The visiting author remembered the name—Azelia, etc., Penn, and found that the lady was now Mrs. Fowkes, 70 years old, living on Sixth street in Hannibal. He lost no time in calling on her.

A clouded day and a drizzling rain this morning prevented any excursion to outlying places which possess a sentimental attraction for Mark Twain. Fatigued by a busy Memorial Day, though he said he enjoyed it greatly, he kept to his room until noon—a proceeding entirely unaccountable to those who remembered Sam Clemens as the boy whose father saw that he rose promptly with the sun.

Returning to his hotel late last night, he was still in the conversational mood, and talked to two or three listeners for an hour or more. At this time he received an unintelligible telegram from New York, which read simply, "Mark Twain, try Hannibal hotels."

"Is the man who sent that a lunatic?" he queried, talking chiefly to himself. "I'm trying one hotel now," he continued. "No, let's see, is it paid for? No, collect. That man is not a lunatic." This last very decisively.

The subject of lunacy suggested, he continued: "I've often been in lunatic asylums—as a guest. I remember once in Belfast, Ireland, where there is an immense institution, the superintendent's idea was that dangerous lunatics should be treated as if they were sane—as if they were not the least dangerous. He allowed them the freedom of the asylum grounds. He was very philosophical, and thought that to humor insane men was the way to cure them. Perhaps it is, but that superintendent was killed by some of his lunatics just a few days after I visited the place."

Probably Mark Twain will never revisit Famous Cave, about two miles south of Hannibal, the cave where he often went as a boy, the cave which housed "Injun Joe," the cave in which Tom Sawyer and his loved Becky Thatcher were lost.

"I know all about that cave," said he. "It is clear in my mind now down to the minutest details. If I go to it now it will be only a sentimental journey. I suppose there is but one thing changed about it. In the old days there hung in it a copper cylinder, filled with alcohol and in the alcohol was a corpse—the corpse of the daughter of a St. Louis doctor, a well-known man of his day, who, however, was not given credit for insanity, only eccentricity. He caused a metal bar to be fixed into the rock walls in a narrow passage, far back under the bluff, and to the bar he attached the cylinder. Never had human being such a mausoleum.[3]

"I guess that the cylinder is now gone. But I am not anxious to investigate into such a ghastly matter."

It is said that "Injun Joe" is still living near Hannibal in the person of a half-breed Indian, who is fully 80 years old.[4] If so, the person who so impressed Mark's imagination that the portrait of "Injun Joe" resulted must not be thought of harshly. Yesterday this person walked a full mile to present Mark with a bouquet, which he did impressively and in silence. Mark's honest thanks made the half-breed's face glow with pleasure.

This morning the hotel was again thronged with visitors who came to see Mark Twain. Among them was Charles Curts, another of the now gray and feeble men who played with Mark when he was a boy.

"I guess," said Curts, "no day passed here fifty years ago when I didn't see Sam Clemens. I went to school with him, played with him, and did everything that he did, I guess. Many a time I have been down to the cave with him—and remember several instances when we were lost for a brief time among its endless windings."

This afternoon I visited "Injun Joe," or Joe Douglas, the half-breed here, who is accorded the distinction of being the genuine Injun Joe by everybody in Hannibal save Mark Twain, who is noncommittal, saying only that he may as well have the honor as anybody else.

"Injun Joe" tells that he has been known by that name since the fifties, when he was taken to Marion County from Mexico. He is half Mexican and half Cherokee Indian. In and around Hannibal he has worked for several families.

When he first came here he was greatly feared by the negroes. Given shelter by a negro family the members of the latter feared that he would cut their throats or scalp them in the night, and guarded him with shotguns. Then again hearing him snore they imagined that he was on the warpath, that the guttural sounds were war whoops. Whether or not he contributed more than the name to the character in Mark Twain's book, facts are to show that the suggestion for such a character lay in his life.

At this late day Joe Douglas is a personality of interest. The only Indian in town, without education, cheated and made game of incessantly, he has accumulated property and money to the extent of several thousand dollars.

He has learned to read and eagerly endeavors to get the newspapers. He married a negro woman, who is now dead, and he has no relative to leave his possessions. He has made no will and says that he preferred that his money go to the State than to anybody he knows.

The afternoon was spent visiting by Mark Twain. His sister-in-law, Mrs. Orion Clemens, came down from Keokuk, Iowa, to meet him, and he spent a portion of his time with her.[5] He paid the promised visit to Mrs. Frazier, and stopped a time with others of whom he knew or who wished to know him. Returning to his hotel at 6 o'clock, he received in the parlors of the hotel the members of the High School class to whom he gave diplomas last night. The young people were accorded a good time by their genial, jolly, fascinating host, which they will remember for life.

He entertained them as usual with reminiscences. This time it was of a momentous occasion in youth that he told, when he worked assiduously to get the measles. Another boy had them; he wanted them, too. The other boy should have no such monopoly. He got into the other boy's house, but was collared by his father and marched back to the little home which still stands on Hill street. Hearing the other boy's father advise his mother to keep him locked in a room, he jumped from a second-story window, landing almost on the head of the father of the boy with the measles, who had just started away from the Clemens house. He was again returned into durance vile, but escaped, penetrated to the bedside of the boy with the measles, got into bed with him, and got the measles.

"They were not what I expected they would be," said he.

At 9 o'clock he prepared to attend the reception of the Labinnah Club.[6] There the society of this city formally welcomed him. He partook of punch, served by Hannibal's handsomest young women, all of whom he claimed as his sweethearts of the third generation. He responded to a welcoming address, holding the assembled admirers for fifteen minutes, midway between tears and laughter. Concluding, he said: "As this is probably my last visit to you, my old, old friends, and you my new friends, and to Hannibal, I want to express my sincerest affection for you all and this town where I spent my boyhood. Goodby."

Notes to Interview 159

1. See n. 13 to interview 157.
2. See n. 2 to interview 155.
3. Joseph Nash McDowell (1805–68), a St. Louis physician, allegedly preserved the body of his teenaged daughter in a glass and copper cylinder in the cave. MT refers to this local legend in the final paragraph of chapter 55 of *Life on the Mississippi*.
4. According to local legend, the mixed-blood Joe Douglas (1821?–1923) was MT's model for Injun Joe.
5. Mary (Mollie) Clemens (1834–1904), MT's sister-in-law and Orion's widow. On Orion, see n. 7 to interview 50.
6. Labinnah is Hannibal spelled backward.

160

Robertus Love,[1] "Mark Twain Takes a Drive with His Schoolmate's Pretty Daughter," *St. Louis Post-Dispatch,* 2 June 1902, 5.

Hannibal, Mo., June 2—Mark Twain this morning enjoyed a drive with a pretty girl, the daughter of one of his schoolgirl friends of nearly 60 years ago. Miss Katheryn Lakenan, of Columbia, Missouri, formerly of Hannibal, called at the hotel, by appointment, and took the humorist out driving.

Mr. Clemens first met Miss Lakenan on the train coming into Hannibal last Thursday. Mrs. Lakenan and her daughter were aboard, and happily were in the same coach with the author. Mrs. Lakenan went to Mark Twain's seat and greeted him.

"Don't you know me" she asked.

"Ye-e-e-es," replied he, "I do-o-o-o-oo know you-u-u, but. . . . "

It was plain that he saw something in the lady's face to remind him of a girl away back in the past.

"I won't tell you who I am at first," said Mrs. Lakenan. "Think awhile."

"I have a name in my mind," replied Mr. Clemens, "of a girl who used to attend the old Cross school in Hannibal, but I'm not sure—I may make a mistake."

"Will you promise—honor bright—to tell me if you are thinking of the right girl or not, when I give my name?" asked Mrs. Lakenan.

"I promise, honor bright."

"Then I'm Mary Moss."[2]

"That's the girl I was thinking of," said Mr. Clemens.

As soon as he learned that Mrs. Lakenan's daughter was aboard, he went back to the young lady and gallantly escorted her to a seat beside him.

Miss Lakenan took advantage of the opportunity to invite him to go driving with her, and thereby made herself the only Missouri girl so honored by the great man.

Mark Twain also took a drive about Hannibal—the Hannibal of 60 years ago, the St. Petersburg of Tom Sawyer—with John Briggs, Sunday afternoon.[3] Mr. Briggs lives in New London, and came in Saturday just to see his old chum. The two boys played together and did other things as comrades and accomplices when they ran about barefooted and sunburnt in the '40s.

John Briggs was one of the young men who joined the Confederate army with Sam Clemens in 1860, undergoing the strenuous two weeks' campaign of keeping away from Colonel Ulysses S. Grant which the humorist loves to tell about.[4]

"Briggs and I," he said, "were the best retreaters in the company."

The two old boys went up over Holliday's Hill in Ghost Hollow and through Soap Hollow, where they dug for buried treasure many years ago and never found it—except in Mark Twain's fiction.

They also drove past the fine new mansion of J. J. Cruikshank,[5] which cost $125,000, the Hannibal people are proud to tell the visitor, and which is located where the Richmond orchard of 60 years ago furnished the finest apples for the loot of Sam Clemens, Johnny Briggs, Billy and Tom Nash, Eddie Pierce, Charlie Curts and Ben Blankenship[6]—the latter dead and gone these many years, being by common consent at least fixed upon as the one and only original of Huckleberry Finn.

"Do you know, John," remarked Sam Clemens yesterday, "I have never had any pangs of conscience for stealing those apples. They were good apples, John."

Tonight Mr. Clemens will be the guest of honor at a reception in the Cruikshank home—the closing entertainment of his trip, for at 10:50 Tuesday morning he takes a train for Columbia, bidding farewell to the old home.

Mark Twain's sermon at the Baptist Church Sunday morning was a little different from what the people had expected. Hannibal folk have come to expect lachrymose scenes when the distinguished fellow townsman arises to talk.

For that matter, the Baptist Church service was lachrymose, but not Mark Twain's part of it. Rev. Everett Gill,[7] the pastor, preceded Mr. Clemens by preaching a short sermon on "A Garland for Ashes," in which he said some things that brought out the trickling tear from hundreds of eyes.

"Life," said Mr. Gill, "is a strange medley of flowers and ashes. One half of the world go along life's highway garlanded with the flowers of joy, tripping along with merriment and song, while the other half sit by the roadside in sorrow, with the ashes of mourning on their heads. Moreover, both of these experiences come into the lives of each of us. No life is one continual song, nor yet one long-drawn sigh, not all flowers nor all ashes. Life is a dappled picture of shadow and sunshine."

The pastor then referred to the guest of the city, the great man who has come back to say good-bye.

"Mr. Clemens," he said, "has not scattered the ashes of his own griefs upon the heads of others. He has kept them to himself, and all through his life has been bestowing garlands of joy. In doing this, he has been doing the work of Christ."

Mr. Gill then invited Mr. Clemens into the pulpit, "not to preach a sermon," he said, "but to say a few words, whatever might come to him to say."

"No," said Mark Twain, arising in the pew where he sat beside his old sweetheart, Mrs. Frazier, the Laura Hawkins of his boyhood.[8] "No, I shall not come into the pulpit. I might do that on a weekday, but I cannot do it on a Sunday without bruising my own sense of the proprieties.

"But I must take issue with Rev. Dr. Gill, who says that I need not preach a sermon. What I say will be preaching. I am a preacher. We are all preachers. If we do not preach by words, we preach by deeds. What we do and say has its influence upon others, and in our daily life, though we be not clergymen, we preach to each other.

"The art of preaching is to influence. From the pulpit and from the mouths of all of us, the preaching goes on all the time. Our words and deeds are like the tidal waves of the seas that encircle the earth.

"They are not for ourselves alone, but for others. We forget that we carry influence, but we should remember it and we should see that our influence is of the good kind.

"Words perish, print burns up, men die, but our preaching lives on. Washington died in 1799, more than a hundred years ago, but his preaching survives, and to every people that is striving for liberty his life is a sermon.

"My mother lies buried out there in our beautiful cemetery overlooking the Mississippi, but at this age of mine, she still cheers me. Her preaching lives and goes on with me.

"Let us see that our preaching is of the right sort, so that it will influence for good the lives of those who remain when we shall be silent in our graves."

Two things were plainly evident in Mark Twain's little sermon. One was that he strove, and with excellent success, not to say anything that could be construed as humor. It was apparent that he felt the sanctity of the place and was determined not to profane it by a word of worldly wit.

The other patent fact was that he had steeled himself against uttering any word which might bring to himself and to his auditors the pathos of his approaching farewell to the old hometown. He knew that he could not touch upon that topic without giving way to his emotion and thereby bringing the sympathetic tears to the eyes of those who listened. Twice before in Hannibal during this visit he has broken down when mentioning the farewell aspect of his visit.

So in this his first Sunday sermon, Mark Twain did what he has done throughout his literary career—he kept the ashes of his own griefs to himself and scattered garlands of good cheer.

And five minutes later, when the benediction had been pronounced, he stood in the aisle and shook hands with the hundreds who passed by, holding a few old schoolmates for a little space to discuss the teachers in the little old schoolhouse.

"Was it Mrs. Horr or Miss Horr?[9] Why, it was Mrs. Horr that I went to school to," he said.

Out on the sidewalk he asked Rev. Dr. Gill to walk down to the hotel with him. "It will give me a better standing in Hannibal," said Mark Twain, "to be seen on the street with a preacher."

Notes to Interview 160

1. See n. 1 to interview 153.
2. See also *Auto* (1959), 70–71.
3. John B. Briggs (1837–1907), MT's childhood friend, the model for Ben Rogers in *Tom Sawyer*. See also *Auto* (1959), 41, 77; and *Auto* (1990), 159, 216.
4. See n. 2 to interview 101.
5. Cruikshank's Rockcliffe, a 28,600-square-foot mansion in Greek revival style completed in 1900, contains nine bedrooms and seven bathrooms.
6. Benson (Bence or Ben) Blankenship (b. circa 1829) was Tom Blankenship's older brother (see n. 6 to interview 158).
7. Everett Gill was pastor of the Fifth Street Baptist Church in Hannibal from 1896 to 1903.
8. See n. 13 to interview 157.
9. Elizabeth Horr (d. 1873). "Mrs. Horr taught the children in a small log house at the southern end of Main street" (*Auto* [1959], 31–32). She apparently became a model for Miss Watson in *Huck Finn*.

161

"Mark Twain Going Home," *Hannibal Morning Journal*, 3 June 1902, 1.

... In the afternoon he, in company with his old chum and playmate, John B. Briggs,[1] of Ralls county, drove over the city and far out in the country. ... On their return Mr. Clemens accepted an invitation to a 6 o'clock dinner at the home of Mrs. Garth[2] and shortly afterward returned to the Windsor hotel and retired to his room, considerably fatigued from the travels of the day.

About 9 o'clock Sunday night a *Journal* reporter called on Mr. Clemens and found him lying in bed puffing away on a black cigar and with a book in his hand. He said he was somewhat fatigued, but he welcomed the reporter and for about thirty minutes talked incessantly. He said that he had greatly enjoyed his visit to Hannibal, the first one really in about forty years, and only regretted that he could not remain here a week or two longer. He said that he had so many engagements that he could not remember all of them, that they often conflicted and that he was obliged to cancel one or two yesterday. Said he: "If my wife had been with me she would not have permitted me to make two engagements for the same time."

Yesterday morning Mr. Clemens paid the *Journal* a pleasant visit and talked entertainingly of Hannibal as the old town was fifty years ago.

Mr. Clemens was shown a "Journal Carriers' Address" that was printed in the year 1850, and he said he was at that time about 15 years old and thought probably that he might have written it. Then reading it carefully he said: "No, I hardly think that I wrote this, although about that time I was thinking of writing a Carriers' address. I was too lazy and left it for someone else." . . .

Notes to Interview 161

1. See n. 3 to interview 160.
2. The widow of John H. Garth. See n. 2 to interview 155.

162

"Good-Bye to Mark Twain: The Last Interview," *Hannibal Courier-Post*, 3 June 1902, 1.

"This visit of mine back to the scene of my boyhood has been one of the happy events of my life," said Mark Twain to a reporter of the *Courier-Post* this morning, as he sat in his room at the Windsor Hotel, after having made all arrangement to take his departure.

"My visit has been a most enjoyable one, and I do not recall a single instance when I ever had a better time. The time was all well spent. I have met many of my boyhood friends and enjoyed pleasant chats with them. My ride with John Briggs[1] Sunday was especially pleasing to me.

"I am glad to know that the people of Hannibal think so much of me. It is not always that a fellow can stay away from his old home as long as I have done, and then return and be received so cordially. I tell you, it [three or four words illegible] have a warm place in his heart [one or two words illegible] such an old home.

"Thank the people of Hannibal for the kind treatment they have accorded me. I can assure you that it could not have been more cordial."

15. Departing Hannibal, 3 June 1902. Courtesy of the Mark Twain Project, University of California, Berkeley.

Note to Interview 162

1. See n. 3 to interview 160.

163

Robertus Love,[1] "Dr. Mark Twain at a Smoke Talk," *St. Louis Post-Dispatch*, 6 June 1902, 2.

And Mark Twain came back.

Friday he is back at his old trade, piloting a steamboat on the lower Mississippi. With the Rochambeau party[2] and other parties he is making an excursion on the city wharfboat, *Mark Twain,* so christened during this voyage.

"Mayor Wells," remarked Mark Twain Thursday night at a smoker in his honor at the home of Dr. and Mrs. James Ross Clemens, his cousin, at 3958 Washington boulevard, "Mayor Wells sent me a threatening telegram today.[3] He said there was a boat here without a name, and if I would come in time to make a trip on it with the other foreigners he would name it after me; otherwise he would name it after somebody else, himself I reckon. The threat scared me. I was doing very well at Columbia, but when I got that threatening message I replied at once, before I recovered from my fright, and accepted the conditions."

"What kind of a boat is it?" somebody inquired.

"I don't know," replied the humorist. "It ought to be a snag boat if it is going to be named after me."

"By the way," said a man from Pike County, "there's a town named for you up in our county. It's—"

"No, it isn't in your county," interrupted Mr. Clemens. "It's in my county—Marion, right in the lower edge of Marion. And it is not a town, either; it's a town site. When I was going up to Hannibal last week on the Burlington the brakeman invited me to stand on the rear platform of the tail-end car and see something. I stood there several miles and saw nothing in particular, until at length we whizzed past a shed with the name 'Clemens' lettered on the end.

"'That's it,' said the brakeman. 'See it?' I saw it. 'It's named after you,' said the brakeman; then he explained that Henry Miller, division superintendent at Hannibal, christened the townsite."

Mr. Clemens learned on the train that the place originally had been named Taylor, but as it was discovered that there are two or three towns in Missouri already named Taylor, a new name was decreed. Thus Marion county honored her most illustrious stepson.

"There are no houses in my town," said Mark Twain, "but the place will grow."

Bearing lightly his burden of the double dignity of two doctoral degrees with the same initials, Mark Twain came in from Columbia Thursday evening at 6 o'clock. James Ross Clemens, M.D., met Samuel Langhorne Clemens, LL.D., Yale; LL.D., M.S.U., at Union Depot.

Dr. and Mrs. Clemens will entertain the author during his stay in St. Louis, which will last until Sunday noon.

Dr. J. R. Clemens was born on Pine street, in St. Louis, but has been in London, England, the past 20 years, studying and practicing medicine. He moved into his Washington boulevard home only last week, and the first social function was the Mark Twain smoker, at which about 50 gentlemen were present.

It is probably that Mark Twain would prefer that all the entertainments in his honor be smokers. He is a smoker himself. Smoke Inspector Jones should have been present last evening in his official capacity, for there is no chimney in St. Louis that smokes more constantly than does Mark Twain.

"How many cigars a week do you smoke?" I asked him last week in Hannibal.

"Just as many as I can," was the reply.

Mark Twain smokes two grades of cigars, both Porto Ricans, three-centers and seven-centers. He prefers the three-centers, because they are "just as good" and cost less.

"I am looking for a man who holds the commercial value of a cigar above its smoking value," he remarked. "At home I have a few cigars that cost $1.66 apiece, and I am keeping them in the hope that I can sell them to somebody who thinks the cost of a cigar has anything to do with its quality." . . .

At 10:30 Walter B. Stevens arrived with an invitation from President Francis[4] of the St. Louis Club for Dr. Clemens (M.D.) and his guests to attend the club's reception in honor of the Count and Countess Rochambeau. The party proceeded to the St. Louis Club, where Mark Twain held an involuntary reception in the garden, gay with lights and lovely ladies' faces.

The great Missourian talked with the count in French and with the countess in English. He talked with the other ladies and gentlemen in any language that came to hand. No language appears to stump Mark Twain; for, though he was not the Latin linguist of the Hannibal public school of half a century ago—the one sole and solitary pupil who knew Latin—he has become a cosmopolite and can palaver many dialects, from Mississippi river patois to Volapuk.

Until midnight the author was the center of groups of admirers.

Dr. Clemens, his host, waited for him until the lights went out. He was then wandering down the garden walk, with a pretty girl's arm in his and two cigars in his right hand, like chopsticks. Just why he held cigars in one hand, smoking one between talks, I am unable to explain; but as the thing happened it should be reported faithfully.

Presumably after midnight Mark Twain smokes in relays. Perhaps he lights the relief cigar with the stub of the one that goes off duty, thereby saving the waste of time which lighting of a match would entail. Otherwise he would be unable to smoke "just as many as I can."

What mattered it to Mark Twain that the lights were turned out in the club garden at midnight?

Was not his cigar still burning and did not the relay cigar await its turn, clasped caressingly between the third and fourth fingers?

"If you don't I'll have my revenge, sure as fate," the pretty girl was saying to him.

Mark Twain likes pretty girls almost as well as cigars.

And that reminds me of a story he told me, anent the prettiest girl he ever saw—that is, before returning to Missouri; for in Hannibal, Columbia, and St. Louis he confesses to having seen a bewildering profusion of the prettiest.

"It was in Boston," he said, "years ago, and William Dean Howells[5] and I were walking down one of those crooked alleys they call streets. We saw her in a window—just glimpsed her. Howells and I both involuntarily clutched each other's arm to draw attention to her, and we looked for a fleeting moment in speechless awe.

"Even Howells felt a thrill," continued Mark Twain. "We walked off, bewildered and after turning the corner we agreed together that we ought to go back and take one more look—a good long, lingering look.

"Well, it was Boston, as I have said, and for the life of us we could not find the house again. We hunted until we were fatigued beyond further endurance, but the girl was gone from us forever." . . .

This evening Mr. Clemens will dine at the St. Louis Club as the guest of honor, Theophile Papin being the host.[6]

Saturday he will visit the World's Fair site and other points of interest,[7] and at noon Sunday he will board the Knickerbocker special for New York, where he will retire to his home at Riverdale-on-the-Hudson and smoke some cigars.

Notes to Interview 163

1. See n. 1 to interview 153.
2. A French delegation led by the Count and Countess Rochambeau was visiting St. Louis.
3. Rolla Wells (b. 1856), mayor of St. Louis from 1901 to 1909.
4. David R. Francis (1850-1927), mayor of St. Louis (1885-89), governor of Missouri (1889-93), and U.S. secretary of the interior (1896-97), was president of the St. Louis World's Fair committee.
5. See n. 2 to interview 2.
6. Theophile (Toto) Papin (1857-1916), a prominent St. Louisan.
7. The St. Louis World's Fair was held between 30 April and 1 December 1904 in Forest Park on the west side of the city to commemorate the Louisiana Purchase and the Lewis and Clark expedition.

164

Ralls County Record, 6 June 1902; rpt. *Hannibal Courier-Post*, 6 March 1935, 5C.

. . . On Sunday afternoon about 2:30 o'clock Mark Twain, John B. Briggs,[1] and the *Record* man rambled over Holliday Hill together. Driving past his old home on Hill street, they went through the alley in the middle of the block, pointing out places where they played in their boyhood days. They commanded the driver to stop and Mark said: "John, the ell of the old house has another story on it. That's about the only change." As we drove by the gas works John said, "Sam, the gas works stand on the site of my old home." Going into Palmyra Avenue, they called to mind house after house where incidents of their early days had occurred. Going up Holliday Hill as far as the carriage could go, we walked the remainder of the way and stood on the summit. Looking up and down the Mississippi river, which spread out in its magnificent grandeur, the hills on either side covered with tall trees, Lover's Leap standing like a huge sentinel in the distance, islands dotting the river here and there, waving fields of wheat glinting in the sunshine in the lowlands along the Illinois shore, Mark turned to Mr. Briggs and said: "John, that is the prettiest sight I ever saw. There is the place by the island where we used to swim. There is where a man was drowned, and there is where the steamboat sank. These things all come to my mind now. 'Twas fifty years ago, John, and yet it seems as yesterday." Pointing to various houses in the city and places among the hills, for the town lay spread out before us, he continued: "There is where the Millerites put on their robes one night to go up to heaven.[2] None of them went that night, John, but no doubt many of them have gone since. John, fifty years have whitened our hair and warned us that we are growing old. We stand today amid the scenes of our boyhood days for the last time. Let us be boys again today, and live over the past for this is one of the happiest days of my life."

And there standing face to face, hands clasped, these two strong men, equally great in strength of character, and each imbued with a love for the other that had sprung up in their childhood and grown with the years, looked into each other's eyes while tears stole down their cheeks. Turning to John he said: "Do you remember the days we stole the peaches from old man Price?" "Yes," said John, "as if it were last week." "Well," resumed Mark, "you know he moved out here from Virginia and he had a raft of bow-legged negroes. He set out a big peach orchard over there" (pointing to the place) "and we invaded it one morning, filled ourselves with peaches, stuffed a lot of them in our shirts and started for home, when one of those bow-legged negroes set the dogs on us. We ran until the dogs came up, then we fought them back. Then we ran again, the dogs still following, when all of a sudden we turned, drove the dogs back and tried to catch the negro, but he was too swift for us and got away. Do you remember, John, that we intended to catch that negro and drown him? Why, of course we did."

Going over the hill, they came to the place where they pried a huge rock from the top of the precipice and sent it crashing down the hill, across the road, over a negro driving a wagon, and into a cooper shop. Arriving at the spot John said: "Sam, here is where we pried the rock loose, after digging the dirt out from under it for three Sundays." Mark said: "John, if it had killed that negro we would have had a dead negro on our hands with not a cent to pay for him. John, I believe there were only four of us in that devilment, yet from all reports there was a gang of forty. It seems we have more playmates today than we had then. After the crash, we escaped and played innocents at home, although the patrolees gave us a close chase." Going down the hill, Mark and John keeping up a rambling chat about old times, of the people who were living fifty years ago, of those who had died and of the few left among the living, we came to a well on Palmyra Avenue with two old oaken buckets in it. Here a boy drew up a bucket of water from the cold depths below, when the lady of the house called to her son: "Tommie, get a glass for the gentlemen," when Mr. Clemens said: "No glass for me, John, we are boys today and we'll drink out of the bucket." So we all took a long draught out of the old bucket, and the water was good, cool, and refreshing. Driving along Palmyra Avenue, John Briggs pointed out the house where Barney Farthing, now of Paris, once lived. Barney is one of the original "Hucks." Then we drove down the river road to old Scipio. As we passed the bridge Mark said: "Here is where I swam the river when I was a boy. When I got near the other shore one leg cramped. I crawled up on the bank and rubbed my leg to get the cramps out of it. The sun was going down and the chill of evening was setting in and I had to swim back. After a while I started and when I got halfway across my leg commenced drawing up, then the other began to cramp, but I swam on. Once, when near the shore, I thought I would let down, but was afraid to, knowing that if the water was deep I was a goner, but finally my knees struck the sand and I crawled out. That was the closest call I ever had." Driving along the road, these boys for the evening pointed out the place where the haunted house once stood, but the house and ghost have long since gone. They told how Scipio was to be a great city and defeat Hannibal, repeating the history of the old Roman and Carthaginian days, but the order was reversed and today Hannibal is the victor and Scipio is only a memory. And thus these boyhood chums, one the greatest writer and humorist of the world, the other a prosperous farmer and good citizen, chatted and laughed, here calling up some incident, there looking for a spring at which they had slaked their boyish thirst, now dried up; casting longing looks at the hills, the river, and scenes here and there, drove back to the hotel and went to Mr. Clemens's room, where the conversation drifted into parting words. They stood up and shook hands, when Mr. Briggs said; "Sam, this perhaps will be the last time we will meet on earth and I reluctantly say good-bye. God bless you. May we meet in heaven and renew our long friendship." "John," said Mark Twain, "I am glad we have been together today. I have enjoyed it. It's been worth a thousand dollars to me. We were like brothers once. I feel that we are just the same today. Good-bye, John. If we never meet again here, I'll try to meet you on the other side." And with tears in their eyes and their voices trembling with emotion, they parted.

Notes to Interview 164

1. See n. 3 to interview 160.
2. A millennial sect named after its leader William Miller (1782–1849), who prophesied that the Second Coming of Christ and the end of the world would occur on 22 October 1844. MT also alludes to the Millerites in chapter 39 of *The Innocents Abroad;* chapter 4 of *What Is Man?* (1906); and book 1, chapter 5 of *Christian Science* (1907).

165

"Renewed Welcome to Mark Twain," *St. Louis Republic,* 6 June 1902, 2.
Wearing the additional honor of Doctor of Laws, conferred upon him by the State University, Samuel L. Clemens returned yesterday from Columbia, Mo., to receive a renewed welcome. As Mark Twain the weight of the newly acquired distinction rested lightly upon him. As Doctor Samuel Clemens, however, he took advantage of the degree.

"I am told that a Doctor of Laws ranks a Doctor of Medicine and other kinds of doctors," he said last night at a smoker given in his honor by his cousin, Doctor James Ross Clemens. . . . "For this reason I propose to remain seated while the other doctors stand." And he did. . . .

166

"Mark Twain at the Wheel Again," *St. Louis Star,* 6 June 1902, 1.
Captain Jenks was at the wheel when the St. Louis harbor boat pulled out with the Rochambeau[1] and Clemens parties aboard Friday morning, but Mark Twain piloted the *Mark Twain* back into port after a cruise up and down the muddy stream Mark knew so well some forty years ago.

The old boat had been given a coat of white paint in honor of the occasion, and folks will hardly recognize the ancient tub with its new name.

The christening of the harbor boat is Mayor Wells' idea, and a splendid one it was. That a *Mark Twain,* as the boat will now be called, had not been plowing the eddies of the Mississippi long before is a wonder.

The party arrived at the wharf in carriages at 11:20 and fifteen minutes later the hawser was cast off and the boat backed away. The band played, the breeze blew and the sun shone brightly.

The Count and Countess Rochambeau occupied the first carriage and were first aboard the steamer, and Missouri's Mark Twain drove up in the second.

As he stepped from the stringpiece of the wharf to the rail of the boat Mark lifted his Panama, as if in salutation to the river, which once was his pride.

The band was playing "Sewanee River," too, and the reminiscences must have crowded Twain's mind.

"Does the river look familiar?" Dr. Clemens was asked.

"Yes, just as wet and muddy," returned he.

"Do you anticipate any difficulty in navigating the boat as pilot?"

"Did you ever know a Missourian who anticipated the difficulty of any undertaking? I am from Mizzoura," and some pride mingled with the jesting words of Mark.

"It has been suggested that the boat be rechristened 'Mark Twain,' in your honor," he was told.

"Honor to he whom honor is due. You must show me the man from Mizzoura who would shrink from thus being honored. Everybody loves a compliment and likes to have them go their way, totally unlike the cat and the bootjack."

"Are you as well acquainted with this part of the stream as the upper—about Hannibal?"

"I used to know every ripple on its entire thousands of muddy miles. These look like the same old ripples and eddies. They might fool me at night, but I guess I could keep this boat from sticking her nose in the mud in daylight."

"Do you think the river could regain its old standing as a navigable stream with proper dredging?"

"Undoubtedly. In my time the river was alive with boats from New Orleans to St. Paul. It can be made to serve commerce in just as heavy a way again, despite the railroads. I'd like to see Congress dig the old Mississippi deeper and pull it out of its slumber." . . .

Note to Interview 166

1. A French delegation led by the Count and Countess Rochambeau was visiting St. Louis.

167

"Mark Twain at Pilot Wheel; Bids Farewell to Mississippi," *St. Louis Republic,* 7 June 1902, 1.

Mark Twain at the pilot-wheel for the last time, on the Mississippi he helped to immortalize, and the Countess de Rochambeau christening the craft with the *nom de plume* of the world-famous Missourian were the stirring sights on the river excursion yesterday in honor of the Exposition's distinguished French guests. . . . [1]

Doctor Clemens's farewell to the historic stream was impressive. Standing in the pilothouse far above the crowd on the decks, the river breezes caressed his frosty hair, the great wheel moved obediently to his master hand,[2] while the kind, blue eyes of the celebrated humorist were lifted dreamily up the lazy current.

Then his hearty voice called: "Lower away lead."

"Mark Twain, quarter, f-i-v-e a-n-d o-n-e-h-a-1-f, s-i-x f-e-e-t," came the response from the lower deck.

"Mark Twain, Mark Twain," shouted the spectators who had surged to the bow and were frantically waving their hats and 'kerchiefs in the breeze.[3]

"You are all dead safe as long as I have the wheel," answered Mark, taking three turns on the wheel." There I have rested you," he said to the pilot,[4] but the party on the deck raised their hands appealing and begged Mark to stand by them, and he did. He steered the harbor boat for a full half hour and enjoyed every minute of his task.[5]

"That is the last time I will ever play pilot," were the serious words which fell from his lips as he slowly descended the steps from the wheelhouse. Something of solemnity cast its shadow over the gay party. Tears stood in the eyes of old rivermen. It was only a snatch of sadness. Doctor Clemens ordered refreshments for the crew.

"Something stronger than river water," he added. "A crew cannot perform its duty without something bracing."[6] The excursionists laughed. A head waiter tried to announce that luncheon was served, but his voice was lost in a chorus of salutation from the deep-toned whistles of passing craft. Bells joined the clamor. The whistles of the harbor boat answered and the river was sonorous with sound. It was the tribute of the rivermen to the distinguished pilot. Mark Twain raised his Panama so that the wind tossed his snowy hair until the crews of other steamers recognize him and cheered their good-by.

The French guests enjoyed the experience. They were unanimous in the expression that it contained more of the true thrill than they had yet encountered on this side of the water. Then came the christening. It happened after the guests had been seated, when Mayor Wells paid an eloquent compliment to the author and announced that it had been determined to commemorate the return of Mark Twain to his native State by christening the boat they were on by that famous name.

Countess de Rochambeau stepped to the open way leading from the cabin to the deck. The guests arose and pressed forward to witness the event. The Countess took a bottle of champagne from the hand of President Francis,[7] and dashing the sparkling wine on the deck exclaimed: "I christen thee, good boat, *Mark Twain*."[8]

Notes to Interview 167

1. A French delegation led by the Count and Countess Rochambeau was visiting St. Louis.
"Twain at the Helm of City Harbor Boat," *St. Louis Post-Dispatch*, 8 June 1902, sec. 4, 1: "Why didn't you talk to the count, Mr. Clemens?" inquired a lady, after the incident. "Because the count does not talk English and I don't talk French—that is, the sort of French one should talk to a count. I might try it on a Parisian shopkeeper, but on a count—no."

2. *St. Louis Post-Dispatch*, 8 June: "I'll rest you a spell," said Mark Twain, with no further ado grasping the wheel hand spokes and giving her a whirl.

3. *St. Louis Post-Dispatch*, 8 June: The white-haired boy gave vent to his youthful feelings by mimicking the leadsman's cry. "Starboard leadsman!" he cried. The crowd almost whimpered in sheer delight.

4. "Mark Twain at the Pilot Wheel," *St. Louis Post-Dispatch*, 7 June 1902, 7: "You can steer now," he remarked loud enough to be heard by the other guests. "Everything looks safe."

5. *St. Louis Post-Dispatch*, 8 June: But Mark Twain was not frightened at the prospect of steering his namesake half an hour. "I'll follow that tug yonder," he remarked to Mr. Tulley. A mile ahead steamed a tug, and the usurper of the wheel followed its track.

6. "French Visitors Afloat," *St. Louis Globe-Democrat*, 7 June 1: "That's good enough water for anyone," said Dr. Clemens. "You couldn't improve it without putting in a little whiskey."
"Mark Twain at the Pilot Wheel," *St. Louis Post-Dispatch*, 7 June: "Mark twain," sang out the distinguished pilot. "Good enough water for anyone; you couldn't improve it without a little whisky."

7. See n. 4 to interview 163.

8. MT's response appears in Fatout, 440–41. MT also spoke at the University Club Friday evening: "If I am not called at least 'Doc' from now on," said Mark Twain, "there will be a decided coolness. This is a university club. No ignorant person can enter here. You are my collegiate colleagues—perhaps I may say collegiate inferiors, those of you who are not doctors yet. I have done a great deal of useful work during the past week, chiefly in the line of giving good advice. I have delivered diplomas and told the graduates what they must do, if they wanted to become doctors like me. I have talked to old soldiers and told them how much I admired them and how glad they ought to be that they had not got into such scraps as I had. I have talked in church on Sunday morning, to my own satisfaction at least. I have piloted a steamboat on the Mississippi river, and by the help of Providence that ship is still safe. When I saw a line in the Mississippi which looked partly like wind and partly like a snag, I simply told the regular pilot I was tired of steering and gave him the wheel. I could have told once what made the line on the water, but a man loses that trick. I would not lose that last week and my visit to Hannibal for anything. My joy has been made perfect by the handshaking of these Missourians. There has not been a cold handshake among them. Some have asked me if I were not tired of all this. That has seemed hardly a proper

question. Missouri cordiality does not tire a man. If it is true, as has been published, that I have made the world laugh, it is also true that Missouri has made me shed tears. . . . Life is just a sandwich of pleasures and heartaches," he said. "You have to have the pains to appreciate the pleasures" (*St. Louis Post-Dispatch,* 8 June 1902).

168

"The Eugene Field Memorial Tablet," *St. Louis Globe-Democrat,* 7 June 1902, 1.

A great living Missourian paid a tribute to a sweet singer of Missouri when Mark Twain, at 4:30 o'clock yesterday afternoon, unveiled a bronze tablet to the memory of Eugene Field at the house on South Broadway where the poet was born.[1] . . . The appearance of Mark Twain as a pilot yesterday marked his first attempt to essay the role of a wheelsman since 1880. In that year he "stood the daylight watches" between Cairo and New Orleans, and he recalled the incidents leading up to the trip yesterday after he had descended from his post at the wheel. He had come West to absorb some Mississippi river fiction for literary purposes.

When asked if the exertion of whirling the wheel was noticeable, he said: "It is good exercise. Do you know that I believe that any unaccustomed exertion is the best exercise? Some years ago I looked ten years older than I do today. That was principally because I was bankrupt at the time. The possession of a lot of debts that one cannot pay is not a disgrace, but it brings an indescribable feeling of humiliation. It crushes the spirit, and our nerves and muscles are fed by the spirit. Well, I undertook that lecturing tour with Cable.[2] The routing was abominable. It called for travel by night and day. It meant moving on railroads when we were not on platforms. I did not expect to survive it, but it rejuvenated me. It was new, and it built me up. It gave me ten years of health. I might do it again, but I do not need ten years of health now, because I shall not live that long. There are some people who are sufficiently lacking in discretion to linger alive until they get to be 80, but I am not one of them. I have been in financial straits, and I have also had dyspepsia. In two years I had cured the former trouble, but it was eight years before I got rid of the dyspepsia, and I don't think I ever would have done so had it not been for the 'starvation process.'"

Notes to Interview 168

1. Eugene Field (1850–95), American poet. MT's address is reprinted in Fatout, 442. See also "Memorial Tablet Unveiled at Eugene Field's Birthplace," *St. Louis Republic,* 7 June 1902, 4: Stepping into his carriage a moment later Mr. Clemens said that he was more than pleased to have been able to take parting this act of homage to the memory of Eugene Field. "He was a lovable fellow. In his death I felt a personal loss."

2. See chapter 2.

169

Hastings MacAdam, "Mark Twain's Return to Hannibal," *St. Louis Republic* magazine, 8 June 1902, 3; rpt. *New York Herald*, 15 June 1902, V, 9.

... From the moment that Mr. Clemens set foot in Hannibal the town was his very own. But such is the contrariness of human nature that some there were who would not surrender to Mark Twain. The trouble was the conflict of fiction and fact again, and an inability to see fiction as truth. Somehow, simple-minded folk had the notion that everything in the books, scenes of which are laid in Hannibal, should be literally true.[1] Finding them not so in some details they confused Mark Twain and Mr. Clemens and held him to be a prevaricator. That the fatted calf should be killed for him was crowning him, declaring him arch-prevaricator. One gentleman, a character all to himself—a subject, it would seem, for the humorist to picture—was jealous. He was aged, had lived sixty years in Hannibal, and I thought should have much information concerning the youthful Sam.

"Know him!" he exclaimed. "Yes, he says he was a pilot. He wasn't. Talk about Mark Twain! I've been on the river for fifty-one years. My brother Abe, now, who lives over to ——, he fit in the Civil War. I can tell you all about Abe and my son is general passenger and ticket agent of the railroad." This was a challenge to Mr. Clemens.

"What!" he exclaimed. "I never was a pilot? I'll venture to say the man who said that is—is—mistaken. If I were going to stay here long enough to have time I'd make him recant."

Unexpectedly, Mr. Clemens stepped from an afternoon train at Hannibal. He avoided committees because the committees could not get ready in time. He was already in his hotel, had had his supper, and was in his room when the first committee arrived. He was too tired to see the gentlemen. He lay in his bedroom, gazing southward through his window where "Lovers' Leap," "Cardiff Hill" of the books, reared skyward, doubtless with many a reflection, and smoking, for he always smokes. "I smoke just as much as I can," said he. "Of course, I cannot smoke when I am asleep, but I think that is the only reason I wake up in the morning."

Next morning, by glancing at the papers, he found that it was Decoration Day. He had forgotten it. He was pleased, saying that he felt it a good time to be in Hannibal. It also was the day of the High School graduation—a happy coincidence also, for last year he had refused an invitation to be present at the commencement exercises. Now he was rested. Now he felt that it was time to meet his old friends. Now he gave himself to Hannibal. If there was aught which could please or amuse these people of his hometown in his long-studied forte of entertaining, they were welcome to it. He threw himself upon the mercies of the committees.

That morning he went for a walk down to his old home. A quaint little two-story frame it stands, very small, very humble, very dingy. It faces upon Hill street, a thoroughfare which has ceased to be a favored residence locally. He gazed upon it in silence. Some hours after, he commented upon it, and there was something of pathos as well as humor in what he said:—

"It seems to have grown smaller," he remarked. "A boy's home is a mighty big place to him. Why, I believe that if I should come back here ten years hence it would be no bigger than a bird house." . . .

His genial humor and imagery brought back the days gone, brought to life men long since dead, and refreshed everybody. His method of distributing diplomas doubtless never has been duplicated. "Take one, take a good one," he said to the graduates. "Now, don't take two, but be sure and get a good one."

He met his early sweetheart, Mrs. Frazier, at dinner at the home of a Mrs. Garth, and again at a reception given by the Labinnah Club—Hannibal's best known social organization.[2] Later he called upon her [Mrs. Frazier]. The talk veered back to the old times, when she was the girl dear to him, who was painted to the life as Becky Thatcher. She was then a dainty bit of femininity, a romping child, on the threshold of beautiful womanhood. Now she is a matron, past 60, wondering if a hoop will not have to be placed around Mark's head after all the adulation which Hannibal has been giving him. And Sam Clemens—he was a romping boy also, and now 67, famous, with knowledge of every country on the globe. She has spent all her long life in Hannibal. His home has been the capitals of Europe and his associates celebrities. It was a contrast which gave them much of which to converse.

Mr. Clemens, having shaken hands with everybody at the Labinnah Club, and having charitably beamed upon the many beautiful young women of Hannibal who beamed at him, retreated. It was reported that he had mysteriously disappeared. In fact, he had sought a table and a chair in Green's saloon. There were several others there, including newspaper correspondents. He sipped mint juleps and talked of every subject under the sun. Perhaps the most astonishing bit of information was that Pudd'nhead Wilson emanated from Florence, Italy. That Pudd'nhead ever could have sojourned, much less have come into being, in Florence seemed on the face of it preposterous.

Explanation, however, cleared matters up. "It's like building a pair of boots over here years before," said he, "and blacking them in Florence. I had worked out Pudd'nhead a long time previous, and at Florence I had the opportunity to dress him up in language." Until 3:30 A.M. Mark Twain chatted at Green's.

Then he was whirled away in a carriage through a driving rainstorm to his hotel, where, staring at the convincing clock, he said: "Well, I am amazed. If my wife knew this! This is the latest I've been up for many a day." ...

He realized that in human probability many more years will not be his and he as much as said that this would be his last visit to the land of the Mississippi in which he had lived so long, in which he had drawn the sinews of his fame. He voiced again and again a deep love for Hannibal, and the smiling face was often saddened by memories of the many whom he had hoped to see, yet of whom he found trace only at the cemetery, and some not even there.

Once he spoke of death, his view of death.

He had received the High School class, to which he had handed "good" diplomas, in the hotel parlor. Talking with them, he told of the time in boyhood when he had had an ambition to get the measles, and after some trouble had gotten them.[3] He spoke of being on the point of death. It terrified him.

"I did not know," said he, "what an easy thing it is to die. I have since learned that it is like falling asleep. The hands and the feet grow cold, but you do not know it. Then you are in a kind of dream or trance, and you do not understand that you are dead at all until you begin to investigate the matter."

Notes to Interview 169

1. See also "Mark Twain's Return to Hannibal," *New York Herald*, 15 June 1902, sec. 5, 9: Speaking of the characters in Tom Sawyer, Mark Twain said:—"They are not absolutely portraits of any one person. Some of the incidents accredited to Tom Sawyer happened to one boy and some to another, and some not at all. Huckleberry Finn was the son of the town drunkard, but it could not be said that literally he was the boy I had in view."

2. Labinnah is Hannibal spelled backward. On Mrs. Frazier, see n. 13 to interview 157.

3. See interview 159.

170

"'Mark Twain' Bids Missouri Farewell," *St. Louis Republic*, 9 June 1902, 3.

After two busy weeks in Missouri, Samuel L. Clemens, Mark Twain, departed yesterday for his home at Riverdale, N.Y., probably bidding a final farewell to the State of his birth and the Mississippi Valley, wherein were spent so many years of his eventful life.

Despite his strength, unusual for a man 67 years old, he was much fatigued after his continued exertions. He returned to the home of Doctor James R. Clemens,[1] No. 3956 Washington avenue, from the St. Louis Country Club, where he was entertained Saturday evening, about 11 o'clock at night. He spent the morning quietly yesterday and left the city at noon on the Big Four Knickerbocker Special.

He was escorted to the train by Doctor Clemens. At Union Station were many citizens who came to bid him good-by or to have the opportunity to shake hands with him. To all, stranger or acquaintance, he was genial and friendly, and at the parting gained additional admirers as he gained them wherever he visited after his arrival "back home."

Mark Twain's slim appetite has been remarked by all who have met him, and he was induced to talk upon the subject after his brief sojourn at the helm of the harbor boat last Saturday, when he once more assumed the role of pilot.[2]

"I have starved for twenty-five years," he said.

The newspapermen who had just watched him say farewell to the wheel looked into the placid face of the humorist and focused their eyes on the pink cheeks of 67 years.

"It has been that many years since I ate more than one meal a day," continued Doctor Clemens. "I do not count breakfast as a meal because it consists of one cup of coffee and a meager allowance of bread. My meal is at 6 or 7 o'clock.

"There is no principle involved in this abstinence, what many persons would call starvation. I discovered long ago that one meal is plenty for the man who does no more work than the brain-worker. Now if I were chopping wood, I probably would eat three times every twenty-four hours. The waste of muscular force in that sort of an occupation requires rebuilding.

"There are many advertisements nowadays that entice the man who does not use his muscles to build them up. There is not any occasion for it. Beyond light gymnastics to preserve healthy circulation, the man who labors with his mind to the exclusion of his muscles need not be alarmed because he cannot put a hundred-pound shot more than three feet.

"Oh, when I was a pilot, that was long before I stopped eating three meals," said Mark, in reply to a question. "The last time I was on the river—hum, let me recollect, it was in eighty, 1880 that Jimmie Osgood,[3] the publisher, and myself made a trip down the river under fictitious names. We were gathering material for *Life on the Mississippi*. Knowing the riverman well, I concluded that the only way to get him to do and say things that would make the sort of material I sought was to catch him off his guard. If they had known it was Clemens, you can depend upon it that he would have gone into his shell and spoiled the whole scheme.

"Well, we were discovered right here in St. Louis. We registered at the Southern. The clerk there wheeled the old book around on its swivel sand and gave me a pen. I think that I wrote down the name, J. Smith, from some place in New Jersey.[4] That fellow turned the book around, just glanced at the name, and called:

"'Front! Show Mr. Clemens up to 236.' The rascal had known me when he was a clerk at a hotel down East. It was a little embarrassing to be caught disowning yourself. But with that incident, the danger of recognition passed. It would have been a little awkward if he had put the newspapers boys on. Down the river I chanced across other old-timers who knew me, and that was the only time I ever adopted disguise.

"But this question of exercise. The general shaking up a man gets at intervals through his lifetime affords all the physical exertion needed by the person of unmuscular avocation. This sort of exercise is a tonic. Now, when I was out with Cable in 1885 we experienced the hardest work I have ever known. It was made up of the most absurd railway jumps from one lecture point to another. Our schedule was inflexible. The dates had to be filled under any circumstances.[5]

"I think that the experience of that trip prolonged my life ten years. I was always tired at night, but I slept the sound, just sleep of the man who has done his work. I would not undertake such a shaking up now. Besides, it would not be necessary. I do not expect to live long enough to justify the adding of another ten years. The man who lives until he is 80, or wants to live until he is 80, has lost his reason. I feel so hearty now that I am really beginning to be afraid that I will live to be foolish."

Notes to Interview 170

1. MT's cousin James Ross Clemens, M.D. (1866-1948), a pediatrician and author.
2. See interviews 166 and 167.
3. See n. 6 to interview 17.
4. See n. 5 to interview 18.
5. See chapter 2.

8

At Large, 1902–1906

Interviews 171–195

In the twilight of his career, Twain hired Isabel Lyon, who soon referred to him as "the King," to be his personal secretary. This period in his life is punctuated most forcibly by the declining health of his wife, Olivia, and her death in Florence on 5 June 1904. In January 1906, he anointed Albert Bigelow Paine his official biographer.

∽

171

"My First Vacation and My Last," *New York World Magazine*, 7 September 1902, 3.

Mark Twain, the great humorist, is spending his vacation at York Harbor, Maine. The place, if Mr. Funston or any of the Denver Library people care to know,[1] is in that exact spot frequently referred to as the southeastern part of the State.

The genial philosopher has been enjoying the summer working there since early in July, and he says that he is going to do his best to hold out at his cottage until the eleventh day of October. As to the reason for the "eleventh" he absolutely refuses to commit himself.

In about a year the reading public, however, will be very thankful to York Harbor. For the novel upon which Mark Twain is now engaged will be issued then and he says that the bracing sea air that comes to him in his retreat is helping him to do fine work.

He hasn't wholly succeeded, though, in keeping care off his porch and the forty acres that surround his cottage, perched high above the waters of York River, for in the early part of August Mrs. Clemens fell sick with heart failure, and since then her famous husband has been nursing her back to health.

The writer for *The World's Sunday Magazine* discovered the author of *Tom Sawyer* the other day walking slowly to and fro on the lawn. Now, Mark Twain has made it a rule to be interviewed only when in a foreign country or when coming from or going to a strange land. But here it was proved beyond all doubt or peradventure that *Huckleberry Finn*'s creator is a humorist, for he laughed at and agreed to the logic of another man's joke.

"I am only interviewed," began the sage, with the deliberate, premeditated and immortal Mark Twain drawl, "in foreign countries."

A most decided and dramatic period after "countries."

"But you know, Mr. Clemens; Misther Dooley speaks in thim furrin' countries, such as Harrlem an' Hoboken an' Maine."[2]

"He does," he said, with his hearty smile, "he does. I guess"—a pause which would easily give him an opportunity to change his mind twenty times—"I guess I have to give in."

Then he led the way into the house, excusing himself for a moment "just to see how Mrs. Clemens was getting along." He returned presently.

"So you want me to tell you about my first vacation," he said.

"My first vacation?"

Very deliberately he took from his vest pocket a long black deadly looking cigar. Then, after groping for an interminable time in his coat pocket, he pulled out three matches and placed them side by side on the table. He was very particular about those matches, for he rearranged them six times.

"That was long ago."

A pause.

"That"—the matches again engage his attention—"was sixty years ago."

He lit the cigar—not placing it in his mouth, but assuring himself that he had a good light before the match was wholly consumed.

A pause certainly of three minutes.

He puffed at his cigar three or four times, but only mechanically. It became very clear indeed that he was away back in his boyhood days again with Tom Sawyer and Huckleberry Finn, wading in the Mississippi or playing leap-frog in the dusty streets of Florida, Missouri.

"Ah, I shall never forget that first vacation," he said. "It wasn't as long as this one, nor in some respects as pleasant, but"—very slowly—"what it lacked in length it made up in excitement.

"Do you know what it means to be a boy on the banks of the Mississippi, to see the steamboats go up and down the river, and never to have had a ride on one? Can you form any conception of what that really means? I think not.

"Well, I was seven years old and my dream by night and my longing by day had never been realized. But I guess it came to pass. That was my first vacation."

A pause.

"One day when the big packet that used to stop at Hannibal swung up to the mooring at my native town, a small chunk of a lad might have been seen kiting on to the deck and in a jiffy disappearing from view beneath a yawl that was placed bottom up.

"I was the small chunk of a lad.

"They called it a life-boat," said Mr. Clemens, "but it was one of that kind of life-boats that wouldn't save anybody.

"Well, the packet started along all right, and it gave me great thrills of joy to be on a real sure-enough steamboat. But just then it commenced to rain. Now, when it rains in the Mississippi country it rains. After the packet had started I had crawled from beneath it and was enjoying the motion of the swift-moving craft. But the rain drove me to cover and that was beneath the yawl. No. It was not a lifeboat, for the manner in which that rain came pouring down upon me from the bottom of that yawl made me wonder if I was ever to return home again.

"To add to the fun the red-hot cinders from the big stacks came drifting down and stung my legs and feet with a remorseless vigor, and if it hadn't been a steamboat that I was on I would have wanted to be safe at home in time for supper.

"Well, it kept on raining and storming generally until toward evening, when, seventeen miles below Hannibal, I was discovered by one of the crew."

A very deliberate pause.

"They put me ashore at Louisiana."[3]

Another pause.

"I was sent home by some friends of my father's.

"My father met me on my return."

A twinkle in the steel-blue eyes. "I remember that quite distinctly."

Then as an afterthought: "My mother had generally attended to that part of the duties of the household, but on that occasion my father assumed the entire responsibility."

Reminiscently: "That was my first vacation and its ending"—he bit his cigar—"and I remember both.

"So now, sixty years after that event," emphasis on "event," "I'm enjoying another vacation at the age, I believe, of sixty-seven.

"Fact of it is," he drawled, "the best part of a man's life is after he is sixty. I feel stronger, mentally, now, than ever before."

He lit another of those ominous looking cigars. Their mere appearance compels comment. You express surprise that the first one was not guilty of murder.

"No. Smoking doesn't seem to affect my health at all. Perhaps though, that's because I only take one smoke a day." A brief pause and with a flash of humor from his eyes—"That commences in the morning and ends just before

I go to bed. But, Lord bless me! I like to smoke and have since I was seven years old. That first smoke was a fine one, but it made me very sick. I rolled a cigar from green tobacco and when my father found out about it he did the rest.

"I find," he added seriously, "that smoking aids me while I am engaged in writing."

He looked far out to sea.

"This bracing salt air makes me do good work," he said. "I work harder in the summer than in any other season of the year. Just at present, because of Mrs. Clemens' illness, I am not doing much writing, but up to the 11th of August I was busily engaged upon the novel that isn't finished yet, though I've been at it for four years. It's to be a fantastic book," he added, "not so serious as *Joan d'Arc*—it took me twelve years to write that—but up to the present I can't tell how the book is going to end. Confidentially, I won't know until it's finished.

"In fact," said the humorist, "that's the purpose of the book."

He placed his hands on the table as he spoke. They are the hands of a strong man, of a worker, prehensile yet artistic and with nails which are kept in beautiful condition. In shaking hands with him you note that while his hands are as soft as a woman's, there is a manly vigor in the grip he gives you that carries with it instantly the mark of good-fellowship and kindliness.

He spoke of his recent trip to the scenes of his boyhood days, and told how he met his chum and playmate, John Briggs.

"Together," said the Mark Twain of *Huckleberry Finn*, in serious tones, "we visited some of the scenes of our former crimes and misdemeanors."

Meditatively—"Stealing apples, though, isn't a crime or a misdemeanor. The elements of danger and self-hero worship are too largely involved in the deed.

"What I consider a crime was the act of John Briggs and myself when we got hold of a boat along the Mississippi at Hannibal and painted it red over its coat of white. Just as we had finished our job the owner of the boat appeared and 'lowed that if that boat had been white he would have sworn that it was his own."

As to whether or not the boat ever got back into the hands of the original owner Mr. Clemens refused to say. He did talk freely, however, about his now famous letter written from his vacation retreat on August 14 to a Denver friend anent the attempt to exclude *Huckleberry Finn* from the Denver Public Library. "Now, that was a very funny thing about that letter getting into print," he said. "You see I sent it to my man marked 'Private,' and that was a sure sign that it was going to be published. That is the reason I don't care to be interviewed, too. You see, it puts it up to the other man."

He lights his fourth cigar. "If I write a letter and then it is published through the carelessness or base intent of the man to whom it is sent, I am not being directly interviewed for the benefit of the readers of a paper, but am only expressing a private opinion, which, however much I might mean it, was only intended for the man to whom the letter was written."

"But as to Denver," he drawled, "it isn't so far removed from Butte, Montana. I subscribe for a weekly paper which gets here every two weeks, and I learn from that that Mary MacLane is exploring the East for *The World*.[4]

"Is the young woman a genie," he asked, "or is her book a composite of thoughts that had been written before?"

It was suggested to the genial philosopher that he take the lady's word for it.

"But I can't," he said, "in view of her frank declarations about her own mendacity."

He sat there smoking his fourth cigar. In the advertising papers of a monthly on the table before him was a picture of Sir Walter Scott. Looking at the picture with evident affection, he said: "There never was a man in the history of all literature who was confronted by so gigantic a task as that undertaken by Scott in his magnificent effort to rid himself of a mountain of debts for which he was not responsible."

Yet, but a few years before, the man who had paid this tribute to Sir Walter Scott had himself won the admiration of the world for a transaction similar in almost every detail.

He went upstairs again "to see about Mrs. Clemens," saying as he left, "Now, make yourself as comfortable as you can."

The room in which much of his writing is done is large and cheery, with everywhere the evidence of woman's taste—and an author's carelessness. An edition of Saintine's *Picciola* lay on a table in the centre of the room.[5] One of the villainous-looking cigars had been left on it, presumably to frighten burglars.

Upon the mantelpiece was a huge bouquet of golden rod, Mrs. Clemens' favorite flower, and on either side of it were pipes and bric-a-brac. In one corner of the room was a tobacco cabinet and on top of it lay the brother of the "Missouri meerschaum" corn-cob pipe that Rudyard Kipling once hungered for.

In another corner was a roomy window-seat, and upon it had been thrown the Panama which, on the lawn, the lord of the demesne had earlier referred to "not as a nearly but a real one." The morning mail—some twenty or thirty letters—had been dumped into it.

"We'll take a look 'round," he said, as he stepped to the veranda, "and then you can take the pictures you've hinted at"—a pause—"I believe."

The blue sea stretched away to the eastward, while between it and the delightful spot where Mark Twain is spending the summer the deep and silent waters of York River glided by.

"This is almost as good as my Tarrytown place," he said, with a chuckle. Evidently he was thinking of the famous over-assessment.

"When a friend of mine," he continued, "heard that I had been assessed $70,000 for the property there that I had paid $45,000 for, he asked me why I didn't sell the property to Tarrytown. That wouldn't be bad, now, would it?

"This is as good a place as any," he remarked, with the kodak prospect still in mind. Then, with the greatest good nature, the King of Humor posed in the pine woods for several characteristic photographs.

Very evidently Mark Twain's sojourn at York Harbor is doing him a world of good.

Bronzed and ruddy, with clear eye and alert step, he is the picture of perfect health. Yet walking is his only exercise. The pleasures of boating, bathing, golfing or driving do not appeal to him.

Notes to Interview 171

1. General Frederick Funston (1865-1917) had engineered the removal of *Huck Finn* from the shelves of the Denver Public Library, apparently in retaliation for MT's ironic "A Defence of General Funston," *North American Review* 174 (May 1902): 613-24. See also "Mark Twain on 'Huck Finn,'" *New York Tribune*, 22 August 1902: "Huck Finn was turned out of a New England library seventeen years ago—ostensibly on account of his morals.... There has been no other instance until now.... A few months ago I published an article which threw mud at that pinchbeck hero, Funston, and his extraordinary morals.... Huck's morals have stood the strain in Denver and in every English, German, and French-speaking community in the world—save one—for seventeen years until now.... Everybody in Denver knows this, even the dead people in the cemeteries. It may be that Funston has wit enough to know that these good idiots are adding another howling absurdity to his funny history; it may be that God has charitably spared him that degree of penetration, slight as it is. In any case, he is—as usual—a proper object of compassion, and the bowels of my sympathy are moved toward him."

2. A satirical Irish American character invented by the humorist Finley Peter Dunne (1867-1936).

3. Louisiana, Missouri, downriver from Hannibal.

4. Mary MacLane (1881-1929), author of *The Story of Mary MacLane* (1902), journalist and actor.

5. Huck Finn also alludes to *Piccolla* (1836) by X. B. Saintine (1798-1865) in chapter 38 of *Adventures of Huckleberry Finn*.

172

James Montague, "Mark Twain: His Wit and Humor," *New York Evening Journal,* 20 December 1902, 5.

"Twain? Mark Twain? Never heard of him. Guess he don't live nowhere's 'round here."

The Riverdale butcher boy spoke as one having authority.

"Clemens, then," suggested Davenport.[1] "Can you tell us where Samuel L. Clemens lives, boy?"

"Nope. Never heard of him, either. These fellows belong in Riverdale?"

"Well, one of them does. Has a house here some place."

"Oh, I guess not. I know everybody in the neighborhood. But hold up"—this as we started on our way—"mebbe they're new boarders up on the hill. No? Well, I can't help you any, gents."

And the butcher cart rattled away, carrying a nine days' wonder—a boy who had never heard of Mark Twain.

But we had come to Riverdale, and early in the morning at that, to see the humorist, and butcher boy or no butcher boy we were going to do it. There was no public conveyance at the Riverdale station. There is one there sometimes, but as near as we could learn its sailing days are Mondays and Fridays.

On other days the populace of the sleepy suburb on the Hudson slide down the hill on smooth shod feet. We met some of them coming down as we toiled upward, but lacking brakes they could not stop to point out the way to the Twain residence.

Davenport was discouraged at the words of the butcher boy. "Maybe there isn't any Mark Twain after all," he said, thoughtfully. "Maybe he's just a syndicate or something. I don't believe just a man could have written those books of his, anyway."

There seemed to be a gleam of reason in that, but I had seen pictures of the humorist, and once I knew a man who knew a friend of a cousin of an old Nevada acquaintance of his. Beside, Major Pond had given Davenport a letter to him. He surely wouldn't have done that, I pointed out, if there wasn't any Mark Twain.

While we were debating a young woman came down the road and Davenport appealed to her.

"Can you tell us, madam," he said, "if you know a man named Mark Twain or Clemens or Clements or—"

"Oh, yes," replied the young woman, without pausing in her flight. "He lives right in here." She mounted a stile as she spoke and sped away down a snow-covered path, sliding whenever she came to an incline in the manner of all the denizens of the place.

So here, right in front of us, was the house of Twain, and Twain really lived in it—a benighted butcher boy who had never read of Tom Sawyer to the contrary notwithstanding.

We followed the young woman down the path, and the butler who answered her ring confronted us and demanded our business.

"Don't you think we'd better ask him if Twain is just a man," whispered Davenport. "I'd hate to have to make pictures of a whole syndicate."

I thought the lady's assurance that Twain lived in the house sufficient for our purpose, so Davenport told the butler that we had come to draw Mr. Twain and hear him talk.

"I'll see if you can," said the butler, looking us over suspiciously. He departed into another room, taking several silver candelabra from the mantle as he went.

We stood in the hall a minute and took note of some pictures on the wall, which Davenport said were either by Carot or Hogarth, he wasn't quite sure which.[2]

"There used to be an artist in Silverton," he began—but at that moment the hall was filled with the perfume of a pipe compared with which those of Pan would have been feeble, and it was Mark Twain himself, in slippers and very comfortable morning attire, who stood before us, looking better than the best pictures of him either of us had ever seen.

"We came to draw your picture, Mr. Twain," said Davenport; "that is, I did. He"—here the cartoonist indicated me "came to hear you talk."

"Ah," said the humorist, in a voice that took several minutes to pass a given point, "come in here."

He piloted us into a little room in one corner of the house, a room filled with books, [piles of?] newspapers, boxes of cigars, corncob pipes, cans of tobacco and matches in about equal proportion.

Through one of the windows we could see the Hudson, with a steamboat passing now and then, to tempt the master of the house to go down there and grasp the spokes of a wheel. The others look out on grass and trees, abundance of both, for the Twain place is a trifle smaller than Central Park.

There is no describing Mark Twain. Davenport's pictures of him are better than descriptions, better than photographs. The shock of hair is not quite so heavy as it used to be, but the eyebrows are just as long, and the moustache just as drooping as of old. Time has written a great many wrinkles on his brow, but it has taken pains with the job, and the wrinkles are like the picture writing on a totem pole.

You can read in them the story of that time when Twain and Higbee struck a blind lead and were millionaires for a week.[3] You can decipher the tale of the little boy who wandered up and down the big Mississippi steamboat and filled himself with joy. You can see the mark of the mining camp, the imprint of the Hannibal newspaper, the lines worn by the intrusions of lightning rod agents, the stupidity of European guides, the heartlessness of city editors, the vandalism of French translators of "The Jumping Frog of Calaveras County."[4]

It is a kindly, gentle face; one would never suspect that grim irony and savage satire lie behind it, ready to rouse at some fresh contact with the shams and affectations of a shamming and affected world.

We sat for a while and said nothing. The humorist puffed steadily on his reeking pipe, now and then stroking the papers on the arm of his chair lovingly, as if he longed to begin work upon them again.

"This hour," he said finally, "between a quarter past 10 and 11—it isn't an hour; only three-quarters of an hour, you know—is the only time I have for visitors. Then people can come and see me. After my breakfast is settled and I am ready to get to work."

There was more silence, which Davenport suddenly broke.

"Do you know, Mr. Twain," he said from behind his Bristol board, "that you kept me from seeing Prince Henry?"

"Well, no; I can't say that that fact is in my collection."

"That's right. You were at the banquet they gave him at the Waldorf, and the minute you came into the room I followed you around and forgot that the prince was there."[5]

"Ah, that was very thoughtful of you." The smoke rose in an opaque cloud and the artist stayed his pencil until it should be dissipated. The silence again became heavy.

At length I found it oppressive, and by way of lightening it asked him if he remembered that story about the Gold Arm, with which he used to terrorize people who came to hear him lecture.[6]

"Now, I'm glad you mentioned that," he said deliberately. "You know, I delight to tell that story. I've retired from all public speaking entirely. I never go any place or appear in public unless I have to, but now and then I do love to tell that story."

And his eyes lighted reminiscently.

"Sometimes I go to the house of friends of mine in New York to get a chance to tell a story or two—I can't help doing it just once in a while. I go on condition that nothing shall be said about it before or afterward in the newspapers, for if mention was made of it people would say, 'That dad-blamed old liar said he was never going on the platform again, and here he is just the same as ever.' But I do love to tell that story. I'm going to talk to some friends before long—I have half an hour to fill—and that will fill up three of six minutes I was short. Now, if I can just get another story for the other three minutes I'll be fixed."

Whoever will have the privilege of listening to that story may esteem themselves among the favored ones of the earth. I heard him tell it in a Western town when he made his trip around the world to get money to pay off his debts.

When he came to the climax the audience jumped back as one person, starting loose every seat in the house, so the janitor had to come around the next morning and screw them down again.

"But I'm out of public life now," continued the author, lighting his pipe and puffing until his white head showed as in a fog, darkly. "I have a very happy time here, all to myself I shall never go far away again.

"I should not have gone to Missouri last June if I had not gone to get a decoration. I think when an institution, especially in a man's native State, offers to confer a decoration on him it is equivalent to a royal invitation; it's a command. He ought to go if he has to go in a hearse.

"But when I see some of these old, these very old fellows, going from one side of the earth to the other to get degrees it does seem hard. Some allowance should be made for their years. The universities ought to mail them the decorations."

Davenport, who had up to this time been shifting from one chair to another, trying to get a firm grip on the elusive features of the speaker, here gave tongue.

"Mr. Twain," he said, "I'll bet you'd have given a good deal to be where I was a few years ago, down in Jackson's Canyon, where you heard them tell that Jumping Frog story."

"Yes," said the humorist, extracting a match from a box on the table and lighting it and his pipe with the single motion known only to the long-seasoned pipe smoker; "yes, I would. How did you happen to go down there?"

"I went down for the *Examiner.* They found a cave full of bones down there. Nothing but bones in it—Indian bones, skulls and ribs and legs and arms. They'd been there so long they'd go to pieces like a played-out horse on the home stretch if you touched one of them."

"And I suppose the scientists out in that country never paid any attention to them?"

"Not so much that they were ever caught at it. The ranchers take them away in sacks full and make fertilizers out of them.

"I suppose not. I wonder what these scientists are for. I know, near Mentone, where there are two caves filled with skeletons in a row, two rooms to the cave, and two rows of skeletons in each room. Not one of those skeletons is less than seven feet tall and one of them is more than that. It would seem the easiest thing in the world for a few scientists to flit over there from France and take steps to protect them; but they don't. Tourists come along, ignorant, wooden-headed to risks, and carry them away bone by bone, and not a scientist to stop them."[7]

"Couldn't those tracks have been made by a bear?" asked Mr. Twain.

"Bear? Never! I could see the grain on the ball of the man's toe. There was a little fellow walking beside him. They were men's footprints, I tell you, and they ought to be enclosed in a glass case. We haven't got any scientists in this country. Never had."

"Well, well!" The humorist grew thoughtful. "Joe Goodman[8] came to my house in Hartford one time and read over a manuscript of mine in which I alluded to those Carson footprints as something like Santa Claus, deserving of a place in fiction, but of no permanent value as truth. He told me it wouldn't do—that they were not to be spoken of lightly. I must see about this. The Metropolitan Museum ought to have those footprints or, if that is impossible, it would be easy for every museum in the country to have plaster casts of them."

I have since discovered that the late Professor Joseph Le Conte of the University of California made a two years' study of the Carson footprints and pronounced them to be those of a giant sloth who prowled around Nevada some time previous to the time of Hank Monk.[9] I didn't know it then, however, so I did not shed any light on the conversation.

The denouncer of scientists was still thinking of the neglected skeletons in the South of France.

"Those caves were right near that gambling place—I can't recall the name of it—"

"Monte Carlo?"

"Yes, Monte Carlo. There, that reminds me of something I can make use of. Monte Carlo, presided over by the Prince of Hall, otherwise known as the Prince of—of—of—"

"Monaco?"[10]

"Yes, the Prince of Monaco, for three hundred years able to marry into any royal family in Europe, simply because he rules a ten-acre lot of royal ground. I can use that, sometime."

"Mr. Twain," asked Davenport, who had now finished his sketches and was cruising around the room admiring the pictures and pipes and other ornaments that were scattered about, "there are two pictures by Phil May, mighty fine ones, too.[11] Great, ain't he?"

"Yes. I am going to make use of those two as soon as I can think of some way to do it; in a book or story of mine, perhaps. He did them for me so quickly that I did not realize for a long time how really great they were. He's a wonderful man."

One of the sketches was a picture of a Chinaman, no art calendar Mongolian, but a real impressive self-satisfied native of the land of flowers. The other was a girl, a street girl, but so natural you could almost see her winking at you.

"May is a great artist," continued the author. "But here," he had seen Davenport carefully rolling up his sheets of bristol board, "I must have a look at those."

Davenport continued to roll them up. "Oh, Mr. Twain, I guess you really don't want to see them, do you?"

"Yes, indeed I do." He jumped out of his chair with the agility of Jim Smiley's Dan'l Webster—Dan'l was the frog's name—and the cartoonist unrolled the sketches.

"Well," said their subject, slowly. "They're bully, but you've made me look two hundred years old. I claim a good many years, but not two hundred."

We had started to go, observing that he was looking wistfully at the door, as if he yearned to know how one or both of us would look framed in it. A photograph of Mr. Twain tossed among some other pictures on the mantel caught Davenport's eye.

"I don't think that does you justice, Mr. Twain," he said.

"Well, possibly not. Here is one I drew of myself."

He fished from a drawer in the table a copper plate with an astounding sketch engraved upon it.

A line in his own chirography underneath explained what was the matter with it. "I never could draw a mouth," it said, "so in making this picture I have left the mouth out. —Mark Twain."

We shook hands and journeyed forth in the direction indicated by the "yes" of our host.

He had been pleasant, agreeable, hospitable, but he had taken the wheel from the moment we came in the room and piloted the conversation in smooth but profitless channels, never foundering once on a pay ledge. He had made us feel that it would be useless to extract any "copy" from him. He is not giving away his humor or his views on men and things.

And neither would you, readers of the *Evening Journal,* if after long years spent in acquiring cheerfulness you had learned to communicate it to others so gracefully that every time you framed a word a silver quarter jingled into your treasury. If words paid everybody as well as that, general conversation would soon become a lost art and only the scratching of millions of pens would break the silence that hung over the world.

As we slid down the hill to the Riverdale Station, following the fashion of the place, the butcher boy came rattling past us in his wagon and leaning far out into space shouted: "Find him?"

Notes to Interview 172

1. This interview was illustrated by the cartoonist Homer Davenport (1867–1912).

2. Henri Carot (1850–1919), French painter; William Hogarth (1697–1764), English printmaker and painter.

3. Calvin H. Higbie (d. 1914), an "Honest Man," "Genial Comrade," and "Steadfast Friend," according to MT's dedication of *Roughing It.* See also *Auto* (1959), 107–12.

4. MT's "Jumping Frog" sketch had been translated into French by Maria Thérèsa Blanc, aka Th. Bentzon (1840–1907), in *Revue des Deux Mondes,* then retranslated by

MT in "Private History of the 'Jumping Frog' Story," *North American Review* 158 (April 1894): 446–53.

5. Some twelve hundred guests were hosted by the *New York Staats-Zeitung* at a reception for Prince Henry of Prussia at the Waldorf-Astoria Hotel on the evening of 26 February 1902.

6. "The Golden Arm," based on a folktale collected by the brothers Grimm, was originally published in 1888 and appears in MT's "How to Tell a Story," *Youth's Companion* (3 October 1895): 464.

7. A brief part of the interview seems to have been deleted here.

8. Joseph Goodman (1838–1917), owner, editor, and publisher of the Virginia City *Territorial Enterprise* during MT's tenure as a reporter for it in the 1860s.

9. Joseph Le Conte (1823–1901), scientist and University of California professor of geology and natural history (1869–96) and cofounder of the Sierra Club in 1892. Hank Monk is a stagecoach driver in chapter 20 of *Roughing It*. See also *Auto* (1959), 144.

10. Monaco, one square mile in territory, was ruled as an absolute monarchy until 1910.

11. Phil May (1864–1903), English caricaturist.

173

Roy L. M'Cardell, "Men of Today Who Make the World Laugh: Mark Twain," *New York Evening World*, 13 April 1903, 11.

It was a tempestuous day in early April in the year of 1903 that a solitary traveler might have been seen trudging up the muddy hillside from the railroad station in the pretty suburban town of Riverdale-on-the-Hudson, where choice building lots on easy terms, to purchasers who intend to build, are obtainable on a small first payment from any of the urbane suburban local real estate agents. . . . I was going to Mark Twain's house. . . . A man servant opened the door that led into an old-fashioned colonial hall. . . . Old fashioned steel engravings hung on the walls in the side hall and up the side of the staircase.

The man servant told a young woman writing in a small room off the hall, and the young woman told the man servant to tell Mark Twain, or Samuel L. Clemens, just as you choose to call him.

Presently the dean and the foremost of American humorists came from his study. He wore a black velvet smoking jacket, gray vest and trousers, white hair and plenty of it, a gray and tawny mustache and carried a fountain pen.

"I am opposed to interviews," said Mr. Clemens. "The whole theory of interviews is wrong so far as it concerns a writer. For a politician an interview is something of inestimable value. But to ask a man who writes for his livelihood to talk for publication without recompense is an injustice. How would it seem to go to a gardener and say, 'Those are fine potatoes you are raising—let me have three or four bushels.'"

I ventured to hint that Mr. Clemens was some potatoes, if it came to that, but that he couldn't keep his light hid under a bushel.

But the serious humorist went on refusing to talk by saying a whole lot of things.

Among the things he said was that to ask a humorist to give an interview for nothing was as incongruous as to ask a great tragedian—Sir Henry Irving, for instance—to go into a circus and act the clown—for nothing.[1]

The interviewer hinted that if it was a question of recompense, that could be arranged, but Mr. Clemens said his contract with a certain publishing house forbade him writing for hire for anyone else.

Then, the interviewer suggested, would the great humorist give one of his celebrated handmade pen-and-ink sketches for publication? This the great humorist said was a request he could not comply with. "If I draw a picture," he said, "I can put some lines to it and get paid for it. The lines might not be funny, but the picture would be.

"This resolution not to be interviewed was made some years ago. There was a time I thought it was of value, but experience has taught me better. Experience has taught me many things."

The unauthorized interviewer reminded Samuel L. Clemens that several interviews with him had been printed, mentioning one illustrated by a newspaper cartoonist some few months ago.[2]

"That interview was obtained from me without my consent and by deceit and fraud. I thought I was entertaining Mr. ——," naming the cartoonist, "as a friend of a young relative of mine, a chum and a workfellow of his in the West. He brought a newspaper writer with him, but that I was being interviewed was kept hidden from me."

"Well, then," said the writer, "you will only be interviewed to say that you won't be interviewed."

"That is it exactly," said Mark Twain. . . .

Notes to Interview 173

1. Sir Henry Irving (1838–1905), English actor.
2. Probably interview 172.

174

"Mark Twain's Door Open to Burglars," *New York Herald*, 15 June 1903, 6.

Undisturbed by the recent activity of thieves in the Bronx, Mark Twain, at his home at Riverdale, in the extreme northern end of the borough, expressed himself yesterday as not averse to the powers that prey on his neighbors.

"I just wish I knew the fellows on my route," said the humorist, his eyes twinkling with merriment. "I have been expecting them about here, and from feelings of brotherhood, if for no more noble reason, I have been intending to give them a warm reception. My larder is open to them, and if they smoke they can have the best in the box. You know all we literary people and second-story men have a good deal akin. We all travel in groups. We work one neighborhood until we feel that we have sapped the lemon dry and then we move on to more fruitful soil. I don't know, but I am ready to believe that the gentlemen who visited Riverdale and stole everything they could lay their hands on are now laying away treasure down in Ohio and some other rich preserve of the Union. These grafters are pretty wise fellows. They know when they have been long enough in one neighborhood and when their victims seem to have become tired of them.

"There is such a thing as despoiling even the fatted calf, and these fellows understand that as well as we do. I'd like to meet the gentlemen who have this route now. I would treat them well. In fact, I fear I might succumb to the temptation to treat them too well. Perhaps that is why they have passed my door without giving me a call, but that's one of the fashionable habits they have—they never come around when you want to see them. I am going to leave here in a little while, and they will have to hustle if they expect to see me.

"Burglary, like many other things, has got to be a science, and the man who is a success at it ought to be respected. He has a family to support, maybe—little babies and a wife, who need nice clothes and things—and it is only fair that he should be given a chance to ply his chosen trade. It is cruel to put him in jail with forgers and common swindlers."

Since the last visit of burglars to Riverdale all of the houses have been provided with burglar alarm systems, and in some of the larger houses watchmen are employed.

On their last sortie they broke into the Appleton mansion, in which the novelist lives, and stole oil paintings and other articles, valued at about $500.

175

"Twain Off Shooting Shafts of Humor," *New York Evening Journal*, 24 October 1903, 3.

Mark Twain sailed for Europe on the *Princess Irene* today for a stay of one year in Florence, Italy, where he and his invalid wife, his two daughters, and friends will reside in Villa Reale di Quarto, one of the most beautiful palaces overlooking the Mediterranean.[1]

The humorist went abroad with joy in his heart because at the banquet given him at the Metropolitan Club, Colonel G. B. M. Harvey made it known that Twain had signed contracts for his writings that assures luxury to his latter days and a fortune to those he remembers in his will.[2]

Bubbling over with good spirits and with his blue eyes twinkling as he gave forth one story after another Mr. Clemens talked to the *Evening Journal* today just as if he liked to be interviewed.

Before leaving the Hotel Grosvenor to take carriage for the Hoboken Ferry, he walked up to the desk and, pulling out a checkbook, observed: "I love to write my name to checks. It gives a man the impression that he can manufacture money."[3]

Then turning to the *Evening Journal* reporter he drawled: "Getting ready to sail for a trip abroad requires a vast deal of trouble. I've always felt sorry for Noah; he had such an awful lot of worry getting all his animals on the Ark.[4]

"Those fellows who gave me that dinner," remarked Mr. Twain, "said that they loved me, but I don't see how anybody could care for a person who was as disagreeable as I am. I have been absorbing the pugnacity of my wife and the audacity of my daughter for years, so that I am ferocious ordinarily.[5]

"After a long séance of heavy dining I am simply unbearable. I guess the United States will be glad to get rid of me for a spell. Pity I can't take Dowie with me."[6]

Then he left the desk and, getting his wife under his arm, he escorted her gallantly to the waiting carriage.

When Mr. Clemens reached the steamship pier in Hoboken he busied himself with various matters connected with his departure and shortly afterward went aboard ship to Cabin de Luxe No. 1, which he had engaged for his party. Emerging in a big Ulster he walked down the gangplank again and was met by Colonel G. B. M. Harvey, who talked with him for several minutes and finally wishing him "bon voyage" departed.

Then turning to an *Evening Journal* reporter he answered a question concerning Aristophanes and Rabelais that had been propounded after he had read an article in which the humorist was heralded as the modern reincarnation of those two distinguished gentlemen.[7]

"Remarkable statement, that," he drawled with a twinkle in his eyes, "and very handsome, very handsome; but if I tell you the truth I can't agree with the statement because I was only an empty vessel at the various times my friend William D. Howells says that Aristophanes lived. So you see, I don't know Aristophanes even if Howells has told me at various times that he was everything from a sailor with Sir John Hawkins in the British Channel to a Greek physician and an Italian virtuoso.[8] But Rabelais! Ah, my dear young sir, I know Rabelais from the head down to the end of his toes and from his toes to the top of his head. Yes, I know Rabelais, and if I had lived in the fifteenth century I would have been Rabelais."[9]

Mr. Clemens was then asked if he had John Alexander Dowie in mind when he wrote the story in *Huckleberry Finn* of "the King" who was painted with leopard's spots and exhibited in the town hall for monetary purposes.[10]

"Well," drawled the humorist, "I can't answer that. I've never seen Dowie with his clothes off![11]

"In fact, I've never seen John Alexander Dowie, but I have a premonition and an awful presentiment that I am going to meet him in the next world.

"If I do meet Dowie in either one of the two places where people go and I see Dowie there, I am going to leave. It don't make any difference to me whether the place I go to is one thousand degrees warmer than the place where I meet Dowie, I am going to leave. I like society, I love society, but not Dowie.

"Yes; neither Dowie nor Mrs. Eddy.[12] In case I meet them in the same place I'll go to the other. If I see Dowie in one place and Mrs. Eddy in the other, I can only then place my trust in Divine providence and go to places I know not of."[13]

Just at this moment an interruption occurred in Mr. Clemens' story, when a man with a Van Dyke beard and an effusive manner rushed up to Mark and introduced himself as a member of the centennial committee of the big celebration at Tarrytown one year from now, [and] asked him if he was going to get back to America in time for the celebration.

"You know, you've been a taxpayer up there," he said, "and we want to have you back."

"Well," said Mark, with ever the same drawl, "I certainly intend returning to America after a year abroad, but I'm not sure whether I am going up to the celebration. I might get taxed for being there. They love to assess you in Tarrytown.

"Now," he declared with great emphasis, "I've hired this fancy villa over in Italy at a fancy price, but it is our house, and I am going to live in it for one year. I've got mighty tired of paying rent and taxes for four places and living in one."

The man with the Van Dyke beard nearly exploded at this sally of the humorist.

"Four houses and properties, that's it exactly, and only a chance to live in one. Let's see. There was the house at York Harbor, Maine; one at Riverdale, another at Hartford, and then the Captain Casey Place at Tarrytown where they love to assess people."[14]

Another interruption occurred here when a number of newspaper men rushed up to Mr. Clemens and asked him if he had heard of the arrival of Henry W. Lucy, the noted English humorist, and famous as "Toby, M. P., of *Punch.*"[15] Lucy said he had come to this country to ask a settlement with Twain in the matter of *The Obituary,* a magazine to be devoted to publishing obituaries of men while they were alive and then selling the subject all the copies he desires, suppressing the rest of the edition.

Twain was shown the following letter that he had written Lucy several weeks ago, and which Lucy had produced on his arrived on the *Lucania* today.[16]

The letter read:

My Dear Lucy—You will arrive on the morning that I depart, and so there isn't going to be any rendering of accounts. *The Obituary* will still continue to be published, but you are out of it. I am firmly convinced that in its earning capacity it is better for Twain than for two. You were the other segment of the "two."[17] Good-by.

Mark Twain.

When the humorist saw the letter his eyes twinkled as he replied: "Can't that man Lucy understand a joke? I wonder if an Englishman can understand a joke."

He was informed that that very question had been propounded to Lucy today and that the Englishman in reply had handed Twain's letter to the questioner as proof positive that an Englishman could understand a joke.

"Well, I'm glad that at least one Englishman can see the point," said Twain. "I was afraid that he wouldn't. You see, this idea of *The Obituary* was mine. I suggested it to Lucy at a dinner given us by Mrs. Edwin A. Abbey in London several months ago.[18] He jumped at the opportunity and we formed a partnership. Now he understands the joke, for he is living on hopes and I am living on accomplished certainties.

"You see," and Mark grew enthuiastic, "this was the greatest money-making contrivance ever devised and, as I was the originator, I naturally in my heart expected to reap the fruits of my originality.

"The scheme was simply this: We were to go to various men and offer to write obituaries of their lives before they were dead, for fifty guineas. There would be no money in a corpse, you know, and he would pay for the obituary while he was alive.

"We would say to the man: We can write a fine obituary of you; you pay us fifty guineas, we give you the right to have as many copies printed for you as you desire and then *we suppress the remainder of the edition.*[19]

"It was great fun to see the way men would come to us. We were able to cover up—we are yet, that is, Lucy and I—all the dark spots in a man's life, and then even artistically shade them so that they resembled the deeds of glory.

"Things went beautifully until a little while ago, when Lucy wanted more profits, and, as I've said, I knew that for the money in it, the proposition resolved itself into the axiom of 'It is better for Twain than for two.'[20]

"Poor Lucy! His predicament reminds me of the story St. Clair McKelway told at the dinner Colonel Harvey gave me at the Metropolitan Club the other night when he said, after the announcement of the signing of the contracts had been made: 'The Harpers are living by faith and hope, while Twain will live on accomplished certainties.'[21] That's the way with Lucy about *The Obituary*—he's living on hope.

"He's a good fellow and I hope he will do well in this country. Even if he lives on hope, I hope he don't meet Dowie."

Notes to Interview 175

I have supplemented this interview as reported in the *New York Evening Journal* with versions of Twain's comments published in other newspapers. All newspaper citations below are from 25 October 1903 unless otherwise noted.

1. Built in 1900 for North German Lloyd, this ship had a capacity for 2,350 passengers, including 268 in first class. MT had leased the sixty-plus-room Villa Reale di Quarto in the hills above Florence. Olivia Langdon Clemens would die there on 5 June 1904. See also Paine, 1209-15. The reporter seems to labor under the impression that Florence is a coastal town.

2. Founded by J. P. Morgan for the New York financial elite, the prestigious Metropolitan Club built its house (1891-94) at Fifth Avenue and Sixtieth Street fronting onto Central Park. Colonel G. B. H. Harvey (1864-1928), American journalist, bought the *North American Review* in 1899 and edited *Harper's Weekly* from 1901 until 1913.

3. The Grosvenor was a luxury hotel at Fifth Avenue and Tenth Street.

4. "Mark Twain Makes Some Parting Remarks," *New York Times*, 9: "Well," he replied, "I always was sorry for Father Noah; he had so much trouble getting all of his animals aboard the ark."

"Twain in Sympathy with Father Noah," *New York World*, 5: "Well, I always felt sorry for Noah," remarked Mark Twain at the Grosvenor, "because Noah had a whole lot of trouble in getting all his animals aboard the ark."

"Mark Twain Sails; Last Word a Joke," *New York American*, 40: "This makes me feel sorry for Noah." "Why?" chorused the reporters. "Because he had so much trouble getting the animals into the Ark."

5. *New York Times*: "But you see I'm peevish today. I have absorbed all of my wife's pugnacity, and all of my daughters' audacity."

New York American: "I feel peevish today," he said. "I'm the bad one of the family now. I've absorbed all my wife's pugnacity and all our daughters' audacity."

"Mark Twain Off for Italy," *New York Tribune*, 7: "I feel very peevish today. In fact, I have absorbed all my wife's pugnacity and my daughters' audacity."

"Mr. Clemens, before Sailing, Talks on Tammany, Dowie and Mrs. Eddy," *New York Herald*, sec. 1, 7: "I feel very peevish today. In fact, I have absorbed my wife's pugnacity and the audacity of my daughters. I hope I shall not come back to find Tammany in power. Certainly all self-respecting people hope that Mayor Low will win. Fusion [a coalition government] must be likened to heaven in comparison with Tammany, which certainly is hell."

"Tammany is Hell—Twain," *New York Sun*, 5: Speaking in serious strain, Mr. Clemens said: "I am of the opinion that the people of New York will return Mayor Low. Fusion must be likened to heaven in comparison to Tammany, which is certainly hell."

6. John Alexander Dowie (1847–1907), Scottish-born founder of the International Divine Healing Association.

7. "Mark Twain," *New York Times Saturday Review of Books*, 24 October 1903, 758: "One of the most daring and ingenious of critics of literature lately has been classifying Mark Twain with Aristophanes and Rabelais."

8. Sir John Hawkins (1532–1595), British admiral.

9. *New York Times*: "Rabelais, yes," he commented. "Aristophanes, no. I never knew Aristophanes personally. All of what I know of him was told me by William Dean Howells. I get quite a confused idea of what he was like. Sometimes I think of him sailing up the English Channel with Sir John Hawkins; again, I think of Aristophanes as the Greek physician, and again as an Italian virtuoso. If I had lived in the fifteenth century I should have been Rabelais. I know him from top to bottom."

New York American: "I don't know very much about Aristophanes," he said. "All I know about him I got from William Dean Howells, and you know you can't depend on anything Howells says. One time he tells me that Aristophanes was with Sir John Hawkins in the English Channel, another time that he was a Greek physician and again that he was an Italian virtuoso. I don't know. As I have no personal acquaintance with Aristophanes, I don't care, and I don't know whether that comparison was intended as a compliment or not. But Rabelais—when anyone calls me the Rabelais of the twentieth century I call that handsome. I know Rabelais all right, and if I'd lived in 1500 I'd have been Rabelais myself. That's a compliment worth while."

10. The reporter refers to the "Royal Nonesuch" episode in chapter 23 of *Huck Finn*.

11. *New York Times*: "I can't trace the slightest resemblance, for I have never seen Dowie disrobing."

New York American: "I've never seen Dowie with his clothes off," he said.

12. Mary Baker Eddy (1821–1910), founder of the Church of Christ, Scientist, which MT indicted in "Christian Science and the Book of Mrs. Eddy" (1899) and in his long essay *Christian Science* (1904).

13. *New York American*: "I'm afraid I'm going to meet him someday, though—he and Mrs. Eddy, both. I don't expect to see them in this world, but probably will in the next. I don't know which place it will be in, but whichever it is I'm going to the other if Dowie's there. I want society, not company."

New York Herald: "Do you know, I have had a premonition of late that I am going to meet Dowie in one place or the other in the immortal world. I like heaven and am fond of society, but if I meet Dowie there, or Mrs. Eddy, I shall go to the other place."

New York Times: "I have a presentiment that I am to meet Dowie in the next world, but I do not know where. If I find him in one place I will go to the other. I don't care how hot or how cold it is, but I do not want to be in the same place where he is. I want society in the next world, but not that of Dowie or Mrs. Eddy."

New York Tribune: "I have been in great trouble the last few days," he said, after he had got a big cigar drawing well. "I have had a premonition that I am to meet Dowie. I don't know where we are going to meet now I have missed him in New York, but I am afraid it is going to be in one place or the other. I shall like Heaven and I want society, but I don't want the society of either Dowie or Mrs. Eddy. If I get to Heaven, wherever it may be, and find Dowie there I'll fight like the deuce to get out."

14. The William Casey Place on Highland Avenue in Tarrytown was built in 1882.

New York Times: "I don't own the Casey House at Tarrytown; I have only rented it for a year. As a matter of fact, I am tired of renting four houses and being able to occupy but one. I don't see that it matters to that fellow at what time I am going to return."

New York World: "I rented it for only a year. As a matter of fact, I have got tired of paying rent for four houses and living in only one house."

New York American: "I've only rented the house for a year. . . . I'm tired of paying rent for four houses and living in only one of them, so I refused hereafter to take any house for more than a year. We are going to the Villa Real de Quarto, Florence, Italy, and I shall do some literary work there while Mrs. Clemens tries to recover her health. One of my daughters will act as my amanuensis, while the other makes snapshots of me in the throes of composition for use in the Saturday literary reviews."

15. Henry W. Lucy (1843-1924), English journalist.

16. Built in 1893 for the Cunard line, this ship had a capacity for two thousand passengers and set speed records between New York and Liverpool.

17. *New York Herald:* "Oh, yes; I remember we were to divide the profits. But when I returned home I discovered that twain was better than two, so I had to drop Lucy out of the project. I had expected to sail before he arrived so as to avoid an accounting."

New York Times: "You arrive this morning, and I sail this afternoon, in order to avoid you."

New York American: "Has Lucy arrived?" he asked, in evident perturbation. "I would never have confessed but that I thought he would not get my letter until after I had sailed. Now that he has let the cat out of the bag, I might as well tell all."

18. Mary Gertrude Mead, W. D. Howells's niece by marriage, wed the painter Edwin Austin Abbey (1852-1911) in 1890.

19. *New York Times:* "That's true, we did talk it over, and I think there never was a better paying institution that could be devised. You see, the idea was to write the most scandalous things about a man while he was alive, and tell him it would be published at the time of his death unless he paid to have it kept out of the papers. If the man paid handsomely, we would allow him to alter the proof and cover up the spots on his career. There are very few men who have not some spots that can be artistically covered. He could cut the proof, add to it, or polish it as much as he wished, but he had to pay for that. He could have as many of the copies of the paper in which the article was printed as he wished, and in the end he could, by paying enough money, get as good a reputation as he wanted, and one of which his family could be proud."

New York Tribune: "That's true, . . . every bit of it. It was plain to us both that there was never a better money making scheme invented. The object was to write up a man while he was alive. There is [no] money in a corpse. What we wanted to do was to write up for *The Obituary* the lives of prominent men, covering all their shady spots, and some of them have an awful lot of spots, you know. The more papers one bought and the larger his contribution to our support, the more spots would be artistically whitewashed. If he didn't fall in with our scheme, well, the result would be too painful to talk about. If he bought up an edition or two, then he would get an obituary of which even his enemies would be proud."

New York World: "That's true. We did talk it over. There never was a better-paying institution that could be devised than that weekly paper *The Obituary*. The object was to write up a man's life while he was living and get money out of him, because you can't write up a man while he's dead. There's no money in a corpse. What we wanted to do was to write up a man very thoroughly, cover up all his spots and cover them very cleverly, for there are few men that don't have spots in their lives that can't be artistically covered. Then we were to send a proof of the obituary and demand $250 for its suppression, $750 for the privilege of cutting and trimming it up and polishing it as much as he pleased, with the privilege of as many copies as he desired."

New York American: "The whole scheme was based on the idea that you can't get money out of a corpse. We proposed to write people's obituaries while they were alive and in a position where we could soak them. The obituaries were to be very thorough, covering every spot in a man's life. Every man has some shady spots, you know, and if he hasn't there are spots that can be artistically shaded. Mr. Lucy is mistaken as to the price of these obituaries—it was 50 guineas each, not 50 pounds."

20. *New York World:* "When I got home to America I concluded that more money was to be made by Twain than by two, so I gently but firmly had simply to eliminate Lucy from the money-making proposition, because I wanted it all myself. I calculated that Lucy wouldn't come ashore until tomorrow, or I should not have sent the note until I was out of the country."

New York Times: "We had no circulation to our paper, for you see the circulation end is the losing end. When I got home I found I could make more money by Twain than by two, so I gently but firmly had to eliminate Lucy from the money proposition. I calculated that he would not land until tomorrow, or else I should not have sent the note until today. But he is a good fellow, and I hope he will do well."

New York American: "Of course, none of you have ever seen a copy of the *Obituary*. That is because it has no circulation—the entire edition is suppressed in advance. It must be clear to you newspaper men that a newspaper without circulation must be a good money-maker, for every newspaper publisher tells me that he loses money on circulation.... When I came back from Europe I thought it over and concluded there was more money in it for Twain than for two, so Lucy has been left."

New York Sun: "It was to be a great money maker. That's the reason I decided to cut Lucy out. I found out that there was more in it for Twain than for two. That pun is British enough to have been made by Lucy himself. I wish you would tell him that I'm sorry I couldn't welcome him to America. I will even authorize you to remark that I regret that I cannot 'linger longer, Lucy.'" MT refers in the final phrase to a popular ballad by Walter Ingram.

21. St. Clair McKelway (1845–1915), American author and editor. See n. 10 to interview 142.

New York Times: "However, his situation reminds me of what St. Clair McKelway said to me when he learned that the Harpers had promised me a pension for life in consideration of work I had promised to do for them. 'Colonel Harvey is living on hope,' he said, 'while you are living on a certainty.'"

New York Tribune: "Lucy is a good fellow," he said, "and I hope he will do well over here, but so far as *The Obituary* is concerned, he must live on hope."

New York American: "I hope Lucy'll do well in this country. I know he has great hopes. He lives on them like Harper & Bros. You know, Dr. St. Clair McKelway said at a dinner the other night that Harper & Bros. were living on hope, but that I was living on an accomplished certainty."

176

"Mark Twain's Pictures," *Ladies' Home Journal* 20 (November 1903): 1.

With regard to two of the photographs of Mark Twain . . . a word of explanation is given here for which proper space could not be found in connection with the photographs.

The cat in Mark Twain's lap in one of the pictures is apparently a wonderful animal. Mark Twain says: "It is a porcelain cat, from a work by a great French sculptor, and is perhaps the only handmade cat in existence that is perfect in form, in attitude, and carries in its face and eyes the right and true charm and spirituality of its race. This is the most satisfactory workroom cat I have ever had, because it does not fuss with the manuscripts nor try to help do the writing."[1]

The colored man in another picture is John T. Lewis, "a friend of mine," says Mark Twain, "these many years—thirty-four, in fact. He was my father-in-law's coachman forty years ago; was many years [a] farmer of Quarry Farm, and is still a neighbor. I have not known an honester man nor a more respect-worthy one. Twenty-seven years ago, by the prompt and intelligent exercise of his courage, presence of mind, and extraordinary strength, he saved the lives of relatives of mine whom a runaway horse was hurrying to destruction. Naturally I hold him in high and grateful regard."[2]

Notes to Interview 176

1. MT probably refers to one of the porcelain cats mass-produced around the turn of the century by Camille Naudor and Co. of Paris.

2. John T. Lewis (1835-1906). Lewis had saved MT's niece Ida, her daughter, and her daughter's nurse. See *MTHL,* 1:195-99.

177

"Mark Twain on the Law of Copyright," *Sketch* (London), 30 March 1904, 376; rpt. *Harper's Weekly,* 14 May 1904, 753.

Half an hour's journey from Florence in the Sesto train, and then another twenty minutes' gentle uphill walk along a lane, will bring you to a small iron gate in a wall—the wall which encloses the grounds of the Villa di Quarto, where Mark Twain has been spending the winter. Here a special representative of the *Sketch* visited the great humorist recently, and obtained the new pho-

16. Mark Twain and John Lewis at Quarry Farm, summer 1903. Courtesy of the Mark Twain House, Hartford, Connecticut.

tograph and interview with him which are herewith reprinted for the benefit of Mr. Clemens's host of admirers in this country.

It was raining dismally when I arrived (writes the representative of the *Sketch*), as it can rain sometimes in Florence; the chrysanthemums round the villa were woefully bedraggled, and there was a general feeling of damp discomfort in the air, so that I was scarcely surprised when I was told that the famous humorist was confined to bed with a sharp attack of rheumatism. Fortunately, however, he sent word that he would receive me. The first thing that impressed me was his eyes. What wonderful eyes Mark Twain has! At times, in repose, seeming to be set far back in his head, dull, dead of expression, and then, of a flash, shining out keen, piercing, full of life. I recognized at once the mass of long hair inclined to curl, the heavy mustache, and the shaggy eyebrows of lighter hue, which go to make up the characteristic head so familiar in portraits. He has extraordinarily expressive hands, full of nervous force, seeming to point his meaning even more than the vigorous "By George!" with which he would introduce a more than usually interesting comment. On my entrance, I made some stumbling apology for my intrusion, and he said, rather severely, that he had made it a rule never to be interviewed between whiles, but that during the twenty-four hours preceding his departure from one country and the twenty-four hours after his arrival in another country he was open to all comers. I ventured to hope that my visit would not result in his undoing, and inquired if he knew Italy well.

"No," he replied, laboring with a recalcitrant pipe; "I should like to very much, but this is the only part of Italy that I know. A very pleasant race the Tuscans are, and I get on well with them in a deaf-and-dumb fashion; not that I did not carry on long conversations with every Italian I met when I was in Settignano eleven years ago, only I spoke English and the Italian spoke Italian, and neither of us understood what the other was saying. But we never bore malice and always parted friends." After applying a fresh match to his pipe he went on: "The world, of course, is the same all over, and I have my singular correspondents here, too. Today I have received a letter from a Florentine gentleman in which, as far as I can make out with the aid of my daughter, he asks me to pay him twenty francs for some copies of his paper which he sent to me and as recompense for five visits which he has made to my house 'at grave risk from your dogs.' I did not ask for his papers, I did not ask him to pay me those visits, and the dogs who threatened his life belong to my neighbor!"

Speaking of the followers of Mrs. Eddy,[1] who do not reason but blindly believe, he said: "For the matter of that, the ordinary followers of any religion may be accused of the incapacity to reason clearly about it. The opinion of 'The Man in the Street' is worthless on a subject of which he has not made a special study. Lawyers, perhaps, and college professors may be listened to with attention on their own subjects, for their training has been long and in one direction, but this is true of scarcely any other men." The pipe was going easier now. "Take, again, the burning copyright question. Why, when I want some plumbing done in the house, do I go to the expense of getting the plumber out of the town, if the village carpenter who lives next door could do the work as well and cheaper? It is just because he does not understand the mysteries of pipes and soldering that I do not ask him for his opinion. And why should we expect the seven hundred or so Members of Parliament or Congress to settle satisfactorily the intricate question of copyright? Perhaps there are twenty-five out of the whole number who have written a book that has achieved success; of these twenty-five certainly not more than five have written a book that will outlast the statutory forty-two years. The remaining six hundred and seventy-five may be gifted with more than average intelligence, but that is not sufficient if they are to adjudicate on a matter outside their own special province. Now the learned Law Lord who examined me when I appeared before the House of Lords made a point that the owner of land, for instance, had a right to perpetual freehold, but not the author of a book, the value of which depended on an *idea,* on something evanescent. I objected at once that the value of real estate was as much dependent on an idea as any book was. Take a simple example: A shrewd traveler in the heart of Africa comes upon some land, which he foresees will some day become the center of a network of railways, and purchases it from the local chief. At that moment it is not worth a cent, but will be valuable in the future, in his children's or his grandchildren's time, years after some wretched writer, perhaps, would have ceased to have any property in a book he had written at the same time. And yet in both cases it was an *idea* which gave the value, and why should there be this discrimination? I cannot understand why Lord Macaulay, who *was* qualified to judge, and whose advice was listened to, favored the forty-two rather than the sixty years' limit in copyright.[2] But, even with forty-two years, the English are better off than we with our twenty-eight years in America. It is true that we can extend our copyright for another fourteen years, but the application has to be made, personally, within the last six months of the term, and it is not always easy to remember dates."

I rose to go, and, looking out of the window at the incessant rain, expressed a regret that Florence was treating him so unkindly with her weather. "Well," quoth the humorist, "it is rather an incentive to imaginary rheumatism. Mother Eddy has not taught me yet to suppress my imaginings." Whereat I laughed, and so ended a long visit in which all my preconceived notions of the great writer had been upset, and a New Mark Twain showed himself to me, not solely humorous, but intensely earnest.

Since Mark Twain published a portion of Adam's Diary a few years ago in *Harper's Magazine,* he has, as he puts it, "deciphered some more of Adam's hieroglyphics," and they now appear in book-form, with comic drawings by the humorous illustrator, Mr. F. Strothmann.[3] *Extracts from Adam's Diary,* "translated from the original MS," and illustrated "with photographic reproductions of the original Diary carved on stone," is conceived in a spirit of broad fun, and yet it is not without its touches of tender seriousness. Adam had his doubts about Eve for a long time, but "after all these years," he concludes, "I see that I was mistaken about Eve in the beginning; it is better to live outside the Garden with her than inside it without her."

Notes to Interview 177

1. See n. 12 to interview 175.
2. Lord Thomas Babington Macauley (1800–1859), English historian and essayist.
3. "Extracts from Adam's Diary," originally published in 1893, collected in *My Début as a Literary Person with Other Essays and Stories* (1903). Frederick Strothmann (1879–1958), magazine and newspaper illustrator.

178

"Mark Twain to Reform the Language of Italy," *New York Times*, 10 April 1904, 11.

Reporter: And how do you like Italy again after your long absence from here?

Oh, Italy is right enough. The best country in the world to live in. Perhaps England runs it rather close, but here all is quiet, town and country alike. In England there is always London with its great unquiet pulse.

Reporter: And the Italians?

Right enough, too. I love to watch them, and to study their gestures and their ways. That is why I do not object to the slow pace of our horses, like my daughter there, even if they do take a time to land us in town.

Reporter: And the language?

I never get hold of an entire sentence. Just a word here and there that comes in handy, but they never stay with me more than a day.

There is one person who always understands me, and that is our old kitchen scrub. She was with us last time, too. We have quite long talks together and exchange no end of compliments. I talk English; she rattles along in her own lingo; neither of us knows what the other says; we get along perfectly and greatly respect each other's conversation.

When the talk turned to books, the reporter said that he had never been able to read a novel by Sir Walter Scott.

Just so. I was once ill and shut up and there was nothing but Scott's novels to read, so I had another try. Well, when I got through *Guy Mannering*, I wrote to Brander Matthews and asked him if he would be good enough to point out to me the literary and stylistic merits of the work, for I could not find them.[1]

Fact is, nothing is eternal in this world, and literature is as much subject to the character of the times as any other intellectual manifestation. Books reflect the mental atmosphere in which they were born, and on that account cannot expect to live forever. Every generation has its own authors. Look at Dickens. At one time nothing went down that was not a little tinted with the Dickens style; now who would allow that? And the same for all the others. Is there a more tiresome and unnatural book than *Pendennis?*[2] All the people are exaggerated, caricatures, with no intention of being so. It's like when they show us some weird old picture and say it's wonderful. I dare say it is wonderful, for its time; but its time is past.

Notes to Interview 178

1. Sir Walter Scott's novel *Guy Mannering* (1815). MT derided the Leatherstocking Tales of Cooper (1789-1851) in "Fenimore Cooper's Literary Offenses," *North*

American Review 161 (July 1895): 1–12. J. Brander Matthews (1852–1929), professor of dramatic literature at Columbia University, was one of the targets of MT's satire.

2. William Makepeace Thackeray's novel *The History of Pendennis* (1848–50).

179

"Will Keep His Feet, as They Are 'My Last and Solely for My Use,'" *Boston Globe* morning edition, 25 August 1905, 12.

New York, Aug. 24—Suffering torture from gout, Mark Twain, who more than a score of years ago solemnly declared, "Rare things are not common," perpetuated another joke in Norfolk, Virginia, yesterday by having the announcement made that he had returned to his home in New York to have both feet operated on. As a result there were numerous callers at the big red brick house, 21 5th avenue, and the flaxen-haired maid was kept busy answering rings at the door.[1]

"Mr. Clemens is out of the city, and will not return till November," said the young woman to each caller. "We have heard of no amputation."

This was repeated time and time again, and "It's mighty funny," came from more than one pair of lips as the callers turned to retrace their steps down the front stairs.

Late in the afternoon, still in Norfolk, Mark Twain, who, in signing checks uses his own name, Samuel L. Clemens, authorized a denial of his self-circulated report that he was in New York.

"I am still here," he said to a friend who met him there, "and probably shall remain here till I get away. As for the gout, I may have a touch of it. In fact, I always have felt a little sore that way, but I am going to keep my feet as long as I can stand. They happen to be my last feet and are solely for my use."

Note to Interview 179

1. Catherine (Katy) Leary (1856–1934) worked for the Clemens family from 1880 until after MT's death in 1910.

180

"In Genial Mood," *Boston Globe*, 6 November 1905, 9.

"A man who is a pessimist before he's 48 is a fool—he knows too much. A man who isn't a pessimist after he's 49 is a fool—he doesn't know enough."[1]

This was one of Mark Twain's reflections yesterday afternoon while chatting with a group of newspaper men at the residence of S. B. Pearmain, 388 Beacon st.[2]

The famous humorist was discussing old age and his approaching 70th birthday, which comes on the 30th of this month, when he made the above remark.

Colonel Thomas Wentworth Higginson was present during the combination interview, which lasted more than two hours and during which time a wide range of subjects were discussed and commented on by Mr. Clemens.[3] He was in a genial frame of mind and with little effort on the part of the reporters he talked on old age and its manifestations, on the copyright laws, on King Leopold and the Congo Free State horrors, on Russia and the present uprising, and on American graft and grafters. He also read a few of his latest aphorisms and a couple of letters from people who had views distinctly opposite to himself and his writings.

Every subject Mark Twain touched on was illuminated by some anecdote or experience or by some caustic observation which usually hit "the nail on the head."

The pallor of his face is perhaps lightened by his thick, white head of hair and moustache, but as he became more and more interested in his subject the excitement drove a slight flush into his countenance and his eyes flashed while he emphasized his remarks by a wave of the hand or a toss of the head.

Mark Twain likes newspaper men, for he claims to be one still himself; in fact, he says he is the dean of American journalists and, as he said, "probably the most respectable, if you ask me about it," but he never cares to be interviewed until the day before he is to leave a place; hence the appointment with the reporters yesterday afternoon—he leaves Boston today.

After the reporters had been introduced by Mr. Pearmain there was a brief, uneasy moment's wait for somebody to break the ice. Colonel Higginson at once came to the rescue by suggesting that as Mr. Clemens was nearly 70 years of age a few reflections on old age from the dean of American humorists—and journalists—might be a proper beginning.

"I don't mind," said Mark, as he settled back in his chair, crossed his legs, and lighted a big cigar. "I'm ready to talk on anything. I never really knew what it was to be old until about five years ago. Now I believe I'm the oldest man in the world.

"At that time I was in London and I met Sir William Harcourt.[4] I hadn't seen him for 30 years and I couldn't see that time had made any change in him. You see, I had then begun to think I was the only old man in the world. I said to Sir William: 'You're a satisfaction to look at. You look just as young as ever. I would like to find someone older than I am.'

"Sir William said there were two dates that he remembered—one was that when he was 9 years of age and crossing London bridge he distinctly heard the bells toll that announced the death of William IV,[5] and the other was his birthday. He was born in 1828, and I was born in 1835. I said to him 'Then I have found the only man older than I am.'"

When asked if he hadn't experienced any of the usual manifestations of old age up to his 65th year—the little pains and aches, the gray hairs, etc.—Mr. Clemens said: "No. As for the gray hairs, I had them when I was 50, and I might have had indigestions, but that is not a sign of age; it is a sign of indiscretion. No, I can't say that I began to feel old until I was past 60."[6]

The next subject touched upon was the copyright laws, a subject which Mark Twain has been deeply interested in nearly all his life, and in the interests of which he has fought very hard.

But before touching on that it might be well to give a few of his latest aphorisms. He said he had been writing aphorisms all his life—on occasion—and some day he hoped to publish a book of them. Here are the latest additions to his stock:

"Taking the pledge will not make bad liquor good but will improve it."

"It's not best to use our morals weekdays. It gets them out of repair for Sunday."

"Don't part with your illusions; when they are gone you may still exist, but you have ceased to live."

"It is noble to be good; it is still nobler to show others how to be good, and much less trouble."

"I like aphorisms," commented the humorist with a twinkle.

The copyright question lies very close to his heart. He believes the author should be protected in this country as he is in Germany, France, and Russia, where the author's copyright holds good through life and seven years thereafter. In this country the copyright law protects the author for 42 years, and it has taken years of agitation to bring it up to that point.

"There are no civilized countries," said Mark, "in which the author isn't protected for life, except England, Labrador, and America.[7]

"Consider what this means in the face of our boasted civilization. Even in Russia the author gets more protection than here. We are trying now to get the same kind of law."

"When do the copyrights begin to expire on your books, Mr. Clemens?"

"In about six years on *Innocents Abroad,* and some others follow very soon after that. It is likely to cut down my children's income, not mine. I'm old and not much interested in the subject of incomes."

Colonel Higginson thought the publisher should be protected also, but he said he could not agree with Mr. Clemens that the author should have a monopoly of his books through life.

Then there was a discussion. Mark maintained that a book was as much the property of an author as a piece of land.

Colonel Higginson couldn't see it in that light. A book represented an idea to which the public was freely entitled after a certain time, for the author owed much to the public for the materials from which he made his book—the characters and situations that inspired him to write it.[8]

Mr. Clemens maintained that all property represented an idea. A number of men go into a new country. One of them is a trained civil engineer, and he sees by the lay of the land the spot where the city will eventually be built. He settles there and the city is built. That property is only so much stone and earth, like the spot where the others settle, miles away, but an idea has made it valuable. The same with all property—it is first an idea; so is a book.

"Take the trademark," said Mr. Clemens. "It give perpetual protection. The government protects the article with its eyes shut. It may be a poisonous patent medicine. The mixture may be deadly, but it is protected by the government, while the propagation of literary poison is protected for only 42 years.[9]

"When the question is brought up in Congress," continued Mr. Clemens, "some Congressman gets up and argues that a copyright makes books dearer and his constituents want cheaper books. That is one of those things where men work on a theory. I never heard of a constituent asking his Congressman for cheaper books. It is a fallacy, because they don't get them cheaper. The publisher gets all the profit and the author none."

He said he was interested in international copyright, but cared less about it than protection at home. He thought in the case of pictures that an artist when he sold a painting or work of art should stipulate in his contract with the buyer whatever was necessary in regard to the sale of duplicates or photographs. If there was no contract the purchaser should have the right to photographs.

The horrors of the Congo Free State, as told by missionaries, have brought down on the head of King Leopold of Belgium all the vials of Mark Twain's wrath and sarcasm. He has no use for King Leopold, and he has just published a little work entitled *King Leopold's Soliloquy,* which shows the monarch of Belgium, who is also monarch of the Congo Free State, in anything but a pleasant light.[10]

He believes the report which has just been made by the committee which the king appointed to investigate conditions in the Congo is a farce and a lie. The missionaries and the photographs which the missionaries have taken give the lie to King Leopold's committee's report, he said.

"Leopold is too well known as a domestic person, as a family person," said Mark Twain, facetiously, "as a king and a pirate, to believe what he says. He sits at home and drinks blood. His testimony is no good. The missionaries are to be believed. I have seen photographs of the natives with their hands cut off because they did not bring in the required amount of rubber. If Leopold had only killed them outright it would not be so bad, but to cut off their hands and leave them helpless to die in misery—that is not forgivable.

"We're interested in all this because we were the first country to give recognition to Leopold's villainous Congo Free State in 1885."[11]

Mr. Clemens commented on some of the brutalities perpetrated by other nations on the natives of Africa and cited the Matabele war, in which the English massacred so many thousands of the Matabeles.[12]

Mr. Clemens apparently never had much use for Cecil Rhodes or the methods which he used in introducing civilization to South Africa.[13] In 50 years he believes the mines in the Rand will be worked out and the country will revert once more to the Boers.

He is deeply interested in the present upheaval in Russia, but he fears it will not amount to anything.[14] The peace of Portsmouth was premature—premature for the Russian people who desired to free themselves of the autocratic yoke. It should have been postponed until the Japs had won one more battle. Then the people of Russia would have with them the sentiment of the soldiers at the front when they returned.[15]

As long as the czar has the army, navy, and treasury in his power, there is no hope for Russia. All the concessions he makes will amount to nothing unless the people have the control of the army, navy, and treasury.

Mark Twain takes little stock in the granting of Finland a constitution.[16] Finland was granted that before and the grant was revoked. This grant will be revoked inside of three years unless something unforeseen happens.

"No one can place any confidence in what Russia says," said he. "She was only going to Khiva to pacify that place, but once there she held it.[17] The same in Manchuria and other places.[18]

"I thought when the czar had granted a constitutional government a few days ago that perhaps I was premature in my opinions about the peace of Portsmouth. But I see from later dispatches that the people have gained nothing that can't be taken from them again tomorrow or any time as long as the czar controls the army, the navy, and the treasury."

The speaker was even skeptical about the resignation of the procurator of the holy synod.[19]

He seems no immediate hope for Russian freedom.

When asked what he thought of the present wave of reform that was sweeping over the United States Mr. Clemens quickly said: "McCurdy business! The McCurdys and the McCalls are a nice lot.[20] It reminds me of the plague they had in Bombay some years ago when I was there. Every day they would discover a new plague center. It was here today, there tomorrow, and somewhere else the next day. What I wanted to find was a center where there was no plague. It's the same with this insurance business. Every day brings to light a new plague center."

"What do you think of the municipal reform wave and the municipal grafters?"

"The grafting seems to be all over the country, and I don't think much of the reforms."

"How about Philadelphia?" interposed Colonel Higginson.

"Well, of course in this country we have one great privilege which they don't have in other countries. When a thing gets to be absolutely unbearable the people can rise up and throw it off. That's the finest asset we've got—the ballot box, which has been exercised in Philadelphia.[21] But graft seems to permeate everything in this country today."

When asked how he thought this new standard of ethics and morals in business had originated and if he thought Rockefeller's success had anything to do with it, Mr. Clemens said: "I suppose it has had something to do with it. It's a new thing. I believe, however, that it began with Jay Gould and Jim Fisk.[22] The operations of these two men dazed people. Here were men who could make a million in a few minutes. This was all new.

"I remember being in the Lotos Club,[23] I think it was in 1869, and hearing some prominent men discuss these things and I heard respectable men say: 'Well, give me the million and I'll take the odium.' The poison began to work then, you see."

It was suggested that perhaps the civil war and the big army contracts and the reconstruction period might have been the origin of these new business ideals, and Mr. Clemens admitted that perhaps it was out of these things that the later business ethics grew.

"We gave," said he, "to the world the spirit of liberty more than 100 years ago and now we are giving the world the spirit of graft. Look at the British army scandals during the Boer war.[24] No British commissioned officer ever did such things before. The spirit of graft has spread."

Colonel Higginson said the sturdy old spirit of honesty still existed among many of the people in the New England towns and he cited one notable example of a man in Dublin, N.H., who did a little job for which he charged eight cents, and after being paid he tramped back in the rain a mile or more and said he had charged too much—the job was only worth six cents. He handed back two cents and returned to his home in the rain.

Mr. Clemens told a story of a burglar who had literary ideals—a New England burglar up at Dublin, N.H.—who when arrested was found deeply absorbed in a copy of *Innocents Abroad*.

Notes to Interview 180

I have supplemented this interview as reported in the *Boston Globe* with versions of Twain's comments published in other newspapers. All newspaper citations below are from 6 November 1905.

1. "Is Same Old Mark Twain," *Boston Herald*, 4: "It is, indeed, a long time to look back to my earlier books, and I still receive letters about them. One man says he's got all my works on his shelves, but regrets having ever read them, and is willing to tell me why if I will ask—stamped envelope enclosed. Then there is another of my recent

correspondents, whose communication I prize, indeed, for while he says complimentary things, he doesn't give his name and address. . . . And as to pessimism," said he, "any man who is a pessimist before he is 48 knows too much, but any man who has passed 48 and is not a pessimist shows thereby that he knows too little."

"Mark Twain, between Puffs, Talks Some," *Boston Journal*, 4: "By the way, I had a letter today a little different from any I ever received before. People often write me that my books are no good and go into details to explain why, but this man encloses a stamped and addressed envelope and paper and says if I'll ask him he will be glad to tell me all my bad points. This is what he says," and Mr. Clemens drew a neatly typewritten sheet from the envelope:

Samuel L. Clemens, Boston, Mass.: Oct. 26, 1905.

Dear Sir—I have had more or less of your works on my shelves for years and believe I have practically a complete set now. This is nothing unusual, of course, but I presume it will seem to you unusual for anyone to keep books constantly in sight which the owner regrets ever having read.

Every time my glance rests on the books I do regret having read them and do not hesitate to tell you so to your face, and care not who may know my feelings. You, who must be kept busy attending to your correspondence, will probably pay little or no attention to this small fraction of it, yet my reasons, I believe, are sound and are probably shared by more people than you are aware of.

Probably you will not read far enough through this to see who has signed it, but if you do, and care to know why I have left your work unread, I will tell you as briefly as possible, if you will ask me.

        (Signed)   George B. Lauder, Concord, N.H.

"Are you going to answer it?" asked a reporter.

"Oh, I believe in reforming other people, but don't believe in reforming myself," replied Mr. Clemens enigmatically.

 2. Sumner B. Pearmain (b. 1859), a Boston stockbroker.

 3. Thomas Wentworth Higginson (1823–1911), Unitarian minister and man of letters, best known today for his correspondence with Emily Dickinson. See also n. 3 to interview 31.

 4. Sir William Harcourt (1827–1904), Liberal member of Parliament 1868–80.

Boston Journal: "Do you know at 50, until I met Colonel Higginson, I thought I was an old man and no one in the world older. Then I went to England and met Sir William Harcourt. He said he remembered when the first man was seen smoking on the street in London and told of walking across London bridge and hearing the bells ringing when they crowned William IV. After 50, when the gray hairs came and I had indigestion, I went to the hilarious Dublin society (Dublin, N.H., where he spends the summer) and since then I have been getting younger right along."

 5. King William IV (1765–1837) reigned from 1830 to his death.

 6. *Boston Herald:* "As to my age," he went on, "that does not affect me, nor does my gray hair, for it was gray at 50; the only thing I suffer from now as regards health is dyspepsia."

Boston Journal: The *Journal* reporter showed Mr. Clemens a newspaper clipping telling of the demolishing of McDougal's cave, immortalized by Mark Twain in *Huckleberry Finn* [sic], by a cement company. "When I was only 15 back there in Hannibal, I suppose I was an incipient rowdy. We boys used to dig in the little plot in front of that cave in emulation of the Forty-niners, who were passing through our town. We'd keep an account of the gold we dug every day, but just think if we'd only dug for cement; I wouldn't be talking to you today. Five thousand barrels of cement a day," he added reminiscently, closing his eyes as he exhaled a cloud of smoke. See also *Auto* (1959), 75.

7. *Boston Herald:* "It irritates me," he said, "to find that Germany gives an author copyright during his lifetime and for 50 years after, and that France and Russia do the same. Indeed, there are no highly civilized countries that do not grant this period as a right except England, Labrador and America. Consider what that means in our day. We who boast of our civilization don't go in [for] copyright as far as even Russia, which of late has been under so much criticism. As to my first books," and here there was a touch of regret in Mr. Clemens' manner, "they will fall in six years from now, for they will reach their 42d year. The excuse made in England and America is that an author has had enough when he has had 42 years' income from his books, and that the government having protected him for that period, the people of the country are entitled to the book."

Boston Journal: "I'm going to Washington in a few days to see what is doing with the copyright laws.... England, America and Labrador are the only civilized countries which don't extend to authors the privilege of a copyright during their lives and for fifty years afterwards," he continued. "I suppose fifty years would be enough. A man will probably be obliged to support his grandchildren, but I don't think as a general rule he will need to support his great-grandchildren. It has been three centuries since the law of fourteen years of Queen Anne's time has been extended to the present forty-two years, and so I suppose if I live long enough I'll see it extended to what it ought to be. I suppose their argument is that after a man gets a copyright for forty-two years he has made enough to last him...."

"Mark Twain Talks of World Affairs," *Boston Post,* 12: He first spoke of the copyright laws of America. He said: "They irritate me beyond measure. All the protection we are given here is 42 years. There is nothing fair about it. In France, Germany, and even Russia every author is protected during his lifetime and 50 years afterwards, thus protecting his heirs. It is only in America, England, and Labrador that the copyright laws are faulty. We boast of our civilization and then do not go as far as Russia in justice to the author. We hope to get it rectified, however, in the near future, and I am going to Washington in a few days to see what can be done in the matter."

8. *Boston Herald:* Colonel Higginson here asked: "But don't you think the publishers of a book have an advantage even after the copyright has expired, since they know the market better than anyone else?" "Yes," replied Mr. Clemens, "but the people of the country don't obtain the book for nothing, for no publisher is going to publish it unless he gets a profit out of it. So far as I am myself personally concerned, I do not care, because I am old enough not to be much interested in copyrights. Why, only the other day—and it is a striking thing to consider—I read that the trademark does not require anything of anybody, and is given for a perpetuity. You don't, for example, have to specify what your patent medicine is made of, yet the government, with its eyes shut, accepts this poison, if it is a poison, and gives a man a trademark which is perpetual. That the government should do this, and yet should limit the producer of a book to 42 years, does not seem fair. As to the obstacles in the way of change, the

only one I ever heard of was when, in 1889 or 1890, being in Washington on copyright matters, a congressman told me that his constituents had the impression—the superstition—that when a book lost its right of protection, people were going to get that book cheaper than before. It was for this reason, therefore, that the congressman could not venture to get copyright extended. That shows how men work upon a theory. The congressman probably never placed the matter before his constituents. I myself never heard a constituent who made any such an objection. Now, I am going down to Washington in a few days to see what they are doing there about copyright. We are trying to do something, and we authors hope to bring about for the United States an extension of the time to the lifetime of the author and for 50 years after. I ought to say that American literature has grown in spite of these obstructing conditions, until today there are issued in this country from 6000 to 7000 books a year. The production in Germany is 24,000, though I suppose that includes pamphlets."

A possible objection to the argument here came from Colonel Higginson. "Is it not, after all," he reasoned, "the community who gives the author his education, his opportunity, his subjects, his illustrations, his stimulus? Is it just for him to argue as if the thing were all on his side? If I were in Congress, I don't think I should vote for such a bill as you suggest, Mr. Clemens. I think it is giving the author and his children too much in consideration of what the public has given him. I think he ought to be willing, even proud, to give a large part of his labor for nothing."

"You see," interrupted Mr. Clemens, "I was born in a more selfish atmosphere than you, colonel."

"You are in Boston now," urged [Higginson] the limner of *Cheerful Yesterdays* [a memoir published in 1898].

"But," retorted the author of *The Innocents Abroad*, "I have not absorbed its atmosphere. I should look at it," continued Mr. Clemens, "in this way. When before the House of Lords in England on this question, I asked what objection there was to make the change to 'lifetime and 50 years after,' and they said: 'You can't have a property in an idea. A book is an idea. That is too much in the air.' But I asked them if they could name any property in this world that was not an idea. The whole basis of any piece of property is an idea, and not any more or less of an idea than is a book. I don't see why the people of a country should take an author's work from him on the pleas that they have given him the material. That occurs in every sort of business, but business men don't give up their property on that account, and I don't think it should be required of an author."

"Mark Twain Talks on 'Graft,'" *Boston Transcript*, 6: "Don't you think it a little unfair for a man to be educated in a community, get his ideas there and then keep them all for himself?" asked Colonel Higginson. "Guess I must have been born in a more selfish atmosphere," replied Mark Twain, blowing out a cloud of smoke and winking at one of the reporters. "Well, you are in Boston, now" retorted the colonel. "Don't believe I have absorbed enough of the atmosphere yet," was the ready response.

9. *Boston Transcript:* He thinks the copyright law should give to authors the exclusive right of their books for life and fifty years afterwards. "Why, just take the trademark law," he exclaimed. "I was reading the other day in the newspapers that a man can register a trademark forever for some patent medicine—just bottled poison—but they limit me to propagating my literary poison to forty-two years. There is none

of my books that I care anything about gone out yet, but *Innocents Abroad* goes out in six years."

10. *King Leopold's Soliloquy* (1905), a dramatic, satirical monologue that indicts King Leopold II of Belgium for profiting by a system of forced labor in the Congo.

11. *Boston Herald:* "I notice," said he, "that King Leopold has received the report of his commission, but that report, saying that everything had been done satisfactorily, is very different from the report of the missionaries. The members of the King's commission are interested persons—one of them is brother of his private secretary—and their report will do the King more harm than good. Leopold is too well known as a domestic person, as a family person, as a King, to get his evidence, or the evidence of any commission of his, accepted by an intelligent public. The missionaries, who go out at the risk of their lives, are much better witnesses than he. Leopold sits at home and drinks blood. The condition of things in the Congo is atrocious, as shown by the photographs of children whose hands have been cut off. Leopold thinks this can go on because the Congo is a distant out-of-the-way country. But once we can get England and America to investigate, and take this matter up, something will be done. We Americans are especially interested, because it was our recognition of the flag there that led to recognition by other powers."

Boston Journal: "Isn't it strange how a man will change when he changes locality? A man will be ever so polite to blacks at home, but when he goes where they predominate he gets overbearing. Take the condition of things in [the] Congo today. Of course, this commission, appointed by King Leopold, don't amount to anything. He is too well known as a domestic man, a family man, a King and a pirate to get his report accepted by any public. But photographs don't lie. A missionary showed me pictures of children with their hands cut off as evidence. King Leopold's soldiers have done their duty, because the natives didn't bring in rubber enough."

Boston Post: "I read in the *Boston Post* this morning about the terrible cannibal work of the natives there and, coming from a lady missionary, one can rely upon it. Against this we read the report submitted to King Leopold, stating that matters are going along calmly. But who is going to believe Leopold? That very report was drawn up by his own relatives and friends. It is just like appointing convicts in Sing Sing to inquire into the behavior of Sing Sing convicts. Leopold's report, to my mind, will do more harm than good. He is too well known. The lady missionary whom the *Boston Post* interviewed is a much better witness. She is one of many who take their lives in their hands. They risk their health, sacrifice their domestic comforts, and what they say, as a rule, one can believe." [MT alludes to "Horrors of Congo Region: Boston Woman Missionary Tells of Cruelty There," *Boston Post*, 5 November 1905, 26.]

12. A war of aggression from July to November 1893 against the Mashona, another Bantu tribe, in South Africa in which the British intervened.

13. On Cecil Rhodes, see n. 2 to interview 116.

Boston Journal: When I was in South Africa the bulletins used to amuse me. They would tell of some battles; of the heroic defense of some 100 white soldiers attacked by 4000 savages, and they would wind up: 'Result, 3000 natives killed and one mule wounded on the white side.' Somehow it seemed ridiculous after a while. They say they must subdue them? Why not go away and let them alone? I suppose England will go away after the mines are exhausted, and then there will be another misfortune and more gold found."

14. MT refers to the aborted Russian revolution in 1905-7.

15. The Russo-Japanese War (1904-5) in which Japan forced Russia to surrender its plans to expand its sphere of influence into Asia. The Treaty of Portsmouth ending the war was signed on 5 September 1905.

Boston Herald: "I did feel," said he, "on hearing the news of peace that another great defeat of the Russian armies would have assured freedom at home. I was afraid that peace at that time was going to fasten the shackles still more firmly on the Russian nation. When we heard recently of the new concessions made by the Emperor I began to think that, after all, peace had come at the right time. But I do not feel so sure of that now, because the later news shows that the Czar has not granted anything valuable, but has kept all the power in his own hands. Inasmuch as he grants legislative privileges without putting the army and navy and the treasury in the hands of a legislature, what he really grants amounts to nothing. Just as soon as he can quiet those people down and get them again into orderly shape he is going to take away again the few little privileges he has granted. While the army and navy and the treasury are in the hands of the Emperor nothing is really accomplished, though I admit there has been a great advance in thought and feeling among the Russian people. If the Russian army were to side with the people then a revolution would come."

Boston Journal: "I was really sorry when I heard there was to be peace between Russia and Japan. I thought if there was another battle the dissatisfaction would be so strong at home the government would have to give in to freedom. A few days ago when I read a constitution had been granted I began to think I had been too hasty, but now I don't feel so sure of it. As long as the army, and navy, and treasury are in the hands of the Czar the constitution don't amount to anything; nothing is accomplished today. If the army comes back from the East there will be different things. This resignation of Poblio—Poblio—Poblio—er—dontcareadamoldstaff (head of the Russian Church [see n. 19 this interview]) is a good thing. When a mild-mannered pirate gets into a conspicuous place there is usually a strong-minded pirate of the old-fashioned kind behind him. The Czar is in a hole, but not a bottomless hole. He's only waiting for a few years till the people get pacified and then he'll take back, one by one, the things he has doled out. Russia is a country by itself. When it talks about honor it is like any other pauper talking about money."

16. The Parliament Act of 1906 would establish a democratically elected parliament in Finland.

17. The region around Khiva, Uzbekistan, was annexed and occupied by Russia in 1873.

18. A battleground between Imperial Russia and Japan during the Russo-Japanese War. In December 1904 Port Arthur in Manchuria had fallen to the Japanese.

19. Konstantin Pobedonostsev (1827-1907), virulently anti-Catholic procurator of the Russian holy synod from 1880 to 1905, was an advocate of absolute monarchial authority.

20. Richard A. McCurdy (1835-1916), president of the Mutual Life Insurance Co., and John A. McCall (1849-1906), president of the New York Life Insurance Co. A New York state legislative committee had recently exposed corporate corruption and overcharging by insurance companies, including secret contributions to Theodore Roosevelt's presidential campaigns.

Boston Transcript: Asked what he thought of the McCurdy disclosures now coming to the front in New York, he said: "They remind me of the plague they had in Bombay some years ago when I was there. Every day they would discover a new plague center. It was here today, there tomorrow, and somewhere else the next day. What I wanted to find was a center where there was no plague. It's the same with this insurance business. Every day brings to light a new plague center. Grafting seems to be all over the country, and I don't think much of the reforms. But in this country we have one great privilege which they don't have in other countries. When a thing gets to be absolutely unbearable the people can rise up and throw it off. That's the finest asset we've got—the ballot box, which has been exercised in Philadelphia."

Boston Journal: "We furnished the liberty sentiment to Europe by our Revolution, and now we are furnishing the graft sentiment. But then an asset we have is that when conditions become unbearable we can arise and stamp them out. I remember reading during the yellow fever scare in New Orleans almost every day of some new center of fever being found, some new swamp where it was bred. We didn't hear of any place where it wasn't. It was all of some place where it was. This McCurdy investigation strikes me just like it. We are finding more and more centers of McCurdy's morals."

21. The reformist City Party, organized in 1905 to oppose the Boises Penrose machine, was defeated in the Philadelphia mayoral election in February 1907.

22. John D. Rockefeller (1839–1937), American oil baron; Jay Gould (1836–92) and Jim Fisk (1834–72), American robber barons. On Gould, see also n. 9 to interview 47.

23. See n. 2 to interview 138.

24. *Boston Transcript:* "We gave to the world the spirit of liberty more than one hundred years ago, and now we are giving the world the spirit of graft," he said. "Look at the British army scandals during the Boer War. No British commissioned officer ever did such things before. The spirit of graft has spread."

Boston Herald: "I am a pessimist, you know, and cannot change. But we have one asset in our country, and it is the finest asset we have. Whenever a condition becomes intolerable, the people will rise up and stamp it out. They did that in Philadelphia. At present look what is happening. We furnished to Europe the sentiment of liberty with our revolution—now we are furnishing Europe with graft."

181

"Mark Twain Would Kill Bosses by Third Party," *New York Herald*, 12 November 1905, sec. 2, 3–4.

Mark Twain has suggested a remedy for bossism, a way to overthrow the Murphys, the McCarrens, the Coxes, and make them stay overthrown.[1] He believes his treatment will not entail the abandonment of that habit, so dear to most citizens of this great Republic, of voting for their party candidates. Under the new order of things a man who cast his first ballot for the democratic nominee, and has done so every election since, because his father and his grandfather were partisan democrats, may continue to vote the democratic ticket and advise his son to vote the same way, with the comforting assurance that he will be honestly following the dictates of his conscience and that the election of his nominee will mean political purity, no bosses and the best administration possible.

Mr. Clemens believes it is simple to bring about this state of political perfection. All that is required is the organization of a permanent third party, call it "mugwump," if you choose, which shall continually hold the balance of power in municipal, State and national elections.[2] It must be a party with no candidates and no political or personal interests to further, and its members may not even suggest the appointment of any of their friends to office.

Mr. Clemens, as he lay propped up in bed in his city home, at No. 21 Fifth avenue, explained his theory yesterday to a *Herald* reporter. He was not ill. In fact, he said he hadn't enjoyed such good health for years. He was only resting in preparation for a trip to Washington next Saturday.

"It is a peculiar condition, but none the less true," said Mr. Clemens, "that the political liberty of which we are so proud is mainly responsible for the existence of the political boss. At any election the people, if they choose, may turn out the whole crowd. This is shown by the re-election of Mr. Jerome by citizens who believe in his honesty of purpose and that his qualifications fit him for the office of District Attorney.[3]

"But this very power which rests with the people is accountable for the laxity which permits the Murphys and the McCurdys and the McCalls and Hegemans to flourish.[4] We know that whenever we get tired of the domination of the bosses or those in office who represent them we have an unfailing remedy. We may apply it at any time, and for that reason we don't until some flagrant act causes an upheaval such as we have just seen in this city and in Philadelphia and in some other places.

"There is a way to escape from the thralldom of bossism, and that is by the organization of a third party, an independent party, made up of those who are generally called 'mugwumps'! I'm a 'mugwump.' I have never tied myself to any party, but have voted for the nominee who appealed to me as being the best man."

Mr. Clemens lighted his favorite pipe and blew a great cloud of smoke into which he gazed thoughtfully.

"What is party, anyway? That fog labeled 'democrat' or 'republican,' which means nothing to the average mind when it is analyzed. The democratic party shouts for free trade while the republican party shrieks for high tariff. Which is right? Why, there is no possible way of deciding which is right. If in the great party politic one-half believe high tariff is right and the other is certain free trade is the proper thing, who is there to settle the question?

"If you ask me what I suggest as a remedy for present conditions, I'll tell you that some one, a man of great executive ability, John Wanamaker, for instance, will have to enlist all his energies in the formation of a permanent third party.[5] It must be composed of men who are willing to give up all affiliations with either of the great parties. No man in it can have any political aspirations. He must not have any friends whom he wishes to push forward for political preferment. The sole reason for the existence of this new third party must be to elect the candidate of either the democratic or the republican party who is believed to be the best fitted for the office for which he is nominated.

"It is not the idea that this independent party is to consist of another fog of non-individualities to be swung in a mass for any candidate at any one's dictation. There would be nobody who could deliver that vote in a mass.

"It is a party made up of separate individualities, each holding and prizing the privilege of voting as he chooses, the rest to vote as they choose. And therefore you have this result, that if the candidate of one of the great parties is conspicuously a better man than the candidate of the other great party it is believable that the independent party would vote as a mass for that man.

"But if both are equally conspicuous for merit it is believable that this would split the independent vote in two with this final result, that, both of these candidates being excellent men, no one would care which was elected.

"If an independent party can obtain the nomination of excellent men on both sides this would certainly justify the organization of a third party."

"What if both the nominees are bad men?" Mr. Clemens was asked.

He turned upon the questioner a look of pity which there was no mistaking.

"Can't you see that if this third party has power to elect whomever it pleases, neither will select for its nominees any but the very best men? Don't you realize with what pains the names of the candidate would be considered before they were chosen for a place on the tickets? There could never be any question about their eligibility. All the 'mugwumps' would have to do would be to decide which man they liked best and vote for him. I admit it would be a mixed government, but that wouldn't matter.

"I have often wondered at the condition of things which set aside morality in politics and make possible the election of men whose unfitness is apparent. A mother will teach her boy at her knee to tell the truth, to be kind, to avoid all that is immoral. She will painstakingly guide his thoughts and actions so that he may grow up possessed of all the manly virtues, and the father of that boy will, when it comes time for his son to cast his first vote, take him aside and advise him to vote for a bad man who is on the democratic ticket because he has always adhered to democratic principles. Could anything be more absurd?

"I see by the newspapers that there has been a switching of affairs in Ohio, and that Boss Cox has thrown up his job. By the way, that was the first time I ever heard of a boss being, as the slang phrase has it, 'too previous.' Then I read of an overturning of things in Philadelphia. Why, I don't believe the new conditions will last the year out. How can they? There is no organized party to hold matters as they are. It has been the history of such political upheavals that as soon as the thing is accomplished those who brought it about settle back and let everything drift until the old conditions return.

"Mr. Hearst's fight for the Mayoralty was evidence of what the people can do if they choose.[6] Just think what it would mean if, instead of a spontaneous uprising of voters who are tired of the conditions existing at present, these same voters were members of an organized third party held together by a leader so that it could be counted on as the deciding factor in our municipal elections. It is probable that these same voters will soon forget all about it and then the boss will pick up his lines again and drive as before.

"Personally I would trust Mr. McClellan as Mayor of the city.[7] I believe he is capable and honest, and gives the best administration possible under the prevailing state of affairs. Free from any possible domination of a boss he would make a good chief magistrate. But we need some one to come forward and offer to lead this army of mugwumps who can set all straight.

"As a matter of fact, we hear of a good deal that isn't so. Recently we were told in the cable dispatches that the Tsar had proclaimed liberty in his country, with freedom of the press and political representation, very large matters in themselves. By the time we had got used to believing that such things could happen it was discovered that the people of Russia hadn't got so much after all, because the half dozen concessions mentioned don't amount to so much when we know the revenues of the country and the control of the army and navy are still in the Tsar's hands.

"When I mentioned Mr. Wanamaker as the man to do this I only need him as an example of the type of man who must stand at the head of such a movement. There are many others who would serve as well, men who have devoted their energies to accomplishing great effects by the employment of remarkable executive ability. He must be a builder up who would prove an acceptable leader of this 'mugwump' party.

"I cannot understand the philosophy of the man who, looked up to as a model citizen, loses sight of the morality of politics when it comes to casting his ballot. Why, it's nothing but a question of morality. And I know lots of men who will throw aside all considerations of morality when they go to the polls and will vote for the man nominated by his party irrespective of his personal fitness for the place. Prejudice influences him. He won't heed the dictates of his conscience.

"This question of prejudice is very important. There are lots of people who don't believe that a slice of ripe watermelon will cure dysentery. It cures my personal friends every time, but I'll bet if I tried to teach the gospel of ripe watermelon to a hospital full of dysentery patients and would sell watermelons for three cents a dozen they'd put me out of the institution."

Mr. Clemens became quite animated as he turned to the subject of cures. There is no gainsaying the fact that the author has improved greatly in bodily strength during the last year. His eyes were bright and his cheeks bear the glow of health. All his motions were vigorous as he emphasized the points of his argument.

"Speaking of indigestion, I've adopted a new method of treatment that has done the business for me. For thirty years I have suffered from that most annoying of ailments. Six months ago I began to try Mr. Fletcher's cure, which is to thoroughly masticate one's food and saturate it with saliva.[8] Within the last two weeks I have begun to realize the full benefits of this simple preventive.

"I have learned that when you have an attack of dyspepsia and you get those awful grinding pains in your stomach it's a sign you're all right. The stomach craves food and wants something to work on.

"Now I keep a glass of milk and some crackers beside my bed and I wait for the signal my stomach gives me. When it comes I eat and feel all right."

Notes to Interview 181

1. Charles F. Murphy (1858–1924), Tammany boss; Patrick H. McCarren (1847–1909), Brooklyn political boss; George B. Cox (1853–1916), Cincinnati political boss.
2. Mugwumps were liberal or reform Republicans who bolted the GOP in 1884.
3. On Jerome, see n. 4 to interview 151.
4. John Rogers Hegeman (1844–1919), president of the Metropolitan Life Insurance Co. See also note 20 to interview 180.
5. John Wanamaker (1838–1922) opened the first department store in Philadelphia in 1876.
6. William Randolph Hearst (1863–1951), American newspaper publisher and politician, ran unsuccessfully for mayor of New York City in 1905 and 1909 and for governor of New York State in 1906.
7. George B. McClellan Jr. (1845–1909), son of the Civil War general George B. McClellan and mayor of Boston from 1903 to 1909.
8. Horace Fletcher (1849–1919), American businessman who advocated a theory of nutrition based on serving small portions and chewing food thoroughly.

182

"Mark Twain at 70," *Hartford Courant*, 25 November 1905, 16.

November 30 is Mark Twain's birthday—that date marks the end of his seventieth year of genial beneficence. It has been a long and undisputed reign for the Prince of humorists, and long may it continue! That it began seventy years ago need not be disputed, for though in his various recollections he has given the public as yet none of his babyhood observations, who will doubt that he could do so if he would? A man who is so miraculously acquainted with the childhood of the race as to be able to reproduce the diaries of Adam and Eve would find anecdotes of his own infancy a mere bagatelle. That such recollections would prove him to have been a humorist from the day of his birth is not to be questioned.

The observant reporter finds that Mr. Clemens' seventy years have been only mellowing in their effect. The wonderful shock of hair has been gray these several decades, and any lines in his grave countenance are only the marks of quizzical observation or perhaps of inward laughter. The year finds him, after as widely varied a life as man could have, a citizen of New York, and this is probably a permanent abiding place. He is domiciled in one of those dignified old mansions of lower Fifth avenue, in sight of the Washington Arch, which hold their own against the encroachments of office buildings and the noise of business streets with a grim determination that earns for them added respect.

Mr. Clemens will tell you, however, that dignified old mansions have their drawbacks at times in the matter of heat. He has surmounted various difficulties in his lifetime, in ways all his own, and callers in the cold days of last spring cherish the memory of being received at his bedside, where the distinguished author carried on his end of the conversation warm and comfortable beneath bedclothes drawn to his chin.

It is a pity that Mr. Clemens has not been moved to give a full record of his householding experiences, summer and winter. His first experience in householding, as a man of family, was in Buffalo, where he began his married life. This was about 1870. He had bought a third interest in the *Buffalo Express*, and the house was a wedding gift from his father-in-law. For a time he was a member of the staff of this paper, but his days of working in harness were past. The demand for his work had so increased that he could choose his own time and place for writing. The inevitable move was made within a year. Samuel E. Moffett, in his biographical sketch, describes the event in interesting fashion.[1]

"There was at that time," Mr. Moffett says, "a tempting literary colony at Hartford; the place was steeped in an atmosphere of antique peace and beauty, and the Clemens family were captivated by its charm. They moved there in October 1871, and soon built a house which was one of the earliest fruits of the artistic revolt against the mid-century philistinism of domestic architecture in America. For years it was an object of wonder to the simple-minded tourist. The fact that its rooms were arranged for the convenience of those who were to occupy them, and that its windows, gables and porches were distributed with an eye to the beauty, comfort and picturesqueness of that particular house, instead of following the traditional lines laid down by the carpenters and contractors who designed most of the dwellings of the period, distracted the critics and gave rise to grave discussions in the newspapers throughout the country of 'Mark Twain's practical joke.'"

Hartford was for many years his home, though in the Summer intervals various mountain or seaside cottages got in some of their dread work, while so recently as a Summer or two ago an Italian villa added strange new items to the sum total of his domiciliary experience.

His latest solution of the Summer question is Dublin, New Hampshire. There he was last Summer, and there he hopes to be again. His own account of how he reached so satisfactory a solution is entertaining, and may be instructive.

"Yes," he said, when asked about the matter. "I have tried a number of summer homes, here and in Europe together.

"Each of these homes had charms of its own; charms and delights of its own, and some of them—even in Europe—had comforts. Several of them had conveniences, too. They all had a 'view.'

"It is my conviction that there should always be some water in a view—a lake or a river, but not the ocean, if you are down on its level. I think that when you are down on its level it seldom inflames you with an ecstasy which you could not get out of a sand-flat. It is like being on board ship, over again; indeed, it is worse than that, for there's three months of it. On board ship one tires of the aspects in a couple of days and quits looking. The same vast circle of heaving humps is spread around you all the time, with you in the center of it and never gaining an inch on the horizon, so far as you can see; for variety, a flight of flying-fish, mornings; a flock of porpoises throwing somersaults, afternoons; a remote whale spouting Sundays; occasional phosphorescent effects, nights; every other day a streak of black smoke trailing along under the horizon; on the one single red-letter day the illustrious iceberg. I have seen that iceberg thirty-four times in thirty-seven voyages; it is always the same shape, it is always the same size, it always throws up the same old flash when the sun strikes it; you may set it on any New York doorstep of a June morning and light it up with a mirror-flash and I will engage to recognize it. It is artificial and is provided and anchored out by the steamer companies. I used to like the sea, but I was young then, and could easily get excited over any kind of monotony, and keep it up till the monotonies ran out, if it was a fortnight.

"Last January, when we were beginning to inquire about a home for this summer, I remembered that Abbott Thayer had said, three years before, that the New Hampshire highlands was a good place. He was right—it is a good place. Any place that is good for an artist in paint is good for an artist in morals and ink. Brush is here, too; so is Colonel T. W. Higginson; so is Raphael

Pumpelly; so is Mr. Secretary Hitchcock; so is Henderson; so is Larned; so is Sumner; so is Franklin MacVeagh; so is Joseph L. Smith; so is Henry Copley Greene, when I am not occupying his house, which I am doing this season. Paint, literature, science, statesmanship, history, professorship, law, morals—these are all represented here, yet crime is substantially unknown.[2]

"The summer homes of these refugees are sprinkled, a mile apart, among the forest-clad hills, with access to each other by firm and smooth country roads which are so embowered in dense foliage that it is always twilight in there, and comfortable. The forests are spider-webbed with these good roads—they go everywhere; but for the help of the guideboards, the stranger would not arrive anywhere.

"The village—Dublin—is bunched together in its own place, but a good telephone service makes its markets handy to all those outliars. I have spelt it that way to be witty. The village executes orders on the Boston plan—promptness and courtesy.

"The summer homes are high-perched, as a rule, and have contenting outlooks. The house we occupy has one. Monadnock, a scaring double hump, rises into the sky at its left elbow—that is to say, it is close at hand.[3] From the base of the long slant of the mountain the valley spreads away to the circling frame of hills, and beyond the frame the billowy sweep of remote great ranges rises to view and flows, fold upon fold, wave upon wave, soft and blue and unworldly to the horizon fifty miles away. In these October days, Monadnock and the valley and its framing hills make an inspiring picture to look at, for they are sumptuously splashed and mottled and betorched from sky-line to sky-line with the richest dyes the autumn can furnish; and when they lie flaming in the full drench of the mid-afternoon sun, the sight affects the spectator physically, it stirs the blood like military music.

"These summer homes are commodious, well built and well furnished—facts which sufficiently indicate that the owners built them to live in themselves. They have furnaces and wood fireplaces, and the rest of the comforts and conveniences of a city home, and can be comfortably occupied all the year round.

"We cannot have this house next season, but I have secured Mrs. Upton's house,[4] which is over in the law and science quarter, two or three miles from here, and about the same distance from the art, literary and scholastic groups. The science and law quarter has needed improving this good while.

"The nearest railway station is distant something like an hour's drive; it is three hours from there to Boston, over a branch line. You can go to New York in six hours per branch lines if you change cars every time you think of it, but it is better to go to Boston and stop over and take the trunk line next day; then you do not get lost.

"It is claimed that the atmosphere of the New Hampshire highlands is exceptionally bracing and stimulating, and a fine aid to hard and continuous work. It is a just claim, I think. I came in May, and wrought thirty-five successive days without a break. It is possible that I could not have done that elsewhere. I do not know; I have not had any disposition to try it before. I think I got the disposition out of the atmosphere this time. I feel quite sure, in fact, that that is where it came from.

"I am ashamed to confess what an intolerable pile of manuscript I ground out in the thirty-five days, therefore I will keep the number of words to myself. I wrote the first half of a long tale—'The Adventures of a Microbe'[5]—and put it away for a finish next summer, and started another long tale—'The Mysterious Stranger.'[6] I wrote the first half of it and put it with the other for a finish next summer. I stopped then. I was not tired but I had no books on hand that needed finishing this year except one that was seven years old. After a little I took that one up ["The Mysterious Stranger"] and finished it. Not for publication, but to have it ready for revision next summer.

"Since I stopped work I have had a two months' holiday. The summer has been my working time for thirty-five years; to have a holiday in it (in America) is new for me. I have not broken it, except to write 'Eve's Diary'[7] and 'A Horse's Tale'[8]—short things occupying the mill twelve days.

"This year our summer is six months long and ends with November and the flight home to New York, but next year we hope and expect to stretch it another month and end it the first of December."

Surely no man has reached his seventieth birthday with a more perfect title to winter comfort and summer rest than Mark Twain. His life has been as full of wandering and varied adventure as an egg is full of meat. In 1835 he was born in Florida, Missouri, and while he was a child the home was moved to Hannibal, in the same state.

His father, a local judge, died when he was twelve years old, and at thirteen he was at work in his elder brother's printing office. But to the care-free boyhood preceding that date we are indebted for those classic histories of small-boydom written very many years later, *Tom Sawyer* and *Huckleberry Finn*. By 1853 he had become a wanderer, working in chance printing offices in New York, St. Louis, Muscatine, and Keokuk. Some memories of those days, softened by the intervening years, are gathered together in the little volume "Editorial Wild Oats," or scattered through his various collections of shorter sketches....

In such varied ways has his life been cast, each year broadening and deepening his experience; and it was long ago that the mere humorist was merged in the philosopher. The effect of such a career on the kindly heart and keen, observant nature of the man has been to build greater things than the present generation has as yet appreciated, generous as its judgment may have been. It will remain for later critics to view his work with a surer vision, knowing nothing, perhaps, of that great part of his contemporary public who asked only that he be "funny," and write him down in his rightful place, between Dickens and Thackeray—America's greatest student of human nature and common life.

Notes to Interview 182

1. Though attributed to Samuel E. Moffett (see n. 2 to interview 127), this essay was written by MT.
2. Abbott Thayer (1849–1921), American painter. George de Forest Brush (1855–1941), American painter. On Higginson, see n. 3 to interview 180. Raphael Pumpelly (1837–1923), director of the U.S. Geological Survey. Ethan Allen Hitchcock (1835–1909), U.S. secretary of the interior from 1898 to 1907, also received an honorary degree from the University of Missouri in June 1902. Ernest Flagg Henderson (1861–1928), American author and historian. Josephus N. Larned (1836–1913), formerly part owner of the *Buffalo Express* with MT. Sumner B. Pearmain (b. 1859), a Boston stockbroker. Franklin MacVeagh (1837–1934), director of the Commercial National Bank of Chicago and subsequently U.S. secretary of the treasury (1909–13). Joseph Linden Smith (1863–1950), painter and expert on Egyptian art. Henry Copley Greene (1871–1951), American playwright.
3. Mount Monadnock in southwestern New Hampshire also figures in the writings of Hawthorne, Thoreau, Melville, Cather, Edwin Arlington Robinson, and Amy Lowell.
4. Alice H. Upton, Sumner B. Pearmain's mother-in-law.
5. Also titled "Three Thousand Years among the Microbes," a forty-thousand-word fragment written in May–June 1905 and narrated by a germ in the "blood of a hoary and mouldering old bald-headed tramp." See also *Auto* (1959), 266.
6. The final version of "The Mysterious Stranger" manuscripts featuring "No. 44," virtually completed in 1905. See also *Auto* (1959), 266.
7. A sequel to "Extracts from Adam's Diary" (1893) written in July 1905 and published in the December 1905 issue of *Harper's*. See also n. 10 to interview 200.
8. Partly told from the perspective of a horse gored during a bullfight, a tale first published in the August–September 1906 issues of *Harper's*.

183

A. E. Thomas, "Mark Twain: A Humorist's Confession," *New York Times* first magazine section, 26 November 1905, 1, 5.

Mark Twain will be 70 years old on Thanksgiving Day, and he has never done a day's work in his life. He told me so himself, sitting in one of the cheerful, spacious rooms of the old-fashioned stately New York house which he will probably call his city home as long as he lives. I probably started upon hearing this unlooked-for statement from the lips of the good, gray humorist, for he repeated emphatically:

"No, sir, not a day's work in all my life. What I have done I have done, because it has been play. If it had been work I shouldn't have done it.

"Who was it who said, 'Blessed is the man who has found his work'? Whoever it was he had the right idea in his mind. Mark you, he says his work—not somebody else's work. The work that is really a man's own work is play and not work at all. Cursed is the man who has found some other man's work and cannot lose it.[1] When we talk about the great workers of the world we really mean the great players of the world. The fellows who groan and sweat under the weary load of toil that they bear never can hope to do anything great. How can they when their souls are in a ferment of revolt against the employment of their hands and brains? The product of slavery, intellectual or physical, can never be great. . . .

"I'm glad you came to see me today, as I'm up and about, which I shouldn't have been if I had been doing anything of consequence. You're surprised at that, are you?

"Well, I've found that whenever I've got some work to do—"

"You mean play, of course," I ventured.

"Of course, of course; but we're all slaves to the use of conventional terms and I'll stick to them to avoid confusing you. Whenever I've got some work to do I go to bed. I got into that habit some time ago when I had an attack of bronchitis. Suppose your bronchitis lasts six weeks. The first two you can't do much but attend to the barking and so on, but the last four I found I could work if I stayed in bed, and when you can work you don't mind staying in bed.

"I liked it so well that I kept it up after I got well. There are a lot of advantages about it. If you're sitting at a desk you get excited about what you are doing, and the first thing you know the steam heat or the furnace has raised the temperature until you've almost got a fever, or the fire in the grate goes out and you get a chill, or if somebody comes in to attend to the fire he interrupts you and gets you off the trail of that idea you are pursuing.

"So I go to bed. I can keep an equable temperature there without trying and go on about my work without being bothered. Work in bed is a pretty good gospel—at least for a man who's come, like me, to the time of life when his blood is easily frosted."

This was queer talk for those virile lips. The only frost you can perceive about Mark Twain is in his hair, and this is a crisp, invigorating frost, like that of a sparkling November morning.

"Well, Mr. Clemens," I said, "what you say about work and play may be true, but a good many people would think that the immense amount of labor you went through to pay the debts of the publishing house of C. L. Webster & Co., after that firm went to smash, was entitled to be called by the name of hard work."

"Not at all. All I had to do was write a certain number of books and deliver a few hundred lectures. As for traveling about the country from one place to another for years—the nuisances of getting about and bad hotels and so on—those things are merely the incidents that every one expects to meet in life. The people who had to publish my books, the agents who had to arrange my lecture tours, the lawyers who had to draw up the contracts and other legal documents—they were the men who did the real work. My part was merely play. If it had been work I shouldn't have done it. I was never intended for work—never could do it—can't do it now—don't see any use in it."

It occurred to me to ask Mr. Clemens to tell the secret of the vital hold he has had for years upon the most intelligent people of the English-speaking world—a grip upon the public mind such as no mere humorist has ever held or ever could hold.

"Well," he answered, "I know it is a difficult thing for a man who has acquired a reputation as a funny man to have a serious thought and put it into words and be listened to respectfully, but I thoroughly believe that any man who's got anything worthwhile to say will be heard if he only says it often enough. Of course, what I have to say may not be worth saying. I can't tell about that, but if I honestly believe I have an idea worth the attention of thinking people it's my business to say it with all the sincerity I can muster. They'll listen to it if it really is worthwhile and I say it often enough. If it isn't worthwhile it doesn't matter whether I'm heard or not.

"Suppose a man makes a name as a humorist—he may make it at a stroke, as Bret Harte did, when he wrote those verses about the 'Heathen Chinee.'[2] That may not be the expression of the real genius of the man at all. He may have a genuine message for the world. Then let him say it and say it again and then repeat it and let him soak it in sincerity. People will warn him at first that he's getting a bit out of his line, but they'll listen to him at last, if he's really got a message just as they finally listened to Bret Harte.

"Dickens had his troubles when he tried to stop jesting. The *Sketches by Boz* introduced him as a funny man, but when Boz began to take him seriously people began to shake their heads and say: 'That fellow Boz isn't as funny as he was, is he?' But Boz and his creator kept right on being in earnest, and they listened after a time, just as they always will listen to anybody worth hearing.

"I tell you, life is a serious thing, and, try as a man may, he can't make a joke of it. People forget that no man is all humor, just as they fail to remember that every man is a humorist. We hear that marvelous voice of Sembrich—a wonderful thing—a thing never to be forgotten—but nobody makes the mistake of thinking of Sembrich as merely a great, unmixed body of song.[3] We know that she can think and feel and suffer like the rest of us. Why should we forget that the humorist has his solemn moments? Why should we expect nothing but humor of the humorist?

"My advice to the humorist who has been a slave to his reputation is never to be discouraged. I know it is painful to make an earnest statement of a heartfelt conviction and then observe the puzzled expression of the fatuous soul who is conscientiously searching his brain to see how he can possibly have failed to get the point of the joke. But say it again and maybe he'll understand you. No man need be a humorist all his life. As the patent medicine man says, there is hope for all."

"You are far from being a bad man; go and reform," thought I reminiscently of "The Man That Corrupted Hadleyburg."

"The quality of humor," Mr. Clemens went on hurriedly—for him—"is the commonest thing in the world. I mean the perceptive quality of humor. In this sense every man in the world is a humorist. The creative quality of humor—the ability to throw a humorous cast over a set of circumstances that before had seemed colorless is, of course, a different thing. But every man in the world is a perceptive humorist. Everybody lives in a glass house. Why should anybody shy bricks at a poor humorist or advise him to stick to his trade when he tries to say a sensible thing?"

"Even the English?" I suggested.

"The English don't deserve their reputation. They are as humorous a nation as any in the world. Only humor, to be comprehensible to anybody, must be built upon a foundation with which he is familiar. If he can't see the foundation the superstructure is to him merely a freak—like the Flatiron building without any visible means of support, something that ought to be arrested.

"You couldn't, for example, understand an English joke, yet they have their jokes—plenty of them. There's a passage in Parkman that tells of the home life of the Indian—describes him sitting at home in his wigwam with his squaw and papooses—not the stoical, icy Indian with whom we are familiar, who wouldn't make a jest for his life or notice one that anybody else made, but the real Indian that few white men ever saw—simply rocking with mirth at some tribal witticism that probably wouldn't have commended itself in the least to Parkman.[4]

"And, so you see, the quality of humor is not a personal or a national monopoly. It's as free as salvation, and, I am afraid, far more widely distributed. But it has its value, I think. The hard and sordid things of life are too hard and too sordid and too cruel for us to know and touch them year after year without some mitigating influence, some kindly veil to draw over them, from time to time, to blur the craggy outlines, and make the thorns less sharp and the cruelties less malignant."

Mr. Clemens doesn't mind being seventy years old, but he isn't especially gay about it.

"When our anniversaries roll up too high a total," he said, "we don't feel in a particularly celebratory mood. We often celebrate the wrong anniversaries and lament the ones we ought to celebrate."

Notes to Interview 183

1. A parody of Christ's Beatitudes in the Sermon on the Mount.
2. Harte's "Plain Language from Truthful James," or "The Heathen Chinee," first published in the *Overland Monthly* 5 (September 1870): 287-88.
3. Marcella Sembrich (1858-1935), Polish American operatic soprano.
4. Francis Parkman (1823-93), American historian, best known for *The Oregon Trail* (1849).

184

W. O. Inglis, "What I Am Thankful For," *New York Sunday World Magazine*, 26 November 1905, 1.

"We have much to be thankful for: most of all, (politically), that America's first-born son, sole & only son, love-child of her trusting innocence and her virgin bed, King Leopold of the undertakers, has been spared to us another year, & that his (& our) Cemetery Trust in the Congo is now doing a larger business in a single week than it used to do in a month fifteen years ago. Mark Twain."[1]

This remarkable sentiment was given to me by Mr. Clemens at the end of an interview. His seventieth birthday will be celebrated next Thursday, and, because his life is an additional reason why the American people should feel grateful, he was asked by the *Sunday World Magazine* to say why we should all be thankful at this particular season.

Mere black words on white paper cannot give the force with which Mr. Clemens uttered the denunciation of King Leopold, whom most people recall in a vague way as the destroyer of Congo negroes and promoter of Parisian orgies.[2] The outburst came as a surprise, for the conversation up to that point had been quite general. No one could think of Mr. Clemens as seventy years old who had seen the burning eyes of the man or heard the slow, irresistible roll of his sonorous voice as he denounced the King of the Belgians for his traffic in human flesh.

We were sitting in the library of Mr. Clemens' home, a stately, spacious old mansion in lower Fifth avenue. The white-haired humorist had been in a delightful mood, now pacing up and down the long room as he talked, again allowing himself a few moments of luxury in a great easy chair before he resumed the busy walk. He had been speaking of Thanksgiving days in general. It is difficult to give an adequate idea of the charm of an interview with Mark Twain. The man breathes the spirit of hospitality, and upon every subject that comes up his quick mind plays with all the brilliance and illuminative power of a searchlight.

The surprising thing about him is the absence of an appearance of age. When one interviews a man about his seventieth birthday one expects to find a certain venerableness. But in Mark Twain the venerableness is lacking.

His erect, supple, well-knit figure and springy step would be creditable to a man of forty. The clear, healthy pink and white of his complexion are unmarred by wrinkles. His hazel eyes are as keen and searching as ever. The great shock of grizzled hair is not yet white, the thick, red-brown mustache is heavily splashed with gray.

"How do you keep so well?" was the question that inevitably suggested itself at the beginning.

"That's only a recent phase," Mr. Clemens replied. "I was until lately subject to the annoyance of attacks of acute indigestion. Never could tell when the miserable, nagging thing was going to pounce upon me and torture me. Midday or 3 o'clock in the morning was all the same to it. I can see now the trouble was due to my habit, of thirty years' standing, of eating only one meal a day.

"Last summer a dear friend said to me: 'Why don't you give up your one-meal-a-day plan? It's enough to give a statue indigestion! You'll notice that doctors tell their patients to eat many times a day, a little at a time. Try it yourself, and you'll get well.'

"I'd have tried anything. As long as I can remember I've been willing to risk any scheme that any one said was good for me. And this time I tried the right one. Three small meals a day, sometimes four, made a wonderful change. The indigestion and the pangs disappeared. The family, returning after an absence of only three weeks, were astonished at the cure. I'm feeling better than I have felt in years.

"Perhaps we Americans eat too much. If we do, I am convinced that the proper cure lies in dividing the food supply into several small meals a day rather than in overloading the digestive machinery at one fell swoop."

"How about your exercise?" I asked.

"No exercise at all," said Mr. Clemens. "For weeks at a time I did not leave my home up in the mountains. Often I lay in bed all day and wrote. It's a great luxury to arrange your desk in bed and write as long as you like. I've spent whole weeks that way. You see, I'm in no hurry for publication. It pleases me to do a certain amount of work every day. I keep some of the manuscript for years. If after lying unread for three, four, or five years, it comes up to the standard I have set, then I publish it; if not, it drops into the waste basket. I write to please myself. No editor is so hard to satisfy as one's own standard."

"But don't you feel the lack of exercise?" I persisted.

"No," replied Mr. Clemens. "Perhaps I am exceptionally lucky. I may not need it. I never fail to run upstairs. That is exercise enough, I find. You know, it's a great mistake to say a fellow is lazy because he doesn't like to rush around and be active in your own kind of activity. The average man whom we call lazy is probably not lazy at all, but is simply storing up energy which he will burn up in some form of work which doesn't happen to appeal to us.

"What a mistake we make in setting up two arbitrary definitions of effort and calling one work and the other play. You can't measure effort that way. Whatever a man likes most to do, the thing into which he puts all his energy heartily without ever thinking whether he is doing enough or too much—that thing is play to him, no matter whether he works at it by way of diversion or to earn his living.

"Look at the idle men and women who live in luxury and give all their energy to what they call amusement. Are they really amused by all their labor or are they tired out, depressed, bored to death?"

Mr. Clemens was walking up and down the long library, smoking a black cigar. In his earnest talk he kept forgetting the cigar and every little while he had to stop and relight it. So each match he struck marked the beginning of a paragraph.

"They apply the same cast-iron conventional rule to everything," he went on. "For years they have regarded me as a trifler, one who is always ready with a joke on any subject. I tell you, there never lived in this world a more serious man than I."

Now, here was a remarkable confession from one who has long been regarded as the greatest humorist in the world. Much has been said and written about the Mark Twain drawl. It is not a drawl. Mr. Clemens takes time to arrange his ideas, hammering them into the exact form he wants, as a good workman hammers metal. Therefore, as he is one of those who think while they talk—rare beings!—the words Mr. Clemens utters march forth slowly and carefully, each falling without haste into its place. Mark Twain's voice, by the way, is as sonorous and robust as when it delighted thousands from the lecture platform.

"What is it that strikes a spark of humor from a man?" Mr. Clemens continued. "It is the effort to throw off, to fight back the burden of grief that is laid on each one of us. In youth we don't feel it, but as we grow to manhood we find the burden on our shoulders. Humor? It is nature's effort to harmonize conditions. The further the pendulum swings out over woe the further it is bound to swing back over mirth.

"I will not give you," he said, suddenly becoming grave, "any humorous trifling for this great and solemn day, for I am anxious not to hurt the feelings of any one to whom this day, with its deep and serious memories, appeals. But I will say this"—and here Mr. Clemens read the denunciation of Leopold.

If it were possible to reproduce on this paper his earnestness, his horror of the tyrant's murderous acts, the depth of indignation, and accusation in his menacing voice, a million readers would arise and demand that the murderer be put on trial.

"I hope," said Mr. Clemens, "that the American people will bring retribution to this unclean, lying murderer who is taking lives day by day in order that he may clutch more and more of the tainted money he wastes. I hope that this Thanksgiving sentiment of mine will sink into the minds of *The World*'s readers, make them think, make them act. In giving it to you I am trying not to do something that will please one, but to do something that will damage that wholesale murderer, that greedy, grasping, avaricious, cynical, bloodthirsty old goat!

"Think of it. Here sits a King in luxury and debauchery, placidly ordering thousands of innocent human creatures driven to death, tortured, crippled, massacred in order that his foul revenues may be increased! If only we could bring home that picture to the minds of the American people how they would rise to destroy that aged, brutal trafficker in human flesh!

"We read the other day of the awful Boston dress-suit-case murder mystery, and as we read of it every decent man was eager to conduct a private, personal auto da fe for the incarnate fiends who wantonly slaughtered that poor girl, butchered her and sought by scattering her tortured body to hide their crime. The horror of the thing thrilled us because it was so close to our homes.[3]

"Yet in these days the steamship and the electric cable have made the whole world one neighborhood. We cannot sit still and do nothing because the victims of Leopold's lust for gold are so many thousands of miles away. His crimes are the concern of every one of us, of every man who feels that it is his duty as a man to prevent murder, no matter who is the murderer or how far away he seeks to commit his sordid crime.

"I wish *The World* would produce the two cartoons I give you, for they summarize better than any words of mine can tell the exact condition of the case.[4]

"When mankind first heard the accusation that Congo negroes were being whipped, slashed, murdered, or mutilated by having hands or feet cut off because they did not bring in enough rubber for Leopold's collectors, the news was so appalling that it could not be believed. Normal minds instinctively rejected such atrocities as impossible.

"The accusation became louder, more people talked of these crimes. Some notice had to be taken of the clamor. It was easy for Leopold and his agents to pooh-pooh the charge, to say it was due to the envy of discontented, jealous missionaries whom they had offended.

"But the cry grew louder and louder and could not be stifled. And then the accusers began to present documents, awful human documents, gathered with the photographic camera. Leopold could no longer brush away the accusation by crying 'Lies! Lies! All lies!'

"Thank God for the camera, for the testimony of the light itself, which no mere man can contradict. The light has been let in upon the Congo, and not all the outcries of Leopold can counteract its record of the truth. Publicity is the weapon with which we shall fight that murderer and conquer him and punish him.

"The cartoons I give you expose at one glance the specious fraud of Leopold's protestations and his panic now that he finds the record of the photographic camera confirming the charge of wholesale murder against him.

"I wish I could show to every American, to every decent, humane man in the world the photographs of these poor creatures starved to mere skeletons by Leopold's order, beaten with lashes, murdered in cold blood. And, worse still, the many cases of little children whose hands and feet are cut off to punish their parents because they have not brought in enough rubber.

"We are sad when we hear of some one going blind; but can anything be more helpless, more hopeless, than one of these little creatures, forever unable to walk, unable even to feed itself. Think of all that this mutilation means!

"The cemeteries of New England send $800,000 every year to maintain missions in remote places of the earth, to spread faith among those who sit in darkness—yet should not something be done to rescue these poor people, so long murdered in darkness? I say the 'cemeteries of New England' because most of the contributions for foreign missions come from New England, and you will find that about $600,000 of the $800,000 comes from estates of dead men.

"And there is a picture not easy to forge—the hungry money-grabber, eagerly piling one dollar upon another as long as his strength remains, no matter how he acquires it; so jealous of his wealth that he will risk his life sooner than part with it; yet hoping by a bequest of perhaps one-tenth of his grabbings, which he gives from the grave, to purchase a little forgetfulness from the Almighty! He takes from his heirs in the hope of shielding himself from the consequences of a lifetime spent in despoiling mankind."

Notes to Interview 184

1. This was MT's handwritten note, which was reproduced in the article.
2. See nn. 10 and 11 to interview 180.
3. On 28 September 1905, a suitcase containing a young woman's torso was found floating in Boston harbor. The murder became a local cause célèbre.
4. This interview was accompanied by a pair of cartoons by David Wilson (1873–1935).

185

Marlen E. Pew, "Samuel L. Clemens Interviews the Famous Humorist, Mark Twain," *Seattle Star*, 30 November 1905, 8.

New York, Nov. 30—Mark Twain is an even 70 years old Thanksgiving day. Maybe it would be more accurate to say 70 years young.

Three score and ten have silvered the beautiful leonine head of the famous American author and humorist, time has brought a slight tremble to the busy hands, but his youth remains in the sparkling eyes, pure rose madder paints the cheeks, while buoyant spirits, crisp thought, with clear and rapid expression, tell of health of body and mind.

This is Samuel Langhorne Clemens at 70.

We went to interview him, my friend Fireman the artist, and I. At the corner of Fifth av. and Ninth st. in the shade of Twain's fine old-fashioned town house we plotted an assault. We would sandbag him and take away funds of knowledge and information which would encompass the Twain version of all questions of the day at home and abroad.

In a small library we opened the attack. We all sat down to smoke.

Twain ran up a white flag for a council of war.

He told us that he believed we were honest. We might go on and talk for an hour, he answering our questions freely. But he defied us to go out and repeat accurately what he had said. No human being could carry away another's thought as expressed in an hour's talk and transcribe it exactly.

Let us be exact in all things and begin today. Let us experiment with this interview just for fun. It would be original, anyway, and he had long wanted to interview himself.

We capitulated unconditionally.

He put me to taking down words verbatim.

Fireman started his sketch.

Mr. Clemens began his interview with Mark Twain: "There have been all kinds of interviews except natural interviews—that is to say, conversations which could occur naturally in real life. Necessarily an interview must be one of two things, question and answer, or monolog. Neither of these is quite what is wanted in an interview. The question and answer process belongs in the court, and the parties to it are a lawyer who wants to find out something, and the witness who often wishes to defeat the lawyer's desire.

"Manifestly this process could not produce a valuable interview since it would lack its most interesting feature, the attempt to conceal what the interviewed person had been questioned about. In the case of the interviewed it is no trouble to conceal, for the accused can decline to answer when you put him in an uncomfortable place, and as there is no compulsion upon him the subject has to be changed. The result must always be a colorless interview, for the subject is changed at exactly the moment when it is about to become interesting.

"But never mind about the forms; the real trouble about an interview is that the matters touched upon are always suggested by the interviewer, and as he cannot know what is of first interest in the prisoner's mind, he is not likely, save by accident, to suggest a topic that the prisoner can talk about with any real warmth.

"It is most unlikely that either of you gentlemen with a week to prepare in could guess the subject which is not only uppermost in my mind this morning, but is occupying and solidly packing to the exclusion of all other interests the whole spacious firmament of it. That subject will seem to you and to everybody else trivial whereas to me for just this day and train only it is of first importance. It is the matter of portraits—portraits of me.

"Many people think I am a happy man, but I am not; it is because my portraits do me justice. I have a highly organized and sensitive constitution and an educated taste in esthetics, and I cannot abide a portrait which is too particular. I am as I was made—this is a disaster which I cannot help and am in no way responsible for; but is there any fair reason why the artist should notice that? I do him no harm, yet he always exercises this wanton and malicious frankness upon my portraits.

"I should like to be drawn once, before I reach 70 again, as I should look if I had been made right instead of carelessly.

"You must not expect me to be calm and collected when I am talking upon the subject which has made my life a bitterness. I could be handsome if the artist would only help, but he has never done this.

"Even the camera has always entered with enthusiasm into this conspiracy to paint me as I am. There is one photograph which has persecuted me for what may be fairly termed a lifetime. Sarony took that portrait and in all these years I see it in print oftener than any other.[1] It arrived once more yesterday with this remark: 'With this I enclose a picture of yourself in the *Detroit Journal*. Of course it is a wood cut, but I presume not a bad picture, in which you can see yourself as others see you.'[*]

"No doubt the presumption is right. That is just the fault I find with it. I have explained that portrait a great many times. It is such a distress to me when I see it, that I always put down my work and explain it. I have explained it to this Lansing gentleman in a dictated letter last night, and if you would do me the kindness to print that letter, maybe I shan't have to explain again for a month."

Twain handed over a letter addressed to Samuel H. Row, of Lansing, Michigan, who in a recent communication recalled to the humorist how "when you were young and handsome I had the pleasure of introducing you to a Lansing audience."[2] Mr. Row recalled that during the lecture Twain was "sweating blood" because Lansing didn't tumble to his humor and Row began to clap his hands, stamp his feet and cheer. The audience fell in line. At the hotel that night Row reminded Twain that he had said: "Mr. Row, you saved me."

"Dear Mr. Row: That alleged portrait has a private history. Sarony was as much of an enthusiast about wild animals as he was about photography; and when Dr. Du Chaillu brought the first gorilla to this country in 1819 he [Sarony] came to me in a fever of excitement and asked me if my father was of record and authentic.[3] I said he was. Then Sarony, without any abatement of his excitement, asked me if my grandfather was also of record and authentic. I said he was. Then Sarony, with still rising excitement and with joy added to it, said he had found my great-grandfather in the person of the gorilla and had recognized him at once by his resemblance to me.

"I was deeply hurt, but did not reveal this, because I knew Sarony meant no offense, for the gorilla had not done him any harm, and he was not a man who would say an unkind thing about a gorilla wantonly. I went with him to inspect the ancestor, and examined him from several points of view, without being able to detect anything more than a passing resemblance. 'Wait,' said Sarony with strong confidence, 'Let me show you.' He borrowed my overcoat and put it on the gorilla. The result was surprising. I saw that the gorilla, while not looking distinctly like me, was exactly what my great-grandfather would look like if I had had one. Sarony photographed the creature in that overcoat and spread the picture around the world. It has remained spread around the world ever since. It turns up every week in some newspaper somewhere or other. It is not my favorite, but, to my exasperation, it is everybody else's. Do you think you could get it suppressed for me? I will pay the limit."

After this letter had been marked in evidence, Mark Twain went on: "This morning I have received another heart breaker in this line. It comes from Webster of the Chicago *Inter-Ocean*.[4] If you will examine that portrait (handing to me a cartoon by Webster) and then look at me you will see, yourself, that it is too exact. This kind of accuracy, continued long enough, can ruin a man who is constructed as I am. In that picture all the imagination is lavished upon the butler, all the cold facts are lavished upon me. My butler is an Italian; the Italian in that picture is idealized, that is what I want."

Webster's cartoon letter, in which was an exaggerated negro, was marked "Exhibit A 2," and Twain turned his attention to the pictures by Fireman, which were then nearing completion.

"These portraits are absolutely satisfactory. What I want is a handsome picture. These are not only good portraits, but they are also handsome. They are dignified. They are intellectual. Let us disseminate these; let us make them popular. Let us use them to drive out Sarony's over-conscientious gorilla. These portraits are right, because they are physically correct and at the same time they are idealizations spiritually. They break the boiler iron law of portrait painting, and therein lies their great value to me.

"I saw a play last night in which you will find this seeming paradox. In that play all the implacable rules of the drama are violated, yet the result is a play which is without a defect. I refer to *Peter Pan*. It is a fairy play. There isn't a thing in it which could ever happen in real life. That is as it should be. It is consistently beautiful, sweet, clean, fascinating, satisfying, charming, and impossible from beginning to end. It breaks all the rules of real life drama, but preserves intact all the rules of fairyland, and the result is altogether contenting to the spirit.[5]

"The longing of my heart is a fairy portrait of myself: I want to be pretty; I want to eliminate facts and fill up the gap with charms."

Notes to Interview 185

1. Napoleon Sarony (1821–96), American theatrical photographer. According to Budd (1996), 90n4, MT sat at least twice—Nov. 1884 and c. 1894—for portraits by Sarony. Paine "inferred that MT meant the earlier portrait. However, the Seattle *Star* printed a pose of the later sitting, which was much exposed, especially during the publicity about his world lecture-tour in 1895–96" (1293).

2. Samuel H. Row, Michigan state commissioner of insurance (1871–83). MT delivered his "Roughing It" lecture in Lansing on 20 December 1871.

3. Paul Belloni Du Chaillu (c. 1831–1903), French traveler and travel writer.

4. Harold T. Webster (1885–1952), newspaper cartoonist.

5. In a letter of 16 November 1905 MT assured the theatrical manager and producer Daniel Frohman (1851–1940) that in an interview on that day for a syndicate of sixty-two western papers he had closed with high praise for James Barrie's *Peter Pan* (Budd [1996], 90n6).

186

"Twain Calls Leopold Slayer of 15,000,000," *New York World*, 3 December 1905, sec. 3, 6.

... Mr. Clemens dictated the following remarkable statement to the *World* reporter on the eve of his seventieth birthday:

Beside Leopold, Nero, Caligula, Attila, Torquemada, Genghis Khan, and such killers of men are mere amateurs.[1]

My interest in the Congo and the Belgian King's connection with that State is not personal further than that I am a citizen of the United States and am pledged, like every other citizen of the United States, to superintend that King as foreman and superintendent of that property. Thirteen Christian nations stand pledged like our own. The thirteen are responsible for that King's good conduct, for his humane conduct; we are all officially committed to see that King Leopold does his righteous duty in the Congo State, or, if he falls short of his duty, to call him to strict account.

By the arrangement in 1884 at Berlin the Christian powers gave the well-being of the Congo State into the hands of the International Association and charged that association with a couple of very important responsibilities. The association was required to protect the natives from harm and to advance their well-being in various Ways; also it was charged with the duty of seeing that the several Christian states have freedom of trade in the Congo State. The King of the Belgians has taken over the whole property; he is acting as an absolute sovereign in that State: He has over-ridden all the restrictions put upon at Berlin in 1884, and by the conference of Brussels in 1890. He has thus, in taking over this vast State, which is twice as large as the German Empire, very rich and very populous before he began his devastation, robberies and massacres of the natives, taken upon himself all the responsibilities which were placed upon the International Association. By the terms of the two conventions it is not only the privilege of those Christian powers to call him to account, but it is their duty to do this—a duty which they solemnly assumed, and which they are neglecting.

The responsibility of the United States may be said to take first place, because we were the first of the nations to recognize the Congo flag, which was done by a Presidential order in 1884. We occupied the office of midwife to the Congo State and brought it into the world.

But we are not any more responsible than are the other powers. There should be a concert of action between them. That concert will be brought about in due time; the movement is on foot on the other side of the water and is making progress, particularly in England, where the Government is becoming more and more interested in the matter, and where the people are strongly stirred and are giving voice to their outraged feelings.

The outlook is that England will presently invite the other powers to join her in demanding a searching inquiry into Leopold's performance, this inquiry to be conducted by a commission, not appointed by him as was the late one, but by themselves. We shall need to take a hand in this righteous proceeding, and it is not likely that we shall be backward about it.

The packed commission appointed by Leopold finished its work and prepared its report many months ago. It was made as mild as possible, but it was nevertheless not the sort of report which the King wanted to spread before the civilized nations. He kept it back several months and issued it lately, and with very proper reluctance.

There is a matter connected with that report history which had a good deal of significance at the time. I speak of the suicide of the chief Congo official, a governor-general or something like that. That man had been representing the King a good many years; his treatment of the natives had been merciless; he harried them with the torch and the sword; he robbed and burned right and left; he was bitterly hated, not by the natives only but by the whites. He read the report of the commission in its original shape there on the Congo before Leopold had had an opportunity to blue-pencil it.

Late that night two white men, one of whom was an Englishman of high character and position, occupied a room next to the Governor General's. They heard a peculiar noise, and one of them said to the other: "Something is happening in that room."

They went in there and found the Governor-General gasping out his life with his throat cut. The noise they had heard was the streaming of his blood upon the floor. His last act had been the writing of a note of a rather impressive character. I cannot quote its language, but in substance it was to this effect:

"I cannot stand up against that report, yet I can only say in all sincerity that everything I have done was by command of the King himself."

That note was brought away, and is now in the possession of that Englishman. I have these facts from an American missionary who was on the spot at the time, and who vouches for their authenticity.

The King has not mended the condition of things in the Congo since he blue-penciled that report and issued it. The atrocities go on just as before, and the world must expect them to continue until the Christian powers shall exercise the right which they have reserved to themselves at Berlin and Brussels to put an end to them.

The pamphlet which I lately issued contains a small part of the twenty-year accumulation of evidence against King Leopold, and this evidence is of an authority which cannot be disputed. It comes from English officials, Belgian officials, and from American missionaries of unimpeachable character. I intend that the pamphlet shall go into the hands of every clergyman in America, and this purpose will be carried out. We have eighty millions of people who will speak, and speak audibly, when they find out the infamies that are being perpetrated in the Congo, and that our whole nation has a personal interest in the matter and is under written engagement to look after it.[2]

In the pamphlet to which Mr. Clemens refers in his signed interview he epitomizes the evidence against King Leopold in the form of a soliloquy by the King. The pamphlet is entitled "King Leopold's Soliloquy," and is published at Mr. Clemens's expense. . . .

Notes to Interview 186

1. Lucius Domitus Nero (15–68), emperor of Rome; Caligula (12–41), emperor of Rome; Attila (c. 406–53), barbarian king of the Huns from c. 433 to 453; Tomas de Torquemada (1420–1498), the inventor of torture methods during the Spanish Inquisition; Genghis Khan (1162–1227), chieftain of the Mongolian empire, which included most of Asia and eastern Europe.

2. *King Leopold's Soliloquy* (1905), a dramatic, satirical monologue that indicts King Leopold II of Belgium for profiting by a system of forced labor in the Congo. See also n. 11 to interview 180.

187

"Mark Twain in 'Uncle Joe's' Lair," *New York Herald*, 30 January 1906, 5.

Mark Twain and "Uncle Joe" Cannon have developed a mutual admiration society.[1] For two days they have been much in each other's company, "swapping lies," according to "Uncle Joe." It started at the Gridiron dinner Saturday night when they sat side by side.[2]

Mark Twain today spent an hour in the Speaker's room at the Capitol, where there was a "gabfest," in the language of the Speaker, and a conversazione, according to Mr. Clemens, that would live in history could everything that was said be told.

The fact of the distinguished author's presence soon became noised abroad. The crowd of members of the House who had important business with the Speaker just at that time was sufficient to call into play all the finesse of the Speaker's secretary, L. White Busbey, to keep the room from being crowded to suffocation.[3]

Colonel "Pete" Hepburn was one of the favored whose presence was desired inside. Former insurgent "Jim" Tawney was permitted as a reward for his recent good behavior.[4] Others were there long enough to be presented to the Speaker's distinguished visitor and then made way for still others.

At the time Mark Twain and "Uncle Joe" and the Colonel talked of the early days on the Mississippi, of which each knew much from personal experience. They talked about the great writers, the great orators, the men great in other lines whom they have known. Henry Ward Beecher was mentioned.[5]

"I knew Major Pond," said "Uncle Joe," "and I went down to the old Willard to meet Beecher. Pond asked me to introduce Beecher the next night at the Old National. 'I'll not do it,' said I. Beecher was embarrassed. 'No,' I said, 'I'll not do it. I can get up and say, "Ladies and gentlemen, I introduce you to Henry Ward Beecher," but everybody in the crowd will be saying "Who is this fool who has the assumption to introduce Beecher?"' So I told Mr. Beecher the thing to do was for him to introduce himself, and he did."

Twain told his story of the boys caught playing cards in the preacher's room. They hid the cards in the sleeve of the minister's robe. A few days later when the preacher was engaged in baptizing a convert by the immersion method, a full hand floated out upon the waters.

"I've heard that before," said "Uncle Joe."

"I reckon you have," said Twain. "I invented that story forty years ago and the newspapers stole it. Why, about ten years later I was lecturing in England and stopping at a country house. What do you think I had to do? Sit by quietly and hear one dude tell that story to another as a personal experience. About twenty years later I was down in Australia on a lecture tour. I told that story and my English experience with it. A big strapping fellow from the brush got up and corroborated me in every detail. He was the dude who had told the story as his own."

Twain told one of a Chinaman of much education and learning, to whom it had been recommended that he read *Innocents Abroad* as the funniest thing ever written by an American. The English edition of this work is published in two volumes, the second being called *The New Pilgrim's Progress*.[6] Not very long after Twain met this Chinaman at his home. With characteristic Celestial frankness he fished a book out of his library.

"I was very much disappointed, Mr. Twain," he said. "I cannot find a joke in the whole book." He had got hold of Bunyan's *Pilgrim's Progress*.

"I wanted to see how you were as a presiding officer," said Twain as the party broke up. "You're no different in the chair from what you are in real life. Methinks thou art truly great, for only a big man can afford to be natural."

Mr. Clemens also visited the Senate gallery. There he listened to a speech of Senator DuBois on forest reserves.[7]

Notes to Interview 187

1. Joseph G. (Uncle Joe) Cannon (1836–1926), Speaker of the U.S. House of Representatives from 1903 until 1911.
2. The Gridiron Club, founded by journalists in 1885 in Washington, D.C., with the sole purpose of hosting an annual dinner.
3. L. White Busbey (1852–1925), Speaker Cannon's private secretary.
4. William Peters Hepburn (1833–1916), U.S. representative from Iowa (1881–86, 1893–1908); James A. Tawney (1855–1919), U.S. representative from Minnesota (1892–1911).
5. Henry Ward Beecher (1813–87), minister of the Plymouth Church in Brooklyn.
6. The subtitle of *The Innocents Abroad*.
7. Fred T. DuBois (1851–1930), U.S. senator from Idaho (1891–97, 1901–7).

188

"Congress Admires Mark Twain's Hair," *New York World*, 30 January 1906, 3.

Washington, Jan. 29—Mark Twain and Congress saw one another today. Before they separated each knew the other fairly well. Mr. Clemens did not shy at Congress, but Congress did shy a little at Mark.

Mark Twain's hair was the first thing that attracted the attention of Congress. From the floor and the galleries he looked like Chief Justice Fuller.[1] After watching the hair for a time the Senate decided to get better acquainted, and Col. George B. Harvey and Mr. Clemens were invited to come down and see the Vice-President. Mr. Fairbanks tried to be cordial.[2] He shook hands with Col. Harvey first. Then he warmed up and gave Mr. Clemens' hand a little squeeze—the kind that is known in Indiana as the "ice tongs." Then Mr. Fairbanks glanced at Mr. Clemens's hair and looked as though he would like to know him better so that he might ask what tonic he used. Thinking it over, Mr. Fairbanks carefully brushed four hairs over his bald spot.

The Vice-President was about to present his visitors with his autographed photographs when other Senators came romping in and insisted that Mr. Clemens and Col. Harvey take luncheon with them in the Senate restaurant.

"We lunched and lied together," Mr. Clemens said in describing the luncheon. "We would take a bite of pie and then indulge in a few flights of the imagination. Oh, n-o-o-o-o, the Senators did not eat pie with their knives, at least none of them that I saw; but of course, you know, I was pretty busy myself and couldn't watch all of them. I was really impressed by those Senators."

Mr. Clemens said he could not discuss the debate intelligently, as he could hear none of it. Senator Tillman, who was talking, will be much surprised at this.[3] He can generally be heard out in the corridors.

"What were the flights of imagination?" said Mark Twain in answer to a question. "Oh, they were said in open session, and nothing ever said by a Senator in open session amounts to much. Had they been said in executive session I would have made notes on my cuff or have written them on the back of an envelope, but before going to the Senate I was warned that nobody, at least no real weighty Senator, ever said anything in open session. I guess that's true. We had a most delightful time, though, and a good luncheon."

After being shown over the Senate part of the building, Mark Twain and Colonel Harvey went over to the House and were shown into the Speaker's room.

"We called on my old friend, the Speaker," Mr. Clemens said. "I say he is my old friend because I met him on Saturday night. Any man who meets another on Saturday night has a right to refer to him as an 'old friend.' We got pretty well acquainted, too. I sat next to Speaker Cannon at the Gridiron Club dinner, and I think if the dinner had lasted half an hour longer I would have been calling him 'Joe' and he would have referred to me as 'Sam.' Members of the House came in and there were flights of imagination, but the Speaker and I stuck pretty close to the truth, except in a few instances the Speaker may have stretched a point or two."[4]

Mr. Clemens held an informal reception on the House side. He was shaking hands with two men at a time, and he admits that he had the time of his life, next to his experiences at the Gridiron dinner.

"I don't know; politics is a little out of my line," Mr. Clemens said, "but I rather think I would like to be a Senator. The title adds such an air of dignity. Then again, when I think it over I think I would like to be a Congressman. A Congressman appears to have such a happy, carefree existence. He slaps the Speaker on the back and says, 'Hello, Joe! How's things?' That's real democracy; but who ever heard of a Senator slapping the Vice-President on the back and saying, 'Hello, Charley. How's things?' He would need a step-ladder or have to stand on top of a barrel."

Mr. Clemens will return to New York tomorrow.

Notes to Interview 188

1. Melville Fuller (1833–1910), chief justice of the U.S. Supreme Court from 1888 to 1910.
2. Charles W. Fairbanks (1852–1918), U.S. vice president from 1905 to 1909.
3. Benjamin R. Tillman (1847–1918), U.S. senator from South Carolina.
4. Joseph G. (Uncle Joe) Cannon (1836–1926), Speaker of the U.S. House of Representatives from 1903 until 1911. The Gridiron Club, founded by journalists in 1885 in Washington, D.C., with the sole purpose of hosting an annual dinner.

"Views of Mark Twain on Being in Congress," *New York Times*, 30 January 1906, 9: [MT was asked why he came to the Capitol.] "Well," he said, "I wanted to see my old friend Joe Cannon." "Is Mr. Cannon a friend of yours?" he was asked. "I call him an old friend," explained Mr. Twain, "because I met him for the first time on Saturday night, and a man you meet on a Saturday night is always an old friend. I sat beside him at the Gridiron dinner, and I gradually came to have a good opinion of him. If the dinner had lasted half an hour longer I think we would have been calling each other Joe and Sam. . . . But it did not," added Mr. Twain, "and so I have not called him Joe yet. Perhaps I will the next time I come. . . . What did we talk about?" said Mr. Twain afterward. "Well, we just swapped lies. . . . And," said Mr. Twain, "there were a good many flights of imagination in what those people said. But the Speaker and I stuck pretty close to the truth." He reflected on this for a moment, and then seemed to fear that he had been too hasty. "At least," he amended, "I did. I don't know whether or not the Speaker stretched a point or two."

189

"Mark Twain Pays Tribute to Servant," *Hartford Courant,* 28 February 1906, 3.

Samuel L. Clemens, once a resident of this city, returned here yesterday to attend the funeral of his old and faithful servant, Patrick McAleer, which takes place this morning.[1] Mr. Clemens will be the guest of Rev. Joseph H. Twichell during his stay here, which will terminate tomorrow afternoon, when he will return to New York.[2] Mr. Clemens, when seen yesterday afternoon, paid a high tribute to his former servant as he said:—

"I have never known a finer human being than Patrick McAleer and I never knew him to be in error but once in my life. That was when, when talking with another of my servants, he said he had been in my employ for thirty-five years.

"Thirty-five years, he said it was, but in reality it was ten years less. In making his calculation Patrick counted in the ten years we spent abroad without him. He seemed to feel that it was his fault that we went away and that our absence ought not to count in reckoning up his term of service.

"In all the time he was with Mrs. Clemens and myself he never ran out. I have had other servants who would say, 'Mr. Clemens, I forgot and there isn't a cigar in the house,' but that never happened with Patrick McAleer, for he never forgot anything and I never had to give him an order.

"He was just the age of Mrs. Clemens and he entered my employ the day before I was married. He was as full of life as a watch spring and he knew everything there was to know about his business. His life ought to rank with that of great soldiers, statesmen, and chief justices, for they were no more proficient in their professions than he was in his.

"He was with me last summer in Dublin, N.H., and it did not seem to me that he was a day older than he was when he first entered my employ. His hair was just as black as it ever was and he was just as efficient. I did not give him an order during the summer and he did not need one; he knew just what I wanted. I shall never find a man more faithful, loyal, and honest than he was."

The regard which the Clemens family had for Mr. McAleer is evidenced by the appearance of the great humorist in this city. Mr. Clemens and his family have sent a large floral wreath to the McAleer home bearing this inscription:—

"In faithful remembrance of Patrick McAleer, faithful and valued friend of our family for 36 years. S. L. Clemens, Clara L. Clemens, Jane Clemens."

While Mr. Clemens was evidently pleased to see Hartford, he seemed fatigued by his journey from New York to this city. He will leave here for his New York home on the 5:05 P.M. train tomorrow afternoon.

Notes to Interview 189

1. Patrick McAleer (1846-1906), the family coachman in Hartford. See also Fatout, 494.
2. On Twichell, see n. 1 to interview 2.

190

"Mark Twain Too Lazy for a U.S. Senator," *New York Herald,* 11 March 1906, sec. 1, 5.

Suggestions having come from various sources that in the event of retirement from Congress of either of the New York Senators Samuel L. Clemens (Mark Twain) would be named as successor, a reporter for the *Herald* called on the humorist yesterday at his home in Fifth avenue to get his expressions on the subject.

Mr. Clemens, who was clothed in his pajamas and busily engaged in shaving when he was asked if he would accept a Senatorial seat, instantly stopped wielding the razor and, turning to his questioner with an expansive smile on his lathered face, said: "If such an offer as that were made to me it would be the most gigantic compliment I ever received. I would not consider myself, however, a worthy successor to Dr. Depew or Mr. Platt, as I am in no way qualified for the post.[1] A Senator needs to know the political history of the country, past and present, as well as its commercial, industrial, and financial affairs. Of these things I am blissfully ignorant. Even if I were qualified, the duties of a Senator would be distasteful to me: My own particular work is the greatest source of pleasure I have, and for that reason I do not consider it as work at all. I regard myself as the most lazy human being on earth. I have absolutely no industry in me whatever, and to 'make good' as a Senator one must be in love with the job and be industrious. If a man is to succeed in any occupation the work to him must be a labor of love. It has always been so with me and my work, and I think I can justly say, without vanity, that my career has been, to a fair degree, a success.

"For five days every week I am busy writing or dictating, and I'm in a modified paradise all the while. Saturdays and Sundays I take off, and during these two holidays, as I call them, I'm in a modified hades."

When reminded that the Senate, as a body, is sadly lacking in humor and needs livening up, Mr. Twain said smilingly: "Well, as 'Falstaff to the Senate' I guess I could fill the bill and earn my salary.[2] But as a 'representative of the people' I would be certain to prove dead timber."

"But can't humorists be serious as well as other mortals, Mr. Twain?"

"Most assuredly. There is no man alive—not even excepting a Scotch Presbyterian minister—who can be more serious than I am. But as a Senator the people would refuse to take me any more seriously than they do in my natural capacity as a humorist, and I would score a failure if I attempted to convince them that I was in earnest. I don't care to make an unattractive exhibition of myself. It's a humorist's business to laugh at other folks, not inspire other folks to laugh at him."

Mr. Twain is now writing his autobiography. He started on the book on January 9, he said, and has now one hundred thousand words of it completed. He devotes one hour and three-quarters to the work every morning, dictating it while in bed.

Notes to Interview 190

1. Chauncey Depew (1834–1928), U.S. senator from New York from 1899 to 1911; Thomas Collier Platt (1833–1910), U.S. senator from New York from 1897 to 1909.

2. Shakespeare's comic character Falstaff appeared in three of his plays.

191

"Huckleberry Finn's End Disappoints Mark Twain," *New York American*, 18 March 1906, magazine section, 11.

"So Huck Finn has died again, has he?" chuckled Mark Twain, whose other name is Samuel L. Clemens. "Well, now that's too bad, too bad. To think that a boy who had so many hair-breadth escapes at an age when life was worth living adventurously should calmly go West and have heart failure! I am disappointed, besides being distressed. I always had a sneaking idea that Huck would come to a more artistic end, such as hanging, though he always was more practical than Tom Sawyer, his partner in crime."

Mark Twain still held in his hand a clipping which bore the startling announcement—startling to millions of boys in all corners of the earth, not to mention many more millions of grown-up children—that the real and only original of the inimitable Huckleberry Finn had died in Murray, Idaho.

Captain A. C. Tonkray is the name on the stone which marks the remote grave.[1]

"There is nothing disrespectful nor even irreverent in my confessing that, up to date, more than a dozen real original Tom Sawyers and Huckleberry Finns have succumbed during the past twenty years," continued the famous humorist. He lapsed into a brown study, the only sign of consciousness being a reminiscent twinkle about the kindly gray eyes. Presently he pursued:

"I wonder how many times the originals of Hamlet or Tom Brown or Robinson Crusoe or Gulliver or David Copperfield or any of the great tragic characters of history were buried and resurrected. I met a man the other day—an inventor—who disabused my mind with regard to Don Quixote being dead. Life is full of deaths and disappointments—full of tragic mistakes, full of comical verities."

"But of Huckleberry Finn?"

"Have you read his biography—yes?" said Mr. Twain with the manner of one on the witness chair, and thereby on oath. "Well, do you remember Jim and the hairball and how they told Huck Finn his fortune?[2] Jim always seemed to me to have given a fairly accurate forecast with respect to young Finn. . . .

"Now," Mark Twain added, "Jim knew Huckleberry Finn pretty well, and there is nothing in the verdict that coincides with the death of Captain Tonkray. Did I know Tonkray? Maybe so, but my memory is not as good as it was. It seems likely that anyone with the reputation Huck Finn had round Hannibal would change his name."

"But this dispatch says: 'Captain Tonkray was a native of Hannibal and sixty-five years of age. In early life he ran on Mississippi and Missouri river steamboats and came in frequent contact with Twain, and tradition has it the author later used Tonkray as his model for Huckleberry Finn,'" was ventured.

"Well," was the drawling rejoinder, "here is another clipping which appeared the other day." And he read:

> The Clemens residence on Hill street (Hannibal) and a portion of Huck Finn's house are the only surviving architectural landmarks of the humorist's sojourn in Missouri. The Finn cottage is tenantless and as dreary-looking as the old mill on Salt River.
>
> Some people say that Tom Blankenship, of this place, was the original of Huckleberry Finn, while over at Stoutsville they lay it on Barney Farthing, of Paris. The latter is a jolly, good-natured fellow of seventy, and says he is willing to stand for anything in reason except Injun Joe.
>
> George Moore, clerk of the United States Court, and known to have been a playmate of Sam Clemens, was asked about him. "I don't re-

member much," said he. "Of course, I was living here when his folks came over from Florida in about 1845, I think, and I was pretty well acquainted with him, but he was a good deal older than me, and I didn't run in his crowd. Suppose you see Judge Bacon—he'll know."

A call on the latter brought this answer. "I don't understand why so many people come to me about Mark Twain. I didn't know much about him. He was much older than I am, and I was not associated with him intimately for that reason. But—you see George Moore. He's about Clemens' age, and he'll tell you more." The attempt to find a man as old as Mark Twain was abandoned.

Again Mark Twain chuckled. Presently he said, in conclusion, that possibly the key to the identity of Huckleberry Finn would be found between the veracious lines of his biographical adventures. As for himself, the following notice, which appears in the introduction of the book copyrighted by Harper & Brothers, was his last, as well as first, word of explanation:

"Persons attempting to find a motive in this narrative will be prosecuted; persons attempting to find a moral in it will be banished; persons attempting to find a plot in it will be shot. By Order of the Author. Per G. G., Chief of Ordnance."

Notes to Interview 191

1. MT had recently received a letter from a childhood acquaintance in Hannibal, Alexander C. Tonkray (or Toncray), asking if his brother, John, or "Captain Tonk" (1842-1906), was the original of Huckleberry Finn (*Auto* [1959], 67; *Auto* [1990], 191).

2. MT alludes to an incident in chapter 4 of *Adventures of Huckleberry Finn*.

192

"Mark Twain on Ocean Scenery," *New York Herald Magazine,* 15 April 1906, 4.

Mark Twain had one of the surprises of his life the other day. The word "had" is used advisedly. Some surprises are enjoyed; most of them are suffered. The expectation of the person who imposed this one upon the humorist was that it would go into the latter category, but the unexpected happened and it did not. It is a truism that humorists always take seriously things that affect themselves, but Mark Twain showed that he really could appreciate a joke.

One morning last week a *Herald* reporter called at Mr. Twain's—or Mr. Clemens'—residence, No. 21 Fifth avenue, and solicited an interview. It was not early morning—in fact, it was rather close to noon—but the reply at the door was that Mr. Twain was still abed. The caller happened to remember, however, that it is one of the eccentricities of the author to spend a good part of his day among the pillows, not in slumber, but in reading and writing, and he pressed his request.

Being one of the most amiable of men, Mr. Clemens presently sent down word that he would see the reporter, and in a few minutes there came down the stairs a vision, the general effect of which was an elaborate dressing gown surmounted by the shaggy white mustache and mass of silver hair, through which peeped a pair of laughing and ever young eyes, which the American public has come to know as a cherished possession. With a word of apology for the intrusion the caller said:—

"Mr. Clemens, I should like to submit to you a speech which you have never delivered."

"There are many," responded the humorist, obviously puzzled. "I believe that William Pitt and Edmund Burke and a few others—"[1]

"No," interrupted the visitor. "This is one of your own speeches," and the manuscript was submitted as an evidence of good faith.

His wonderful eyes blazed on it for a moment. Then he smiled, and it all came back to him like Mississippi River sunshine, with flags flying and the band playing.

"How in the name of all that is holy—pardon me, I have been reading my daily chapter in the Book of Job—but how, I say, did you happen to get hold of that?"

He was told, as the facts are recounted below. "The speech is genuine, and it is quite true that I did not deliver it," he said, at the end. "*The Herald* has my permission to print it."

The circumstances of that never-delivered speech are these:—The steamship *St. Paul,* of the American line, was to have been launched from Cramp's shipyard in Philadelphia on March 25, 1895,[2] and, according to custom, a company of prominent persons was present to witness the ceremonies. Ordinarily at the functions the launching is followed by a luncheon in the great sail loft of the shipbuilding works, where addresses appropriate to the occasion are made.

While the crowd was assembled on the stand awaiting the final word that should send the ship shooting into the stream a reporter observed Mark Twain standing a little apart from the others and asked him if he had prepared anything in the way of a speech for the luncheon. The humorist replied that he had, and, to facilitate the work of the reporter, consented that he should make a copy of it in advance, which he did from typewritten sheets handed to him by Mr. Clemens.

It happened, however, that when the blocks were knocked away from the great hull and the sponsor raised aloft the conventional bottle of champagne to break on the bow, the big ship refused to budge and no amount of labor could move her an inch. She had stuck fast upon the ways. As a result the launching was postponed for a week or two, when it was successful, but in the meantime Mr. Clemens had started on a tour of the world and his speech was never heard. This is it.[3]

Notes to Interview 192

1. William Pitt the younger (1759–1806), British statesman and prime minister from 1801 to 1804; Edmund Burke (1729–97), Irish-born British statesman and philosopher.
2. One of the largest shipyards in the world, on the Delaware River, with origins dating back to the mid-nineteenth century.
3. The speech is reproduced in Fatout, 274–76.

193

"Gorky Evicted Twice in a Day from Hotels," *New York World*, 15 April 1906, 1–2.

Maxim Gorky's time yesterday was completely taken up by events arising from the announcement that the woman whom he brought to this country as his wife was not Mme. Gorky, but Andreeva, a Russian actress. . . .[1] The admirers of the Russian, with a few faithful exceptions, stayed away from him yesterday, apparently not having quite made up their minds how to regard the matter.

Mark Twain was authority for the information that the grand dinner which was to be given two weeks hence "by purely literary folks" in homage to Gorky's eminence in the world of literature had been called off, but he explained that it was solely because it had been impossible to find a date which would accommodate everybody.

The humorist is a member of the American committee whose object is to make the Russian revolution succeed. He talked at some length last night on Gorky's case as he saw it.

"Now I'm a revolutionist," he said, "by birth, breeding, principle, and everything else. I love all revolutions no matter where or when they start.[2]

"I sympathize with these Russian revolutionists, and, in common with some other people, I hope that they will succeed. So when the committee asked me to become a member, I did. I told them, as I am constantly telling other people, that I am always glad to lend my name if they won't give me anything to do. I love to be an ornament and a figurehead. I'd like to be an ornament and a figurehead all over town.

"Well, when Mr. Gorky came here, it seemed to us that he was going to be a prodigious power in getting the American people interested. I don't think it had ever occurred to him that any objection like this would be raised. The people in Russia had always made him feel that his acts were just as they should be.

"But every country has its laws of conduct. It is right that it should, and when anyone arrives from a foreign land he ought to conform to those laws.[3]

"It seems to me that Mr. Gorky has seriously impaired—I was about to say destroyed—his efficiency as a persuader. He is disabled, and the propaganda by so much loses the help of his great genius and tremendous personality.[4]

"I don't know what the committee will do. I can tell better after I have had a chance to speak to some of the members. Meanwhile, I believe in sticking by the flag until the last minute."[5]

Notes to Interview 193

I have supplemented this interview as reported in the *New York World* with versions of Twain's comments published in other newspapers. All newspaper citations below are from 15 April 1906.

1. Maxim Gorky (1868-1936), Russian dramatist and revolutionary. Maria Andreeva, Gorky's mistress, was a Moscow Art Theater actress.

2. "Gorky Sent from Hotel," *New York Tribune*, 2: "I am said to be a revolutionist in my sympathies, by birth, by breeding, and by principle. I am always on the side of the revolutionists, because there never was a revolution unless there were some oppressive and intolerable conditions against which to revolute [*sic*]."

"Hotels Turn Gorky Away," *New York Sun*, 1: "I am a revolutionist by birth, breeding, and principle," said Mr. Clemens, "and I am therefore in sympathy with any kind of a revolution anywhere. . . . There is never a revolution unless there is oppression to instigate the people. . . . I am one of those impulsive persons who like to be an ornament and figurehead when it comes to matters of public note. I always am willing to lend my name to any organization so long as they don't give me anything to do. That was the way in which I consented to serve on this committee."

3. *New York Tribune*: "Every country has its laws of conduct and its customs, and those who visit a country other than their own must expect to conform to the customs of that country."

New York Sun: "I am in hearty sympathy with the Russian revolutionists, but I fear that Gorky has been ill advised. Whatever may be the way of looking at these things in Russia, we have certain conventions and standards of conduct and Gorky should have been made aware of the views the American people hold in this matter." (See also MT's essay "The Gorky Incident" [1906]).

4. *New York Tribune*: "Gorky came to this country to lend the influence of his great name—and it is great in the things he has written—to the work of raising funds to carry on the revolution in Russia. By these disclosures he is disabled. It is unfortunate. I felt that he would be a prodigious power in helping the movement, but he is in a measure shorn of his strength. Such things as have been published relate to a condition that might be forgivable in Russia, but which offends against the customs in

this country. I would not say that his usefulness has been destroyed, but his efficiency as a persuader is certainly impaired."

5. *New York Sun:* "As for the dinner which was to be given to him by the writers and literary people of the country it has been found impossible so far to find a date on which a representative gathering of American authors might be got together to do honor to the Russian. As a literary figure Gorky is certainly deserving of all the honors that can be given him."

194

"Mark Twain's Position," *New York Times,* 15 April 1906, 3.

Much adverse criticism has arisen here through the formation of a committee to purchase arms to aid Maxim Gorky in his revolutionary movement. Many prominent men are on the committee. Mark Twain, one of the members, was questioned on the matter yesterday at his Fifth Avenue home.

"Why," he was asked, "should this country assist in any way the Russian people in their revolutionary movement?"

"Because we were quite willing," he replied, "to accept France's assistance when we were in the throes of our Revolution, and we have always been grateful for that assistance. It is our turn now to pay that debt of gratitude by helping another oppressed people in its struggle for liberty, and we must either do it or confess that our gratitude to France was only eloquent words, with no sincerity back of them."

"But do you think it consistent that Americans, with their so-called love of peace, should aid in a movement to throw Russia into a bloody revolution, particularly in view of the fact that America was chiefly instrumental in bringing to an end the Russo-Japanese war?"[1]

To this Mr. Twain replied: "Inasmuch as we conducted our own Revolution with guns and the sword, our mouths are closed against preaching gentler methods to other oppressed nations. Revolutions are achieved by blood and courage alone. So far as I know there has been but one revolution which was carried to a successful issue without bloodshed."

"In lending, then, our assistance to the Russian people for the overthrow of their despotic form of government, why should we not also start active propaganda seeking the abolition of all similar forms of government?"

"Simply because," replied Mr. Clemens, "we have not been invited to do it. Should the invitation come, as in the present case, we will put our shoulder to the wheel."

Note to Interview 194

1. Russo-Japanese War (1904–5); the Treaty of Portsmouth ending the war was signed on 5 September 1905.

195

"Mark Twain's Memories of City," *New York Tribune*, 20 April 1906, 5.

Samuel L. Clemens, after his lecture at the Carnegie Hall for the benefit of the Robert Fulton Memorial Association fund,[1] said: "The poor, smitten city.[2] I have no close friends there at present, although I have some at Alameda. I see that all of the district around Montgomery street is destroyed. The place where I lived while there and the place where I boarded is gone. I knew the district very well, as I was a reporter on *The Call*, and so of course got around pretty well. I worked first as a reporter on *The Virginia City Enterprise* and in September or October 1862 went to San Francisco. I was on *The Call* until 1866.

"I was there when they had one healthy earthquake, however. It was the worst I ever heard of. It was one Sunday afternoon hot and close. I was walking along the street when I was juggled. I did not know what had happened. I thought there had been a quarrel or something between the houses. I saw the front of a six-story brick house fall across the street and form a bridge. I sprung up against a wall. But say, that was the only house in town that did such a thing. I don't know how it happened. No one else saw it but me. I never told anyone about it.[3]

"The last time I was there, I think, was in 1868. The town then had 118,000 people. That is 18,000 Chinese and 100,000 people. I was there in 1863 and wrote *Roughing It* in sixty days.[4] It would take me six months now. The town has grown from what it was when I was there to what it was two days ago since I left. There were no big buildings there then."[5]

After his address at Carnegie Hall he made an appeal to the audience to remember in their hearts and with their purses the people in "San Francisco, the smitten city."

Notes to Interview 195

1. The Robert Fulton Memorial Association had been organized earlier in 1906 to erect a monument to Fulton (1765–1815), who proved the practicality of steam power. See also Fatout, 515.

2. MT refers to the devastating earthquake in San Francisco on 18 April 1906.

3. MT described the San Francisco earthquake of 8 October 1865 in chapter 58 of *Roughing It*.

"Mark Twain Appeals for the 'Smitten City,'" *New York Times*, 20 April 1906, 11: "I remember one day I was walking down Third Street in San Francisco. It was a sleepy, dull Sunday afternoon and no one was stirring. Suddenly as I look up the street about three hundred yards the whole side of a house fell out. The street was full of bricks and mortar. At the same time I was knocked against the side of a house and stood there stunned for a moment. I thought it was an earthquake. Nobody else had heard anything about it and no one said earthquake to me afterward, but I saw it and I wrote it. Nobody else wrote it, and the house I saw go into the street was the only house in the city that felt it. I've always wondered if it wasn't a little performance gotten up for my especial entertainment by the nether region."

4. In fact, MT returned to San Francisco in 1868 to polish the manuscript of *The Innocents Abroad*. See also n. 6 to interview 46.

5. *New York Times*: "I haven't been there since 1868," he said, "and that great city of San Francisco has grown up since my day. When I was there she had 118,000 people, and of this number 18,000 were Chinese. I was a reporter on the *Virginia City Enterprise* in Nevada in 1862, and stayed there, I think, about two years, when I went to San Francisco and got a job as a reporter on the *Call*. I was there three or four years."

9

"Dean of Humorists," 1906–1907

Interviews 196–220

Twain began to dictate episodes of his autobiography during this time, planning to publish some of them and withhold others until long after his death. Twenty-five installments appeared in the *North American Review* between September 1906 and December 1907. Although he was suffering from gout, chronic bronchitis, and dyspepsia, he lobbied Congress on behalf of a more progressive international copyright.

196

William A. Graham, "Mark Twain—Dean of Our Humorists," *Human Life* 3 (May 1906): 1–2.

It was a few months more than seventeen years ago that I first heard the slow, drawling voice of Samuel L. Clemens, whom, in spite of his weight of years and the dignity of his snowy locks, the public still affectionately calls, and will continue to call Mark Twain.

It was soon after I had come to Hartford in the way of newspaper work, and duty took me to a Thanksgiving-day dinner provided by the local Y.M.C.A. The spread was for young men in the city who had no family attachments, and who were supposed to have nowhere particular to go for this annual New England feast. Mr. Clemens was down as the star after-dinner speaker. He filled the role to the delight of all who heard him. Mr. Clemens' topic was "How to speak extemporaneously on any subject," and he set out to prove his theorem.

"Now," said Mr. Clemens, speaking with much deliberateness and with that drawl which is characteristic of his speech under all circumstances, after a few introductory words, "to show how easy it is to speak on any subject, I will ask someone to suggest a topic."

A topic was suggested, and later, several other topics. Say the first was "Thanksgiving Day," and the humorist started off something like this: "To many of us there is no season of the year that brings fuller suggestions than this we are now observing, and that reminds me of a man I once knew," and with a witty story he started off on a ramble. So with his other topics. There was simply a brief reference to each at the start, and then he told whatever stories and got off whatever quips and cranks of humor came into his head. It was a clever and good natured little satire on the after-dinner speaker, and in its humor, brightness, and sparkle it was in every way worthy of the reputation of the man.

Only a few days ago I recalled this incident to Mr. Clemens.

"Oh, yes," he said. "Now that you speak of it I remember the occasion, but I had forgotten I had ever got that off in Hartford. I thought I had done it only once, at a dinner in New York a short time before that.[1] I remember now that I did the same thing at the dinner you speak of."

For fifteen or sixteen years Mr. Clemens has been only an occasional visitor to Hartford, but it was only three or four years ago that that famous house of his was sold. But no one who knows Mr. Clemens intimately will doubt or deny that the happiest years of his life were passed in this city. He came in 1871 and it was here that his three daughters were born and grew to womanhood. It was here that he formed his dearest friendships and it was here that he and his beloved wife lived in beautiful harmony and trustfulness through the years from their early married life until the snows of many winters had whitened the heads of both.

The home life in the hospitable Clemens house was one of peculiar charm. It possessed an all-pervading hospitality, gentleness, sympathy, and consideration. Father, mother, daughters, and guests were infected with it. The whole house was filled with sweetness and unselfishness, and it is no wonder that in a city of charming homes there was attracted to the Clemens home all that was best in Hartford.

When Mr. Clemens was in Hartford a few weeks ago—having come to attend the funeral of his coachman, of whom I shall speak later—a friend in a joking way remarked:—

"I think I know what really brought you to Hartford. You are looking around for a house. You are coming back here to live, and we will give you a hearty welcome."

"Old friend," said Mr. Clemens, even more slowly and deliberately than usual, "if I should come back I would want the old house again."

"I suppose there have been some changes in it. Have you been inside of it since coming to town?"

"No," he said. "I don't want to see it. It is peopled with spirits, not only of my own family, but of the old friends whose faces I used to see so often and who are now gone. Strangers come in with rough shod feet and walk over holy ground. No, I don't want to see inside the old house now," and his voice choked with feeling and little tears came into his gentle gray eyes. A wife and a daughter, who were so much a part of the old household, have gone to the land beyond since the Hartford home of the family was broken up.

It was business that brought Mark Twain to Hartford. It was the strong friendships and the intimate associations formed by him and his family that established him here and made this city more a home than any other place in which he ever lived. To Rev. Joe Twichell, the beloved pastor of the Asylum Hill Congregational Church, Mr. Clemens was bound by stronger ties of affection than are usually found between two men. There was a friendship scarcely less deep and strong between Mr. Clemens and the late Charles Dudley Warner, and back of whose house around on Forest Street looked into the back yard of Mark Twain's house on Farmington Avenue.[2] Hard-by was the home of Mrs. Harriet Beecher Stowe, and only a few steps away that of Mrs. Stowe's sister, Mrs. Isabella Beecher Hooker.[3] William Gillette's home was in the same neighborhood and there were many other cultured and intellectual people on all sides.[4] Mark Twain found congenial surroundings in Hartford, and a circle of friends who loved him and gave early appreciation to his literary quality.

Mr. Twichell's house was not so near as some of the others, but the space between was only a short walk, and a walk that Mr. Clemens frequently trod. Mr. Twichell, who himself possesses so broad a sympathy and so pervading a kindliness that he can understand almost any sort of nature and tolerate almost any kind of vagary, had, perhaps, a more complete understanding of Mark Twain's somewhat complex nature than any other man in Hartford—than any other person in Hartford except Mr. Clemens' wife. . . .

It was only a few days ago that Mr. Clemens was in Hartford. He came because Patrick McAleer had died.[5] McAleer was for many years the coachman of the Clemens family, and even last summer he was with them in Dublin, New Hampshire. The funeral occurred on the last day of February. On that day Mr. Clemens said:—

"I have never known a finer human being than Patrick McAleer and I never knew him to be in error but once in my life. That was when, in talking with another of my servants, he said he had been in my employ for thirty-five years.

"Thirty-five years, he said it was but in reality it was ten years less. In making his calculation Patrick counted in the ten years we spent abroad without him. He seemed to feel that it was not his fault that we went away, and that our absence ought not to count in reckoning up his term of service."

Notes to Interview 196

1. Probably in February–March 1883.
2. On Twichell, see n. 1 to interview 2; on Warner, see n. 2 to interview 28.

3. Isabella Beecher Hooker (1822–1907), half-sister of Harriet Beecher Stowe and a Hartford feminist.
4. On Gillette, see n. 4 to interview 49.
5. See interview 189.

197

"Mark Twain Well Again," *New York Tribune,* 13 May 1906, 16.

Mark Twain, who has been confined to his house for the last two weeks by a mild attack of bronchitis, has entirely recovered, and will leave this city on Monday for Dublin, N.H., where he will remain until late in November.

Mr. Clemens spoke jokingly of his illness, saying: "The trouble was confined exclusively to my throat. I hope it will be a long time before I get it in the neck."

198

"Mark Twain's Guide to Health," *Boston Sunday Post,* 20 May 1906, 30.

"I was shaving when your card was brought to me," said Mark Twain, the prince of American humorists, to the *Sunday Post* reporter on Wednesday at his country home, the Upton Place, at Dublin, N.H., by way of explaining a delay in receiving the caller.

It was the day after the arrival of the famous author at the magnificent summer home, and by way of further explanation he said:

"I have to be very slow and careful nowadays, for my beard is like a barbed wire fence, the points of which must not be rubbed the wrong way.

"In that respect I am very different from my friend Tom Bailey Aldrich,[1] for he takes a razor, slaps it this way a couple of times up and down," suiting the action to the words, "and then in two scrapes, this way and that, takes a continent of fur off."

These were the introductory sentences that bubbled from the mind of the man who has made every American laugh at one time or another during his long life of spreading cheer among his fellow men.

He had just completed a late, very late, morning toilet that began with the shaving process and was rapidly completed with the donning of a suit of black, rough goods which set off in extraordinary contrast the ascetically pale features and great leonine head of pure white hair that the author wears carelessly.

And how happy he was over the outlook for a glorious first day in the country after his busy fall, winter, and spring in the cities!

As he stood on the veranda of his beautiful home with stick in hand, he raised his arm, and slowly sweeping the point in a three-quarter circle, said, with an honest and enthusiastic ring in his voice:

"There is a sight of nature's magnificence that cannot be equaled in the world. See that lake there," hesitating as he pointed to Dublin Lake; "what foreign country could give us the equal of that setting?"

And there is Monadnock, great, stately, and the first in the long range of magnificent mountains that we can see from here on a fine and clear day.[2]

Here was the man who had come to the New Hampshire hills for his health, scorning the beauties of other health spots of the world for this corner of New Hampshire and descanting on its marvelous charm as if this one panorama of scenery was the only one that had ever attracted his eyes.

Beside him on the veranda was his daughter, Miss Jean Clemens, and his secretary, Miss I. V. Lyon, who for the past four years has been the literary guardian of the aged humorist.[3]

His frank admiration of the scenery about the home caused the reporter to ask the veteran as to whether he would change his regime of living to any great extent with the change to the air of the country.

"Change my way of living, did you say?" exclaimed Mr. Clemens. "I am going to live and eat while up here just as I found last year that good old Mother Nature wanted me to live.

"And now, my dear friend, as long as you come from Boston, let me tell you of the little secret about my health that a Boston woman taught me. I was suffering with that affliction that others call indigestion at the time I was spending two weeks in Boston at the home of Mrs. S. B. Pearmain,[4] and that lady asked me: 'Mr. Clemens, won't you let me feed you as you should be fed for a week or two and allow me to prove that your dyspepsia can be cured or helped?' It was agreed.

"During the remainder of the time that I stayed at that house I was offered the opportunity of gorging every two hours or oftener as the fit of hunger or working of my jaws happened to seize on me.

"If it was 12 o'clock at night and if I felt I had room down below for any more food it was given me, and do you know, young man, that the gnawing and tearing away at the insides began to give me a chance to feel as other folks are supposed to feel.

"She told me that I needed plenty of food, as I had been starving an excellent digestive apparatus, and there is not a doctor that lives today who can tell me that she was not right in the cure.

"When I left her I of course fell back into the old rut of things in New York, and had to take what they would think right for me there.

"The change that the woman brought about in me was so marked that it would not take even a fool long to find out that she was right, so that digestive machinery is going to get all the work that it is capable of during the long summer that I intend putting in among these hills.

"But I want to prove to you that there is nothing in the nature of fun in this thing. When we got back to our home in New York, a little Italian maid servant that we had brought from Italy said to another the first morning on entering the dining-room: 'Oh, you would not know the Padrone now, he looks so good.'"[5]

There was a twinkle in the eyes of the rare old author as he told of the maid's enthusiasm over his improved looks and he topped this proof by telling of trouble with his tailor, who said after the vacation period that Mr. Clemens was positively beginning to look gross, and that he was evidently trying to fit the clothing made for him rather than to let the clothing fit his form.

Getting back to the reason for his selection of New Hampshire for a permanent summer house, Mark Twain said: "For many of those foolish years I thought that the Adirondacks were the only mountains among which the lazy man could live and really enjoy life.

"There were many of my friends who thought differently, however, and Albert Thayer, that good lover of old New England, was one of them.[6] He asked me to come over to Dublin three years ago, but at first we only got as far as Cornish, where other of the literary firmament conjure and bottle up thoughts for the surprise of the people.

"I found that I could hire a place there for a few months in the summer at a price that would pay for the place, and then would have to pack up and get out before September, so that the owner might enjoy the most glorious part of the vacation that you had prepared for yourself.

"If there was to be any glorious good coming when I paid the price, then I wanted to have it, so I could not make any terms with those people which would strike a pleasing note with me.

"Thayer had said, 'Come along over and see the good fellows and their people who live in Dublin,' and of course I came along.

"I saw, liked, and hired.

"My, but were not the people here good to me!

"I got Mrs. Copley Greene's home,[7] Lone Tree Hill, for last summer, and maybe I didn't hang around the old woods like any boy would.

"I simply did as I pleased and kept the folks all anxious about me. Get as much health as there was abounding around me, I could not fully rid myself of this indigestion.

"We have spent our summers in all lands, in our country and in the homes of foreigners, but here at last I have found the spot that I have longed for, but never until now realized that it existed in fact."

Sprightly as a man half his age, the author then arose, saying: "Come along up to my rooms and let me show you what I have to look upon when I wake in the morning."

17. Isabel Lyons, Jean Clemens, and Mark Twain on the veranda of the Upton House in Dublin, N.H., 16 May 1906. A large St. Bernard is lying at their feet. From the *Boston Post*, 20 May 1906, 30. Courtesy of the Boston Public Library.

It was a great airy room, finely lighted on two sides with broad windows opening on the view about the premises, and near the center of the floor, just under the electrolier, was the huge brass bed that Mr. Clemens had selected for himself.

Its standing in the center of the room was also for his comfort, where he might read under the light until he fell asleep, as is his custom.

A bunch of cigars lay at one side of the pillow that had been placed at the lower end of the bed.

"Those cigars were placed there handy," Mr. Clemens said, "so I won't have the trouble of getting out after them."

On the other side of the pillow was an open volume which the owner had been studying while the early morning hours were on, and before the other folks in the house had arisen.

When the suggestion was made that the visitor be allowed to take a group picture on the porch of the house, Mr. Clemens readily replied: "Why, certainly, my boy. We are all up here for health and a good time, so I see no objection to having a picture taken that will show me as I am."

Down on the veranda Miss Clemens and Miss Lyon were engaged in correspondence, but when Mr. Clemens insisted that they join the group with him, one of them pleaded for the great St. Bernard's company to fill out the setting indicative of the easy and well-guarded country life that he is leading among the hills.

After a couple of pictures had been snapped, at the hint of taking him alone Mr. Clemens spoke up, saying: "Yes, one of them all alone would be the real thing now, for it would not do for you ladies to become too well known as moving with the great and famous, eh, Jeannie, dear?" as he turned to his youngest daughter.

"I have never had a good profile taken, so now will this gentle picture man," turning to the reporter, "go ahead with the operation?"

As he talked there was a laugh in every sentence, humor in the features, and merry twinkles in the eyes that gave absolute indication that the one day in the country had worked a change in the convalescing author that no physician's medicine could outdo.

While in Dublin Mr. Clemens expects to devote about two hours at various times each day dictating to Miss Lyon the material for his autobiography, for as he says, "that autobiography is the only work I expect to do the rest of my life."

But they insist that this summer shall be a restful one with him, for last winter was one of the busiest periods of his life.

The present home that he has hired for the summer was of his own choosing and about the first of May his daughter Jean came on from New York with three servants to prepare it for his occupancy.

Back from the village of Dublin it is located on an avenue leading from the Jaffrey road, and has long been considered the finest location on the hills overlooking the lake and mountain.

The house is a new one set in the midst of wide farm land, and bounded by the country estates of many rich New York professional men, who consider it one of the greatest honors that could be paid to the town to have the dean of American humorists among them.

Practical affairs of the world he wants to let remain a dead letter while getting that digestive apparatus into shape, and on saying this he turned the conversation to a cut on the lower lip which he inflicted while shaving.

"Now, a little cut like that I inflict quite often, for while I am using the razor every emotion makes itself felt in the use of my hand.

"It might be hate, affection, laughter, or any other in the whole gamut of emotions, but on the instant of its force striking me away goes the hand with a jerk and usually blood will pour, as occurred in this case.

"The cut is there now, but what the emotion was I cannot tell."

This was the Mark Twain of envied reputation in the literary affairs of the world as he was to be found with tension relaxed, in his secluded house of the New Hampshire hills.

Notes to Interview 198

1. On Aldrich, see n. 4 to interview 28.
2. See n. 3 to interview 182.
3. Isabel Van Kleek Lyon (1863–1958), MT's private secretary from 1902 until 1909.
4. Alice Whittemore Upton Pearmain, wife of S. B. Pearmain (b. 1859), a Boston stockbroker.
5. Padrone, the owner of an Italian inn or an employer.
6. Albert Thayer (d. 1955), a New England landscape artist.
7. Henry Copley Greene (1871–1951), American playwright.

199

"Polk Miller's Visit to Mark Twain," *Chattanooga Times*, 7 July 1906, 7.

From his home in Richmond, Va., under date of the 18th, Polk Miller,[1] the well-known platform entertainer, sends out the following letter:

On reading the account of a banquet given to Mark Twain in New York, on the occasion of his seventieth birthday, it recalled to my mind a visit which I paid him in his room a short while ago at the Grosvenor hotel.[2] As I had been with him on several occasions in the clubs in New York, and had appeared with him on the platform of one of his delightful entertainments at Madison Square Garden in 1894, I was anxious to meet him again. I was told by a mutual friend of ours that he was in the city, but did not visit or receive company, but it was suggested that I call at the hotel and leave my card. After handing my card to the bellboy, with no thought of seeing the great humorist, I loitered in the hallway looking at some pictures which had attracted my attention. The boy came down the elevator with a rush and said: "Mr. Clemens says come right up; he wants to see you." On going into his room, I found him in a recumbent position in the bed, smoking a cigar, "one at a time," with a huge pile of newspapers, magazines and writing material on all sides. He greeted me most cordially, and, although I tried to go, fearing that I was taking up time that was valuable to him, he wouldn't hear of it, and for nearly four hours we talked about the time when we first met; when he, James Whitcomb Riley, and I faced the great crowd of New Yorkers in an entertainment at Madison Square.[3] He never grew tired of talking about the old south, and laughed and cried, alternatively, when I would tell him of something which

18. "Looking over the hills," 16 May 1906. From the *Boston Post*, 20 May 1906, 30. Courtesy of the Boston Public Library.

recalled his boyhood days in Dixie. Mark Twain is a southern man, with a heart full of love for his native section, but broadened as he is by intimate contact and long association with the people of the north, he is an American of the highest type, with the ability to see the peculiarities which differentiate the people of both sections of our great country, without losing in any way his affection for and identity with both.

During my stay with him, when we spoke of that grand civilization which was destroyed by a war in the south and the baneful influences of the carpet-bag reign which followed, and from which we are still suffering, a stranger looking in on us would have thought that we were weeping over the departure of some near relative. When I brought up some little incident characteristic of southern plantation life, which none but those who had been reared here could appreciate, Mark's eyes would fill up, and for several minutes a dead silence prevailed. His long absence from us, so far from dulling his sensitive southern nature, has intensified his love for those things which a cold, calculating, money-making and money-loving people are pleased to call "sickly sentimentalities." I told him of a thing which happened to me when I was at the Mary Baldwin seminary in Staunton, Va., a few months before, lecturing on the "characteristics of the Old South."[4] In this school nearly all of the states of the union are represented, but the majority of the girls are from the south. During my talk I had something to say about the people of Kentucky, and sang "My Old Kentucky Home." The very minute that I struck the air a perfect flood of tears came from the Kentucky girls, and it broke me up. The telling of it broke Mark Twain up, too, and when he had recovered from its effects, he said: "Polk, the next time you go to that school, telegraph me, and I'll be on hand, for I am anxious to witness one more time a scene which could have happened nowhere else but in the south."

Long may this good man live to brighten the lives of the people, not only of this country, but of all lands, and when he dies we should raise a monument to his memory as one who has drunk deeply of the fountains of nature, and who comes nearer knowing human nature than any other man who has lived since the days of Shakespeare.

Notes to Interview 199

1. Polk Miller (1844-1913), American dialect humorist.
2. The Grosvenor was a luxury hotel at Fifth Avenue and Tenth Street.
3. James Whitcomb Riley (1849-1916), American poet.
4. The school, founded in 1842 as Augusta Female Seminary, is known today as Mary Baldwin College.

200

"Twain Awes Capitol," *Washington Herald*, 8 December 1906, 1, 7.

"I belong to the ancient and honorable society of perfection and purity. I am the president, secretary, and treasurer. I am the only member. In fact," drawled Mark Twain, stretched out in an easy chair in the press gallery, with his toes turned up to the crackling fire on the grate, "I am the only person in the United States who is eligible."[1]

Previously, the humorist had sauntered through the Capitol, talking to some of his legislative friends about the copyright bill, which he is anxious should pass, to save his family from starvation. Attired in a snow white serge suit, which matched almost to perfection the crowning glory of his noble head, he needed but a palm-leaf fan to complete his personification of the tropics. A white cravat was held in loose folds with a creamy moonstone, his polished teeth gleamed below a grizzled mustache, his skin was like a baby's, a very vision from the equator. And outside the wintry wind whistled around the dome of the Capitol and cut with nipping zeal the legs of statesmen, whose fur coats could not keep out the frigid blasts, and carried gusts of snowflakes that beat upon the panes.

"Honest," said Mark Twain, "I can't get over the abomination of the American clothes. The garments the average man wears are a fright; but I have reached that age of discretion which gives to years the right of individuality in dress. I wear my white serge not as clothes. No, it's my uniform.[2]

"I have seen but one man dressed the way I would like to dress—dressed in the best way to dress. He was a Sandwich Islander, and he wore—let me see, it was a special occasion—a pair of spectacles. You may talk about clothes, but, after all, the human skin is the best thing in that line I have ever struck.[3]

"Now, there's the plug hat. Whenever I see a man in a plug hat I begin to suspect him of something. Time was when a man couldn't be dressed in the United States unless he wore a plug hat. Now a man can't be dressed if he does wear one.[4] I don't like to see men in black.

"Oh, now, I don't care for the gaudy effects. Something with color in it, though, catches my fancy. I love the women. They know how to get themselves up to capture the heart and eye, and I don't see why, as the ladies are constantly borrowing ideas in clothes from men—whenever they get any good ones—the men shouldn't borrow from the ladies.

"Were there ever any styles like the peek-a-boo waist, the low-cut gown, the short sleeves? Wouldn't man look gorgeous in that kind of a rig? Why not? Of course, I believe in it. For men? Certainly.[5] I like to look over the theaters, the opera houses; but do you think I care about the men? Not by a considerable sight. They speck the landscape like a lot of crows. But with the women, it's different.[6] There is something gay, and festive, and full of life and color, and warm and pleasing and artistic about a woman. They don't get themselves up like delegates to an undertaker's convention, with no more atmospheric fitness about them than a ham. No, sir; a woman knows how to blend herself with the scenery, and if there happens to be an aurora borealis or a rainbow around, it doesn't give her any chills. She comes right up smiling with the goods, and she sails in and makes the aurora borealis look sick. But with a man, it's different, and he couldn't shake off a waiter's coat unless— unless he should have attained the age of seventy-one, as I have."

Mark Twain lolled back in his chair the picture of contentment, and the correspondents who had rescued him from the crush in the lobby below, and had installed him in the chair of honor in the lounging room of the press gallery, forgot the debate in the House and crowded around him.

"The ideal dress doesn't exist now," he drawled. "You've got to go back to the Middle Ages for that. Now, I don't mean the tinned-goods era. I mean the doublet and hose period, the silk-and-velvet age, when the men decorated their heads with hats like the swinging garden of Babylon and drooping plumes. There weren't any anesthetic buttons in those days, and a man laced his pants on. It must have taken 'em some time to dress—and—I—guess—proved—embarrassing—when—the—house—caught—fire."[7]

"But, Mr. Clemens," said one of the correspondents, "what made you dress your Yankee at King Arthur's Court in armor and a silk hat?"

"Because when I wrote that book the plug hat was all the rage in America. I did it to cater to popular clamor.[8] Now, there's William Dean Howells. He knows better, and his own taste tells him not to wear a plug hat. But he listens to what other people say. Why, when we came over from New York to attend this copyright hearing, Howells wore a plug hat. It was the only one on the ferry-boat. He looked like an ass. But, then, I didn't have to see him in a plug hat. I know that, anyhow.[9]

"These are just some of the reasons why I wear white clothes in midwinter; I've got my real clothes underneath. It suits me, and I'm getting to be an old man now. So is Howells; he's seventy, and he ought to know better, but he never seems to learn.

"Why, we went over to the hearing on the copyright bill at the Congressional Library this morning. The mechanical musical instrument people, who want to get a copyright on the perforations in a roll of paper, had the floor. So I didn't go in. But Howells did, and he's there yet. He's the most diffident man I know, and if I had offered him a week's wages to leave that meeting he wouldn't have accepted. He hasn't got the nerve to quit. He's getting full of facts about musical instruments—and he won't remember a bit of it next week."

Somebody asked the venerable humorist his opinion about the public library board of Worcester, Mass., that barred his book, *Eve's Diary*.[10] He smiled contentedly and drawled: "The whole episode has rather amused me. I have no feeling of vindictiveness over the stand of the librarians there—I am only amused. You see they did not object to my book; they objected to Lester Ralph's pictures.[11] I wrote the book; I did not make the pictures. I admire the pictures, and I heartily approve them, but I did not make them.

"It seems curious to me—some of the incidents in this case. It appears that the pictures in *Eve's Diary* were first discovered by a lady librarian. When she made the dreadful find, being very careful, she jumped at no hasty conclusions—not she—she examined the horrid things in detail. It took her some time to examine them all, but she did her hateful duty! I don't blame her for this careful examination; the time she spent was, I am sure, enjoyable, for I found considerable fascination in them myself.

"Then she took the book to another librarian, a male this time, and he, also, took a long time to examine the unclothed ladies. He must have found something of the same sort of fascination in them that I found. Now, if the pictures were so good as to occupy their attention so long, it seems to me that they were a little selfish not to permit the rest of the city a chance instead of shutting the volume out.

"Seriously, the pictures in the book are graceful and beautiful; they show fine and delicate feeling. So far from being immodest, I thought them chaste and in good taste. To the library that barred them it would, no doubt, have been satisfactory had the ladies in Eden been garbed with a fig-leaf each, but to my mind that sort of thing is only advertising immodesty."

Mr. Clemens was asked if he had any opinion as to the theory of Mrs. Parsons, promulgated in her book, advocating short-term marriages.[12]

"It is no new thing," he said; "but as I have no idea of marrying, I guess I shan't be required to try it.

"That sort of a trial marriage was a common thing in Scotland 300 years ago—I wasn't there then, but I've heard so. A couple would unite for a year, and if at the end of that time they did not agree, they separated, without prejudice to either. I have never heard how the plan worked. At any rate, it did not continue, so there may have been something wrong with it. We should have to know all about how the project affected things in Scotland before we could venture to try it here."

Some of the correspondents asked Mark Twain questions bearing on timely issues, and, merely to accommodate them, he consented to be semi-serious for five whole minutes. But he didn't express any very weighty opinions. He said: "On the Japanese question, so called, I have no knowledge.[13] In my day, in California, we never had any Japanese; so there was no question. If I, without any knowledge of the subject at all, save that I have gathered secondhand, should express my opinion one way or the other it might do harm—an opinion based on such lack of knowledge could hardly do any good."

"With your interest in all educational matters, what do you think," he was asked, "of that part of the President's message relating to teaching the boys marksmanship in the public schools?"[14]

"An excellent idea," said Mark Twain. "Both physically and metaphorically, let us 'teach the young idea how to shoot!' They have done it for a long time in England; that is, they have done everything possible to organize the youth of England into shooting societies and clubs, so as to make good marksmen out of them; so that they have a large body of men who are in this way qualified for military service anytime.

"A little while ago my daughter wrote to me asking my opinion as to the discharge of the colored soldiers at Brownsville, Texas, asking me if I did not think it was wrong.[15] I replied that I had no opinion on the subject. Before I could express an opinion I should have to study the facts and have a knowledge of military law and custom and civil law, which I do not possess. I told her, too, that she ought not to have an opinion on the subject. She could not possibly have mastered the facts."

Then Mr. Clemens got down to the copyright bill that brought him to Washington.[16] He said: "We want to have this copyright bill dissected—divided. The musical fellows should drop out, and there should be a law for authors of books only, and another one for the musical piano players.[17] We want the copyright during the author's life, and for fifty years after.[18] A few years ago I remember that in one year only two books were re-copyrighted, for the additional fourteen years allowed—only two books, which were to go on for a full forty-two years. One of these was *Innocents Abroad* and the other was Mrs. Eddy's Christian Science book.[19] There have been 250,000 books published in this country since the establishment of the government, and not more than 1,000 books have been re-copyrighted. Out of the thousands of books published every year, ten will live, and the copyright law we want is aimed to protect the writers of those ten books that live.[20] To remove the copyright doesn't give the people cheaper books, but it gives more money to the publishers.[21]

"A few years ago the copyright on one of my books expired, while I was following the equator, and wasn't here to have it extended. In a couple of years or so the renewed copyright will expire on *Innocents Abroad*. That will be some more bread and butter out of my children's mouths. When a man reaches the age of forty, he isn't working for himself any more; he's working for his wife and children. Under the present copyright law, when a man dies, and leaves his family requiring his support—why, that's just the time his copyrights run out.[22]

"The trouble is, Congress is composed of lawyers and agriculturists. No authors or publishers. That's why it's hard to get a good law passed.[23] When the present international copyright bill was up in the House it looked as though it would fail. I went to Sunset Cox, and told him I wanted the privilege of going on the floor.[24]

"'Why, that's impossible,' replied Cox. 'Have you ever received the thanks of Congress?'

"'No,' said I, 'but I hope to.'

"'If you are caught by the Speaker and sentenced to Siberia, will you go quietly?'

"'I will,' said I.

"'All right,' said Sunset Cox. He took me on the floor, and introduced me to all the Democrats. I told them about the bill. They said they'd vote for it. John D. Long introduced me to all the Republicans.[25] They promised to vote for it. And the next session they did. "

Mr. Clemens almost caused a riot when he went in to make a call on Uncle

Joe Cannon, and that worthy gentleman thought he was seeing things. Before the two old friends—they met one Saturday night at a Gridiron dinner, and Mr. Clemens asserts that that makes them old friends—had really settled down into a confidential conversation, Sereno Payne dropped in. He seemed pained and shocked when he saw the white suit.[26]

"Look here," he said, after a few preliminaries; "aren't you afraid you'll catch cold with that white suit on?"

"Oh, no," said Mr. Clemens. "It doesn't matter about the weight or the color of your suit if your underclothes are all right. My underclothes are quite heavy. Why, you can wear steel armor and not get cold, if your underclothes are heavy."

"Well, I'd hate to make the experiment," said the Republican floor leader, thinking, perhaps, of how he would look in armor.

The talk passed on to legislation.

"The way to do a thing is to do it," said Twain. "It's all nonsense, this business of writing to members of the Senate and House and asking them to vote for this bill or that. The thing to do is to go after them."

Then Uncle Joe told his distinguished visitor how regrettable it was that nobody could get him in on the floor of the House. "But, you see," he explained, "when your friend Tom Reed was Speaker he got through a rule which not only forbids the extension of the privilege of the floor to an outsider, but prohibits a member from moving that such a privilege be extended.[27] If it were not for that, there is not a member who wouldn't be proud to ask for the honor of having Mark Twain in there with them during a session.

"Tell you what I'll do, though," said Uncle Joe, after some more conversation. "I'll invite you to make yourself at home in my private rooms down on the next floor. There's plenty of space there, and I think you will be comfortable."

So Secretary Busbey steered Mr. Clemens to the Speaker's gallery,[28] where he sat awhile, the observed of all the observed, and then took him to the Speaker's apartment, where he remained most of the afternoon, writing. "It reminds me of the time, forty years ago, when I was a Washington correspondent," he said. "Things were a little different then, though."

Notes to Interview 200

I have supplemented this interview as reported in the *Washington Herald* with versions of Twain's comments published in other newspapers. All newspaper citations below are from 8 December 1906.

1. "Mark Twain in Cream-Colored Summer Flannel," *New York World*, 1-2. "I suppose everyone is wondering why I am wearing what I am," he said modestly, referring to the flannel outfit. "This is a uniform. It is the uniform of the American

Association of Purity and Perfection, of which I am president, secretary, and treasurer, and the only man in the United States eligible to membership."

"Mark Twain in White Attire," *New York Sun,* 4: "Oh, I find this flannel suit comfortable," he began. "You see (illustrating) I wear heavy underclothing. This suit I may say is the uniform of the Ancient and Honorable Order of Purity and Perfection, of which organization I am the president, secretary and treasurer, and sole member. I may add that I don't know of anyone else who is eligible."

2. *New York World:* "I was seventy-one years old last Saturday, and when a man reaches that age he has a right to arrogate to himself many privileges to which younger men cannot aspire. When you are over seventy-one you are privileged to dress in the fashion that conforms most to your comfort and enjoyment. I have reached the age where dark clothes have a depressing effect on me. . . . Clothes, in our modern civilization, are to preserve decency, and for us to get as much comfort out of as possible. But how any man can get comfort out of the clothing made for men today I cannot see. Nothing is more absurd, ungraceful, and uncomfortable than modern men's clothing, day or night, and at night man wears the most ridiculous of all garb—evening clothes."

New York Sun: "You see, when a man gets to be 71, as I am, the world begins to look somber and dark, and I believe we should do all we can to brighten things up and make ourselves look cheerful. You can't do that wearing black, funeral clothes. And why shouldn't a man wear white? It betokens purity and innocence."

"Mark Twain in White Amuses Congressmen," *New York Times,* 5: "Why don't you ask why I am wearing such apparently unseasonable clothes? I'll tell you. I have found that when a man reaches the advanced age of 71 years as I have, the continual sight of dark clothing is like to have a depressing effect upon him. Light-colored clothing is more pleasing to the eye and enlivens the spirit. Now, of course, I cannot compel everyone to wear such clothing just for my especial benefit, so I do the next best thing and wear it myself."

3. *New York Sun:* "There is absolutely no comfortable and delightful and pleasant costume but the human skin. That, however, is impossible. So when you are seventy-one years old you may at least be pardoned for dressing as you please."

New York World: "What, in your judgment, is the most comfortable costume?" Mr. Clemens was asked. "There is no more delightful costume possible than the human skin. The most satisfactory costume I ever saw was worn by the natives of the Sandwich Islands, whom I saw forty years ago. When they wanted to adorn themselves beyond what nature gave them they put on a pair of spectacles."

New York Sun: "The most beautiful costume is the human skin, but since it isn't conventional or polite to appear in public in that garb alone, I believe in wearing white. I don't know of anything more hideous and disgusting in men's attire than the black clawhammer coat. A group of men thus adorned remind me more of a flock of crows more than anything else. About the most becoming getup I ever saw in my life was out in the Sandwich Islands thirty years ago, where a native who wanted to appear at his best usually appeared in a pair of eyeglasses."

New York Times: "The best-dressed man I have ever seen, however, was a native of the Sandwich Islands, who attracted my attention thirty years ago. Now, when that man wanted to don especial dress to honor a public occasion or a holiday, why he occasionally put on a pair of spectacles. Otherwise the clothing with which God had provided him sufficed." See also chapters 67 and 72–73 of *The Innocents Abroad.*

4. *New York World:* "I can go up and down the streets of New York—I never have, but I know I can do it—and never see a plug hat on the best-dressed people. If I did see a plug hat on a fellow I would suspect him of something."

5. *New York World:* "What would you suggest for men—peekaboo waists, with short, fluffy sleeves?" "Certainly," replied Mr. Clemens, running his fingers through his hair. "The women take and wear our clothes, don't they? Why should we not learn from them? They always have beautiful fabrics, splendid colors, and, moreover, women's clothes are always pretty."

New York Sun: "I'm in favor of the peekaboo waists and the décolleté costumes."

New York Times: "Of course, I have ideas of dress reform. For one thing, why not adopt some of the women's styles? Goodness knows, they adopt enough of ours. Take the peek-a-boo waist, for instance. It has the obvious advantages of being cool and comfortable, and in addition it is almost always made up in pleasing colors, which cheer and do not depress."

6. *New York World:* "I prefer light clothing, colors, like those worn by the ladies at the opera. Whenever I go to the opera and see the men sitting around with those beautifully-gowned ladies they are no more cheering than a lot of old crows. If nobody else will wear colors that cheer me up I shall wear them myself. Man's clothing is bad in color and generally uncomfortable."

New York Times: "Of course, before a man reaches my years, the fear of criticism might prevent him from indulging his fancy. I am not afraid of that. I am decidedly for pleasing color combinations in dress. I like to see the women's clothes, say, at the opera. What can be more depressing than the somber black which custom requires men to wear upon state occasions? A group of men in evening clothes looks like a flock of crows, and is just about as inspiring. After all, what is the purpose of clothing? Are not clothes intended primarily to preserve dignity and also to afford comfort to their wearer? Now I know of nothing more uncomfortable than the present day clothes of men. The finest clothing made is a person's own skin, but, of course, society demands something more than this."

"Mark Twain's Views," *New York Tribune,* 3: "For instance, I like the colors of the costumes that women wear. They are lively and not so depressing as the dark suits of men. At the opera house in the evening when I look around at the men in their black evening clothes I am disagreeably impressed with the fact that they are no more cheerful and no more pleasant to look at than a lot of crows. Man's dress of the present day is absurdly awkward and ungraceful."

7. *New York World:* "I would go back to the Middle Ages for the gorgeous, glorious, gaudy costumes of that time. Then we could wear colors. Back to the days before buttons were invented, when they laced their clothing up, and it took a little time to do it; back to the days of tights and helmet! Yes, I admit that it might be uncomfortable for a bald-headed man wearing a tight-screwed on helmet, with a bee or a fly imprisoned therein."

New York Tribune: "I am in favor of going back to the splendors in dress of the Middle Ages. Those were the days when a man could wear bright raiment that was a pleasure to the eye. The Chinaman wears comfortable and bright looking clothes, but I am not prepared to say I would favor that kind of dress altogether, though they certainly have an advantage in the kind of shoes they wear."

8. *New York World:* "But the Yankee at King Arthur's Court was not dressed that way," was suggested. "No, I dressed the Yankee in the costume of twenty-five years

ago, when it was customary for a man who wished to be well-dressed to wear a plug hat. Now, when a man wants to be dressed up he does not wear a plug hat. He leaves it at home in the tightly-tied box in which it came from the hatter's."

New York Times: "It is true that I dressed the Connecticut Yankee in King Arthur's Court in a plug hat, but let's see, that was twenty-five years ago. Then no man was considered fully dressed until he donned a plug hat. Nowadays I think that no man is dressed until he leaves it home. Why, when I left home yesterday they trotted out a plug hat for me to wear. 'You must wear it,' they told me. 'Why, just think of going to Washington without a plug hat!' But I said no; I would wear a derby or nothing. Why, I believe I could walk along the streets of New York—I never do—but still I think I could—and I should never see a well-dressed man wearing a plug hat. If I did I should suspect him of something. I don't know just what, but I would suspect him."

New York Tribune: "And yet there has been a decided change in the style of man's dress in recent years. Why, twenty-five years ago I remember when a man was not considered dressed unless he wore a high hat, and now—well, I know I wouldn't wear one of them myself."

9. On Howells, see n. 2 to interview 2.

"Twain Would Like to Dress Like Adam," *New York American,* 1, 4. "The plug hat is a farce. When I left New York, the one man on the ferryboat that sported a plug hat was William Dean Howells. William didn't want to wear that lid, but someone cajoled him into mounting it on his head. I can go through the streets of New York and not find a plug hat on the best-dressed men. The tights and helmet of by-gone days are superior raiment. Mr. Howells mightn't look dignified and literary in a helmet and tights, but I quarrel with him about that plug hat because he's old enough to have better judgment than to take the advice of other people about plug hats and things."

New York Sun: "They tried to get me to wear a plug hat when I started to come down to Washington, but I rebelled against it. Of all styles of headgear I think the plug hat is about the limit, and I'm glad to see that it has become obsolete. You might walk up and down Broadway all day and you would never see any of the best dressed men wearing plug hats. I always suspect a man I see wearing a plug hat these days. Coming down here the only man I saw wearing one was William Dean Howells." "Did you suspect Mr. Howells?" someone asked. "Yes, I suspected him of being an ass," replied the humorist. "Howells just let someone persuade him into wearing that plug hat, and any man who will let another do that is an ass. Of course, Howells is a mighty fine old fellow—he is 70, and therefore old enough not to be bamboozled into wearing a hat of that sort."

"Mark Twain Bids Winter Defiance," *New York Herald,* 4: "Whenever I see a man wearing a plug hat I always suspect him. I remember W. D. Howells showed up in one not long ago. Howells was not made to be ridiculous, but he certainly had his opportunity on that occasion. Did I suspect him? Yes. I suspected him of being an ass and I didn't have to inquire about it either, for I knew he was one in wearing that hat. Howells is over there in the library now sweating it out with the committee in charge of the copyright bill. He has no business there today, but he is too diffident to come away. You couldn't get him out of there with an offer of a week's wages. He won't hear anything that will do him any good or that he will want to remember next week."

New York World: "There's William Dean Howells. He's seventy years of age, and he was the only man on the ferryboat on which I left New York that wore a plug hat.

He didn't want to wear it, but someone persuaded him. I hold that when a man is seventy years old he ought to know his own mind and not take advice from other people."

New York Times: "Why, when I got up on the second story of that Pennsylvania ferryboat coming down here yesterday, I saw Howells coming along. He was the only man on the boat with a plug hat, and I tell you he felt ashamed of himself. He said he had been persuaded to wear it against his better sense, but just think of a man nearly 70 years old who has not a mind of his own on such matters!"

10. A sequel to "Extracts from Adam's Diary" (1893). "Eve's Diary," *Harper's Monthly* 112 (December 1905): 25–32; rpt. *Eve's Diary Translated from the Original Manuscript* (New York: Harper and Bros., 1906). In a letter on 7 February 1907 MT insisted that "when a Library expels a book of mine and leaves an unexpurgated Bible lying around where unprotected youth and age can get hold of it, the deep unconscious irony of it delights me and doesn't anger me."

11. Lester Ralph (1877–1927) supplied fifty illustrations for the 1906 edition of *Eve's Diary,* some of which depicted Adam and Eve naked.

12. The sociologist Elsie Clew Parsons (1875–1941) discussed "early trial marriage" in *The Family: An Ethnographical and Historical Outline* (1906).

13. In his annual message to Congress on 3 December 1906, President Roosevelt criticized a decision of the San Francisco school board to require children of Japanese descent to attend segregated schools.

14. In the conclusion to his annual message to Congress on 3 December 1906, Roosevelt recommended that in case of a national emergency the U.S. Army recruit volunteers "who already know how to shoot. . . . We should establish shooting galleries in all the large public and military schools, should maintain national target ranges in different parts of the country, and should in every way encourage the formation of rifle clubs throughout all parts of the land."

15. Budd (1977), 99n62: "It is now generally agreed that President Roosevelt acted unjustly in ordering that 159 black enlisted men be dishonorably discharged from the U.S. Army because of a shooting incident in Brownsville, Texas." See also John D. Weaver, *The Brownsville Raid* (College Station: Texas A&M University Press, 1992).

16. *New York World:* "But I am not here to talk fashions but copyright law. If you had ten authors and an equal number of publishers in Congress more would be known of copyright laws. With 25,000 bills in Congress coming in, I don't see how members have an opportunity to even read the titles."

New York Sun: "We poor authors who are giving the world the benefit of our brainwork at a royalty of so much per volume want protection, and I believe that if we can properly impress and interest members of Congress we will get it."

17. *New York World:* "We came down here expecting only to talk about book copyrights, and when we got inside we found they were discussing music gramophones, perforated rolls, and automatic musical instruments, with very little or nothing about books."

18. *New York Sun:* "Under the present laws an author obtains a copyright for twenty-eight years, with the privilege of renewing it within six months before it lapses for another fourteen years. There is no reason why it should not be perpetual, but all we are asking is that it shall continue during the life of the author and fifty years thereafter. That will give him and his family all the protection required. Why, under

the present law I won't be in heaven but a few years before my children will lose my royalties and be going hungry, and the publishers will be getting the benefits which should accrue to them."

19. Mary Baker Eddy's *Science and Health* (1875), copyright renewed in 1890, 1894, 1901, 1902, and 1906. See also n. 12 to interview 175.

New York World: "I shall hardly get into Heaven before my children will have no book on which to live. Out of all the 150,000 books published during the last half century, but two have been extended to the 42-year-term period. One of them is *Science and Health* by Mrs. Mary Baker G. Eddy, and the other is my own *Innocents Abroad*."

New York Sun: "Several years ago, when the copyright on some 5,000 books expired, there were only two out of that number which were renewed—Mrs. Mary Baker Eddy's *Science and Health* and *Innocents Abroad*, the name of whose author I am too modest to mention."

20. *New York World:* "There are women who write, idiots and well-meaning persons who write, who know nothing about copyrights, but I profess to have some knowledge on this subject. There are between 5,000 and 7,000 books issued every year. Ten may live twenty-eight years, the first period of the present copyright, and two be renewed to bring them up to the forty-two-year limit. Then the author dies and his children starve."

New York Sun: "The copyright on my first book ran out while I was 'following the equator,' and I failed to get it renewed. Now the publisher is drawing the royalties which should be coming in to me. Of the 7,000 books copyrighted every year now there are not more than ten which outlive their copyright, so it cannot be contended that the reading public obtains any benefit from the lapse of a copyright. The benefit accrues only to the publisher and the author suffers."

New York American: "You cannot name twenty persons in the whole United States," he declared, "who in the past 100 years have produced books which have outlived the copyright limit."

21. *New York World:* The expiration of a copyright, he explained, did not inure to the benefit of the public, but to the publisher, "who lives forever and rears families in affluence and enjoys from generation to generation these ill-gotten gains."

22. *New York World:* "I am particularly interested in the portion of the measure which concerns my trade," he continued. "I like that extension to the life of the author, and fifty years thereafter. I think that ought to satisfy any reasonable author, because it will take care of his children—let the grandchildren take care of themselves. It will satisfy me because it will enable me to take care of my daughters. After that I don't care. I have long been out of the struggle, independent of it, and indifferent to it. It is not objectionable to me that all the trades and industries of the United States are in the bill and protected by it. I should like to have the oyster culture added, and anything else that might need protection. I have no ill feeling. I think it a just and righteous measure and I should like to see it passed. . . . But," he added, "I understand it must have a limit because that is required by the Constitution of the United States, which sets aside that prior constitution we call the Decalogue. The Decalogue says you shall not take away from any man his property—I will not use that harsher word. But the laws of England and America do take away the property from the author. They all talk handsomely of the literature of the land, then they turn around to crush and wipe it out of existence. . . . My copyrights produce to me a great deal more money

than I can spend. However, if I did not have them I could take care of myself. I know half a dozen trades and if those ran out I would invent a half dozen others. But, for my daughters, I hope Congress will extend to them the charity which they have failed to get from me."

23. *New York World:* "Congress is made up of lawyers, agriculturists, and all sorts of persons with all sorts of opinions, gained by experience, but men will not study the copyright laws unless they have been both author and publisher. I have been both author and publisher and have been smashed."

24. On Cox, see n. 1 to interview 45.

25. John D. Long (1838–1915), governor of Massachusetts (1880–82), Republican member of Congress (1883–89), and president of the Authors Club of Boston.

New York Sun: "Several years ago through the assistance of the late Sunset Cox and ex-Senator Long, then a member of the House, I was instrumental in bringing the necessity of an international copyright law to the attention of Congress, with the result that we have the present law on that subject. It is good as far as it goes, but it does not go far enough, and the measure which is now pending seeks to correct its errors of omission."

26. Joseph G. (Uncle Joe) Cannon (1836–1926), Speaker of the U.S. House of Representatives from 1903 until 1911. The Gridiron Club, founded by journalists in 1885 in Washington, D.C., with the sole purpose of hosting an annual dinner. Sereno E. Payne (1843–1914), U.S. representative from New York (1883–87, 1889–1914).

27. Thomas B. Reed (1839–1902), Speaker of the U.S. House of Representatives, 1889–91 and 1895–99. See also Fatout, 349.

28. L. White Busbey (1852–1925), Speaker Cannon's private secretary.

201

"Mark Twain Demands Thanks of Congress, and Right Away, Too,"
Washington Times, 8 December 1906, 1.

With the thermometer down to twenty degrees above zero, Mark Twain today discarded his white flannel clothes, which were the attraction at the Capitol yesterday, and journeyed to the White House in a heavy dark suit.

"It's too bleak," he said.

Mr. Twain arrived at the White House at 11:30. He was accompanied by his private secretary, and both were evidently very "green" at the White House. "Where do I go?" asked the humorist. Then Congressman Sereno E. Payne of New York grabbed his arm and introduced him to a friend from Albany.[1] "I remember listening to your address before the Sanitary Committee several years ago," said the Albany man.

"I don't remember it," said Mr. Clemens, looking perplexed.

"Not in Washington. It happened in Albany," explained the man from the Empire State capital.

"Oh, yes, I do remember that,"[2] said the author of *Tom Sawyer.* "But you see this is the first time I have been in Washington for twenty-two years. I don't often come here on depredation expeditions like the one I'm on now.

I'm here on this copyright business and want to see the President about it." Then he walked over to Major Loeffler,[3] the President's doorkeeper, and exclaimed: "I want the usual thing. I'd like to see the President."

Mr. Clemens was not in the President's office more than five minutes. When he came out he said: "The President is one with us on the copyright matter."

Just at this moment the correspondent of a Boston paper asked him if he would not give his views on simplified spelling. "Well, as I have written an article on that subject for a certain magazine, I do not feel that it would be fair to the magazine to tell you what I think of it. Besides that, I doubt if your paper will pay me 30 cents a word for the matter anyway."[4] . . .

Notes to Interview 201

1. Sereno E. Payne (1843–1914), U.S. representative from New York (1883–87, 1889–1914).

2. MT had testified before the Assembly Committee on Public Health in Albany on 27 February 1901.

3. Major Charles Loeffler, a German immigrant and Civil War veteran, served on the White House domestic staff for nearly forty years.

4. MT's article on simplified spelling, written in 1899, remained unpublished until its appearance in *Letters from the Earth* (1962). MT had also joked about simplified spelling in an address at the Associated Press annual dinner in New York on 18 September 1906 (Fatout, 522–27).

202

"Heard at the Capitol," *Washington Post,* 12 December 1906, 4.

Samuel L. Clemens (Mark Twain) was at the Capitol yesterday and took an informal leave of Speaker Cannon and Vice President Fairbanks and other prominent members of the national legislature.[1] He told "Uncle Joe" that he was sorry to depart without receiving the thanks of Congress he had requested, as he needed it in his business; but it had been intimated to him that, if he would get out of town and leave Congress alone, the deferred thanks might be forthcoming at once. If the surmise should prove true, Uncle Joe, it is understood, will forward the "thanks" to the noted humorist by special delivery letter.

Mr. Clemens said he felt he had accomplished all he could for the copyright cause for the present and that no good would result from his remaining here any longer; in fact he thought he might undo all of his missionary work if he continued to longer haunt the halls of legislation.

"I have found out several things since I have been in Washington," said Mr. Clemens yesterday. "I could write a book on my discoveries and not enumerate all of them. I have learned among other things that legislation is a much more complicated proposition than I ever dreamed it to be. It looked very simple and easy at a distance, but a closer view has given me quite a different impression.

"The mistake the authors made was to permit those mechanical fellows— the makers of musical instruments, phonographs, &c.—to break into our game. There appears to be no opposition in Congress to extending the copyright on books to one hundred years, and if the proposition stood alone it would go through both Houses, I think, by a practically unanimous vote. But I learn that there is serious opposition to granting such a long copyright to mechanical devices, phonographs, photographs, and other things of that character. Whether anything will be done at this session toward amending the copyright laws is doubtful. I was opposed to letting the mechanical fellows join hands with us at the time we held our copyright congress in New York, but my advice was disregarded. We now know what a dangerous thing it is to ignore my advice!"

Note to Interview 202

1. Joseph G. (Uncle Joe) Cannon (1836-1926), Speaker of the U.S. House of Representatives from 1903 until 1911; Charles W. Fairbanks (1852-1918), U.S. vice president from 1905 to 1909.

203

"Twain's Plan to Beat the Copyright Law," *New York Times,* 12 December 1906, 1.

Washington, Dec. 11—Mark Twain has the copyright law beaten to a frazzle. It is from pure altruism, pure interest in authorship as a profession, that he is here booming the Copyright Extension bill; it doesn't affect him. He has a scheme which puts his children beyond the reach of want till they shall be old ladies and makes the present copyright law look like a very sick and discomfited pirate, indeed.

The weapon whereby Mark Twain has vanquished the copyright law is his much heralded autobiography. Hitherto the manner of publication of that work has been shrouded in mystery. It has been given out that it would not be published in book form or published at all in its entirety until after Mark Twain's death. He consented to the publication of a few extracts in the *North American Review,* where it is now running.[1]

Mark Twain looks upon the copyright law as pure robbery. He believes that it is not designed in the interest of the public, but is simply a mechanism whereby after the author has enjoyed the fruits of his labor for forty-two years his property can be taken from him and handed over to a lot of publishers who had nothing to do with it. He considers it a law for the robbery of an author's children in the interest of the publishers. This is a tolerably conservative statement of his views—a radical statement of them would cause this issue of *The Times* to be excluded from the mails.

For years Mark Twain has devoted his intellect to the question how to beat this law, how to foil this robbery, how to insure to his children the profit of their father's labor, and prevent it from being handed over by the Government to some publishers who have never done anything for Mark.

And he has devised a way. He has written between a quarter and half a million words of his autobiography, and is adding to it continually. As soon as the copyright expires on one of his books Mark Twain or his executors will apply for a new copyright on the book, with a portion of the autobiography run as a footnote. For example, when the copyright on *Tom Sawyer* expires, a new edition of that book will be published. On each page a rule will be run about two-thirds of the way down the page, and below these lines will be printed the autobiography, or so much of it as is designed for publication in that volume. About one-third of this new edition of *Tom Sawyer* will be autobiography, separated from the old text only by the rules or lines. The same course will be followed with each book, as the copyright expires.

So far as possible the part of the autobiography will be germane to the book in which it appears. For instance, the part which is printed with *Innocents Abroad* will be mostly that section which relates to the trip of the Innocents and to Mark Twain's other European visits. The part printed with *Tom Sawyer* will be made up chiefly of Mark Twain's early life in the little Missouri town where he, the real Tom Sawyer, lived. The part printed with *Roughing It* will consist largely if not entirely of the author's life in the West.

All arrangements and provisions for the carrying out of this plan, which Mark Twain means as seriously as any man ever meant anything, have been made, and long after his death the autobiography will continue to appear in this form. It is not true that no part will be published in his lifetime. If he is living in 1910, and he certainly looks as if he intended to be alive and lusty then, the first part of the autobiography will appear in that year, for in 1910 the copyright on his first book, *Innocents Abroad,* will expire. It is true that "The Jumping Frog" was published first, but that was only a collection of sketches not lending itself to Mark Twain's present purpose. The copyright on *Innocents Abroad* will expire late in that year, and the new edition will appear as soon as it does.

A new copyright can be obtained on each of these books. Of course it will not entirely prevent piracy, but Mark Twain figures that it will vitiate the sale of editions which do not contain any of the autobiography as it would be to sell an edition which contained only half or two-thirds of the chapters in the original *Innocents Abroad*.

He is confirmed in this by the experience of Sir Walter Scott, from whom he got the germ of his idea. Scott kept his copyrights alive by publishing new editions with commentaries. The result was that all editions which did not contain the commentaries were a drug on the market; nobody would buy them. Mark Twain is certain that what was done with mere commentaries can be done in a much surer fashion with an autobiography.

There is no compunction in Mark Twain's mind for the dismay his scheme will spread among the publishers. He holds that they are waiting for his copyrights to expire to rob his daughters, and that after much thought he has devised a way to save his daughters. About its success he has no doubt in the world, and he has planned its execution in a most methodical and elaborate way. He believes his scheme will insure a copyright of eighty-four years instead of forty-two, and, as he said the other day: "The children are all I am interested in; let the grandchildren look out for themselves."

He finished his legislative work in behalf of the copyright bill today and will return to New York tomorrow morning.

"My duties as an occasional, unsalaried, professional lobbyist are at an end for the present," he said.

He spent the day seeing Senators, Mr. Lodge having turned over his committee room for the purpose, as Mr. Cannon had turned over his own room yesterday.[2] In the afternoon he and Albert Bigelow Paine, his secretary, went out to Rock Creek Cemetery for a drive.[3]

His stay here has been a sort of triumph. Wherever he has gone crowds of people have hurled themselves upon him to shake his hand. He cannot appear in the lobby of the Willard without becoming instantly the center of a swarm of men and women, strangers to him, who fairly paw him in the exuberance of their joy.[4]

This morning he registered his opinion of the elaborate thingumabobs out of which one has to pour cream in high-toned hotels.

"Paine," he said, after he had tried to pour some cream into his cup and had landed it in the saucer, "Damn this—damn—Paine, I am frightfully short of adequate profanity."

Notes to Interview 203

1. MT published twenty-six installments of a version of his autobiography in the *North American Review* between September 1906 and December 1907.

2. Joseph G. (Uncle Joe) Cannon (1836–1926), Speaker of the U.S. House of Representatives from 1903 until 1911; Henry Cabot Lodge (1850–1924), Republican U.S. senator from Massachusetts from 1893 until his death.

3. Albert Bigelow Paine (1861–1937), MT's official biographer and first literary executor. The eighty-six-acre Rock Creek Cemetery in northwest Washington, D.C., was established in 1719.

4. The Willard was a fashionable hotel at the corner of Fourteenth Street and Pennsylvania Avenue adjacent to the White House in Washington. Established in 1847 and rebuilt in 1904, it was considered the first skyscraper in D.C.

204

Ervin Justice, "Mark Twain Actually in Earnest," *New York World,* 16 December 1906, E3.

"Nearly seven thousand books appear in America every year. Ten may live twenty-eight years, and by the renewal of their copyright their lives may be extended to forty-two years. The author dies about that time. His copyright expires just in time to permit his children to starve, which is not quite fair.

"It is a fallacy that the public gets the benefit when a copyright expires. There is a vague idea in the Congressional mind that it is not a fallacy, and that by placing the present restriction on the author a benefit is being conferred on the nation. The member of Congress thinks that by the restriction he is making the nation a present of a book, but as a matter of fact he is making a publisher a present of a book.

"If all books lived this would be all right. But when there are only a few, what's the use of taking away the little scrap of bread and butter which the author's children get from a copyright?

"In the early '90s, I remember, the record showed that of the books launched twenty-eight years before only two had been re-copyrighted. In those years 5000 books were published each year, and only two of them lived! These two books were *Christian Science and Health* by Mary Baker Eddy and my *Innocents Abroad.*

"I am inclined to think that the copyright on the latter will expire before the bill is passed. I shall hardly be in Heaven before my children will not have a book to live on.

"When you have passed forty you are not laboring for yourself anymore. You are laboring for the wife and the children. This is true of everybody except the author, who is stopped by the Government at a certain time. His income is restricted, while the publisher, under the present copyright law, may take the profit that properly belongs to the author and add it to his own.

"The publishers ought to learn by experience that the very minute the copyright on a published book expires half a dozen publishers are ready to rush in to bring out a cheap edition, with the result that nobody gets any profit.

"The books which have been profitable right along under the copyright law cease to be so when the copyright expires. After the half-dozen publishers have rushed in it is very likely that the book will be left alone for some years;

no publisher wants to take hold of it and burn his fingers again. Sometimes a publisher will be hardy enough to bring it out, but the book no longer has the vigorous life it would have had its prosperity remained unbroken.

"A limited copyright law damages literature just as much as it damages the author.

"There are few books that live forty-two years. I should really like to know how many books this country has produced since it became a Republic which sill live. There are certainly not a great many, although we have published in America in that time 220,000 books.

"What is the use of putting a limit on the American books that have been published during the last century, when not more than 1000 of the total number have survived?"

205

"Twain and the Telephone," *New York Times,* 23 December 1906, 2.

"The trouble with these beautiful, novel things is that they interfere so with one's arrangements. Every time I see or hear a new wonder like this I have to postpone my death right off. I couldn't possibly leave the world until I have heard this again and again."

Mark said this as he lounged on the keyboard dais in the telharmonium music room in upper Broadway, swinging legs, yesterday afternoon. The instrument had just played the "Lohengrin Wedding March" for him.[1]

"You see, I read about this in the *New York Times* last Sunday," said he, "and I wanted to hear it. If a great Princess marries, what is to hinder all the lamps along the streets on her wedding night playing that march together? Or, if a great man should die—I, for example—they could all be tuned up for a dirge.

"Of course, I know that it is intended to deliver music all over the town through the telephone, but that hardly appeals as much as it might to a man who for years, because of his addiction to strong language, has tried to conceal his telephone number, just like a chauffeur running away after an accident.

"When I lived up in Hartford, I was the very first man, in that part of New England at least, to put in a telephone, but it was constantly getting me into trouble because of the things I said carelessly. And the family were all so thoughtless. One day when I was in the garden, fifty feet from the house, somebody on the long distance wire who was publishing a story of mine wanted to get the title.

"Well, the title was the first sentence, 'Tell him to go to hell.' Before my daughter got it through the wire and through him there was a perfect eruption of profanity in that region. All New England seemed to be listening in, and each time my daughter repeated it she did so with rising emphasis. It was awful. I broke into a cold perspiration, and while the neighborhood rang with it, rushed in and implored her to desist. But she would have the last word, and it was 'hell,' sure enough, every time.

"Soon after I moved to New York; perhaps that had something to do with my moving. When I got there and asked for a fire-proof telephone the company sent up a man to me. I opened up all my troubles to him, but he laughed and said it was all right in New York. There was a clause in their contract, he said, allowing every subscriber to talk in his native tongue, and of course they would not make an exception against me. That clause has been a godsend in my case."

Note to Interview 205

1. The "Wedding March" from the opera *Lohengrin* (1845–48) by Richard Wagner (1813–83).

206

"Mark Twain in White Greets 1907," *New York Tribune*, 1 January 1907, 2.

Dressed in the suit of spotless white which attracted so much attention in the streets of Washington a few weeks ago, Mark Twain (Samuel Clemens) celebrated the birth of the new year last night with a few friends in his home, at Fifth avenue and 9th street.[1]

"This is the famous suit I wore when I went to interview the copyright committee of Congress in Washington," said the humorist to several newspaper men during the festivities.[2] "Yes, I insist that white is the best color for men's clothes. If men were not so near insane they would appreciate the fact."

A three-act entertainment called "Champagne" was the feature of the evening. It closed with a temperance lecture by Mr. Clemens. The first act was a satire on grand opera, in which a man and woman with cracked voices screeched as they sang the high notes from various operatic selections. This was the "sham." The second act, which represented the "pain," had as its only characters a nurse holding a screeching baby. In the last act Mr. Clemens appeared bound with a red ribbon to another man, and they were labeled the "Siamese Twins."[3]

While Mr. Clemens was lecturing and decrying the evils of drink and begging his friends with tears in his eyes not to touch, taste, nor handle strong drink, his twin was drinking bottle after bottle of champagne. The liquor imbibed by Mark Twain's twin entered his system and the lecture ended with a "Hic, hic."[4]

"The selection of Mr. Hughes as Governor was the result of a political convulsion," said Mr. Clemens after the entertainment.[5] "The time may come when they will have to call upon me to become Governor. I am the real man. I am sure I would make a great Governor."

Notes to Interview 206

1. "Mark Twain in White Greets 1907," *New York Herald,* 1 January 1907, 5: A moment before the old year died Mr. Clemens became so serious that his friends were alarmed. "Listen," he commanded. An instant later there pealed through the rooms the sweet music of the chimes. "It's the telharmonium," he explained. "Auld Lang Syne" and "The Star-Spangled Banner" followed the notes having all the richness of a great orchestra.

"Twain Gives 1906 a Merry Funeral," *New York World,* 1 January 1907, 2: "I'm going to be the first man to have music on tap at his home over the telephone wire," said Mr. Clemens.

"Twain Gives Guests Music by Wire," *New York American,* 1 January 1907, 4: "Every once in a while I think I have seen it all and get ready to die, and then I see something else that looks so good that I want to live to see it completed.... Next to the day I was put in trousers," said Mr. Clemens, "this is the happiest occasion of my life."

2. See interview 200.

3. Conjoined twins were a recurrent source of humor in MT's writings from the early sketch "Personal Habits of the Siamese Twins" (1869) to *Those Extraordinary Twins* (1894).

4. "Mark Twain and Twin Cheer New Year's Party," *New York Times,* 1 January 1907, 1: "We come from afar," said Mark. "We come from very far; very far, indeed—as far as New Jersey. We are the Siamese twins, but we have been in this country long enough to know something of your customs, and we have learned as much of your language as it is written and spoke as—well—as the newspapers. We are so much to each other, my brother and I, that what I eat nourishes him and what he drinks—ahem!—nourishes me. I often eat when I don't really want to because he is hungry, and, of course, I need hardly tell you that he often drinks when I am not thirsty. I am sorry to say that he is a confirmed consumer of liquor—liquor, that awful, awful curse—while I, from principle, and also from the fact that I don't like the taste, never touch a drop. It has often been a source of considerable annoyance to me, when going about the country lecturing on temperance, to find myself at the head of a procession of white-ribbon people—so drunk I couldn't see," he said. "But I am thankful to say that my brother has reformed." At this point the Siamese brother surreptitiously took a drink out of a flask. "He hasn't touched a drop in three years." Another drink. "He will never touch a drop. Thank God for that." Several drinks. "And if, by exhibiting my brother to you, I can save any of you people here from the horrible curse of the demon rum!" Mark fairly howled, "I shall be satisfied." Just then apparently some of the rum or the influence of it got through the pink ribbon. Mark hiccoughed several times. "Zish is wonderful reform—" Another drink. "Wonder'l 'form we are 'gaged in. Glorious work—we doin' glorious work—glori-o-u-s work. Best work ever done, my brother and work of reform, reform work, glorious work. I don' feel jus' right." The company by this time was hysterical with laughter. Mark was staggering about on the improvised stage, apparently horribly under the influence. His brother still held the bottle and was still putting it to the use for which it was made.

New York World: While Mr. Clemens was talking a wagon was drawn upon the stage. In it sat a bewhiskered old gentleman whom Mark immediately recognized as the year 1906. "There he comes butting in," said Twain. "He doesn't know when to quit."

5. Charles Evans Hughes (1862–1948), governor of New York from 1907 to 1910; associate justice of the Supreme Court from 1910 to 1916; Republican candidate for president in 1916; U.S. secretary of state from 1921 to 1929; and chief justice of the Supreme Court from 1930 to 1941.

New York Herald: "For New York for the New Year," said Mr. Clemens, "my best wishes are for a good government. If it is better now than it has been it is a matter for congratulation. It's very seldom that we have a Mr. Hughes in the Governor's chair, and then only because of a popular convulsion. And how long can we expect to have a Hughes? Why, you can't tell but what you'll have to vote even for me before long."

207

"Little Old N.Y. Is Good Enough for Me—Twain," *New York Evening Journal,* 9 January 1907 (late edition), 4.

Mark Twain, accompanied by his secretary, Miss Isabel Lyon, and the Rev. Dr. Joseph Twichell, arrived on the Bermuda line steamship *Bermudian,* which docked today.[1] The celebrated humorist, with several friends, left New York about two weeks ago for a pleasure trip to Bermuda.

"I went away for pleasure, and I got a broadside of it," he said as he left the steamer. "We had a pleasant voyage both ways, spent enjoyable days in Bermuda, and the trip altogether was satisfactory.

"Bermuda may be all right," continued the white flannels exponent, "but you may say that little old New York is good enough for Mark Twain.

"Oh, yes. My health! Why, it was never worse in my life," he concluded, with a chuckle.

The large crowd which had gathered to greet the humorist was considerably disappointed when he made his appearance. The cause of this was the fact that his white flannels, which recently created such a furor in Washington, were conspicuous by their absence.

"No; I have not abandoned them," he said in explanation. "I wore them while in Bermuda, and they proved very comfortable.[2]

"I intend remaining in New York for some time to come," he said as he hurried away with Dr. Twichell. . . .

Notes to Interview 207

1. Isabel Van Kleek Lyon (1863–1958), MT's private secretary from 1902 until 1909. On Twichell, see n. 1 to interview 2. The 5,530-ton *Bermudian* was built in 1904 for the Quebec SS Co.

2. "Mark Twain Back, Symphony in Gray," *New York Herald,* 10 January 1907, 7:

"Don't say I went to Bermuda for my health," said Mark Twain yesterday, as he stepped ashore from the steamship *Bermudian,* just in from the green isle: "I went down there for a rest. I have plenty of health—health enough to give away, health that I have never used, health in [the] bank. It was a rest I wanted and I went to Bermuda to get it."

The humorist returned a symphony in gray. He was asked about the white suit, the one that startled Washington so much.

"Oh, I wore that all the time I was in Bermuda," he explained, "and all said it exactly suited my complexion and style of beauty."

"Where are you going now, Mr. Clemens?"

"New York; no further. I'll probably stay here the rest of my life."

208

"Tributes to Poet by Men of Letters," *New York Times* pictorial section, 24 February 1907, 4.

It was about the time of the publication of *The Innocents Abroad* that Mark Twain came East to lecture. His lecture tours took him to New England, where he soon came in contact with the poet Longfellow.[1] To a *Times* reporter he relates as follows his recollections of the latter:

"I first lectured in New York in '67. The next year I lectured in Boston—I was always lecturing in those days. But on that first Boston occasion there was no Longfellow present, so far as I can remember. On that visit I called on Holmes. Again, another time, soon after that, my wife and I called on Emerson. Nothing happened. But—yes, yes, we went once, Mrs. Clemens and I, just about that time, and took luncheon with Longfellow at Craigie House. And then there was another time, during the same visit, when I was present at a little dinner given in Boston to Wilkie Collins.[2] Longfellow was there, and [Ralph Waldo] Emerson, Whittier, Holmes, Whipple, J. T. Fields, and J. T. Trowbridge.[3] Trowbridge survives. I also survive—ostensibly. The others are dead. I used to meet all those men with some little frequency—before they had passed away, of course—in those early days at Fields' house, both before and after Fields' death. Unhappily for the purposes of this Longfellow reminiscence, there was no striking incident, so far as I can recall, connected with my contact with Mr. Longfellow; whereas, with those others it was different. In my various contacts with them things happened to happen that have left little landmarks in my memory and which might be edifying to relate if we were not on the subject of Longfellow.

"In my mind's eye, however, I only see Mr. Longfellow. I see his silky white hair, his benignant face, as he appeared to me surrounded by his friends. But I don't hear his voice. It may be that things happened in his case, also, that left an impression in my memory. But at the present moment I can't recall them.

"I remember that there were dinners in those days, just as there are now.

One dinner that I especially recall took place just thirty years ago. This dinner was given in honor of Whittier's seventieth birthday. I was invited to attend. I thought I was going to do one of the gayest things in my whole career. But things happened differently, and before I left I had turned that dinner into a funeral. What did I do? The time has not yet come for a recital of those painful events.[4] I will publish a full account of it, however, in my *Autobiography*, which is running along indefinitely in the *North American Review*. The feeling of remorse for the part I took on that festive occasion has gone away now. But I confess that for two years after that dinner I used to kick myself regularly every morning for half an hour on account of what I had done.

"Speaking of affairs of this kind, I have one most poignant recollection connected with Mr. Longfellow. This was not a dinner. It was a thing that happened not long after his death, when there was a Longfellow Memorial Authors' Reading in the Globe Theatre, in Boston. This reading was to begin at 2 o'clock in the afternoon. I was number three in the list of readers. The piece I was to read would ordinarily take twelve minutes to finish; but by art and hard work I reduced its length to ten and a half minutes before I carried it to Boston. My train was to leave Boston for New York at 4 o'clock. I vacated the stage of that theatre the moment I had finished my brief stunt, and I had only barely time left in which to catch that train. When I left, third in the list, as I have said, that orgy had already endured two hours. Six other readers were still to be heard from, and not a man in the list experienced enough in the business to know that when a person has been reading twelve minutes the audience feel that he ought to be gagged, and that when he has been reading fifteen minutes they know that he ought to be shot. I learned afterward—at least I was told by a person with an average reputation for trustworthiness, that at 6 o'clock half the audience had been carried out on stretchers, and that the rest were dead—with a lot of readers still to hear from."

Notes to Interview 208

1. Henry Wadsworth Longfellow (1807–82), American poet.
2. Wilkie Collins (1824–89), English novelist.
3. John Greenleaf Whittier (1807–92), Quaker poet and abolitionist. Oliver Wendell Holmes (1809–94), American poet and novelist and author of *The Autocrat of the Breakfast Table* (1858). E. P. Whipple (1819–86), American critic and lecturer. James T. Fields (1817–81), a prominent Boston publisher and editor of the *Atlantic Monthly* from 1861 to 1871. J. T. Trowbridge (1827–1916), American novelist and poet.
4. At a dinner on December 1877 hosted by the *Atlantic Monthly* to honor the poet John Greenleaf Whittier on his seventieth birthday, MT narrated a tale about a visit to a Nevada miner's cabin by three bums named Ralph Waldo Emerson, Oliver Wendell Holmes, and Henry Wadsworth Longfellow—with the three men actually in the audience. See also *Auto* (1990), 230–37; and Paine, 607–10.

209

"Mark Twain Sails South," *New York Herald*, 17 March 1907, sec. 1, 12.

Few persons who yesterday gathered at the pier of the *Bermudian* to see that vessel and her voyagers start on their way for the breezy Bermudas, failed to recognize in a white flannelled, white haired man who strode up her gangplank America's humorist, described on the passenger list as "The Honorable Samuel L. Clemens," and known to the rest of the world as Mark Twain.

"I am in search," said "The Honorable Samuel L.," "of rest, British humor, and an opportunity to appear logical in March in a suit of white flannels."

Mr. Clemens said he expected to be absent for several weeks and would then return to look after that farm of his which he recently bought in Connecticut.

210

"Mark Twain's Wanderings at an End," *New York Times*, 31 March 1907, 3.

Mark Twain is at last to have a home of his own building. He has wandered around the world for fifty years. Some of the time he had no home at all. In other years Missouri, Nevada, London, Paris, Berlin, Florence, and Vienna claimed him as their own. For a long time he had houses in Buffalo, New Haven,[1] and New York, where his family lived. Still he wandered around the world, writing and lecturing. So numerous were these abiding places that a reporter sought him at his residence in lower Fifth Avenue one evening last week to straighten the matter out. The famous author explained the doubtful points. He chatted of art for awhile. He exploded some of the stories told about himself—or rather put them in a way that robbed them of their traditional point.

Mark Twain, or Mr. Samuel L. Clemens in private life, made a distinction between a dwelling place and a home.

"If a man spends a month or two in a place," he said, "the surroundings grow to be familiar. Yet he may not feel at home. If he spends a couple of years there he may come to look on the place as his home." . . .

"The Celebrated Jumping Frog of Calaveras," one of Mark Twain's most noted stories, brought him fame in 1867. The chat drifted to this little masterpiece.

"You attribute much of your success in telling the story to the pause before the last words, do you not?" asked the reporter.

"There is a knack in telling such a story," Mr. Clemens replied. "You must know exactly how long to hold your audience before coming to the point of the joke. After some experience I could tell how long the pause should be to the moment. The length of such a pause differs from time to time and with different audiences. Circumstances may alter it. Even such a little thing as a person coughing in an audience will hurry the point."

"It is the same principle, then, that governs an actor when he gains the attention of an audience by moving, or 'holding a scene,' as he calls it?"

"That is the idea exactly. One of the best examples I remember was Mr. Herne's acting in the last scene of *Shore Acres*.[2] You remember there was a long silence before the curtain fell. The actor's movements and expression were telling the story. Then came the final moment—an absolute pause, a final impression conveyed by it. That is the best way I can illustrate the value of a pause."

The conversation turned again to the home in Buffalo. . . . "Most of your admirers when they think of the Buffalo house," said the reporter, "will recall a favorite story about your life there. Mrs. Clemens, so the anecdote goes, urged you to pay a neighborly call on a family living across the street. You put it off from day to day. Finally you strolled across the street to visit them. It was summer, and several of the family were sitting on the front veranda. They rose to welcome you. 'We're so glad you called,' one of them said. Then you replied: 'I should have come before. I've dropped over now to say your house is on fire.'"

"It didn't happen in exactly that way," Mr. Clemens replied. "I certainly did tell them their house was on fire. Perhaps I did stroll across the street. Nowadays I would probably run. Age makes a lot of difference when you're telling your neighbors about a fire." . . .

The Hartford home is the one most closely identified with his name. So is a story of Mark Twain and Mrs. Harriet Beecher Stowe,[3] one of his neighbors. Mr. Clemens' version of this anecdote exploded the popular conception of the yarn. It also gave an insight into a humorist's idea of humor.

"The version I've heard," said the reporter, "is that you called on Mrs. Stowe one day to find on your return that you had neither a collar nor a necktie on. Then, it is said, you wrapped a collar and a necktie in paper and sent it to Mrs. Stowe with the message that 'here is the rest of me.'"

"The incident was not like that," replied Mr. Clemens. "Mrs. Stowe and my family were neighbors and friends. We lived close to each other, and there were no fences between. I had a collar on when I made the call, but found when I got back that I had forgotten my necktie. I sent a servant to Mrs. Stowe with the necktie on a silver salver. The note I sent with it was ceremonious. It contained a formal apology for the necktie. I'm sorry now I didn't keep a copy of that letter. It had to be ceremonious. Anything flippant on such an occasion and between such close friends would have been merely silly." . . .

Mark Twain's declaration twelve years ago that he would pay his debts by a lecture tour around the world is well remembered. He was a man of 60 at the time. In some ways his task was more difficult than that of Sir Walter Scott when he wrote some of his greatest novels under a burden of debt.[4]

But Twain was very popular as a lecturer. Theaters and halls were not large enough to hold the crowds that gathered at the doors. The proceeds of the lecture tour, the book *Following the Equator* that grew out of it, and his other publications not only paid his debts but replenished his fortunes. After his lecture tour came the years of residence in Europe.

"I suppose you could call the dwellings we occupied in Europe our homes. In England we lived near London and the home of Mr. Gladstone.[5] Two years were spent in Paris. That house was a fine one. It had been built by a man who was both an architect and an artist. What fine large rooms there were! And everywhere were suggestions of a painter's home.

"Then there were the two years in Vienna and about the same time in Berlin. It was while we were living there in 1891 that the Emperor William asked me to dinner. Yes, I meant what I wrote about that dinner. The Emperor did most of the talking. If I could entertain him I would feel I had a right to talk most of the time, too.[6]

"In Florence we spent about two more years. We occupied La Capponcina, a villa near the city with a beautiful view of the Pistoria Mountains. *Joan of Arc* was written at Florence. The villa is now occupied by the Italian poet D'Annunzio."[7] ...

Notes to Interview 210

1. Hartford, not New Haven.
2. *Shore Acres* by the American playwright James A. Herne (1839-1901) was first produced in 1893. See the stage direction at the end of Act 4 (New York: French, 1928), 121.
3. Harriet Beecher Stowe (1811-96) was the author of *Uncle Tom's Cabin* (1852).
4. After the failure of John Ballantyne and Co. in 1826, Sir Walter Scott (1771-1832) pledged to repay the firm's indebtedness of £130,000.
5. William Ewart Gladstone (1809-98), former prime minister of Great Britain.
6. MT was the guest of honor at a dinner hosted by Kaiser Wilhelm II in Berlin on 20 February 1892. See Paine, 940.
7. Gabriele D'Annunzio (1863-1938), Italian poet, novelist, and playwright.

211

"Cub Reporter Has Interview with Mark Twain: Humorist Asks Himself One Question," *Elmira Advertiser*, 4 April 1907, 5.

For an hour last evening the youngest reporter on the *Advertiser*, first by hints, then by pleadings, and finally by a direct demand sought an assignment to interview Mark Twain.

"What do you wish to ask Mr. Clemens?" inquired the city editor.

"Oh, I don't know; I'll think of something on the way up to General Langdon's,"[1] answered the scribe. "Wherever Mark Twain goes, they always interview him, don't they?" and to this argument there was no convincing defense.

So away started the reporter, smiling joyfully at his success in securing the assignment.

"Ask him what he thinks of the new forward movement in Elmira," finally directed the city editor.

"Ask him what progress is being made with the movement toward the monument to Adam," yelled a man at another desk.

"Ask him to write an article on 'How Best to Keep Elmira Going Ahead,'" came another voice from an inner corner of the office.

"Ask Mr. Clemens if he wore his white suit from New York to Elmira," said the telegraph editor, as the reporter, filled with the importance of his mission, finally fled from the office.

But to obtain the much desired interview was found to be quite another matter. Resting after the fatigue of the day, Mr. Clemens was found in the handsome library of General Langdon's Main Street home. Members of the family and Mr. Clemens had just finished dinner and the humorist was now smoking.

To the *Advertiser*'s representative it was explained that Mr. Clemens positively could not be interviewed.

"I have really nothing to say," said the well-known former Elmiran. Then seeing the look of disappointment spreading over the face of his inquisitor, the hero of many a good story appeared to relent.

"Will you really be badly disappointed if you can't get something from me?" asked the veteran author, kindly.

"Yes, I will," came the answer stoutly, but with an uncontrollable quaver.

"Well, then, I'll tell you what we'll do. I have not been 'interviewed' in a long time. In fact, I stopped being interviewed some time ago, but you just ask any questions you wish and answer them for yourself, and we'll see how you manage it. But wait—ask me what I think of the new forward movement in Elmira, and I'll tell you that I think it is one of the most gratifying things I have known of in a long time. I am delighted to observe the greatly changed aspect of things here, and I can to some extent, appreciate the effort it has cost. I think Elmira is the ideal location for our big new organ industry as well as for all the other new concerns you are endeavoring to bring here. I appreciate the spirit in which the *Advertiser* seeks to obtain my views, and I deeply appreciate the honors that all wish to do me, but really, I would rather have my time to myself while here. I am just making a family visit and want to have all my time undisturbed."

Note to Interview 211

1. Charles Langdon (1849–1916) was the brother of MT's wife. The Langdon family mansion was at the corner of Church and Main streets in Elmira.

212

"Mark Twain Is Going to Be a Buccaneer," *New York American*, 23 April 1907, 5.

Mark Twain is going to be a buccaneer!

That is the startling act he made known down on old West Eighth street yesterday morning, between determined puffs at one of his celebrated cheroots. He emphasized his declaration by laying stress on the fact that the Peace Conference had just ended.[1]

"Yes, I'm going to be a buccaneer," said the humorist, with only the faintest twinkle of his eye. "No pirate of finance, but just a carefree ocean searcher for havens of pleasure aboard the yacht of a friend of mine.

"And I'm a young buck, too," Mr. Clemens continued. "I never felt better in my life, and I'd have you know that I'm over seventy-one years young at that.

"The bucks and buccaneers on this cruise to the Spanish Main will be the guests of Henry H. Rogers, aboard his yacht *Kanawha*.[2] We expect to have a bully time, and our first port of entry will be Jamestown, where we go to see the naval review."[3]

Mr. Clemens became grave a moment after this last remark when he was asked if attending a naval review almost immediately after the termination of the Peace Conference did not smack of warlike leanings.

"You see, it's this way," he said solemnly. "I don't know a thing about peace, so how can I attempt to either extol or decry the efforts of those estimable persons who fought their way into the convention at Carnegie Hall.

"Of course, people always love to get up and shout about things they don't really know anything about. That's human nature, and as long as there are people on the earth there are always going to be esoteric discussions about the beauties of peace.

"But I am afraid that I will have to attend that naval review. There's something inspiring about seeing a lot of big warships that seem to say: 'Now, be good and there won't be any trouble, but if you aren't good and peaceful, then look out.'

"And I tell you," said Mr. Clemens, as he paused and lifted his right arm, "human nature hasn't changed in the past five thousand years. Mankind hasn't changed a whole lot, and the millennium of universal peace isn't very much nearer than a year or so ago, when the Russians and Japs were at each other's throats.[4] Even opera-bouffe revolutions, where a few hundreds are shot down in Central America, give an intimation of what all this talk about peace really amounts to. I guess the people that attend the peace conventions haven't been in such positions yet.

"It seems to me the nations are a good deal like the little boy who knocked the chip off the other little boy's shoulder—somebody was very apt to get hurt. Of course, it all depends, though, upon whether the little boy with the chip on his shoulder really wants to fight. But he has the desire to hit the other little boy, even if he doesn't do it for matters of policy.

"As far as I'm concerned, I don't know whether I'm a man of peace or not. Certainly I could get up and shout for peace, whatever that means, just as well as any of the rest of us. Then I might get mad afterward and do just what I had been declaring, with the utmost positiveness, that I wouldn't and oughtn't to do.

"But peace conventions are a good thing for the world. They set a shining example of what people think they will do before the occasion arises that might precipitate the unleashing of the martial canines.

"Meanwhile, I guess it's a mighty good thing to have a whacking big navy. In times of peace prepare to have peace continued. Anyway, this old buccaneer is going down to Jamestown to see the naval review and I wouldn't be a bit surprised if some of the peace delegates are there, too, thinking after all that Uncle Sam can lick all creation.

"I shall never forget the great naval review I attended at Portsmouth, England, several years ago.[5] We were aboard one of the inspection boats, and most of the war vessels were of the old-fashioned square-rigged variety. We passed through a long lane of water flanked on either side by England's former fighting ships, with the sailors ranged along the yardarms. It was an example of a great fighting race, which has survived by being able to fight for its rights and its own."

Notes to Interview 212

1. The National Arbitration and Peace Conference was held at Carnegie Hall in New York 14-17 April 1907.

2. Henry H. Rogers (1840-1909), vice-president of Standard Oil Co. and one of MT's best friends since 1893, helped to sort out MT's finances after his bankruptcy. See also *Auto* (1959), 259-60: "Mr. Rogers was a great man. . . . He was great in more ways than one." Built in 1899 and bought by Rogers in 1901, the *Kanawha* was, according to MT, "the fastest steam yacht in American waters" (*Auto* [1959], 326).

3. The naval review at Jamestown on 2 May 1907, part of the Jamestown Exposition to mark the three hundredth anniversary of the founding of the settlement, featured sixteen U.S. battleships.

4. The Russo-Japanese War (1904–5).

5. MT described the naval review at Portsmouth in "Mark Twain Hooks the Persian out of the English Channel," written on 26 June 1873 during the visit to England of the Shah of Persia and published in the *New York Herald* on 11 July 1873. See also note 3 to interview 15.

213

"Marooned Mark Twain," *Norfolk (Va.) Ledger-Dispatch*, 1 May 1907, 7.

Mark Twain was marooned at Old Point Comfort on the yacht *Kanawha*, and so far from Fifth Avenue that he says he will never look upon the Washington Monument again;[1] that was the whisper that went around the lots or at the Hotel Chamberlin yesterday.[2]

Mark himself held a reporter with his glittering eye and drowned the blare of the loud basso in the dining room in recounting his modern version of the ancient mariner's tale.

"Here I am," said the author, nervously flicking a bit of cigar ashes from his copyrighted white flannel suit. "Here I am alone on Mr. H. H. Rogers' yacht *Kanawha* anchored out there and not one saint to look down in pity.[3]

"Rogers has gone home. His son, Harry, has gone and the only remaining guest that came down to this merry exposition opening last Friday says he is going back to New York tonight. But I cannot go. For two days we have been held up by the fog out by the Capes, and the navigation officer says that he won't risk the passage.

"I simply will not go back by train, so here I remain, pacing the boards of the *Kanawha* or the carpets of the Chamberlin, utterly, unforgivably alone. I think of that Fifth avenue and of the dear omnibus trundling up and down from the monument and I feel that I am without a country."

Mr. Clemens bit deep into his cigar end and went on to explain that he had come down as Mr. Rogers' guest on the *Kanawha* to witness the opening of the exposition, believing in his innocence that he would straightway be carried back to New York and his work after the show was over.[4] But when the fogs of the last three days chained up the Capes and the navigation officer on the yacht would not move anchor one inch, Mr. Clemens had the alternative of taking the train back with his host or waiting on the pleasure of the weather bureau. Since he detests railroad travel, he says that there is no alternative, and that he will remain a marooned mariner until the fog lifts. . . .

Notes to Interview 213

1. The arch in Washington Square Park, designed by the architect Stanford White (1853–1906) and dedicated in 1896, was a short walk from MT's home at 21 Fifth Avenue.

2. One of the most fashionable resorts in Virginia, opened in 1896.
3. See n. 2 to interview 212.
4. See n. 3 to interview 212.

214

"Twain Hesitates to Admit He's Dead," *New York American,* 5 May 1907, I, 6.

Sitting comfortably in his armchair at his home, No. 21 Fifth avenue, Mark Twain yesterday puffed at a big, black cigar and genially talked of how he wasn't lost at sea. *The Times* had printed a dispatch from Virginia[1] stating that Mr. Clemens, who was on H. H. Rogers's yacht *Kanawha,*[2] probably had been drowned, it being supposed—according to the paper—that the *Kanawha* had been wrecked.

The venerable humorist gravely strode to a mirror, looked at himself, pinched himself, found his name in the directory, and then, just as gravely, turned to the reporter and said: "You may tell those friends of mine who are quaking and preparing to write my obituary that, in my opinion, the rumor of my having been lost at sea is somewhat overdrawn. I do not honestly believe that I was drowned, but I shall inaugurate a most rigorous investigation to determine whether I am alive or dead, or if I have been lost or stolen.[3]

"To the best of my knowledge and belief, I arrived Wednesday night from Norfolk on the yacht. Should I find that I have been killed or have strayed away, I assure you that I shall at once inform the public.

"It is my sincere hope that I am not dead or lost."

Mr. Clemens then took another big puff at the huge cigar, settled back in his chair and added, "We shall now ponder this matter."

Notes to Interview 214

1. See "Twain and Yacht Disappear at Sea," *New York Times,* 4 May 1907, 1. MT refers in the dispatch to the delay in his return to New York: "Here I am, all alone on H. H. Rogers's yacht anchored out there, and not a saint to look down in pity. Rogers has gone home, his son Harry has gone, and the only remaining guest that came down to this Exposition opening says he is going back to New York tonight, but I cannot go. . . . I simply will not go back by train," he remarked. "I declare that I feel like 'the Man Without a Country.' I pine for Fifth Avenue and the dear old coaches, to say nothing of the arch in Washington Square."

2. See n. 2 to interview 212.

3. "Not Lost, Says Twain," *New York Tribune,* 5 May 1907, 6: "However," he told a group of reporters yesterday, "you can assure all my friends that I will make an exhaustive and rigid investigation of the rumor, and if there is any foundation for the story I will at once apprise an anxious public of the facts."

"Mark Twain Investigating," *New York Times,* 5 May 1907, 2: "You can assure my Virginia friends . . . that I will make an exhaustive investigation of this report that I have been lost at sea. If there is any foundation for the report, I will at once apprise the anxious public. I sincerely hope that there is no foundation for the report, and I also hope that judgment will be suspended until I ascertain the true state of affairs."

215

"'I'm Not Lost at Sea,' Says Twain," *New York World*, 5 May 1907, 9.

... Mr. Twain got back to New York on Wednesday evening last on the *Kanawha*,[1] and his arrival was duly reported the following morning. Until yesterday he was at his home at No. 21 Fifth avenue, when he went into the country to stay until tomorrow.

"I see you are lost in the fog, Mr. Twain," said a neighbor yesterday morning, who met him in front of his house.

"Lost in a fog? What do you mean?" The neighbor passed him the paper which contained the Norfolk dispatch.[2]

"Well, I'll—." Then he broke out into a laugh and added:

"If the young man that wrote that ever comes to New York he will make a hit writing fiction for the ten-cent magazines."

Notes to Interview 215

1. See n. 2 to interview 212.
2. See n. 1 to interview 214. See also "Not Lost, Says Twain," *New York Tribune*, 5 May 1907, 6: It was just this way. Mr. Rogers saw that there was a heavy fog and that the trip home would be delayed, so he jumped on a train, the humorist deciding to stay aboard even if she went down. He got chummy with the skipper, and the skipper said it was all right, the yacht would poke her nose under Williamsburg Bridge a few minutes after 9 Wednesday night.

216

"Mark Twain Tells Literary Secret and Many Other Things," *Baltimore News*, 10 May 1907, 13.

Samuel L. Clemens is 71 years old. Stored in his brain are the memories of two generations and the acquired recollections of a world's history. He looks more than his years. He has been a very busy man. He has accomplished much, and he has much yet to accomplish, for, waiting for his train connections at Camden Station yesterday morning, he said that he expected to work until the end of his life. He came into Baltimore on the train arriving at 2:47 o'clock yesterday afternoon, accompanied by Miss Lyon, his secretary.[1] On the platform were Governor Warfield and Colonel E. L. Woodside to escort him to Annapolis on the 3:30 train.[2] Senator Rayner was there,[3] waiting for his train to Washington, and he and the Governor stood apart and chatted until it came in, and the hospitality committee hurried toward the rear to Mr. Clemens' car. The famous man had hardly set foot on the platform when

Colonel Woodside grasped his hand, and then Governor Warfield came up and beamed. The Governor introduced the newspapermen. Among them was one who covers the Governor's office in Baltimore.

"The city editors of the papers," said Governor Warfield, "assign their various men to various parts of the work, and here's one from each paper whose duty it is to call at my office every day and inquire what news there may be in administrative circles. These men are faithful, very faithful, about it."

"Exactly," murmured Mr. Clemens, who, like the Governor, was formerly a newspaperman.

Mr. Clemens preferred not to use the elevator from the tunnel level to the upper platform. Thank you very much, but he shook his head emphatically, put his hands defiantly into the pockets of his white flannel coat and stepped forward, with his hand on the Governor's arm. A few curious ones upstairs watched him as he passed, his shoulders erect, his tangled hair floating, the white mane of a literary lion. Around by the Annapolis track a photographer had set his camera. He took his hat off and approached the party. Half of this reverence was for Mark Twain, the other half for Mr. Warfield. The Governor listened and then turned to his guest.

"Mr. Clemens," he said, "these young men have heard of your coming and would like to take your picture."

Mr. Clemens looked bored. He had probably had his picture taken before. But he turned the thing into a big laugh, and stood up with the Governor, while all others kept off the artistic grass. Then, while the Governor stood solidly and officially, and Twain's face was all wrinkled up in a huge laugh about something, there was a click of the shutters, then another, and the photographer gratefully whispered that he'd send him a copy. Mr. Clemens was overpowered.

"If this train isn't ready to move," said the humorist at the car platform, "I believe I'll stand out here and get some fresh air."

"Hey! boy," shouted the Governor to one of half a dozen scurrying deck hands, who seemed to be chiefly interested in the executive's guest, "have you got all those parcels on?"

"Yes, sir, Mr. Governor."

"Very well, then," and the Governor asked Mr. Clemens his opinion about cornbread.

"Ah! there's no cornbread in the North," said the humorist. "You can get it anywhere in the South, but in the North they don't seem to know how to make it," and this was with a lingering drawl, characteristic of the man.[4]

"Mr. Clemens"—from a ubiquitous journalist—"is it true that you were lost as sea on H. H. Rogers' yacht, after leaving Norfolk?"[5]

"Well, that is a matter of some conjecture, but I am looking into it. There was a very peculiar coincidence about that. I was lost, I believe, on May 2, and the news of the disaster reached New York the next day. While I was battling with the waves in my study I read all about it in the dispatches.[6] On the same day I had cabled an acceptance to Whitelaw Reid, in response to a cabled offer of the degree of bachelor of letters in Oxford[7]—an honor which, I believe, is a rare one extended to any man on this side of the waters—and I have no doubt that over in the Embassy at London they received my cablegram after having the news of my disappearance, which must have puzzled them. They may be figuring yet how the drowning man managed to cable.[8] Perhaps I struck a merman station down below and tapped the cable. Anyhow, that would have been a very ingenious expedient."

One of the charter members of the American Press Humorists, an organization which meets this fall in Los Angeles, was present and delivered a formal invitation to Mr. Clemens to be the special guest of that body this year.

"No, indeed!" said Mr. Clemens. "I would like to be there, but I have made my last long land journey. I never expect to go farther than from New York to Washington by rail. I may have said that I would never take another sea trip, but if I ever did I'll make an exception of this Oxford journey. I don't like the trains. They wobble. I intend to leave on June 8 for Europe, to take my Oxford degree on June 26, and I shall go in a cattle boat because it is the most comfortable. The cattle down below naturally sway their bodies against the motion of the boat, keeping it steady. Yes, I shall go on a cattle boat, and I shall travel on the main deck."[9]

The train was ready to move.[10] The Governor piled aboard; Mark Twain piled aboard; the newspapermen piled aboard. Up in the center of the car there was a sacred section saved for the party. The Governor and the humorist's secretary took the seat facing front, and gave Mr. Clemens the seat riding backward, because the humorist would rather ride backward on the Annapolis Short Line. Someone remarked that riding backward on the Short Line was much like riding frontward on any other road. Mr. Clemens smiled, but refused to commit himself. He began to talk shop, and very interesting shop it was. He was asked if it was true that he had given up writing forever.

"I shall never write with the pen again," he said. "I am dictating my autobiography, and that is not literature; that is narrative.[11] You can't write literature with your mouth. And in my autobiography I have invented what William Dean Howells says is the most unique thing in the history of recent letters by combining autobiography and diary, without any reference to chronological placing of events.[12] It makes me sick to pick up a narrative that works you all up to the highest pitch and then runs into a paragraph: 'But of this we shall speak further in its proper place!' There you've got your reader worked up to that very incident, looking for what is going to happen next, and then you throw a pitcher of ice water down his back! I am jumping from 1847 to 1902, back to 1864 and then into the time of the Pilgrim fathers, to take a dip into the future about 2000, and then come back home again. That is the natural form of narrative. Here in our hour's chat we will jump all over the country and the century, which simply proves the point. I have to see the interest from my reader's standpoint. What interests me will interest him."

"But was there no objection on the part of your publishers as to the innovation?"

Mr. Clemens laughed. "If there had been, it would have been pitched out the window. No, I hardly expect any objection."

The conversation wandered through every subject from boiling cabbage to raising babies, and rambled into journalism.

"You know, Mr. Clemens," said Governor Warfield, "I was once a newspaperman. Yes, indeed, I owned a country newspaper and used to get potatoes and wood in lieu of cash. A trick the advertising agents had in those days was to send us a check far below our advertising rates, with a blank year's contract, and they'd always send it toward the end of the week, knowing we would be hard up for cash."

Then Mark Twain told a secret. "Everything I have ever written," he said, "has had a serious philosophy or truth as its basis. I would not write a humorous work merely to be funny. In *Yankee in King Arthur's Court*, for instance, the fun is all natural to the situations, but the underlying purpose is a satire on the divine right of kings. My *Joan of Arc*, published in 1892, was the first of the historical novels, and it was not a pretense of history; it was real history; and after it came the school of historical novel writers, with their deluge of historical tales. But *Joan of Arc* started it all."

"Will you leave any unfinished works?"

"Oh! yes; five of them. What are they, Miss Lyon?"

The humorist and his secretary cudgeled their memories and searched the salt barrel of literature for the titles. This was the result:

"Which Was It?"

"The Mysterious Stranger."

"The Adventures of a Microbe."

"Refuge of the Derelicts."

"Captain Stormfield's Visit to Heaven."[13]

"They are all unfinished and will be left to my daughter, who will be my literary executor. They will never be completed, excepting possibly 'Captain Stormfield's Visit,' which I shall complete by chopping off the last chapter and letting it go. It was written 39 years ago, and all that time I have been afraid to publish it, because it is a satire on the work of a man who still lives. Were he dead, so that it would not injure him, I would publish it."

The chat drifted naturally back to country papers, and Mr. Clemens told of his observation of the keen local interest which keeps the oft-repeated personal item in constant limelight.

"It is like the Court Circular," he said, "and in just that degree interesting. Where everyone knows everyone and is interested in the individual, the court circular of the country town is the newspaper of the community."

Mr. Clemens referred to the collapse of the Webster publishing house, his publishers, and his eyes filled with tears as he recounted the famous struggle which ended only when he, by his personal efforts, involving a lecture tour of the world, paid penny for penny more than $100,000 of liabilities.

"The payment of that debt," he said, "was the happiest incident of my life. I value its memory more than all my work; more than all my royalties; more than fame, name, or anything material. When the publishing house failed letters began to pour in upon me from people I had never heard of, and, although I was already broke, it kept me broke again paying postage on checks which I returned to the generous senders. The first day after the failure I received two checks of $1000 each from men I did not know. Then creditors came to me and offered to settle at a discount, but I had to refuse them. Our home—I thought we could save that; my daughter was born there"—and his lip trembled as the tears started afresh—"but it went, too. Everything went. But it all came right in the end."

Incidental to the general talk, the subjugation of the Hereros in South Africa by the German Government was introduced by a casual reference to Lord Calvert's former estates made by Governor Warfield.[14]

"It makes my blood boil," said the humorist, "to think of the titled robbers of Europe who could give a man a piece of paper granting him vast estates not yet stolen from their real owners, but just about to be stolen. Think of Calvert in Maryland, Penn in Pennsylvania,[15] and the rest—freebooters of the worst type—coming into a country, with no right but the right of superior force, and daring to claim possession of whole States! The German thieves, directed by the sceptred thief of all, go into South Africa with a force of 30,000 men and drive a handful of the Hereros from their possessions simply because they want the territory. The Hereros made a bold and brilliant fight, considering their numbers, but they were nothing to the murderers sent by a scoundrel in ermine to cut their throats and pick their pockets. We claim to be a democratic people—a square-dealing people—but we have bought our way into the Society of Sceptred Thieves by paying $20,000,000 to a country that didn't own it for an island group [the Philippines] that we had no right to purchase. It was the stupendous joke of the century when the United States, after conquering Spain and acquiring the islands by right of conquest, gave Spain $20,000,000. What for? For the islands? Spain didn't own them. Then, what for? Why, just for this: An American goes abroad and sells his daughter to a title and buys his way into noble circles. Uncle Sam paid that $20,000,000 for his entrance fee into society—the Society of Sceptred Thieves. We are now on a par with the rest of them. We dare to turn what should be a benevolent protectorate into an autocratic monarchy!"[16]

"And you think—"

"I think that if a man has anything any government wants he might as well give up. England stole, by thievery, plunder, murder, arson, and rapine, the diamond fields of Africa, and the same brave system of government would make short work of an individual who would steal a single precious stone from a jewelry store window."

That wasn't all. He talked on a variety of subjects—enough to make a book.[17] But this is not a book.

Notes to Interview 216

I have supplemented this interview as reported in the *Baltimore News* with versions of Twain's comments published in other newspapers. All newspaper citations below are from 10 May 1910.

1. Isabel Van Kleek Lyon (1863–1958), MT's private secretary from 1902 until 1909.
2. Edwin A. Warfield (1848–1928), governor of Maryland from 1904 to 1908.
3. Isador Rayner (1850–1912), U.S. senator from Maryland from 1905 until his death.
4. "Mark Twain in Clover," *Baltimore Sun*, 14: Governor Warfield . . . asked him if they had fried chicken up North in the same way Maryland had it. . . . "No," he said slowly and with a shade of regret. "They don't know how to fry chicken north of here. The art hasn't spread there yet. You can't get anything like it anywhere except in the South." "Cornbread?" the Governor suggested. "Ah!" he replied, and anybody would have guessed that his mouth watered as he thought of it, "you can get that all over the South. They know how to bake it down here. Missouri is the place for that, but any place you go in the South the cornbread is good. I remember once when I stayed a week at a hotel in Baltimore," he continued, and his face had the look of a man who tells you how he once shook hands with the President or won a 100-to-1 shot. "When I came here I tasted perch, and I found out that it was a Baltimore specialty. I liked it. Then they gave me some kind of duck—it wasn't canvasback—and I don't remember what the name of it was, but they told me it was another one of Baltimore's good things. Well, I stayed here, doing nothing but eating and sleeping, for one week, and I didn't eat anything but perch and duck. . . . Another funny thing is that the farther South you go the better the chicken. How do you account for that? Wonder if the climate has anything to do with it? You know I believe chicken and cornbread have got a lot to do with Southern hospitality. You take a healthy man and give him a good dish of fried chicken and cornbread, and how can he feel anything else but friendly toward his fellow man? Why, a man full of chicken couldn't be anything else but liberal."

"Mark Twain an Honored Guest," *Baltimore American*, 16: "It has been some years since I was in Baltimore," continued Mr. Clemens. "This was while I was lecturing. I've forgotten the name of the hotel and what I ate, but I know the eating was good. I cannot recollect whether it was canvasback duck, or birds, or terrapin, but I was here for a week, and I know I had it, whatever it was, for every meal. I seemed to enjoy whatever it was because I had my meals in bed and they seemed to go good. I cannot recall just what I did have. I wish I could." "I remember, Mr. Clemens, in reading your memoirs, you said that nowhere in the country could they make cornbread as they do in the South," said Governor Warfield, who joined the party on the platform. "That's so," answered Mr. Clemens; "that's the only section where it is made good, and they make it better in Missouri, where I came from, than in any other section of the South."

5. See n. 2 to interview 212.

6. *Baltimore American:* "I was so busy after my return to New York from Jamestown that I did not get a chance to investigate the rumors of my death at sea, but I hope to get an opportunity soon. I will say, though, that the drowning has not discommoded me in the least. I have felt no inconvenience thus far, but I feel that in justice to my friends that I must look into the matter further. I think the report originated in this way. We had attended the Jamestown opening on Mr. Rogers' yacht and Mr. Rogers and his son having business in New York took a train for home. I didn't relish the idea of a long railroad journey and decided to remain on the yacht and go to New York with it. The afternoon of the night I was drowned a party of us were sitting in the Hotel Chamberlin, at Old Point. There was a fog outside. The yacht was anchored in full view of the hotel and could be plainly seen. At night I went aboard and the fog was still heavy. I turned in and knew nothing more until morning when I awakened to find we were on the ocean, bound up the coast. The fog had lifted at 4 A.M., so the captain told me, and we had gotten under way. When the people at Old Point missed the yacht they imagined we had sunk in the night. I wonder what my friends in England thought of my unfortunate fate when the next day they read in the papers that I had been drowned, and then on top of that receiving a cablegram from me announcing that I would sail for England on June 26? . . . However, I will look thoroughly into the matter of my death as soon as time affords."

Baltimore Sun: "I didn't know I had been drowned until they told me about it," he said. "I must have been drowned without knowing anything at all about it. I'm sure it did not discommode me any. I suffered no inconvenience at all and I really did not know I was drowned until I arrived at New York and people asked me about it. . . . The yacht was anchored in front of Old Dominion, or Old Point Comfort—whatever it is," he said, "and everybody saw her there when evening fell. The fog came up in the night," he continued, "and nobody could see the yacht. We got away at 4 o'clock the next morning, before anybody was up. The fog was clearing, and by the time it lifted we were away. Then, I suppose, they concluded that we were lost because they couldn't see us. I did not know a thing about being drowned until I got to New York."

7. On Reid, see n. 4 to interview 9; on the honorary degree from Oxford, see chapter 10.

8. *Baltimore Sun:* "I got a cablegram from the other side telling me that if I went over to Oxford University the degree of doctor of letters would be conferred on me. I wrote a telegram accepting the honor and saying that I would sail on June 28. The telegram was not sent until after I was reported drowned, and now I wonder if those Englishmen are worrying about me."

Baltimore American: "While at Old Point I received a cablegram from Whitelaw Reid, our Ambassador to England, asking me to be in that country by July 6 to receive the degree of doctor of letters from Oxford University. I replied to this from New York, naming the date. Those at the American Embassy must have figured that while on my way down to Davy Jones I had stopped long enough to tap the cable and send them the message."

9. *Baltimore Sun:* The humorist said that he intended sailing on the *Minneapolis*— "a nice, comfortable cattle ship, with only a few passengers. It's the first time I've ever gone over on a cattle boat, although I have often come back on them," he went on. "Of course, they never brought back any cattle except me," and the smile broadened and the wrinkles deepened. [Hardly a cattle boat, the *Minneapolis* was a 13,443-ton luxury passenger ship launched in 1900 by the Atlantic Transport Line.]

10. *Baltimore American:* "Near train time, isn't it?" asked Mr. Clemens, feeling for his timepiece. He fished out an open-faced gold watch with guard and gold fob and said: "It's a quarter past three. I don't know if that's the correct time. I haven't set it since noon. Yesterday it was 15 minutes fast and the day before a half hour. It's one of these go-as-you-please watches and often takes advantage of time. Miss Lyon set it right at noon and I guess it hasn't changed much."

11. *Baltimore Sun:* When asked if he intended to write any more after finishing his biography he replied: "I hardly think so, but can't tell. Writing is a relief for me. I get ideas into my head and naturally they must come out. So I just lay in bed and dictate my 'stuff' and when those thoughts are out of my head and on paper I feel better. Besides, my pocketbook feels heavier. Now, in writing my biography I don't commence with the date of my birth and continue straight through until the present day. I jump about from one happening to another, just as people do in conversation. The most aggravating thing that can happen, I think, is for a lecturer to be just about to divulge some interesting fact and then tell his hearers that he was a little bit ahead of his story and start out on something else. If it's funny or interesting tell it while it's hot and while your hearers are anxious to get it."

12. On Howells, see n. 2 to interview 2.

13. "Which Was It?" a long dream-disaster fragment begun in 1899 and abandoned in 1906. See also *Auto* (1959), 265. "The Mysterious Stranger," see n. 6 to interview 182. "The Adventures of a Microbe," see n. 5 to interview 182. "Refuge of the Derelicts," a novel fragment written in 1905–6. See also *Auto* (1959), 265–66. "Captain Stormfield's Visit to Heaven," MT worked intermittently on this incomplete satirical book for some forty years. He published "Extracts from Captain Stormfield's Visit to Heaven" in the December 1907 and January 1908 issues of *Harper's* and a fuller fragment in book form in 1909. See also *Auto* (1959), 277.

14. The Herero, the main indigenous tribe in southwestern Africa in present day Namibia, retaliated against German colonialists in 1904, prompting a genocidal German response.

Baltimore Sun: "My sympathies are also with the Hereros down in South Africa," said Mark. . . . "They are a poor downtrodden people, and they are all right, too. The atrocities that are being inflicted upon the Congo natives by the Belgians should be stopped. It's cruel, I tell you. I have lectured down in the Congo State, and I know those people. They are a simple, law-abiding race."

15. The Calverts and Penns were the proprietary families of Maryland and Pennsylvania, respectively.

16. See also note 5 to interview 133. *Baltimore Sun:* "The funniest thing [that ever happened]," he said, "was when at the close of the Spanish-American War the United States paid poor decrepit old Spain $20,000,000 for the Philippines. It was just a case of this country buying its way into good society. Honestly, when I read in the papers that this deal had been made, I laughed until my sides ached. There were the Filipinos fighting like blazes for their liberty. Spain would not hear to it. The United States stepped in, and after they had licked the enemy to a standstill, instead of freeing the Filipinos they paid that enormous amount for an island which is of no earthly account to us; just wanted to be like the aristocratic countries of Europe which have possessions in foreign waters. The United States wanted to be in the swim, and it, too, had to branch out, like an American heiress buying a Duke or an Earl. Sounds well, but that's all."

17. *Baltimore Sun:* When asked if he was going to wear his famous white dress suit at the dinner given at Government House in his honor he said: "Now, that's funny, too," and the humorist threw back his head and laughed. "Why, of course, I'm going to wear it. Why not? You just ought to see me in it. I look at least 10 years younger. Oh, no; I don't wear it because of that fact, but simply because I like the bright colors. What's the use of a man wearing mourning clothes at a reception or dance? Why isn't a white dress suit just as appropriate? It certainly would be more becoming to most men. . . . When are we going through the academy? I have been all through West Point several times and I am sure this will prove interesting. I never in my life saw such college buildings. Say, Governor, the people of this grand old Commonwealth have many things to be proud of. . . . This is a beautiful, quaint old city you have here, Governor."

217

"As Mark Twain Watched Drill," *Baltimore American,* 11 May 1907, 15.

In the first place, be it understood by the gentle reader, or the reader not so gentle for that matter, that any grammatical or rhetorical mistakes that may occur in the course of the following sentences were not perpetrated by Mr. Samuel L. Clemens or, to give him the name which he has made famous, Mark Twain. In the second place, the aforesaid sentences are not an interview; they are simply snatches of Mr. Clemens' conversation caught by the would-be interviewer and offered to the public under the impression that they are a little more interesting than many and many a labeled "interview."

The would-be interviewer traveled down from Baltimore yesterday to the quaint, picturesque and historical town of Annapolis, on the banks of the Severn River, to the Executive Mansion, where, as the guest of the Chief Executive of the State of Maryland, Governor Warfield,[1] the author of *Huckleberry Finn* is stopping. Lots of questions surged into the interviewer's mind, the subjects ranging from Mr. Clemens' opinion of the Peace Congress to his opinion of Maryland oysters. And then, when Mr. Clemens was reached, he announced that he was never interviewed, and did not express opinions without carefully thinking the subject over and writing the results down himself.

"And why do you object to being interviewed?" was the plaintive query.

"Because," and will the gentle reader remember the warning in the opening paragraph, "it is impossible for any reporter to get my exact language, my exact expression or my exact thoughts. I have often been quoted, but never, unless I have written out the interview myself, have I been quoted accurately. I do not know how it is with other writers, but my English is perfect, not through any merit of my own, but because I am a writer, and to speak and write perfect English is my profession or trade. I never use slang nor bad constructions, yet you will find that, with the exception of a very few persons who know me very well, and know what I have stated to be a fact, no one will believe this because there have been published articles which purport to be interviews from me that seem proof to the contrary. So, if I desire to give an opinion upon any subject in which I am interested, and I feel that I cannot wait a couple months until it can be published in magazine form, I write it myself and get it out.

"Then, I am under contract to Harper Brothers not to write for newspapers or to give out interviews upon any subject. To break the contract I incur a fine of $500, so, you see, I must be very much interested in a subject to be willing to do this." Mr. Clemens speaks so slowly and distinctly, it seems a pity he cannot be quoted correctly.

But that is the reason this article is not an interview with Mr. Clemens, and mistakes in English must be accredited to the would-be interviewer. Anent Mr. Clemens' remarks about perfect English, the reporter wanted awfully to ask him what he thought of Henry James' English, but he was afraid he had not given it sufficiently deep thought.

However, in answer to a query, Mr. Clemens admitted that in the majority of cases, when the interviewed was not a literary man and had not had the practice in English that the professional author necessarily has had, his expressions are apt rather to gain in quality as they pass through the hands of the newspaper writer. He also said that, while the interview was a phase of newspaper work that is receiving, perhaps, too much attention, it is a valuable phase for the lawyer or business man, whose business is benefited through his getting his opinions and interests before the public.

And with this the interviewer had to be content, to salve professional pride.

Mr. Clemens had delivered this opinion as he sat in a carriage with Governor and Mrs. Warfield and Miss Isabel Lyon, his private secretary,[2] at the drill grounds at the Naval Academy just before the afternoon drill. The early afternoon he had spent sleeping and was inaccessible, and upon his appearance at the parade grounds to see the drill he was surrounded. In the white suit that has become renowned, with his long white hair and bushy eyebrows, the veteran author was a picturesque and attractive sight. The only somber item of apparel was a black derby, which he wore only when necessary, as he apparently dislikes hats.

After he had talked for a little time Mr. Clemens wanted to smoke. Twice during his exploration of the Naval Academy grounds in the morning had he been admonished not to smoke, and he was sorely tempted to break the rule.

"I will fill the world with crime if I don't smoke," he announced, and Governor Warfield, perhaps awed at this terrible threat, said he would take unto himself the whole blame of Mr. Clemens' misdeeds. But international difficulties were averted by Mrs. Sands, the wife of Admiral Sands,[3] who at that moment drove up and invited the party to see the drill from her porch.

"Can I smoke there?" asked Mr. Clemens, and, upon being answered in the affirmative, eagerly made for the portico.

"Yes, I have smoked practically all my life," he announced, when placidly puffing a cigar, "and it has never done me any harm. I suppose I was only about 10 or 12 years old when I was commenced. It all depends upon a man's constitution what he can do."

Mr. Clemens likes automobiles, they are "so comfortable," he says, but he will never be arrested for exceeding the speed laws—he likes them to go about eight miles an hour.

"But you'd never get anywhere," was objected.

"Then I'd never go," he announced decidedly.

And he does not use a typewriter, he uses a pen for all the work he does, and dictates his autobiography. "I am accustomed to the pen, and am too old to try a typewriter now," he explained.

Mr. Clemens has a great deal of trouble because he looks like his photograph. In answer to a remark to that effect he told a story of a young girl whom we met at an evening reception. "Oh, Mr. Clemens," remarked this charmingly ingenuous demoiselle, "did anyone ever tell you how much you look like Mark Twain?" And then, there was the gentleman on the railroad train who, after gazing admiringly at the author, came up to him and said: "I feel as if I must tell you that you are enough like the pictures of Mark Twain to be his brother."

"Is that so? How interesting," was Mr. Clemens' polite rejoinder.

Then Governor Warfield told a joke that, as far as the reporter could remember, was not in any one of Mr. Clemens books. In telling the joke he set at rest any doubts as to whether it was proper to tell jokes not written by the literary celebrity present. It was told apropos of the remark made by the Governor that after seeing the splendid drilling of the soldiers Mr. Clemens would take as much interest in the Naval Academy as West Point. The story was about an old colored preacher who was interested in getting a member of his own race to join the "army of the Lord."

"Is yo' a member of the army?" he asked the colored brother.

"Yes, I is," was the answer.

"What denomination is yo'?"

"I'se a Baptist."

"Sho' yo' doan belong to de army; yo' belong to de navy."

Then Mr. Clemens talked politics—at least he said he was a "mugwump." There was a little discussion about what a "mugwump" was, especially among the ladies present, several thinking it was a renegade Democrat and several others deciding it was a renegade Republican. Mr. Clemens' definition was that it was a man who changed his mind.[4]

"There have been mugwumps ever since the world began," he said, "men who were not affiliated with any party. I would not think of attaching myself to any party; I want to change my mind every day if I feel like it. I vote for the men, not for their principles—sometimes I doubt if he has any principles."

Mr. Clemens enjoyed the drill very much. The class on parade was that which has been selected to be President Roosevelt's guard at Jamestown on President's Day, and for that reason has been given the name "Teddy Bears."[5] The music of the band at times inspired the veteran author into a slight swinging motion that led one to believe that, in spite of his 70 years, he would like to march with the boys. It was just about the close of the drill that Mr. Clemens was betrayed into what might be interpreted as an expression of opinion.

"That is a sight somewhat incongruous with the principles of the Peace Congress," was remarked.[6]

"Yes," was the answer, "but that means peace, too. Give two big nations armies and navies so large that they will be afraid of each other and they are not likely to get into a fight. I believe in a big army to preserve the peace." . . .

Mr. Clemens does not mind autograph hunters. He writes a lot of autographs, turns them over to Miss Lyon, and upon her shoulders come the requests from all over the country.

"I don't mind them—they just want a name," was the comment.

Mark Twain spoke last night in the hall of the House of Delegates, at Annapolis, to about 500 persons. His address was for the benefit of the Presbyterian Church of Annapolis, his visit to Annapolis being upon the invitation of Governor Warfield and for that purpose. Governor Warfield introduced Mr. Clemens, and said that he was one of the world's most distinguished citizens.

The humorist said he had too good a knowledge of the proprieties to dispute the words of Governor Warfield. "I believe that he is right," he added. The speaker then laid several volumes on the roster, announcing that he would read to the audience from his own works, but would first read something in the nature of a sermon—an extract from the work of another, which had impressed him deeply.

"It is a matter for the profoundest apprehension and the most gloomy forebodings," he read, "to contemplate the contrast between private American morals and public American morals." He continued to read that private morals of Americans were generally above reproach, and this sentiment suggested his first ramification from his subject. He said that private morals were not always beyond exception, and that he had known several persons whose private morals might be the subject of criticism to some extent. "Every now and then," he said, "I come across a person whose character is not perfect. I know several such persons. I am not perfect." This opened the way for the first story, and a great moral principle which it illustrated.

Mark Twain told how he had once stolen a watermelon, but withdrew the verb as too harsh, "withdrew," "retired," "extracted," he suggested as more appropriate, the last-mentioned word being the one selected as exactly fitting the case. He had done it, he said, when the man was waiting on another customer, and he had taken the watermelon to a shady alley, where he opened it and found it green. He reflected, he said, and with reflection began a struggle, his better nature striving for the mastery. He returned the watermelon. He chided the man with his falseness to the public. He obtained a ripe watermelon. He felt uplifted, the speaker said; the dealer had been made to see the error of his ways and right morals had triumphed.

"It is a matter of the profoundest apprehension and the most gloomy forebodings," resumed Mark Twain, and then he launched forth into the relation of another incident of his early youth illustrative of the struggle and the triumph of private morals.

This story concerned an incident which happened in the office of his father, who was justice of the peace, coroner, sheriff and chief of police in the local village, in fact, the personification of government. This unreasonable parent objected to his son going fishing on school days, and one day, when the latter had done so, the youth decided to spend the night on an ancient settee in his father's office. He did not know that a man had been stabbed to death and that the body had been placed in that office for the exercise of his father's duties as coroner the next day. Young Mark gained the settee without incident, but as his eyes became accustomed to the faint light of the room he thought that he perceived an unusual occupant. He firmly resolved to dismiss the idea by the exercise of moral courage. He turned to the wall, resolved to count a thousand and hoping that the vision would disappear. He turned again towards the object, and in the square of light formed by the rays of the moon through the window pane, he perceived a marble hand. He again turned to the wall, but for a short period only, and upon another gaze the square of light had traveled so that an arm and a part of a head could be seen. Again and again moral courage struggled with terror, but upon a last glance the full torso and face were revealed, lying ivory white in the moonlight. Moral courage disintegrated, amid breaking glass and cracking window sash. . . .

Notes to Interview 217

1. Edwin A. Warfield (1848–1928), governor of Maryland from 1904 to 1908.
2. Isabel Van Kleek Lyon (1863–1958), MT's private secretary from 1902 until 1909.
3. James H. Sands (1845–1911), superintendent of the U.S. Naval Academy at Annapolis from 1905 to 1907.
4. Mugwumps were liberal or reform Republicans who bolted the GOP in 1884.
5. By refusing to kill a bear on a hunting trip in Mississippi in November 1902, President Theodore Roosevelt (1858–1919) inspired a stuffed toy known as the "teddy bear."
6. The National Arbitration and Peace Conference was held at Carnegie Hall in New York 14–17 April 1907.

218

"Mighty Mark Twain Overawes Marines," *New York Times*, 12 May 1907, 4.

Annapolis, May 11—"Yes," said Mark Twain, with an air of conscious importance, "I have been arrested.[1] I was arrested twice, so that there could be no doubt about it. I have lived many years in the sight of my country an apparently uncaught and blameless life, a model for the young, an inspiring example for the hoary-headed. But at last the law has laid its hand upon me.

"Mine was no ordinary offense. When I affront the law I choose to do so in no obscure, insignificant, trivial mariner. Mine was a crime against nothing less than the Federal Government. The officers who arrested me were no common, or garden, policemen; they were clothed with the authority of the Federal Constitution. I was charged with smoking a cigar within a Government reservation. In fact, I was caught red-handed. I came near setting a stone pile on fire.

"It is true that the arrest was not made effective. One of the party whispered to the marines what Governor Warfield was going to say, and did say, in introducing me to the audience at my lecture—that I was one of the greatest men in the world. I don't know who proposed to tell that to the marines, but it worked like a charm. The minions of the law faltered, hesitated, quailed, and today I am a free man. Twice they laid hands upon me; twice were overcome by my deserved reputation.

"Perhaps I ought not to say myself that it is deserved. But who am I to contradict the Governor of Maryland? Worm that I am, by what right should I traverse the declared opinion of that man of wisdom and judgment whom I have learned to admire and trust?

"I never admired him more than I did when he told my audience that they had with them the greatest man in the world. I believe that was his expression. I don't wish to undertake his sentiments, but I will go no further than that—at present. Why, it fairly warmed my heart. It almost made me glad to be there myself. I like good company.

"Speaking of greatness, it is curious how many grounds there are for great reputations—how many different phases, that is to say, greatness may take on. There was Bishop Potter.[2] He was arrested a few months ago for a crime similar to mine, though he lacked the imagination to select United States Government property as the scene of his guilty deed. Now, Bishop Potter is a great man. I am sure he is, because a street car motorman told me so. A motorman is not a Governor of Maryland, but then Bishop Potter is not a humorist. He could hardly expect a certificate like mine.

"I rode with the motorman one day on the front seat of his car. There was a blockade before we got very far, and the motorman, having nothing to do, became talkative. 'Oh, yes,' he said, 'I have a good many distinguished men on this trip. Bishop Potter often rides with me. He likes the front seat. Now there's a great man for you—Bishop Potter.'

"'It is true,' I responded. 'Dr. Potter is indeed a mighty man of God, an erudite theologian, a wide administrator of his great diocese, an exegete of—'

"'Yes,' broke in the motorman, his face beaming with pleasure as he recognized the justice of my tribute and hastened to add one of his own. 'Yes, and he's the only man who rides with me who can spit in the slot every time.'

"That's a good story, isn't it? I like a good story well told. That is the reason I am sometimes forced to tell them myself. Here is one of which I was reminded yesterday as I was investigating the Naval Academy. I was much impressed with the Naval Academy. I was all over it, and now it is all over me. I am full of the navy. I wanted to march with them on parole, but they didn't think to ask me; curious inattention on their part, and I just ashore after a celebrated cruise. While I was observing the navy on land," said Mr. Clemens, "I thought of the navy at sea and of this story, so pathetic, so sweet, so really touching. This is one of my pet stories. Something in its delicacy, refinement, and the elusiveness of its humor fits my own quiet tastes.

"The time is 2 A.M., after a lively night at the club. The scene is in front of his house. The house is swaying and lurching to and fro. He has succeeded in navigating from the club, but how is he going to get aboard this rolling, tossing thing? He watches the steps go back and forth, up and down. Then he makes a desperate resolve, braces himself, and as the steps come around he jumps, clutches the handrail, gets aboard, and pulls himself safely up on the piazza. With a like manouvre he gets through the door. Watching his chance, he gains the lowest step of the inside staircase, and painfully makes his way up the swaying and uncertain structure. He has almost reached the top when in a sudden lurch he catches his toe and falls back, rolling to the bottom. At this moment his wife, rushing out into the upper hall, hears coming up from the darkness below, from the discomfited figure sprawled on the floor with his arms around the newel post, this fervent, appropriate, and pious ejaculation, 'God help the poor sailors out at sea.'

"I trust this matter of my arrest will not cause my friends to turn from me. It is true that, no matter what may be said of American public morals, the private morals of Americans as a whole are exceptionally good. I do not mean to say that in their private lives all Americans are faultless. I hardly like to go that far, being a man of carefully weighed words and under a peculiarly vivid sense of the necessity of moderation in statement. I should like to say that we are a faultless people, but I am restrained by recollection. I know several persons who have erred and transgressed—to put it plainly, they have done wrong. I have heard of still others—of a number of persons, in fact, who are not perfect. I am not perfect myself. I confess it. I would have confessed it before the lamentable event of yesterday. For that was not the first time I ever did wrong. No; I have done several things which fill my soul now with regret and contrition.

"I remember, I remember, it so well. I remember it as if it were yesterday, the first time I ever stole a watermelon. Yes, the first time.

"At least I think it was the first time, or along about there. It was, it was, must have been, about 1848, when I was 13 or 14 years old. I remember that watermelon well. I can almost taste it now.

"Yes, I stole it. Yet why use so harsh a word? It was the biggest of the load on a farmer's wagon standing in the gutter in the old town of Hannibal, Missouri. While the farmer was busy with another—another customer, I withdrew this melon. Yes, 'I stole' is too strong. I extracted it. I retired it from circulation. And I myself retired with it.

"The place to which the watermelon and I retired was a lumber yard. I knew a nice, quiet alley between the sweet-smelling planks and to that sequestered spot I carried the melon. Indulging a few moments' contemplation of its freckled rind, I broke it open with a stone, a rock, a dornick, in boy's language.

"It was green—impossibly, hopelessly green. I do not know why this circumstance should have affected me, but it did. It affected me deeply. It altered for me the moral values of the universe. It wrought in me a moral revolution.

I began to reflect. Now, reflection is the beginning of reform. There can be no reform without reflection—

"I asked myself what course of conduct I should pursue. What would conscience dictate? What should a high-minded young man do after retiring a green watermelon? What would George Washington do?[3] Now was the time for all the lessons inculcated at Sunday School to act.

"And they did act. The word that came to me was 'restitution.' Obviously, there lay the path of duty. I reasoned with myself. I labored. At last I was fully resolved. 'I'll do it,' said I. 'I'll take him back his old melon.' Not many boys would have been heroic, would so clearly have seen the right and so sternly have resolved to do it. The moment I reached that resolution I felt a strange uplift. One always feels an uplift when he turns from wrong to righteousness. I arose, spiritually strengthened, renewed and refreshed, and in the strength of that refreshment carried back the watermelon—that is, I carried back what was left of it—and made him give me a ripe one.

"But I had a duty toward that farmer, as well as to myself. I was as severe on him as the circumstances deserved: I did not spare him: I told him he ought to be ashamed of himself giving his—his customers green melons. And he was ashamed. He said he was. He said he felt as badly about it as I did. In this he was mistaken. He hadn't eaten any of the melon. I told him that the one instance was bad enough, but asked him to consider what would become of him if this should become a habit with him. I pictured his future. And I saved him. He thanked me and promised to do better.

"We should always labor thus with those who have taken the wrong road. Very likely this was the farmer's first false step. He had not gone far, but he had put his foot on the downward incline. Happily, at this moment a friend appeared—a friend who stretched out a helping hand and held him back. Others might have hesitated, have shrunk from speaking to him of his error. I did not hesitate nor shrink. And it is one of the gratifications of my life that I can look back on what I did for that man in his hour of need.

"The blessing came. He went home with a bright face to his rejoicing wife and I—I got a ripe melon. I trust it was with him as it was with me. Reform with me was no transient emotion, no passing episode, no Philadelphia uprising. It was permanent. Since that day I have never stolen a water—never stolen a green watermelon."

Notes to Interview 218

1. MT was arrested and jailed overnight in San Francisco, ostensibly for public drunkenness, probably in January 1866 (Edgar M. Branch, *Clemens of the Call* [Berkeley: University of California Press, 1969], 314).

2. Henry Codman Potter (1835-1908), American Episcopal bishop.
3. See n. 3 to interview 123.

219

"Mark Twain's Visit Ends," *Baltimore News,* 11 May 1907, 9.

Samuel L. Clemens, who made a large audience, composed of many people from Annapolis and a few from Baltimore, laugh by a lecture in the House of Delegates at Annapolis last night, left that city today for New York. Mr. Clemens, or Mark Twain, for most persons know him by his Mississippi river name, had been the guest of Governor and Mrs. Warfield at the Executive Mansion,[1] at Annapolis, and his visit was due to his desire to help Mrs. Warfield buy a new organ for the Presbyterian Church. About 500 persons, who paid $1 each for the privilege, heard the celebrated man of letters, who is about to be granted the bachelor's degree by Oxford University, an extremely rare honor for an American.[2]

"I will think it over carefully and possibly deliver a written opinion sometime later," said Mark Twain, in his inimitable drawl, when asked this morning to express an opinion as to what he thought of Annapolis and her hospitality.[3] The question had been qualified with an inquiry as to whether or not Mr. Clemens could depart from his policy, which he announced yesterday, of not jumping at conclusions hastily. The man who last night made all Annapolis laugh was standing on the station platform preparing to take his train back to New York. He almost fell from grace, and departed his custom, however, by continuing. "I cannot give an opinion properly. When a man is full of good impressions he thinks inwardly so much that he does not see outwardly." This was pretty close to a compliment to Annapolis. . . .

After the talk in the House of Delegates last night—for it was merely a talk—Mr. Clemens went into an anteroom, and there met several newly found friends.[4] There were only a few so honored. As he shook hands with these lucky ones he remarked: "I am poor and cannot leave you money, but I want you to come to New York and attend my funeral, and I want you to be one of my honorary pallbearers."

"Oh! Thank you so much," exclaimed one young lady. "With pleasure," was the impulsive acceptance of one man.

"Not at all; the pleasure is all mine," said Mr. Clemens, and it didn't dawn upon the man that the pleasure to Twain was doubtful.[5] . . .

Notes to Interview 219

1. Edwin A. Warfield (1848-1928), governor of Maryland from 1904 to 1908.
2. MT was awarded a doctoral degree, not a bachelor's degree. On the honorary degree from Oxford, see chapter 10.

3. "Mark Twain at Annapolis," *New York Tribune,* 12 May 1907, 7: "I cannot give an opinion properly. When a man is full of good impressions he thinks inwardly so much that he does not see outwardly. I will really think it over, and possibly deliver a written opinion sometime later."

4. MT's "Dinner Speech at Annapolis" is reprinted in Fatout, 550–54.

New York Tribune: At his lecture Mr. Clemens, among other things, said: "I haven't been on the platform for eleven years, and never expect to be again."

5. *New York Tribune:* In bidding goodby to some of his newly made Annapolis friends Mr. Clemens said: "I am poor and cannot leave you money, but I want you to come to New York and attend my funeral, and I want you to be among the honorary pallbearers." "Oh, thank you so much!" exclaimed one young woman. "With pleasure!" was the impulsive acceptance of one man. "Not at all; the pleasure is all mine," said Mr. Clemens. He did not set a date for the funeral.

220

"Mark Twain Departs," *Baltimore Sun,* 12 May 1907, 20; excerpted in "Mark Twain Tells the Secrets of Novelists," *New York American,* 26 May 1907, 7.

Mr. Samuel L. Clemens, the greatest living humorist, who had been the guest of Governor Warfield since Thursday,[1] left for New York yesterday breathing benisons upon Maryland hospitality and remarking almost momentarily [i.e., instantly] upon the things dear to his heart which he met here and which are not found in the North.

The last place visited, save for a brief stop at the Governor's office, was to the Sun Building. The surroundings seemed to awake a flood of memories, and he grew eloquent in contrasting the most modern of newspaper establishments with those he had known.

"My, what an evolution!" he exclaimed. "Just think of the old *New York Tribune* editorial compartments in contrast with this! Peanut-stand editorial accommodations were the idea in those days, it seems to me—the least possible comfort in the least possible space, with the utmost amount of dirt and confusion."

Of the editorial rooms and library he said: "This is a sanctuary, not a sanctum. Beautiful! fine! I even believe I could even write something good in here myself!"

Passing through the spacious business office and up the marble stairway, Mr. Clemens had expressed his admiration at almost every step. The introductions in the private offices of the A. S. Abell Company[2] had scarcely been completed when Mr. Clemens' eye was attracted by an oil painting in which a slice of watermelon almost gleams in its crispness.

"Let me see that first," he exclaimed. "Doesn't it look lifelike and luscious! You cannot get any watermelon fit to eat north of Mason and Dixon's line.[3] Anywhere else it is either spoiled by ripening after being plucked immaturely or by the effects of exportation after ripening properly on the vine. Once in India I one time ate a piece of fairly good melon. But the Southern watermelon on its native heath is the only real thing in that line."

Just then the visitor seemed to miss something necessary to his comfort. Those about him remembered that smoking is his favorite diversion and the one almost unchangeable rule in the Sun Building "No Smoking Permitted" was suspended. Among all the thousands of guests who have visited the new building—Governors, Senators, the Cardinal, prelates, and citizens—no one had smoked in the main portion of the building. By proclamation of Governor Warfield, who was personally escorting him, the law was waived in favor of Mr. Clemens. With a word of thanks for the unusual privilege, and a smile, he produced a long cigar and was soon blowing out wreathes of smoke, christening the new Sun Building with the incense of St. Nicotine.

Laying off his gray overcoat, he threw his leg over a desk, and seated upon the flat top, breathed the balm of contentment. He was enjoying himself. He wasn't being bored or wearied or lionized.

"I have not known the present generation of the family of the founder of the *Sun*," he said, "but I recollect well members of the second generation of the family. You must remember that I have been in Baltimore in years gone by, several times to lecture here.

"I guess I am beyond dispute the oldest journalist in the country, for ever since the time I first began the business with my little paper at Hannibal, Missouri, I have been in newspaper work, with scarcely any interval whatever, in one form or another—if not actively writing or making material for the press, then figuring in interviews or as the subject of newspaper comment."

"I was reared on Tom Sawyer and Huckleberry Finn," said one of those present. "Were they real boys of your own boyhood acquaintance?"

Throwing one knee carelessly across the top of the desk, the other dangling until the foot nearly touched the floor, the twinkle in the humorist's eyes ceased for a moment and the furrows in his forehead became somewhat more pronounced. In a most serious way, he said: "Authors rarely write books. They conceive them, but the books write themselves. This is practically true of all characteristics intended to be portrayed. A sketch is begun in one locality. It may be with one view in sight. Soon, however, the dialogue surrounds the individual and he or she is carried away beyond the point at first intended."

Here Mr. Clemens indicated his meaning by placing his index finger at one end of the desk and rapidly shifting it to another.

"Who can tell what is going to become of a character once created? It goes hither and thither as fancy dictates, much as an individual would do in the daily course of the lives of many. The start may be made with the view of meeting only certain classes or assumed conditions. These change rapidly and the first thought may evolve into something entirely different from the first conception.

"This is what I mean to imply when I say the book writes itself. This does not mean that the physical labor does not rest somewhere. It always does. But the character goes on in its evolution; creates its own surroundings and makes its dialogue conform to these varied changes as they progress.

"I never deliberately sat down and 'created' a character in my life. I begin to write incidents out of real life. One of the persons I write about begins to talk this way and one another, and pretty soon I find that these creatures of the imagination have developed into characters, and have for me a distinct personality. These are not 'made.' They just grow naturally out of the subject. That was the way Tom Sawyer, Huck Finn, and other characters come to exist. I couldn't to save my life deliberately sit down and plan out a character according to diagram. In fact, every book I ever wrote just wrote itself. I am really too lazy to sit down and plan and fret to 'create' a 'character.' If anybody wants any character 'creating,' they will have to go somewhere else for it. I'm not in the market for that. It's too much like industry."

Turning to Miss Isabel Lyon, his secretary,[4] one of the group remarked: "I expect he doesn't mean half of that, does he? He is industrious enough when he has to be, isn't he?"

"Oh, I wish you could see him," she replied, "and see the tremendous pile of manuscript he has produced. It is simply marvelous.

"But there do come times when he winds a thing up that he is working on; won't go any further; just simply stops and puts it by. I remember when he was dictating the manuscript of 'Eve's Diary' we found one day that he had apparently concluded it.[5] 'Oh, don't stop,' I exclaimed. 'Do let her say some more.' 'No, no,' he responded, with a wave of his hand. 'That is all of it.' I persisted, and then he said he would see how matters were in the morning. The next morning he came in from the porch after smoking a cigar and I started at him, with pencil and notebook in hand ready for action, only to be met with another wave of his hand, this time in all positiveness, and the exclamation, 'No, no more! Eve hasn't spoken.'"

A pleasant incident occurred on the way from Annapolis, where Mr. Clemens had delivered a humorous address in the House of Delegates Friday night for the benefit of the First Presbyterian Church.

On the arrival of the *Sun* at the Government House there had been much favorable comment on a poem by the "Bentztown Bard," in which the serious side of Mark Twain's work, not so generally appreciated as his humorous productions, was referred to in these lines:

Humorist? Author? Not merely! Although he has made us all laugh
Although he has turned us away from our care so often with light-
hearted chaff,
Deep down in the core of his spirit, the calm suaviter of his soul,
The thunders that shook the crusaders in terrible earnestness roll!
Ho, fakir, get out of this way there! Ho, fraud, you had better beware
When Elijah goes after his Ahab with bristles of wrath in his hair!

The lines pleased Mr. Clemens and he expressed his desire to meet the author. Governor Warfield suggested a visit to the *Sun* office. After the farewells had been said the Governor and his guests started for Baltimore in a Short Line train. At Robinson Station the "Bentztown Bard," who in private life is Mr. Folger McKinsey, boarded the train.[6] The Governor sent for him and introduced him to Mr. Clemens, who expressed his delight with the poem.

Miss Lyon, his secretary, spoke enthusiastically of it as the work of someone who had at last discovered the real thing in Mark Twain, the spirit that makes him more than merely a great humorist, a great writer.

"A beautiful poem," chimed in Mr. Clemens, "beautiful poem. I was going to the *Sun* office specially to see you and thank you for it."

At Camden Station Reverend and Mrs. John Timothy Stone,[7] who had been members of the party, bade Mr. Clemens and his secretary goodbye and Governor Warfield and his guests drove to the *Sun* office.

Governor Warfield called Mr. Clemens' attention to the beginning of the burnt district line and pointed out in a general way the vast area that had been devastated by the fire and so rapidly rebuilt.[8] "The fire," said Mr. Clemens, "did for Baltimore what the great fire of London did for London—it led to the building of the new city, the city of the new spirit and the new force and energy."

Everywhere that the carriage went the white-haired visitor was gazed at through the windows and in many instances recognized by the onlookers. . . .

Notes to Interview 220

1. Edwin A. Warfield (1848–1928), governor of Maryland from 1904 to 1908.

2. The family of Arunah Shepherdson Abell (1806–88), founder of the *Philadelphia Public Ledger* (1836) and the *Baltimore Sun* (1837), owned a controlling interest in the *Sun* until 1910.

3. The border between Pennsylvania and Maryland surveyed between 1763 and 1767 by Charles Mason and Jeremiah Dixon. The Mason-Dixon Line is a popular designation for the boundary between the North and the South, or before the Civil War, between the free states and the slave states.

4. Isabel Van Kleek Lyon (1863–1958), MT's private secretary from 1902 until 1909.

5. See n. 10 to interview 200.

6. Folger McKinsey (1866–1950) was known as the Bentztown Bard (from a neighborhood in Frederick, Maryland, called Bentztown after the Bentz family who owned a farm at that site). For forty-two years (1906–48) he wrote a column, "Good Morning," for the *Baltimore Sun*. He also wrote the city anthem for Baltimore.

7. John Timothy Stone (1868–1954), pastor of Brown Memorial Presbyterian Church in Baltimore, later president of McCormick Theological Seminary in Chicago. His first wife was the former Bessie Parsons.

8. The Great Baltimore Fire of 7–8 February 1904 consumed four hundred acres, some seventy-two square blocks, of downtown Baltimore, and took thirty-two hours to contain.

10

Visit to Oxford, 1907

Interviews 221–235

The greatest honor of Twain's life was his receipt of an honorary Litt.D. conferred by Oxford University on 26 June. He sailed from New York on 8 June, and while in England he played well the part of the literary lion, attending a royal party at Windsor Castle, meeting members of Parliament, and lunching with George Bernard Shaw. A gaggle of fifteen reporters met him at the dock upon his return to New York on 22 July.

∼

221

"Mark Twain Sails; Shiest Man Aboard," *New York American,* 9 June 1907, I, 3.

Mark Twain sailed on the Atlantic Transport Liner *Minneapolis*[1] yesterday for what he said was probably the last trip he would make to London from this sphere. He felt certain that, having led so exemplary a life, he would be permitted to go to London when he died. Just at present, though, he was in excellent health.

The humorist did not wear his white suit, but he did appear in the lightest of gray suits with an overcoat to match and a white tie. The white dress suit was in his trunk.[2]

As soon as Mr. Clemens went on deck he took a cigar from his overcoat pocket and carefully peeled off its several wrappers. There was a smile of anticipation on his face, until he found the crowd had broken it.

"There," he said. "Just for that I will not smoke a cigar on the whole voyage."

Two minutes later he slipped away from his friends and searched out the deck steward.

"Get me the blackest cigar you have," he said.

As the ship slipped from the dock he was seen lighting it and his smile returned and expanded with each puff.

"I am going to Oxford University to receive the degree of Doctor of Literature on June 26, and shall spend two days in London before I return," he said. "I am booked to come back on this same ship on June 29, that is, I expect to return then. But you never can tell. I lived eight years in London and the boys there may tempt me to stay longer. I do not know what they will do with me.[3]

"However, I shall do my part. I am always ready to take my proper share of dissipation to teach other people how to be better than I am myself.

"I have given up all work, you know. I did so on my seventieth birthday and that was so long ago I have almost forgotten it. Now my idleness consists in dictating two hours a day for five days a week. I am writing my autobiography, and it is not to be published until I am well and thoroughly dead.

"It has in it all the caustic and fiendish and devilish things I want to say. It will be many volumes, I cannot say how many, because that depends on how long I live.

"It is not to appear until the people in it are dead and their children and their grandchildren also. I would hate so to hurt anybody's feelings. In fact, it will not appear in print until I am canonized."[4]

Mr. Clemens was asked who the people were who had come to see him off.

"Oh, I do not know," he answered. "The fact is, I am the shyest person you ever saw. Most people are shy, but mine is of a peculiar sort. I never look people in the face, because they may know me and I not know them. And that is so embarrassing.

"I never observe anybody or anything. I gave that up years ago. I do not know what goes on around me until it happens and then I get away as soon as I can. If you do not use an ability it will atrophy. That is what has happened to me. All my powers of observation are dried up and withered."

Notes to Interview 221

1. See n. 9 to interview 216.
2. "Mark Twain Sails for Oxford Honors," *New York Times,* 9 June 1907, sec. 1, 9: "Where is the white suit? We had been looking for the suit and quite overlooked you." "Well," said the author, "I have discarded the suit for the moment, but your fears may be set at rest, for I am going to wear it again. I am wearing this overcoat to keep out the heat which isn't here, and as for the style of my clothes they are always selected with due regard to my peculiar style of beauty."
3. *New York Times:* "I may never go to London again," he said, "until I come back to this sphere again after I am dead, and then I would like to live in London. I spent seven years there, and I am going back to see the boys."
4. *New York Times:* "Do you enjoy idleness?" he was asked. "Splendidly. I put in two hours a day dictating my autobiography, but I don't want it published until after I am dead. And I want to be thoroughly dead when it is published. No rumors, but really dead. I have made it caustic, fiendish, and as devilish as I possibly can. It might

be what you call a sensation, for I have spared no one. It will occupy many volumes, and I will go right on writing until I am called to the angels and receive a harp. The story of my life will make certain people sit up and take notice, but I will use my influence not to have it published until the children of some of those mentioned in it are dead. I tell you it will be something awful. It will be what you might call good reading." "Have you included all of Mrs. Eddy's friends?" "Yes, you will find them all there all right." [On Eddy, see n. 12 to interview 175.]

222

"Mark Twain in London," *Westminster Gazette,* 18 June 1907, 7.

Mark Twain arrived in London this morning. He crossed the Atlantic in the *Minneapolis,*[1] which was berthed at Tilbury Docks at about 4 A.M.

Mr. Clemens came up to town with the special boat-train, and was received at St. Pancras Station by Mr. J. Y. W. MacAlister, editor of the *Library.*[2] The distinguished visitor was accompanied by Mr. Ashcroft, and is staying at Brown's Hotel.[3]

An incident of interest, but wholly accidental, occurred at the railway station. Among the few persons parading the platform was Mr. George Bernard Shaw,[4] who was surprised to learn from a Pressman that, traveling in the train whose arrival he was awaiting, was Mark Twain. Mr. Shaw responded to an invitation to express an opinion on the great humorist. "He is by far the greatest American writer. America has two great literary assets—Edgar Allan Poe and Mark Twain. I understand Americans do not say much about Edgar Allan Poe. Mark Twain does not give you the chance of ignoring him." Mr. Shaw added that he spoke of Mark Twain not as a humorist, but merely as a sociologist.

When the train steamed into the station, Mr. Shaw busied himself in looking for Professor Archibald Henderson,[5] who has come over to write Mr. Shaw's biography.

Mr. Clemens was immediately surrounded by a crowd of ladies on stepping on to the platform. He was dressed in a smart grey suit and bowler hat, and he chatted very cheerily.

Speaking to a Central News representative, he said he had come over for an Oxford degree. He would not say anything on the State subject of Anglo-American relations. "It is ancient; there is no vitality in it. The relations have been long established."

"Do you know that Mr. George Bernard Shaw is on the platform, Mr. Clemens?"

"Oh! is he? I want to see him."

"Then you don't know him?"

"No, I have never met him," answered Mr. Clemens.

"Would you express an opinion on Mr. Shaw?"

"No," was the reply. "I never give an opinion unless I have studied the matter. I only give an opinion on my own deductions, and not somebody else's."

Mr. Clemens said he would stay in England for about a fortnight. He wanted to see the processions at Oxford.

"What do you think of these great pageants?"

"I have never seen one."

"But what do you think of the idea?"

"Oh! the idea is excellent."

"Don't you have them in America at all?"

"Why, yes," he replied. "In 1876, you know, they had a series at the 100th anniversary of the Declaration of Independence; and then, just as it happened here, any town or place that had some events in its history that connected it with the American Revolution all followed, one after the other. That was in our 100th year, but you are in your thousands. It is good, you know, to revive history and impress the people. It does not take us long, for there is not much of it; but you have got to concentrate in six days the history of a thousand years."

To a question whether he was at present engaged in another work, Mr. Clemens replied: "No; I have not written for two years; but I do dictate autobiography for one or two hours a day on five days a week, and that is sufficient to keep me alive and the blood circulating."

"When do you expect to finish that work?"

"Just when they send for the undertaker, and not sooner!"

"To judge from appearances, that time is a long way off," said the interviewer. "I don't know about that," replied the humorist, with a shake of the head; "all the palmists and clairvoyants tell me I am going to die, but they don't state any date."

At this point "G. B. S." came walking down the platform, and the distinguished pair were introduced. "Do you know," said Mr. Shaw, "these Pressmen were asking me before the train came in if I thought you were really serious in writing 'The Jumping Frog,'" and both laughed heartily.

"I answered for you," said "G. B. S.," "and I gave the correct answer."

Mr. Shaw was with Mr. Clemens for a couple of minutes and, after handshaking, the interrupted interview was resumed. Mr. Clemens was asked for his impressions of England. The answer was most emphatic: "If I had impressions of England so intense that I could not contain them I would write them. I do not write anything until I am inspired with a very 'Fire! fire! fire!'" and Mark hammered an imaginary table. "Everybody has got their impressions," he went on; "but I have got to perceive that my impressions are superior to any other people's before I put them on paper. I would not have commonplace impressions proceed from this source and damage my reputation."

"You have not said what you think of the palmists who say you have lived long enough."

"Well, except that I feel an admiration for people who make a prediction like that, but fail to convince me it is true. I should think a little more of the prediction if they had given me the date. However, I don't much care about that because I have got myself insured."

Mr. Clemens has accepted an invitation to attend the Lord Mayor's banquet on the 29th inst. to the Savage Club.[6]

Notes to Interview 222

1. See n. 9 to interview 216.
2. John Young Walker MacAlister (1856-1926), Scottish journalist, editor, and librarian.
3. Ralph W. Ashcroft (1875-1947), MT's business adviser from 1907 to 1909, married Isabel Lyon (MT's personal secretary) in March 1909. Founded in 1837, Brown's Hotel in Mayfair had hosted Alexander Graham Bell, Rudyard Kipling, and Theodore Roosevelt over the years.
4. George Bernard Shaw (1856-1950), Irish man of letters. See also *Bernard Shaw: Collected Letters, 1898-1910,* ed. Dan H. Laurence (New York: Dodd, Mead, 1972), 696-97.
5. Archibald Henderson (1877-1963), University of North Carolina professor, later one of MT's biographers (1911).
6. MT was elected to honorary membership in 1899 in this "gentlemen's club" founded by Richard Savage in London in 1857.

223

"Mark Twain on the Secrets of Youth," *Leader* (London), 19 June 1907, 1.

The good ship *Minneapolis*[1] yesterday brought to these shores a cheery, white-haired old gentleman, described in the passenger list as "Mr. Samuel L. Clemens, of New York City, U.S.A.," but better known to millions of readers as Mark Twain—soon to become Dr. Mark Twain.

The famous humorist has come to England to receive a doctor's degree from the University of Oxford.

It is to be a very short visit, but it promises to be a merry one, for Mark Twain solemnly and seriously declares that he is here incidentally to gather ideas for his funeral—and can anyone believe that a funeral, as planned by Mark Twain in his festive and flippant moments, would be any other than a merry undertaking?

Mark Twain was serenely shaving in his cabin when the interviewers, like a horde of pirates, clambered up the sides of the *Minneapolis*. At last he braved the dangers of the note-books and cameras, and dashed to the breakfast-saloon, where he sat beside a pretty young American girl.[2]

Breakfast over, however, he delivered himself body and soul to the *Morning*

19. Mark Twain and British reporters aboard the *Minneapolis* after docking at Tilbury, London, 18 June 1907. Courtesy of the Mark Twain House, Hartford, Connecticut.

Leader representative and the other interviewers, and, resting his back on the iron bulwarks of the boat, he chatted to the group of them in a playful fashion—hardly ever serious for a moment.[3]

White as snow, his hair and moustache were in striking contrast to the sunburnt bronze of his complexion. Everyone had hoped to see him appear in the famous suit of white, the costume that set two continents talking, but the genial Mark had tucked it into his wardrobe, and wore instead a pale-grey lounge suit and an orthodox black bowler hat.

Before he had finished greeting the journalists a donkey-engine, not half a dozen yards away, set up a fearful clatter. The humorist's eye twinkled as he noticed the interviewers straining their ears to catch his words amid the roar and rattle, and he poked a little fun at them.

"Do you object to being placed with the *other* donkey-engines?" asked Mark, in tones of simulated sympathy.[4] The journalists laughed at their own expense, and persuaded the humorist to lead them to a quieter corner of the boat.

With the inevitable cigar in his mouth, he confided (in a hushed whisper) that this visit is only a "preliminary vacation necessary before my funeral."

"Funeral!" gasped one of the audience, horror-stricken.

"Yes, funeral," replied Mark Twain, with mock gravity. "I'm making arrangements for my funeral now. I'm inviting hosts of people—it's a friendly sort of thing to do, don't you think?"

The palmists and fortune-tellers, he explained, told him recently that he was to die. "And as it's going to be a nice, large, showy funeral, one that will attract attention in the newspapers, I've got to hurry up and arrange for it. A little early, you think? Well, all the better. We shall be able to have a rehearsal."

Someone asked him to outline the program, and he boldly launched out on the task. "I hope the procession will be about five miles long! There'll be brass bands by the score—say, a brass band every 50 yards, and every one of 'em playing a different tune! It ought to be one of the greatest things ever seen!" Again he laughed at the prospect.[5]

The Oxford Pageant, which Mr. Clemens is determined to attend—though it means lengthening his stay beyond his original intentions—is to supply him with some ideas for his funeral.[6] "We haven't settled the time or the place of the funeral yet," he confessed to the disappointed interviewers, all athirst for hints; "but the American fortune-tellers say I'm going to die in a foreign land—it may be in New Jersey."

Then he told a little story. There was a dear little young lady on the boat, he said, who had interested him, and as they grew quite confidential the little girl and he formed a solemn compact—that if he would go to her wedding she would go to his funeral. "At first the prospect didn't seem to appeal to her," he added, "but when I described it she grew keener, and now she's a little more eager to go to that funeral than ever I could desire!"

A reference to his cigar-smoking habits drew from him a story of Rudyard Kipling. "Did Kipling ever steal one of my corncob pipes? Never," said Mark; "and if he says so he's wrong. He tried to steal one and failed; then he tried to steal another, but I prevented the theft and gave it to him—probably the only pipe that Kipling ever got honestly!"[7]

The famous White Suit came out of the wardrobe on the voyage. "I wore it three days on the boat," confessed the humorist to the *Morning Leader* representative, "but I'm not intending to wear it in London. This white suit stands for a Purity Campaign," said he. "I am that Purity Campaign. I'm the only one in it—in fact, I'm the only one who's eligible!"[8]

He is not fond of globe-trotting, he declared. Out of all his 37 voyages to different parts of the world, only two voyages has he taken from absolute free choice.[9]

"Do you hope to come to England again?" asked the *Morning Leader* interviewer.

"Not unless I come over to take another degree," replied the humorist. "For such distinction one would be willing to walk two or three thousand miles."[10]

At present busy with his autobiography, and having already written "The Diary of Adam and Eve," he is not contemplating at the moment the publication of more family history such as "The Diary of Cain and Abel."[11]

"Cain is a delicate subject to handle," he said confidentially. "You see, Cain was one of my ancestors. You here may be descendants of the other branch, but we in the family never speak of that branch! Our side of the family began with murder and quiet assassination, and then descended into quiet theft and burglary, and things of that sort, but it got a bit too noticeable, and the family became noted for piety—which is always a characteristic of the family, even yet!"[12]

Though a big reader (especially of books that he has read before and forgotten),[13] he does not read novels; he does not like the phonograph, because it lacks expression, and because you can hear it "grating its teeth" when it talks;[14] and he believes that he owes the fact that he feels only 14 years old, instead of 72,[15] to his habit of taking plenty of rest and spending plenty of time in bed, even in the middle of the day.[16]

"How many cigars do you smoke a day?" asked someone.

"As many as I can—one at a time as a rule," came the answer, almost before the question was finished.[17]

Though he had never met George Bernard Shaw, or seen his plays, Mark Twain said he was eager to meet and talk to Mr. Shaw in London.[18]

With a parting injunction that none of them must miss his funeral, and a regret that he could not name the date, the playful humorist left the interviewers, and with his secretary, Mr. R. Ashcroft, took train to St. Pancras, en route for a West End hotel.[19]

Curiously enough, at St. Pancras he accidentally encountered Mr. Bernard Shaw, and the two humorists of international reputation exchanged greetings for two or three minutes.

"He is by far the greatest American writer," remarked Mr. Shaw to an interviewer.

Notes to Interview 223

I have supplemented this interview as reported in the *Leader* (London) with versions of Twain's comments published in other newspapers. All newspaper citations below are from 19 June 1907.

1. See n. 9 to interview 216.
2. Frances Nunnally (1891–1981), Atlanta schoolgirl who became one of MT's

"angelfish." See also *Mark Twain's Aquarium*, ed. John Cooley (Athens: University of Georgia Press, 1991), 137-38, 140.

"Mark Twain," *Chronicle* (London), 7: We trooped to the ship's side, and as we walked the photographers darted in, presented their cameras, and fired. "Why, you're even worse than the reporters," said the genial Mark. "My characteristic smile? Well, I usually charge extra for that. But here you are."

3. "Mark Twain in London," *Express* (London), 1: Mark Twain, as the steward said, is "a bright lad" and there are not many subjects on which he is not an authority. Thus he talked of—

Gramophones	The "Tuppenny Tube"
Mrs. [Mary Baker] Eddy	Old age
Cigars	Humor
[George] Bernard Shaw	The Twain family
King Leopold	Himself
White suits	
The Purity campaign	

But through all these topics it was evident that there was one matter dearest and nearest to his heart—and that it was his funeral. Every time Mark was coaxed away to another subject he sighed heavily, and, regarding his long cigar with a thoughtful, faraway look, said: "But about this funeral of mine—"

"Mr. George Bernard Shaw Greets Mark Twain," *New York Herald*, 9: Anglo-American relations he declined to speak about, as being too ancient a subject and one that lacked vitality.

Express (London): "Mrs. Eddy? I have been discussing her a very long way back in that book of mine. I can't stay interested in Mrs. Eddy for more than five minutes." [On Eddy, see n. 12 to interview 175.]

Chronicle (London): "No, I'm afraid I can't say anything more about Mrs. Eddy. I said it all five years ago. She was constituted like some people. When I say a thing I've no further use for it." . . . "Going to Italy any more?" "No, I shan't go to Italy. Since my last attempt to reform the Italian language I understand there have been difficulties with the police."

Edgar Wallace, "Mark Twain in London," *Mail* (London), 5: Do you remember how Mark Twain started to learn Italian? Not exactly to learn it, but to speak it. It was while he was living in his Italian villa. He got the language from the local Press. "Dolce far niente" and "conversazione," and "per bacco," and similar foreign expressions flowed from his lips as naturally as though he had been born in the country. Then the Italian police intervened. The man who created The Man Who Corrupted Hadleyburg was corrupting the language. A strange, weird, new Italian was rapidly spreading through the land. Mark Twain was the guest of a friendly nation; the situation was complicated. Washington stepped in and telegraphed to the American Ambassador in Rome. "Stop Twain speaking Italian—send the bill to us." [In "The Man That Corrupted Hadleyburg," published in the December 1899 issue of *Harper's*, MT satirically attacked civic complacency and hypocrisy.]

4. *Express* (London): When the *Express* representative suggested that a quiet place might be found, Mr. Clemens said blandly: "I see you don't like being mixed up with the other donkey-engines."

Chronicle (London): "Come along, sir," said the journalists. "Let's get away from this donkey engine." Mark Twain saw his opportunity. "Ah, you don't like the other donkey engines, eh?" (Loud laughter.)

5. "Mark Twain Invades London; Meets Shaw," *Chicago Inter-Ocean*, 3: "I have come, first," he said, "to receive an honorary degree from Oxford; second, to see an Oxford pageant and get some notions for my funeral; and, third, to issue invitations for my burial procession. You see, a palmist recently predicted my approaching end. As a rule I don't go a cent on palmists, but internal evidence convinces me that this one knew what she was talking about, especially as she concealed the date. I admire a palmist who makes a prediction of that kind. The only point definitely settled is that the procession will be five miles long, with brass bands every fifty yards. The invitations would read: 'Mark Twain will give an entertainment and lunch, free drinks included; room for all; be in time for the return ride,' or something like that."

Express (London): A clairvoyant has told him that he is going to die in a foreign land ("Maybe England; maybe New Jersey," says Mark), and so he is making arrangements for his funeral now, in case he is too busy afterwards. "I think this funeral is going to be a great thing. I shall be there," he drawled. "I'm stopping for the Oxford pageant, and I guess I shall pick up a few hints from it. I only wish I could make it last six days," he mused ruefully. "Shall I have a band? Land! I shall have fifty bands falling over one another at every fifty yards, and each playing a different tune. It'll be a showy funeral, with plenty of liquor for the guests. I shall issue invitation cards something like this: 'The late Mr. Mark Twain requests the pleasure of ——'s company. Mourning dress.' I haven't decided on the route yet, but it will be somewhere in a parallel latitude. . . . Now, with regard to this funeral, I'd like you to know that the hearse . . . Oh, yes; I was there when they opened the 'Tuppenny Tube.' So they've made it the 'Thripenny Tube.' Well, I guess the stockholders won't mind sacrificing euphony if the stock goes up. . . . But this funeral of mine. The procession will be five miles long. It'll be one of the biggest shows of the time. Why, there was a lady on board asked me to come to her wedding. 'Yes,' I replied, 'I will, if you'll come to my funeral.' I told her all about it, and now she's quite eager for it to happen."

Chronicle (London): "So you intend to die?" "Yes, as soon as ever they send for the undertaker. Where is it to be? Ah! Now you're prying into private affairs. But I may tell you that I have been assured that I shall die in some foreign country—New Jersey, perhaps. Anyhow, people are so fond of discussing my last moments that I'm sending out the cards of invitation now." "Mr. Mark Twain presents his compliments . . . ?" "Yes," he replied, catching the humor of the situation, "something of that kind. An attractive card, mind you. A real hearty invitation to all my friends. Including my tailor? Why, certainly. I want a great funeral, with as many brass bands as possible all playing different tunes. As for refreshments, I promise to see that there's enough for everybody—something for those who don't drink, and something for those who do. Don't be afraid"—Mr. Clemens paused to size up the reporters—"I'll see that there's enough for everybody. You'll be made as comfortable as possible. The tickets will be numbered, and there'll be seats for those who won't be standing. The Press? Well, gentlemen, make your own arrangements, as you usually do. It has just struck me that instead of sending out the invitations gratis I might sell them. I must think that over. I might even form the concern into a company and float it."

Mail (London): "Will there be a band?" asked a reporter with musical leanings. A band! Mark Twain was mildly amused at the puerility of the question. One band!

One mean, contemptible orchestra for a funeral of that class? As a matter of fact, there will be a band at every fifty yards, and the procession will take hours passing a given point. "May I suggest," asked a serious reporter with a wide range of knowledge, "that refreshments should be provided?" The suggestion was received with favor. Invitation cards will be issued very shortly. They will not be given away. There will be no deadheads at Mark Twain's send-off. No rival humorist shall pass the cemetery gates and sneer: "It's only a paper funeral, anyway!" The tickets will be sold and a liberal commission allowed. The backs of the tickets will be let to advertisers. It will be an unrivalled opportunity. "If he had worn a Toffey's mackintosh he might have been alive today." "Prolong Your Life—Eat Oat Nuts." "Why Pay Rent?—Ashley will bury you for Ten Dollars," and the like.

6. [W. B. Northrop?] "Mark Twain's Quest," *Dispatch* (Manchester), 5: "One of the things I want to see while in England," he said, "is the forthcoming pageant at Bury St. Edmund's. Of course, we Americans cannot go in for pageants of this kind so extensively as you in England do, because, you see, we haven't the history to back us up. Some time ago we did celebrate the Declaration of Independence; but then we were only able to retrospect a hundred years or so. What I do not quite understand is how your pageant is going to be managed in merely a week. It must be difficult to crowd centuries into a single week like that." "How are you so interested in the pageant?" he was asked. "Well, you see, I want to get some good ideas for my own funeral," answered Twain. "Certain palmists have predicted that I would die abroad; but they omitted the exact date. I don't really care about that particularly, however," he continued, "as I am fully insured. But the funeral idea appeals to me more or less," he added.

Chronicle (London): "And the pageant?" "Yes, I shall see that. I did intend to sail in about two weeks, but I must not go away without seeing the pageant. Your pageants, gentlemen, *are* pageants, I understand. You have processions that last six days. They must be like funerals. Why"—smiling at the very thought of it—"I shall be able to get some ideas for my own funeral."

New York Herald: "But surely, Mr. Clemens, you aren't thinking of death?" interpolated one of his hearers. "Sh!" replied the humorist. "All the clairvoyants and palmists I have consulted tell me I am going to die, but I may add they would have impressed me more had they named the date."

Mail (London): "What did he say?" asked the reporter on the edge of the crowd. "Says he's going to witness the Oxford pageant to pick up a few tips for his funeral," repeated the informant.

7. For the Kipling interview, see interview 50.

Express (London): Mark Twain had something to say about the famous Kipling interview, when Kipling, as a young man, tried to steal one of his corncob pipes. "I gave him the pipe," he said. "It's about the only one he ever came by honestly."

Chronicle (London): "What about the corncob, Mr. Clemens, that Rudyard Kipling stole from you?" Mark Twain greeted the question with a hearty laugh. "You're mistaken. He didn't steal that; I gave it to him. He did try to get another, I believe. But the one you mention I certainly gave him—and it's the only thing I knew him to come by honestly."

8. *Express* (London): As for the all-white suit which created such a sensation in New York, he declared that he had worn it three times during the journey with great success. "Of course, I had plenty of things underneath," he explains. "As a matter of

fact, that suit is the emblem of the purity campaign. I'm the campaign, because I'm the only eligible member," he added, with a sly smile.

New York Herald: "Yes, I brought white suits with me, but I don't expect to wear them in London," he said. "You see, I had to wear them on shipboard, but I was terribly disappointed. It takes more than a white suit to make a person conspicuous on an ocean steamer."

Mail (London): There was no white suit on view yesterday. The emblem of the new purity campaign which Mark Twain has started in America is packed away in a capacious steamer trunk. Perhaps he won't wear it in England, but he might compromise and wear a white mackintosh. He is the only wearer of the Blameless Suit in America. He admits that. There is nobody else in America who is worthy to wear it. He admits that, too. He does not make the admission sadly. "Bumptiously" would be a better adverb. He wore the Blameless Suit once on the voyage over, and ran the gauntlet of fourteen cameras—which was discouraging.

9. "Mark Twain Tells Sea Tales," *New York Sun,* 3: "My trip over was delightful. The captain was most courteous, but firm. As I felt that he needed my assistance in running the boat I used to go up on the bridge in a nice neighborly fashion when he wasn't there and tell the other officers what to do. This lasted just three days. At the end of that time Captain Gates came to me and said very courteously: 'Twain, this is the third time I have found that while I was lunching you have gone to the bridge and altered the course of the ship and haven't told me about it. As it's up to me to get the *Minneapolis* to Tilbury would you mind quitting and allowing me to earn my money well?' Of course, after the man had shown a spirit like that it rather discouraged me giving him my invaluable assistance, so I let him manage the ship himself. And somehow the *Minneapolis* managed to arrive safely at Tilbury."

Chronicle (London): "Well, Mr. Clemens, what sort of a passage have you had?" The genial old man beamed like a boy. "Splendid. Beautiful weather all the time. I'm looking forward to my visit to Oxford, where I'm going to get a degree, you know. I want to show them at home what a real American college boy looks like."

10. *Dispatch* (Manchester): "I suppose this is your last visit to England, Mr. Clemens?" I asked, as he again shook hands with me. "Well, I don't know," he replied. "Perhaps it is; unless, of course, they are going to confer some more degrees on me."

Chronicle (London): "And when are you coming to London again?" "As soon as you offer me another degree."

11. On the diaries of Adam and Eve, see n. 3 to interview 177 and n. 7 to interview 182.

12. *Express* (London): "Future work? Well, there's my autobiography—it's going on till the undertaker finishes it. Oh! by the way, that funeral of mine . . . the autobiography? It's going on forever, like Tennyson's brook. [MT alludes to Tennyson's poem "The Brook" (1853).] I dictate it for one and a half hours a day for five days a week." Mark Twain was asked whether he was going to write a diary of Cain and Abel to follow the delightfully irresponsible diaries of Adam and Eve. "No," he replied seriously. "You see, Cain was an ancestor of mine, and I try to hush up that affair of his with Abel."

Dispatch (Manchester): Before taking my departure I asked the humorist if he were engaged in any serious literary work just at present. "Yes," was his reply. "I am writing my own biography. I dictate some of it every day to my secretary—working two or three hours a day. This is sufficient to keep the blood in circulation." "And when will the biography be concluded?" he was asked. "The day my funeral comes off," he replied, with a merry nod.

New York Herald: "And your autobiography—when do you expect to finish that?" "Oh! I calculate just before they send for the undertaker."

Chronicle (London): "I'm doing very little writing now—nothing beyond my biography. When shall I have that written? When the undertaker calls. But most of my book is done through dictation. I give it an hour and a half each day, from 10 o'clock in the morning till 11:30. The arrangement has this advantage: One need not be out of bed to dictate. However, I'm always up for lunch, but it is not long before I am again resting."

New York Sun: "I am very glad that the stories are being circulated that I spend twenty-six hours daily on my autobiography. It is well to have such a reputation for work, but somehow I feel for once obliged to tell the truth and admit that three hours a week, at most, constitutes my period of labor."

13. *Express* (London): As far as reading is concerned, Mark Twain confessed that he never reads novels. There are half a dozen books which he reads over and over again. "And I'm kept pretty busy reading the books I like," he concluded.

Chronicle (London): "And what am I reading? Just the five or six books I've been reading all my life." "Are you as fond of encyclopædias as ever?" "Just as fond."

14. *Express* (London): "Gramophones? I haven't spoken into one yet, though we've had the house full of machinery.... And, talking about them, this funeral business ought to bring in a fair amount from the sale of tickets and programs with advertisements, such as 'Why die? Eat ——'s food and beat Methuselah,' or 'Wear ——'s galoshes at the funeral.' If I get sufficient money from this I might buy a new set of teeth. I'm a little tired of my own teeth, for I've worn them for seventy-two years."

Chronicle (London): The conversation drifted to gramophones. "I don't mind them away back two or three rooms," remarked Mr. Clemens, "but I don't like to be close beside them when they're talking through their teeth. They never really represent the human voice, and for that reason I've always declined to talk a record into one."

15. *Chronicle* (London): "Mr. Clemens," solemnly said the youngest of the journalists, "do you think the world's improving?" "Well, now, that's difficult to answer." Puff, puff, puff went the cigar whilst Mark Twain thought about the world. Then he said slowly: "I think I can safely say this, that my latest impressions of it are better than my first."

Mail (London): "Do you think—do you think, Mr. Clemens," asked a reporter in spectacles, "that the world is growing better or worse?" It was a foolish question, because Mark Twain had already admitted his seventy-two years of useful work.

"Shaw Meets Twain and Explains Him," *New York Times,* 1: "Is the world growing better?" one youthful scribe inquired, and Twain solemnly answered. "Yes, I think so. You know, I have been here almost seventy-two years, and—but, really you must not ask me to say more on this subject. I am a very modest man, and prefer not to speak of my achievements.... I always like to read the *New York Times,*" he said. "It prints only the news that's fit to print, and as I have been told I am in my second childhood, I like to read a paper which I know will not exert a contaminating influence on me. Old men cannot be too careful, you know."

16. *New York Times:* "Every morning," said he, "as soon as I'm up, I smoke a cigar, and then have breakfast at 8 o'clock. After breakfast I smoke another cigar, and then go back to bed. At 10:30 I smoke another cigar and start dictating to my stenographer.

I finish at 12 o'clock and doze off till 1. I smoke another cigar and eat lunch. Then I go back to bed and read what the newspapers have to say about me. I smoke more cigars until half past 6. Then three assistants dress me for dinner, evening parties, etc., after which I associate with elite society till 1 o'clock in the morning. I never go to bed till my daughter turns out the lights, and then I smoke in the dark. My constitution is improving all the time."

New York Sun: "With all these affairs, how am I to get my usual quota of sleep, which is about twenty-two hours daily, is something that's puzzling me. I usually spend most of the time in bed, rise about 10 o'clock and very seldom have lunch, so that I can go back to bed again by 2 o'clock. If I have no engagements on, why I can then remain in bed until noon the next day."

Express (London): Mark Twain's advice for those who wish to live to an old age is "Sleep." "I lie abed, and I lie when up," he said. "The best way to keep young is to sleep a lot. I never do anything in the middle of the day, so I have only to lie about. I breakfast at eight, and then get back to bed again. The stenographer comes, and I talk my autobiography to him. . . . Now, as far as this funeral of mine is concerned—Land! I wish I could see the entertainment myself."

Chronicle (London): "I get as much rest as I can. . . . For a man of my age rest is essential. I believe in giving way to the body as soon as it feels tired, just as I always obey my eyes when they suggest sleep. For dinner in the evening I always dress, but 11 o'clock generally sees me in bed, where I read and smoke till, perhaps, 1 o'clock in the morning."

17. *Dispatch* (Manchester): Asked how many cigars he smoked a day, he replied: "Not more than one barrelful."

Express (London): He was asked how many cigars he smoked a day. "All I can get," he replied tersely. "One at a time."

Chronicle (London): "How many cigars a day do you smoke, Mr. Clemens?" "As many as I can get for six dollars a barrel."

18. *Dispatch* (Manchester): "I hope to see Mr. Shaw when in England," said Mr. Clemens. "What do you think of his work?" he was asked. "I never give an opinion on the writing of another, unless I have had an opportunity to draw my own deductions; but I can better answer that question after Mr. Shaw and I have met."

New York Sun: His meeting with Mr. Shaw gave him great pleasure. "I like his face," he said. "I want to see more of him." Some one suggested that it would be nice to have Mr. Shaw answer questions on Mark Twain's views and vice versa. Another with more acquaintance with Mr. Shaw said the latter would want to do both, whereupon Twain spoke up, saying: "That's even better still. It makes me more anxious to meet him again. It would save me a lot of trouble if some one would give my opinions for me."

Mail (London): Bernard Shaw? No, he had not read much of Bernard Shaw, but he knew of him and hoped to meet him.

Chicago Inter-Ocean: "I have read everything that Mark Twain has ever written, and I consider him the greatest American literary asset and he and Poe America's two greatest men," said Mr. Shaw in reply to a question. When Mark stepped on the platform he was asked whether he had read Shaw's works. "No," he replied. "I never read any of them, but I would like to meet him." They were introduced and Mr. Shaw said: "Mr. Clemens, do you know that one of these English newspaper men has been asking me whether you were serious when you were writing 'The Jumping Frog.'" "I guess you made it all right for me," rejoined Mark. Mark, being asked his opinion of Shaw, said: "I never give an opinion unless I have studied the matter. My opinion is based on my own deductions, not on other people's."

New York Times: "A number of these pests," said Bernard Shaw to Mark Twain, indicating by a gesture that he was referring to a great congregation of English newspaper reporters who stood around him and Twain in a great circle, "just asked me whether you were really serious when you wrote 'The Jumping Frog.' Yes," Shaw went on, "these pests asked me that, and I told them what I thought to be the truth." "No doubt," broke in Twain, "I'm sure that you did me full justice. I have every confidence that I was quite safe in your hands." "Certainly you were," asserted Mr. Shaw. "I told them that I read everything good that you had written, and I was able to give them the fullest assurance that you always wrote seriously." "Mr. Shaw," said Twain, "I assure you that I can return the compliment."

19. Ralph W. Ashcroft (1875–1947), MT's business adviser from 1907 to 1909, married Isabel Lyon (MT's personal secretary) in March 1909.

Express (London): At this moment Mr. Ashcroft, who is acting as secretary to Mark Twain, reminded him that the train was about to steam out. As he passed along the promenade deck some dock laborers caught sight of him and recognized him. They cheered him as one might cheer a king, and the man who has made millions laugh raised his hat, bared his magnificent white head to them, and waved his hand, echoing the words of another American: "So long!" [The interviewer alludes to the American poet Walt Whitman (1819–92).]

Dispatch (Manchester): At Brown's Hotel, later in the afternoon, Mr. Clemens was again besieged by friends and would-be interviewers. He was dressing to go out, and considered that he had had a pretty hard day of it. "I cannot see everybody in one day," he remarked, as the latest card came up to his room. He then turned to his genial secretary, Mr. Ralph W. Ashcroft, and remarked: "Look here—can't we go out by some secret entrance from this hotel?—isn't there an underground passage, or something of that kind, by which we can emerge without being further interviewed?"

224

"Mark Twain at Windsor," *Evening News* (London), 20 June 1907, 1.

Mark Twain will be one of the guests of the King on Saturday at the afternoon reception at Windsor.

The great humorist, who had risen from his bed at the abnormally early hour (for him) of noon, told the *Evening News* representative today that he was gratified at the opportunity he will have of conversing with his Majesty again.

"Many years ago," he drawled, "I wrote an article—an article that appeared in a magazine—some magazine or other—and I said I had met the Prince of Wales, as he was then, in the Strand.[1]

"This article remarked on the fact that we didn't stop to speak. He happened to be in a carriage, and I happened to be on top of a 'bus.

"Three years later I met the King at Homburg. He remembered the matter—not that meeting but that article. He spoke to me about it."[2]

And, placing his spectacles on the tip of his nose so that he could only see through them with the greatest difficulty, Mark Twain threw back his head, and in a few expressive gestures conveyed the impression that his Majesty had very much regretted not seeing him on the top of the penny bus, but that he, Mark Twain, had not been too impulsive in forgiving the omission.

Mr. Clemens asked the *Evening News* to deny the statement that he will sail before the date of the Lord Mayor's dinner to the Savage Club at the Mansion House.[3] He intends to be there even if he misses the soup, or even the fish.

The American Ambassador gives a dinner tomorrow, at which Mark Twain will be the chief guest among a gathering of well-known literary people. No ladies will be at the dinner.

"On Sunday I break the Sabbath for the first time in my life," said Mark Twain. "I call on Archdeacon Wilberforce."[4] . . .

Notes to Interview 224

1. "A Letter to the Queen of England," *Harper's* 76 (December 1887): 922–26. See also Paine, 852–54.

2. MT and Twichell met the Prince of Wales at Bad Homburg in August 1892 (see interview 225). On Twichell, see n. 1 to interview 2.

3. MT was elected to honorary membership in 1899 in this "gentlemen's club" founded by Richard Savage in London in 1857.

4. Albert Basil Orme Wilberforce (1841–1916) was appointed chaplain of the House of Commons in 1896 and Archdeacon of Westminster in 1900.

225

"Mark Twain Again Meets His Former Chum Edward," *New York American*, 23 June 1907, 1–2.

Windsor, England, June 22—Mark Twain has renewed his acquaintance with King Edward. The first time he "met" the King was when he really did not meet him, and when the King was not the King at all. Today the humorist met the monarch at the Windsor Castle garden party to which Mark Twain was invited immediately on his arrival in England.

Mark Twain wrote in a magazine a dozen years ago how he first met King Edward. "We were going down Piccadilly," he wrote; "the then Prince of Wales was riding in a State chariot at the head of a procession, going to some State function. I was on top of a bus. Our eyes met, and at that moment I felt that the Prince and I understood one another, that our souls were one."[1]

Mark Twain said today that this incident is true, and he gave this very interesting sequel: "I really met the King for the first time at Homburg ten years ago. He was traveling incognito as the Duke of something or other. He was taking the baths, and an Englishman well up in the diplomatic circle who knew me asked me if I wouldn't be presented. I said 'Sure,' and he took me up to the Prince, who was sitting with one or two friends chatting and drinking at a café table.

"The Prince began to chat with me as glibly and familiarly as though he had known me for years. I was enjoying myself hugely, as you always do, you know, when you meet somebody that you can really treat as your equal. Presently the Prince asked me if I did not feel like taking a little stroll in the Park. 'Sure,' I said, and we strolled out and spent about half an hour in the park near the baths. I think he talked about every subject in the world except the most interesting one in the world—myself, and at parting he said, with a warm clasp of the hand, 'I am really delighted to have met you again.'[2]

"'Damn Bishop Potter,' I said to myself.[3] The Bishop was in Europe at the time, and people were constantly taking me for him. I was sort of riled that the Prince of Wales should have made that common mistake, and I said to him, 'But your Royal Highness, I never had the pleasure of meeting you before. Your Highness has mistaken me for—' The Prince interrupted: 'I am afraid,' he said, 'that I have a better memory than you. Is it possible that you have forgotten our meeting in Piccadilly?'

"The Prince had read that old magazine article and had not forgotten it."

Mark Twain, who wore the regulation frock coat and silk hat, was the center of attraction at the garden party at Windsor this afternoon, and besides meeting the King and the royal party had a handshake with several hundred notables during the afternoon. Upon his return from the garden party he declared that he was not a bit tired and had thoroughly enjoyed himself.

He was accompanied to Windsor by John Henniker Heaton, the "Father of Imperial Penny Postage," who introduced him to many of the King's guests on his way to the party, including Sir Henry Campbell-Bannerman, Fridtjof Nansen, Sir Henry Mortimer Durand, and Ellen Terry.[4] He heartily congratulated Miss Terry on her recent marriage, the two shaking hands enthusiastically.

After tea, which was served on the lawns, Ambassador Reid presented Mark Twain to King Edward and Queen Alexandra,[5] and the King and the humorist spent a quarter of an hour in conversation, the King laughing heartily at Twain's jokes. The Queen also joined in the conversation, and was much amused when Twain jokingly asked if he could buy the Windsor Castle grounds from Her Majesty.[6]

Then the King called on him to meet the other guests. He introduced Twain to the King of Siam, the Duke of Connaught, Prince Arthur of Connaught, and others.[7] Prince Arthur is to receive a degree at Oxford at the same time as the American humorist, and he remarked that he would collapse if called upon for a speech. Thereupon Twain offered to undertake to speak for him.

William Crooks, labor member of Parliament for Woolwich, appeared in company with Mr. Burns, attired in a sack coat [line dropped] most representative social assemblage of all varieties of persons prominent during King Edward's reign.[8]

The royal party had their headquarters in two large marquees, where the visitors thronged to pay their respects. The bands of the Horse Guards and Grenadier Guards furnished the music. The company was massed on the east lawn, a splendid stretch of grass, around which are the Castle golf links, and made a most impressive theatrical scene.

Many tons of flowers were used in the decoration of the tents in which refreshments were served. Ten special trains brought the London guests, and all the roads leading to Windsor were crowded with motor cars throughout the afternoon.

After his interview with the Royal Party, Mark Twain said: "I think the Queen looks as young and beautiful as she did thirty-five years ago, when I saw her first. I didn't say this to her, because I learned long ago never to say an obvious thing. That she still looks to me as young and beautiful as she looked thirty-five years ago is good evidence that ten thousand people have noticed this and have mentioned it to her. I have kept the remark unuttered, and that has saved Her Majesty the vexation of hearing it for the ten thousandth and one time.

"All that report about my proposal to buy Windsor Castle and its grounds is a false rumor—I started it myself."[9]

Mr. Clemens has announced that he will be a passenger on the steamer *Minnetonka*, sailing for New York July 13.[10]

Notes to Interview 225

1. "A Letter to the Queen of England," *Harper's* 76 (December 1887): 922–26. See also Paine, 852–54.

2. MT and Twichell met the Prince of Wales at Bad Homburg in August 1892. On Twichell, see n. 1 to interview 2.

"Twain Amuses King and Queen," *New York Times*, 23 June 1907, sec. 3, 3: "His Majesty was very courteous," he said. "In the course of the conversation I reminded him of an episode of sixteen years ago, when I had the honor to walk a mile with him, at the time he was taking the waters at Homburg. I said that I had often told about that episode, and that whenever I was the historian I made good history of it, and it was worth listening to, but that it had found its way into print once or twice in an unauthentic way, and was badly damaged. I said I should like to go on repeating this history, but that I should be quite fair and reasonably honest, and while I should probably never tell it twice in the same way, I should at least never allow it to deteriorate. His Majesty intimated his willingness that I should continue to disseminate that piece of history, and he added a compliment, saying that he knew good and sound history would not suffer at my hands, and that if the good and sound history needed an improvement beyond the facts he would trust me to furnish these embellishments."

3. Henry Codman Potter (1835-1908), American Episcopal bishop.

4. Sir John Henniker Heaton (1848-1914), journalist and Tory MP; Sir Henry Campbell-Bannerman (1836-1908), liberal English politician; Fridtjof Nansen (1861-1930), Norwegian scientist and explorer, recipient of the Nobel Peace Prize in 1922; Sir Henry Mortimer Durand (1850-1924), British ambassador to the United States from 1903 to 1906; the English actress Ellen Terry (1848-1928) had recently married fellow actor James Carew (1876-1938).

5. On Reid, see n. 4 to interview 9. King Edward VII and Queen Alexandra, the former Princess Alexandra of Denmark (1844-1925), were married in 1863. See also n. 2 to interview 1.

6. "Mark Twain a Royal Jester," *New York World*, 23 June 1907, 4: "I like your castle, Your Majesty, and will make you an offer for it."

7. King Rama V of Siam (1868-1910); Arthur William Patrick, Duke of Connaught (1850-1942), son of Queen Victoria; Prince Arthur of Connaught (1883-1938), grandson of Queen Victoria and son of the Duke of Connaught.

8. William Crooks (1852-1921), Labour MP from Woolrich; John Elliott Burns (1858-1943), prolabor MP.

9. *New York World:* "I am treating with the King for the purchase of his little place at Windsor. I am ahead of my other fellows on that proposition, anyway. The King was looking fine and the Queen looks as young as she did when I saw her some years ago."

10. The *Minnetonka*, weighing 13,400 tons, was built in 1902 for the Atlantic Transport Line.

226

"Mark Twain Meets King Edward," *Leader* (London), 24 June 1907, 1.

Mark Twain lay back in his armchair. There was a cigar stuck in each corner of his mouth, and one bristled out in the middle. Above his head there writhed a heavy halo smoke. But he smiled the smile of tolerance.

"Take a chair," he said to the interviewer. "Sit right down there.... No, it isn't a lethal chair. I don't kill interviewers. It's too cheap and easy. And sometimes—sometimes they amuse me."

The interviewer bowed and sat down.

"Conversing about dreams," continued Mark, "reminds me of one I had the other night. I dreamt that I had at last achieved the next existence. It was a pleasant spot where you could wear plush pajamas in the street and be respected. There were, too, I remember, no interviewers—no newspapers—"

"—and no humorists," murmured the interviewer.

"Now I come to think of it," went on Mark imperturbably, "there were no humorists either. Perhaps that was what made the place so pleasant and habitable.

"Well, as I was saying, I enjoyed the King's Garden Party immensely—immensely. And next to being myself I should now like to be an Indian Maharajah. They have a tremendous advantage over me. They can apparently wear what color-scheme of clothes they like; whilst I—However, I don't think I allowed my annoyance to be noticeable."

At this point Mark Twain threw away the butts of his three cigars and said, "Excuse me, I think I will go to sleep for a little while. I invariably go to sleep when I can help it."

"You mean," said the interviewer tolerantly, "when you can't help it."

"I mean," said Mark, "what I said. I go to sleep when I can help it. I can help it now to the extent of closing my eyes."

And he did.

It was during this interval that the *Morning Leader* representative learnt of what had transpired at the garden-party. Mark Twain, it seems, was presented to the Queen, who was sitting at a table, by Mr. Whitelaw Reid, the American Ambassador.[1] Mark was talking away to the Queen, and making her laugh, when her Majesty touched him on the arm, and, turning, Mark saw that another interested spectator had joined the group. It was the King.

Mark Twain at once turned to the King and held out his hand, which his Majesty warmly shook. And then for a full ten minutes they chatted and laughed together.

In particular, Mark asked the King if he remembered a former meeting between them some 16 years ago at Homburg.[2] The King said that he certainly did, and Mark then told the King what excellent "copy" he had made out of it, at which the King smiled and then laughed.

Hearing the merry laughter, the Duke of Connaught walked up and introduced himself, and then introduced Mark to Prince Arthur, who at once had a very frank, hearty laugh at something Mark said to him. Then the King introduced Mark to the King of Siam, who in turn presented him to one of his sons.[3]

Mark had far more of the King's time than anyone else, and he was undoubtedly the Lion—or, perhaps, it should be the Eagle—of the occasion.

At this juncture in the narration of Saturday's history, Mark woke up again, and instantly resumed smoking.

"Won't you give me a joke or two to take away?" pleaded the interviewer.

"Joke," said Mark, becoming invisible for a moment behind a cloud of smoke. "I never joke except when someone mentions funerals, jumping frogs, or white suits to me. No, sirree. Musing of white suits, however," he added, bending confidentially forward, "reminds me of something I brought over with me, which, to me, knocks big lumps off the white suit. Promise me that you won't say a word about it, and I'll tell you. It's a bathrobe—a white bathrobe, with a beautiful, pale, convalescent blue stripe running all down it. As a bathrobe, it's a cinch—the extreme edge."

Although the bathrobe is a secret, it is not such a secret as all that. And anyone with an eye for the beautiful might do much worse than take a stroll down Dover street a little after breakfast time, when he, or probably she, might be rewarded by seeing Mark, garbed in the bathrobe, setting forth for the Bath Club, which is adjacent. He will be accompanied by his secretary, Mr. Ashcroft,[4] and the opportunity might be embraced to purchase from the latter some of Mark's funeral tickets. They are, quite apart from the ceremony, well worth the outlay, being very handsome and ornate in the early Gothic type.

Notes to Interview 226

1. On Reid, see n. 4 to interview 9.
2. See interview 225.
3. Arthur William Patrick, Duke of Connaught (1850-1942), son of Queen Victoria; Prince Arthur of Connaught (1883-1938), grandson of Queen Victoria and son of the Duke of Connaught; King Rama V of Siam (1868-1910).
4. Ralph W. Ashcroft (1875-1947), MT's business adviser from 1907 to 1909, married Isabel Lyon (MT's personal secretary) in March 1909.

227

"His Hat on before the King: Mark Twain Kept Covered, but by the Queen's Order," *New York Times,* 24 June 1907, 1.

London, June 23—"Is it true that you kept your hat on when you met the King yesterday, and slapped him on the back while you were talking and laughing with him?" I asked Mark Twain this afternoon, directing his attention to a paragraph in a London Sunday paper, in which these solecisms were good-naturedly alleged against him.

"I'll tell you just what took place," said Mark Twain. "When I renewed my acquaintance with the Queen I took off my hat and made my lowest bow. 'Put on your hat; put on your hat,' said the Queen, fearing, I supposed, I'd catch cold. But I didn't obey her, and we continued our conversation, I remaining uncovered.

"Presently the Queen told me again to put on my hat, and her tone was such that I couldn't, with gallantry, longer disregard her injunction.

"Almost immediately thereafter I was presented to King Edward, and, remembering the Queen's command, kept my hat on. I didn't feel at liberty to do anything different."

"And did you slap the King on the back?"

"No; of course I didn't. The King put his hand on my arm, and, not to be outdone, even by a sovereign, I went a bit higher and laid my hand on his shoulder. Each of us meant to honor the other in this laying on of hands."

Mark Twain has received a number of letters from English people who don't understand his humor, or, rather, the sorry remains of it that get into their newspapers through the medium of the English reporters. After showing me several letters of this sort he had received, in some of which he is strongly upbraided, Mark Twain smilingly remarked:

"It all comes to this: England is the home of wit; America the home of humor."

228
"Oxford Pageant: What Mark Twain Thought of the Show," *London Daily News,* 28 June 1907, 8.

There will be many sore throats in Oxford tomorrow morning. Yet the pageant has been an artistic, a commercial, even a historic success....

"It's been grand—simply grand. Just that!" Mark Twain told me with the smile of a man who has never so much as mentioned his own funeral. "The only difficulty, I may say, in connection with this unique experience is adjectives. I am a man of few words," he said. "There is one word—grand—that serves many purposes. You may take that and publish it.

"I'd have crossed the Atlantic right away to see this pageant. America can do a few things well, I will admit, but it hasn't history, and it hasn't this—" with a wave of the hand towards the rain-dimmed scenery.

"America," observed Mark Twain, "has neither Oxford nor that weather which may be said to inspire a man to noble fortitude."

229
"Mark Twain Living Up to His Degree," *New York Times,* 30 June 1907, sec. 3, 1.

"I was much impressed by my reception here. However, I have refused to be interviewed up to this point, and don't feel any more like it now than before. Naturally, I am much impressed. 'Naturally' is a good word. Take it down.

"The ceremony was all most venerable and beautiful, and I was greatly moved by it. I have met hundreds of people here and have been touched, deeply touched, by their various welcomes. They have all greeted me with great heartiness. From the Sheldonian Theatre, where the degrees were conferred, to All Souls, where luncheon was served, the way was lined with spectators.[1] Of all things, I was most moved to see how the walk was walled in with people of both sexes and all classes.

"The actual number of my books circulating here may very well be greater than in America. The reason is the difference in price. A book costs a shilling or two here and a dollar or two in America.

"Palmists, clairvoyants, seers and other kinds of fortune tellers all tell me that I am going to die, and I have the utmost admiration for their prediction. Perhaps they would convince me a little more of its truth if they told me the date. But I don't care so much about that. It was enough to know, on their authority, I was going to die. I at once went and got insured.

"I think this funeral is going to be a great thing. I shall be there. I'm stopping for the Oxford pageant, and I guess I shall pick up a few hints from it. I only wish I could make it last six days.

"Shall I have a band? Land! I shall have fifty bands, falling over one another at every fifty yards, and each playing a different tune. It'll be a showy funeral, with plenty of liquor for the guests. I shall issue invitation cards something like this: 'The late Mr. Mark Twain requests the pleasure of ——'s company. Mourning dress.' I haven't decided on the route yet, but it will be somewhere in a parallel latitude Why, there was a lady on board asked me to come to her wedding. 'Yes,' I replied, 'I will if you'll come to my funeral.' I told her all about it, and now she's quite eager for it to happen.

"No, I'm afraid I can't say anything more about Mrs. Eddy.[2] I said it all five years ago. She was constituted like some people. When I say a thing I've no further use for it I get as much rest as I can. I'm doing very little writing now—nothing beyond my biography. When shall I have that written? When the undertaker calls. But most of my book is done through dictation.

"I give it an hour and a half each day from 10 o'clock in the morning till 11:30. The arrangement has this advantage: One need not be out of bed to dictate. However, I'm always up for lunch, but it is not long before I am again resting.

"For a man of my age rest is essential. I believe in giving way to the body as soon as it feels tired, just as I always obey my eyes when they suggest sleep. For dinner in the evening I always dress, but 11 o'clock generally sees me in bed, where I read and smoke till perhaps 1 o'clock in the morning.

"In 1876, you know, they had a series [of pageants] at the hundredth anniversary of the Declaration of Independence, and then, just as it happened here, any town or place that had some events in its history that connected it with the American Revolution, they all followed one after the other. That was in our hundredth year; but you are in your thousands. It is good, you know, to revive history and impress the people. It does not take us long, for there is not much of it, but you have got to concentrate in six days the history of a thousand years."

Notes to Interview 229

1. The Sheldonian Theatre, designed by Sir Christopher Wren (1632–1723) and erected at Oxford University between 1664 and 1668. College of All Souls of the Faithful Departed, established at Oxford in 1438.

2. On Eddy, see n. 12 to interview 175.

230

"Mark Twain," *Chronicle* (London), 2 July 1907, 7.

... [A] *Daily Chronicle* representative had the privilege yesterday of just a few minutes' talk with Dr. Clemens in his own rooms at a time when the necessity for the humor was not uppermost. In point of fact, though it was midday, old Mark was very tired. The ceaseless outburst of affectionate ovation that has greeted him since he stepped on shore at Tilbury has been pleasing enough, but almost too much for his strength.

This very morning a photographic séance—in the Oxonian robes—had been demanded. Mark had just survived the ordeal, and now he was going to bed. This, by the way, is his habit at any time of the day when he feels tired. The amount—and quality—of writing he has done in bed would probably startle many sticklers for the rigor of the desk!

However, he cheerfully forwent his rest for a moment or two, not least as he expressed himself particularly touched by Mr. David Wilson's *Chronicle* cartoon, showing the figure of Mark Twain bearing the laurels of "worldwide appreciation," while Mrs. Eddy and King Leopold of Belgium confabulate maliciously in a corner.[1] Of this the original had been sent him by request. Old Mark sat and conned it through his gold-rimmed spectacles with unfeigned delight.

"Now that's bully," he said, in his own simple-hearted way. "That's mighty good! What I like about it is that it takes me just a bit seriously. You see, though I love England from my heart, and I'd go over many seas for the welcome that you've given me, you generally seem to expect a joke if I'm anywhere by. In America I reckon they've got a bit used to my jokes, and they look out for something else now and then.

"Birrell Was Bully![2]

"Don't think that I mind!" the genial old philosopher went on. "I'll do all I can. But nowadays joking isn't quite the same thing as it used to be with me. In times gone by I never cared where or when or how it was. I'd do my best and think no more about it.

"Now, somehow or other, it's different. I am an old man, and have to be in the mood. Take after-dinner speeches, for instance. I feel nowadays I'd like to prepare them beforehand. But I can't bring myself to do it. It wouldn't be honest. So I'm anxious all the time about what I'm going to say. Some people manage to find it in the jug. My jug's generally empty.

"Everything depends," he continued, "on previous speakers. Very often I go down to a public dinner hoping and praying that somebody may let fall any little bit of inspiration—just a crumb. But it's no good. On the average, one's only hope is in God Almighty."

Notes to Interview 230

1. On Eddy, see n. 12 to interview 175; on Leopold of Belgium see n. 10 to interview 180. David Wilson (1873-1935) published in the *Chronicle* for 20 June 1907 a cartoon about MT, King Leopold, and Mary Baker Eddy. Two of his cartoons also accompanied interview 184.

2. Augustine Birrell (1850-1933), British author and Liberal politician, chief secretary for Ireland at the time of MT's visit.

231

"Mark Twain for Penny Post," *New York Sun*, 2 July 1907, 2.

London, July 1—Mark Twain will endeavor tomorrow to prove that the *Saturday Review*'s designation of him as Ambassador to Great Britain is founded in truth, as after luncheon at the House of Commons he will accompany Henniker Heaton to the Postmaster-General to urge the establishment of penny postage between the United States and Great Britain.[1] Speaking to the correspondent of *The Sun* tonight, Mark said:

"I have gone into this subject thoroughly with Mr. Heaton, and I am convinced that the present postal arrangements are absurd. Why should parcels of printed matter be carried between the two countries for a mere nothing and letters charged at the rate of a dollar a pound? The whole burden of postal cost comes upon the senders of letters, and to my mind it is nothing but downright robbery to extort a dollar a pound for letters.

"If the Post Office is in the robbery business let it be on a decent scale, and if it is going to rob the public let it do it for $10 instead of $1. Magnitude in crime may be forgiven, but petty larceny is always abhorrent.

"One stock argument employed against cheap postage is that a reduction of rates would decrease the revenues, but curiously in postal affairs this has never been found to be true. In fact every reduction in rates has increased the revenue.

"Speaking postally my mind goes back to the old days when it cost as much as a quarter to send letters to New Orleans. We had no stamps in those days. My father used to give me letters with money to take them to the post office. This constituted my one source of income, as it did for most youths in Missouri. I pocketed the money. The letters went just the same, only the receiver had to pay. I believe this system did more to undermine the moral fiber of boys in Missouri than anything I know. Fortunately, my moral character has since been rehabilitated.

"When England introduced stamps in 1848 my feelings were decidedly anti-English as America took up the system and my income disappeared, as my father used to buy stamps and put them on the letters and I had to trudge to the post office and mail them without recompense. At that time, when the proposition was advanced to reduce the postage to five cents for short and 10 cents for long distances, the same cry was made which is now raised, that reduction would ruin the post office.

"But the cry was false. Reduction increased the revenue, and a reduction of the postage between the United States and Great Britain to a penny would have the same effect. I am taking up this matter on this side because it is a curious commentary on our Government that once England introduces a new system it is very easy to get the United States to follow suit. The mere fact that England has done this or that acts with wonderful effect on Congress, and if we glance back along the line of governmental reforms and ideas we find that America only adopted them after England had tried them and found them desirable."

Mr. Clemens is full of his Oxford experience. He relates one amusing mistaken impression which he obtained on the evening of his arrival at Oxford. His host said: "Come to Jesus?" Mark says: "I thought I was in for a revival meeting or something of that sort, but, being polite, I made no objections. Nevertheless, it was a great relief to find that my host meant Jesus College, where I had a mighty fine time." . . .

Note to Interview 231

1. Sir John Henniker Heaton (1848–1914), journalist and Tory MP, dubbed the "Father of Imperial Penny Postage."

232

"Sleepy, But Happy: Mark Twain's Regretful Farewell," *London Daily News*, 12 July 1907, 7.

Mark Twain has come back to London a graver and extremely grateful man. He was overwhelmed by the warmth of his reception in Liverpool, and now he is quite cast down by the fact that he must leave the shores of hospitable England tomorrow.

"Can't you give one little joke?" pleaded a *Daily News* representative yesterday.

Mark said he couldn't think of one at his own expense just then, and he didn't like to make one at anybody's else's.

"Did you bring a cup from Liverpool?"[1] asked the interviewer.

"No," declared Mark.

That unfortunate affair at Ascot, he explained, had been a lesson to him, and he was trying to redeem his reputation. Professor Boyce telegraphed to Mark whilst he was at Liverpool to ask what he had done with the Irish Regalia.[2]

"Now, I can assure you," Mark declared earnestly, "I haven't got the Irish

Regalia. It is true that Lord and Lady Aberdeen invited me to go over to Dublin,[3] and if I had been able to accept I should have been there on the very day the jewels disappeared. Why must you always bring a man's past up against him? I'm not even a confederate this time—and they're very fine jewels, too, I'm told," he murmured regretfully.

There is one thing he intends to steal, however, at the earliest opportunity. That is another visit to England. He is quite enthusiastic about things English, and so grateful for all the nice experiences he has had, that he declined even to admit that we had lost our summer.

"What impressed you most?"

He found it very hard to say, but—here is a little secret—he has found some of the most beautiful ladies he has ever seen in England. He was discreetly silent when the interviewer asked where to look for them.

"I am inviting them all to my funeral," he observed. "It will be the greatest gathering of beauty and magnificence that the world has ever seen."

"And what," asked the *Daily News* representative, "is the funniest thing you have seen in England?"

Mark looked hard at the interviewer, but to the interviewer's relief forbore to laugh.

"That," he said, "I am saving for my autobiography." When he gets back to America he will make the autobiographical fur fly. He thinks nothing of turning out 10,000 words a day, thanks to the help of a gem of a lady stenographer whom he discovered when he thought the perfect note taker could not exist.[4]

One of the joys of Mark Twain's life in England has been the English strawberry. It is, he says, both refreshing and spectacular. He is particularly keen on the spectacular. American strawberries are spectacular, but somewhat flavorless. Soon after reaching Brown's Hotel yesterday he went to bed and slept for hours and hours. He leaves Tilbury on the *Minnetonka* for America tomorrow.[5]

Notes to Interview 232

1. The gold cup awarded the winner of the two-and-a-half-mile race for three-year-old and older horses at Ascot Hearth, Berkshire, was stolen during the race on 18 June 1907 and has never been recovered.

2. Sir Rubert William Boyce (1863–1911), chair of pathology at University College, Liverpool, from 1894 to 1911. The Irish Regalia, or crown jewels, were stolen between 11 June and 3 July 1907 and are still missing.

3. John Hamilton-Gordon (1847–1934), Seventh Earl of Aberdeen and governor-general of Canada (1893–98), and Ishbel Maria Marjoribanks (1857–1939) were married in 1877.

4. Josephine Hobby, formerly a stenographer for Charles Dudley Warner and Mary Mapes Dodge.

5. The *Minnetonka*, weighing 13,400 tons, was built in 1902 for the Atlantic Transport Line.

233

"Twain Postpones Funeral," *New York Times*, 13 July 1907, 1.

London, July 12—Mark Twain (Samuel L. Clemens) spent the last day of his visit to England quietly, being free at last from the engagements which have filled almost every hour of his time since his arrival. During the morning he went over the National Gallery under the guidance of the Director, Sir Charles Holroyd, and after lunching with friends returned to his rooms, where he will remain until his departure early tomorrow for Tilbury to embark on boar the Atlantic Transport Line steamer *Minnetonka* for New York.[1]

Many persons called to bid farewell to the humorist, whose reception in England has exceeded in warmth that of any visitor in many years. Mark Twain, naturally, is greatly pleased, and expresses himself as having had the best of times.

In an interview tonight Mr. Clemens said: "I have led a violently gay and energetic life here for four weeks, but I have felt no fatigue, and I have had but little desire to quiet down. I am younger now by seven years than I was, and if I could stay here another month I could make it fourteen.

"This is the most enjoyable holiday I have ever had, and I am sorry the end of it has come. I have met a hundred old friends and made a hundred new ones. It's a good kind of riches—there's none better, I think.

"For two years past I have been planning my funeral, but I have changed my mind and have postponed it.

"I suppose I won't see England again, but I don't like to think of that."[2]

Notes to Interview 233

1. Sir Charles Holroyd (1861-1917), English artist and director of the National Gallery. The *Minnetonka*, weighing 13,400 tons, was built in 1902 for the Atlantic Transport Line.

2. This farewell message was also published in the *Tribune* (London), 13 July 1907, 7; *Lloyd's Weekly News*, 14 July 1907, 2; and in the *Leader* (London), 16 July 1907, 5.

234

"Twain Home with English Jokes at 30 Cents a Word," *New York American*, 23 July 1907, 5.

Dr. Mark Twain returned from England yesterday on the Atlantic Transport Liner *Minnetonka*, high-browed under the degree of Doctor of Letters, which he received from Oxford University, and which he declared was no joke.[1]

He cautiously admitted that he still had the famous King's Ascot Cup, which vanished from an English race track just after he landed in London.[2]

He denied any knowledge of the stolen Dublin Jewels, declaring that some one else had turned the Irish trick.[3]

A search of the humorist's baggage at the pier supported his statement about the jewels. The customs officers found no false bottoms in his trunk, although they struck a veritable gold mine of notes on English jokes, which Mr. Clemens intends to translate, diagram, and spring as his own.

The customs officers did find an Ascot Cup, but they did not have it sent to appraisers to discover that it was not the valuable one King Edward held out as a track prize. It was a gaudy imitation presented to him by the Savage Club.[4]

The American reporter who boarded the *Minnetonka* at Quarantine found the humorist in one of his famous white suits, sprawled on a steamer chair, gazing at the Staten Island shore.

"I was looking for the first mosquito," he pouted. "Not one to welcome me."

"What do you think of America?" was the first question.[5]

"Ask my keeper," said Mark Twain, indicating little nine-year-old Dorothy Quick, of Plainfield, N.J., who adopted her distinguished fellow passenger the first afternoon out and guarded him closely during the voyage.[6] She sat in his lap and leaned her head trustfully against his shoulder. "You can tell them," she consented, patting his cheek by way of encouragement.

"How do I like America?" repeated the humorist. "I don't know; I've been away six weeks. Now ask me what I think of the tall buildings."

"Suppose you tell us your latest joke instead," was suggested.

"I get thirty cents a word," he returned.

"Tell us one at night rates," was offered.

"No night rates on my jokes or cut rates either," said Mark Twain shrewdly. "It's thirty the word."[7]

The fifteen reporters made a pool, raising ninety cents. They offered it for a three-word joke. Mark Twain delivered the goods promptly: "Hist! I've got the Ascot Cup."

That was rejected because it was an old joke and had more than three words.

"I met King Edward, all right," said Mr. Clemens. "He enjoyed it.[8] But he wouldn't sell me Windsor! Fine place, that castle. Better than the bungalow I've been paying rent on out at Tuxedo. I'm going out there now, but I've been away so long I'll have to sit up nights to get even with the rent."

"I really have got the Ascot Cup on board. I'd like to arrange with one of you reporters to sneak it ashore for me. No, I haven't got the Dublin Castle jewels. I proved it to them on the other side, despite the bad character they worked up for me. I just told them that it couldn't have been me, for I'd have stolen the safe, too."[9]

"Have the British a sense of humor?" was one of the leading questions.

"They certainly have a humor," Dr. Twain answered promptly. "I have come to the conclusion that every nation has a sense of humor and that all senses of humor are equally developed. An Englishman can make a jolly fine joke and laugh at it immediately. You may not understand it because you are not on the inside. They let me get on the inside and it was great. I am now the proud possessor of two senses of humor, British and American. Next to my degree my new sense of humor is the most sensible thing that happened to me on the trip. Make this plain—it is nonsense that one nation has a better sense [of humor] than another. Just get on the inside."[10]

King Edward told him a ripping joke, he said, a regular twister—but unfortunately he is saving it for thirty cents a word. It was a long joke, and he didn't think the reporters could buy it.[11]

"Now what about the English women? How did they compare with the ones you made so much of at the Actors' Club Fair, just before you started?"

"A leading question, young man," returned Mark Twain. "Decidedly too leading. Don't know where it would lead me to, so I'll sidestep it and ask for more time."[12]

"Don't you dread these reporter men?" asked little Miss Quick, who had stuck bravely to her post.

"No, my dear child," he smiled. "I've prepared myself for the next world."

He was told that "Big Tim" Sullivan on his return had declared, in referring to King Edward, "Ed's all right," and, asking his estimate of the British ruler, "I don't want to come into competition with 'Big Tim,'" he evaded.[13]

A long wicked looking scrape on the starboard side of the *Minnetonka*, a jagged hole and several bent plates told of her narrow escape in a fog by collision with an English bark. Mark Twain had reported the accident to *The American and Journal* by wireless.[14] Asked why he turned reporter, he said: "The collision came at 6 in the morning. I had not left a call for that hour, but I went on deck. It turned out that I was too late for the collision, too late by several seconds. I wanted something to excuse my pink pajamas and bathrobe, so I turned reporter.[15]

"Do you know that, after hitting us that bark was different from any vessel I ever saw. It had the peculiarity that another ship wouldn't have. You couldn't tell her bow from her stern. You see, she had left us her bowsprit."[16]

He was reminded that he had shocked London by crossing from his quarters in Brown's Hotel to the Bath Club in a bathrobe.

"Shocking! nothing," he said, shaking his shaggy white mane. "That was one of the privileges granted to one in his second childhood. Accumulated privileges form the chief advantage of old age.[17] I'll be seventy-two in November.[18] At 2 A.M. I feel every year of it, but at 8 in the morning, when I'm shaving, I feel twenty-five."[19]

"Did you ever take a Fairbanks cocktail?" asked the irreverent one.[20]

"I take anything that's offered," he returned. "If you can find anything that will make me blush, bring it along."

Someone showed him a newspaper report that his old homestead at Hannibal, Mo., was about to be sold.

"The newspapers have burned that old homestead four times, without my getting a cent of insurance, and now they're trying to sell it."[21]

On the program of the Saturday evening concert Mark Twain's name is printed "(By courtesy of Miss Dorothy Quick)." He made a plea for more assistance for the adult blind, and told a story of a friend who lives on Seventy-second street, who reached his home late one night with blind staggers and an inability to climb the stairs.

"The world was going round and round for him, and as he tumbled from stoop to pavement a second time he cried out: 'God pity poor sailors out at sea on a night like this.'"

After Miss Quick's mother had pried her loose from her self-adopted charge, Mark Twain with his secretary and manager was driven to his home at Fifth avenue and Ninth street. He will go to Tuxedo today and write reams of English humor at thirty cents the word.

Notes to Interview 234

I have supplemented this interview as reported in the *New York American* with versions of Twain's comments published in other newspapers. All newspaper citations below are from 23 July 1907 unless otherwise noted.

1. The *Minnetonka*, weighing 13,400 tons, was built in 1902 for the Atlantic Transport Line.

"Mark Twain Home, Captive of Little Girl," *New York World*, 18: "Doctor Twain, if you please," he said. "That is the only title I am using now. My dinner with the King? Did he enjoy it? How do I like America? What do I think of the English women? Did I get away with the Ascot Cup? The Dublin jewels, too? What's the best story I heard in England? Whoa—one minute, boys. Give me a chance to think. I haven't had any practice for nine days, and you remind me of work.

"Twain Glad He's Back," *New York Tribune*, 7: "I was pleased and elated, but I was most pleased because the honor was intended for my country and only secondarily for myself, as was the case. I found among Oxonians, as amongst the English everywhere, a strong regard for America and a deep interest in things American. I had all sorts of questions fired at me and was surprised at the intelligent knowledge shown of things on this side of the water."

"Mark Twain Home in Good Humor," *New York Times*, 7: "Just how my old friends are going to get away from calling me 'Mark' is something they will have to work out for themselves," he said, "and when they see me in my new cap and gown they will be bound to fall."

2. On the Ascot cup, see n. 1 to interview 232.

"English Know a Joke, Says Mark Twain," *New York Evening World*, 22 July 1907,

2: "Did you bring the Ascot gold cup with you?" "It's in the hold. I want you boys to help me smuggle it past the Customs officials. I honestly believe that some people believe I did steal that cup. If I had been on robbery bent I could have cleaned up a lot of things."

New York Times: "Oh, yes; I have the cup on board, and I hope some of you reporters are slick enough to help me smuggle it through the Custom House. It would be too bad to give it up after getting so close to home with it."

"Dr. Mark Twain Home with His Honors," *New York Herald,* 6: Mr. Clemens confessed to taking away the Ascot Cup, which was missed the day he arrived in England. "In fact," he said, "I've got it with me here, but this customs business bothers me. Do you think I ought to declare it? Perhaps you can give me a hint as to the best way to get into the country."

New York World: "As to the Ascot Cup, I don't mind taking you all into my confidence. Sh! It's on board this ship, and I expect to get ashore with it if I have luck and use diplomacy."

3. On the Dublin jewels, see n. 2 to interview 232.

New York World: "As to my lifting the Dublin jewels, the idea is absurd. Wasn't the safe left? Can it be thought for a moment that I would take the jewels without taking the safe?"

New York Times: "But I didn't get the Dublin jewels. With the character they gave me over on the other side I should certainly not have left the case. I would have taken both," he said.

4. MT was elected to honorary membership in 1899 in this "gentlemen's club" founded by Richard Savage in London in 1857.

5. *New York Times:* "How do you like America?" the reporters all asked at once. "I was afraid I would be asked that question," began Dr. Clemens, but before he got any further another was fired at him. "Have you seen the Statue of Liberty?" "I decline to commit myself, young man; you cannot trap me into any damaging admissions."

New York Herald: "Well, go ahead, gentlemen," he said. "I rather expected that you would come to inquire how I like America."

New York World: "I like America very much. I was prepared for that question and nearly all the others, but being a good Christian I do not dread the worst."

New York Evening World: "Are you glad to get back to America?" inquired the reporters. "I ought to be," was the reply. "This is my country. Before my departure for England—where, I must say, I had a great time—I paid the rent of a house at Tuxedo. It is my intention to spend the summer there."

New York Tribune: "Young man, you're right. Whether I sighed or didn't there's no place like a man's own home, unless it be heaven."

6. Dorothy Quick (1900-1962). See also Quick's memoir *Enchantment: A Little Girl's Friendship with Mark Twain* (Norman: University of Oklahoma Press, 1961).

7. "Mark Twain Comes in White," *New York Sun,* 7: "But, Mr. Clemens," said a hopeful young reporter, "we are willing to do the fair thing. Far be it from us to beat down your rates. If we club together and make up a pot can't we buy about $10 worth of conversation at the market rates? Or perhaps you might be willing, since you are on vacation, to come down a few cents per word or even per jest—say from thirty to twenty-seven, or to twenty-five. Does that appeal to you?" "Impossible," said Mark. "And I have no cheap rates."

8. *New York Evening World:* "I knew you would ask me how I enjoyed dining with

King Edward. To that question I will reply that the King enjoyed himself considerably."

New York Herald: To the question "How did you enjoy dining with the King?" he replied, "The King enjoyed it."

New York World: "Well, the King enjoyed the dinner and that is enough."

New York Times: "Did you enjoy the dinner very much?" "The King did."

New York Tribune: When informed that Jacques Lebaudy, the king of the Sahara, was now his next-door neighbor, the humorist replied: "If the king calls upon me, I will return his favor. That is the way I was trained in Missouri. I found the King of England to be a pretty good fellow; in fact, I am partial to kings, so to speak." [Jacques Lebaudy, aka Jacques I (1868–1919), French colonialist and self-proclaimed Emperor of the Sahara. See also Richard A. Winsche, "Jacques Lebaudy: Nassau County's 'Emperor of Sahara,'" *Nassau County Historical Society Journal* 57 (2002): 28–37.]

9. *New York Sun:* "You probably heard about the theft of the Ascot cup and the crown jewels later in Dublin. . . . I was accused all over England of being the culprit, and since I have no character left, I seldom took the trouble to deny it. I merely told them that any good detective knowing my habits would never put the crime on me, because he would have figured out instantly that if I had been on the job I would have taken the safe as well as the jewels and would have stolen the grandstand at Ascot as well as the gold cup."

10. *New York Evening World:* "England has a sense of humor, no matter what may be said to the contrary. English humor is hard to appreciate, though, unless you are trained to it. The English papers, in reporting my speeches, always put 'laughter' in the wrong place."

New York Tribune: "How about the English sense of humor?" he was asked. "We are told that you are the first American humorist to drive a joke home to the British mind." "No! No!" he replied. "I had no trouble in doing that thirty-five years ago. It is all nonsense, this talk that there is more humor in one part of the world than another. Human nature is the same in that respect everywhere—I presume even in China. I can understand an English joke—when all the details are explained," he added, and the bystanders swore he smiled grimly.

New York Herald: To the inquiry if it were really true that Englishmen could appreciate a joke he answered, "Certainly. I found that out in the case of my jokes thirty-five years ago. It is nonsense to say that one nation surpasses another in a sense of humor. To fully appreciate an English joke you must have all the details, and when you know them all you are sure to appreciate it."

New York Sun: "It isn't fair, by the way, to say that the English are not on bowing terms with a joke. I know, because I tried them first thirty-five years ago and got away with it. They are merely a little slow, but when things are explained to them and they comprehend the plot and get an idea of the mechanism of the joke, and are perfectly sure it isn't the kind that will kick back or go off unexpectedly, why, they are strong for it."

11. *New York Evening World:* "I knew also that you would ask me what were the best jokes I heard in England. I heard some good ones, but I am keeping them. Later on I will sell them for 30 cents a word."

New York Times: Dr. Clemens said that it was all a mistake that the English could not understand a joke. "I had not the slightest trouble in getting mine through their heads," he said. "What was the best joke you told them?" "That will cost you 30 cents a word, and I am having no bargain days now." "Did they laugh?" "Why, surely; but if you want to hear it you must be prepared to pay heavily for it. At this time of life one must get all one can for one's wits. I have been interviewed a great deal while away, but many of the interviews, when they appeared in print, were grossly exaggerated."

New York Herald: "What was the best story exclusive of any you told yourself that you heard in England?" he was asked. "That is one which I haven't told yet." One of the newspaper men asked him to tell it. "Can't," was the reply. "I get thirty cents a word for them." He declined an offer for a three-word story on the spot.

New York World: "The best story I heard in England is not one that I am going to tell now. I get thirty cents a word for stories." "What's the best joke you heard?" "My rate is the same for jokes—no rebate. Did the King crack a joke at the dinner? Yes; but I'm keeping that, too. I've got a place in the country, you know, that I have to pay rent for. No, I wasn't interviewed much in London, but my secretary was. Someone has asked me if anybody else ever succeeded in getting a joke through the English hide. Now that does not suggest a broad view of the situation. Humor isn't a thing of race or nationality. So much depends upon the environment of a joke. To be good it must absorb its setting. The American joke does this, so does the English. Believe it or not, I have met English jokes that were funny."

12. *New York Times:* "Are the Englishwomen as attractive as those in America?" was another question. "That is too leading, and I refuse to commit myself," was the diplomatic reply.

New York World: "As to English women, I will not commit myself just now. This is so sudden. I must have time to consider these great questions."

13. Timothy Daniel (Big Tim) Sullivan (1862–1913), a Tammany Hall politician and later a U.S. Representative; he was also elected to the U.S. Senate but was killed in an accident before taking his seat.

New York Sun: "Oh, I'm not competing as a humorist with Big Tim," said Mark. "I might finish back of the flag; but King Edward was very courteous and pleasant to me and he said a number of complimentary things. He remembered taking a walk with me sixteen years ago at Homburg, and when I told him that I often recounted that incident and never told it twice the same way he merely said he was content to leave himself in my hands—that he thought I was a capable and veracious historian." [On MT's meeting the king at Bad Homburg, see interview 225.]

New York Times: "What did you think of the King? When Tim Sullivan returned a short time ago he said 'Ed's all right; I like him. He is the goods.'" "I am not competing with Mr. Sullivan."

14. Among the many printings of MT's report of the *Minnetonka*'s collision with a bark off the coast of England is "Mark Twain's Wireless Message from the Sea," *New York World,* 18 July 1907, 9.

New York Evening World: "How about the collision in which the *Minnetonka* figured, news of which you sent to England by wireless?" was the next question. "It didn't amount to much," said Mark. "I sent that wireless message merely to keep in touch with the world and to give the people an idea that I knew what was going on."

15. *New York Sun:* "And yet," said he, discussing the incident, "my costume was a model of propriety and modesty compared to some that I merely glanced at in passing. Of the collision I saw nothing, because I dressed very leisurely. I was disappointed because I felt that I should have been notified beforehand."

16. *New York Tribune:* The humorist presided last Saturday at a concert on board and edited some resolutions drawn up and signed by the passengers, in which Captain Layland and Chief Officer Woolcock were commended for the admirable manner in which they handled the vessel in the collision between it and the French bark *Sterling*, on July 15. The preamble to the resolutions read in part:

"Steamer *Minnetonka*, at sea, July 20.

"This sixtieth voyage westward by the steamship *Minnetonka* has been marked by an occurrence which will never be forgotten by those now on board. During the morning watch on Monday, July 15, the fog which had enveloped the ship more or less all night became very dense. Suddenly, without any warning note of horn or bell a towering mass of canvas loomed up on our starboard bow, and was borne swiftly toward us. It seemed impossible for a moment or two to avoid either cutting down or being cut down by the bark which carried it, but instantaneously arising to the emergency, Captain Layland, who had been on the bridge for nearly thirty-six hours, and his chief officer, Mr. Woolcock, were able, owing to our greatly reduced speed, to maneuver the *Minnetonka* so admirably that the bark, losing only her bowsprit and head sails, merely struck us a glancing blow and dragged along our starboard side without seriously wounding the ship.

... "I saw from the deck," he said, "that her bowsprit had been carried away, and she looked to be considerably damaged, and I feared that she might possibly be in bad condition."

17. *New York Times:* Asked about his appearance in the lobby of Brown's Hotel, in London, in his pajamas and bathrobe prior to walking across the street to the Bath Club, he said: "When a man reaches my age he has certain privileges that younger men cannot have. I did that, and there was absolutely nothing improper in it."

18. *New York Times:* Dr. Clemens [was asked] if he objected to telling his age. "Not in the least. I shall be 72 in November. I do not mind it. Every year that I gain furnishes a new privilege, and all I want to dodge is second childhood."

New York Tribune: Some one asked him if he did not dread the assault of England's Fourth Estate. "No," he replied. "I have lived for seventy-two years of varying luck and adventure, and I am now ready to face anything, even the hereafter, and, anyway, you may be able to help me pass the Ascot cup through the customs."

19. *New York Tribune:* "Had it occurred at 2 o'clock in the morning, instead of 6," said the humorist, "I might have been frightened, for you know what Napoleon said of '2 o'clock courage.' When I wake up at that hour I feel old—seventy-two years old, as I will be in the latter part of November." [Napoleon Bonaparte (1769–1821) reputedly claimed that he had rarely seen moral courage at two o'clock in the morning.] "When do you feel youngest?" he was asked. "Oh, when I shave at 8 o'clock in the morning," was the reply. "From that time on I am never older than twenty-five years."

New York Sun: "At 2 o'clock in the morning I feel old and sinful," said he, "but at 8 o'clock, when I am shaving, I feel young and ready to hunt trouble. There is this about old age, though—every year brings one a new accumulation of privileges, a greater capacity for enjoyment. Maybe that's the only advantage of second childhood, but it isn't a bad one."

New York Times: "At 2 o'clock in the morning I feel as old as any man. At that time you must know that life in every person is at its lowest. At that hour I feel as sinful, too, as possible. But the rest of the time I feel as though I were not over 25 years old. You know one gets back both youth and courage by 6 o'clock in the morning."

20. Charles W. Fairbanks (1852–1918), U.S. vice president from 1905 to 1909. Apparently a topical joke at the expense of Fairbanks, who was a teetotaler.

New York Sun: "Do I ever take a Fairbanks cocktail? Boys, I'll take anything that is offered me, and like the girl in a show I saw before going to England, I'll do anything that won't make me blush. However, I'd like to see anybody make me blush."

New York Tribune: "Do you ever take a Fairbanks cocktail to help out?" was the next question. "I take anything that is offered me," was the quick reply.

21. *New York Herald:* Mr. Clemens betrayed no emotion when asked concerning the report that the house in Hannibal, Mo., in which he was born [sic] is to be sold. "It is about time it was," he observed laconically; "it has been burned down four times." [MT was actually born in Florida, Missouri.]

235

"'Mark Twain' Recalls Happy Days in 'Frisco," *New York Evening World,* 23 July 1907.

Samuel L. Clemens, known better to nearly every reader of the English language on two continents as Mark Twain, while returning home yesterday afternoon on the Atlantic Transport Liner *Minnetonka*,[1] said to a bevy of reporters who had boarded the vessel at Quarantine in reply to the query, "Are you glad to get back to America?"

"I ought to be. This is my country."

That the venerable humorist had uttered a loyal truth was evidenced by an incident.

He had sought a sequestered portion of the ship's rail, where he could obtain a view of the harbor with his charming little companion of the passage, Miss Dorothy Quick, whom he was heard to refer to affectionately as "mon amie" (pretty friend—and certainly a most appropriate term of endearment).[2]

His left arm was thrown paternally around the child's shoulder. Every lineament of his countenance expressed supreme appreciation of the peerless harbor.

An *Evening World* reporter who had spent his earlier years in California approached the grand old man and said: "Mr. Clemens, does this sight remind you at all of another beautiful harbor on the other side of the continent?"

"Ah, you mean San Francisco Bay. Dear old California! Yes, I spent some of the happiest days of my life there. That was many, many years ago. Let me see. I left there in the early '60s. But what happy days they were. Days when dear old Bret Harte and Henry George and myself used to sell our little tales to the old *Sacramento Record-Union*.[3] They are all gone now, and dear old 'Frisco, too. We shall never know the like of any of them again.

"Why, once I remember someone pointed out to me a little girl there—one just like my little companion here," and he indulged in a fond little hug. "They told me she was born in 'Frisco. It was so odd then to see a girl that

20. With Dorothy Quick at Tuxedo Park in early August 1907. Courtesy of the Mark Twain Project, University of California, Berkeley.

had been born in that wild region. And now here I am. Back home again after receiving the greatest ovation of my life. I have been what you call 'lionized.' But am I happier than in the dear, dead Bohemian days of long ago? I wonder! I wonder!" and this wonderful genius, in whose ears must have still been ringing the cheers of all England, turned to the rail and seemed lost in reveries. His eyes peered into space dreamily, and his thoughts must have gone back to those halcyon days in the Golden State which his old friend and confrere Bret Harte has pictured so admirably and so well. . . .

Notes to Interview 235

1. The *Minnetonka*, weighing 13,400 tons, was built in 1902 for the Atlantic Transport Line.
2. Dorothy Quick (1900–1962). See also Quick's memoir *Enchantment: A Little Girl's Friendship with Mark Twain* (Norman: University of Oklahoma Press, 1961).
3. Henry George (1839–97), who knew MT in San Francisco, best known as the author of *Progress and Poverty* (1879). On Harte, see n. 5 to interview 84. MT wrote twenty-five travel letters for the *Sacramento Union* from the Sandwich Islands in 1866. There is no evidence either Harte or George contributed to the paper, though George worked as a typesetter for it between 1861 and 1864.

11

The Long Goodbye, 1907–1910
Interviews 236–258

Depressed and lonely, Twain organized an "aquarium" of "angelfish," prepubescent girls with whom he regularly corresponded and who sometimes visited him. Twain moved into his last home, Stormfield, near Redding, Connecticut, in mid-1908. In a pique of anger and suspicion, he fired both his secretary, Isabel Lyon, and business manager, Ralph Ashcroft, in April 1909, convinced by his daughter Clara that they had swindled him in the construction of the house. Suffering from heart disease, Twain twice traveled to Bermuda in hopes of recovering his health, the second time soon after the death of his daughter Jean on Christmas Eve 1909.

∽

236

Channez Huntington Olney,[1] "'It's an Awful Thing to Get a Reputation for Being Funny,' Says Mark Twain," *New York World Magazine,* 25 August 1907, 7.

Mark Twain certainly made a perfect picture as he lay propped up on his brass bed, his long white, curly hair and mustache, his white negligee shirt, with its white tie, forming a strong contrast to his bright, merry blue eyes and healthy pink coloring. On either side of his bed was a large window, looking out on the green trees, the sunny sky, the smooth lawns and flowers of Tuxedo Park. He held out his hand in greeting, and gave a cordial, friendly handclasp.

"You must excuse me," he said, "but I caught cold on the ship coming over, and can't seem to throw it off, so I decided the best place for me, at present, was in bed. This bronchial trouble gets a hold and hangs on. But the air up here will soon drive it away. Yes, this winding road, up the mountain, does look like the road that leads up the mountain at Florence, to Michelangelo's old home. Yes, Italy is a beautiful country.

"Let me see, how many times have I been abroad? Thirty-seven times, and

I'm always glad to get home again, although I am a first-class sailor. Never sick in my life on shipboard. Oh, that statement that the papers printed about each word I spoke being worth thirty cents. That was my little joke. I was tired out when I reached New York, and, not feeling well, I couldn't think of anything interesting to say. I can't talk to order. Thoughts only come by inspiration, and I had really nothing to say.

"It's an awful thing to gain a reputation for being witty and humorous. Every time you talk people expect you to tell a story or say something funny. You can't always live up to it. We are all only human beings. Well, the day after that article appeared in the paper about my getting thirty cents for every word, an enterprising editor telephoned me that he would give me double that amount, or sixty cents a word for a talk."

Here Mr. Clemens laughed; a hearty, merry, infectious laugh that you couldn't help joining in to save your life. His private secretary, who was sitting opposite, laughed also. She is a very attractive young Englishwoman, with lovely, large, intellectual dark eyes; very gentle, very charming, very capable.[2]

Mr. Clemens's manner is perfect—so hospitable, so unassuming, so cheerful. Kindness just breathes from him. I have noticed that the more talented a man is the more tactful and charming he is. As Mr. Clemens himself remarked: "It's only the man who is climbing up, and isn't sure of his position, who is rude. He hasn't learned to discriminate. Everybody is a stepping-stone to him, up to heights above him. When he arrives at the top then he has time to be affable. His worry is gone. He has arrived."

He said: "Aren't my hands steady for a young man of seventy-two?"

He held out two smooth, shapely, beautiful, artistic hands.

They were as steady, as firm as those of a man of twenty-five.

"There," he said, "what do you think of them? And I have been promised a long life, too—to be exact, until I am ninety-six, eleven months and two days old. And I hope I do live until then, if I have all my faculties. I wouldn't want to live and be feeble-minded or a burden to myself or others."

Speaking of a man who is eighty-two and gives the credit to out-of-door exercise, he replied: "Now, on the contrary, I do not take any out-of-door exercise. Instead, I stay at home and rest, and attribute my good health and long life to that. Of course, if a man's work has carried him out of doors, then it agrees with him all his life, but if he has nothing but brain work he doesn't need the physical exercise. I think brain work is the most fatiguing work in the world. It makes you physically more tired than manual labor. It isn't so much what a man does, it's how he does it, that counts in this world. I have just as much respect for a man who excels at one thing as another, so long as he excels—so long as he is a master of his art.

"Yes, I believe firmly that the hand expresses the character of the person. I think it a great idea.

"Now, what does my hand indicate?"

He held out both white hands—hands to be very proud of, hands that showed care, pride.

They represented, above all things, an artist, a sensitive man, proud, firm willed, impulsive, clear headed. A man splendidly equipped mentally, with great imagination, great love of travel, great love of humanity. No melancholia, no brooding. Just good cheer, optimistic in the extreme. The hands of a poet, a writer, a physician, a humorist. The ideal and the mental, large, predominant. Going without a meal wouldn't bother Mr. Clemens half as much as missing a beautiful song, or a beautiful painting, or a beautiful statue.

His hands show tact, very good luck, and increasing fortunes, gained in two different ways. When that was mentioned he replied:

"Yes, I made money first by writing, then by lecturing. Oh, I've been all through it. I know what hard work means, what newspaper work means. It hasn't all been a joke, by any means."

His hands, his general appearance, all seem to promise a very long, healthy, prosperous life. His wonderful magnetism, influence over others, whatever one may call that something that attracts one person to another willy-nilly, seems to radiate from his whole being. You couldn't help like Mark Twain, or Mr. Samuel Clemens, as his secretary calls him, any more than you could help breathing.

His hands are beautiful; a great object lesson to anybody who has his artistic talents. To a young boy or ambitious man or woman his hands are a study.

See if yours are like them, or if they are not, try to be as like them as you can. When he had completed a beautiful impression of his hand and had signed his famous name to the paper, he said the friendliest of goodbys.

And he never even tried to say anything funny or spring a joke!

Notes to Interview 236

1. Channez Huntington Olney (1873–1908), journalist and aspiring actor.
2. Isabel Van Kleek Lyon (1863–1958), MT's private secretary from 1902 until 1909.

237

"Mark Twain's Ideal Pipe," *New York Press,* 15 September 1907, sec. 2, 1.

Samuel L. Clemens (Mark Twain) is looking for the ideal smoking pipe. He cannot understand, he declared in an interview the other day, why, in this twentieth century and the marvelous things that the brains of man has produced, the ideal pipe has not yet been realized. The pipe has been Mark's favorite means of enjoying the soothing influence of tobacco during his long and active life.

"It seems to be impossible on this fair earth of ours, with all the subtle resources of a complex civilization, to produce one perfect pipe," said Mr. Clemens with a somewhat serious look. "Natural laws evidently do not permit of it. It is of no use to rebel against them. We can only fold our hands and endure. And for want of a better pipe, our smoke is but a shadow of what it might be.

"In the first place, the ordinary pipe has not a sufficiently large bowl. To the superficialist that may seem easy of remedy. 'Then,' he says, 'make a pipe with a larger bowl.' If we did that the smoke passing through the tobacco would render the latter part of the pipe foul and fetid. Even with the bowl of an ordinary size the last of the pipeful is not so good as its commencement. The larger bowl would also make the pipe too heavy; a pipe bowl must be of thick, porous wood or clay. Besides, the prolonged smoking would render the bowl too hot.

"A pipe that would give a man a sufficiency of smoke, or regular and invariable sweetness and coolness, would be perfect; there is not and there never can be such a pipe. No one can make the ideal pipe, but it is possible to imagine it. It smokes for two hours without refilling, and it is good all the time. It never needs a brush or string to be drawn through its mouthpiece. It cakes a little inside the bowl, but only a little—enough to give it a friendly, used appearance, but not enough to require that hideous operation for the excision of cake to be performed with a pocket knife. It never breaks or cracks, and it cannot be lost or mislaid. It is not a patent. No patent pipes are good for anything. Their anatomy is so complicated that a diagram is sold with them. You have to unscrew things, and take out cylinders and put in wads. There is no sort of restfulness about a patent pipe.

"The ideal pipe would not look clever or perplex people in any way. But it is of no use talking about it. We shall probably go on smoking as well as we can, and as much as we can; and even at the best, how far we shall be from perfection? I am 71 years old now, so I entertain no hope that the ideal pipe—if such thing is really possible—will be realized during my remaining years."

238

Isidore Harris,[1] "A Prince of Humorists: Interview with 'Mark Twain,'"
Great Thoughts from Master Minds, 5 October 1907, 136–38.

It is not easy at any time to secure an interview with Mark Twain; the difficulties were well nigh insuperable on the occasion of his recent visit to England.

He has denied himself to most interviewers ever since he reached the age of seventy—two years ago—when he publicly announced that he would never again hold forth on any stated subject unless he had given that subject proper reflection beforehand. This announcement was intended to keep interviewers at a distance, since they seldom give the person interviewed an opportunity of thinking out what he has to say. As he humorously remarked: "Even on such a subject as the weather, when I feel inclined to observe to Mr. Ashcroft, my business representative and traveling companion, that it is a fine winter morning—I believe it's supposed with you to be midsummer—I hardly like to commit myself to such a statement without adequate preparation." While he was in England an enterprising newspaper asked him for an interview which they wished to "marconigraph" to some American liners in mid-ocean.[2] "Why, that's work," replied Mark Twain, "and I've retired from work long ago." All the same, the great humorist has not exactly retired. At the present time he is engaged in writing his autobiography. One of the most interesting chapters in this work will be the last, containing the experiences and impressions of his latest visit to England.

"Was your visit to England in 1897, on the occasion of the Diamond Jubilee of the late Queen Victoria, the last time you visited this country?" I asked.[3]

"Not exactly. On that occasion I made a trip round the world, which occupied three years, and I returned to England. So I was here three years ago."

"And you have noted a good many changes that have come about in the appearance of things since that time?"

"Indeed I have. Seven years ago there were no motor-buses and motor-cars, and very few electric vehicles. Today people seem to ride nothing else. And, concurrently with this change, I have observed a noticeable absence of bicycles. When I was here before all sorts of people used bicycles. Even titled persons did not disdain them; but now, if they are used at all, it is only by the humbler classes. It has struck me also that London has been greatly altered and beautified in the meanwhile. The Strand, with the Kingsway thoroughfare, and the neighborhood of Pall Mall have been changed out of all recognition. New hotels and playhouses have sprung up, new thoroughfares and palatial public offices; vast series of flats have been erected, and, altogether, London is becoming a second Paris. Yesterday afternoon, being one of the few lovely days with which we have been favored of late, I drove out to Dollis Hill, which I used to know as the occasional summer residence of Mr. Gladstone. It has now become a public recreation-ground, but it struck me as being, if anything, more beautiful that it ever was. I have not had any occasion to go eastward into the City, so I am unable to say what changes have been made there."

"But you appear to have been almost everywhere?"

"I have done and seen a great deal. I have been to Windsor, where, as you know, I was received by the King and Queen. I have been to Oxford to receive my degree, by the right of which I am privileged to doctor the English literature as much as I please. At Stratford-on-Avon I visited Shakespeare's birthplace, and Miss Marie Corelli.[4] I have been the guest of the Pilgrims and the Savages, and of my American fellow-citizens at the Cecil on the occasion of Independence Day."[5]

"How does the welcome you have everywhere received strike you?"

"I feel it has been a welcome of sincere admiration and love and not a merely polite reception. And it has often occurred to me that visits such as I and other public men from time to time pay to your country do more to cement good fellowship between nations than any number of Hague Conferences and ambassadorial negotiations.[6] But this conversation is getting rather too egotistical; you had better ask Mr. Ashcroft what he thinks of the effect of my visit."

"I think," said Mr. Ashcroft, "that the English race have been led to realize more fully, even than they did before, that they are part-owners with the American nation of Mark Twain."[7]

It will, probably, surprise many readers to learn that Mark Twain prefers to be considered as, before all things, a philosopher, and only secondarily as a humorist. . . . His polemic against Christian Science . . . though humorously written, he regards as a serious piece of work.[8] And he is careful to explain that he does not condemn Christian Science out and out. There is something in the theory that mind can exert a powerful influence upon the body in conditions of disease. A striking instance of the power of mind over body came under his notice in the course of his early experiences as a Mississippi pilot. The boat on which he was voyaging collided with another vessel. The crew rushed to the other end of the boat for safety, and no one ran faster than a helpless cripple, who threw away his crutches and just raced for his life. The underlying idea of Christian Science is right enough; it is the use which people have made of it which is all wrong. Mrs. Eddy and her satellites have exploited it as a business proposition for all and much more than it is worth, and it is their dishonest methods which one of the most upright of men has lashed with all the power of his scornful humor.

Mark Twain does not even believe that *Science and Health* was written by Mrs. Eddy. "The known and undisputed products of her pen," he says, "are a formidable witness against her. I think she has been claiming as her own another person's book, and wearing, as her own property, laurels rightfully belonging to another person."

"Why has not that other person protested against such literary piracy?" I ask.

"Because her work was not exposed to print until after he was sagely dead." ...

Speaking of *The Innocents Abroad,* Mark Twain assured me that this, one of his most humorous books, was taken so seriously by a prominent English journal when it first made its appearance that the review proved to be more deliciously funny than the book itself. The ingenious critic charged Mark Twain with displaying shocking ignorance and an utter disregard of truth.[9] Now what the American writer had to say about his own country was both interesting and instructive, as, for instance, when he mentioned the quite new fact that in America the small farmers carry their farms away on wheelbarrows overnight to avoid paying the taxes! "I should think that was a new fact," said Mark Twain, "considering I made it up myself. And the reviewer took it for gospel truth, because it referred to America, which I was supposed to know all about.

"Nor was this writer alone in taking *The Innocents Abroad* seriously. The first time I visited England was in 1872. It was while I was riding up in the train from Liverpool to London, thoroughly enjoying the novel scenery, that I observed my fellow-passenger. He was so painfully absorbed in a book he was reading that he never once looked up. Curious to know what it was that could so take a man's attention to the exclusion of everything else, I looked over his shoulder and discovered that he was reading *The Innocents Abroad.* From that time I felt miserable. The man looked so solemn, and I had intended that book to make people laugh. Just as I wished that I was anywhere but sitting next to such a serious personage, the train slowed down. As we arrived at Crewe my fellow-passenger appeared to have reached the end of his volume. He put it in the rack and jumped out. Now, I thought, I should be able to resume the interrupted enjoyment of the scenery. But alas! presently he returned, reached into his handbag for the second volume, and all the way up to London he continued to read, but never smiled. Neither did I.

"Talking of humor," says Mark Twain, "there is no success in the literature of fun equal to what is attained by ignorant schoolchildren, without intention of being funny, in their heroic efforts to set forth hard facts and sober statistics. As, for instance, when a pupil sets forth the following meanings of words:—

Amenable, anything that is mean.
Plagiarist, a writer of plays.
Equestrian, one who asks questions.
Mendacious, what can be mended.
Irrigate, to make fun of.

Emolument, the headstone to a grave.
Parasite, a kind of umbrella.
Tenacious, ten acres of land.

"Or his knowledge of mathematics in this form:—
"A straight line is any distance between two places.
"Parallel lines are lines that can never meet until they run together.
"Things which are equal to each other are equal to anything else.
"A circle is a round straight line with a hole in the middle.
"Or his conceptions of geography thus:—
"The United States is quite a small country compared with some other countries, but is about as industrious.
"Russia is very cold and tyrannical.
"The two most famous volcanoes of Europe are Sodom and Gomorrah.
"Climate lasts all the time, and weather only a few days."[10]

Notes to Interview 238

1. Isidore Harris (1853–1925), assistant minister of the West London Synagogue of British Jews in Westminster from 1881 until his death.

2. To "marconigraph" was to send a wireless communication, or radio telegraph. Named for Guglielmo Marconi, who was granted the first patent for a system of wireless telegraphy and was the corecipient of the 1909 Nobel Prize for Physics.

3. Queen Victoria celebrated her Diamond Jubilee, or sixtieth anniversary, on the British throne in 1897.

4. Marie Corelli (1855–1924), English romance writer. See also *Auto* (1959), 350–53.

5. The Pilgrim Club hosted a dinner in honor of MT on 25 June 1907 at the Savoy Hotel in London. See also Paine, 1389–90. MT was elected to honorary membership in 1899 in the Savage Club, a "gentlemen's club" founded by Richard Savage in London in 1857. The American Society hosted a dinner in MT's honor at the Hotel Cecil in London on the Fourth of July.

6. The Second International Peace Conference at the Hague would conclude on 18 October 1907.

7. Ralph W. Ashcroft (1875–1947), MT's business adviser from 1907 to 1909, married Isabel Lyon (MT's personal secretary) in March 1909.

8. MT's two-volume *Christian Science* (1907). See also n. 12 to interview 175.

9. MT apparently refers to the review of *The Innocents Abroad* in the *Saturday Review,* 8 October 1870, 467–68: "He parades his utter ignorance of Continental languages and manners. . . . He exhibits that charming ignorance of all languages but English which is so common amongst his fellows. . . . Perhaps we have persuaded our readers by this time that Mr. Twain is a very offensive specimen of the vulgarest kind of Yankee." Reprinted in *Mark Twain: The Contemporary Reviews,* ed. Louis J. Budd (New York: Cambridge University Press, 1999), 83–86.

10. A similar set of satirical definitions appears in chapter 61 of *FE*.

239

Frederick Boyd Stevenson,[1] "Mark Twain on the Scope of the Children's Theater," *Brooklyn Eagle* news special, 24 November 1907, 1.

"When I saw the performance of those children and heard the perfect rendition of the parts assigned to them," began Mark Twain, "one thing came uppermost in my mind: That was their perfect enunciation."

He shifted his position a little in the big Venetian bed—where he receives some of his visitors and does much of his writing—took a good pull at his pipe and blew a cloud of smoke ceilingward. The night before the dramatization of his book *The Prince and the Pauper* had been presented at the Children's Theater of the Educational Alliance,[2] where he had been the host to a fashionable audience.[3]

"Now, if there is one particular thing which Americans should learn to do," he went on, "it is to speak their native language correctly. We have certain acquaintances who visit us occasionally and whom we in turn visit, as you and other people have, no doubt. One of these persons whom I have in mind pronounces his words so indistinctly that I can hardly understand him, although he may not be sitting farther from me than you. That one defect destroys all the pleasure of his visit. But he is not the only offender. The blurring of our words, the curtailing of our syllables and running them into other syllables of other words is one of the most disagreeable characteristics of the American method of speech. And it is not a characteristic that belongs alone to the uneducated. It is quite common—yes, I think I may say, it is common—with the educated classes. One thing is certain: incorrect enunciation is a great bar to the true enjoyment of conversation. Why, the man who cannot talk correctly—the man who cannot talk correctly—"

He raised himself from his pillows, took his pipe from his mouth, waved his hands threateningly above his head and ejaculated fiercely: "He ought not talk at all."

A little tiger-striped kitten that came from Tuxedo took a quick run across the room, and with one agile jump was on the big bed. Mark Twain stroked its soft fur caressingly. The fierceness had gone from his voice as he continued: "And now it seems that we Americans may learn how to speak the English language from the East Side, nearly all of whose citizens came to this country unable to speak the tongue of which they so soon become master. This fine enunciation of many of the young people of the East Side is due to the work of the Educational Alliance, and a great part of it is brought about by the training received at the Children's Theater, under the auspices of that organization. The work of this institution is one of the most remarkable educational developments in the country. Its influence has already spread throughout the lower East Side. I believe it will spread to all parts of the country and be universally adopted as an educational factor."

"President Eliot of Harvard,[4] who was there last night, as you know," I said, "told me that he had witnessed with a great deal of pleasure a dramatic performance in Cambridge where the poet Longfellow's granddaughter took the part of Shylock.[5] He said he believed that such instruction was of inestimable educative benefit, and that the same methods ought to be introduced in every public school in the United States."

"President Eliot is entirely right," said Mr. Clemens. "In this method of instruction you have the first incentive for obtaining knowledge—that is, personal interest. With that comes concentration and ambition to excel. It is not the theatrical idea that is aimed at. In fact, as Miss Herts, the manager of the theater, says, the idea of the theater as a profession is discouraged rather than encouraged.[6] The scope of the movement is to interest these young people of the East Side in wholesome and classic dramas, to instill in them a love for good literature and a knowledge of the true motives of life. There is a great deal of the dramatic in the makeup of every human being. By the dramatic we can appeal to one's sympathies, to one's highest sentiments, to one's sense of justice and right and to one's ambition to progress. Not only are the mental attributes quickened by this method of instruction, but the esthetic attributes are developed also. I have in mind an instance that occurred not long ago at that little theater which illustrates this point. They were putting on a play requiring fifteen or twenty characters to be represented by young girls. The costumes were plain and somber. To many of the East Side people there remains that relic of savagery—a love of gaudy colors and display in dress; and on this occasion that bit of hereditary fondness made itself apparent. Several of the mothers of the young girls who were to take part in the performance were anxious to make costumes for their daughters of striking patterns and colors that would accord more with their ideas of fine dress than the subdued garments of the play. But the manager was firm. The play must be presented on conventional lines. And this decision resulted in the formation of a more refined taste in the households that were represented at the play and in the households whose members attended the play. So it is in all lines of action and of thought. The improvement comes not only to the young people who take part in the plays, but extends to their families and friends. They rehearse their parts in the homes, and the plays become known to every one of the immediate family and acquaintances. So you see, this education is an education for all the people of the East Side.

"There is another point—perhaps it is the most important of all; yes, I am sure it is the most important," he continued slowly. "A point that we should all attend to—a point that America has good reason to attend to."

The strong face of my host assumed a thoughtful, a serious expression. He sat erect in bed and ran his hands through his long, white hair. His white robe with its turned down collar was open at the throat. The pillows were clustered behind him against the high mahogany headboard of the bed. He spoke more earnestly than he had spoken before.

"This chief point of importance," he said, "relates to citizenship."

Again he paused for just an instant. Then he said quickly, sharply: "Citizenship? We have none! In place of it we teach patriotism, which Samuel Johnson said a hundred and forty or a hundred and fifty years ago was the last refuge of the scoundrel—and I believe that he was right.[7] I remember when I was a boy I heard repeated and repeated time and time again the phrase, 'My country, right or wrong, my country!'[8] How absolutely absurd is such an idea. How absolutely absurd to teach this idea to the youth of the country."

He was speaking calmly and deliberately, but his voice showed the indignation that he felt.

"And this seems to be the sole idea of patriotism," he went on. "Not long ago I saw fifteen or more boys drilling. They assumed a military air, and went through the evolutions of trained soldiers. This was to teach them patriotism, but what incentive with our ideas of patriotism is there for the young man of today to shoulder his gun and fight for his country? I can imagine one situation—even under the present state of affairs—where a man could feel that he ought to fight for his country. That situation might be an invasion. In such a case a man should fight, but he should fight under protest, and for this reason: When a country is invaded it is because it has done some wrong to another country—some wrong like the United States did in taking the Philippines—a stain upon our flag that can never be effaced. Yet today in the public schools we teach our children to salute the flag, and this is our idea of instilling in them patriotism. And this so-called patriotism we mistake for citizenship; but if there is a stain on that flag it ought not to be honored, even if it is our flag. The true citizenship is to protect the flag from dishonor—to make it the emblem of a nation that is known to all nations as true and honest and honorable. And we should forever forget that old phrase—'My country, right or wrong, my country.'"

Mark Twain refilled his pipe carefully; he applied a match and pulled away vigorously till the tobacco on top was aglow. The little tiger kitten climbed upon his shoulders and walked familiarly around his neck. For a few moments Mark Twain puffed in silence.

"It may be," he continued, "that we must learn our lessons of citizenship on the East Side in the Children's Theater. There the true principles of true life which mean true citizenship are being taught to those boys and girls who are to be the future citizens of America. First of all they are taught self-respect and confidence. They are taught that the true motives of life are to reach for the highest ideals. The dramas that they play have morals that tend toward this aim. And best of all, they are taught to act for themselves and to think for themselves. It is his self-thinking that goes to make up the true public opinion. We say we have public opinion in America. We have none. We only think second hand. How many of us are there today who know whether it is better for the country to have a tariff or free trade? The only opinions most of us have on this subject are the opinions derived second hand from certain men who seek to influence us to their way of thinking, and their way of thinking is generally in a direction that will subserve their own private ends or the ends of the party which they represent. So, you see, we have no citizenship, and our so-called patriotism is a patriotism that is employed for the benefit of political parties and is made a party cry.

"Now, then, is there a new cult forming on the East Side? Are we to learn what true citizenship means and what true patriotism means from this new cult? Is the beginning here to extend universally? For fourteen years Isidor Straus, the president of the Educational Alliance, has devoted himself to educating these future citizens.[9] The Educational Alliance greets them at the steamship landing and from that time onward never loses track of them. Their morals are watched; they are educated in the practical things of life—the things that make for this very citizenship which we, as a nation, have lost. We have good reason to emulate these people of the East Side. They are reading our history and learning the great questions of America that we do not know and are not learning, and they are learning them first hand and are doing their own thinking. They are not backward in studying the statistics that many of us seem to abhor, because we think they are dry, yet if we only studied them the right way statistics are intensely interesting."

The fire in the grate was burning low. Mark Twain arose and tossed three or four logs upon it. The flames wrapped around the dry wood and lighted up the room.

"Your life has been a busy one," I ventured. "The public owes much to you. But perhaps the most important work of your life is the work of helping this movement of the Children's Theater."

"It is the most important work of my life," he said emphatically.

The serious look had left him. The brightness of the flames on the logs was reflected in his face.

Notes to Interview 239

1. Frederick Boyd Stevenson (1869–1938), American journalist.
2. A revised version of Abby Sage Richardson's script. See also note 2 to interview 49.

3. The Children's Theater of the Educational Alliance, founded in 1902 and dissolved in 1909, was located on Jefferson Street at east Broadway on the Lower East Side.

4. Charles William Eliot (1834–1926), president of Harvard University from 1869 to 1909.

5. Probably Frances Appleton Dana de Rham (1883–1933).

6. Alice Minnie Herts (Heniger), author of *The Children's Educational Theater* (1911).

7. Attributed in *Life of Samuel Johnson, LL.D.* (1791) by James Boswell (1740–95).

8. A phrase coined in 1816 by the U.S. naval officer Stephen Decatur (1779–1820) and later amended by Carl Schurz (1829–1906), U.S. senator from Missouri (1869–75) and secretary of the interior from 1877 to 1881: "Our country, right or wrong. When right, to be kept right; when wrong, to be put right."

9. Isador Straus (1845–1912), German Jewish émigré and U.S. representative from 1894 to 1895.

240

"Twain Out $32,000 in Plasmon Failure," *New York American,* 21 December 1907, 1–2.

Mark Twain is a sufferer to the extent of $32,500 by the involuntary bankruptcy which was thrust upon the Plasmon Company of America in the United States Court yesterday.

Twain was acting president and vice-president of the concern, an independent branch of which is flourishing in England. It manufactures milk products, and until mismanagement forced it to the wall the American concern was doing a rushing business.

Twain thought it was a good thing anyhow, and put $32,500 into it. Disregarding his former business experience, he permitted himself to be inveigled into the marts of trade once more, like the comedian who simply can't resist Hamlet.

While acting president of the concern, an office which he accepted in the hope of saving it from final destruction, someone served on the humorist the preliminary papers in an action to recover more than there was in the treasury. Mark carefully put the notice in his pocket. That was his day to be literary. Next day he completely forgot the circumstance, and a few days later judgment was taken by default. That started the run on the bank. Yesterday the end came.

It isn't altogether a funny story, for there is reason to believe Mr. Clemens has been deliberately swindled. He admits that he has, anyhow. His faith in the product of the company—which cured him of dyspepsia, he says—was so strong that he was disinclined to adopt harsh measures. Somebody played on his good nature and his artistic contempt for sordid details. Anyhow, he's $32,500 out.

At his home, No. 21 Fifth avenue, last night, the humorist, whose second venture in business has thus turned out disastrously, wagged his head dolefully over the upset. A big black cat sat on the top step and yowled dismally as the reporter walked up. Miss Lyon, Mr. Clemens's secretary, saw the reporter first.[1]

While they discussed the affair there were sounds of sardonic laughter in the room beyond. Then a pen scratched viciously over a sheet of paper. Just when the reporter had abandoned all hope of seeing the humorist, the acting president and vice-president of the Plasmon Company of American strode out into the hall. He had discarded his customary suit of white flannel and wore solemn black. He shook hands after the manner of one welcoming the mourners.

Pressed to tell all about it, however, Twain seemed too full for utterance. He pointed out that he mustn't talk for publication, alleging a fear that the reporter wouldn't quote his language exactly as he said it. In substance the interview was as follows:

"Your friends say that you were outrageously swindled. Were you?" asked the reporter.

"I was."

"Out of how much?"

"Oh, about $32,000."

"How did it happen?"

"Well"—and here the reader can imagine a characteristic drawl—"I hold $25,000 worth of stock, and one of the members of the company swindled me out of $12,500 later."

"Did—"

"But I don't mean that I was swindled out of the $25,000. The company failed because of bad management."

"Who was the man that got your $12,500?"

Mr. Clemens here mentioned the name, with a hideous laugh, and turning to Miss Lyon, said: "Well, I guess that will fix Mr. —— of ——."

"Was this the first time that you were ever swindled?" asked the reporter.

"In my life? The first time in my life?" The humorist looked pained. He seemed to regard the question as a slight on his world-wide experience. He laughed outright.

"Why, I have been swindled out of more money than there is on this planet," he replied, triumphantly.

"But," he resumed, with a reminiscent air, "I oughtn't to say I was swindled out of all the money. Most of it was lost through bad business. I was always bad in business."

Mr. Clemens wound up the chapter by cautioning the reporter not to confound the bankrupt company with the English Plasmon Company.

"That is paying five or six per cent," said he, "which is doing well for an English company. I hold $80,000 worth of stock in the English company."

Curiously enough, it was while Twain was laboring prodigiously to retrieve the losses sustained in his other business venture that he made the acquaintance of plasmon. That was eight years ago, when he was "following the equator" on his famous lecture tour. He was suffering horribly from indigestion when he met in Vienna a Professor Siebold, who had discovered plasmon.[2]

Twain claimed to have been cured by it, and when he went to London some time later and discovered that a plasmon company was being organized he took stock in it. Similarly, when, after the success of the staple in England, John Hays Hammond, the well-known engineer,[3] and others decided to organize a plasmon company in America, Twain again invested.

Hammond's associate in the venture was a man named H. A. Butters, of California.[4] The new company was organized with a capitalization of $750,000, of which one-third of the issue went to the English company, one-third was paid-up capital, and the remaining third was to be given as bonus to the subscribers who put up the money.

Twain subscribed $25,000, for which he was entitled to 50,000 shares, but as it turns out someone manipulated the books and he was never credited with more than the original 25,000 shares at a par of $1, and these are now valueless. The remainder of his loss was sustained through money advanced at odd times to the promoter, whose name he gave to the reporter last night.

Bad management has characterized the life of the company here from the beginning. There have been constant fights in the courts, the directors have been divided, litigation has followed litigation until a much better businessman than Mark Twain would have found himself nonplussed to locate the exact financial standing of the concern.

According to Ralph W. Ashcroft,[5] whose claim was included in those which have reduced the concern to bankruptcy, the bad management of Butters was responsible in the first instance for the wreck of the company. Butters is now in California.

Ashcroft also places considerable blame on Harold Wheeler, who succeeded Butters as manager of the company.[6] John Hays Hammond tried to make something out of it, and he, too, failed.

It seemed to be the fate of the concern, perhaps because of the blighting influence of Twain, never to prosper, and finally, after its counsels had been divided for more than a year, Hammond, a year ago, gave up in disgust and turned it over to Twain and Ashcroft.

Notes to Interview 240

1. Isabel Van Kleek Lyon (1863-1958), MT's private secretary from 1902 until 1909.
2. Siebold patented his invention under the name "Plasmon-Milch-Eiweiss." Plasmon was a food supplement made from dried milk.
3. See n. 3 to interview 115.
4. Henry A. Butters (d. 1908), prominent mining man and rancher. MT described Butters as "my heart's detested darling" (*MTE*, 356).
5. Ralph W. Ashcroft (1875-1947), MT's business adviser from 1907 to 1909, married Isabel Lyon (MT's personal secretary) in March 1909.
6. Harold Wheeler, Hammond's agent in the plasmon venture. See also *Auto* (1959), 205.

241

"Rival Jokesmiths Off for Bermuda," *New York World*, 23 February 1908, 3.

Mark Twain and his friend, H. H. Rogers, sailed on the *Bermudian* yesterday for Bermuda. Years ago Mark Twain warned "my young friend Harry Rogers to mend his ways" or he would "come to some bad end."[1]

"I see we're discovered," said Mark Twain, when the reporters appeared. "That's what I get for being in bad company."[2]

"You've got no edge on me," returned the Standard Oil's chief jester. "Some of my methods may be bad. The public says so, at least. But they're no worse than your jokes, Sam."

"Listen," said Mr. Twain. "I'll sell you a joke for a dollar and Rogers will sell you financial information for another dollar. I keep my jokes to sell, just as he keeps his knowledge on finance to sell."[3]

"I'm going because Mark is paying my fare," said Mr. Rogers. "I'm broke again."

"Yes; I'm paying his fare, but I'm $2 shy," said the other. "I'm going to shake him down for that $2 when we get out to sea."[4]

"That's one of his jokes," returned Mr. Rogers, "but it isn't worth $2, is it? My picture? I'll pose, but only on condition that Twain will promise not to pick the photographer's pocket when the cloth is over his head."

"I'm rather particular about who poses with me," drawled Mark Twain between puffs at his cigar. "Of course it will be a step down to pose with Rogers, but I suppose I'll have to take a couple of steps down like that before I die. Rogers usually has his picture taken up in Mulberry street, but—well, I'll submit."[5]

"That kind of financiering is too high for me," said the author.

"I'm as near to you as I want to stand," remarked Mr. Rogers.

"I'm really going along to keep Rogers straight," said Mr. Twain in a stage whisper.[6]

Wheeling and surveying the cloudless horizon, Mr. Rogers said the financial outlook didn't differ very much from that. "The horizon is bright," he added, looking far away.

Notes to Interview 241

I have supplemented this interview as reported in the *New York World* with versions of Twain's comments published in other newspapers. All newspaper citations below are from 23 February 1908.

1. On Rogers, see n. 2 to interview 212. The 5,530-ton *Bermudian* was built in 1904 for the Quebec SS Co.

2. "Rogers and Twain Sail," *New York Times,* 1: "This is what I get for being in bad company," said Mark Twain, humorist, pointing to H. H. Rogers, financier....

3. "Twain and Rogers Off for Bermuda," *New York Herald,* sec. 2, 3: "I sell my jokes to the highest bidder. Rogers sells his information on finance to the highest bidder."

"Two Jokers, One Deck," *New York Tribune,* sec. 1, 8: When it was suggested that he was seeking the seclusion of the sea to swap jokes for stock tips with Mr. Rogers, Mr. Clemens replied: "No; not that at all. You see, I keep all my jokes to myself and sell them in lots to the highest bidder, just as Rogers does with his financial information."

4. "'Rogers is Busted'—Twain," *New York American,* 1: "For heaven's sake, stake me to two dollars! Rogers is busted, and I haven't a thing my uncle will take from me. ... I have my doubts about Rogers. You know the market has sagged, and my poor friend here has suffered heavily. He's like a man in the midst of plenty, yet devoid of appetite. 'Tis a sad case—yes, a very sad case." "You don't mean to say that Mr. Rogers has had grave reverses of fortune, do you?" Mr. Twain was asked. "Yep. Rogers hasn't any more money than the Swiss navy has ships. I'm the good Samaritan in this affair."

New York Times: [Rogers noted that he was traveling to Bermuda because MT had offered to treat him.] "That's true," said Mark Twain, "but I'm $2 shy of the amount, and I'm going to shake him down for it when we get to sea."

5. *New York Herald:* "I'll pose only on one condition," said Mr. Rogers. "That is that Twain will promise not to exact money from the photographer for the job." "Huh, it's a step down for me to pose with such a man as Rogers!" the humorist rejoined. "However, one must encounter a step down like this once in a while.

New York Tribune: "I'll pose," broke in Mr. Rogers, "on condition that Twain will not take the money for giving consent." "And so will I," said the author dryly, "but before this thing is over Rogers will make you pay me $10 for the picture, get $14 from me; give it to you, and then make believe that I still owe him $5. I am not up to that scale of financiering."

6. *New York American:* "I feel like someone who isn't out for the Presidential nomination, and that means I'm contented and not worried." "Why are you going to Bermuda, then?" was the next question. "Oh, just to keep old Rogers here straight. He's a sly one, is Rogers, and he needs a chaperon," said Mr. Clemens. "If he behaves himself, maybe I'll beat it back to New York in a few days after we inflict our celebrated persons on the citizens of Bermuda. But I don't know."

New York Herald: "I am going to Bermuda just to keep Rogers straight.... If I succeed I'll sneak back home pretty quickly. If I don't, I'll have to stay."

New York Tribune: "I'm simply going to keep Rogers straight. If he behaves all right I'll sneak back; if not, why, I shall have to stay awhile."

242

"Mark Twain Faced 2 Perils," *New York American,* 14 April 1908, 3.

After an escape from being washed overboard while gallantly showing a young lady how a log works at the taffrail of the Quebec steamship *Bermudian,* Mark Twain with his friend, H. H. Rogers, arrived from Bermuda yesterday.[1] Both men were looking extremely well, and while the former did not go away exactly for his health, Mr. Rogers was willing to admit that his own had been improved. Mrs. Rogers accompanied her husband on the homeward voyage.

Miss Dorothy Sturgis of Boston is the young woman who had the honor of being drenched with the world-famous humorist. She is a granddaughter of Russell Sturgis.[2]

It was on Sunday. The ship was pitching heavily. Mr. Clemens and Miss Sturgis were watching the revolving of the little wheel that tells how fast the ship is going.

Suddenly and without warning a huge wave came up from behind the ship and the two were engulfed in it. The young lady was lightly dressed and Mark Twain had on his famous white suit. When the water receded and they could be seen again they looked as if they had been in swimming.[3]

The humorist, in speaking of the incident yesterday, said: "Miss Sturgis, being from Boston, is always in the swim, but at my time of life I have lost interest in surprise parties. I prefer something more formal than a slap in the back, even from my old friend Neptune."

Continuing, Mr. Clemens said: "My other old friend, Rogers, has improved very much as a result of our trip. He is not any heavier, but he takes more interest in life and is rather steadier on his feet than when he went away. Financially he is just as bad as ever. I had to help him out repeatedly. At one time I was so careless as to offer to lend him $2. He did not take me up, so I am in $2, but it was a terrible risk.[4]

"Yes, it is true I have joined the anti-noise society. Having made all the noise I could, and getting tired of it, I have decided that nobody else is to make any at all hereafter. I have given up the lecture platform and banquets, and now everybody else has got to be still. Mrs. Rice came to me just at the proper moment. The anti-noise society is an excellent thing. I am going to be quiet hereafter and so must everybody else."[5]

Mr. Clemens was asked about the plan of digging a deep water channel through the length of the Mississippi, and he declared that he was unalterably against it.

"I would rather follow things that are reasonably substantial than this will-o'-the-wisp," he said. "In the first place if the channel were dug it would never be maintained, and to dig it fourteen feet deep would require all the money in fourteen banks in England, and then it would not last.[6]

"I see that they have invited the President to view the project, which is very much wiser for them to do than to invite the Mississippi pilots to see it."

Mr. Clemens said he would remain at his Fifth avenue house for five weeks and would then repair to the new home he is building on a farm at Redding, Conn., four miles from Danbury.[7] He had written nothing, he said, during his stay in Bermuda, but would resume work when settled in the country. . . .

Notes to Interview 242

I have supplemented this interview as reported in the *New York American* with versions of Twain's comments published in other newspapers. All newspaper citations below are from 14 April 1908.

1. The 5,530-ton *Bermudian* was built in 1904 for the Quebec SS Co. On Rogers, see n. 2 to interview 212.

"Mark Twain a Hero? He Won't Admit It," *New York World*, 16: "He was in rare good humor and when his friend Rogers balked at the camera brigade Mark said: "Let the boys take a shot at you, Rogers."

"Twain and Rogers Back from Bermuda," *New York Times*, 9: "Birds of a feather," said Mark Twain, as he appeared on the deck of the steamer *Bermudian* yesterday holding H. H. Rogers by the arm. "You know the rest of it," and both humorist and financier laughed heartily.

2. Dorothy Sturgis Harding of Boston was another of MT's "angelfish." See also "Mark Twain Lands an Angel Fish," *Columbia Libraries Columns* 16 (February 1967): 3–12. Russell Sturgis (1836–1909), design artist, architect, and art critic.

3. *New York World:* "You are safe in saying that I was soused," said the humorist. "I never knew the ocean was so wet before."

"Twain Was 'Soused,'" *New York Tribune*, 6: "But I—well, I must confess that I was 'soused' on the second day out from Bermuda. It was the first time in my life that I have had the misfortune, but I wasn't alone. There was a young lady with me, clad in white, just as I was, who became 'soused' under the same circumstances and at the same time."

"Not a word of truth in it," interposed Mr. Rogers.

"Oh, you don't know a thing about it," returned the humorist. "I will explain. I was standing on the main deck aft, looking at the patent taffrail log, in the company of Miss Dorothy Sturgis, sixteen years old and from Boston. As we were watching the line take up its slack a beautiful blue comber broke on the rail and 'soused' the two of us from head to foot. I guess I forgot to tell Henry about that."

"Mark Twain Gets a Sea Souse," *New York Sun*, 3 "The weather was certainly very rude during this last trip," declared Mark.

4. "Mark Twain Rescues a Girl as Huge Sea Sweeps the Bermudian," *New York Herald,* 5: "Of course I've had a great time," said Mr. Clemens; "if I hadn't I should not have remained seven weeks. Yes, my friend Mr. Rogers was caught short of money several times and I had to make him small loans, but I guess he's good for the amounts and I am not worrying."

New York Times: "It's a terrible strain, this being a financier," he said, nodding his head in the direction of Mr. Rogers. "It is also a strain traveling with one. I offered to loan Rogers $2, though I knew I was taking an awful risk. Rogers thought it was simply a courtesy and so did not take me up. Now I am $2 ahead.

New York Tribune: "Yes, Rogers was a good boy," said Mr. Clemens, "and he has taken a new lease on life and affairs." "Anything else happen to you on the way from Bermuda?" asked a reporter. "Yes, two things," said the humorist, with a smile. "I offered Henry a $2 bill as we came close to Sandy Hook, and he refused it. Said he didn't need it. That was one thing important, and the other was a scare I got while sitting aft with a number of passengers suffering from *mal de mer*. The weather was rude, but they look out for one's comfort on board, and that is how I got my little scare. I had a good black cigar about half smoked as I sat among the seasick ones. They could not understand how I weathered the gale, but a young woman who was recovering called my attention to a sign that advised passengers who would avoid seasickness to refrain from smoking on the after deck. The suggestion was well taken and I went forward to forget it."

5. Julia Barnett Rice (1860–1929) was the founder and president of the Society for the Suppression of Unnecessary Noise, established in 1906.

New York Sun: "Since I left New York I have joined the Anti-Noise Society," he said. "I've been a big scream long enough and have made all the noise I am going to. I have abandoned the lecture platform and I shall make no more after dinner speeches. Mrs. Isaac L. Rice is all right and I agree with her perfectly that there should be less noise."

New York Herald: The humorist announced that he had decided to ally himself with Mrs. Isaac L. Rice's Anti-Noise Society. "You see," he said, "since I have retired permanently from the lecture platform I am not making any more noise myself than I have to, and I don't see why anybody else should."

New York Times: "I have returned from my trip a reformer. I have joined the ranks of the anti-noise society. I have retired both from the making of after-dinner speeches and the lecture platform. No one can tolerate noise, you know, unless they are the noisemakers. I am through making a noise and so I now insist on quiet. Mrs. Rice started her crusade at the right time for me."

New York Tribune: "Oh, I am a member of the anti-noise society now," he continued. "I am a disciple of quiet for evermore. I have made all the noise allotted to me, and now I intend to be quiet. I have flung to the four winds all lecture tours and all overtures for after-dinner speeches, and will lead henceforth the simple life."

New York World: "I'm done lecturing. I'm not going to make any more noise and I'm going to see that no one else does, either. I'm going to join Mrs. Rice's anti-noise crusade. Noise is only to be tolerated when you are making it yourself."

6. *New York Times:* "I have no sentimental interest in such a project, and I have too many realities to deal with to be chasing a will-o'-the-wisp. When the Almighty built this earth He knew very well that a fourteen-foot channel from Chicago to the Gulf would have been a very excellent and much needed thing, but he also knew that

it would tax even His resources. If there were fourteen Banks of England behind the scheme, and fourteen more behind them, there would not be enough available money to finance the scheme.... I know the Mississippi Valley and its cozy soil too well. The digging of the channel would be but the beginning. A thousand dredges could not keep it clear."

7. MT moved into Stormfield, his home near Redding, in June 1908. Built in the style of an Italian villa, it contained nineteen rooms and five baths.

243

"Mark Twain Meets the Cardinal," *New York American,* 10 May 1908, 1W.

... After the parade was over and the stand was about deserted, Mark Twain and his secretary, Miss Lyons, started away together.[1] The humorist politely inquired of a lieutenant the way out, but the latter merely pointed his finger at the street.

A second later, upon being told who the white-haired gentleman was, the officer hurried after him and made amends by escorting Mr. Twain to Broadway.

"Yes," drawled Mr. Clemens as he climbed in his cab. "It was a fine parade. I always liked the police, but I suppose that was because they always seemed to take such a great interest in me and what I was doing.

"Did I meet the Cardinal?[2] Oh, yes, I met His Eminence, and found him a very nice old gentleman. He told me he had read my books. He didn't say with approval, I must admit, but he looked like an intelligent man and one who approved of high class literature, so I took it for granted that he read my books with approval." ...

Notes to Interview 243

1. Isabel Van Kleek Lyon (1863–1958), MT's private secretary from 1902 until 1909.
2. Michael Cardinal Logue (1840–1924) of Armagh, Ireland, was visiting New York.

244

"Mark Twain Cannot 'Bubble Humor,' He Says, as Demanded," *New York American,* 8 September 1908, 3.

Samuel L. Clemens (Mark Twain), who has deserted New York, has moved into his new nineteen-room house one mile from Redding Center, in Connecticut. Speaking yesterday to an American reporter, he said:

"I came to Redding because I became too tired to stay in New York. When I first came up here and had a glimpse of the Berkshire range in the distance I was charmed. It all seemed so restful. It was what you might call a feeding view, for every time you look away across the hills and vales you see some new point of interest to feed upon and enjoy. I am not going to vegetate, because

21. Mark Twain and Michael Cardinal Logue, 9 May 1908. From Isabel Lyon's photograph book: "This divides the sheep from the goats." Courtesy of the Mark Twain Project, University of California, Berkeley.

to vegetate means to rust, and I don't intend to treat myself in any such rusty fashion.

"You see in New York, where I had to attend social functions and dinners, I generally had to speak.

"Now when a humorist rises to speak he is expected to simply bubble humor, and there are times when one does not feel the bubbling process as strongly as at others. I felt that I needed rest, and here I am going to get it. We shall have small weekend parties here, and I shall be glad to see my friends."

Mark Twain had not even heard yesterday of the reported engagement of his daughter, Miss Clara Clemens, to Charles Wark, of this city.[1] Miss Lyons, the novelist's private secretary, denied the report.[2] Miss Clemens, she said, had no thought of marriage. Instead, it is possible that she may become a grand opera star. Her voice is a contralto of great power and has gained much praise in her concert tour in Europe.

Notes to Interview 244

1. Charles E. (Will) Wark, Clara's accompanist and later her fiancé. The *New York World* reported the rumor of their engagement on 7 September 1908. On Clara's wedding to Ossip Gabrilowitsch, see interview 255.

2. Isabel Van Kleek Lyon (1863–1958), MT's private secretary from 1902 until 1909.

245

"Burglar Chase at Mark Twain's Ends in Shooting," *New York World*, 19 September 1908, 3.

Mark Twain's Notice to His Next Burglar. There is nothing to be had in this house henceforth but plated ware. You will find it in that brass thing over in the corner by the basket of kittens. If you want the basket put the kittens in the brass thing. And do not make a noise; it disturbs the family.

You will find gum shoes in the front hall by that thing that has umbrellas in it—the thing they call a chiffonier or pergoia, or whatever it is. Please close the door when you go away. Affectionately, S. L. C.

The above is the notice that Mark Twain—Samuel L. Clemens—wrote yesterday and hung up in the dining room of his beautiful country home in the hills near Redding, Conn.

The reason for the notice was potent. For burglars—bold bad burglars, who are now languishing in the jail at Bridgeport—invaded the Clemens home early yesterday morning and stole $300 worth of real silverware and some considerable amount of near-silverware. The latter they disdained and threw away—the plated stuff—and the real silver they kept and had taken away from them when Sheriff George Banks, of Fairfield County, and H. A. Lounsbury,[1] of Redding, a neighbor of Twain's, fell on the pair in a New York, New Haven, and Hartford train at Bethel and beat them up. They also arrested them.

Mark Twain thinks that if he had had the thumbprints that Pudd'nhead Wilson discovered, the capture and identification of the burglarious couple might have been quick and more complete; but the Sheriff and Mr. Lounsbury, who started on the trail as soon as Miss Lyon, Mark Twain's secretary,[2] and Miss Clara, the daughter of the famous humorist, gave the alarm, had something "equally as good" to aid them.

One of the burglars wore rubber heels. His track in the dust was distinct. They trailed the rubber heels and captured the two robbers.

The sheriff was shot in the leg by one of them and the burglar was hit on the head with a club. Incidentally, the battered burglar shot four or five holes in the roof of the New Haven car in which the fight took place.

Mark Twain was quite delighted with the burglary. He was in rare good humor last night when he talked to a *World* reporter. First he insisted—as is his wont—that he positively must not be quoted—that he would not have any quotations marks used in reporting him. And then he settled back in the chair in the handsome big library of his residence and puffed contentedly on a black cigar before starting to relate the story.

He was attired in a white linen suit and a white tie and white shirt—suggesting, somehow, a new schooner with all sails set.

Mark Twain said he was very, very glad to receive burglars—that he had always found them to be most amiable people, and that he had had so much experience with them in his lifetime that he had come to like them greatly.

"And, Father didn't get downstairs until ages after it was all over," said Miss Clemens. "And then he came sauntering down at 2 o'clock in the morning, mind you, in a bathrobe, smoking a pipe and asking what all the commotion was about.

"And then he said that it was silly to get scared about burglars, and that he wished they'd be more quiet about it and not wake people up. He said that he heard the pistol shots—you know Claude, the butler,[3] shot several times at the men—but Father said that he didn't know what the sounds were, and didn't care."

Mr. Clemens broke in at this juncture to say that the sounds reminded him of popping corks and that he had a vague desire to join the party, but that he remembered that he had a bottle of Scotch in his room and that it would therefore be very foolish to go downstairs to get a drink.

And champagne didn't appeal to him much anyhow. He said that if future robbers would just do as he suggests in his notice, they won't trouble anybody in the house; and while they'll get no profit, they'll suffer no losses. He added that he had never met a burglar that bothered him, especially if the burglar was thoughtful enough to leave the premises three or four hours before he (Twain) knew he was around.

Then Mark Twain, shaking his snow capped dome, sagely stated that if he were to wake up and find a burglar in his room he'd invite him to have a drink, make himself at home, and that he would tell Mr. Burglar to take what he wanted and go away and let other folks sleep. Why fuss with a burglar? was a suggestion. Why quarrel with him or annoy him?

He said that the young folks around the house had got all worked up about burglars, but that was because they hadn't had his experience with them.

Down at the City Hall in Redding, when the two thieves, who gave their names as Huffinan and Williamson, were arraigned before Judge Nickerson, of Fairfield County, and bound over to the grand jury, Mark Twain was on hand. He was just as unperturbed as usual and drawled in the same old way when he lectured the "yeggs" [criminals].

"You are a disgrace to your race," said he, "and you ought to be ashamed of yourselves. I have been at the front as a defender of the Jewish people all my life. I have written defenses of you and have contended that Jews have never, as a rule, been guilty of big crimes—crimes of violence.

"The Jews as a people are law-abiding and seldom do anything such as you have done."[4]

The Twain country home is splendidly isolated. It is half a mile from the nearest neighbor, Mr. Lounsbury, and is surrounded by forest and flowered field. There are goldenrod and smilax: and beds of asters and tangles of berry bushes about it.

It was this place that the two robbers entered.

It was past midnight when Miss Lyon, Mr. Clemens's secretary, heard a noise downstairs. She says that it sounded as though someone had stumbled. Miss Clara Clemens heard it also.

Miss Lyon rushed boldly downstairs. In the dining room she found confusion. A heavy mahogany table, in which $300 worth of silver was kept, was gone. A small taboret was upset. Some liqueur glasses were broken. The door was open. Miss Lyon rushed to the telephone and called up Mr. Lounsbury.

"Burglars have been here and stolen the furniture," she wailed.

"And when I heard her say that I thought she'd gone mad," observed Miss Clara, in relating it.

Claude Beuchotte, the French butler, heard the racket and rushed downstairs with a revolver in his hand. The butler shot four or five holes in the yielding fog of Redding Hills, and it was these shots that reminded Mark Twain of "popping corks."

The burglars had broken in by prying open a kitchen window. Then they took the dining room table out into the night. They put the good silver in the bag subsequently recovered by Sheriff Banks and Neighbor Lounsbury.

They broke one spoon in two, to see if it was the real thing. The plated ware they evidently threw away, because none of it was recovered.

As soon as Mr. Lounsbury got word over the telephone from Miss Lyon he started for the Clemens home. Sheriff Banks was notified by 'phone also, and he arrived there within half an hour with his son Will.

Assisted by Claude, the butler, the Sheriff and his son and Mr. Lounsbury started on the trail. They soon found it. One of the burglars wore rubber heels. They were easily trailed and the clue led to Redding and from there to Bethel. At 6 o'clock Mr. Lounsbury telephoned to the Clemens home that he was still on the job. Half an hour later he telephoned that he had met the enemy and that they were his'n.[5]

Sheriff Banks stopped at Redding when the sleuthing party arrived there; Lounsbury went on to Bethel. At the latter place two men boarded the train. They carried a satchel, were covered with dust and seemed to be somewhat winded. The conductor of the train was consulted. He didn't know them. Then Lounsbury asked one of them who he was.

"Haven't I met you somewhere?" was the query. The stranger replied in the negative and rather abruptly at that. He was in no communicative mood. Mr. Lounsbury saw that he wore rubber heels. When the train stopped at Redding Sheriff Banks boarded it.

As he came up to the seat which Lounsbury occupied, the latter said, "Here are the men we want." As he did so one of the "yeggs" bolted for the door and jumped off. The train was running rapidly by that time. The other burglar pulled a revolver, but Banks landed on him first.

A general fight resulted, and Lounsbury, Banks, two brakemen, several passengers, a telegraph operator named Andy, George Brunson, a section hand, and a few others mixed it up in the aisle while the conductor stopped the train.

The sheriff was on top of the burglar and the rest of the crowd was on top of the sheriff, as nearly as can be ascertained. The burglar managed to get out a revolver and, twisting his arm up, shot five times. Four of the bullets hit the sides and ceiling of the car. The fifth one hit the sheriff in the right leg and inflicted an ugly wound.

A brakeman procured one of the sticks used to turn the car ventilators and hit the burglar across the head with it, laying his scalp open for four inches and putting him completely out of business. Then Lounsbury, the brakeman, the operator, and the section man started after the yeggman who had escaped from the train. They caught him a short distance away, he having injured himself when he jumped.

Both of the men were taken back to Redding, while the Sheriff was removed to his house and a physician summoned. The wound in his thigh is a serious one, but unless blood poisoning sets in he will recover.

The prisoners were subsequently arraigned before the local justice and it was during the hearing that Mark Twain delivered them the lecture.

The men were then removed to Bridgeport. It is believed that they are New York crooks, although they gave their residences as South Norwalk. Neither one is known there. One of the local police said that the smaller of the two men was "Red" Rooney, a noted crook. This has not been corroborated. Neither of the men would talk.

"Father says that he is glad the men didn't take the kittens," said Miss Clemens. "He says that he would rather lose all the silverware in the house than those kittens." And she proudly displayed a half dozen fluffy little balls of fur that aren't more than two weeks old and that are the pride of the Clemens household. "And they were right in the dining room where the burglars were," she said.

It is a matter of record that after Mark Twain had sauntered down to hear what the fuss in his house was about, and after he had finished a pipeful of tobacco, he promptly went back to bed and allowed the rest of the family to sit up and await returns from the burglars.

Notes to Interview 245

1. Harry A. Lounsbery, the general contractor who built Stormfield.
2. Isabel Van Kleek Lyon (1863–1958), MT's private secretary from 1902 until 1909.

22. From Isabel Lyon's photograph book, 10 November 1908: "[MT] showing how he would attack the burglars." Courtesy of the Mark Twain Project, University of California, Berkeley.

3. Claude Joseph Beuchotte (1877–1941?).
4. MT expresses similar philo-Semitic opinions in his essay "Concerning the Jews" (1898).
5. Commodore Oliver Perry (1785–1819) in 1813: "We have met the enemy and he is ours."

246

Charles Henry Meltzer,[1] "Twain Says He Told Her 'Book a Mistake,'" *New York American*, 27 September 1908, sec. 2, 1.

When I placed a copy of the pamphlet in the hands of Mark Twain, he accepted it in the philosophic attitude so characteristic of the man, and began to read it and make his comments as the reading progressed.[2] He then dictated the following statement to me for publication in *The American*:

"This is not an important matter. I can say in two minutes all it is worthwhile to say about it. Let me dictate it to you, and you write it down. Proceed:

"I am not well pleased with her conduct in publishing in a printed pamphlet (as charged by you) a private conversation which I had with her; also for making me talk in the first person, when she could not by any possibility reproduce the words I used, since she did not take me down in shorthand.

"She put into my mouth humiliatingly weak language, whereas I used exceedingly strong language—much too strong for print, and also much too indelicate for print—a fact which she has fully recognized by not reproducing any of it.

"Inadequate as was her report of my sermon, she got at a good part of the substance of it, but she left out its only worthwhile feature—which was the argument I offered that her book was a mistake, since, while it uttered a very large truth, it was a sort of truth which the world for wise reasons lets on to be unaware of and does not talk publicly about—a sort of truth which is best suppressed, because it is not a wholesome one and its discussion is much more likely to do harm than good.

"I think Mrs. Glyn originated the idea of getting you to publish that private conversation. It has the look of it. I think she gave you that typewritten report of it. It looks like the very one she showed to me the time I told her it was a quite extraordinary piece of misreporting, and much below her literary capabilities.[3]

"I am afraid she wants another advertisement of her book. I am sorry, for it is a very harmful and very readable book, though I did not pay it the extravagant compliments which she has put into my mouth.

"There, I think of nothing further to say. And it is just as well, for your space is valuable and so is my time."

Notes to Interview 246

1. Charles Henry Meltzer (1853–1936), translator and playwright.
2. The English writer Elinor Glyn (1864–1943) had depicted an adulterous affair in her novel *Three Weeks* (1904). In her short pamphlet *Mark Twain on Three Weeks* (1908), she recorded an interview with MT he repudiates here.
3. See also *Auto* (1959), 353–57: "Some days afterward I met [Glyn] again for a moment and she gave me the startling information that she had written down every word I had said, just as I had said it, without any softening or purifying modifications, and that it was 'just splendid, just wonderful.' . . . She begged me to let her publish it and said it would do infinite good in the world, but I said it would damn me before my time and I didn't wish to be useful to the world on such expensive conditions."

247

"Owner of Virginian in Excellent Health," *Norfolk (Va.) Ledger-Dispatch*, 2 April 1909, 1.

Henry H. Rogers and his party, who came down from New York on the Old Dominion line steamer *Jefferson* to attend the celebration of the opening of the Virginian Railway, debarked on the pier here about 10 o'clock.[1] . . . According to pre-arrangement with Mr. Du Puy,[2] a reporter for the *Ledger-Dispatch* met the Rogers party upon their arrival at the hotel, and gained audience with Mr. Rogers and Mark Twain, whom Mr. Rogers said should be given his proper name and title, which is, Rogers said, Doctor Samuel L. Clemens. . . .

One of the most gratifying things observed during the sorting out and stowing away of something like a couple car loads of luggage which the visitors brought along was the fact that both Messrs. Rogers and Clemens, notwithstanding each is well along in years and the latter confessed a couple of years ago to having then "rounded pier 70," appeared to be in as good health as ever in their lives. . . .

Hardly a more democratic man than Mr. Rogers is may be imagined. . . . He laughed when he said that the newspaper men should be particular about addressing his close friend, Mark Twain, as Doctor Clemens, and there seemed to be some joke in connection with this, which was not explained. . . .

Mark, being a mine, was next worked.

"Mr. Twain, I beg your pardon, Dr. Clemens, will you say a few words for publication in the *Ledger-Dispatch,* but before you begin will you kindly mention what your price per word is; I have heard that it is thirty cents, but want to be sure about it before ordering," said the newspaper man in an unbroken stream of words.

Then he was informed that his newspaper wants only the highest class of literary word and has heard of some writers who lately have charged a dollar a word.

"I have raised my price," the only one said, "and am as high as the highest of them now."

Here Mr. Rogers observed: "They call you Mark Twain, Incorporated," apparently alluding to an editorial which recently appeared in this newspaper.

"Yes," said Mr. Clemens, "the newspapers may treat that matter humorously, but it is no laughing matter. Do you know that I have received a letter from the German Government about that and my incorporation of myself is probably going to break the present international copyright system all to smash?"

Next, Mr. Clemens, who it is known by some was a pilot on the Mississippi river a little earlier in the game of life and knows all about the bars and snags and other nightmares of navigators, was asked whether he is going to pilot the river steamer *Nanticoke* from Franklin, Va., to Venezuela, which steamer was said in a recent press report to have been sold to one who perhaps is an agent of former President of Venezuela Castro.[3]

"What does the job pay?" he inquired. "It is altogether a question of how much there is in it and the security."

With this evasive answer Mark ported his linguistic helm and sheered off.

Notes to Interview 247

1. On Rogers, who funded the construction of the Virginian Railway, see n. 2 to interview 212. The *Jefferson* was built in 1899 for the Old Dominion line.
2. Raymond Du Puy (1860–1933), vice president and general manager of the Virginian Railway.
3. Cipriano Castro Ruiz (1858–1924), president of the Republic of Venezuela from 1899 to 1909.

248

"Mark Twain Delighted the Little Ones," *Norfolk (Va.) Ledger-Dispatch,* 5 April 1909, 1, 13.

Dr. Samuel L. Clemens heard a considerable number of younger children somewhat haltingly but nevertheless delightfully repeat today a certain story written by one whom they have been taught to look upon as illustrious.

The story is the story of Joan of Arc, by Mark Twain, and the telling of it to Dr. Clemens was held by the Norfolk women interested in the kindergarten. . . .

The ladies were at the Lynnhaven Hotel preparing to transport Dr. Clemens to the kindergarten in a Rambler bubble which he had just blown,[1] when Superintendent of Public Schools R. A. Dobie and School Committeeman H. B. Bagnall called at the hotel to ask Mark to address the High School scholars. They found that the kindergartners had him booked, but proposed to let the high school scholars have him after the kindergarten visit, which was imminent, was over. They, therefore, took Messrs. Dobie and Bagnall into partnership and all bundled into the auto with Mark and Secretary of Mark Twain, Incorporated, Ralph Ashcroft;[2] and set off on the expedition. . . .

Dr. Clemens, who declined to go out on the inspection tour of the Virginian Railway with his friend, H. H. Rogers,[3] and party, yesterday but decided to return with Mr. Ashcroft to New York tonight aboard the Old Dominion liner *Hamilton,* spent several hours yesterday watching the Sunday school children and the church-goers traversing Freemason street. . . .

His triumphant progress about Norfolk yesterday, during which he was introduced to many folks here, was attended by many diverting incidents and his brilliant wit flashed at brief intervals.

When he returned to the Lynnhaven, after his walk, to say good-bye to Mr. Rogers, . . . Mr. Rogers saw him pick up his overcoat and immediately charged him with attempting to make off with another man's coat.

Mark protested that the coat was his, as it really was, but Mr. Rogers said that he knew Mark's coat and also his other one and that this was neither. This badinage which was much enjoyed by everybody in the neighborhood did not end until Mr. Rogers bade Mark an affectionate farewell, inquiring, first, however, his plans, and ascertaining that Mr. Ashcroft was to remain with him and look after his comfort.

"You are going straight to New York, are you," asked Mr. Rogers. "You are going right to my house, aren't you?"

"No," said Mark, "I have an engagement which I must fill and then I shall go right on to Redding." Redding, Conn., where he has his home . . . also is the place where he put out the famous notice to burglars asking them to take what they wanted without waking him.[4] During the chafing between him and Mr. Rogers yesterday, Mark asked his friend to speak to Manager Johnston, of the hotel, and assure him that Mark was a nice man and probably would pay his hotel bill some time.

"Where is the manager?" inquired Mr. Rogers.

"He is hiding behind a screen," said Mark.

The manager does not seem today to be apprehensive over his bill. Indeed he has placed a big automobile at the service of his famous guest.

A visitor who was received at the Lynnhaven today and whose call was highly appreciated by Dr. Clemens is Evelyn Harris, son of the late Joel Chandler Harris, "Uncle Remus," whose close friend and admirer Dr. Clemens is.[5] There has been a stream of callers today. It is suspected that he will have something of an ovation at the Old Dominion pier, when he sails tonight.

Dr. Clemens' absolute disregard for conventionality was never better shown than yesterday. With his private secretary, he had been taking a stroll along Freemason street, the street of the churches, in Norfolk, and happened to pass the Freemason Baptist Church just as services had been concluded.

Dr. Livius Lankford,[6] one of the deacons of the church, was one of the first to spy the eminent humorist, and he promptly introduced himself, concluding the introduction with an invitation to dinner. Dr. Clemens as promptly accepted.

"But, Dr. Clemens," protested his secretary, "you have an engagement at half past four this afternoon."

"Guess I am man enough to break it," said Mark Twain. . . .

Notes to Interview 248

1. In the *Rambler* for 27 November 1750, Samuel Johnson (1709-48) described a fragile hope as "a mere bubble, that by a gentle breath may be blown" to almost any size.

2. Ralph W. Ashcroft (1875-1947), MT's business adviser from 1907 to 1909, married Isabel Lyon (MT's personal secretary) in March 1909.

3. On Rogers, see n. 2 to interview 212.

4. See interview 245.

5. Evelyn Harris (1878-1961), reporter and city editor of the *Atlanta Constitution;* Joel Chandler Harris (1848-1908), Atlanta journalist and author of *Uncle Remus: His Songs and Sayings* (1881) and other dialect tales narrated by Uncle Remus.

6. Dr. Livius Lankford (1854-1917).

249

"Mark Twain, Rockefeller and Others Pay Tribute to the Dead," *Boston Herald*, 20 May 1909, 1.

New York, May 19—Conspicuous among those who arrived early at the home of Henry H. Rogers, after the death today, was Samuel L. Clemens (Mark Twain), for many years one of the most intimate friends of Mr. Rogers.[1] Mr. Clemens left his country place, near Redding, Ct., this morning, intending to visit the Rogers home, only to be confronted with the sad news of his old friend's death when he arrived at the Grand Central station. Mr. Clemens was too moved to fully express his feelings. "It is terrible, terrible," he said. "I am inexpressibly shocked.

"It is too much of a shock for me to be able to say anything now. I cannot talk about it. Mr. Rogers was my dearest and closest friend for years. And I only heard of his death a few minutes ago, when I got off the train at the Grand Central. He was a great man (tears were streaming down Mr. Clemens' face at the time), but it is too much for me to say anything.

"The shock has been too great for me to think of anything to say befitting so great a man as Mr. Rogers. I can't talk any more. Mr. Rogers was as close to me as a brother."[2]

Notes to Interview 249

1. See n. 2 to interview 212.
2. "Mark Twain on Way to See Friend," *New York Tribune*, 20 May 1909, 1: "It is terrible. It is terrible. I can't talk about it. I am inexpressibly shocked. I don't know what I shall do. . . . I can say nothing now. . . . It is terrible. I feel it very much."

"Mark Twain Grief-Stricken," *New York Times*, 20 May 1909, 2: "This is terrible, terrible, and I cannot talk about it. . . . I am inexpressibly shocked and grieved. I do not know just where I will go."

250

"Mark Twain's High Esteem for Dr. Hale," *Baltimore News*, 10 June 1909, 4.

Mark Twain (Samuel L. Clemens) was standing this morning on the broad lawn, near a clump of shady old trees, at St. Timothy's School, Catonsville, when the news was brought to him of the death of his old friend, Rev. Edward Everett Hale.[1] . . . "I had the greatest esteem and respect for Edward Everett Hale, and the greatest admiration for his work. I am as grieved to hear of his death as I can ever be to hear of the death of my friends, though my grief is always tempered with the satisfaction of knowing that for them the hard, bitter struggle of life is ended."

Note to Interview 250

1. Edward Everett Hale (b. 1822), Unitarian minister and author, best known for his story "The Man without a Country" (1865).

251

"Twain Puts Blame on the Typesetter," *Baltimore News*, 10 June 1909, 14.

Protesting his innocence of all guile, his love of pretty girls and Baltimore spring chicken, his horror of dirty streets and his admiration of Providence, Mark Twain, whose name is given in Redding (Conn.) City Directory and on the church calendar as Samuel L. Clemens, gazed out of a window at the Belvedere this morning and awaited orders.[1]

Mark—as he is known at the Arundell and Journalists' Clubs—had an appointment at Catonsville, and he was waiting for the signal to take up his hat and his reputation and go there and to say funny things to a group of young folks who had done nothing more serious than to graduate from St. Timothy's School. The great American humorist arrived in Baltimore yesterday evening, but refrained from any public function except a shave in the barber shop patronized by the common herd.

One of the first themes that occupied his attention was the charge that has been spread broadcast that he pilfered for *Is Shakespeare Dead?* a chapter from another distinguished gentleman's book. Mark made an extensive explanation of this. The sum and substance of his defense is that the whole thing was a regrettable mistake, and that the publishers of the other fellow's book are now trying to make capital out of the matter at Mark's expense.

Referring to the stories of plagiarism Mr. Clemens made the following statement: "In this, the first statement which I personally have given to the press, I wish to say that in writing my book I took the liberty of using large extracts from Mr. Greenwood's book *The Shakespeare Problem Restated*.[2] I made use of the extracts because of the great admiration which I have for that book, and with the full permission of the publishers. I added a footnote in which I gave full credit to both author and publishers.[3] The book was put through the press in great haste and somewhere, nobody seems to know where, the footnote was lost, probably in the composing room. That is the sum and substance of the whole story.

"But of course the John Lane Publishing Company of England, the publishers of Mr. Greenwood's book, are good advertisers and have only one object in life and that is to make money. Now one of Mark Twain's books, so they tell me, is considered worthwhile reading. I know, at any rate, that my books have always sold well. But to have a man like Mark Twain steal portions from another man's book makes that book something extraordinary. Messrs. Lane are well aware of this fact, and it is to be regretted that a mistake in the mechanical department of another publishing house should be made much of to accuse falsely one who has already won fame in the literary world and to put in a false light another who is the most modest and retiring of men."

The humorist had been real serious for five minutes, and it was natural he should pine for a lighter vein.

"Let's talk about something pleasant," said he. "Baltimore? Oh! I like Baltimore—always have. One of the most interesting things I know about Baltimore is in regard to spring chickens. You may not believe it, but it is a fact that you can't get real spring chickens like you get in Baltimore anywhere else in the world. You could put a fresh spring pullet in a basket, and a Baltimore cook also; put the basket in a box and nail the lid down, and take them both to New York, and let the same cook do the chicken nice and brown in the metropolis, but I declare the chicken wouldn't taste the same by any means in New York. I don't know why it is, but if you don't believe it, well—you just try it.

"What a lot of weather you are having in Baltimore! I never saw anything like it. I don't mind a little bit of rain, but I certainly do not want to run the risk of another Johnstown flood.[4] But there is a Providence over all things, they say, and I suppose the rain has been sent to accomplish one good purpose in Baltimore, for of all the places I have seen I can't recall where I ever saw so much mud and dirt in the streets. If we could only have another week of heavy rains like the last week, I am sure that Providence would accomplish what the Street Department cannot."

Mr. Clemens said he likes the ladies very much, especially the young ladies. "That is why I am going to the commencement his morning at St. Timothy's," he added. "They are all very sweet, and make one feel young again to be with them. Not that I am old, of course, or even think of getting old. No, indeed; I am just as young now as I was 40 years ago. Why, I don't see any reason why I shouldn't live another hundred years. There's nothing funny about that. You know Methuselah lived for 999 years. Scripture doesn't record that he lived a better life than the rest of mortals. We never know what is in store for us."

Mr. Clemens was the star figure at St. Timothy's School, where the commencement exercises were held this morning. Accompanied by A. B. Paine,[5] Mr. Clemens arrived at the Catonsville school about 10 o'clock and was one of the speakers. With his eyes a-twinkle and a smile playing about his face, Mr. Clemens, with his peculiar drawl, gave the girls some advice.

"There is nothing for me to do but to tell you young ladies what not to do. There are three things that you should never do on any occasion.

"First—Don't smoke—that is, not to excess. I am 73 and have always smoked during my 73 years to excess.

"Second—Don't drink—that is, to excess.

"Third—Don't marry—that is, to excess.

"Now, if you young ladies refrain from all these things you will have all the virtues that anyone will honor and respect.

"Another thing I want to say, and that is that honesty is the best policy.

"I remember when I had just written *Innocents Abroad* when I and my partner wanted to start a newspaper syndicate. We needed $3 and did not know where to get it. While we were in a quandary I espied a valuable dog on the street. I picked up the canine and sold him to a man for $3. Afterwards the owner of the dog came along and I got $3 from him for telling him where the dog was. So I went back and gave the $3 to the man whom I sold it to, and I have lived honestly ever since."

Mr. Clemens was received with great enthusiasm.

Notes to Interview 251

1. The Belvedere was a sixteen-story hotel in downtown Baltimore modeled on the Plaza Hotel in New York and opened in 1903.

2. Sir Granville George Greenwood, *The Shakespeare Problem Restated* (1908). "Mark Twain No Plagiarist," *Baltimore American,* 10 June 1909, 14: "He virtually admits . . . the use of Greenwood's ideas in the chapter under question. 'Just say for me,' said he, 'that it was entirely an oversight.' Only this, and nothing more, would the great man say."

3. Not only did MT acknowledge his admiration for Greenwood's book in chapter 1 of *Is Shakespeare Dead?* (1909), but later printings of the book included a footnote on page 79 in which he admits borrowing much of his chapter 8 from Greenwood's chapter 13.

4. The Johnstown Flood, known locally as the Great Flood of 1889, occurred on May 31, 1889, in Johnstown, Pennsylvania. More than twenty-two hundred people were killed. It was the first major disaster relief effort handled by the American Red Cross, led by Clara Barton, and remains one of the greatest disasters in U.S. history.

5. Albert Bigelow Paine (1861–1937), MT's official biographer and first literary executor.

252

"Mark Twain Their Guest," *Baltimore Sun,* 11 June 1909 13.

His eyes twinkling, the inevitable long cigar clenched between this teeth and with a springy step that belied his 73½ years, Samuel L. Clemens, who likes to be called Mark Twain, jumped into an automobile yesterday morning in front of the Belvedere Hotel and went to see his "granddaughter," Miss Frances Nunnally of Atlanta, graduated at the commencement of St. Timothy's School at Catonsville.[1]

"I call her 'granddaughter,'" he said between puffs, "because she called me 'grandpa' when I met her on the *Minnehaha* in 1907, when I was being steamed over to King Edward's Island."[2]

Mr. Clemens made the long journey from his home in Redding, Conn., with Mr. Albert Bigelow Paine,[3] a biographer and novelist and close friend of the great humorist, just to hand Miss Nunnally her diploma and incidentally tell the other five graduates some things they should avoid in after life. He arrived in town Wednesday afternoon, took a shave, a light lunch, and went to bed. But he was up early to be ready for the trip to "granddaughter's" school. On the trip to the school he was accompanied by Mrs. James H. Nunnally,[4] mother of the author's "grandchild," and Mr. Paine, whom he has designated to write his biography when he dies.

"But Mr. Paine will have a long wait," he said to a friend, who was talking of the biography. "I'm going to fool him worse than he thinks."

During the trip down Charles street the venerable humorist made serious remarks about the Baltimore girls. He sat comfortably back in his seat, gazed with undenied admiration at the passing girls and women and declared that they are as pretty as ever.

"Pretty girls—and you almost have a monopoly of them here—are always an inspiration to me," he smiled through his gold-rimmed glasses. "The Baltimore type still upholds the reputation the city has, and it's a fine reputation to have."

When Mr. Clemens reached St. Timothy's School the animated gathering of prettily gowned young ladies, six academically robed graduates, and a host of friends and relatives of the students bade him a warm welcome. When he stepped from the big touring car in his white flannels, big Panama hat, cigar, and smile he sought his little "granddaughter." Miss Nunnally was there to receive him. The pretty young graduate, with cheeks tinted like the pink roses she carried, hurried out to greet "Grandpa Twain." She was the little Southern girl the humorist took such a fancy to on his recent trip to England, when he received the degree of doctor of literature from Oxford University.

Surrounded by the graduates and friends, Mr. Clemens walked into the assembly hall of the school, took a seat on the stage in a corner and listened to the singing of the girls. When Mr. Edward S. Martin of New York,[5] an essayist whose daughter, Miss Lois Martin, was among the graduates, gave a talk to the young women on what they should do in later life the humorist paid rapt attention.

"I don't know what to tell you girls to do," said Mr. Clemens, rubbing his hand through his thick gray, silvery hair. "Mr. Martin has told you everything you ought to do, and now I must give you some don'ts.

"There are three things that come to my mind, which I consider excellent advice. First, girls, don't smoke—to excess. I am 73½ years old and have been smoking 73 of them. But I never smoke to excess—that is, I smoke in moderation, only one cigar at a time. Also, never drink—to excess."

The third admonition—"don't marry—to excess"—created much amusement among the newly qualified alumnæ, the students, and the audience.

Turning from "don'ts," Mr. Clemens began a more serious discourse on honesty. He told a story from his own experiences, which he said proved that it was just as cheap to be honest as otherwise. While he related the anecdote in his inimitably witty manner, the students did not fail to appreciate its serious import, although everyone enjoyed a huge laugh over the then struggling writer's mishap.

After his talk Mr. Mark Twain, as he is accustomed to being addressed, gave the diplomas to the graduates, the presentations being accompanied by a handclasp and a few cheering words of advice and congratulation. The exercises concluded with singing by the girls. . . .

When Mr. Clemens appeared on the lawn the sun came out and said good day to him, and immediately the humorist was the center of a group of kodaking girls. With good grace he posed for them, and then he and his "granddaughter" had their picture taken. Miss Nunnally stood with her big bouquet of roses and academic cap and gown, while "Grandpa Sam" removed his cigar from his mouth and looked mischievously at the photographer.

While on his way to an adjoining building where luncheon was served, a heavily built, ruddy-cheeked man, appearing to be 65 years old, approached him and said: "Mr. Clemens, here's a young man who wants to meet you."

"Where is he?" said Mark.

"Why, you're shaking hands with him now," said the man, who was Mr. Elias Livezey of Catonsville. "I just celebrated my ninetieth birthday a few days ago and want to meet another young man like myself."

"We're well met," said the humorist smiling, as they walked off to the dining room together. . . .

Notes to Interview 252

1. On the Belvedere, see n. 1 to interview 251; on Nunnally, see n. 2 to interview 223.

2. Actually the *Minneapolis*. MT returned from England on the *Minnehaha* in October 1900.

3. Albert Bigelow Paine (1861-1937), MT's official biographer and first literary executor.

4. Cora Nunnally, wife of James H. Nunnally (d. 1938), a candy baron in Atlanta.

5. Edward S. Martin (1856-1939), poet and essayist.

• 253

"Twain Pokes Fun at Union Station and Pities City," *Baltimore Star*, 11 June 1909, 1, 12; excerpted in "Why Not Baltimore?" *Baltimore American*, 12 June 1909, 13.

When Mr. Samuel L. Clemens, better known as Mark Twain, America's foremost living author, is left in the seclusion of his room in his palatial New York home tonight he is going to pray that the people of Baltimore may soon procure a union station really worthy of the name. He said he would.

Mr. Clemens shook the city's mud from his feet this morning, caught a 10:40 o'clock train for New York over the Pennsylvania Railroad and is scheduled to arrive there this afternoon.[1] He was accompanied by Mr. Albert Bigelow Paine, the man who has been engaged to write his biography.[2]

The poor accommodations at Union Station caused the humorist to depart from Baltimore in a sorrowing mood. Had he not seen the station, he declared (humorously, of course) there would have been no occasion for prayer, and he could have trusted Baltimoreans to take care of themselves. But now that he has seen with his own eyes the small, inadequate building used as a station by the Pennsylvania Railroad to accommodate the great Baltimore public, he just felt that it would be the basest ingratitude on his part not to intercede on their behalf.

"Poor Baltimore! Poor Baltimore!" remarked Dr. Clemens, sympathetically, as he strolled by one of the small gates at the station and witnessed 100 persons struggling to get to their proper trains. "It's too bad that she hasn't a better station. Why don't the people say something? Why don't they speak their minds? Yes, it's too bad. And this for Baltimore."

The humorist was numbered among the 100 persons, more or less, who attempted to jam through the gate to the New York express train. He finally did get through by making a center rush, which verified the fact that he once played football in the old college days.[3] When he managed to wriggle his way through the gate he knocked the ashes from the black cigar he was smoking and took one deep breath for relief.

"My, but that was a squeeze," he remarked to Mr. Paine. "This city deserves something better. How does Baltimore stand it? Possibly she isn't but remains sitting holding her hands. She should arise and do some kicking.

"And look at the tracks," he said sarcastically. "Every chance of getting hurt. But, then, I suppose all the passengers, or prospective passengers, have their lives insured. But that's no way to send people to incoming and outgoing trains. Why don't they let the passengers climb over the roof and slide down poles to the track on which their train is standing? Now, that is rather an odd way, but, to me, it is less dangerous. A slide is easier than a run and especially when the latter is attended with the danger of being hit by a locomotive while running.

"Ah, but wouldn't it be better," exclaimed Dr. Clemens, growing serious, "if the Pennsylvania Railroad would construct stairs leading down to the trains? That would remove all danger. Yes, why don't they give Baltimore a better station? Other cities have much better stations. Why not Baltimore?"

Dr. Clemens was a busy man prior to his departure. He was one of the first to arise at the Hotel Belvedere,[4] and up to the time he was ushered into his cab which conveyed him to the station, hadn't a minute to spare.

The first thing he did when he awoke was to look out the window to see if it was raining. Much to his surprise he discovered that it was not and that a few streaks of mellow sunshine were attempting to stream through the window of his room.

"That sunshine was a surprise to me," he remarked as he came down on the elevator and walked leisurely about the hotel lobby, puffing away at a cigar. "I thought it did nothing but rain in Baltimore. I did not know that Baltimoreans ever saw the sunshine.[5]

"And I wonder," he continued, while a smile broke over his countenance, "if my visit is responsible for this rain. While I was in Sydney, Australia, there hadn't been any rain for six weeks, and the Christian people began praying for rain. They prayed night and day, and finally one day, after supplications had been offered for about a month, a shower came up which lasted for about two hours. Now take me, for instance, one who is referred to as an infidel. I came here to Baltimore and produce more rain than those Christian people in Australia could in weeks of fervent prayer. Funny, isn't it?"[6]

After finishing his cigar, the humorist was escorted to the dining room, where he breakfasted with Mrs. James Nunnally and her daughter, Miss Nunnally, the latter being the young woman responsible for Dr. Clemens' visit to Baltimore.[7] From the dining room he returned to his room and later departed for the station.

At Union Station Dr. Clemens was the center of attraction, although he endeavored to keep out of public gaze as much as possible. With Dr. Paine keeping close by, the humorist sought the rear platform and promenaded up and down it until train time. Dr. Paine saw that every fancy was gratified. Turning around Dr. Clemens happened to see the scales standing by.

"I want to weigh," he said, "to see how well Baltimore has been feeding me." Stepping upon the scales, Dr. Paine dropped a penny in the slot and the indicator pointed to 150 pounds.[8]

"Well, well," Dr. Clemens exclaimed, "I have gained one pound. They do feed well here, and I will go back home in good shape."

Inside the waiting room the humorist was approached by a bevy of pretty girls from the Carter school in Catonsville. The girls wanted to bid him farewell and had taken an early car for Baltimore. Dr. Clemens shook each one by the hand and told them how he had enjoyed his visit.

"My visit to Baltimore," he said, "has been most delightful, and I especially enjoyed the exercises at Catonsville yesterday. It was the sanest commencement I ever witnessed. I mean by that the girls were not required to read long, tiresome essays. No, there was none of that. The exercises were splendid.[9]

"Then Baltimore is such a delightful place, too," he continued, "and her people, well, we haven't their equal. The city appeals to me because of its delightful Southern atmosphere. I am a Southerner, and that is why I like to come to Baltimore. I was born in Missouri, and some of my happiest years were spent right in the South."

Dr. Clemens discussed the charge of plagiarism slightly, the only important thing coming from him being the announcement that Messrs. Harper & Co. were now printing an edition of the book *Is Shakespeare Dead?* which will give the Greenwood people credit for the excerpts taken from the book in England.[10]

"I think," he remarked, "that I have explained the situation to the satisfaction of the public, but I don't mind saying that in the future full credit will be given for all quotations from the Greenwood book. It was my intention that this should be done in the edition heretofore published."

Dr. Clemens is taking a great deal of interest in the biography that is being written of himself by Dr. Paine. Every now and then he reviews what has already been written, but the author declares it will be many, many years before the public sees it.

"It will be a long time," he declared, "because I am not going to die until I am at least 100 years old, or possibly older. Why, I am a boy, and Dr. Paine will have to wait several years before he can finish the closing years of my life. He has already written some of the biography, but not all, and he can't conclude his work until I am put under the ground. I am making no promises when that will be."

Dr. Clemens referred lightly to his belief, he stating that it was the general impression that he did not believe in a God. All on this score he would say was that he believed in a great intellectual force which ruled this great universe. He emphatically stated that he did not concur in the belief of some that this big world came here by chance.

Dr. Clemens is not contemplating writing any more new books just at this time. He will remain in New York for a few days, and will then go to his home at Redding, Conn., where he will remain all summer.

Notes to Interview 253

1. "Two Dozen White Suits Are Twain's," *Baltimore News,* 11 June 1909, 3, 12: "I prefer the gray for traveling," he said apologetically. "My white suits are all in my trunk." "How many white suits have you?" he was asked. "About two dozen," was the reply. "Enough to keep one week ahead of washday. You see, everything I wear is white. . . . Hey! you!" he called out to a darky porter on the platform near the carriage entrance. "Are you sure you put my grips in the 'club smoker'?" "'Deed, sah, I don't know what no club smoker is. I done put 'em inside till de train heave in sight." "What! Didn't Paine attend to all that?" said Mark. "He is not near so intelligent as he looks, is he?" Thereupon the darky began to laugh loudly, and upon being asked by Mark as to the cause of his mirth replied: "It ain't nuffin, sah; only it struck me sort of funny about Mr. Twain and Mr. Paine going to take a train."
2. Albert Bigelow Paine (1861–1937), MT's official biographer and first literary executor.
3. Of course, MT never played football, nor did he attend college.
4. See n. 1 to interview 251.
5. *Baltimore News:* "When I awoke this morning I was somewhat undecided as to whether to go or not, but when I saw signs of clearing I made up my mind at once to go north with the storm."
6. *Baltimore News:* "Speaking of weather puts me in mind of an experience I had once in Sydney, Australia. There had been a long drought there lasting seven weeks. The farmers and people were all praying for rain, special services were being held in the churches, and experimenters were trying all sorts of schemes to induce the heavens to rain. I landed in Sydney one morning after the seven weeks were up, and though I am supposed to be an infidel, I brought a great downfall of rain with me that neither prayer nor explosives had been able to bring. In fact, I frequently bring long periods of rain when I arrive at a place. That is why I have to have so many linen suits." Just as he finished speaking the gates were opened, and waving his hands to the newspapermen, Mark remarked that he could remember the time 50 years ago when he ran a race with a train in Missouri. "Now I couldn't beat an elephant," he exclaimed as he went through the gate.
7. See interview 252.
8. *Baltimore News:* Spying the penny-weighing machine, he climbed on. Mr. Paine dropped a cent in the slot and the needle swung around to 155.
9. *Baltimore News:* "I feel fine after my experience yesterday," he said. "You see, I always like the young ladies, and would go a long way to be in their company. It was too bad for the ladies that the weather was so bad, but, as I told you yesterday, I was rather glad to see it rain hard in Baltimore."
10. See nn. 2 and 3 to interview 251.

254

"Mark Twain's Smokes," *Danbury (Conn.) Evening News,* 3 August 1909, 6.

Mark Twain, who has been known for years as an inveterate and incessant smoker, has had to reduce his smokes to four a day, by the order of his physician. This is one of the means by which he is with the aid of the physician combating a heart trouble with which he has been afflicted for two months or more, he told a reporter of *The News* who called upon him at his country home yesterday afternoon.

Danbury as well as Redding has now a personal interest in Dr. Samuel L. Clemens, the aged humorist, of Stormfield, as his Italian villa in Redding is now known, and the people of this vicinity are gradually becoming familiar with his real name. It will be with a great deal of regret, therefore, that the people of this vicinity will learn that he is not in good health. Dr. Clemens was seen by a reporter at his home yesterday afternoon, and to him in a half-humorous way the famous author of humor spoke of his health and his four smokes a day.

He was seated in the loggia of his Redding home, reading one of the late magazines and enjoying what was probably a third smoke of the four smokes a day which he is allowed, when the reporter called and asked for a few minutes' interview. Dr. Clemens smiled a bit whimsically and extended his hand in greeting, then motioned the reporter to a chair nearby. He was cordial, yet a trifle restrained in his conversation. Although he consented to talk about himself a little he remarked in the course of the conversation that he did not like to be interviewed.

He wore the immaculate white flannel suit with which the people of the entire world are familiar through the many pictures which have been made of him during the last few years. Seated in the open porch, which the cement construction of the house gave a soft gray tone, his white clad figure, surmounted by the snow white locks which gave him a peculiar dignity and charm of appearance, outlined against the green of the opposite hills, he was a more unique and picturesque personality than he has been made in any of the pictures which have been taken of him in the same or other surroundings. He was a trifle pale and haggard, but he was calm and his hand was steady as he relighted the pipe which he had been smoking, and which had burned out, in the evident hope of securing from it a few more puffs of the delectable smoke.

The pipe itself was unique. It was evidently a favorite pipe, for it was an old one, with a bowl partially burned away and a generally dilapidated appearance.

In speaking of his condition of health, Dr. Clemens said that he was condemned by his physicians to keep perfectly quiet and to indulge in no more than four smokes a day, which to one who had been accustomed all his life to forty smokes or more was a reduction which was about as easily accomplished as a total prohibition.

"In fact I did quit entirely for a time," said Dr. Clemens, "but the doctor said that was not necessary. The object would be accomplished just as easily with not more than four smokes a day. And I am not sure but there is just as much pleasure to be derived from the four smokes as from forty, in the more complete enjoyment of the four and the delight of anticipating the approach of the time for one of the smokes."

Dr. Clemens said that he was not able to walk three hundred yards or to take a couple of extra smokes in a day without paying the penalty in a severe pain in his heart. The humorist spoke quite whimsically of the fact that he had lived almost seventy-four years in the belief that a man could smoke any time or all the time without any injury to his health, only to have that belief shattered at last by the condition in which he now found himself.

During the conversation he made some comments upon the criticism offered upon his conduct in smoking at Oxford while waiting to receive his degree of LL.D., in violation of the rules of the institution, criticisms made recently by Dr. James L. Tracy in *American Medicine*, referring to Mark Twain's description of the incident in his autobiography.[1] He did not seem to be disturbed by the criticisms but he explained the incident a bit in detail.

"I was not responsible for that incident," he said. "There were several of us who were there for the degree of letters and some for science degrees, who had to wait a long time for the ceremonies in which we were interested, perhaps an hour. As we stood around there was a group of four of us of which I was one. I asked if smoking was allowed and Mr. Kipling said that it was forbidden. Then some one of the four said that we could go around to a certain corridor and no one would see us and there would be nothing said. We went down there and no one said anything and no one came near us except some photographers. I was not the chief criminal; there were four, one American and three Englishmen, so you see that the crime was pretty well divided up."

Dr. Clemens said that he did not mind what was said about him; he was quite accustomed to it.

Note to Interview 254

1. In "The Psychology of the Tobacco Habit," *American Medicine* n.s. 4 (July 1909): 366-67, Dr. James L. Tracy criticized MT's "humorless conduct" in smoking while waiting to receive his Oxford degree. MT had described the incident in the October 1907 installment of his autobiography in the *North American Review*. See also *Auto* (1990), 218.

255

"Miss Clemens Weds," *New York Tribune*, 7 October 1909, 7; excerpted in "Twain in Oxford Gown at Daughter's Bridal," *New York World*, 7 October 1909, 5.

... Mr. Clemens prepared the following characteristic interview "to avoid any delays at the ceremony," as he expressed it. Speaking of the bride and bridegroom Mr. Clemens said: "Clara and Gabrilowitsch were pupils together under Leschetitzky in Vienna ten years ago.[1] We have known him intimately ever since. It's not new—the engagement. It was made and dissolved twice six years ago. Recovering from a perilous surgical operation, two or three months passed by him here in the house ended a week or ten days ago in a renewal of the engagement. The wedding had to be sudden, for Gabrilowitsch's European season is ready to begin. The pair will sail a fortnight from now. The first engagements are in Germany. They have taken a house in Berlin."

Speaking of the guests, Mr. Clemens said: "These guests are kinsfolk and old special friends. The Reverend Joseph H. Twichell, of Hartford, is a friend of mine of forty-two years' standing.[2] He married this bride's mother and me thirty-nine years ago. Mrs. Crane (sister of Mrs. Clemens), who is present now, was present then.[3] Mrs. John B. Stanchfield, a schoolmate of my wife, is present now.[4] She was present then. She has grown-up children now; she was a slim young girl then, preparing for Vassar. This bride is named for her. Jervis Langdon and Mrs. Julie Loomis, nephew and niece of mine, were playmates of Clara in childhood.[5] Dr. Quintard is present, a very old friend.[6] Miss Ethel Newcomb, pianist, was a fellow pupil of Clara and Gabrilowitsch under Leschetitzky in Vienna.[7]

Mrs. Wood is Mr. Twichell's daughter.[8] I knew her when she had only one tooth and preferred a nursing bottle to the Constitution of the United States. She is a mother in Israel now. But this is merely figurative—she really lives in Brooklyn. Mrs. Crane and I have been comrades forty-one years, and our ages are the same. United they foot up 148 years, though you wouldn't think it to look at us. The Gilders are old friends, though not very old in the matter of years.[9] William Dean Howells will arrive at any time.[10] He is seventy-one or seventy-nine years old, or along there. I have known him since he was a child. Age has no age. The word has no definite meaning.

"Howells and I pitied James Russell Lowell when he reached fifty,[11] and Lowell pitied himself, too, not being aware that he had not yet crossed the boundary line of youth. It distressed him to have us mention the subject of age. At fifty a person is really very young, but he will not find it out until later."[12]

"The marriage pleases you, Mr. Clemens?"

"Yes, fully as much as any marriage could please me or perhaps any other father. There are two or three tragically solemn things in this life, and a happy marriage is one of them, for the terrors of life are all to come. A funeral is a solemn office, but I go to it with a spiritual uplift—thankful that the dead friend has been set free. That which follows is to me tragic and awful—the burial. I am glad of this marriage, and Mrs. Clemens would be glad, for she always had a warm affection for Gabrilowitsch, but all the same it is a tragedy, since it is a happy marriage with its future before it, loaded to the Plimsoll line with uncertainties."[13]

Notes to Interview 255

1. Ossip Gabrilowitsch (1878-1936), Russian concert pianist and composer. On Leschetitzky, see n. 25 to interview 133.
2. See n. 1 to interview 2.
3. See n. 1 to interview 4.
4. Clara L. Spaulding (1849-1935) married the lawyer John Barry Stanchfield (1855-1921) in 1886. "My wife's playmate and schoolmate from the earliest times" (*MTL*, 2:182n6).
5. Jervis Langdon (1875-1952) and Julia Olivia Langdon Loomis (1871-1948), children of Olivia Langdon Clemens's brother Charles.
6. Edward Quintard (1867-1936), graduate of the Columbia Medical School in 1887 and the Clemens family physician.
7. Ethel Newcomb (b. 1879), pianist for Clara and the author of *Leschetitzky as I Knew Him* (1921).
8. Julia Curtis Twichell (1869-1945) had married the Brooklyn lawyer Howard O. Wood (1866-1940) in 1892.
9. Jeanette Gilder (1849-1916), critic, editor, and author, founded the *Critic* with her brother Joseph Gilder in 1881. She described the wedding in her column "The Lounger," *Putnam's* 7 (December 1909): 369-70. She was accompanied by her brother Richard Watson Gilder (1844-1909), poet and editor of *Century*.
10. W. D. Howells (1837-1920), American novelist and critic, MT's closest literary friend, and editor of the *Atlantic Monthly* from 1871 to 1881.
11. James Russell Lowell (1819-91), American poet and author of *The Biglow Papers* (1848; second series 1867).
12. At this point in the version of this interview that appeared in the *New York Times,* MT was asked about the Redding Mark Twain Library ("Miss Clemens Weds Mr. Gabrilowitsch," 7 October 1909, 9): "The village did me the honor to name it so. It flourishes. The people come to it from a mile or so around. We are all engaged in propagating the building fund, in a social and inexpensive way, through picnics, afternoon teas, and other frolics in the neighborhood, with now and then a full strength concert in my house at ostentatious prices. We had one last week with a team composed of Gabrilowitsch, David Bispham, and his bride, with me as introducer and police. We had an audience of 525. When I have a male guest I charge him a dollar for his bed and turn the money into the fund and give him an autographed receipt, which he carries away and sells for $1.10." "Are you at work now?" "No, I don't work. I have a troublesome pain in my breast which won't allow it, and won't allow me to stir out of the house. But I play billiards for exercise. Albert Bigelow Paine, my biographer and business manager, plays with me. He comes over every day for two or three hours. He has a farm half a mile from here upon which he raises hopes." "Do you like it here at Stormfield?" "Yes, it is the most out of the world and peaceful and tranquil and in every way satisfactory home I have had experience of in my life." [David Bispham (1857-1921) was an American operatic baritone.]
13. A line on the side of a ship that indicates the safe loading level, named after Samuel Plimsoll (1824-98).

256

"Mark Twain Feeling Blue," *New York Sun,* 21 December 1909, 5.

Mark Twain, who has been a month in Bermuda, where he celebrated his seventy-fourth birthday on November 30, returned yesterday by the Quebec Line steamship *Bermudian* somewhat out of sorts physically and even disinclined to jest.[1] He was amiably sad and his familiar drawl lacked the humorous note. He said he did not like the transition from the pleasant temperature and green fields of Bermuda to the chill atmosphere of New York. He put his hand on his left breast, indicated that his trouble seemed to be chiefly there and attributed it to indigestion. He was accompanied by Albert Bigelow Paine, who is assisting him with his autobiography.[2]

"I have spent most of my time in Bermuda riding," said Mr. Clemens. "I am getting too old to play golf and tennis and I have not the inclination to do much work. When I got down to Bermuda that pain in the breast left me; now, on my return, I have got it again. I have five or six unfinished tasks, including my autobiography, and I do not know when I will finish them. I have done almost nothing in the last three years. I may take up my autobiography again in a few weeks. I have already published 100,000 words and expect to have 500,000 published, most after I am dead."[3]

In regard to the challenge of Major Charles Gonter of St. Louis to play with him and Mathias Dougherty the continuation of a game of euchre they had played when all three, the last surviving members of the St. Louis Euchre Club, sat up all night at St. Louis away back in 1867, the humorist said: "I read that challenge in a dispatch from St. Louis. I am not going to continue the game. I am not well enough and I have not time."[4]

He had this to say about woman suffrage: "I not only advocate it now, but have advocated it earnestly for the last fifty years. As to the militant suffragettes I have noted that many women believe in the militant methods. You might advocate one way of securing rights and I might advocate another, and they both might help to bring about the result desired. To win freedom always involves hard fighting. I believe in the women doing what they deem necessary to secure their rights."[5]

Mr. Clemens said he had been invited to lecture on women suffrage by women's organizations. They knew where he stood on the matter. "I cannot oblige them," he said, putting his hand over his left breast; "I am troubled too much here. I would not have the strength to deliver a lecture. I won't lecture any more. My work is over in this life and this world."

It was not with his usual firmness of step that the humorist came down the gangplank. Among those who met him at the pier was Mr. Martin W. Littleton and his daughter.[6] He will spend the holidays at his home in Redding, Conn.

Notes to Interview 256

1. The 5,530-ton *Bermudian* was built in 1904 for the Quebec SS Co.
2. Albert Bigelow Paine (1861-1937), MT's official biographer and first literary executor.
3. "Mark Twain Done with Work," *New York Times,* 21 December 1909, 1: "Of course, I may do a trifle on my autobiography. There is still much to be done on it, but most of it will appear after my death as is known. I like to have some uncompleted work about me. It gives me something to do when the humor for work seizes me. The last few years have found me seldom in the humor to write."
4. "Mark Twain Home," *New York Tribune,* 21 December 1909, 7: "Yes, I know about that challenge," he said, "but I cannot accept. The major expected an easy victory, but has forgotten how badly he was beaten." Asked what his favorite card game was now, Mr. Clemens said: "S-s-h! That's private." See also MT's "Happy," (San Francisco) *Alta California,* 13 May 1867. MT wrote from St. Louis on 15 March 1867 that "twelve to sixteen or twenty gentlemen, composing the Euchre Horns' Club, meet once a week at each other's residences and play euchre" with the "partners first scoring seventeen games" winning. "Two gentlemen may then challenge them for the next meeting."
5. *New York Tribune:* "I have been an advocate of woman's suffrage for fifty years," said Mr. Clemens. "My views on the subject have been set forth clearly in my books."
6. The lawyer Martin W. Littleton (1872-1934) had been elected Borough President of Brooklyn in 1903.

New York Tribune: "I must live close to the law," said Mr. Clemens as he was about to leave the pier. "I might get into trouble, and I want a good lawyer to advise me. That's why I am going to Mr. Littleton's house."

257

"Mark Twain Hastily Returns to Bermuda," *New York World,* 6 January 1910, 2.

Mark Twain sailed again unexpectedly for Bermuda on the *Bermudian* yesterday for a four weeks' stay. His name was not on the passenger list.[1]

On December 20 the humorist returned from Bermuda to celebrate Christmas with his daughter, Miss Jean Clemens, at his home in Redding, Conn. While preparing for the Christmas festivities Miss Clemens, who was subject to fainting spells, suddenly met her death, having been found on Christmas eve drowned in her bath.[2]

It had not been Mark Twain's intention to go back to Bermuda before April, when his daughter was to have sailed with him. The pain in his left chest, he said yesterday, was still annoying, and he thought Bermuda was the best place for him.

"It is a digestive pain," said he, "and does not alarm me at all."[3]

"Naturally I am not pessimistic; I certainly was not feeling pessimistic then, for I was returning to spend what I anticipated as a very merry Christmas. I had small idea of the blow which was soon to come.

"This is my only companion and solace," he added, holding up a long black cigar. "It is about all I care for now, and I have been warned about making it too constant a companion. I detest the idea of shaking him though, for he and myself have been companions such a long time."

Notes to Interview 257

1. The 5,530-ton *Bermudian* was built in 1904 for the Quebec SS Co.

"Mark Twain Goes Back to Bermuda," *New York Herald*, 6 January 1910, 15: "Found me, did you? Thought I could fool you and slip away quietly this time," he said. "I didn't expect to go away so soon, but my side pains me and Bermuda seems to be the best place for relief.... I want to be quiet for a time," said Mr. Clemens. "I want to take it easy, and the weather is better for me in Bermuda."

2. On 24 December 1909 Jean Clemens suffered an epileptic seizure while bathing and drowned.

3. Rather than "digestive pain," MT suffered from angina pectoris, a symptom of the congestive heart failure that would kill him ten weeks later.

"Mark Twain Leaves Home," *New York Tribune*, 6 January 1910, 7: "I still have that pain in my left breast," he said yesterday, "but I am going back to Bermuda to see if I cannot get rid of it. I am not troubled with the pain when on the island, but as soon as I return to this city it attacks me again. I was not as ill as the reporters perhaps imagined when I came back to New York a few weeks ago."

"Mark Twain Goes South," *New York American*, 6 January 1910, 10: "I have a pain in my breast that made it advisable for me to seek the Bermuda climate," he said, on the ship. "It is not true that I am very ill. I am afraid an exaggerated idea about my bad health has gotten about. I am just taking care of myself, that is all."

"Mark Twain Ill, Hurries Back to Warmer Climes," *New York Evening World*, 6 January 1910, 10: "It is a digestive pain," he said, "and not pulmonary, and does not alarm me at all. I was rather surprised that my old newspaper friends took it so seriously when I came to read their accounts on my arrival."

New York Herald: "My friends, the reporters, seemed to think I was seriously ill when I arrived here last time. I told them about the pain I had and they seemed to be anxious. My trouble is not serious, however. The pain comes from indigestion and is not pulmonary as some seemed to suspect. I'll be back in April."

Unidentified newspaper, 6 January 1910; rpt. Milton Meltzer, *Mark Twain Himself: A Pictorial Biography* (1960; rpt. Columbia: University of Missouri Press, 2002), 286: "I do not know exactly why the 'boys' got the impression that I was seriously ill or incapacitated before Christmas," said the humorist. "I have still some of my old trouble in my left side and chest and am going away for a month to clear it up. When I was here just before Christmas I certainly did not expect what happened a little later."

258

Mildred Champagne,[1] "Mark Twain at Bermuda," *Human Life* 11 (May 1910): 15–16.

"Far from the madding crowd," "the world forgetting," perhaps, but "by the world forgot" never;[2] in a low, rambling, white stone house over two hundred years old, nestling in a semi-tropical garden, on a point of land jutting out into the sea, lives Mark Twain in strict retirement.

The house is reached from the main road by a long avenue of cedars. They extend to the thick hedge of oleanders that encircles the house and garden, hiding both from view of the casual passerby or the solitary stroller that comes upon this sylvan retreat.

At the hotel where Mark Twain had been stopping, before his recent bereavement, I was told in a cautious whisper, with many side glances lest someone might overhear, of his present abode, for the secret is zealously guarded from the host of curious visitors who, upon setting foot upon Bermuda soil, eagerly inquire, "Where is Mark Twain stopping?"

So it was with fear and trepidation that one bright, sunshiny morning I guided my pony down the cedar-lined path. The thick, overhanging branches made an archway that was almost somber, if it weren't for the stray bits of dazzling sky that peeped through the branches and cast fantastic shadows on the road. But for the chirping of the scarlet songsters among the branches and the soft lapping of the sapphire sea on the coral reefs, Nature's sweet stillness enveloped the scene.

Not a soul was in sight when I drew rein before the oleander hedge, hitched my horse to a post, and cautiously let myself within the iron gates. Then I was somewhat startled to find the big black eyes of a pickaninny staring reproachfully at me through the bars. He had sprung up from the road somewhere. He had an abnormally large head and a small, shrunken body, clothed in remnants of a shirt and torn pantaloons. One bare foot crossed the other and was resting upon it. He was sucking a huge sugar cane. In fact, he was all big, black, sad, reproachful eyes, and sugar cane. So might Huckleberry Finn have looked, but for his color.

He didn't want to see anybody.

He evidently regarded me as an intruder. I felt strangely uneasy and sought to mollify him.

"Who lives in this house, sonny?" I inquired.

He was silent for a while. Then he answered reluctantly, "Mr. Allen, the vice-consul."[3]

"And who else?" I persisted.

"Mrs. Allen."

"And who else?"

Again the boy was silent. Then he said in a scarcely audible whisper, "Mr. Mark Twain," and he added eagerly, "he don' lak nobody for to come see him."

I thanked the boy, passed him a couple of huge English pennies through the gate, and told him to run away and hide.

In another moment he had disappeared as mysteriously as he had come, and again I was in stillness and alone.

I stood in the midst of a semi-tropical garden, half natural, half cultivated. Thick masses of bamboo palms, sage brushes, and ferns everywhere, with natural arches of bougainvillea, and in the middle of the garden a clearing of velvety lawn and a tennis court. The path leading to the house was lined with beds of Easter lilies and a luxuriance of the delicate waxen frezia, their heavy, sickly sweet fragrance scenting the air.

The house was a long, low, one-story stone bungalow, with a wide veranda running around the front and side and a whitewashed gabled roof to catch the rainwater.

The rich pinkish-purple bougainvillea masses against the white stone walls, and the scarlet hibiscus and pink sage bushes cluster around the veranda, almost hiding it from view.

To the right in the distance, beyond the oleander hedge, the gleaming blue sea. To the left, and around the front of the house again the oleander buses, and beyond, the avenue of cedars. And over all an intensely blue, fair sky, and a vast stillness. Nature at her best and loveliest. An ideal place surely for a sorrow-stricken soul to find comfort and rest.

I stood on the veranda at the front door, irresolute for a moment. No one was in sight. I rapped timidly once or twice, but no one responded. I made up my mind that the family was not at home, and that, hence, the servants were off duty.

Then I walked around to the side of the veranda and paused in astonishment before a glass door. Through it I peered into the room. A white iron bed stood within three feet of the door, and upon it, full length and face downward, lay a familiar figure in a white linen suit, with a band of black crepe around his arm. A number of books were spread out before him on the bed, and he was poring into them, bearing his weight on his elbows and resting his shaggy white head in his hands. It was Mark Twain.

I knocked at the door very gently. He lifted his head, as if listening, without turning his face. I knocked again. He listened as if undecided whether to open the door or not. He turned his face slightly and I could see his lips move, and I judged it must be a gentle benediction for the knocker. Then he turned and saw me.

He rose hastily from the bed and came toward the door. A beautiful smile lit up his face, which I noticed at once was scarlet, almost livid, against its shaggy frame of silvery hair. His face looked small and pinched and ill. His frame was bent and his walk unsteady. He opened the glass door and with both hands extended he gave me a joyous welcome. And to the creator of Huckleberry Finn and Tom Sawyer and all the other people who have made me and so many others glad, my heart went out in love and sympathy. For just as no human being can read Mark Twain without laughing with him, so none can see him without loving him. For Mark Twain is intensely, vividly, lovingly human.

He shook my hands cordially and said in his kindest, most joyous way, "I'm so glad to see you. How do you do? Come right in. Let me take you right through to the parlor, and then I'll call the family."

"Oh, please don't call the family," I begged. "I haven't come to see the family. I've come to see you—only you."

And then, oh, Horrors! Instead of being, like the rest of mankind, pleased at this frank bit of flattery from a petticoat, Mark Twain's smile faded into a look of reserve and sadness, with perhaps a shade of annoyance. And then he started to cough, a miserable, nerve-racking cough that shook the whole of his slight frame and left him nervous and trembling and a trifle irritated. He held his hand on his chest.

"I don't see anybody," he said. "Nobody, nobody. I'm not—er—extravagantly well. I—er—I bark, bark, bark all the time. I can't talk to anybody. Now, mind you, I didn't get this cough in Bermuda. Somebody kindly imported it for me from the United States."

I expressed my sympathy. He was sweet again and mollified.

"Have you seen the crystal cave yet?" he asked. "Or the aquarium?"[4]

I said, "No. I came to see you first."

A sparkle of humor was in his keen, blue eyes.

"Well, you shouldn't have seen me first," he said quickly. "I run an opposition show to the Crystal Cave and the Aquarium. But they're not shucks to me. I'm lots better. I give them their money's worth. But you should see them. Then you will appreciate me."

I told him that I appreciated him anyway. That I considered him the best show on the island. That I should recommend him to all sightseers and that, furthermore, I considered him a good writer. That I loved Huckleberry Finn and Tom Sawyer as my own soul. That they could entertain and delight me and take me out of myself when no other characters in fiction could. And he replied earnestly, "They're fine books. They're to be recommended. You ought to like 'em. I like 'em. Everybody likes 'em. They're very, very fine works of fiction. I guess I ought to know." I agreed heartily.

"You just recommend them," he continued eagerly. "But don't recommend me to sightseers. I'm too old a bird to be caught. Besides, I'm going to charge an admission fee. It's a shilling a look." He coughed again that terrible, racking cough that left him weak and gasping after each onslaught. "The price is going up—up—all—the time—," he continued weakly. "Tomorrow it will be two shillings—the next day—three—"

He raised his head and squared his shoulders. There was a faraway look in his eye. I felt a lump in my throat and my heart ached.

He took my hand again and smiled into my face.

"What has impressed you most on the island, besides myself?" he asked jocosely. I answered with a will, "A certain Englishman, who said to me, 'George'—er—George—yes, that was it—my word, yes—George—er—Let me see—what was the chap's last name—'Washington'—er—was it not? Yes—er—I believe it was Washington—or something. By the way, who was this—er—George Washington?'"

Mark Twain laughed and seemed to enjoy himself.

"Mr. Clemens," I said, "will you see Professor ———, who has been in Bermuda three weeks now and has made about thirty unsuccessful attempts to see you, and will go away a broken and disappointed man if he doesn't see you? He tells me pathetically that his wife and your sister have been intimate friends and that he taught your sister's children. And so he thinks you ought to see him."

"But I won't!" cried Mark Twain, wrathfully. "My sister has a million intimate friends and my sister's children had a million teachers, and I won't see any of them, and I can't see any of them," he reiterated, between fits of coughing.

Just then Mrs. Allen, wife of the vice-consul, rushed in upon us. Mark Twain is her especial care. She looked anxiously at us. His smile reassured her and we were introduced.

"I'm very glad I saw you," said Mark Twain, shaking my hands cordially. "I'll leave you now to Mrs. Allen. Good-bye, good-bye. Remember the Englishman was selling you. Good-bye."

He kissed his hands to me repeatedly and then receded within his own chamber and softly closed the door, leaving us in the parlor.

Again and again I heard him cough, as Mrs. Allen chatted pleasantly about the various points of interest on the island and about their own house, which she assured me was over two hundred years old. But all I heard was that pitiful cough in the next room, and all I saw was that dear, familiar old face in its shaggy frame of silvery hair.

Mark Twain has experienced many a heartrending sorrow, but it is said the loss he feels most keenly is that of his friend Henry H. Rogers, who spent so much of his time in Bermuda with him.[5]

A good story is told of their visit to the Bermuda Aquarium. They stood in front of the tank containing a huge octopus, when a keeper with a big stick stirred up the tank in order to show the distinguished visitors the octopus in motion. Suddenly Mark Twain turned to Rogers and cried, "There you are, H. H. The Big Stick is after you, even down here."[6]

I saw Mark Twain again before I left Bermuda. His face was paler than when I had first seen him and he was more composed. I inquired solicitously after his health and he thanked me.

"I am much better," he replied. "I suppose I am as well as could be expected of a man of my age and circumstances. Fairly well—but not extravagantly well—you understand. Not—extravagantly—well—"

He smiled sadly and waved his hand to me as I left him.

Notes to Interview 258

1. Mildred Champagne (b. 1885), American romance writer.

2. The first quote is from Thomas Gray's "Elegy Written in a Country Churchyard" (1751); the next two, from Alexander Pope's "Eloisa to Abelard" (1717).

3. The U.S. vice-consul William H. Allen. The house, called Bay House, was at 4 Old Ship Lane.

4. The crystal cave was discovered in Hamilton Parish in 1904 and opened to the public in January 1908. The Bermuda Aquarium was established c. 1905 on the small Agar's Island in Pembroke Parish near the city of Hamilton by the Bermuda Natural History Society.

5. On Rogers, see n. 2 to interview 212.

6. Theodore Roosevelt claimed his antitrust and foreign policy was to "walk softly and carry a big stick."

Appendix

Interviews Published Originally in Translation

"Ein Besuch bei Mark Twain." *Neue Freie Presse* (Vienna), 1 October 1897, 1. Translated and reprinted in *American Literary Realism* 10 (winter 1977): 77–78. Excerpted in *Viestnik Inostrannoi Literarury* (St. Petersburg) 11 (November 1897): 316–17.

Fererro, Felice. "Una Vista a Mark Twain." *Corriere Della Sera* (Milan), 5 October 1899.

Horwitz, Max. "Mark Twain in Berlin." *National-Zeitung* (Berlin), 15 November 1891, Sonntags-Beilage, no. 46.

"Mark Twainnel Galantatol Budapestig." *Pesti Naplo* (Budapest) 24 March 1899, 4–5. Translated and reprinted in Anna B. Katona, "An Interview with Mark Twain," *Hungarian Studies Review* 9 (spring 1982): 73–81.

Ranneye Utro (St. Petersburg). 10 April 1910, 2. Excerpts translated and reprinted in Abraham Yarmolinsky, "The Russian View of American Literature," *Bookman* (New York) 44 (September 1916): 47–48.

Paladini, Carlo. "Un'intervista con Mark Twain." *Corriere Della Sera* (Milan), 12 November 1903. Translated and reprinted in Robert Luscher, "Italian Accounts of Mark Twain: An Interview and a Visit from the *Corriere Della Sera*," *American Literary Realism* 17 (1984): 216–24.

Randon, Gabriel. "Mark Twain." *Figaro* (Paris), 5 April 1894, 2. Translated and reprinted in *American Literary Realism* 10 (winter 1977): 49–51.

Schlesinge, Sigmund. "Eine Viertelstunde bei Mark Twain." *Neues Wiener Tageblatt,* 2 October 1897.

"S. L. Clemens in Budapest." *Magyar Hirlap,* 24 March 1899.

Untitled interview in Berlin newspaper. 24 November 1891. Mark Twain Papers, scrapbook 25, 31.

V[alenti]n, H[ugo]. "Ett Besök hos Mark Twain." *Afronbladet* (Stockholm), 13 July 1899, 3. See also Carl L. Anderson, "Mark Twain in Sweden: An Interview and a Commentary," *American Literary Realism* 11 (spring 1978): 80–91.

Z——ich, P. *Odesskye Novosti*, 8 October 1897. Translated and reprinted in M. Thomas Inge, "Ten Minutes with Mark Twain: An Interview," *American Literary Realism* 15 (autumn 1982): 258–62.

Index

Abbey, Edwin A., 486, 489
Abell, A. S., 605, 608
Aberdeen, Lord and Lady, 636
Able, Dan, 425, 426
accusations of plagiarism, 110–11, 113, 679–81, 686
Adams, Charles Francis, Jr., 6, 7
Adams, George W., 96, 97, 100
Adams, Henry, 7
Adams, John Quincy, 61
Addison, Joseph, 205, 207
Adelaide, Australia, 235–39
Adeler, Max, 110–11, 11
Æsop's Fables, 221
Aix-les-Bains, 143, 356, 362
Alameda, Cal., 544
Albany, N.Y., 99, 567
Aldrich, Thomas Bailey, 63, 64, 77, 78, 135, 146, 322, 549
Alexander II, Czar, 11
Alexander, James, 29
Alexandra, Queen, 626–30, 652
Allahabad, India, 284
Allen, Elizabeth Akers, 154
Allen, William H., 695
American Press Humorists, 589
American Publishing Co., 31, 192, 317, 339
American Revolution, 314, 316, 501, 507, 543, 613, 632
Amiens, France, 311
Andreeva, Maria, 541, 542
angelfish, 618, 647, 665
Annapolis, Md., 587, 588, 589, 595–04
Ann Arbor, Mich., 73, 74

Appleton, William H., 403, 405, 409
Aristophanes, 484, 488
Arthur, Chester A., 52, 53
Arundel Castle (steamship), 300
Ascot Cup, 635–38, 640–42
Ashcroft, Ralph W., x, 612, 614, 617, 624, 630, 643, 647, 651, 652, 654, 661, 662, 676, 677
Atlantic Monthly, 2, 3, 36, 37, 62, 64, 70, 422, 425, 578, 691
Attila the Hun, 529, 531
Auckland, N.Z., 255–57, 264
Australia, 151, 156, 158, 160, 165, 166, 171, 172, 185–87, 197–246, 252, 253, 263–68, 271, 273, 278, 296, 297, 317, 359, 362, 363, 416, 417, 532, 685, 687
Authors Club of Boston, 567
autobiographical dictation, 537, 546, 589–90, 594, 597, 611–13, 621–23, 632, 636, 651, 692, 693

Babcock, Oliver E., 6, 7
Bacon, Francis, 204
Bad Homburg, Germany, 624, 625, 627, 629, 643
Baldwin, Joseph G., 153
Baldwin, Sandy, 152
Ballarat, Australia, 240–41
Baltimore, Md., 11, 13, 53–54, 251, 587–600, 605–08, 679–87
bankruptcy of MT, 182–83, 185–86, 192–93, 317, 355, 360, 580–81, 584, 591
Banks, George, 669, 671, 672
Barr, Robert. *See* Sharp, Luke

Barrie, James, 247, 249, 528
Barton, Clara, 681
Bass, Edgar Wales, 363
Batavia (steamship), 24, 25
Beard, Dan, 105, 237, 238
Beard, William Holbrook, 386–87, 391
Beck, William, 377, 378
Becke, Louis, 213, 215, 231, 266
Beecher, Catherine, 113
Beecher, Henry Ward, 45, 47, 136, 137, 176, 178, 532, 533
Beecher, Rev. Thomas K., 93, 94
Belknap, William W., 6, 7
Bell, Alexander Graham, 256, 614
Bell, George, 209, 213
Bellamy, Edward, 302, 303
Benares, India, 283–89
Benton, Thomas Hart, xi, 279, 280
Bentzon, Th., 480
Berlin, Germany, 356, 362, 529, 579, 581, 690
Bermuda, 245, 576, 577, 579, 647, 662–66, 692–99
Bermudian (steamship), 576, 577, 579, 662–65, 692–94
Besant, Walter, 231, 232
Beuchotte, Claude, 670, 671, 673
Bigelow, Poultney, 191, 192, 351, 352
Billings, Josh, 255, 257
Birrell, Augustine, 633, 634
Bishop, F. A., 426
Bismarck, Otto von, 396, 398
Bispham, David, 691
Bixby, Horace G., x, 35, 37, 415–17, 421, 425, 426, 431, 433–34, 435
Black Hole of India, 289, 290
Black, William, 18
Blackmore, R. D., 64
Blackstone, William, 319, 320
Blaine, James G., 303, 312
Blake, Edward, 171
Blanc, Maria Thérèsa, 480
Blankenship, Ben, 449, 451
Blankenship, Tom, 443–44, 538
Blathwait, Raymond, 130, 136
Bloomington, Ill., 389
Boer War, x, 351, 390, 501, 507
Bok, Edward, x, 130

Bombay, India, 156, 158, 160, 165, 268, 270–81, 284, 287, 289, 292, 293, 297, 299, 307, 362, 437, 500, 506–07
book sales, 74, 80, 248, 290–92, 298, 302, 322
Booth, Edwin, 143
Booth, William, 294, 296
Boston, Mass., 2–4, 9, 11, 47–50, 56, 73, 98, 111, 249, 386, 387, 456, 497, 514, 523, 525, 550, 568, 577, 578, 664, 665
Boswell, James, 659
Bourget, M. Paul, 162, 200–01
Boxer Rebellion, 346
Boyce, Sir Rubert William, 635, 636
Boynton, Henry Van Ness, 96, 100
Bridgeport, Conn., 3, 669, 672
Briggs, Artemisa, 428
Briggs, John B., 449, 451, 452, 456–59, 472
Brockville, Can., 86
Bromley, Isaac H., 422, 425
Bronx, N.Y., 404, 409, 482
Brooks, Noah, 420, 422–23, 425
Brown, Curtis, 340
Brown, F. Gordon, Jr., 376, 377
Brown, J. B., 427
Browne, Charles Farrar. *See* Ward, Artemus
Browning, Robert, 101, 113, 301, 303
Brownsville, Tx., 559–60, 565
Brush, George de Forest, 513, 516
Bryan, William Jennings, 353, 358, 359, 368, 391
Bryne, Michael, 378, 380, 382–84
Buchanan, Charley, 427
Buckle, Charles R., 293, 296
Buffalo Bill. *See* Cody, William F.
Buffalo Express, 512, 516
Buffalo, N.Y., 89, 167, 512, 579, 580
Bunyan, John, 246, 355, 359, 360, 373, 532
Burckhardt, Jean Louis, 134, 136
Burdette, Robert Jones, 322, 329
Burke, Edmund, 220, 222, 409, 540, 541
Burnard, F. C., 55, 56
Burns, John Elliott, 627, 628
Burns, Robert, 31
Burton, Nathaniel J., 369, 370
Busbey, L. White, 531, 533, 561, 567
Bushnell, Horace, 369, 370
Butler, Samuel, 222

Butters, Henry A., 661, 662
Byington, A. Homer, 96, 100
Byron, Lord, 440

Cable, George Washington, x, 49–86, 154, 183–84, 207, 208, 215, 216, 302, 303, 423–24, 425, 463, 468
Cairo, Ill., 36, 463
Calavaras County, Cal., 12
Calcutta, India, 281–95, 297, 307, 362, 363
Caledon, Lord. *See* Alexander, James
Calhoun, John C., xi, 279, 280, 301, 303
California gold rush, 12, 315
Caligula, 529, 531
Calvert, Lord, 591, 594
Calvin, John, 107
Campbell, Thomas, 440
Campbell-Bannerman, Sir Henry, 626, 628
Cambridge, Mass., 2
Cannon, Joseph G., 531–35, 560–61, 567–69, 571
Cape Town, South Africa, 290–92, 313–16, 362, 363
Carew, James, 628
Carew, Kate, 204, 364–67
Carey, William, 166, 167, 168
Carleton & Co., 180
Carnegie Hall, 544, 583, 584
Carot, Henri, 476, 479
Carroll, Lewis, 106, 113, 205, 243
Carson City, Nev., 67, 153, 155, 180
Carter, John Henton, 37–41, 435
Castlemaine, Lady, 103, 105
Castro Ruiz, Cipriano, 675, 676
Cather, Willa, 516
Catonsville, Md., 678–81, 683, 686
Century Magazine, 62, 77, 78, 110, 166, 247, 381, 691
Cervantes, 355, 359, 360, 373
Ceylon, 156, 158, 160, 165, 166, 238, 268–70, 277, 289, 290, 310, 362, 363, 437
Chace Bill, the, 102, 232
Chace, Jonathan, 105
Champagne, Mildred, 694–99
Chandler, Zach, 8, 9
Charles II, King, 105
Charles L. Webster & Co., 49, 87, 100, 104, 105, 112, 113, 190, 192, 517, 591

Charleston, S.C., 99
Chatto and Windus, 103, 105, 280, 281, 322, 335, 339
Chatto, Andrew, 103, 105, 281, 329, 334
Chicago, Ill., 42, 43, 78, 88–90, 137–38, 167, 200, 320, 323, 324, 609, 666
Children's Theater of the Educational Alliance, 655–59
Choate, Joseph, 341, 345
Christchurch, N.Z., 249–55, 261, 264
Christian Science, 652. *See also* Eddy, Mary Baker
Churchill, Charles Spencer, 228, 232
Cincinnati, Ohio, 65–68, 433
City Club of New York, 391
City of Baton Rouge (steamboat), 35, 37, 42
Clapp, Henry, 180, 181, 260
Clark, Charles Heber. *See* Adeler, Max
Clarke, Marcus, 224, 228, 233, 242, 248, 266
Clemens, Clara (daughter), 3, 89, 90, 93–94, 156–58, 164–66, 170, 176, 192, 194, 195, 199, 209, 210, 223, 232, 235, 249, 255, 268, 269, 273, 277, 290, 291, 316, 345, 356, 368, 369, 394, 397, 483, 487–88, 493, 535, 547, 571, 572, 590, 647, 668–72, 689–91
Clemens, Henry (brother), 443, 444
Clemens, James Ross (cousin), 317, 318, 413, 417, 424, 425, 453–55, 459, 466, 467, 468
Clemens, Jane Lampton (mother), 88, 390–91, 420, 425, 439, 443, 450, 471
Clemens, Jean (daughter), 89, 90, 93–94, 156–59, 210, 356, 394, 397, 483, 487–88, 535, 547, 549, 552–54, 571, 572, 591, 647, 693, 694
Clemens, John (father), 188, 443, 471, 515, 599, 634
Clemens, Molly (sister-in-law), 447, 448
Clemens, Olivia Langdon (wife), 3, 14, 24, 25, 28, 29, 69, 88, 89, 94, 98, 143, 144, 158, 164–66, 170, 176, 177, 185, 186, 190, 192, 194, 195, 199, 200, 209, 210, 214, 215, 218, 223–24, 227, 232, 235, 249, 251, 255, 268, 269, 273, 277, 287, 290, 291, 313, 316, 317, 320, 328, 356, 368, 369, 390, 394, 395, 432, 451, 469,

472, 473, 483, 487–89, 535, 547, 548, 577, 580, 690
Clemens, Orion (brother), 122, 126, 259, 443, 444, 515
Clemens, Pamela (sister), 698
Clemens, Samuel L. *See* Twain, Mark
Clemens, Susy (daughter), 89, 90, 93–94, 156, 158, 210, 317, 547, 548
Cleveland, Grover, 67, 151, 155, 190, 191, 279, 281, 301, 303, 312, 338, 354, 359
Cleveland, Ohio, 151, 155, 190, 191, 319
Clive, Robert, 289, 290, 294, 296
Cody, William F., 227, 232
Cogswell, Henry Daniel, 58, 59
Coleridge, Samuel Taylor, 355, 361
Collins, Wilkie, 577, 578
Colombo, Ceylon, 268–70, 289, 291, 292, 295, 307
Columbia University, 403
Columbia, Mo., 412, 413, 417, 419, 424, 436, 448, 454, 459
Columbian Exposition, 138
Conkling, Roscoe, 20, 22
Connaught, Duke of, 626, 628–30
Connaught, Prince Arthur of, 626, 628–30
Cook, James, 248, 249
Cook, Thomas, 136, 137
Cooper, James Fenimore, 165, 166, 280, 495
copyright (international), 17–19, 22, 69, 70, 80, 99, 102–03, 120–21, 229–30, 232, 280, 298–99, 364, 493–94, 497, 498–99, 503–05, 546, 558, 560–61, 565–67, 568–71, 574
Corbett, Griffith Owen, 90
Corelli, Marie, 652, 654
Cornhill Magazine, 64
Corwin, Tom, 40, 42
Cosby, Arthur F., 410–11
Cox, George B., 507, 509, 511
Cox, Sunset, 95, 96, 560, 567
Cozco (steamship), 249
Crane, Stephen, 85
Crane, Susan Langdon (sister-in-law), 7, 25, 91, 94, 690
Crane, Theodore (brother-in-law), 7, 24, 91, 94
Crawford, Jack, 167, 168
Crockett, S. R., 247, 249

Croffut, W. A., 1
Croker, Richard, 403, 404, 407–09
Crooks, William, 627, 628
Crookston, Minn., 164
Cross, Sam, 436, 437, 440, 444, 448
Crounse, Lorenzo L., 96, 100
Cruikshank, J. J., 427, 430, 449, 451
Curtis, George William, 302, 303
Curts, Charles, 427, 439, 446, 449
Curzon, George, 228, 232

Daly, Augustin, 303–06
Danbury, Conn., 687–89
Davenport, Homer, 475–80
D'Annunzio, Gabriele, 581
Decatur, Stephen, 659
Defoe, Daniel, 260, 261, 263
Delagoa Bay, South Africa, 299–300, 310, 362, 363
Delano, Columbus, 6, 7
DeLong, George W., 37
Denny, William R., 262, 263
Denver, Col., 469, 472–74
Depew, Chauncey, 536, 537
De Quille, Dan, 167, 168
Derby, George Horatio. *See* Phoenix, John
de Rham, Frances Appleton Dana, 659
Des Moines, Ia., 99
Detroit, Mich., 60, 82–85, 154, 186
Devery, William S., 409
de Vinci, Leonardo, 261, 263
Dewey, George, 358
Dickens, Charles, x, 11, 18, 21–22, 60, 61, 90, 135, 183, 205, 206, 208, 212, 224, 243, 256, 302, 303, 495, 516, 518
Dickinson, Emily, 502
Dodge, Mary Mapes, 636
Doesticks, Q. K. Philander. *See* Thomson, Mortimer Neal
Donald, Robert, 101, 105
Dougherty, Mathias, 692
Douglas, Joe, 446–48
Dowie, John Alexander, 484–85, 487–89
Dresden, Germany, 23, 31
Du Chaillu, Paul Belloni, 527, 528
du Maurier, George, 213, 291, 303
Du Puy, Raymond, 675, 676
Dublin jewels. *See* Irish Regalia

Dublin, Ireland, 636
Dublin, N. H., 501, 502, 513, 514, 535, 549, 551, 553
DuBois, Fred T., 532, 533
Duke of Marlborough. *See* Churchill, Charles Spencer
Duluth, Minn., 89, 167
Duncan, C. C., 43-47
Dunedin, N.Z., 246-49, 264
Dunn, Arthur, 416, 417
Dunne, Finley Peter, 474
Dunraven, Lord. *See* Quin, Windham T. W.
Durand, Sir Henry Mortimer, 626, 628
Durban, South Africa, 296-300, 303, 307

Easter Island, 250
Eddy, Mary Baker, 485, 487-89, 493, 494, 560, 566, 572, 612, 618, 632-34, 652
Edinburgh, Scotland, 128
Educational Alliance of New York, 655-59
Edward VII, King, 1, 624-30, 638-43, 652
Eggleston, Edward, 99, 101
Eisler, Effie, xi, 157
Eliot, Charles W., 656, 659
Eliot, George, 18
Elmira, N.Y., 4, 6, 26, 31, 87, 90, 91-94, 108, 117-19, 127, 151, 207, 581-82
Emerson, Ralph Waldo, 11, 147, 577, 578
Estes & Lauriet, 69, 70
Euchre Horns' Club, 693
Evarts, William M., 285-86, 288
Everett, Sherman, 377, 382, 388, 391

Fairbanks, Charles W., 533, 534, 568, 569, 640, 645
Farthing, Barney, 458, 538
Field, Eugene, 425, 426, 463
Fields, James T., 62, 64, 577, 578
Fiji, 165, 269, 270, 289
fishing, 396
Fisk, Jim, 501, 507
Fisk, Pliny, 247, 249
Fitch, John, 99, 101
Fletcher, Horace, 511
Florence, Italy, 247, 306, 307, 356, 362, 363, 465, 469, 483, 487, 489, 491-94, 579, 581, 647
Florence, William J., 113

Florida, Mo., 428, 445, 470, 474, 515, 539, 645
football, 375-77
Forbes, Archibald, 33, 34
Ford, Bob, 61, 62
Ford, John T., 13
Fort Madison, Ia., 74-76
Francis, David R., 455, 461
Frankfurt, Germany, 362
Franz Josef, Emperor, 333-34, 336-37, 339-40
Frazier, Laura, 438, 440, 444-45, 447, 450, 465, 466
free trade, 19, 209, 213, 508, 658
French revolution, 278, 315, 316
Frohman, Daniel, 528
Frost, A. B., 178
Fuller, Melville, 533, 534
Fulton, Robert, 99, 101, 544
Funston, Frederick, 469, 474

Gabrilowitsch, Ossip, 668, 690, 691
Gage, Lyman J., 363
Gallia (steamship), 22, 23, 25, 28, 29
Galton, Francis, 149, 150
Garfield, James A., 300
Garibaldi, Giuseppe, 241
Garrick, David, 205, 207-08, 243, 277
Garth, Helen, 426, 430, 438, 439, 445, 451, 465
Garth, John H., 426, 430, 452
Gascoyne-Cecil, Robert A. T., 312, 313
Gatling guns, 404
George, Henry, 209, 213, 403, 645, 646
Gerhardt, Karl, 136, 137
Gilbert, Sir William, 30, 205, 208, 242-43
Gilder, Jeanette, 690, 691
Gilder, Joseph, 691
Gilder, Richard Watson, 99, 101, 377, 381, 690, 691
Gill, Everett, 449-50, 451
Gillette, William, 114-15, 117, 548, 549
Gillis, Steve, 152, 153
Gladstone, William, 581, 651
Glyn, Elinor, 673-74
Gobright, Lawrence A., 96, 100
Gold Dust (steamboat), 40, 42
Goldsmith, Oliver, 208

Gonter, Charles, 692, 693
Goodman, Joseph, 478, 481
Gordon, John B., 202, 203
Gorky, Maxim, x, 541-43
Gottschalk, Louis Morgan, 52, 53
Gould, Jay, 104, 105, 501, 507
Gowen, Franklin, 91
Graham, William A., 546-48
Grand Forks, N.D., 164-65
Grant, Julia D., 112, 113
Grant, Ulysses S., 7, 42, 49, 112, 113, 136, 137, 183, 202, 206, 207, 243, 259, 263, 305, 332, 441, 449
Gray, Thomas, 699
Great Baltimore Fire, 608, 609
Great Sioux War, 12, 13
Greene, Henry Copley, 514, 516, 551
Greenwood, Sir Granville George, 679, 681, 686
Gridiron Club, 531, 533-35, 561, 567
Griffin, George, x, 101, 105, 107, 134
Gurlitz, Augustus T., 392-94
Gutenberg, Johan, 108, 113
G. W. Carleton & Co., 180

Habberton, John, 204, 323, 329
Haggard, H. Rider, 106, 113
Hale, Edward Everett, 678-79
Hale, Perry, 376
Hall, Frederick J., 104, 105, 112, 185, 191
Halstead, Murat, 14, 16, 24, 26, 30-31
Hamersley, William, 369, 370
Hamilton (steamship), 676
Hamilton-Gordon, John, 636
Hammond, John Hays, 305-07, 316, 661
Hammond, Natalie Harris, 307, 308
Handy, Moses P., 425
Hanna, Mark, 417, 418
Hannibal, Mo., 37, 42, 124, 412, 420, 424, 426-30, 432, 433, 435-60, 464-66, 470, 471, 476, 502, 515, 538, 539, 599, 602, 606, 640, 645
Harcourt, Sir William, 497, 502
Harmston circus, 295, 296
Harper & Bros., 192, 389, 487, 490, 491, 539, 596
Harper's Magazine, 118, 153, 298, 494, 516, 618

Harper's Weekly, 409, 487
Harris, Addison C., 333, 334
Harris, Evelyn, 677
Harris, Isidore, 650-54
Harris, Joel Chandler, 77, 78, 136, 677
Harte, Bret, x, 12-14, 66-68, 100, 120, 132, 135, 136, 147, 202-04, 215, 217-19, 238, 240, 247, 289, 415, 417, 420, 425, 518, 520, 645, 646
Hartford, Conn., 2-4, 7, 8, 10, 15, 29, 33, 35, 42, 58, 69, 76, 80, 87, 93, 94, 98, 101-06, 112, 115-17, 124, 125, 130, 156, 158, 160, 164, 182, 183, 279, 306, 317, 346, 347, 351, 356, 361, 369, 370, 372, 405, 420, 478, 485, 512, 513, 535-36, 546-48, 573, 580, 581, 690
Harvard University, 163, 377, 656, 659
Harvey, G. B. M., 484, 487, 490, 533, 534
Hastings, Warren, 289, 290
Hawaii, 27, 33, 34, 126, 139, 156, 160, 165, 166, 274, 557, 562, 646
Hawkins, Sir John, 484, 488
Hawthorne, Julian, 178
Hawthorne, Nathaniel, 11, 62, 63, 70, 203, 516
Hay, John, 98, 100-01
Hayes, Rutherford B., 5, 6, 7, 10
Hearst, William Randolph, 510, 511
Heaton, John Henniker, 626, 628, 634, 635
Hegeman, John Rogers, 508, 511
Heidelberg, Germany, 23, 25, 28, 31
Hemans, Felicia Dorothea, 440
Henderson, Archibald, 612, 614
Henderson, Ernest Flagg, 514, 516
Hendricks, Thomas, 6, 7
Henry, Ambrose, 374, 375
Henry, Arthur, 96, 100
Henry, Charles W., 148-50
Henry, Patrick, 437, 440
Henry, Prince, of Prussia, 477, 481
Hepburn, Williams Peter, 531, 533
Herero, 591, 594
Herne, James A., 580, 581
Herts, Minnie, 656, 659
Higbie, Calvin, 238, 239, 476, 479
Higginson, Thomas Wentworth, x, 70, 497, 498, 501-04, 513, 516
Hitchcock, Ethan Allen, 514, 516

Hobart, Tasmania, Australia, 228, 241–46
Hobbes, Thomas, 207
Hobby, Josephine, 636
Hogarth, William, 476, 479
Holahan, Maurice F., 403, 404
Holmes, Oliver Wendell, 11, 39–40, 42, 61, 62, 70, 110–13, 136, 137, 211–13, 577, 578
Holroyd, Sir Charles, 637
Holsatia (steamship), 14, 16, 29
Honolulu, Hawaii, 99, 112, 172, 434
honorary degree from Oxford University, xi, 17, 589, 593, 594, 604, 610–46, 652, 682, 689
honorary degree from University of Missouri, 412, 413, 417, 419, 424, 436, 448, 454, 459
Hood, Thomas, 82
Hood, Tom, 54–56, 142
Hooker, Isabella Beecher, 548, 549
Hope, Anthony, 247, 249
Horowitz, Johannes, 339
Horr, Elizabeth, 451
Hotten, John Camden, 120, 126
House, Edward H., 113–17, 128
Howe, Julia Ward, 70
Howells, W. D., x, 2, 3, 14, 43, 63, 64, 68, 77, 78–79, 111, 156, 158, 215, 302, 303, 323, 456, 484, 488, 558, 564–65, 589, 594, 690, 691
Hughes, Charles Evans, 574, 576
Hugo, Victor, 18
humor, 60, 131–33, 145–47, 166, 187, 204–06, 212–13, 255–57, 302, 321, 322, 518–19, 522–23, 638–39, 642–43, 653
hunting, 396
Huntington, Clara, 105
Huntington, Collis P., 105
Hutton, Laurence, 375, 377

immigration, 655–58
imperialism, x, 317, 350–51, 353, 358, 391
impersonators of MT, 98–99
India, 156, 159, 160, 165, 166, 172, 186, 238, 245, 249, 277, 281, 283–84, 286–87, 289–93, 295–96, 317, 322, 338, 417, 605
Inglis, W. O., 520–24
Ingram, Walter, 490

international copyright, 17–19, 22, 69, 70, 80, 99, 102–03, 120–21, 229–30, 232, 280, 298–99, 364, 493–94, 497, 498–99, 503–05, 546, 558, 560–61, 565–71, 574
Irish Regalia, 635–36, 638, 640–42
Irving, Henry, 63, 64, 414, 417, 482

Jackson, Thomas J. (Stonewall), 202, 203
James, Henry, 596
James, Jesse, 61, 424
Jameson raiders, 307, 310, 314, 354–55, 359, 360, 373
Jameson, Leander Starr, 299, 300, 310
Jamestown Exposition, 583–86, 593
Jefferson (steamship), 674
Jerome, William Travers, 411, 508, 511
Jesus College, Oxford, 635
Johannesburg, South Africa, 299–08, 310, 314, 315, 362, 363, 373
John Ballantyne and Co., 183, 184
Johnson, Andrew, 97, 100
Johnson, Cuthbert W., 31
Johnson, Samuel, 657, 659, 677
Johnstown, Pa., flood, 680, 681
Jolly, Beck, 435
Jousaye, Marie, 168
Joyce, John A., 98, 101
Justice, Ervin, 572

Kanawha (yacht), 583–88, 593
Keller, John William, 404
Kellogg, William Pitt, 8, 9
Keokuk, Iowa, 74, 88, 89, 443, 447, 515
Khan, Genghis, 529, 531
Kimberley, Australia, 309, 310, 313, 315, 316, 362, 363
King, Clarence, 135, 136
King, Thomas Starr, 202, 203, 206–07
Kingsbridge, N.Y., 405
Kingsley, Charles, 169, 171
Kipling, Rudyard, x, 117–29, 135, 159, 203, 207, 212, 236, 238, 243, 248, 275–66, 277, 288, 299, 338, 339, 392, 393, 473, 614, 616, 620, 689
Kiralfy brothers, 83, 85
Knights of Labor, 250, 251
Koontz, Ben, 124–25

Krüger, Paul, 355, 361, 362, 373
Kubelik, Jan, 414, 417

Lafayette, Ind., 78, 81–82
Lakenan, Katheryn, 448, 449
Lake Saranac, N.Y., 394–400
Lamb, Charles, 205, 207, 438, 440
Langdon, Charles J. (brother-in-law), 25, 92, 94, 118, 119, 582, 583, 691
Langdon, Ida (niece), 491
Langdon, Jervis (father-in-law), 491, 512
Langdon, Jervis (nephew), 690, 691
Lankford, Livius, 677
Lansing, Mich., 527, 528
Larned, Josephus N., 514, 516
Lathrop, George Parsons, 69, 70
Lawley, Beilby, 294
Le Conte, Joseph, 479, 481
Leary, Katy, x, 377, 381, 382, 496
Leary, William, 407, 409
Lebaudy, Jacques, 642
Lecher, Otto, 331
lecturing, 32–33, 50, 54, 65, 73, 183, 187–88, 192–93, 199, 217–19, 251, 254, 272–74, 356, 361, 463, 468
Lee & Shepard, 111
Leopold, King, of Belgium, 497, 498, 505, 520, 523–24, 528–31, 618, 633, 634
Leschetitzky, Theodor, 362, 363, 690, 691
Leslie, Elsie, xi, 114, 117, 157, 158
Levering, A. R., 427
Lewis, Charles Bertrand, 322, 329
Lewis, John T., 491, 492
Libbey, Laura Jean, 140, 143
Library of Congress, 558, 564
Lincoln, Abraham, 5, 70, 101, 259, 356, 361
linotype machine, 248, 249, 326, 327
Lippincott, Dave, 427
litigation, 69, 70, 90–91, 113–17, 392–93
Littleton, Martin W., 692, 693
Livezey, Elias, 683
Livingstone, David, 189
Lodge, Henry Cabot, 571
Loeffler, Charles, 568
Logue, Michael Cardinal, 667, 668
London, England, 17, 23, 25, 31, 55, 127, 142, 166, 202, 203, 206, 231, 243, 251, 254, 261, 282, 284, 317, 318, 333–35, 340, 345–47, 351, 362–66, 415, 432, 454, 495, 497, 579, 581, 589, 610, 611, 621, 622, 630, 639, 651, 653, 654
Long, John D., 560, 567
Longfellow, Henry Wadsworth, x, 11, 61, 62, 577, 578, 656
Loomis, Julie (niece), 690, 691
Los Angeles, Cal., 589
Lotos Club, 375, 501
Louis XV, King, 105
Louisiana, Mo., 441, 444, 471
Louisville, Ky., 49, 68–70
Lounsbury, H. A., 669, 671, 672
Love, Robertus, 418–24, 426–30, 435–40, 448–51, 453–56
Low, Herbert, 199, 201, 204, 208, 223
Low, Seth, 400–10, 488
Lowell, Amy, 516
Lowell, James Russell, 11, 40, 42, 61, 62, 690, 691
Lucania (steamship), 486, 489
Lucy, Henry W., 486–87, 489–90, 491
Lyon, Isabel, x, 469, 550, 552–54, 576, 587, 589, 592, 594, 596, 598, 600, 607, 608, 614, 624, 630, 647–49, 654, 660, 662, 667–69, 671, 672–73, 677
Lyons, Sam, 441

M'Cardell, Roy L., 481–82
MacAdam, Hastings, 440–48, 464–66
MacAlister, J. Y. W., 612, 614
Macaulay, Thomas Babington, 18, 283, 288, 494
MacGregor, William, 269, 270
MacLane, Mary, 473, 474
MacVeagh, Franklin, 514, 516
Madras, India, 290–96
Mann, William D'Aton, 95, 96
Mararoa (steamship), 241, 243, 246, 263
Marconi, Guglielmo, 654
Maritzburg, South Africa, 296, 305, 306
Marjoribanks, Ishbel Maria, 636
Marsham, Charles, 29
Martin, Edward S., 682, 683
Martin, Lois, 682
Martin, William H., 95, 96
Mary Baldwin College, 556
Mason and Dixon line, 605, 608

INDEX / 711

Matabele war, 500, 505
Matthews, Brander, 495, 496
Mauritius, 290, 295, 307, 363
May, Phil, 479, 481
McAdam, John, 175
McAleer, Patrick, x, 535-36, 547-48
McAllister, Ward, 221, 222
McCall, John A., 500, 506, 508
McCarren, Patrick H., 507, 511
McClellan, George B., Jr., 510, 511
McCullagh, John, 408, 409
McCurdy, Richard A., 500, 506, 507, 508
McDaniel, James, 442-44
McDowell, Joseph Nash, 446, 448
McGinley, F. E. D., 82
McKay, John W., 176, 178
McKelway, St. Clair, 391, 487, 490, 491
McKinley, William, 101, 301, 303, 351, 358, 359, 391
McKinsey, Folger, 607-09
McLaren, Ian, 247, 249
Mead, Mary Gertrude, 486, 489
Mee, Mark, 296
Mein, Thomas, 316
Melbourne, Australia, 219, 223-34, 241, 245, 248, 254, 260, 270, 299, 363
Meltzer, Charles Henry, 673-74
Melville, Herman, 516
Memphis, Tenn., 323
Mergenthaler, Ottmar, 249
Metropolitan Club of New York, 484, 487
Metropolitan Museum of Art, 387, 391, 479
Michelangelo, 647
Miller, Joaquin, 19
Miller, Polk, 554-56
Miller, William, 459
Millerites, 457, 458
Milwaukee, Wisc., 79-82
Minneapolis (steamship), 594, 610-12, 614-15, 621, 683
Minneapolis, Minn., 76-79, 159
Minnehaha (steamship), 346, 351, 356, 682, 683
Minnetonka (steamship), 627, 628, 636-40, 643-46
minstrel shows, 207
Missouri State University. *See* University of Missouri

Mitchell, Margaret Julia, 45, 47
Moffett, Annie (niece), 100, 192, 698
Moffett, Samuel E. (nephew), 190, 192, 339, 512, 516, 698
Mohammed, 222, 257
Mohican (steamship), 182, 184
Monadnock, 514, 516, 550
Monday Evening Club, 369, 370
Monroe Doctrine, 278-79, 280
Monroe, James, 280
Montague, James, 474-80
Montreal, Can., 32-34, 49, 80
Moody, Dwight L., 11
Mookerjee, Onoocool Chunder, 287-88
Mookerjee, Sambhu C., 296
Moore, George, 538, 539
Morgan, J. P., 487
Morse, Samuel, 295, 296
Moss, Mary, 448
M. Quad. *See* Lewis, Charles Bertrand
mugwumps, 207, 208, 353, 358-59, 508, 509, 511, 598, 600
Munich, Germany, 23, 25, 31
Munro, Thomas, 294, 296
Murphy, C. A., 235
Murphy, Charles, 507, 508, 511
Murray, John, 262, 263
Muscatine, Ia., 515
Muybridge, Eadweard, 391

Namibia, 594
Nansen, Fridtjof, 626, 628
Napoleon I, 355, 361, 644
Nash, Billy, 427, 437-41, 449
Nash, Tom, 439, 449
National Arbitration and Peace Conference, 583, 584, 595, 598, 600
Nero, 529, 531
New England Club of New York, 9
New Haven, Conn., 304, 376, 579
New London, Mo., 441, 449
New Orleans, La., 4, 38, 42, 76, 77, 80, 99, 153, 155, 179, 183, 185, 215, 431, 433, 434, 463, 507, 634
New York (steamship), 138, 143, 320, 321
New York, N.Y., 7, 23, 26, 54, 73, 112, 128, 165, 192, 203, 241, 245, 282, 305, 307, 317, 329, 345, 347, 351, 355, 361-63,

366, 367, 369, 382-83, 385-88, 394, 410-11, 414, 416, 418, 424, 432, 445, 477, 489, 496, 506, 511-16, 536, 547, 549, 553, 554, 563, 564, 574, 576-79, 582, 585-87, 589, 593, 594, 604, 605, 610, 614, 637, 648, 667, 668, 674, 677, 678, 680, 684, 686, 692
New Zealand, 156, 160, 165, 166, 172, 242, 245, 246-64, 317, 362, 363
Newcomb, Ethel, 690, 691
Newton, Mass., 2, 3
Nicholas I, Czar, 11, 12, 13
Nicholas II, Czar, 506
Noah, Jacob J., 96, 100
Norfolk, Va., 496, 586-88, 676-77
Norham Castle (steamship), 310
Norman (steamship), 316
North American lecture tour (1895), 151-96
North American Review, 63, 64, 162, 409, 481, 487, 495-96, 546, 569, 571, 578, 689
North, John W., 152, 153
Northrop, W. B., 394, 620
Nunnally, Cora, 682, 683, 685
Nunnally, Frances, 614, 616, 617, 681-83, 685
Nunnally, James H., 682, 683, 685
Nye, Edgar W. (Bill), 159

O'Rell, Max, 162, 198, 200, 201, 238, 265
Oceana (steamship), 268, 269
Ollendorf's German Grammar, 23, 25
Olney, Channez Huntington, 647-49
Olympia, Wash., 172, 173, 178, 181
Oom Paul. *See* Krüger, Paul
Osbourne, Lloyd, 216
Osgood, James R., 42, 423, 425, 567
Ottawa, Can., 86
Oxford University, xi, 17, 589, 593, 594, 604, 610-46, 652, 682, 689

Paderewski, Ignace Jan, 176, 178, 201, 206, 414, 417
Page, Thomas Nelson, 215, 216
Paige, James W., 249
Paige typesetter, 87, 248, 249, 324-27
Paine, Albert Bigelow, x, 469, 571, 680-87, 691-93
Painter, Uriah, 96, 100

Palazzo Vecchio, 306
Palmer, Barbara, 105
Palmer, Potter, 43
Papin, Theophile, 456
Pardee, Dwight Whitfield, 369, 370
Paris (steamship), 144
Paris, France, 17, 23, 25, 28, 31, 143, 145, 148, 210, 273, 311, 320, 363, 366, 458, 538, 579, 581, 651
Park, Edwin J., 91
Parker, Harvey D., 11
Parkes, Sir Henry, 210, 213
Parkman, Francis, 519
Parsloe, Charles, 13, 14
Parsons, Elsie Clew, 559, 565
Patrick, Arthur William, 628, 630
patriotism, 657-58
Paul Jones (steamboat), 433
Payne, Sereno, 561, 567
Pearmain, Alice Whittemore Upton, 550
Pearmain, Sumner B., 496, 497, 502, 514, 516
Pease, Lute, 172, 173, 182, 184
Penn, William, 591, 594
Penrose, Boises, 507
Pepys, Samuel, 349
Percy, Florence, 154
Perry, Oliver, 673
Petoskey, Mich., 155
Pew, Marlen E., 525-28
Phelps, Roswell H., 42, 43
Philadelphia, Pa., 52-53, 64, 90-91, 110, 125, 319, 418, 420, 501, 507-09, 540
Philippines, 350-51, 353, 358, 389-91, 591, 595, 657
Phoenix, John, 256, 257
Pierce, Edwin, 427, 439, 443-44, 449
Pietermaritzburg, South Africa, 296, 305, 306
Pilgrim Club, 652, 654
Pitt, William, 540, 541
Pitts, W. R., 427
Pittsburgh, Pa., 60-65
plagiarism, accusations of, 110-11, 113, 679-81, 686
plasmon, 370, 659-61
Platt, Thomas Collier, 536, 537
Players Club, 143
Plimsoll, Samuel, 691
Pobedonostsev, Konstantin, 500, 506

Poe, Edgar Allan, 63, 147, 612, 623
Poisson, Jeanne-Antoinette, 105
Pomeroy, Brick, 145, 148
Pompadour, Madame de, 103, 105
Pond, J. B., 59, 65, 67, 68, 70, 82–86, 151, 154, 157, 159, 164–66, 172, 173, 175–78, 187, 189, 192, 195, 196, 361, 372, 475, 532
Pond, Ozias W., 65, 68
Ponte Vecchio, 307
Poona, India, 282
Pope, Alexander, 184, 206, 699
Port Elizabeth, South Africa, 309–12
Porter, Jane, 94
Portland, Me., 117
Portland, Ore., 172–73, 175, 178, 362, 363
Port Louis, Mauritius, 291, 292
Potter, Henry Codman, 96, 100, 385, 391, 601, 604, 626, 628
Pötzl, Eduard, 330, 331, 340
Pretoria, South Africa, 296, 300, 307, 310, 354, 359, 370, 373
Primrose, Archibald Philip, 255, 257
Princess Irene (steamship), 483, 487
Princeton University, 375–77
prohibition and temperance, 219–22, 498, 574, 575
Puck, 209, 213
Pumpelly, Raphael, 513–14, 516
Punch, 55, 56, 209, 213, 486

Quaker City (steamship), 15, 16, 25, 26, 30, 46, 47, 94, 260, 261, 319, 338, 339, 348
Quarles, John Adams, 134, 136
Quarry Farm, 4, 6–7, 91–94, 108–09, 118–19, 125, 148, 151, 491, 492
Queenstown, South Africa, 309
Quick, Dorothy, 638–41, 645, 646
Quin, Windham T. W., 24, 28
Quintard, Edward, 690, 691

Rabelais, 484–85, 488
racial attitudes, MT's, 237–38, 287
Ragsdale, Bill, 33, 34
Raleigh, Walter, 267, 268
Ralph, Lester, 558, 565
Rama V of Siam, King, 626, 628–30
Ramsdell, Hiram J., 96, 97, 100

Rayner, Isador, 587, 592
Reade, Charles, 18, 266, 268
Reagan, John Henniger, 99, 101
Redding, Conn., 647, 665, 667, 669–72, 677–79, 682, 686, 688, 691–93
Reed, Thomas B., 95, 96, 561, 567
Reid, Whitelaw, x, 15–17, 96, 589, 593, 594, 626, 628, 629
religious belief, MT's, 686
revolution, MT's attitude about, 541–43
R. F. Fenno & Co., 392, 393
Rhodes, Cecil, 300, 306, 308, 316, 500, 505
Rice, Julia Barnett, 664, 666
Rice, Thorndyke, 63, 64
Richardson, Abby Sage, 114, 116, 117, 128, 658
Richmond, Va., 554
Ries Theresa Feodorowna, 331, 332
Riley, James Whitcomb, 438, 440, 554, 556
Riley, John Henry, 97, 100, 316
Riverdale, N.Y., 400, 401, 404–06, 408, 409, 456, 466, 475, 479, 481–83, 485
RoBards, George, 430, 436, 440
RoBards, John, 427, 430
Robbins, William, 444
Robinson, Edwin Arlington, 516
Robinson, Henry C., 369, 370
Rochambeau, Count and Countess, 453, 455, 456, 459–62
Roche, David, 378, 380–83
Rochester, N.Y., 57–59
Rock Creek Cemetery, 571
Rockefeller, John D., 501, 507
Rodney, Lord. *See* Marsham, Charles
Rogers, Harry, 585–86, 593, 698–99
Rogers, Henry H., x, 583–88, 593, 662–66, 674–78
Rollingpin, Commodore. *See* Carter, John Henton
Rome, Italy, 252, 348
Roosevelt, Theodore, 101, 411, 559, 565, 568, 598, 600, 614, 699
Root, Elihu, 44, 47
Rosebery, Lord. *See* Primrose, Archibald Philip
Rosetta (steamship), 268, 269
Ross, Malcolm, 246, 249
Row, Samuel H., 527

Royal Geographical Society, 203
Ruskin, John, 108, 113
Russell, Sol Smith, 425, 426
Russo-Japanese war, 500, 506, 543, 583–84, 585
Russo-Turkish War, 11–12, 13

Sacramento Union, 645, 646
Sacramento, Cal., 274
Saintine, X. B., 473
Saint-Simon, 146, 148
Sala, George Augustus, 55, 56, 142, 143
sales of MT's books, 74, 80, 248, 290–92, 298, 302, 322
Salisbury, Lord, 312, 313
Sands, James H., 597, 600
Sandwich Islands. *See* Hawaii
San Francisco, Cal., 4, 66, 97, 100, 125, 152, 173, 177, 182, 192, 202, 213, 215, 258, 274, 348–49, 362, 363, 388, 420, 544–45, 603, 645, 646
San Francisco earthquakes, 544–45
Sankey, Ira David, 11
Sarawati, Bhaskara Nand, 284–85, 288
Sarony, Napoleon, 526, 527, 528
Saturday Club of Boston, 11
Saturday Press, 180–81, 260
Savage, Richard, 56, 614, 625, 641, 654
Savage Club, 54, 56, 341, 345, 614, 625, 638, 641, 652, 654
Schlegel, Frederick von, 222
Schreiner, Olive, 308, 309
Schurz, Carl, 659
Scipio, Mo., 458
Scott, Walter, 121, 183, 184, 212, 230, 335, 360, 473, 495, 571, 581
Seattle, Wash., 172, 182, 186
Second International Peace Conference at the Hague, 652, 654
Sellers, Isaiah, 80, 153, 155, 180
Sembrich, Marcella, 518, 520
Shah of Persia, 33, 34, 585
Shakespeare, William, 68, 95, 120, 140, 152, 160, 205, 212, 256, 259, 343–44, 537, 652, 656, 679, 681
Sharp, Luke, 82, 85
Shaw, George Bernard, x, 610, 612–14, 617–18, 623–24

Shaw, H. W. *See* Billings, Josh
Shepard, Edward Morse, 409, 411
Sheridan, Philip, 202, 203
Sherman, William T., 36, 45, 47, 173, 175
Shields, John A., 392, 393
Siebold (chemist), 370, 661, 662
Skrine, Francis H. B., 294, 296
Slote, Dan, x, 15–16, 23–24
Smith, George Williamson, 163, 164
Smith, Haskett, 261–63
Smith, Joseph L., 514, 516
Smith, Roswell, 78
Smythe, Carlyle, 238, 239, 242, 249, 250, 296
Smythe, R. S., 235, 238, 242, 249, 268, 270
Society for the Suppression of Unnecessary Noise, 664, 666
South Africa, 156, 158, 165, 166, 172, 186, 238, 249, 290, 295, 296–316, 317, 350, 362, 390, 417, 505, 591, 592, 594
Spaulding, Clara, L., 690, 691
Spencer, Herbert, 140, 143
Spokane, Wash., 165–67
Squibob. *See* Billings, Josh
Stanchfield, John B., 691
Standard Oil Co., 305, 584, 662
Stanley, Henry M., 188, 189, 202, 203, 206, 243, 279
Stead, William T., 177, 178, 227, 308, 309, 320
Stedman, Edmund Clarence, 96, 100, 102
Stephen, James, 281
Sterner, W. E., 160
Stevens, Ed, 441, 444
Stevenson, Frederick Boyd, 655–58
Stevenson, Robert Louis, 212, 215, 216
Stewart, William Morris, 97, 100
St. Louis, Mo., 34, 38, 42–43, 70–74, 89, 188, 189, 193, 215, 317, 323, 412–26, 430–35, 453–56, 459–63, 466–68, 515, 692
St. Louis Country Club, 455, 456, 466
St. Louis Euchre Club, 692
St. Louis University Club, 462
St. Louis World's Fair, 456
St. Nicholas, 236, 238
Stockton, Frank, 302, 303
Stoddard, Charles Warren, 130–31, 136, 420, 425
Stone, John Timothy, 608, 609

Stormfield, 647, 667, 688, 691
Story, William Wetmore, 19
Stowe, Harriet Beecher, 93, 94, 101, 112, 113, 157, 159, 256, 548, 580, 581
St. Paul, Minn., 37, 42, 49, 87, 88, 159, 166, 460
St. Paul (steamship), 540
Stratford-on-Avon, England, 652
Straus, Isidor, 658, 659
Strothmann, Frederick, 494
Sturgis, Dorothy, 664, 665
Sturgis, Russell, 664, 665
suffrage, MT on women's, 222, 692-93
Sullivan, John L., 85
Sullivan, Sir Arthur, 30, 208
Sullivan, Tim, 403, 404, 407, 639, 643
Swift, Jonathan, 184, 395, 398
Swinburne, Algernon, 423
Swinton, William, 97, 100
Sydney, Australia, 171, 192, 197-219, 223, 224, 226, 228, 230, 232, 249, 250, 254, 263-67, 362, 363, 685, 687

Tacitus, 222
Tacoma, Wash., 172, 175, 177, 182, 191
Taft, William Howard, 61, 70
Talleyrand, 146, 336, 339, 342
Talmage, T. DeWitt, 37, 38, 234, 286, 288
Tammany Hall, 5, 7, 312, 317, 391, 401-11, 488, 643
Tansey, George Judd, 412, 413, 417, 432
Tarrytown, N.Y., 474, 485, 489
Tasman, Abel Janszoon, 248, 249, 253, 255
Tasmania, 156, 158, 160, 165, 241-46, 362, 363
Tauchnitz, Baron Christian, 19, 230, 232
Tawney, James A., 531, 533
Taylor, Bayard, 14-16, 23, 26, 27, 30, 31, 136
Taylor, Douglas, 191
Taylor, Howard P., 116, 117
telephone, 161, 573-74, 575
temperance and prohibition, 219-22, 498, 574, 575
Tennyson, Alfred Lord, x, 18, 133-34, 621
Terry, Ellen, 626, 628
Thackeray, William Makepeace, 18, 182, 184, 205, 212, 302, 303, 496, 516
Thayer, Abbott, 513, 516

Thayer, Albert, 551
Thomas, A. E., 516-20
Thomson, Mortimer Neal, 40, 42
Thoreau, Henry David, 516
Tilden, Samuel, 5, 6, 10
Tillman, Benjamin R., 533, 534
Tonkray, Alexander C., 538, 539
Tonkray, John, 539
Toole, John L., 55, 56
Toronto, Can., 59, 73, 117, 170
Torquemada, Tomas de, 529, 531
Townsend, George Alfred, 14, 54, 96, 97
Tracy, James L., 689
Treaty of Paris, 353, 358
Treaty of Portsmouth, 500, 506, 543
trial marriage, 559
Trinity College (Hartford), 164
Trollope, Anthony, 90
Trollope, Frances, 90
Trollope, Thomas, 90
Trowbridge, J. T., 577, 578
Trumbull, James Hammond, 369, 370
Turini, Giovanni, 241
Tuxedo, N.Y., 374, 638, 640, 641, 646, 647, 655
Twain, Mark: on African Americans, 287; on automobiles, 597; on bankruptcy, 182-83, 185-86, 192-93, 317, 355, 360, 580-81, 584, 591; on banning of "Eve's Diary," 558-59, 565; on banning of *Huckleberry Finn,* 474; on bicycles, 324, 651; on biography, 343; on euchre, 692, 693; on exercise, 648, 692; on fashion, 557-58, 562-65; on fishing, 396; on football, 375-77; on free trade, 19, 209, 213, 508, 658; on golf, 374, 692; on gramophones or phonographs, 136, 275, 569, 617, 622; on hazing, 384-85; on human nature, 583-84; on humor, 60, 131-33, 145-47, 166, 187, 204-06, 212-13, 255-57, 302, 321, 322, 518-19, 522-23, 638-39, 642-43, 653; on hunting, 396; on immigration, 655-58; on imperialism, x, 317, 350-51, 353, 358, 391; on international copyright, 17-19, 22, 69, 70, 80, 99, 102-03, 120-21, 229-30, 232, 280, 298-99, 364, 493-94, 497-99, 503-05, 546, 558, 560-61, 565-67, 568-71, 574;

on interviews, x, 35, 65, 131, 143, 218, 235–36, 276–77, 371, 385, 400, 481–82, 525–26, 582, 595–96, 650–51, 688; on Judaism, 670, 673; on lecturing, 32–33, 50, 54, 65, 73, 183, 187–88, 192, 193, 199, 217–19, 251, 254, 272–74, 356, 361, 463, 468; on Mugwumps, 207, 208, 353, 358–59, 508, 509, 511, 598, 600; on Native Americans, 287, 519, 520; on *nom de plume*, 80, 153, 155, 180; on nudity, 557, 562–63; on opera, 390, 574; on palmistry, 224, 227; on party platforms, 5, 507, 508, 509; on patriotism, 657–58; on phonographs and gramophones, 136, 275, 569, 617, 622; on photographs, 389, 391; on prohibition and temperance, 219–22, 498, 574, 575; on protective tariff, 508, 658; on race, 237–38, 287; on religious belief, 686; on revolution, 541–43; on simplified spelling, 568; on smoking, 275, 454–44, 471–72, 597, 606, 610–11, 617, 623, 649–50, 681, 683, 687–89, 693, 694; on tariff, 508, 658; on telephone, 161, 573–75; on temperance and prohibition, 219–22, 498, 574, 575; on trial marriage, 559; on typewriters, 275, 327, 400, 597; on women's suffrage, 222, 692–93

Twain, Mark, books of
—*Adventures of Huckleberry Finn*, 1, 49, 56, 61, 69, 70, 74, 78–81, 91, 93, 106, 126, 131, 134–36, 146, 148, 154, 159, 162, 168, 174, 219, 236, 265, 301, 302, 322, 354, 360, 370, 416, 429, 432, 442, 451, 470, 472, 474, 485, 488, 502, 515, 537–38, 539, 595, 606, 607, 696, 697
—*Adventures of Tom Sawyer*, 1, 44, 46, 57, 64, 69, 118, 121–22, 146, 148, 154, 156, 157, 159, 162, 168, 172–74, 175, 265, 272, 301, 322, 329, 354, 370, 407, 429, 430, 440, 442–46, 449, 451, 465, 466, 469, 470, 475, 515, 567, 570, 606–07, 696–97
—*American Claimant*, 440
—*Autobiography*, 49, 88, 101, 126, 153, 159, 239, 352, 333–34, 336, 339–44, 349–50, 357, 359, 430, 444, 451, 480, 481, 503, 516, 569–71, 578, 584, 594, 654, 674
—*Celebrated Jumping Frog of Calaveras County, and Other Sketches*, 560, 566
—*Christian Science*, 459, 488, 654
—*Connecticut Yankee in King Arthur's Court*, 87, 103–07, 110, 111, 113, 116, 126, 133, 209, 233, 234, 265, 303, 558, 563–64, 590
—*Europe and Elsewhere*, 34
—*Following the Equator*, 32, 171, 173, 177, 232, 246, 269, 270, 283, 288, 290, 297–98, 300, 306–09, 317, 319, 581, 654
—*Gilded Age*, 1, 26, 27, 64, 214, 215
—*How to Tell a Story and Other Essays*, 163
—*Innocents Abroad*, 9–11, 15–17, 22, 23, 25–27, 39, 45–47, 74, 80, 95, 97, 100, 109, 112, 113, 129, 136, 160–61, 163, 164, 166, 173, 216, 233, 245, 246, 248, 257, 260, 263, 275, 291, 296, 302, 309, 319, 321, 322, 392, 404, 411, 416, 459, 498, 501, 504, 505, 532, 533, 545, 560, 562, 566, 570, 572, 577, 653, 654, 681;
—*Is Shakespeare Dead?* 679, 681, 686
—*King Leopold's Soliloquy*, 498, 505, 530–31
—*Letters from the Earth*, 568
—*Life on the Mississippi*, 1, 37, 42, 43, 80, 90, 265, 267, 423, 431, 433–35, 448, 467
—*My Début as a Literary Person with Other Essays and Stories*, 494
—*Personal Reminiscences of Joan of Arc*, 153, 155, 229, 356, 363, 472, 581, 590
—*Prince and the Pauper*, 1, 32, 34, 39, 43, 113–17, 128, 135, 162, 219, 224, 229, 262, 265, 272, 302, 655
—*Pudd'nhead Wilson*, 32, 87, 148, 150, 228–29, 231, 232, 354, 356, 359, 362, 363, 465, 669
—*Roughing It*, 1, 26, 27, 34, 36, 44, 74, 80, 93, 153, 155, 166, 167, 233, 238,

239, 259, 262, 296, 302, 322, 391, 480, 481, 544, 570
—*Sketches, Old and New,* 394
—*Stolen White Elephant, Etc.,* 394
—*Those Extraordinary Twins,* 575
—*Tom Sawyer Abroad,* 236, 238
—*Tramp Abroad,* 1, 16, 17, 22, 23, 25–29, 31, 39, 56, 74, 80, 166, 167, 233, 248, 303, 309, 321, 322, 411
—*What is Man?* 459
Twain, Mark, drama of: *Ah Sin,* 12, 13
Twain, Mark, stories and essays of
—"About All Kinds of Ships," 25, 144
—"Adventures of a Microbe," 515, 590, 594
—"Aix-les-Bains," 361
—"Awful German Language," 5, 57, 321
—"Babies, The" 42
—"Baker's Blue Jay Yarn," 142, 143, 167, 168
—"Captain Stormfield's Visit to Heaven," 590, 594
—"Christian Science and the Book of Mrs. Eddy," 488
—"Concerning the Jews," 673
—"Defence of General Funston," 474
—"Editorial Wild Oats," 515
—"Encounter with an Interviewer," 1, 52, 59, 74
—"Eve's Diary," 511, 515, 558–59, 565, 607, 617, 621
—"Extracts from Adam's Diary," 494, 511, 516, 565, 617, 621
—"Fenimore Cooper's Literary Offenses," 495–96
—"Fishwife and Its Sad Fate," 56, 57
—"Golden Arm," 477, 481
—"Great Dark," 25
—"Horse's Tale," 515, 516
—"How I Edited an Agricultural Paper Once," 67, 68, 263
—"How I Escaped Being Killed in a Duel," 74, 142, 143, 153
—"How to Tell a Story," 481
—"Jerome Reviews His Official Years," 411
—"Jim Smiley and His Jumping Frog,"
25, 98, 180, 197, 238, 239, 259, 260, 296, 404, 427, 430, 476, 478, 480–81, 570, 579, 613, 623, 624
—"Jim Wolfe and the Cats," 98, 101
—"Letter to the Queen of England," 625, 627
—"Literary Nightmare," 425
—"Little Note to M. Paul Bourget," 163, 200
—"Man That Corrupted Hadleyburg," 519, 618
—"Mark Twain Hooks the Persian Out of the English Channel," 585
—"Mark Twain's Wireless Message from the Sea," 639, 643
—"Miss Clapp's School," 440
—"Mysterious Stranger," 352, 515, 516, 590, 594
—"Old Times on the Mississippi, 1, 36, 37, 161, 163
—"Open Letter to Commodore Vanderbilt," 37
—"O'Shah," 34
—"Personal Habits of the Siamese Twins," 575
—"Post-Mortem Poetry," 184
—"Private History of a Campaign That Failed," 216, 263, 444
—"Private History of the 'Jumping Frog' Story," 481
—"Refuge of the Derelicts," 590, 594
—"Riley—Newspaper Correspondent," 100, 316
—"Shem's Diary," 109, 113, 128, 129
—"Stirring Times in Austria," 331
—"Three Thousand Years among the Microbes," 516
—"To the Person Sitting in Darkness," 346
—"What Paul Bourget Thinks of Us," 162
—"Which Was It?" 590, 594
Tweed, William M., 6, 7
Twichell, Rev. Joseph H., 2, 3, 94, 535, 536, 548, 576, 625, 627, 690
"Twins of Genius" reading tour (1885–86), 39–86

University of Missouri, 412, 413, 417, 419, 423, 432, 436, 454, 459, 478, 516
Upton, Alice H., 514, 516

Vancouver, B.C., 151, 165, 166, 171, 172, 186, 187, 189, 353, 355, 362, 363
Vanderbilt, Consuelo, 228, 232
Vanderbilt, Cornelius, 35, 37
Vanderbilt, William K., 232
Vedder, Elihu, 141, 143
Venezuela, 278, 281, 297, 312, 359, 354
Venice, Italy, 23, 25, 81, 214
Verestchagin, Vessilli, 414, 417
Verne, Jules, 85
Victoria, B.C., 151, 172
Victoria, Queen, 280, 628, 630, 651, 654
Vienna, Austria, 31, 329-40, 352, 362, 363, 366, 370, 579, 581, 690
Villard, Henry, 96, 100
Villiers, Barbara, 105
Virginia City, Nev., 66, 93, 95, 151-53, 167, 182, 274, 424, 481, 544, 545
Visscher, Will L., 167, 168
von Hatzfeldt, Francis Edmund, 105

Wadhams, Albion V., 182, 184
Wagner, Richard, 574
Wagstaffe, W. de, 391
Wainwright, W. A. M., 369, 370
Walker, John Brisben, 328, 329
Wallace, Edgar, 618
Wallace, Lew, 298, 300, 303
Walpole, Horace, 207
Wanamaker, John, 91, 508, 510, 511
Wandering Jew, 144
Ward, Artemus, 151, 153, 163-64, 180, 215, 259, 260
Ward, Mrs. Humphry, 126
Wardha (steamship), 290, 291, 295, 296
Warfield, Edwin A., 587-90, 592-93, 595-98, 600, 601, 604-06, 608
Wark, Charles, 668
Warner, Charles Dudley, 1, 27, 63, 64, 101, 105, 112, 113, 117, 214, 368-69, 420, 548, 636
Warner, Susan, 369
Warrimoo (steamship), 171-72, 187, 194-95, 197, 199

Washington Square Park, 241, 512, 585
Washington, D.C., 13, 52, 53, 95-101, 121, 249, 503, 504, 508, 531, 533-35, 556-67, 574, 576, 577, 589
Washington, George, 322, 329, 450, 603, 698
Watson, John, 247, 249
Watson, Joseph Warren, 101
Webb, C. H., 100
Webster, Charles L., 100, 192
Webster, Daniel, 301, 303
Webster, Harold T., 527, 528
Webster, Noah, 31
Weekly Californian, 66
Weems, Mason Locke, 329
Wellington, N.Z., 258-63, 264
Wells, Rolla, 453, 456, 459, 461
Wenlock, Lord, 294
West Point, 384-85, 595, 597
Weston, Edward Payson, 2, 3, 4
Wheatstone, Charles, 295, 296
Wheeler, Ella. *See* Wilcox, Ella Wheeler
Wheeler, Harold, 661, 662
Whipple, E. P., 577, 578
Whitcher, Frances M., 257
White, Frank Marshall, 317, 318
White, Horace, 96, 100
White, Stanford, 585
Whiteing, Richard, 17, 22
Whitely, L. A., 96, 100
Whitman, Walt, 100, 624
Whittier Birthday Dinner, 578
Whittier, John Greenleaf, 11, 61, 62, 577, 578
Wilberforce, Albert Basil Orme, 344-45, 625
Wilcox, Ella Wheeler, 98, 101
Wilhelm II, Kaiser, 581
Willard, Emma Hart, 154
William IV, King, 497, 502
Williams, Mary. *See* Carew, Kate
Wilson, David, 525, 633, 634
Winans, Edward R., 411
Winans, William, 411
Windsor Castle, 610, 624-28, 638, 652
Windus, W. E., 103, 105, 281, 329
Winnipeg, Can., 160-64, 168-71, 179
Wolf, Benjamin E., 113
women's suffrage, MT on, 222, 692-93
Wood, Howard O., 691
Wood, Julia Curtis Twichell, 690-91

Woodside, E. L., 587, 588
Worcester, Mass., 386, 558-59
Wren, Sir Christopher, 632
Wright, George Frederick, 369, 370
Wright, William. *See* De Quille, Dan
Wycoff, W. C., 425

Yale University, 306, 375-77, 427, 454
York Harbor, Me., 469, 485
Young, Jim, 96, 100
Young, John Russell, 96, 100

Zola, Emile, 266, 268, 299